THE COMPLETE JOURNAL
OF
TOWNSEND HARRIS

TOWNSEND HARRIS IN 1847

From a Bronze Tablet by Albert P. D'Andrea, of the Art Department of the Townsend Harris Hall High School—the Preparatory High School of The College of the City of New York. It is a gift presented by the Class of January, 1924, of the High School, and was unveiled on Charter Day, May 20, 1925, by H. I. M.'s Ambassador, His Excellency Tsuneo Matsudaira.

The Complete Journal of
TOWNSEND HARRIS
*First American Consul
and Minister to Japan*

INTRODUCTION AND NOTES BY
MARIO EMILIO COSENZA, PH. D., L.H.D.

*Dean Emeritus of Brooklyn College
and formerly Director of
The Townsend Harris Hall High School
in New York City*

WITH A PREFACE BY
DOUGLAS MacARTHUR II
United States Ambassador to Japan

(REVISED EDITION)

PUBLISHED WITH THE COOPERATION OF
THE JAPAN SOCIETY, INC., NEW YORK

CHARLES E. TUTTLE COMPANY
Rutland, Vermont & Tokyo, Japan

THIS BOOK IS A SELECTION OF
THE AMERICAN CLUB OF TOKYO
Such selections are published with the support and
cooperation of the Club; are recommended to its
members and friends, and are made in order to further
cultural relations between the United States and Japan.

*Published by the Charles E. Tuttle Company
of Rutland, Vermont, and Tokyo, Japan
with editorial offices at
15 Edogawa-cho, Bunkyo-ku, Tokyo*

*Library of Congress
Catalog Card No. 59-9397*

*First edition, 1930
(Published for Japan Society, New York
by Doubleday, Doran & Co., Inc.)*

Second edition (revised), 1959

PRINTED IN JAPAN

"I shall be the first recognized agent from a civilized power to reside in Japan. This forms an epoch in my life and may be the beginning of a new order of things in Japan. I hope I may so conduct myself that I may have honorable mention in the histories which will be written on Japan and its future destiny."

TOWNSEND HARRIS

Journal, August 19, 1856

PREFACE TO REVISED EDITION

THE history of embassies and consulates, like that of all international relations, is inseparable from the stories of individual men. Nowhere is one reminded of this more forcibly than in observing the short and very active century of intercourse between the United States and Japan.

While there have been many personalities of high distinction charged with the weight of representing each of these countries, none, perhaps, has had more demanded of him in courage, ingenuity, discipline, and solitary decision than Townsend Harris, the first consular officer accredited from the United States Government to that of Japan.

It is a source of much satisfaction that the journal of this pioneer, which has been long out of print, has been made available again to the public through the enterprise of the Charles E. Tuttle Company, with the support of the Japan Society of New York and the American Club of Tokyo.

Any important figure in history gathers about him some elements of legend. Stories, whether true or apocryphal, attach themselves to the names of heroes. This is inevitable, and by no means is it always to be deplored. But the sober truth is sometimes more heroic than fiction, and for those who wish to understand, the unvarnished items of fact are indispensable.

It is for this reason that, in a time when the meaning of Japan and the United States to one another, and of their, mutual relationship to the world are of such absorbing concern, we are grateful for the initiative, among others, of Mr.

Juji Kasai, a lifelong friend of the editor, Dr. Cosenza, for causing the original journal of Townsend Harris to be reprinted.

DOUGLAS MACARTHUR II.

U.S. Embassy, Tokyo.
February 25, 1959.

PREFACE

IN 1916, the writer of this preface was appointed Deputy Director, and later Director, of Townsend Harris Hall, the Preparatory High School of The College of the City of New York. Immediately he became interested in learning why the school had been named after Townsend Harris. Preliminary researches revealed the two outstanding achievements of Townsend Harris's life: the first, that, as President of the Board of Education of New York City, he had been the driving force and chief inspiration for the founding of The College of the City of New York; and the second, that, by a particularly happy turn of the wheel of fortune, he had later been appointed our first Consul General for Japan, and had been successful in opening Japan and bringing her into the larger family of nations.

The writer surrendered himself whole-heartedly to the alluring subject of the life and work of Townsend Harris. As a loyal alumnus of The College of the City of New York, he turned first to the study of Townsend Harris's connections with his Alma Mater, and accordingly, in 1925, he published a volume entitled *The Establishment of The College of the City of New York as The Free Academy in 1847. Townsend Harris Founder.*

It soon became apparent that the available information about Townsend Harris was scanty, with much of it inaccurate. An irresistible urge to undertake the pres-

ix

ent task lay in the mass of source material at the writer's disposal. Some years ago, Miss Bessie A. Harris, the niece of Townsend Harris, presented to The College of the City of New York all the original letters, documents, and papers of Townsend Harris then in her possession. The more the writer looked into this material, the more he became aware of the possibilities that lay in it.

Here were four volumes of Townsend Harris's manuscript *Journal;* a dozen historic documents in the original Japanese and Dutch languages; a complete collection of Townsend Harris's various appointments, letters of credence, passport, etc.; five large letter books, containing a complete file of his official correspondence not only with the authorities at Washington and at Yedo, but also with all persons who approached him on topics closely connected with his official duties; and, finally, hundreds of original manuscript letters received from many of the great men of the day—the ranking officers of our navy, the representatives of all the foreign powers accredited to Japan and to China, the many business men of all nationalities who early established themselves in China, in Siam, in Japan, and generally in the Far East; as well as the early British and American missionaries to those countries, etc., etc.[1]

This hasty enumeration is not by any means intended to be a full description of the priceless historical material owned by The College of the City of New York. Enough has been said, however, to indicate the wealth and the importance of this Townsend Harris collec-

---

[1]Townsend Harris did not keep copies of the letters he wrote to his friends. It is very sincerely hoped that readers of this work will be good enough to send to the writer all manuscript material (or copies thereof) that they may possess, for use in future works on the diplomatic relations between the United States and Japan.

tion, practically every item of which is historic and diplomatic material yet unpublished. Large use has been made of these tempting sources in the notes of this volume, but only in so far as they properly illustrate passages of the *Journal*.

In these days of ever-expanding foreign relations, when American destiny in the new Pacific is so closely linked with that of the nations on the western border of that ocean, the story of the beginning of our friendly relations with Japan is an all-absorbing one. That story is here reproduced directly from the original manuscript. Words underlined by Townsend Harris have been printed in italics, and abbreviations have been spelled out in full, but there have been no omissions from the text. The transcription is a faithful and complete one.

The earlier portion of Mr. Harris's *Journal* (which includes his mission to Siam, and which is approximately one third of the entire manuscript) is here published for the first time. The portion of the *Journal* relating to Japan was published (with omissions) in 1895 by Dr. William Elliot Griffis in his book *Townsend Harris, First American Envoy in Japan*. By express understanding with Houghton Mifflin Company, publishers of Dr. Griffis's book (long out of print), the text of the Japanese portion of the Harris *Journal* is now for the first time given to the public in its full and complete form.[2]

The publication of the present volume is due to the kindly and continued interest which the officers of the Japan Society in New York have taken in it, and to their very natural desire that the complete *Journal* of Townsend Harris be made available to students of American

---

[2]The Houghton Mifflin Company book is Copyright 1895, by William E. Griffis.

relations with Japan and the Far East, as well as to the general public. It was, furthermore, peculiarly and historically fitting for the Society to undertake this publication through its Townsend Harris Endowment Fund Committee—a Committee that bears the name of the man whom this volume delighteth to honor. It would be difficult for the writer adequately to convey his sincere thanks to the officers of the Society and to the members of this Committee individually. He trusts they will feel that they are all included when he expresses his deep appreciation of the kindness shown, and of the courteous assistance given, by Mr. Jerome D. Greene, the Chairman of the Committee; by Mr. Douglas L. Dunbar, its Secretary; and, above all, by Mr. Alexander Tison, the President of the Japan Society.

This work, finally, has been signally honored by His Excellency Prince Iyesato Tokugawa, who has graciously contributed a silken scroll on which he has inscribed an appropriate saying of Confucius. The present Head of the House of Tokugawa and the legal successor of Tycoon Iyesada Tokugawa, who made the Treaty with Townsend Harris, by this courteous act establishes still another spiritual contact with the deeds of his ancestors. To him, too, the writer expresses his sincere appreciation and gratitude.

In 1891, Dr. Inazo Nitobe said that four thick quarto volumes had made known to the world the minutest details of Commodore Perry's expedition, but that sufficient justice had not yet been done to the memory of Townsend Harris, whose candle was still kept under a bushel. It is hoped that the present volume may make a beginning of rendering unto Harris the justice that is due him in recognition of his great achievement—a task that was perhaps the most difficult in the history of

xii

American diplomacy. It is a source of high satisfaction to reflect that the establishment of friendly relations between the United States and Japan was providentially placed in the hands of Townsend Harris—a New York City merchant, endowed with so great skill and patience and with so sympathetic an understanding.

In his careful evaluation of the pioneering but quiet and unheralded diplomatic work of Townsend Harris in Japan, Dr. Nitobe further says:

"An oak falls noisily crashing through the forest; the acorns drop with scarce a sound. To generations after, the acorns prove the greater blessing. Men have not yet learned what conquests there are in peace and in silence."

As the years glide silently by, the seeds of sympathetic understanding that were sown by Townsend Harris so many years ago—in a foreign, but congenial and fertile soil—are indeed proving the greater blessing to later generations. The human family, after the passing of countless ages since its migrations from the plains of central Asia, is meeting again on the far-flung coasts of the greatest of waters. The Ocean Sea—first named from its mere size—is no longer an estranging sea. The modern argosies of commerce and of trade, as they cross and recross it from west to east and from east to west, are daily vindicating the prophecy of Magellan, who, as he emerged from the stormy Strait and found himself wafted by gentle breezes, glanced over the quiet waters ahead and hailed them as the *Mar Pacifico*.

MARIO EMILIO COSENZA.

The College of the City of New York.
January 25, 1930.

xiii

CONTENTS

LIST OF ILLUSTRATIONS

Townsend Harris in 1847   *Frontispiece*

From a Bronze Tablet by Albert P. D'Andrea, of the Art Department of the Townsend Harris Hall High School—the Preparatory High School of The College of the City of New York. It is a gift presented by the Class of January, 1924, of the High School, and was unveiled on Charter Day, May 20, 1925, by H. I. M.'s Ambassador, His Excellency Tsuneo Matsudaira.

Townsend Harris's Seal   *Title page*

This impression of Mr. Harris's stone seal shows three Chinese characters—Ha, Ri, S—somewhat conventionalized by the engraver who made the seal.

FACING PAGE

Townsend Harris's First Commission as Consul General for Japan   24

Dated, Washington, D. C., August 4, 1855.

A Holograph Letter from the Second King of Siam   110

Dated, Palace of the Second King, Bangkok, Siam, April 22, 1856.

Townsend Harris's Manuscript *Journal,* August 19, 1856, in vol. 3, p. 25   196

At the top of the page may be read his hope to receive honorable mention in the "Histories which will be written on Japan."

View of Shimoda, from Kakizaki   212

From a drawing in India ink by Mr. H. C. J. Heusken, whose signature in the lower right-hand corner is clearly legible in the original. This drawing was enclosed by Townsend Harris in a letter to "Kate" Drinker (later Mrs. Thomas Allibone Janvier), dated Shimoda, Japan, November 21, 1856. For this letter and drawing, see the Janvier *Letters and Papers,* in the Manuscripts Division of the New York Public Library.

xviii

LIST OF ABBREVIATIONS USED IN THE NOTES

L. & P.: Refer to the volumes of manuscript *Letters and Papers of Townsend Harris.*

L. B.: Refer to the volumes of manuscript *Letter Books of Townsend Harris.*

In referring to the volumes of the *Congressional Series,* the numbers 35–2 (for instance), refer to the 35th Congress, 2nd Session.

All other abbreviations and references in the notes are, it is thought, clear in themselves.

THE COMPLETE JOURNAL
OF
TOWNSEND HARRIS

Introduction

The Appointment of Townsend Harris as Consul General for Japan

INTEREST in the strange and secluded country to which the American squadron under Commodore Perry was proceeding was very great and very general. Consequently many persons, both in the United States and elsewhere, moved either by scientific interest or by keen curiosity, importuned Perry for permission to go aboard the ships of his fleet and so have one of the earliest peeps at the people who, for more than two centuries, had kept the doors of their island empire so tightly shut.

Commodore Perry met these importunate advances with dignity and with firmness. His position in the matter was clearly stated in the Second General Order which he issued while at sea, on December 23, 1852:[1]

"Entertaining the opinion that the talents and acquirements of the officers of the squadron, if properly directed and brought into action, will be found equal to a plain and practical examination and elucidation of the various objects pertaining to the arts and sciences that may come under their observation during the present cruise, and being aware of the limited accommodations of the vessels under my command, I have invariably objected

[1]Perry, *Narrative*, 33-2, S. Ex. Doc., no. 79, vol. 1, p. 88.

to the employment of persons drawn from civil life to conduct those departments more immediately connected with science."

In spite of the fact that these invariable objections of the commanding officer were well known, requests to accompany the Japan Expedition continued to pour in on Perry. Townsend Harris was in China at the time the American fleet reached that country. Perry first stopped at Hongkong and at Macao; from there he went to Shanghai, where he arrived on May 4, 1853, leaving again towards the end of the same month. It was during Perry's stay at Shanghai that Townsend Harris made his first definite effort to reach Japan. In a letter dated Macao, June 18, 1859,[2] Mr. S. Robertson congratulates Townsend Harris on his then recent and brilliant successes both in Siam and in Japan. In the course of his congratulations there appears this interesting paragraph:

"I often smile to myself when I recollect how anxious you were at Shanghai to accompany Commodore Perry on his first visit to Japan, and your annoyance at his refusal. The 'C.' little thought at the time, that he was then refusing a man who would accomplish greater achievements and acquire more renown in Japan [than Commodore Perry himself] while he would at the same time throw additional lustre on the name of Perry. But so wags the world."

This refusal to be permitted to accompany Commodore Perry did not discourage Townsend Harris. At

[2] *L. & P.*, vol. 1, no. 175.

about the same time (the spring of 1853), he applied for the position of American Consul at either Hongkong or Canton, describing himself a resident of Hongkong.[3] In his letter of recommendation addressed to the Hon. William L. Marcy, and dated New York, December 28, 1853, General Wetmore says that he had never met Harris's "superior in a thoroughly educated and accomplished merchant," and says of him: "I think from his unusually extensive acquirements on all commercial subjects and his acquaintance with several foreign languages (such as Spanish, French, Italian) that he could not fail to render himself useful in a consular office."[4]

Instead of either of these posts, President Pierce, by letter dated Thursday, July 27, 1854, nominated Townsend Harris Consul, at $1,000 per annum, for the treaty port of Ningpo, China, to succeed Charles W. Bradley, who was being transferred to Singapore. This nomination was received by the Senate on Tuesday, August 1st, and was duly referred to its Committee on Commerce. On Wednesday, August 2, 1854, the Senate consented to the appointment.[5]

And here we begin to approach rather closely the matter of Townsend Harris's later appointment as Consul General for Japan. On Sunday, April 29, 1855, returning from his travels in India, Harris reached the home of his dear friend, Mr. Charles C. Currier,

---

[3]Dennett, *Americans in Eastern Asia*, p. 348.

[4]Files of the Bureau of Appointments, Washington, D. C.

[5]S. Ex. J'l, vol. 9, pp. 369, 373, 379. Lamb's *Biographical Dictionary* and the *American Encyclopedia* are both wrong in stating that Townsend Harris was appointed only Vice-Consul for Ningpo.

United States Consul at Pulo Penang, in the Strait of Malacca—Penang, "the primeval Paradise not altered at the Flood," as he himself says in the *Journal* entry for May 21, 1855. At Mr. Currier's residence he must have found awaiting him his commission as Consul for Ningpo. Instead, however, of proceeding to this post, which seems to have had no attractions for him, he set sail for the United States on May 21, 1855, after having appointed the Rev. Dr. Daniel Jerome Macgowan his Vice-Consul for Ningpo. This gentleman, a medical missionary of the Baptist faith, carried on for a short while, but with great difficulty and under protest, as his long letters of complaint to Townsend Harris clearly prove. Harris himself never served a single day as Consul at Ningpo.

In the meantime Townsend Harris's friends had been exerting themselves in his behalf. Mr. Sandwith Drinker, whose hospitality Commodore Perry and his officers had enjoyed both at Hongkong and at Canton, was a sailor of the old school and the most intimate friend that Townsend Harris had in the Far East. There is no doubt in our mind that Mr. Drinker improved every opportunity to praise Townsend Harris to Commodore Perry, who had already received Townsend Harris's personal letter expressing a sincere desire to accompany him to Japan. In the United States Harris could count on the active assistance of Mr. W. H. Topping, of General Prosper M. Wetmore, and, through him, of the Hon. William L. Marcy, Secretary of State.

4

We believe the following to have been the course of events. His appointment as Consul for Ningpo must have suggested to Harris the possibility of the far more responsible consulship to Japan—an ambition which could not have been much out of his mind since the days of Perry's Japan Expedition. There, in Japan, lay the greatest opportunity of the century for truly great and pioneer diplomatic work. The Perry Treaty received the approval of the Senate on July 15, 1854, and was signed by the President on August 7th. Ratifications were exchanged at Shimoda, February 21, 1855; and the Treaty itself was proclaimed June 22, 1855. On July 27, 1855, at 4 P. M., Townsend Harris passed the buoy on the Bar of New York, reaching home from far-off Pulo Penang in the Strait of Malacca after a voyage of more than two months.

The appointment of an American representative to Japan was now in order. The Perry Treaty (concluded March 31, 1854) clearly stated (Article XI):

"There shall be appointed, by the Government of the United States, Consuls or Agents to reside in Shimoda, at any time after the expiration of eighteen months from the date of the signing of this treaty; provided that either of the two Governments deem such arrangement necessary."

The President undoubtedly consulted with Commodore Perry as to the best available man, and we have subsequent official testimony to the effect that the Commodore was one of the men who recommended Harris for the post.

Townsend Harris's claims for consideration were truly outstanding and unique. He had resigned as President of the Board of Education of New York City on January 26, 1848. In 1849, he sailed from New York and journeyed around Cape Horn to California as supercargo of his own merchant vessel. With this voyage began his wandering trading expeditions from port to port—expeditions which extended over a period of six years and brought him into close contact with the many different races of the South Seas and of Asia. In the course of these voyages, he visited many islands of the Pacific, and many points on the mainland of the oldest of continents. He visited far-off New Zealand and the Philippines; he crossed the China Sea; he lived and carried on business in both North and South China, in Shanghai, Ningpo, Canton, Macao, and Penang; in Singapore, in Ceylon, and in India.

These statements may seem of minor importance, but they become facts of primary importance when we consider their real significance in connection with the great life work which was to follow. This commercial wandering from place to place gave Townsend Harris the ideal training and preparation for his later diplomatic intercourse with the Japanese. It helped remove that feeling of shock or of puzzled attitude which takes hold of so many men when suddenly brought face to face with a different civilization and with strange manners and customs. It taught Harris to be tolerant and sympathetic,

6

and, above all, to be patient—for patience has ever been the supreme and special prerequisite for all successful intercourse with the peoples of the East. Finally, it gave him a knowledge of the life and the mind of the Oriental that even an extended course of reading of selected books could scarcely have given him.

To repeat, then, these qualifications of Harris could not, we venture to assert, have been duplicated anywhere in the United States of 1855. The Perry Treaty was not a commercial agreement, but merely a "wood and water" treaty, and it provided (as we have seen) for the appointment of consuls or agents. Harris's friends presented and urged his really exceptional claims to the post. On July 31, 1855—only four days after his arrival in New York—the following letter was written to the President of the United States and signed by eight of the foremost citizens of New York:[6]

New York, July 31, 1855.

To the PRESIDENT OF THE UNITED STATES:

SIR:

We desire to recommend for your most favorable notice Mr. Townsend Harris, formerly for many years an active merchant in this city, but more recently a resident in various parts of China and India.

Mr. Harris possesses great business experience, extensive and varied information on commercial subjects, and is unusually well qualified to discharge the duties of a consular or diplomatic situation in the East. Feel-

---

[6]Files of the Bureau of Appointments, Washington, D. C.

ing confident of the great capacity and personal merits of Mr. Harris, we unite most cordially in commending him to your favor.

With high respect

(signed)   Brown Brothers Co.
Herman J. Redfield
Isaac Townsend
Schuyler Livingston
R. Withers
John J. Cisco
John Romeyn Brodhead
C. W. Lawrence

It is interesting to note that Mr. John R. Brodhead, one of the signers of this letter, had himself been nominated Consul General for Japan by President Pierce on Saturday, March 3, 1855.[7] And on August 1, 1855, Mr. John J. Cisco wrote this special letter of recommendation:[8]

New York, August 1, 1855.

In addition to what is contained on the preceding page, I desire to state that Mr. Harris, while residing here, occupied and deservedly a high position in the community. He was an active member of the Chamber of Commerce, trustee of a savings bank, and for several years President of the Board of Education. These duties were all discharged with credit in the intervals of an active commercial life.

As a politician he was a sound, reliable, and influential Democrat, and I have reason to know that his views have

---

[7]S. Ex. J'l, vol. 9, pp. 440, 441.
[8]Files of the Bureau of Appointments, Washington, D. C.

8

undergone no change; that he is a true Democrat now as ever before. I give this testimony with much pleasure.

JOHN J. CISCO.

Townsend Harris now went to Washington and had the privilege of several personal interviews with President Pierce. We are not in a position to give the details of these busy days in the nation's capital. There are extant, however, other extremely interesting documents re lating to this historic appointment.

From Willards Hotel, Townsend Harris addressed to the President a very frank and touching letter:[9]

Willards Hotel,
Washington

August 4, 1855.

SIR:

In consequence of letters which reached me last evening, I have postponed my return to New York, and remain at this hotel, anxiously awaiting Your Excellency's decision on my application.

I have told Your Excellency that I have long had a strong desire to visit Japan; and so deep has this feeling become that, if I was offered the choice between Commissioner to China or Consul to Japan, I should instantly take the latter.

I have a perfect knowledge of the social banishment I must endure while in Japan, and the mental isolation in which I must live, and am prepared to meet it. I am a single man, without any ties to cause me to look anxiously to my old home, or to become impatient in my new one:—You may rely, Sir, that I will not ask for leave

---

[9]Files of the Bureau of Appointments, Washington, D. C.

9

to visit my friends, or resign the place for any reasons of dislike to the country, but will devote myself, zealously, to the faithful discharge of my duties.

I have only to add, that I shall be much obliged by your early decision on my application.

I have the honor to be
With great respect
Your obedient servant,
TOWNSEND HARRIS.

To HIS EXCELLENCY FRANKLIN PIERCE
President of the United States.

The references in this letter to social banishment and mental isolation were a prophetic look into his future life in Japan—a presentiment of the long-continued isolation which later caused him such great pain and sorrow.

The Secretary of State, William L. Marcy, who was at Old Point Comfort enjoying a brief respite from the oppressive heat of the capital, had known of the President's indecision for some days; and on August 4, 1855—the very same day on which Townsend Harris wrote his letter to the President—Secretary Marcy wrote a confidential letter to General Prosper M. Wetmore (an intimate friend of Townsend Harris), giving a clear picture of the President's hesitation—even quoting the President's own words from a letter which he had recently received from the White House. The letter proves that General Wetmore had enlisted the hearty coöperation of Secretary Marcy. The communication is marked "Confidential," but its presence to-day in the Harris *Letters and Papers* simply means that, after reading it,

General Wetmore (in accordance with Secretary Marcy's expressed wish) turned it over to Mr. Harris with his compliments. The letter[10] reads as follows:

(Confidential)

O. P. Comfort
August 4, 1855.

MY DEAR GENERAL:

Your letter notifying me that Harris intended to come here arrived the next day after he left this place for Washington. Some days before I left home, the President had assented to Harris's appointment, but when I sent him a commission to sign he hesitated, and I thought he was inclined to bestow the office on another. I think he retained that view when Mr. Harris had his first interview with him, but it appears by a letter I have just received from him that Harris has carried his point. From that letter I make the following extract, which I do not doubt will be very gratifying to you.

"I had a short interview with Mr. Harris yesterday and he dined with me to-day. He is evidently a man of high character, and his large intelligence derived both from books and observation impresses me forcibly. My consultations with him have been very satisfactory, and you have not in my judgment overestimated his qualifications for the position of which we have spoken. I shall appoint him at once and think he had better sail as soon as possible."

I rejoice as heartily as you can at this result. I cannot doubt that he will justify the favorable opinion we enter-

---

[10]*L. & P.*, vol. 1, no. 5.

tain of his eminent qualifications. Should Harris get the appointment,—as I think it is beyond contingency he will,—I have no objection you should read to him the above extract from the President's letter to me. Beyond that I wish it to be regarded as strictly confidential. I have been here nearly a fortnight and may remain some time longer. I brought work with me. The President says in his letter it is hot in Washington and urges me to remain until the weather changes, unless some emergency calls for my return. We are here "under an ardent Southern sun," as old Mr. Ritchie would say, but we are surrounded by water and nearly all the time fanned by ocean breezes. These breezes and the bathing are our comforts,—perhaps fish[ing] ought to be added thereto.

Yours truly,
W. L. MARCY.

GENERAL P. M. WETMORE.

President Pierce, then, had reached a final and favorable decision before he received Townsend Harris's letter of August 4, 1855. Indeed, on that same day, Mr. W. Hunter, Assistant Secretary of State, sent Harris the following notice of his appointment:[11]

Department of State
4th August, 1855.

DEAR SIR:

I have the pleasure to inform you that the President has signed your commission as Consul General to Japan. He is desirous of conversing with you upon the

---

[11]*L. & P.*, vol. 1, no. 10.

subject and will receive you for the purpose at any time when he may not be otherwise engaged.

Very respectfully
Your obedient servant,
W. HUNTER.

To TOWNSEND HARRIS.

Townsend Harris must have been in New York City by this time, as is proved by another interesting note by Mr. W. H. Topping, written August 5, 1855, which was addressed to him at New York, and which reveals two more persons who strove for the appointment of Harris as our first representative to Japan.[12]

Washington, August 5, 1855.

MY DEAR SIR:

Permit me to congratulate you on your success in obtaining the appointment you desired.

I called on Mr. Webster, as I promised I would, and was informed by him that the President had concluded to give you the appointment, and I then called in at the Hotel, but you had flown.

It is more than probable that you will be obliged to return here to receive your instructions, and, if so, I shall have the pleasure of seeing you again either here or in New York, at which latter place I shall be in the course of a few days. Present my regards to General Wetmore and his brother, and believe me to be

Very respectfully and truly yours,
W. H. TOPPING.

TOWNSEND HARRIS, ESQ.,
etc. etc. etc.,
New York.

---

[12]*L. & P.*, vol. 1, no. 11.

his letter brought added joy to Townsend Harris, who must have hastened to communicate the good news to some of his dearest friends—for this we interpret to be the meaning of the names written in his own hand on the back of this letter—namely, Topping and Marcy (at Washington), Currier (at Penang), Barstow (S. L. M. Barlow?), and Drinker (in China). Mr. Sandwith Drinker, indeed, was particularly well informed about Harris's appointment. Writing from Canton, China, on December 3, 1855,[18] he says to Harris:

"Mrs. Drinker received your note mentioning your appointment to Japan, and we shall all be glad to see you back again. . . . Your secrecy about your mission to Siam is rather amusing, as you say you do not wish it to reach China. We know all your movements better than people at home do. I have received two letters about your going to Siam, and have seen two or three others giving an account of your mission. I also knew, before you wrote, of your appointment to Japan, and knew Marcy consulted Commodore Perry about it. I knew Perry's answer. So you see we are well posted up here."

As Mr. Drinker said, Secretary Marcy had in fact consulted Commodore Perry as to a properly qualified person for the post to Japan. But we are in a position to-day to give more authoritative information than Mr. Drinker had been able to gather from the letters which he had received. Curiously enough, it is information that Townsend Harris himself received only years later—

[18]*L. & P.*, vol. 1, no. 23.

after he had officially sent in his resignation as
Resident to Japan. In regretfully accepting th
of resignation, the then Secretary of State, Will
Seward, bears testimony not only as to the person
actually had recommended Townsend Harris fo
position, but also to the satisfaction of the United S ___s
Government at the pioneer work he had accomplished
in Japan.[14]

No. 24   Department of State
             Washington, October 21, 1861.

SIR:

Your dispatch of July 10 (No. 29) has been received.

You perhaps are informed now for the first time that
your appointment as the first commissioner to Japan was
made by President Pierce upon the joint recommendation of Commodore Perry and myself.

You will do me the justice, therefore, to believe that
I sincerely sympathize with you in your suffering from
ill health, and that I regard your retirement from the
important post you have filled with such distinguished
ability and success, as a subject of grave anxiety, not only
for this country, but for all the Western nations.

The President [Lincoln] instructs me to say that he
accepts your resignation with profound regret, and to
present to you an assurance of his entire satisfaction with
the manner in which the responsibilities of your mission
have been discharged.

Mr. Robert H. Pruyn has been appointed to succeed
you, and, I presume, will reach Yedo as early as January

[14]*Dipl. Corr.*, 1862, pt. 2, p. 816.

next. You will, of course, remain in the discharge of official duties until relieved by his arrival.

I am, Sir,

Your obedient servant,
WILLIAM H. SEWARD.

TOWNSEND HARRIS, ESQ.,
etc. etc. etc.,
Yedo.

So closes the history of Townsend Harris's appointment as Consul General for Japan. He thus became the first representative of any country at any time to be accredited to the Island Empire of the Far East; and it was an extremely fortunate choice—fortunate not only for Japan but for the United States and the world in general. Japan feels deeply the debt of gratitude which she owes to the United States for all that Townsend Harris did for her in those early and troubled days when she first opened her ports to the Western world; and, on the other hand, the world has greatly profited from the fact that Townsend Harris built the diplomatic relations of Japan with the United States and the other members of the family of nations on the firm foundation of friendliness, mutual trust, and sympathetic understanding.

Journal No. 1

Commencing May 21, 1855
Ending April 13, 1856—on page 60[1]

At Penang, 1855. Having arrived here on the 29th ult. from my Indian trip, and being soon to start on my homeward voyage overland, I shall only record a few of the points and dates in my journey.

May 21, 1855. Bade adieu to my most kind and hospitable friend Charles C. Currier, Esq., a true American and an honor to his country; his praises are in the mouth of every gentleman who has visited Penang.[2] Dear Penang! a part of the primeval Paradise not altered at the Flood: here, an everlasting spring reigns; fresh flowers scent the air on each morning; its luscious fruits,—the pisang, mangosteen, durian, ramput, mango, rambutan, kachao, orange, golden fig, among others,— and the whole family of palm fruits are some of them constantly in season. What lovely views! What a panor-

---

[1]This legend is written in Townsend Harris's own hand, on the first page of vol 1 of the manuscript *Journal*. As a matter of fact, *Journal* no. 1 ends (on p. 60 of the manuscript) with the entry for Monday, Apr. 14, 1856.

[2]U.S. Consul at Penang; sailed for the United States on July 1, 1859: *L. & P.*, vol. 1, no. 256.

A thorough search of Hasse's *Index* has failed to find any mention of Mr. Currier as U. S. Consul. In a footnote to his letter to Charles Huffnagle, U. S. Consul General for British India, and dated Shimoda, July 6, 1857 (*L. B.*, vol. 2, p. 39), Townsend Harris distinctly mentions Mr. Currier as U. S. Consul at Penang.

ama from the West Hill 2,800 feet high! What rides in its sweetly shaded valleys! It is a land of delight, and the people are simple, warm hearted and hospitable; so long as memory continues I can never forget them and their terrestrial Paradise. Go on board the steamer *Singapore,* Captain Baker, my old friend who commanded the steamer *Pekin,* when we were in fearful danger from a typhoon in the China Sea, October 2, 1851.

May 29, 1855. Arrive off Point-de-Galle (Ceylon) at 7 P. M. Cannot enter the harbor except by daylight, therefore we lie off and on all night, and enter at daylight on the 30th.

May 30, 1855. Go on board the small steamer *Bombay* for Suez,—horribly crowded, and any quantity of ill-tempered children, speaking Hindostanee, Bengalee, Malay and "Pigeon English"—anything in fact but English—sallow-looking things they are, but time and the temperate zone will give them rosy cheeks, red lips and bleach the yellow stain of bile out of their skins.

June 11, 1855. Reach Aden, created by Shaitan[3] and abandoned by God. Is the most fearfully desolate place I ever saw. Volcanic in its origin, it looks as though it had not yet got cool. Go out to the cantonments five miles, situated on the actual bottom of the old crater. The side to the north is broken down, and through this opening runs the road to the neck which unites it with the land. Finish coaling at 8 P. M. and start for Suez. The weather is oppressive beyond anything I ever knew —it utterly prostrates one.

[3]An Arabic word meaning Satan.

18

June 12, 1855. Last night will always be fixed in my mind as a night of horror. As we ran up the Straits of Bab-el-Mandeb (truly to us the "Gate of Tears") the simoon began to blow; at 1 A. M. the thermometer stood at 104°; the air did not appear to possess any oxygen. Men—strong men—gasped for breath,—for something to satisfy the craving of their lungs. At last we passed the Gate at 5 A. M., and, joy of joys, we saw the blue waters of the Red Sea curling under a fresh breeze from the west. The relief was instantaneous—all were like men raised from a sick bed—and the thermometer fell to 87°. About two years ago, three females died from exhaustion alone, during a passage like that of last night. I would advise any friend to avoid the Red Sea from April to November.

June 19, 1855. Reached Suez early this morning. I had the good luck to draw Van No. 1, consequently I leave in the first caravan of five carriages at 2 P. M. The other passengers will follow at intervals of four hours between each caravan. The *Van* is half an omnibus on two wheels, and drawn by two horses and two mules. Guards on horseback go with each party. The Arabs drive furiously and treat their brutes with great cruelty.

About five miles from Suez, I had a fine sight of the "Moving Sand Pillars" so graphically described by Bruce.[4] There were four that I saw. They are simply occasioned by a small whirlwind which lifts up the burn-

---

[4]James Bruce (Dec. 14, 1730–Apr. 27, 1794), African traveller and explorer. The passage referred to is in *Travels to Discover the Source of the Nile, in the Years 1768–1773*, Dublin, 1790–91, in vol. 5, bk. VIII, ch. XI, pp. 318–19, 321.

ing dust of the desert, and, from its being confined to the vortex of the whirlwind, gives it the appearance of a solid body of great height and moving more or less rapidly over the desert. This no doubt is the origin of the Arab fables of the *Jin* whose heads reach up to the clouds. Afterwards had a fine mirage—the deception was perfect—a beautiful sheet of water—a noble and extensive palace raised its lofty white walls—palm trees were waving—and the green fields refreshed the eye. How much like the future of life in the eye of youth with its glowing anticipations! Alas! how much were the facts like the realities of life!

The water was the sandy desert—the palace simply the low white stables where our horses stood—the palm trees a poor stunted "thorn acacia" and the green fields a few leaves that *will* grow in the desert despite its aridity. We have sixteen relays of cattle and eat three times on the road between Suez and Cairo. The coffee must be drunk to be appreciated. Distance, 83 miles; time, 16 hours. On reaching the hills that overlook Cairo, I saw the Great Pyramid by the light of the rising sun— a grand sight. It looked like a mountain.

June 20, 1855. As the cholera was raging in Cairo, we drove at once to the steamer at Shubra, about three miles below Boulak. Here are a fine palace and beautiful gardens belonging to the Pasha, Said-Pasha. Not fearing the cholera [we] went to Cairo and visited the Citadel and the Tomb of Mehemet Ali. As Cairo is no novelty nowadays I do not describe it, merely remarking that the Mosque or Tomb of Mehemet Ali brought the glories of Agra and Delhi to my mind from the similarity of style; but what a difference! Go and see the Taj Mahal and Moote Musjeed,[5] the Tomb of Ackbar and the Jumma Musjeed and twenty other fine buildings at Agra; then visit Delhi, both old and new, and see her glories, and you would at once say that Mehemet's Tomb is mere *cutcha*.[6]

Having time, I went to the Great Pyramid and went through the whole process of donkey bargaining with its attendant noise and cheatery; was dragged up to the top of the Pyramid by four cutthroat looking rascals, and then came down again, woefully out of breath. I am sorry I ever saw it under any other light than that from the hills at sunrise.

I would advise any friend visiting Cairo to go out there to see the sight. It will pay—as we say in America. Passed the night miserably enough in the small, dirty, hot and crowded steamer. The last passengers arrived at 8 P. M.

June 21, 1855.　Left Shubra at 6:30 A. M. for Kafirlis, or Cafferlis—seventy-five miles below Cairo. Pass through the great hydraulic work called the *Barrage,* intended to secure the inundation of the lands above it.

It is a bold and noble work, but not yet complete. Reached Kafirlis at 4 P. M. and took the railway! Shade

---

[5]*Musjeed* (or *masjid, mesjid, musjid*): a Mohammedan mosque. "Moti Masjid, or Pearl Mosque, is an equally perfect example of the Mahommedan style"; *Encycl. Brit., s. v. Agra.*

It will be noticed that here, and generally so, Townsend Harris anglicizes the spelling of foreign words: *e. g.,* the long "i" of *masjid* he represents by a double "e."

[6]The meaning is quite clear, even without knowing that *cutcha* is an Anglo-Indian word meaning a cheap lime used in building.

of Cheops! A railway in Egypt! Cars new and capital, we spun over the eighty-three miles to Alexandria by 8:30 P. M. Rose early and got a vapor bath—the first bath since leaving Ceylon.

June 22, 1855. Went on board the steamer *Euxine* at 11 A. M. for England ho! via Malta and Gibraltar. View of Alexandria Harbor as you leave it is very fine.

En route to Malta saw Cape Bon near Tripoli, and Captain Weeks like a good fellow sheered in so that we could make out the houses at Algiers as we passed.

June 25, 1855. Arrive at Malta, visit the Church of St. John with its magnificent roof and pavement and noble monuments of the old knights; also the old palace and armory of the knights; about one hundred suits of their armor are preserved in the armory. I was surprised at the smallness of it, but few of the corselets were large enough for my chest, although I am not very large.

July 1, 1855. Arrive at Gibraltar early in the morning. Visit the fortifications, which I think might be truly called impregnable,—so long as ammunition and food hold out, nothing but treachery or cowardice can cause its surrender. Capital apricots and other fruits. Pleasant to my ear it was, to hear the rolling sounds of the majestic Castilian language. I should have noted that, on our voyage from Malta, we saw snow on the peaks of the Sierra Nevada, and that among other places we had capital views of Velez-Malaga, Malaga itself, and the beautiful country between. Malaga must be a capital place for an invalid. We left the same day for our last stage,—Southampton.

July 6, 1855. On our voyage from Gibraltar we sighted Cape Trafalgar, Cape Finisterre and Ushant, of course observing Europa Point and Cape Spartel.

We reached Southampton at 4 P. M. having passed between the Isle of Wight and the villages of New Forest. I would here remark that, from leaving Penang until our arrival here, the weather has been good, so far as wind is concerned, and that we never had any sea that would endanger a common ship's boat. Passed my luggage at the Custom House and went to Radley's Hotel, a very good house, where we had beefsteaks, strawberries and other things that do not figure in the Asiatic bills of fare.

July 7, 1855. Went up to London and on going to Baring Brothers & Co. I met the welcome of letters from my dear friends in New York. I had intended to go to Paris, but my letters were so urgent for my immediate return[7] that I took my passage for the *Atlantic* to leave Liverpool on the 16th inst. Went down to Liverpool on the 14th, passed the 15th in calling on Mr. and Mrs. Miller and Mr. and Mrs. Whittemore, and early on the 16th went on board the noble steamer *Atlantic,* Captain West; and, being so placed and surrounded by plenty of countrymen, I felt as though I had already reached home.

---

[7]Though there is no manuscript evidence, the writer feels sure that among these urgent letters from dear friends in New York there was at least one from General Prosper M. Wetmore, and perhaps one from William L. Marcy, the Secretary of State. The writer is even more sure that the reason for the urgency of Townsend Harris's return was that he might be present in the United States to plead his own cause and to make sure of receiving the appointment as first Consul General to Japan.

We had a singular-mirage on our voyage home. We saw Cape Race early in the morning, and at 3 P. M. land appeared nearly directly ahead and apparently some ten miles distant. Suddenly the line of the land stretched along nearly across our course and extended a long distance. Now, in reality, the nearest land in that direction was Cape Breton (I think) then some one hundred and ten miles (not knots) distant. The land soon began to show remarkable changes. Sometimes it would shoot up into high sharp peaks; then the peaks would change to rounded hills; then the line of coast would be changed into distinct islets as quick as the changes of a kaleidoscope. It continued until 9 P. M.

July 27, 1855. At 4 P. M. we passed the buoy on the Bay of New York, which completed my voyage around the world.

I expressed a hope to some of the passengers that I should never be required to leave New York for two hundred and fifty miles in any *direction*.[8]

I omit the details of what I did while in the United States, merely noting that on the 4th of August I was appointed Consul General[9] for Japan.

---

[8] The hope here expressed by Townsend Harris must have been due to the exuberance of his joy at reaching home again,—"dear old, inflammable New York" (as he elsewhere calls it),—after an absence of seven years, dating from the spring of 1849, when he left for California as supercargo of his own trading argosy. (See note 7.)

[9] See illustration. It will be noticed that the word *General* was inserted by hand on a form intended for consuls only; secondly, that this first commission was addressed to "His Imperial Majesty, The Emperor of Japan," although, as a matter of fact, it was ultimately delivered to the Shogun at Yedo; and thirdly, that W. Hunter signed as Acting Secretary of State, in place of Secretary William L. Marcy, who was then at Old Point Comfort enjoying a short vacation.

THE PRESIDENT OF THE UNITED STATES OF AMERICA.

TO ALL WHO SHALL SEE THESE PRESENTS, GREETING:

KNOW YE, That, reposing special trust and confidence in the abilities and integrity of *Townsend Harris of New York*

I do appoint him **CONSUL,** of the United States of America, for *Japan to reside at Simoda*

and do authorize and empower him to **HAVE AND TO HOLD** the said office, and to exercise and enjoy all the rights, pre-eminences, privileges, and authorities, to the same of right appertaining, during the pleasure of the President of the United States, for the time being, and until the end of the next Session of the Senate of the United States, and no longer: he demanding and receiving no fees, or perquisites of office whatever, which shall not be expressly established by some law of the United States. And I do hereby enjoin all captains, masters, and commanders of ships and other vessels, armed or unarmed, sailing under the flag of the said United States, as well as all other of their citizens, to acknowledge and consider him, the said *Townsend Harris* accordingly.

AND I DO HEREBY PRAY AND REQUEST *His Imperial Majesty the Emperor of Japan No Governors or Officers of Townsend Harris* and officers, to permit the said *Townsend Harris* fully and peaceably to enjoy and exercise the said office, without giving or suffering to be given unto him any molestation or trouble; but, on the contrary, to afford him all proper countenance and assistance; I offering to do the same for all those who shall, in like manner, be recommended to me by *His Imperial Majesty.*

In testimony whereof, I have caused these letters to be made Patent, and the Seal of the United States to be hereunto affixed.

Given under my hand, at the City of Washington, the *fourth* day of *August*

In the year of our Lord one thousand eight hundred and *fifty five* and of the Independence of the United States of America, the *eightieth*

Franklin Pierce

BY THE PRESIDENT

W L Marcy
Secretary of State.

TOWNSEND HARRIS'S FIRST COMMISSION AS CONSUL GENERAL FOR JAPAN
Dated, Washington, D. C., August 4, 1855

During the same month the President was pleased to entrust me with the making [of] a commercial treaty with the Kingdom of Siam,[10] a matter in which Mr. Balestier was unsuccessful in 1851.[11]

[10]The first information Townsend Harris received of this additional assignment was contained in a letter from Secretary W. L. Marcy, dated Washington, Sept. 6, 1855 (*L. & P.*, vol. 1, no. 14). He was informed that he was to visit Siam with a view to negotiate a treaty, and was requested to go to Washington as soon as possible in order to make the necessary arrangements. As is so often the case, the most interesting part of this letter is the postscript, which reads:

"I advise that nothing should be said about the Siam negotiations. If it should become public, obstacles may be thrown in the way of it."

We have already seen (in the Introduction) how well this state secret was kept. Townsend Harris informed Mr. S. Drinker of it by letter of Sept. 15, 1855. For, writing from Canton, China, on Dec. 3, 1855, Mr. Drinker was already in a position to say to Harris:

"Your secrecy about your mission to Siam is rather amusing, as you say you do not wish it to reach China."

Incidentally, there seems to have been no exception made in this instance to the rule affecting secrets. For, just as Townsend Harris, in spite of Secretary Marcy's injunctions, had within ten days seen fit to confide in his intimate friend Mr. Drinker, so had others (at least the "two or three others" referred to by Mr. Drinker) similarly confided in their friends in China.

The two "Full Powers," authorizing Townsend Harris to conclude commercial treaties with Siam and Japan, are dated September 8, 1855, and are signed by President Franklin Pierce and by Secretary of State William L. Marcy. The special passport, signed by Secretary Marcy, is dated Sept. 12, 1855. (These three originals are at The College of the City of New York; *cf.* also *L. & P.*, vol. 1, no. 15.) The President's letters to the King of Siam and to the Emperor of Japan (countersigned by Secretary Marcy), are dated Sept. 12, 1855 (*L. & P.*, vol. 2, nos. 14 and 15). These five documents were sent to Townsend Harris enclosed in Secretary Marcy's Letter of Instructions, bearing date of Sept. 12, 1855, and directing him:

Firstly, to revise the existing treaty with Siam, concluded by Edmund Roberts on Mar. 20, 1833; and

Secondly, to make sure that missionaries from the United States would henceforth be free from molestation. (Dispatch No. 1 from the Department of State: *L. & P.*, vol. 2, no. 16.)

[11]Joseph Balestier, of Massachusetts. He was nominated U. S. Consul for Rhio, Island of Bintang, Malagan Sea, on Jan. 21, 1834; referred to the Committee on Commerce; consented to, Feb. 10, 1834 (Hasse, *Index*, pt. 3, p. 1720).

He was nominated U.S. Consul for Singapore, July 2, 1836; referred to Committee on Commerce; consented to, July 4, 1836; served in this capacity from 1836 to 1852 (*ib.*, p. 1712).

From Aug. 16, 1849, to Feb. 15, 1851, he acted as Special Commissioner of the

It was arranged between the State and Navy Departments, that the Steam Frigate *San Jacinto* would call at Penang, to which place I wished to proceed *overland,* and then take me to Siam and afterwards to Japan. I soon made the acquaintance of Commodore Armstrong[12] whose flag is on the *San Jacinto,* and Captain Bell[13] of the frigate. I put on board of her the presents for the Kings of Siam with my heavy luggage for Japan, with some few stores. I found the Commodore and Captain Bell very kind and accommodating, and I hope we shall prove to be good messmates.

October 17, 1855. Embark on board the steamer *Pacific,*[14] Captain Nye, for Liverpool. For reasons that

---

United States to Cochin China. Mr. Balestier's report to the Secretary of State of his unsuccessful efforts to conclude a commercial treaty with Siam is to be found in 32–1, S. Ex. Doc., no. 38—in Serial no. 618—a report which, ith the accompanying documents, fills 125 pages.

[12]Commodore James Armstrong: born at Shelbyville, Kentucky, Jan. 17, 1794. His official career was as follows: Midshipman, Nov. 15, 1809; Lieutenant, Apr. 27, 1816; Commander, Mar. 3, 1825; Captain, Sept. 8, 1841; Commodore, Retired List, Apr. 4, 1867; died, Aug. 25, 1868 (*cf.* Callahan, *List;* and T. H. S. Hamersly, *General Register*).

In 1814, he was captured by the British while serving in the *Frolic;* from 1855 to 1853, he commanded the East India Squadron, during which time (in 1857) he destroyed the Barrier Forts at Canton.

[13]Captain Henry Haywood Bell: born in Orange County, North Carolina, in 1808. His official career was as follows: Midshipman, Aug. 4, 1823; Passed midshipman, Mar. 23, 1829; Lieutenant, Mar. 3, 1831; Commander, Aug. 12, 1854; Commodore, July 16, 1862; Rear-Admiral, July 25, 1866; Retired List, Apr. 12, 1867; Drowned at the mouth of the Osaka River, Japan, Jan. 11, 1868. (*Cf.* Callahan, *op. cit.;* and Hamersly, *op. cit.*)

In early life he served on the *Grampus* in the expedition against the pirates on the coast of Cuba. In the destruction of the Barrier Forts at Canton, he commanded the *San Jacinto*. During the Civil War, he did distinguished service in the West Gulf blockading squadron under Admiral Farragut. In 1865, he commanded the East India Squadron with the rank of commodore.

[14]This steamer (300 feet long and 46 feet wide) was a ship of 3,500 tons. The New York *Tribune* of Thursday morning, Oct. 25, 1849, in reporting the installation of her engines the preceding day, speaks of her as the largest steamer in the world and the future monarch of the ocean.

I will omit, the voyage was the most unpleasant I ever made. From unavoidable exposure I took a violent cold on the 24th. We arrived at Liverpool at 2 A. M. of Sunday, October 28th. I visited Mr. and Mrs. Miller and Mr. and Mrs. Whittemore, and transacted some business with Messrs. Brown, Shipley & Co. and left for London at 4 P. M. of the 29th. Arrived at the Euston Square Station[15] and thence went to the Clarendon Hotel. I was very happy to meet here Colonel Osborne of the Madras Army, an old fellow passenger on the Indian side. The 30th and 31st were passed in arranging my money matters with the Messrs. Baring, calling on Mr. Buchanan[16] and making some small purchases.

November 1, 1855. Went to Paris via Dover and Calais, Lisle, Amiens, etc. etc. Reached Paris at 11 P. M. and went to the Hotel Meurice, where with great difficulty I got a room up 132 steps of staircase at five francs per day! I ordered some properly ornamented clothes to wear at the Court of Bangkok[17], etc. etc., and

---

[15]Townsend Harris arrived in London the same day—Monday, Oct. 29, 1855. (*L. & P.,* vol. 2, no. 119.)

[16]James Buchanan, then Minister to Great Britain, later President of the United States.

Townsend Harris called at the American Legation on Tuesday, Oct. 30, 1855. Among other reasons, he called to have his passport duly viséd—which was accordingly marked, *Bon pour La France,* and was signed by John Appleton, Secretary of Legation. On the same day, he visited also the Consulate General of France in London, and for the same purpose. His passport was here marked *Bon pour un an pour France.* The next day, Oct. 31, 1855, he paid Mr. Buchanan a visit of leave. (*Journal,* Monday, Mar. 9, 1857.)

By a strange coincidence, Buchanan was destined, as President of the United States, to receive officially, at Washington, the first Japanese Embassy that, in 1860 and at the instance of Townsend Harris himself, left the Island Empire for a visit to the Western countries—seeing America first.

[17]On a small scrap of blue paper (endorsed "Uniform Regulations"), Town-

purchased a good supply of shoes. I visited the great Exhibition, the Louvre and all the great collections of works of art, besides going to the opera as often as I could.

November 15, 1855. The great Exhibition was closed to-day, with all the imposing ceremonies that the French know so well how to arrange. On arriving in London I found the steamer for India was full and that a passage could not be had at any rate. I therefore took my passage by the steamer of the 20th from Southampton (I to go via Marseilles), although this will compel me to wait in Ceylon some fifteen days. I should have reached Penang just as soon by taking the steamer of the 4th of December, but I wished to avoid even the appearance of loitering, though, for that matter, the steamer of the 4th of January, 1856, would have taken me to Penang in ample time for the *San Jacinto*[18], as Captain Bell told me he did not expect to reach Penang before the 20th of February.

---

send Harris wrote the following memorandum of the uniform he was to wear at Court (*L. & P.*, vol. 2, no. 7):

UNIFORM

A blue coat lined with white silk, straight, standing collar embroider[e]d with gold, single breasted, straight or round button holes, slightly embroider[e]d—Navy button—cuffs embroider[e]d in the manner of the collar, white cassimere breeches, gold knee buckles, white silk stockings, and gold shoe buckles—a chapeau bras, black cockade and gold eagle—sword.

[18]The *San Jacinto* left New York for Pulo Penang on Oct. 25, 1855, eight days after Townsend Harris sailed on the *Pacific* (William Maxwell Wood, *Fankwei: or the* San Jacinto *in the Seas of India, China and Japan*, p. 15. London and New York, Harper & Bros., 1859). She arrived at her destination on Mar. 21, 1856, at 11 A. M., 149 days out from New York (*L. B.*, vol. 1, p. 14), having on board Mr. Heusken, Townsend Harris's Dutch Secretary for Japan, and the numerous presents for the two Kings of Siam and for the Emperor of Japan. (P. J. Treat, *The Early Diplomatic Relations between the United States and Japan*, p. 56.)

November 26, 1855. My cold, contracted in the *Pacific,* has not left me, indeed I do not know how it could, as I have only seen the sun twice since I have been in Paris,—fog, drizzle, rain, mud and misery. I am glad to start for the clean skies and bright suns of the tropics once more.

I called frequently on Mr. Mason[19] and Mr. McRae,[20] our Consul at Paris. I was most happy to meet Mr. Vesey,[21] our Consul for Havre, and Charles Huffnagle, Esq.,[22] United States Consul General for British India. The latter is an old Indian acquaintance, and we passed many happy hours together in Paris.

Mr. Huffnagle left on the 19th to go to the Crimea, promising to join me at Alexandria and so go on with me to Ceylon.

I left Paris early this evening and travelled all night

---

[19]John Young Mason, of Virginia: Apr. 18, 1799–Oct. 3, 1859; Envoy Extraordinary and Minister Plenipotentiary to France, 1853–59.

He was Secretary of the Navy (President Tyler), Mar. 14, 1844 to 1845; Attorney General (President Polk), Mar. 5, 1845, to Sept. 9, 1846; again Secretary of the Navy, Sept. 10, 1846–49; commissioned Minister to France (President Pierce), Oct. 10, 1853; nominated Minister on Dec. 6, 1853, in place of William C. Rives, who was recalled at his own request; died at his post in Paris, Oct. 3, 1859. (Hasse, *Index,* pt. 3, p. 1798, and *Encycl. Brit.*)

[20]D. K. McRae, of North Carolina, Consul at Paris, 1854–55.

He was nominated on Feb. 4, 1854, in place of S. G. Goodrich, recalled; consented to, Feb. 13, 1854. (Hasse, *Index,* pt. 3, p. 1723.)

[21]William H. Vesey, of New York, Consul for Havre, France, 1853–59.

He was nominated Consul on Mar. 9, 1853, in place of L. Draper, recalled; reported, Mar. 14th; consented to, Mar. 21st. (Hasse, *Index,* pt. 3, p. 1722.)

[22]Charles Huffnagle, of Pennsylvania.

He was nominated Consul for Calcutta on Dec. 22, 1847, in place of J. B. Higginson, recalled; reported, Dec. 23, 1847; consented to, Jan. 3, 1848; served till 1853.

He was nominated Consul General for British India on Mar 7, 1853; renominated, July 7, 1856; consented to, July 31, 1856; served till 1861. (Hasse, *Index,* pt. 3, p. 1704.)

to Marseilles—passing Lyons, Vienne, Avignon, etc., etc.,—arriving at 5 P. M. Next day called at the American Consulate—the Consul, Mr. Hodge,[23] I left in Paris. Got my passport, etc., *en regle* and finally left Marseilles on the 29th. The new harbor of Marseilles is a noble work; passed quite close to the celebrated Chateau d'If or Monte Cristo's Island. I am in the *Vectis,* a small but very fast steamer which is commanded by Captain Norris, an old China acquaintance.

November 29, 1855. Pass between Corsica and Sardinia and have a fine view of both islands, and on the morning of the 30th we see the coast of Sicily. Pass the Island of Maritima, celebrated for its prison for political offenders of the olden time. It looks bad enough, but it is a pleasure garden when compared with Aden. Have a capital view of the town of Marsala and afterwards some other places on the coast,—coast high and picturesque. At 3 P. M. passed Girgenti, and on the 30th of November at 6 A. M. reached Malta. Called at once on Mr. Winthrop,[24] U. S. Consul; afterwards went on another pilgrimage to the noble church of St. John and to the ramparts of Cività Vecchia.

---

[23]J. L. Hodge, of Pennsylvania, Consul for Marseilles from 1850 to 1856.

He was nominated Consul on Jan. 4, 1850, in place of D. C. Croxall, recalled; reported, Aug. 2, 1850; consented to, Aug. 27, 1850. (Hasse, *Index,* pt. 3, p. 1722.)

[24]William Winthrop, of Massachusetts, Consul for Malta from 1834 to 1869.

William Winthrop was the same individual as W. W. Andrews. As Andrews, he was nominated Consul on Dec. 10, 1834, in place of P. Eynard, removed; referred to the Committee on Commerce, Dec. 15, 1834; consented to Dec. 30, 1834. He changed his name to William Winthrop about Sept. 2, 1845; died at his post, July 3, 1869. (Hasse, *Index,* pt. 3, p. 1709.)

The U. S. Frigate *Constellation* left yesterday for Sicily. We leave at noon for Alexandria.

December 4, 1855. We reached Alexandria at 3 P. M. and am sorry to learn my friend Huffnagle has not arrived, so I shall lose his agreeable company. Mr. De Leon,[25] the U. S. Consul General for Egypt, is in Cairo. The Vice-Consul called on me in the evening.

December 5, 1855. Leave Alexandria per railway at 7 A. M. for Cafferlis. Had we been one day later we should have been able to go all the way to Cairo by rail, which would have been more agreeable than the small dirty Nile steamers. The steamer from Southampton (November 20th) reached Alexandria one hour before us. This shows that a person saves eight days by going to the East via Marseilles. Among my fellow passengers is the Hon. Chisholm Anstey,[26] late M.P., now Attorney General for Hongkong, and Mr. Gregory, M. P. for Dublin, both agreeable persons. Arrived at Cafferlis at half-past ten and did not leave till half-past twelve. A

---

[25]Edwin De Leon, of South Carolina, Consul General for Alexandria, Egypt, from 1854 to 1861.

He was nominated Consul General on Feb. 4, 1854, in place of R. B. Jones, recalled; reported, Feb. 13, 1854; consented to, Apr. 18, 1854. (Hasse, *Index*, pt. 3, p. 1752.)

He was author, journalist, and diplomat. Born May 4, 1818, in Charleston, South Carolina, he resigned his office in 1861 in order to go with the Confederacy. In his *Thirty Years of My Life on Three Continents,* he gives many pleasing reminiscences of distinguished persons whom he met in Europe and in the East. He died in New York City, Dec. 1, 1891. (*Nat. Cycl. Amer. Biogr.*, vol. 4, p. 94.)

[26]The Hon. Thomas Chisholm Anstey, 1816 to Aug. 12, 1873. After a stormy career in English home politics, which scarcely gave him any claim to government office, he was none the less appointed Attorney General for Hongkong in 1854. His endeavors to reform radically the entire administration of Hongkong brought him into serious collision with Sir John Bowring, the Governor; and finally, in 1858, he was suspended from his post by Sir John—a suspension later confirmed by the home government. (*Dict. Nat. Biogr.*)

most unpleasant trip—steamer small, dirty and crowded; and, going upstream, do not reach Cairo until half-past two on the next morning. I found Mr. De Leon at the hotel and am indebted to him for a most agreeable day. Revisited the Citadel, Tomb of Mehemet Ali, and some of the chief bazaars. Leave Cairo at midnight.

December 7, 1855. Reached Suez at 4 P. M. and, after three hours' search after luggage, I go on board the fine steamer *Bengal*. I had applied for a sofa when I was in London, but they were all engaged and I was compelled to take an upper berth, which is very unpleasant in a hot climate. I was most agreeably surprised, on going on board, at being told that sofa No. 95 was assigned to me—one of the best places and cabins in the ship. I find a large and pleasant company on board; but the steamer is so large and roomy and so well ventilated, that we are very comfortable. I here meet Mr. Stirling, late Attorney General for Hongkong, who is going to Ceylon as Puisne[27] Judge. He has Mrs. and Miss Stirling with him. Among the passengers whose names I wish to preserve were Mr. Mitford, Civil Judge, Ceylon; Major Durand,[28] Bengal Engineers; General Lockyer, Commander of the forces, Ceylon, with his amiable wife and daughters. We left Suez during the night.

The sunsets in the Red Sea are glorious beyond any description I can give. At 5 P. M. the atmosphere appears to be composed of liquid gold—more glorious even than

---

[27]Junior, younger or inferior judge. From the old French *puis-né;* Latin, *post natus,* meaning therefore "born later," and giving our English word "puny."

[28]Sir Henry Marion Durand, 1812–1871. (See *Dict. Nat. Biogr.*)

Turner's landscapes which excited so much criticism. It then changes to green, violet, purple and other hues that make a combination "that must be seen to be appreciated."

December 13, 1855. Off Mocha; pass the Calcutta steamer *Oriental* bound to Suez. She is forty-eight hours behind her time. Have a capital view of Mocha. I omitted to state that both in going up in June last, and now in coming down the Red Sea, I had a very good view of the peak of Mount Sinai and of Mount Hor.

Arrive at Aden December 8th, 8 A. M. I did not intend to land, but at nine o'clock I received a letter from Mr. Alley, an American who has established himself here in business. He invited me to his house and said his carriage was waiting for me at the wharf. I accepted his kind offer and passed some hours very pleasantly with him. We left Aden at half-past two P. M. with a fresh breeze from the south. Thermometer 81°. What a contrast to my visit here last June!

Sunday, December 16, 1855. Divine service in the morning by Mr. Brown of the Scotch Kirk, and in the afternoon by the Rev. Mr. Daintree, son of the Bishop of Madras. Among our passengers, beside those noted before, are Colonel Chester, Bengal; Colonel Spottiswood,[29] do.; Major Tombs,[30] Bengal Cavalry; Mr. Farquarson, Bengal Civil Service; and Captain Crish, of Maulmain. A Miss De Quincey, daughter or sister (?) of the "Opium Eater"; she is going out to India to meet

---

[29] Arthur Cole Spottiswoode, 1808–74. (See *Dict. Nat. Biogr.*)
[30] Sir Henry Tombs, 1824–74. (*Ib.*)

her betrothed. She has a sweet voice and sings charmingly. I shall long remember her intelligent face.

Miss Stirling gave the following as a good reason for. not marrying: E. E. xx Matrimony, e e XX.

December 24, 1855. At 6:30 anchor off Point-de-Galle to wait for daylight. The next morning I take leave of Captain Black of the *Bengal,* with thanks for his attentions, and go on shore and proceeded to my old quarters at Bogar's Mansion House. Call on Captain and Mrs. McDonald. The *Bengal* leaves for Madras and Calcutta at 5 P. M. I dine with Dr. Clarke (LL.D.), Acting Judge. The guests, besides myself, were Judge Mitford, Mr. Clarke, the Presbyterian clergyman, Mr. Black,[31] U. S. Consul, and wife. Mr. Clarke is a tee-totaler,—of which class the number is increasing in the East. While in France I drank the delightful mild wine of the South, but after leaving Marseilles I came back to my old Asiatic habit—tea and cold water.

December 26, 1855. Call on John Black, Esq., U. S. Consul—he [was] absent at Colombo. Saw Mrs. Black and her three fine children. Afterwards I see Staff Surgeon Cowen and the Rev. Mr. Garstin, Colonial Chaplain, and Mr. W. C. Forbes, all of whom called on *me first.* What a difference a *title* of office makes in this world of ours! Mr. Forbes invited me to dine with him on New Year's Day, which I accepted.

December 27, 1855. Breakfast *chez moi.* Afterwards go to reading room, where my name has been kindly inscribed. See a grand match at billiards played between

---

[31]John Black (*cf.* entry for Dec. 26, 1855).

Major Lilly, Commander at Point-de-Galle, and Captain Vanderspaar, of the Ceylon Rifles. A deal of betting by the players and bystanders. How fond the English are of a bet! Home to dine and early to bed. Sleep well. *December 28, 1855.* Breakfast and dine with Captain and Mrs. McDonald, my old Hongkong friends. They kindly give me a standing invitation to breakfast with them every day and also to dine, when they are not engaged out themselves.

Write to Judge Mitford and J. O'Halloran, Esq. Mr. H. Sonnerkalb, Consul for Hamburg, called on me today.

Friday, Saturday and Sunday, December 28, 29 and 30, 1855. Did not leave the hotel. Read *The Newcomes.* This, like the other works of Thackeray, leaves a very unpleasant sensation. In his eyes the whole world is base, black and faithless; he ignores everything like benevolent action based on principle, and disbelieves any other motive of action than egoism. On Monday the 31st the steamer from Calcutta for Suez comes in. Mr. Baker, formerly of the Sandwich Islands and now of Calcutta, desires to be remembered to S. N. Greene,[32] (fat Sam), of Penang. Write to N. Dougherty of New York.[33]

---

[32]Samuel N. Greene, an intimate friend of Townsend Harris, of whom we shall hear more later. He was a business partner of Charles C. Currier, U.S. Consul at Penang. (Wood, *op. cit.,* p. 133.) Mr. Greene's wife and two children sailed for Scotland on the P. & O. *Malabar* on Oct. 22, 1859 (*L. & P.,* vol. 1, no. 256). He was a cousin of Captain W. C. Nicholson, of the U.S.S. *Mississippi.* (*Ib.*)

[33]Nathaniel Dougherty, a very intimate friend of Townsend Harris. He served as Townsend Harris's clerk while the latter was in the earthenware business in New York from Oct., 1838, till the winter of 1847–48. (See Nathan-

Monday, December 31, 1855. The steamer from China comes in. Hear of the death of Commodore Abbott,[34] U. S. N., at Hongkong. Call on Mrs. Black and Mrs. McDonald.

Go to reading room; look over China and India newspapers; return *The Newcomes,* and take out *The Caxtons.*

January 1, 1856. Happy New Year! I would much like to be in New York to-day to call on the few friends that Death has left me. This bids fair to be an important year to me. I have important matters entrusted to my charge, and, *if I am successful,* I may connect my name with the history of my country. But, if unsuccessful, no matter what ability I may display in my negotiations, I shall sink just as much in proportion as I should rise if successful. In other words, the world judges solely by results. *Finis coronat opus* is the motto of our day and generation. The steamer from China *(Norna)* sailed for Bombay at 6:30 A. M.

Call on Captain and Mrs. McDonald. Finish and return *The Caxtons.* How much the later works of Bulwer excel his early productions; what a difference in the

---

iel Dougherty's letter to General Prosper M. Wetmore, dated New York, Mar. 24, 1855, now in the files of the Bureau of Appointments, Washington, D. C.) During the early part of 1847 Townsend Harris devoted very much of his time to the establishment of The College of the City of New York, to the neglect of his own business. He resigned as president of the Board of Education of New York City by letter dated Jan. 26, 1848, and in May, 1849, sailed for California. Mr. Dougherty continued independently as an importer of earthenware at 101 Water Street, New York; and during Townsend Harris's absence in Japan frequently acted as his American agent in financial matters. (*L. B.,* and *L. & P., passim.*)

[34]Commodore Joel Abbott, of Massachusetts; died at Hongkong, Dec. 14, 1855. (Hasse, *Index,* pt. 1, p. 7.)

morals and philosophy of *My Novel* and *The Caxtons* and that of *Pelham, Eugene Aram, Paul Clifford,* etc., etc. Dine with Mr. Forbes, Governor's Agent for this place. His bungalow is outside the Fort, on a pretty hill overlooking the Fort and Harbor. Met Captain and Mrs. McDonald, Major Lilly and two subaltern officers. These military men cannot talk anything but *shop.* The Indian officers are, many of them, much better informed than those of Her Majesty's service. The latter talk only of horses, dogs, billiards and cards—that is, beyond the gossip of the regiment and station.

Mrs. Forbes is a very charming person, daughter of a judge, born and educated in Ceylon; she has never been one hundred and fifty miles from her birthplace, yet she is well informed and most pleasing in her manners. The dinner was somewhat different from the usual English one in the colonies. A great number of excellent Cingalese *plates* made their appearance: among others, the *cabbage,* as it is called, of the cocoanut tree, dressed half a dozen different ways,—the meat of the cocoanut which has just begun to germinate, in which state the cavity is quite filled up with a sweet, crisp, vegetable substance that is quite agreeable. The Malay curries of Mrs. Forbes were unexceptionable. *Hulwah,* an Arab sweetmeat, made of rice, sugar and camel's milk, figured at the dessert among a regiment of Cingalese and Hindostanee preparations of fruit and sugar.

January 2, 1856. I meet for the first time with the works of the Rev. C. Kingsley: *Alton Locke, Yeast, Hypatia,* and *Westward Ho!* I shall read these. I took

37

out the *Adventures in the Punjab* by Major H. M. Lawrence, the most remarkable man of India at the present day. He resembles Lord Clive in energy, fertility of resources and indomitable courage, while he has none of the vices that stained the glory of Clive. Also took [out] *Anti-Coningsby.*[35]

January 3, 1856. Up at 5 A. M. and go out to a rock temple (*wiharree*), sitting and recumbent figures of Budh—the last, twenty-five feet long. Plenty of the sacred *tulsi* of the Hindoos growing here. This plant is the "sweet basil" of Europe and America—the purple variety. The Hindoo legend is that "Tulasi," beloved of Krishna, was changed by him into this plant. The first avatar of Vishnu was in the form of a fish, and a fish forms a part of the Royal Arms of the Great Mogul, the King of Oude, and other potentates of the East. When a new Governor General comes out to India, that "shadow of a shade," the "Great Mogul," presents him with a patent of nobility giving him various titles, among others that of "Bahaudor"[36] or "Lord of the Sword." This patent bears the impress of two crossed fishes as a seal. Sacred trees here, as in India, are decorated with red and yellow flags. I cannot but admire the brilliancy and blue tinge of Sirius, the Dog Star, as seen both in India and Egypt. It shines more brightly than Venus with us. Major Durand told me that when he was stationed at

---

[35]*Coningsby: or The New Generation* is the title of a novel written in 1844 by Benjamin Disraeli, Earl of Beaconsfield.

[36]*Bahaudor,* or *Bahadur*: an Anglo-Indian title of ceremony, given to European officers in India State papers; or to high officials, in the common language of Hindus and Mahommedans.

Peshawur, in the Punjab, he had frequently seen the hour by his watch from the light of this star. It is the most agreeable in idea of all the host that was worshipped by the ancient Egyptians, who called him Anubis, and he figures as a Dog-headed Deity. The Hindoos say that the constellation Rishi—our Great Bear—is composed of seven Hindoo Fakeers, who were so placed by Siva or Ram.

The *Neem* tree (Persian lilac) is planted near the temples; leaves are on racemes; are pointed, about three inches long by half an inch wide. In appearance it is like our mountain ash; when in flower, the fragrance is charming. Here also is the henna tree—*Mendee* in Hindostanee. It is the *Lawsonia* of botanists. The leaves are small and the flowers are like those of the clematis; if placed close to the nose, they have an unpleasant vegetable smell, but at a short distance the perfume is charming. The henna dye is produced by bruising the leaves and moistening them with water and lime juice. When applied to the nails and palms, it produces a bright orange tint. The extraordinary custom of *polyandry,—i.e.,* one woman having several husbands,—is practised in Ceylon and also in Thibet and parts of Nepal. The husbands are usually (but not always) brothers, and exercise their marital rights for one week at a time. On the road from Point-de-Galle to Colombo, the rest house where coach passengers breakfast is kept by three Cingalese brothers, who have one wife. On stopping there the second time, I asked the woman which she would like the best: to be one of many wives to one man, the sole wife of one man, or her present situation. She spat at the idea of polygamy, shook her head at a single union, and was emphatic in praise of polyandry. After some pressing she said the youngest of her husbands was her favorite, but that all were kind to her.

January 4, 1856. Major Lilly invites me to dine with him to-morrow. At reading room; finish Guizot's *Charles I,* and first volume of *Coningsby.* Lieutenant Griffith, R.N., and Admiralty Mail Agent, is a fellow lodger at the hotel with me. He is an enthusiast with the microscope, examining flowers, flies, beetles, etc., etc.

January 5, 1856. Finish *Coningsby* and *Anti-Coningsby;* query, Who wrote the latter work? Dine with Major Lilly. Guests: Captain McDonald, Judge Clarke, Mr. Forbes, Mr. Sonnerkalb and Mr. Vanderspaar. Left at 10 P.M., leaving the whole party playing short whist at sovereign points. I never bet on any game of chance—not even sixpenny points, and the older I grow the more am I satisfied with this resolution which I took some eight years since.

Sunday, January 6, 1856. At church, where, to my surprise and annoyance, I found myself occupying a "high place in the synagogue." Dr. Garstin gave a capital sermon. Dined at the McDonalds. Yesterday I took from the library Kay's *Life of Lord Metcalf;* a very readable book.

Monday, January 7, 1856. Steamer *Cadiz* from Bombay for China arrived. By this steamer I shall proceed to Penang, where I am to be taken up by the *San*

Jacinto, but the *Cadiz* must wait the arrival of the steamer from Suez to take the mail on to Penang, Singapore and China. Went on board the *Cadiz* and found my old friend Captain Baker. Captain Franceville and Mr. Newman (Americans) are passengers.

Tuesday, January 8, 1856. Returned *Life of Lord Metcalf.* Write to A. H. Fryer, my kind host at Colombo in 1854, during my visit to that part of Ceylon. Mr. Ronaine, Collector of this Port, was introduced to me to-day. Call on Mrs. McDonald, Mr. Clarke, Major Lilly, and the Rev. Dr. Garstin. Ride with the Collector to Garstin's hill, where he has a pretty bungalow, beautifully placed, charming views from all sides of it.

Dine with Mr. Sonnerkalb, Hamburg Consul.

January 9, 1856. Mr. Ronaine takes me out for a drive. It was charming and such an one as only can be found in the tropics. Palms of every kind shaded our road. The bright sweet-scented flowers were seen on all sides; bright plumaged birds flitted about, and monkeys mimed and grimaced at us on all sides. Our road lay across a stream over which the government engineer had thrown what *he* called an American truss-bridge; but, from some slight errors in his architecture, the bridge, instead of presenting a fair level roadway, formed an *inverted arch* of rather steep descents and ascents. It is a crazy looking affair, and I was glad when I was safely over it. Dine with Mr. Black, U.S. Consul; Captain Baker, Rev. Dr. Garstin and Mr. Ronaine were the guests. It is the custom of all who do not ride

41

or drive out to walk on the ramparts from half-past five to six P.M. The views are beautiful and you have a fine fresh air. I always walk here unless occupied by a drive.

Thursday, January 10, 1856. Breakfast at Captain McDonald's and dine with Mr. Forbes. It is a shame to *nembu* a dinner, no matter how good, when the table is graced by such a woman as Mrs. Forbes, but I must say that her dinners, for my palate, excel all I have partaken of in Ceylon.

Friday, January 11, 1856. Mr. Forbes drives me out to the Paramendr *wiharree*. The High Priest Darmasalmkase Sirisoman Tisse is a clever man. He showed me a number of letters from the First King of Siam *written in English* by the King himself, and a number of presents from him. The High Priest has some curious books in the Pali character, inscribed on leaves of the talipot palm, with a steel style. After thus *engraving* the letters, the surface is rubbed over with blue, red or black, according to taste; and, falling into the marks of the style, the letters remain of the color of the powder applied. This priest built the Burmese wat at Ayer-Etam, Pulo Penang. He speaks Cingalese, Burmese and Malay, and understands English very well—altogether an uncommon man. I had a good deal of conversation with him,—he answering my English by Malay. He said he would not take life under any circumstances; that, if threatened by a cobra capello or tiger, he would not attempt to secure [his life] by destroying either of them; that if it were God's will that he should escape

42

or die, that will would take effect notwithstanding *his* efforts. He said he would not catch a fish or kill a fowl, yet he would eat of both when they were cooked for him; that the sin lay not in the eating but in the slaying. In answer to my remark, that if there were no eaters of fish or fowl none would be killed, he said those things were settled by an overruling power. The Cingalese use the sacred *Aum* of the Hindoos. This word is composed of the initial letters of the three unknown and ineffable names of the Deity. In Thibet the lamas use *Aum, mani pani aum,*[37] and also *Aum! mani pami aum! Heu! jemma lotus heu!* The Chinese use *Aum meto Foo! Amidah Budh!*[38] repeating these thousands of times; and this dull repetition forms the principal occupation of the life of a Chinese recluse. When I was wandering among the picturesque hills and the sacred groves of Tien-Tung in China, I came one day to a hermitage seated high up the gorge of the hills. A little streamlet of water ran near it, and made everything verdant in its vicinity. On approaching the hermitage, its tenant, a pleasant looking old man, came out and saluted me kindly.

On looking about I saw a little water-wheel, such as boys make from shingles in America, placed over the brook, where it was revolving merrily.

---

[37]Still another form of this formula is *Om mani padme hum*—which "by repetition bars the door of the various worlds of delusion and permits pure meditation": Talbot Mundy, *Om, The Secret of Ahbor Valley,* pp. 274 (especially the nòte) and 289.

[38]The Chinese form of this invocation to Buddha is given as *O-me-to-Fuh* in Jos. Hergesheimer's *Java Head,* pp. 84-85. (New York, Knopf, 1919.)

I could not help smiling, as it brought back my boyish days when I used to construct similar pieces of machinery. On looking at it closely, I discovered that the gudgeon or shaft was square, and that it had Chinese characters on each of its four sides, and a further examination showed the inscription to be the same on all the sides. Through my Chinese servant I asked for an explanation and was told that the characters stood for *Aum meto Foo—Amidah Budh,* and that, when the wheel revolved, each time one of its square sides came up, it answered the same as if it had been uttered by the priest; in other words, that he was praying by water. I believe wind wheels are used for a similar purpose.

I may here remark that, while the Chinese Buddhists have retained the *sound* of these pious ejaculations, they have entirely lost the meaning of the words, and this remark will apply to all the books they have in the Pali character. They have preserved the sound by writing it in Chinese, but the sense is lost. The same has taken place with the Mahometans at Ningpo with the *Koran,* and with the Jews and the *Pentateuch.*

The following lines, translated from a Cingalese poet, show that females do not occupy a high position in their estimation:

> I've seen the *udumber* tree in *flower;*
> *White* plumage on the *crow;*
> And *fishes' footsteps* o'er the *deep,*
> I've seen through ebb and flow;

44

If man it is who this asserts,
His word you may believe;
But all that woman says, distrust,
She speaks but to deceive.

The *udumber,* almost alone of the Cingalese trees, *never blooms.* In my wanderings in almost every part of the world I have applied one test, which I find to be unvarying, and that is, that the social position of women in any nation will indicate the amount of its civilization. Therefore, given her social status and you can at once find the mental state of the men.

Saturday, January 12, 1856. No steamer yet from Aden. The *Oriental* is now five days behind her time. Captain Bond of Madras Artillery desires to be remembered to Captains Danen and Macpherson at Penang. Captain Bond is ordered to the Tennessarim provinces at a post back of Maulmain. At library from 11 A.M. to 5 P.M. Steamer from Suez arrived at 11:30 P.M.

Sunday, January 13, 1856. Meet my friend Huffnagle; take him to breakfast at Captain McDonald's. At noon good-bye to all kind friends at Galle, and go on board the *Cadiz* and start for Penang; not crowded. Among the passengers are the Hon. Chisholm Anstey and Captain Twiss, R.A.,[39] both for Hongkong. Captain Twiss is a son of Horace Twiss, a former Tory whipper-in and small poet. I am most happy to meet

---

[39]The father, Horace Twiss, lived from 1787 to 1849. He married twice, and his only son (by his second wife) was Quintin William Francis Twiss, who therefore must be the Twiss here mentioned by Townsend Harris. (*Dict. Nat. Biogr.*)

45

my old friend the Bishop of Batavia, on his return with his health quite restored.

Thursday, January 17, 1856. We have beautiful weather, and expect to be up to Pulo Rondo (off north end of Sumatra) by midnight.

The Bishop has told me some wonderful stories, among others that not long since a soldier bathing in the river at Samarang, Java, suddenly cried out and hastened on shore, when, to his horror, he found the *head* only of a very venomous snake was fastened to his thigh. The head had the appearance of having been recently severed from the body of the snake. All possible aid was given to the poor man, but all was in vain; he died shortly after being bitten. Not long after the man was bitten, the headless body of the snake was seen floating down with the tide. Further inquiry discovered that the snake had been killed some hours before the accident by a native who, having severed its head, threw the head and body into the river. A good *snaik* story!

The Bishop said the sagacity of the elephants in Sumatra was very surprising, for when they heard the sound of the beating out of rice, which is done with a heavy *pestle* in a species of trough or canoe made of a very hard and resonant wood, the elephants would approach the place and, if only a few women were present, they would drive them away and devour the paddy! Well done, Bishop!

Friday, January 18, 1856. The Portuguese Governor of Timor is a passenger with us. I give to Mr. Anstey a parcel for Mrs. Drinker of Macao, which I received from Mr. Walker at New York. Write to Mrs. Drinker,[40] and Armstrong and Lawrence of Hongkong.[41]

Saturday, January 19, 1856. Arrive at Penang at 8 P.M. I am at once approached by my old friend Currier's *khansamar*,[42] who cannot salaam me enough or express his happiness at seeing me. I leave him in charge of my luggage, take leave of my fellow passengers, and at the jetty am received in the most cordial manner by Mr. Currier. On arriving at the house I find the whole family paraded to welcome me. *Bhusties*,[43] *syces*,[44] *bobbachees*,[45] bearers, *misaulchers, kitmagars*,[46]

---

[40]The Drinkers were Townsend Harris's dearest friends. The Mrs. Drinker here referred to was Mrs. Susannah Budd Drinker, the wife of Mr. Sandwith Drinker, a captain and sailor of the old school. Townsend Harris knew intimately their four little children, mentioned in his letters as "Kate," "Harry," "Mortie," and "Elizabeth"—the last born in China while Townsend Harris was in Japan. The little "Harry" mentioned in Townsend Harris's correspondence is (1928) the President Emeritus of Lehigh University; "Mortie" is Morton, who became a student of divinity; while "Kate," with whom Townsend Harris carried on a voluminous correspondence (unfortunately destroyed by fire during a spring house-cleaning), was Catherine Ann Drinker, who became the wife of Thomas Allibone Janvier, and who died July 19, 1922

[41]Bankers. At the end of 1856 this firm was dissolved and was succeeded by the firm of Davis & Lawrence, the new member having been bookkeeper with the banking house of Wetmore & Co., of Canton, which had branches at Shanghai, Foo-Chau, and New York (*Journal*, July 17, 1856), and which had recently failed. *L. & P.*, vol. 1, no. 62.)

[42]*Khansamar* (or: *khansamah, khansuma, consumah, consumar*): an Anglo-Indian word meaning a servant combining the functions of house steward and butler. (*Funk & Wagnalls.*)

[43]*Bhusties* (or: *bheestee, beastee, beestie, bheestie, bheesty*): an Anglo-Indian word meaning a water-carrier, especially one who furnishes water for domestic purposes, carrying it from the tanks in skins. (*Ib.*)

[44]*Syces* (or: *saice, sice, sais*): a groom or horseman's attendant; a horse-keeper. (*Ib.*)

[45]*Bobbachee* (or: *bobachee*): a male cook. (*Ib.*)

[46]*Kitmagars* (or: *kitmutgar, khitmutgar, kitmudgar*): a table servant; an underbutler. (*Ib.*)

and even the poor old *mehter*[47] with the grass cutters were there and help to swell the chorus of *Slamat Allah!! Tuom! Tuom!* etc., etc.[48]

It was not unpleasant to be thus welcomed at the antipodes of New York.

Find three Americans at Mr. Currier's: Captain Hollis and Captain Parker of the American ships *Chilo* and *Daniel Sharpe,* also a Mr. Dow.

Sunday, January 20, 1856. Visit Père Martin[49] at the Cochin-Chinese College; am warmly welcomed by him and his confrères.

Afterwards call at Mrs. Wallace's and T. Mitchell's.

Monday, January 21, 1856. Call on W. T. Lewis, Esq., President Councillor and Acting Governor. Afterwards on Mrs. Rose, Madame du Thune, Mrs. Palmer (who has become a widow since I left here), Mr. Mitchell Sr., Captain Danen of the Artillery, Commandant of Fort Cornwallis; Captain Cross, an

---

[47]*Mehter* (or: *mehtar*): in the original Persian, this word meant a high official in the royal household; here it means a groom or house-sweeper. (*Ib.*)

[48]*Slamat:* a corruption of the Arabic greeting from one Mahommedan to another—a different form of salutation being used to a non-Mahommedan. The usual greeting was: *As-salam 'alaikum*—Peace be unto you; to which the obligatory reply was: *Wa-'alaikum as-salam*—And unto you peace. (*New Int. Encycl.*)

[49]Père N. Martin, head of the Roman Catholic Collège Général at Penang. We know very little about him. In the manuscript *Letters and Papers* of Townsend Harris, there is extant only one letter, and that one is written by P. Martin to Townsend Harris, who was then at Shanghai, on a short visit from Japan. This French letter (*L. & P.*, vol. I, no. 159) is dated Penang, Apr. 27, 1859. It describes P. Martin's visit to the U.S.S. *Powhatan,* which had entered the harbor of Penang to await the arrival of the United States Commissioner to China; it gives news of the different members of the Collège Général, consisting of six teachers and 129 pupils; and announces the victories in Cochin China of the French forces commanded by Vice-Admiral Rigault de Genouilly, etc., etc.

For a short description of the Roman Catholic Mission at Penang, see Wood, *op. cit.,* pp. 137–38; and *Journal,* Jan. 27, 1856.

48

old Indian veteran, seventy-nine years old, has been in India sixty-three years and rose from the ranks, fought under Wellington, has led three forlorn hopes, has been active in storming some thirty fortresses and in more than a hundred actions, or rather under fire more than a hundred times. A noble-minded man, with the simplicity and kindliness of a child. He is now enjoying an extra pension, the just reward of his long service and universal good conduct. Afterwards [call] on Captain Clarke, another veteran who has risen from the ranks, but not so old as Captain Cross.

Tuesday, January 22, 1856. Visit Père Bigandet,[50] George [Charles] Scott of Ayer Rajah, Walter Scott at Scotland Nutmeg Gardens, and Alexander Brown of Sans Souci.

Wednesday, January 23, 1856. It is the custom for the stranger arriving at any place in the East which is held by the English to make the first visit. If he does not do so, it is considered that he declines going into society. It is many times excessively awkward for the poor stranger, who is entirely ignorant of the family he visits, their tastes, habits, etc., etc., but he dashes on and runs through the list his resident friends have given him of people he *must visit*.

Called to-day on Mr. Caunter, Mr. Nairne, Captain Mann, two Captains Hazlett, Ensign Dickson, Rev. Mr. Bland and Captain Boulderson.

---

[50]In *Journal,* Mar. 30, 1856, Townsend Harris tells us that Père Bigandet was that day consecrated a bishop *in partibus infidelibus,* and that he was soon to leave for Burmah. Père Martin, in his letter to Townsend Harris (*L. & P.,* vol. 1, no. 159), adds: *"Mgs. Bigandet est à Rangoon."*

January 24, 1856. Home and wrote letters to W. L. Marcy,[51] Joseph Evans,[52] Mrs. Langlois, Mrs. Drinker, Heerjeebhoy Rustumjee, S. Drinker, D. J. Macgowan[53] and P. M. Wetmore.[54]

Miss Lewis, daughter of W. T. Lewis, Resident Councillor, died yesterday and was buried to-day at 5 P. M.

Friday, January 25, 1856. The steamer *Madras* with the mails from China arrived this morning. Get letters from Mrs. Drinker, Kate Drinker, S. Drinker, and Dr. Macgowan.

------

[51] William L. Marcy, Secretary of State of the United States. The letter referred to is to be found in *L. B.,* vol. 1, p. 12. The two chief items of this letter are: first, that before leaving the United States he had upon the recommendation of the Rev. Dr. De Witt and others of New York, appointed Mr. Heusken of New York to be his Dutch interpreter for Japan at $1,500 per annum and free passage to Japan, "he paying his mess," while Townsend Harris advanced him $750; and second, that the English officers he had met on his journey to the Far East had condemned the spirit and the tone of anti-American articles in the London *Times,* and that they "deprecated even the idea of a war between the two countries."

[52] Mentioned elsewhere in the *Journal.* In a letter to Townsend Harris dated Deshima, Feb. 18, 1859 (*L. & P.,* vol. 1, no. 142), Mr. Jan Hendrik Donker Curtius, the Netherlands Minister to Japan, speaks of the English and the American firms that were establishing themselves at Nagasaki; and he mentions Mr. Joseph Evans as the Nagasaki agent of Dent & Co., of Shanghai.

[53] Daniel Jerome Macgowan, a medical missionary to China, sent out by the American Baptist Union, of Boston, Massachusetts. He had already spent many years in China when Townsend Harris appointed him Vice-Consul for the treaty port of Ningpo, China. It will be remembered that Townsend Harris was then at Penang, and that, instead of going to Ningpo, he returned to the United States and obtained the appointment of Consul General to Japan.

In the *Letters and Papers* of Townsend Harris there are numerous letters by Dr. Macgowan, clearly describing the difficulties of trying to be a missionary, a consul, and a general translator at the same time, until he was driven, on June 22, 1855, to send in his resignation to Secretary Marcy and to Townsend Harris (*L. & P.,* vol. 1, nos. 8 and 9). It was later the ambition of his life to have Townsend Harris appoint him to some post in Japan—the sealed empire to the east of China.

[54] General Prosper M. Wetmore, an exceedingly prominent citizen of "little old New York," and one of the men who had exerted themselves to obtain Townsend Harris's appointment to Japan.

Write to C. W. Bradley, Esq., U.S. Consul at Singapore.[55]

Mr. Murphy,[56] U.S. Consul at Shanghai, is a passenger by the *Madras*. He called on me and informs me that he is on his way to the United States.

Saturday, January 26, 1856. The steamer *Lightning* arrived from Calcutta at 7 P.M. She brought me a letter from S. Drinker at Canton dated December 15, 1855, and sent per steamer *Fiery Cross*,[57] but, as she did not stop here, the letter went on to Calcutta. The *Lightning* leaves to-morrow at 6 A. M.

Sunday, January 27, 1856. At St. George's Church this morning. The Rev. Mr. Bland, Colonial Chaplain, officiated. I never was so much displeased at church as this morning.

From *gross affectation* Mr. Bland sank his voice so low that I could not hear one word in twenty though

[55]Charles William Bradley, Sr., of Connecticut. Consul for Amoy, 1849–54. He was nominated on Jan. 26, 1849, in place of T. S. Peachey, resigned; consented to, Feb. 7, 1849. (Hasse, *Index*, pt. 3, p. 1714.) He was nominated Consul for Ningpo on Jan. 23, 1854; consented to, Jan. 31, 1854. (Hasse, *Index*, pt. 3, p. 1716.) He was nominated Consul for Singapore on Mar. 8, 1854, in place of J. H. Adams, declined; consented to, Mar. 14, 1854. (*Ibid.*, p. 1712.)

The letter referred to was received by Consul Bradley on Jan. 29, 1856, and was answered the following day. (*L. & P.*, vol. 1, no. 28, dated Singapore, Jan. 30, 1856.) In answer to what must obviously have been Townsend Harris's request, he sends him a copy of Sir John Bowring's Treaty with Siam and a list of books on that country. He adds important information on the French mission to Siam. Then he applies for the position of Secretary to Townsend Harris and hopes that he may be sent back to the United States as the bearer of the treaty about to be concluded with Siam. He concludes with the courteous offer of his home when Townsend Harris should arrive at Singapore.

[56]Robert C. Murphy, of Ohio, Consul at Shanghai, 1854–57. He was nominated, in place of J. N. A. Griswold, recalled, on January 23, 1854; consented to, January 31, 1854. (Hasse, *Index*, pt. 3, p. 1716.)

[57]This English steamer was later purchased at Yedo by Shimadzu Saburo for his son-nephew, the Daimyo of Satsuma, at a time when he did not entertain toward foreigners any feelings of hostility. (J. R. Black, *Young Japan*, vol. 1, p. 99.)

I was not thirty feet distant from him. This feeble utterance does not arise from disease or physical inability, for at a dinner party he can talk loud enough, and perhaps a little too loud. From dissatisfaction the congregation of St. George's is not one-half as large as I left it in May last. Penang is well supplied with churches: 1st, St. George's; 2nd, Church of the London Church Missionary Society; 3rd, Scotch Free Kirk; 4th, Armenian Church; 5th, 6th, 7th, three Roman Catholic Churches. The Roman Catholic Cochin-Chinese College is a noble institution. It has about one hundred pupils, nearly all of whom are from Cochin-China. They here receive such an education as will fit them to perform the duties of a priest in their own country, with such instruction in astronomy, natural philosophy, etc., etc., as will enable them to detect the popular errors of their countrymen. In dress, food, manner of living, etc., etc., they follow the exact fashions of their own country, so far as they are compatible with good morals—so that, when the youth returns home after his eight years' absence, there is nothing in his dress or manners to point him out as one who has long been among foreigners. On his return home, the youth bears a report from the head of the College addressed to the Bishop which shows the pupil's attainments, disposition, conduct during his residence, with an opinion as to his fitness for the priesthood. If, after his return home, he wishes to enter the priesthood, his Bishop puts him under a two years' probation; and if his conduct is good and his desire continues, he is then consecrated as a deacon, priest, etc., etc. It does not require any argument to show how preëminently priests so prepared, and of the people themselves, are qualified to be missionaries in a country where the persecution is so fierce and so fatal as it is in Cochin-China. Remain at home in the afternoon with a bad earache.

Monday, January 28, 1856. Gave Mr. Currier thirty-three sovereigns for my account. Ear very bad —number of calls on me, do not see anyone from that cause.

Thursday, January 31, 1856. Write a letter to Commodore Armstrong of the U.S. Frigate *San Jacinto,* now daily expected to arrive here, and gave it to the pilot who is to watch his arrival.

February 5, 1856. Chinese New Year. Talk of keeping New Year's Day by the Americans, the French, or any other people, and it sinks into child's play when compared with that of the Chinese. It is a Saturnalia for all, for three days, and is kept up by the wealthy until the full of the then new moon, and by some until the next new moon.

All work is suspended; the smith pulls down his furnace; other handicrafts renew their tools or workshops; the house is furnished with new cooking and eating appliances. The man, his house, his clothes, his children, are all thoroughly washed and dressed up in their best and gayest clothing. The house, shop or workshop shine with new vermilion papers inscribed with all sorts of wisdom from Confucius, Mencius and other philosophers. The Chinaman gives himself up to the enjoyment of his favorite weakness, gambling; and for three days the anti-gambling laws are suspended. He drinks *samshew*[58]—he fires off uncounted crackers—he beats tom-toms, gongs and his bamboos with their *click clock*. He visits, with all the forms laid down in the books of ceremonies, his friends, and pays his greetings; presents are exchanged; children gaily dressed are now drawn about the streets in pretty little carriages. "Motions,"[59] to use an old English phrase, swarm in the streets, performing before each house. Here is the great dragon trying to swallow the world. There some of the heroic demigods of China are showing how they did it in their day and generation. Yonder is a dance of peacocks—and vastly well done it is. Men are disguised under the plumage and form of the proud bird (except the legs). In the breast is a pretty oval mirror—the tail is spread in all its glory, and now and then the bird flutters its wings, as it "walks the stately pavisse." Now come the bands of music led off by an instrument that looks like a hoboy and sounds like a distracted bagpipe (may its inventor burn in Jehannenn), with tom-toms, gongs, bamboos, and all the noisy appliances that the Chinese delight to call music. Add to this the unceasing explosion of firecrackers, some of which are as loud as a *three-pounder cannon* (fact), and then think for

[58]*Samshew* (or: *samsho, shamshoo*) : a Chinese word for an alcoholic liquor distilled from boiled and fermented rice or millet; loosely, any kind of spirits. (*Funk & Wagnalls*.)

"Only one distillation is made for common liquor, but when more strength is wanted, it is distilled two or three times, and it is this strong spirit alone which is rightly called *samshu,* a word meaning 'thrice fired.'" (S. Wells Williams, *Middle Kingdom*, vol. i, ch. 14, p. 808 [s. '83].)

[59]Puppets, or puppet shows.

seventy-two hours this din never lags—never stops, and you have an idea of "New Year" as celebrated by the Chinese at Penang.

Sunday, February 10, 1856. The American screw steamer *Caroline* arrived in forty-five hours from Singapore. Passengers: Mr. Charles K. Tuckerman, Supra Cargo, and Mr. Shaw of Singapore.

Receive a letter from C. W. Bradley, U.S. Consul at Singapore, dated January 30, 1856.

Monday, February 11, 1856. The *Caroline* sailed to-day for Calcutta; wrote to C. Huffnagle, Esq., U.S. Consul General for British India.

Invited to dine with Captain Boulderson and the officers of 27th Regiment Madras Native Infantry at their mess house—have a prior engagement for that day,—*i. e., Friday next.*

Tuesday, February 12, 1856. Dine at Mr. Charles Scott's, Ayer Rajah. What a glorious house!—worthy of its situation in the center of nutmeg and clove gardens. The approaches to the house are shaded by glorious palm trees of different varieties, among which figures that most graceful of trees, the areca palm, with its straight slender stem and its waving panache of green plumes to ornament its head, while just below hangs its golden fruit, that look like apples of Paradise. What a dining room! Some sixty feet by eighty feet!! Think of *that, Fifth Avenue.*

Saturday, February 16, 1856. Dine with Mr. A. Brown of Sans Souci. We were, greatly to the discomposure of our host, thirteen at table. The belief here

55

is strong that, when thirteen dine in company, some one of them will die before twelve months come round —and hence the discomposure of my good host. Mr. Walker, Judge at Point-de-Galle, who is here for the benefit of hill air for Mrs. Walker, who is an invalid, came down the mill to-day and took quarters with Mr. Currier. As there is no hotel at Penang, strangers are dependent on the hospitality of the Penang people, who, to do them justice, are never backward in showing it. Among the first in the rank of hospitality stands our countryman, Mr. Currier.

Monday, February 18, 1856. Go up the hill on invitation of Mr. S. N. Greene to his bungalow "Bellevue" situated over twenty-six hundred feet above the plain. This hill is one of the delights of Penang. You ride in your palkee[60] to the foot of the hill four and a half miles, and then mount one of the pretty, active and sure-footed Sumatra ponies, who takes you some three miles up the hill in less than an hour, so that in an hour and a half you leave the heat of the plain and reach a point where a covering on your bed is always acceptable at night. The thermometer ranges here from 65° to 81°.

The panorama from "Bellevue" is charming: overlooking the plain and town of Penang—the nutmeg and clove gardens—the varied groves of palms surrounding the spacious and elegant mansions of the Europeans, the view extends out towards the Bay of Bengal and sometimes Pulo Bouton, sixty miles distant,

---

[60]An East Indian word for "palanquin."

can be seen. Directly west you see Elephant Mountain in the Kingdom of Quedah[61] which pays tribute to Siam. To the right you see the mountains that form the backbone of the Malayan Peninsula and are, in fact, a prolongation of the Himalaya range.

"Europe ships," country crafts, Malay prows,[62] and China egg-boats are seen moving or lying at anchor in all directions. Due south you look into the Strait of Malacca, and see the high lands of the dominions of the independent Rajah of Perak. I was warmly welcomed by Mrs. Greene, who resides here the greater part of the year for the health of her two children, a boy and girl—the latter Miss Maggy, my god-daughter.

The children speak only Malay, it being found easier to teach them English as a foreign language than to get them to unlearn the broken lingo they acquire from native servants who pretend to speak English. For this reason most families refuse to employ servants who speak English. Mr. Greene leaves his house at half-past five A.M. and returns at 6 P.M., and he does not find it fatiguing, as the good rest he always enjoys on the hill amply makes up for the extra fatigue of descending and ascending the hill six times a week. There are eight bungalows on this part of the great hill, which makes a little society; besides, each resident has always some guests up from the plain.

As this is my seventh visit to Penang I have fre-

---

[61]Quedah (or: Kedah, Kedda): a state in the Malay Peninsula.
[62]Prows (or: *Proa, prau, prahu*): a swift Malaysian vessel sailing equally well in either direction. (*Funk & Wagnalls.*)

57

quently been on the hill, and every part of it is quite familiar to me.

Tuesday, February 19, 1856. Up at daylight to see the beautiful changes of light and shade produced by the rising sun; indeed, it is a constant source of enjoyment to watch the effect of those changes during the day; now, the light cloud, passing quickly over the sun, seems to *race* down the mountain, across the plain, across the water over to Province Wellesly; where now it darkens for a moment the golden paddy fields—next seems to deepen the green of the canes growing on the various sugar estates. Next dark masses of clouds rise up over Elephant Mountain. The leaden color of its advanced edge does not leave you in doubt for a moment as to its nature—it is a thunder squall. Soon the vivid lightning begins to dart about—next you hear a faint mutter of thunder; the cloud hurries on; the lightning plays incessantly; the crash of the thunder is distinct; you see the curtain formed by the falling rain, down to the tops of the palm trees at a distance of twenty miles—on it comes—now the tall white chimneys of the sugar boiling houses are shut out—now it strikes the shipping—the town—the plain—palm trees and houses are shut out from view. You hear a low sound like an angry roar and it has reached the hilltop. You are in the cloud itself. What blinding lightning—the roll of the thunder never ceases. It continues half an hour, an hour, or three hours, and then the clouds roll away to the southeast and the sun comes out once more. In all parts of the tropics the thunder is heavy and the lightning vivid, but I never saw such grand displays of God's pyrotechnics as I have seen at Penang. On one night that I was on the hill, the storm lasted six hours. It was the most magnificent sight I ever witnessed. I saw on that occasion what indeed I have seen since, the descending stream of lightning, divided into a great number of lines and curved around and upwards, forming an "inverted weeping willow."

Very good bridle paths are cut in various directions on the top of the hill, and you can gallop away for more than a mile without any ascent to check you.

The ferns here are both rich in number, and many rare and beautiful ones are found. Among the sixty and odd varieties that have been catalogued by botanists as having their *habitat* here, the grandest is the tree fern, more than twenty feet high, with branches like the fronds of the cocoanut palm. The rattan is also found here and extends its tendrils, armed with hooks like steel, that forbid all passage until a path is cut. The rattan is a *climber*. It is covered with a great number of husks, so that the body is sometimes five or six inches in diameter. The part used is the *core* or center. As it is attached in the strongest possible manner by the *hooks* before named to every tree or shrub that comes within its sphere, and as it sometimes climbs the tallest trees and thence stretches itself from tree to tree for a great distance (for, some have been found five hundred feet long!), it would be all but impossible to detach it from its place. It is collected for use in the following manner. The natives find its root and then cut it off near the ground; they then strip off the husky covering for some six or eight feet, and of the part so cleaned they form a loop through which they pass a stick some eight or ten feet long. Six or eight men now apply their strength to this stick, surging backwards from the direction the rattan has grown. By thus pulling it backwards, the sutures of the husks that are attached to the rattan at distances of two to five feet are easily broken, and this done, the men have only to pull in and coil away the rattan as they would a rope. If the attempt was made to pull out the rattan from the top, no force could be applied that would accomplish it. The milk tree (so called from its juice being the color of milk and thickness of cream) is the largest of the jungle trees of Penang. One of these measures forty-three feet in circumference some fifteen feet above the ground, and the *boll* rises up one hundred and twenty feet without a limb. The branches and top of this tree are very small when compared with the enormous size of the trunk or boll.

The cinnamon, clove and nutmeg trees grow in the jungle, and my dinner has often been cooked with the wood of these precious trees.

The *cayu-puti*[63] (white wood), corrupted into our cajeput, produces the oil once considered as a specific for Asiatic cholera, also grows here. A great variety of other trees are found in the jungle, but even their names would not be understood if I was to write them

---

[63]*Cayu-puti* (or: *kajeput, cajaput, cajuput*): from the Malay *kayu-putih, kayu* meaning tree, and *putih* (or *puteh*) white. (*Funk & Wagnalls.*)

here. Coffee flourishes on the hill and produces a berry almost equal to that of Mocha. Some tea shrubs are growing here, bearing innumerable small yellow white roses. The rose of Shiraz is cultivated here, and in the early morning the fragrance is delightful. The *ipeca-cuanha* shrub is used to form hedges for the hill gardens and grounds. It produces a pretty flower. The *ipeca-cuanha* is a certain cure for the bite of the centipede and sting of the scorpion; and, if applied immediately, prevents any of the dreadful pain that is sure to follow the neglected wounds made by these insects. The powder is simply made into a poultice with cold water and applied to the wound. I should like to hear of a trial of this remedy for the bite of venomous snakes. It is at least worthy of a trial. Some few vegetables of the temperate zone are raised on the hill, but they do not succeed so well as they do at Calcutta, Bombay or Macao. This may arise in part from unskillful cultivation.

The air plants, parasites and climbers, are without number, and the blossoms of some of the two first are exceedingly beautiful. The nepenthe or pitcher plant —that curious creation of nature with its pitchers filled with sweet potable water—grows here in vast numbers. Happily no tigers, elephants or rhinoceros are found in this happy island, although they abound on the mainland not one mile distant. Wild hogs are numerous and a host of animals of the fox and weasel tribes, that are sad enemies to the poultry. Monkeys caper and grimace and mow in every direction on the hills. Lizards of all sizes, from the smallest up to the *gekko,* which is sometimes four feet long, abound. Scorpions, both black and gray, and centipedes are numerous, but they do not give any uneasiness to the residents here, as, if you let them alone, they will not molest you. A great variety of snakes are found; some are very curious and even beautiful. The cobra capello is also here. The boa constrictor is also found. There is hardly any one production of the East concerning which so much error prevails as concerning this serpent. It will not kill an elephant, or a buffalo, or a man. It is sluggish in its movements and perfectly harmless. The natives are always glad to have them in their rice fields where they destroy the rats, frogs and other things that injure the rice crop. I have made inquiries constantly in India, Ceylon, Java, Borneo, Siam, Burmah, Arracan,[64] and, in fact, in all the countries where the boa is found, and never found any *good* authority for the exaggerated tales of its size and ferocity which are so widely disseminated. I have never seen the skin or body of one that measured more than twenty-five feet long, nor could I ever meet any respectable evidence of the actual existence of longer ones. The stories of boas being fifty, seventy-five, or even one hundred and twenty feet long, are the simple exaggerations of heated imaginations. So again, no reliable account of man or any of the larger animals being attacked by the boa can be found. The skin that was twenty-five feet long I saw in the Museum of the Asiatic Society of Calcutta, and its preservation

---

[64]Arakan, a division of Lower Burmah, on the Indian Ocean.

there is a proof that it is one of the largest that is known.

The beetles are a numerous and interesting family. The *trumpeter* sounds his ra-ta-ta-ta-ta-ra in loudness, tone and length of note precisely like the penny trumpets of children at home. Others resemble the sound of the carpenter sawing his boards, and another is exactly like the knife grinder in sound. The stick insect is a curious affair. It is sometimes eight inches long—legs very long—wings preposterously short—the color gray, or like a decayed stick or twig. When it flies, its long legs are folded closely and parallel to the body, and it looks precisely like a withered stick passing quickly before you. The leaf insect is a curiosity; some of them look like beautiful flowers. I once captured a *flying lizard* on the hills of Penang. It was about six inches long and had integuments or filaments of its skin extending on each side from the fore to the hind legs—precisely like our flying squirrel; and, like him, the lizard can dart from tree to tree on a *descending plane* to a considerable distance.

In this reptile we have the rudiments of the fabulous dragon, exaggerated by the utmost powers of invention.

Many beautiful birds are found here. The toucan and great grosbeak among others build their nests here. The Penang lark has a great many very sweet notes. Snipe are abundant and good, being large and always fat. There is a small bird always found on the snipe ground whose note sounds like the words "did you do it? did you do it?" When the sportsman fires his gun, scores of these birds scream out "did you do it? did you do it?"—sometimes to the great annoyance of the sportsman, especially if he often misses his aim.

Wednesday, February 20, 1856. The Malay is not a handsome person, nor is the Chinese good-looking, yet the children of a Malay woman by a Chinese are really quite good-looking. The high cheek bones of the mother disappear, the oblique eye of the father is displaced by a round, bright and not snaky looking eye. The face is round and the skin like satin; color like a solution of gold laid on a rose colored ground. They are always plump.

It is a singular fact that the children of the Chinaman by the Malay, Burmese or Siamese women are far better looking than the progeny of the white man by women of those nations.

The children of Europeans by native women are a queer race—always warmhearted and hospitable, they are never more happy than when showing their hospitality to white persons. They resemble our negroes in the love of stilted expressions, considering magniloquence and eloquence as synonyms. They always try to secure the hand of a white for their daughters, and to this end the mother has her tiffin spread with curries that only can be made by them, and their beer is always of the coolest. Young men are fond of visiting them from the ease that they can there enjoy and from the pleasure of romping, which is carried to a certain extent. One of the difficulties of the foreigner is to learn how to use certain descriptive words. For example: it is a gross insult to call one of them "half-caste." You may ask them if they are "country born," and no offence is given, but to use the word *liplap* (Dutch for mixed blood) or to call the girls *chee chees* is very offensive—the latter comes from the constant use of the Hindostanee word *chee!* (fie!) which the girls scream out when romping.

But the name most affected by them is *Eurasian*—being a compound of the nouns Europe and Asia. This word is of Calcutta origin.

A young Englishman had long visited a house where the Eurasian daughter, Miss Harriet, was quite a favorite with him. He had sung with her, romped with her, and talked mock sentiment with her, and was rewarded with capital tiffins and now and then a pleasant romping bout. The mother, having asked her daughter how matters stood between her and her admirer, resolved herself to bring the young man "to book." Accordingly, at his next visit and after tiffin was over, Miss Harriet disappeared from the room; and the mother, seating herself near the young man, addressed him as follows:

"You rice and curry eat 'em; hand you squeeze 'em; fum fum pinch 'em. What for you no propose?" The young man evaporated.

Another case is quoted to show how recklessly these poor creatures rush into the cares of matrimony.

A young Eurasian, who was employed in a government office as a *writer* at some sixty rupees ($27) per month, being smitten with the charms of the fair Rosa Matilda, made her an offer of his "hand, heart and fortune." Miss Rosa Matilda simply asked him: "Silver tea pot got?" Yes. "Have buggy got?" Yes. "Can ask mamma."

However, many of these Eurasians are quite well educated (some being sent to England for that purpose), and behave with perfect propriety and decorum. I have passed many satisfactory hours with this class of Eurasians.

As a general rule, the English officials do not neglect the children they have by the illegitimate connections they form with the women of the country.

Mr. Blundell,[65] Governor of Penang, Singapore and Malacca, has eleven children (illegitimate) born of a Burmese woman. He has given them as good educations as were to be had in Singapore, Penang or Calcutta (some of the younger ones are now in England). Has given them his name, introduced them to his own table, and at last opened the State Ball, given on the Queen's Birthday, with one of his illegitimate daughters, thus making her the *Burra Beebe*[66] or Great Lady of the Ball. It was a bold and defiant step and gave offence to many of the Englishwomen, wives of high officials and military men at Singapore, but Governor Blundell carried the matter out with a high hand, and his bastard mulatto sons and daughters have the *entrée*

---

[65]From a letter written by Sir John Bowring to the King of Siam and dated Apr. 5, 1855 (*L. & P.*, vol. 2, no. 9f), we learn that Blundell succeeded Colonel Butterworth in this office when the latter returned to England. Governor Blundell is mentioned as Governor of Singapore in 1854, also in 33–2, S. Ex. Doc. no. 34, p. 182.

[66]*Burra* means great and honorable; and *Beebe* (or *Bibi*) means wife or lady. Both are Anglo-Indian words. (*Funk & Wagnalls.*)

of Singapore society. Three of his girls are married to Englishmen. He gives them 10,000 rupees as a marriage portion ($4,500), and they will receive more at his death.

The circumlocution used in Asia to avoid the phrase "half-caste" reminds me of a similar state of things that existed in Australia before the gold discoveries in that country;[67] up to which period 499 persons out of 500 were transports. But you could not use the word "convict" or "transport" without danger of a row. The questions were put as follows: "What ship did you come out in?" for all the ships were transports for convicts; or, "Are you a Government man?" *i. e.,* a convict. "Are you an old hand?" *i. e.,* have you been reconvicted of crime in the colony? Sydney has a very pretty theater situated in George's Street. The opening address of this theater was written by the celebrated Barrington, the notorious pickpocket. It was very witty and full of allusions to the conditions of the then inhabitants of the place. One couplet has been often repeated, and by many who were ignorant of the author, or of the circumstances under which it was written. It is as follows:

True patriots we, for, be it understood,
We left our country for our *country's good.*[68]

---

[67]Gold was first discovered in Australia at Summerhill Creek, twenty miles north of Bathurst, in the Macquarie plains, in Feb., 1851, by Mr. Edward Hargraves, a gold miner from California.

[68]George Barrington—a truly strange character, born May 14, 1755, at Maynooth, Ireland. He was a robber, confirmed pickpocket, and historian of Australia. His real name was Waldron. After a chequered career in England, Scotland, and Ireland, he was finally shipped to Botany Bay, in New South Wales. On this long voyage, he prevented the success of a mutiny among the convicts on board, and, on arriving at his destination, he received a pecuniary

Friday, February 22, 1856. Came down to the plain to be ready for the mail from China, en route for England.

Sunday, February 24, 1856. The steamer *Cadiz* with the mails arrives from China. Write by this mail to W. L. Marcy, Secretary of State, Washington;[69] N. Dougherty, New York.

Received a letter from Captain John Pope,[70] of the U.S. Corvette the *Macedonian,* now at Singapore. Captain Pope wishes to know when I expect the Commodore to arrive here. He will await his arrival at Singapore.

Monday, February 25, 1856. Steamer *Norna* with the mails from England arrived here to-day. Mr. Harry

---

reward from the captain of the ship and in addition was favorably recommended to the governor of the colony. He was freed in 1792.

A few years later, Governor Hunter authorized the opening of a theater at Sydney. The chief actors were convicts, and the price of admission was meal or rum. The theater opened on Jan. 16, 1796, with Dr. Young's tragedy, *The Revenge,* and George Barrington wrote the celebrated prologue, beginning:

"From distant climes, o'er widespread seas, we come,
Though not with much éclat or beat of drum;
True patriots we, for, be it understood,
We left our country for our country's good.
No private views disgraced our generous zeal,
What urged our travels was our country's weal;
And none will doubt, but that our emigration
Has proved most useful to the British nation."
(*Dict. Nat. Biogr.*, s.v., *Barrington.*)

[69]This is his second dispatch to the Secretary of State. (*L. B.*, vol. 1, p. 13.) He informs his superior that the French Government has appointed a commissioner to negotiate a treaty with Siam; and that Captain Pope is waiting at Singapore for the arrival of the *San Jacinto.*

[70]John Pope, of Maine, United States Navy, 1816–76. Midshipman, May 30, 1816; Lieutenant, Apr. 28, 1826; Commander, Feb. 15, 1843; Captain, Sept. 14, 1855; Retired List, Dec. 21, 1861; Commodore on Retired List, July 16, 1862; died, Jan. 14, 1876. In 1845–47, commanded the *Dolphin,* of the African Squadron; in 1853–54 and 1856–57, commanded the *Vandalia* of the East India Squadron. (Hasse, *Index,* pt. 2, p. 1303; Hamersly, *op. cit.*)

68

S. Parkes,[71] H.B.M. Consul for Amoy, China, and his wife are passengers by the *Norna*. Mr. Parkes is the bearer of the ratified treaty with Siam and will proceed from Singapore to Bangkok for the purpose of exchanging the ratifications.

Mr. Parkes was Sir John Bowring's private secretary when Sir John[72] negotiated the treaty. Sir John spoke to the King seated and uncovered,—made some six official visits. Guard not wanted. Siamese cooks good enough. House comfortable.

---

[71]Sir Harry Smith Parkes, 1828–85. He was one of the really outstanding men in the history of Far Eastern relations. Left an orphan at a young age, he went out to Macao, China, to join his cousin, who was the wife of the Rev. Charles (Karl) Gutzlaff, the famous missionary to China. Dr. Gutzlaff had spent a lifetime travelling in China and in Korea and was one of the few foreigners who knew the Chinese language well. Under his tutelage the young Parkes likewise learned Chinese, and this, together with his intimate acquaintance with things Chinese, proved of great value to the distinguished men under whom he served in almost every capacity—men such as Sir Henry Pottinger, Sir Rutherford Alcock, Lord Elgin and Kincardine, etc. In 1855, Parkes was secretary of the mission to Bangkok headed by Sir John Bowring, and in 1865 he became Minister to Japan, succeeding Sir Rutherford Alcock. The best and standard *Life of Sir Harry S. Parkes* is by Stanley Lane-Poole and Dickins, London, 1894.

[72]Sir John Bowring, 1792–1872: another of that endless chain of wonderful and trained statesmen that Great Britain has always seemed to have at her beck and call for service either at home or abroad—capable, patient, energetic, faithful. There is no doubt that the history of Great Britain's expansion in the Far East is summed up in the lives of her representatives to that region, whether consuls, ministers, plenipotentiaries, chief superintendents of trade, governors, or missionaries.

Sir John was philologist, philanthropist, linguist (in the same class with Mezzofanti), poet, philosopher, statesman, chartist, and voluminous writer on all these subjects. There are extant a number of letters by him to Townsend Harris. The best work in connection with his mission to Siam is: *The Kingdom and People of Siam, with a Narrative of the Mission to that Country in 1855*, in two volumes, 8vo, London, 1857—a very comprehensive work which, though published so long ago, is still one of the standard works on Siam.

The Treaty of Friendship and Commerce between Great Britain and Siam was concluded at Bangkok on Apr. 18, 1855, and was to go into effect Apr. 6, 1856. Sir Harry (then Consul) Parkes had brought the Treaty to England and was now returning with the ratified copy. (*L. & P.*, vol. 2, nos. 26, 30, 31, 32.)

Wrote per *Norna* to Captain John Pope and C. W. Bradley, U.S. Consul, both at Singapore.

February 27, 1856. Visited Alexander Brown and Charles Scott, Esquires.

February 28, 1856. The American ship *Daniel Sharpe,* Captain Parker, sailed for Singapore.

Saturday, March 1, 1856. The Honorable Company's steamer *Pluto* arrived here from Rangoon via Maulmain.

Monday, March 3, 1856. The steamer *Chusan* from Calcutta en route for China arrived yesterday; left Calcutta February 25th.

The *Chusan* brings news, telegraphed to Calcutta from Bombay, that a Treaty of Peace between France, England and Russia was signed at Paris on the 18th of last January. Write to Captain Pope, Singapore, and to S. Drinker, Hongkong.

Tuesday, March 4, 1856. The steamer *Pluto* left for Rangoon. On the 1st, 2nd and 3rd of this month, the wind blew very fresh from North by West to East North East. At 5:30 A.M. on the second, the thermometer in Mr. Currier's verandah stood at 76°; the coolest I ever knew it here.

Wednesday, March 5, 1856. At 2 P.M. the thermometer in Mr. Currier's verandah stood at 90°. This heat is the greatest I ever knew at Penang, and the range of 14° in three days is quite unexampled. (See record March 4th.)

Friday, March 7, 1856. At the sessions of Penang, just closed, a Chinese was convicted of murder and sentenced to be hanged on the 10th of this month. The cause of this murder, and the evidence of one of the Chinese witnesses, shows how little they regard the beastly crime of sodomy. It appeared that the murderer had a catamite paramour who was seduced from him by the murdered man.

The witness to prove the murder was the degraded wretch of a catamite, who coolly told the tale of his own degradation and the fact of his seduction, without any hesitation or apparent knowledge that he had committed any offence against the laws, or against good morals. The authorities here always avoid taking any notice of this crime, if they can avoid it; but this case was so flagrant that the wretch is to be prosecuted.

The crime of sodomy is almost universal among the Chinese, whether they are in China or in any other part of the world; in fact, it is the universal practice of all the people of Asia, as well as those of Arabia, Egypt, Asia Minor, etc. The Cingalese are the least obnoxious to this charge of any of the nations of the East.

Monday, March 10, 1856. News has reached here of the annexation of the Kingdom of Oude to the possessions of the East India Company. It was done by a proclamation of Lord Dalhousie,[73] Governor General of India, dated February, 1856.

This proceeding excites no surprise, as the preliminary measures have been progressing for the last four

---

[73] James Andrew Broun Ramsay, First Marquess and Tenth Earl of Dalhousie, 1812–60. One of the master builders of the Indian Empire of Great Britain. The proclamation annexing the Kingdom of Oude (or Oudh) was dated February 13, 1856.

71

years. It is the old story—Naboth's Vineyard and the Wolf and the Lamb. The lands of Oude are rich and fertile, and the people industrious; and, when I was in Oude (Lucknow, January, 1855), they were more prosperous and thriving than the adjoining lands of the Company at Cawnpore, or in the Doab generally.

The proclamation charges the King of Oude with misgovernment and with oppressing his people. But who made Lord Dalhousie a judge in this case, or the guardian of the people of Oude? It also charges him with the religious feuds of the kingdom which have led to bloodshed. Were none of these feuds excited by British emissaries? Were not the inflammatory papers, which were abundantly circulated in Oude, printed at Calcutta or some other place in the Company's territory? Was there any printing press in Oude except that of the King at Lucknow?

Time will answer these questions, and also *Truth is the daughter of time.*

The Government of Oude has been at peace with the Company since 1765. It did not join the Nepalese in 1816, when there was an apparent prospect that the British could be driven out of Bengal. When the disasters of Cabul took place in 1847, the Indian Government was shaken to its center. The prestige of its military power had received a grievous blow, and it had neither money nor credit, not a rupee would the banyans[74] of Calcutta or Benares advance to the Govern-

---

[74]Hindoo merchants or traders, especially those in the foreign trade, acting also as brokers or bankers.

ment. The troops from Bengal, destined for the Bolan Pass,[75] could not even reach the Punjab. It was in this time of gloom and trouble that this very King of Oude, unsolicited, advanced fifty lacs of rupees (five millions) to the Government of India. The troops then marched —recovered their reverses in Cabul and restored their shaking power. What would have been the present state of the British power in India but for the generous assistance of the King of Oude, is a wide question.

There has been a constant interference in the affairs of Oude by the Indian Government during the last forty years. It dates particularly from the late Nepalese War.

When a British Resident is forced on any Asiatic power, it is only a question of time how long that power shall be permitted to exist, before the fiat of annexation goes forth, and the government of the native sovereign annihilated.

Oude contains 25,000 square miles and 6,000,000 of inhabitants, principally of the Rajhpoot caste.

Tuesday, March 11, 1856. Again up to "Bellevue," Mr. Greene's bungalow.

Friday, March 14, 1856. The American ship *Anna Maria,* Captain Rhodes, arrives here in six days from Singapore.

Saturday, March 15, 1856. Thermometer 71° at

---

[75]A narrow gorge in the southwestern corner of British Baluchistan leading into Afghanistan.

6 A.M. Visit Mr. and Mrs. Mackenzie[76] at Strawberry Hill, the late residence of poor Sir William Jephcott, who died suddenly shortly before my arrival here from Point-de-Galle. The furniture, pictures, etc., etc., of the bungalow remain as they were in his time, and strongly bring him and the many pleasant hours I have passed with him to my mind. Mr. Buttery comes up to Mr. Greene's. Write to S. Drinker, Hongkong, to go by mail now daily expected from Point-de-Galle on her way to China.

Monday, March 17, 1856. Mr. Buttery goes down this morning. Mr. Mackenzie and Lieutenant Corbit call and pass two hours this morning.

Mr. White comes up this evening. Catch a flying lizard—body five inches, head one inch, tail five and a half inches; total, eleven and a half inches. Tail is flat and broader at the end than in any other part.

Thursday, March 20, 1856. The mail in from Point-de-Galle. Hear that the *San Jacinto* has been at Galle and that she left one day before the mail.[77] She is more than a month behind her time. Go down the hill at

---

[76]Mr. K. R. Mackenzie, a business man in China, who later, after Townsend Harris had concluded a treaty with Japan, sought to visit Yedo on business. Townsend Harris, in whom the Japanese placed complete faith to keep traders away from Yedo, held out no encouragement, and wrote him from Shimoda, on February 7, 1859 (*L. B.*, vol. 4, p. 7):

"The creation of a large commerce with Japan must of necessity be the work of time. The rich latent resources of the country must be developed; the labor of a large surplus population must be directed to useful employments, and lastly, artificial wants must be created among the masses."

About ten days later, February 18, 1859, the Dutch Minister, J. H. Donker Curtius, wrote Townsend Harris from Nagasaki stating that several gentlemen had arrived from Shanghai on a visit, among them Mr. K. R. Mackenzie. (*L. & P.*, vol. 1, no. 142.)

[77] The *San Jacinto* arrived at Galle on Mar. 6, 1856. (Wood, *op. cit.*, p. 105.)

1 P. M.; get letters from Captain McDonald and Mr. Forbes at Point-de-Galle.

Good Friday, March 21, 1856. At noon the *San Jacinto* is telegraphed but does not come in to-day.

Saturday, March 22, 1856. The *San Jacinto* comes in at 11 A. M. She left New York October 25, 1856, [1855]. Consequently she has been 149 days on her passage. Two ordinary merchant ships that left the United States after the *San Jacinto* both arrived out before her—one in 87 days, and the other [in] 94 days. Our men-of-war never hurry.

Go on board the *San Jacinto* and am warmly welcomed by all. On leaving am saluted with thirteen guns. The steamer *Fiery Cross* from Calcutta for China comes in. Write to S. Drinker and Captain Pope.

Tuesday [Monday], March 24, 1856. Mail steamer from China for England arrives. Write by her to W. L. Marcy[78] and P. M. Wetmore, also to Captain McDonald and Mr. Forbes at Ceylon.

Wednesday [Tuesday], March 25, 1856. Dine with the Hon. W. T. Lewis, Resident Councillor and Acting Governor, with Commodore Armstrong, Captain Bell, Purser Bradford,[79] Fleet Surgeon Wood[80] and Lieutenant Tyler of the marines. Wilson,[81] Lord Bishop of

[78]Dispatch No. 3, dated Pulo Penang or Prince of Wales Island (*L. B.,* vol. 1, p. 14), informing the Secretary of State of the arrival of the *San Jacinto,* and closing with the statement that in his next dispatch he hoped to be able to inform the Secretary "on the result of my mission to the Court of Bangkok."

[79]T. O. Bradford.

[80]William Maxwell Wood, M.D., already referred to in these notes as the author of *Fankwei.* This work is indispensable for all that relates to Townsend Harris and his mission to Siam (pp. 147–260), but has very little on Townsend Harris's work in Japan (pp. 295–320).

[81]Daniel Wilson, 1778–1858, Fifth Bishop of Calcutta. (*Dict. Nat. Biogr.*)

Calcutta, was among the guests. He is a venerable, charitable and excellent man, but outrageously eccentric. He has a most awkward habit of thinking aloud, and as his private thoughts are very queer, the utterance of them sometimes leads to ludicrous scenes.

He is equally odd in the pulpit. On one occasion, when he was preaching at the Cathedral, Calcutta, his subject was the sin of a lust of money. After illustrating in a very ample manner the social and moral evils that grow out of this sin, he wound up by saying:

"There is my brother the venerable Archdeacon" (pointing at him); "he once sold me a horse for 500 rupees and the brute was not worth an *anna*" (twopence), "and I am very much afraid, my brethren, *that my venerable brother knew it when he sold him to me!*" Imagine the scene.

Thursday [Wednesday], March 26, 1856. The Commodore and Captain Bell go up the Hill to Mr. Greene's, and in the evening Mr. Currier takes a number of officers up to his bungalow "Mount Ellenborough." Repairs are required to the engines of the *San Jacinto* that will keep her here until the 1st or 2nd of next month.

Saturday, March 29, 1856. Mr. Currier comes down the Hill, and Lieutenant Lewis and Dr. Semple[82] go up.

Sunday, March 30, 1856. My old friend Père

---

[82]Assistant Surgeon of the *San Jacinto,* of whom Captain (later Rear-Admiral) Andrew Hull Foote, of the *Portsmouth,* speaks to Townsend Harris in *L. & P.,* vol. 1, no. 75, dated Hongkong, Nov. 5, 1857.

Bigandet is to-day consecrated a bishop *In partibus infidelibus*. He leaves soon for Burmah.

Monday, March 31, 1856. Wrote to C. Huffnagle, Esq., U. S. Consul General for British India at Calcutta. Had the nightmare very bad last night.

Tuesday, April 1, 1856. Gave in charge of Purser Bradford of the *San Jacinto* eleven bags of dollars containing $5,420.

Make all the calls I can and leave cards P. P. C. for all kind friends at Penang—the cards will be sent after I leave by Mr. Greene.

Wednesday, April 2, 1856. Early on board the *San Jacinto,* which gets under way at 9:30 A. M. I am now fairly on my way to the scene of my diplomatic labors.[83]

Friday, April 4, 1856. Arrive at Singapore at 9:30 P. M. Were directed into the harbor by the blue lights and rockets thrown up from the U. S. Corvette *Macedonian*.

Saturday, April 5, 1856. Go on shore to the house of C. W. Bradley, Esq., U. S. Consul. Call on Governor Blundell in company with Captain Bell and the Commodore. The Governor not at home. Afterwards I call on M. Gautier,[84] Consul de France. Monsieur absent,

[83]*Cf.* Wood, *op. cit.,* p. 142; and *L. & P.,* vol. 2, no. 119, in which Townsend Harris, on Mar. 7, 1861, certifies (obviously for the use of the Department of State) to the principal dates of his voyage from the day he sailed from New York to that of his arrival at Shimoda, Japan, Aug. 21, 1856.

[84]Townsend Harris must have been particularly eager to make M. Gautier's acquaintance. Charles Wm. Bradley, Sr., U.S. Consul for Singapore, had written to Townsend Harris a very interesting letter on Jan. 30, 1856. (*L. & P.,* vol. 1, no. 28.) Among other important information, he wrote:

"Mr. Gautier, French Consul at this port, called on me yesterday, and in the course of conversation informed me that his Government were about to demand a commercial convention from the Siamese; and that for that pur-

see Madame and pass an agreeable half hour. Make some small purchases of stationery, etc., for Siam, and a satin cover[85] for the President's letter.

Monday, April 7, 1856. Wrote W. L. Marcy,[86] N. Dougherty, S. Drinker and Dr. Macgowan. Am invited to attend a ball and supper to be given by the citizens of Singapore to the French Commodore Montravel (see private letter book).[87] Send excuse, as I hope then to be in Siam.[88]

pose the diplomatic gentlemen already designated by H.I.M. would proceed to Bangkok about the end of next month (February). Mr. Gautier will be one of the mission,—probably its Secretary, and the bearer of its fruits to France."

[85]In *L. B.*, vol. 1, p. 7, there is the following entry in Townsend Harris's hand: "At Singapore. Paid on Diplomatic a/c Whampoa & Co.'s bill for satin cover for the President's letter, and sundry small articles of stationery—$7.40."

[86]Dispatch No. 4 (*L. B.*, vol. 1, p. 14), by which he informed the Secretary of State that a French squadron of two corvettes and one steamer was at Singapore awaiting the arrival of the French Envoy to Siam, who would then proceed to Bangkok with a fleet of four vessels. Townsend Harris then voices his fears as follows:

"I hope I shall be able to close my negotiations with the Siamese Court before the arrival of the French mission, as its presence would cause much delay, if no other embarrassment should arrive.

"I shall therefore use my best exertions to bring my negotiations to a close as speedily as possible."

In the meantime, ratifications of the English Treaty with Siam (concluded by Sir John Bowring on Apr. 18, 1855) had been exchanged at Bangkok by Harry S. Parkes on Apr. 5, 1856 (*L. & P.*, vol. 2, no. 26), and had gone into effect on Apr. 6, 1856 (*L. & P.*, vol. 2, no. 32). By letter of the same date (Apr. 6, 1856), Commodore James Armstrong was urging Townsend Harris to be quick in selecting the person (Consul Bradley) to be the bearer to Washington of the American Treaty to be concluded with Siam (*L. & P.*, vol. 1, no. 34).

[87]The letter to which Townsend Harris refers is lost. Commodore Perry had met Commodore Montravel (whose fleet lay at anchor in the roadstead of Macao, China) in Aug. 1853, when Perry put in there after his first visit to the Bay of Yedo. (See Perry, *Narrative,* in 33-2, H. Ex. Doc., no. 97, vol. 1, p. 300; and W. E. Griffis, *Perry,* p. 344.)

[88]Though Townsend Harris was only about to begin negotiations with Siam, the Americans in China had long been on the lookout for the arrival of his ship. Commissioner Parker, in writing to Secretary of State Marcy (Macao, Apr. 10, 1856) says: ". . . and am most solicitous for the arrival of the *San Jacinto* (reported by the last mail as having left Point-de-Galle on or about the 20th ult.), . . ." (35-2, S. Ex. Doc., no. 22, pt. 2—in Serial no. 983—p. 761.)

Tuesday, April 8, 1856. San Jacinto leaves at 3
P. M. for Bangkok. Have delightful weather—no dates
—perfect calm all the way. Pulo Panjang has a small
islet near it quite covered with guano. Passed Pulo Way
at midnight. Vast quantities of snakes in the Gulf of
Siam. Water *blue* at only sixteen fathoms soundings!
Sunday, April 13, 1856. We anchored at the bar of
the River Menam at 11 :30 A. M. in six fathoms water.[89]
We can just see the tops of the trees on shore.

The Honorable Company's steamer *Auckland* is
here with Mr. Parkes, who has not yet completed his
labors with the Siamese. I fear his presence may delay
me. Write a letter to the Minister of Foreign Affairs[90]

---

[89]Wood, *Fankwei*, p. 150. In his letter to the Rev. Stephen Mattoon, written
on board the *San Jacinto* the same day (*L. B.*, vol. 1, p. 9), Townsend Harris
says that the vessel "anchored here about 2 P. M." It will be remembered that
Perry, when he reached Point-de-Galle on his way out to Japan, wrote a letter
to His Royal Highness Prince Phar-Pen-Clow of Siam (dated Mar. 14, 1853),
and that, as the result of the courteous answer he received and of other private
information, "he would have gone to Siam had not uncontrollable circumstances prevented." (Perry, *Narrative*, in 33–2, H. Ex. Doc., no. 97, vol. 1,
p. 122.)

[90]His name, as it appears in the treaty later concluded by Townsend Harris,
is: His Excellency Chau Phaya Rawe Nongee Maha Kosa Dhipade, the
Phra Klang—the last two words meaning "Minister of Foreign Affairs."
Townsend Harris's letter was dated: "Legation of the United States of
America to Siam. U. S. Steam Frigate *San Jacinto,* at anchor off the Menam.
[Sunday], April 13th, 1856." (*L. B.*, vol. 1, p. 10, Dispatch No. 1.)
In addition to the statement in the text, Townsend Harris expresses his
desire to deliver the President's letter, of which he is the bearer; gives the
names and ranks of those who will compose his suite; asks for proper con-
veyances to move a number of large packages; and trusts that all facilities
will be afforded the Rev. S. Mattoon to enable him to reach the *San Jacinto*
as speedily as possible.
In signing this letter, Townsend Harris describes himself as: "Envoy Plenipotentiary of the United States of America to Siam, and American Consul
General for the Empire of Japan."
Townsend Harris had learned from the experiences of the two Americans
who had preceded him as envoys to Siam—namely, Edmund Roberts and
Joseph Balestier; and he began immediately to surround himself with all the
pomp and ceremony and dignity which have everywhere so much weight, but
particularly in the Far East.

announcing my arrival and requesting boats, etc. Also write to the Rev. Mr. Mattoon, an American missionary residing at Bangkok, requesting him to come to me, as I wish him as my interpreter.[91] I sent to him a letter from the Rev. Mr. Lowera of New York, requesting him to assist me.[92]

The Captain and Supra Cargo of the American ship *Ino* come on board. The *Ino* has loaded rice here for China and sails to-day. Mr. Stone of the house of King & Co. also came on board. He says the King has prohibited the exportation of rice and salt. By Mr. Stone I send up all the letters and parcels for Bangkok. I also give him the letter for the Minister of Foreign Affairs, and desired him to show it to the Governor of Paknam and offer to carry it up to Bangkok if the Governor

---

[91]The Rev. Stephen Mattoon, an American Presbyterian missionary long resident at Bangkok, who became indispensable to Townsend Harris and of whom we shall therefore hear a good deal. We quote from the letter referred to in the text (*L. B.*, vol. i, p. 9):

"I am most anxious to secure your valuable aid not only as interpreter but as my adviser in many things, for which your long residence here and knowledge of public men peculiarly fit you. . . . Of course I shall expect to repay you all your expenses for boats, etc., as well as for your services."

Dr. Mattoon's home was visited by members of the American party on May 4, 1856, and is described by Wood, in *Fankwei*, pp. 215, 220.

[92]The reference is to Senator Walter Lowrie, born in Edinburgh, Scotland, Dec. 10, 1784, died in New York, Dec. 14, 1868. His family moved to the United States, where the young man was educated for the ministry, but went into politics instead. He was successively State Senator in Pennsylvania, United States Senator, and Secretary of the Senate. His early training and his earnestly religious nature now led him into the field of foreign missions, and in 1836 he was elected Corresponding Secretary of the Western Foreign Missionary Society, later known as the Presbyterian Board of Foreign Missions. This post he held for more than thirty years, and it was as Secretary of the Presbyterian Board that he recommended Townsend Harris to the Rev. Mattoon, a Presbyterian Missionary in Siam.

This letter introducing Townsend Harris, who, although not personally known to Mr. Lowrie, was "highly appreciated" and cordially recommended, is dated at the Mission House, New York, Oct. 12, 1855. (*L. B.*, vol. i, p. 8.)

wished him to do [so], but to be careful to fully understand the wishes of the Governor before he took it from Paknam.

Gar fish abundant and very large, pretty gulls, also shrike or Indian kite, called *jheel*. Now make out houses of the fishing stations.

Commander Drought of the *Auckland* comes on board. He cannot salute the Commodore, as he has only six guns, and vessels of that number and under are not allowed to fire salutes. The *Ino* sailed this evening—a lovely night—the land breeze is very refreshing. Thermometer 85°.

Monday, April 14, 1856. The Commodore and Captain Bell return the call of Commander Drought of the *Auckland*.

Mr. Richards, of H. B. M. Surveying Schooner *Spartan,* came on board and kindly promised to send me his copy of Admiral Stirling's Treaty with the Japanese.[93]

For continuation of *Journal* in the order of dates, see *Journal* No. 2.

---

[93]Sir James Stirling ("Knight, Rear-Admiral and Commander-in-Chief of the ships and vessels of Her Britannic Majesty in the East Indies and Seas adjacent") signed a Convention with the Japanese at Nagasaki, on Oct. 14, 1854; it was ratified by Queen Victoria (Lord Clarendon) on Jan. 23, 1855; and ratifications were exchanged at Nagasaki on Oct. 9, 1855—the very day on which Hotta, Bitchiu-no-Kami, was appointed to the Japanese Cabinet! (Akimoto, *Lord Ii Naosuke,* p. 137.)

This Convention was concluded for the purpose of "regulating the admission of British ships into the ports of Japan." There is a manuscript copy of the full text in **L. B.,** vol. 1, pp. 176–78, which is followed, on pp. 178–81, by Admiral Stirling's own explanation of the various articles of the Treaty. The *Hongkong Government Gazette,* dated Victoria, Saturday, Oct. 27, 1855, carried the same material, with the addition of a "Copy of the English Act of Ratification." (*L. & P.,* vol. 2, no. 22.) More accessible references are: Perry, *Narrative,* 33-2, H. Ex. Doc., no. 97, vol. 1, pp. 388–89; and J. H. Gubbins, *The Progress of Japan,* Appendix 3, pp. 232–33.

Journal No. 2

Commencing April 15, 1856
Ending July 6, 1856

Tuesday, April 15, 1856. On board the *San Jacinto* off the Menam.[94] At 9 A. M. a small steamer belonging to the King appeared in the offing and soon anchored alongside. She is about forty tons and has a small, high-pressure engine or locomotive brought out from the United States. She was otherwise wholly built and set agoing by the Siamese. She is called *The Siamese Steam Fleet.* Dr. Mattoon came on board[95] in company with Phra Nai Wai (brother of the Prime Minister[96]), who informed me that he was sent down by the King to welcome me on my arrival.

I soon learned that the Prime Minister was on board and would visit the ship, provided he could come in a private capacity, or incognito. A boat was sent for him, and he came on board with four younger brothers. After a little conversation I learned that the house occupied by Sir John Bowring when here was now occu-

[94]In his manuscript, Townsend Harris breaks off at this point to say: "For *Journal* from May 21, 1855, see Journal no. 1."

[95]This visit is fully described also by Wood, *op. cit.,* pp. 151–54.

[96]His name, as it appears in the treaty later concluded by Townsend Harris, is: His Excellency Chau Phaya Sri Suriwongse Samuha, Phra Kralahom—the last two words meaning "Prime Minister."

pied by Mr. H. Parkes, and that they wished me to send up two officers to inspect the house prepared for me to see if it would suit me, or whether I would prefer waiting until Mr. Parkes should leave. On inquiry I found that the new house, although sadly deficient, was really the best they could give me until Mr. S. Parkes leaves. I determined that I would not send anyone up as it would lead to a great delay, and I was most anxious to get to Bangkok as speedily as possible—that I would take the house they had prepared, and that I was to be removed to the other and better house as soon as it was vacated by Mr. Parkes.

The Minister said he was not prepared to enter into business, so that what I got from him was rather from incidental than direct remarks. I gather that the King is rather inclined to undervalue our mission, as it does not come from a crowned head, etc., etc. By his advice I wrote letters to the First and Second Kings (see copies).[97]

The flag of Siam (white elephant on red ground) was then saluted with a royal salute of twenty-one guns. The [Prime] Minister, whose name is Phra Kalahom,

[97]The letter to the First King of Siam is to be found in *L. B.*, vol. 1, pp. 15–16. Townsend Harris informs the King of his desire to present the President's letter, thanks him for his kindness to Americans in Siam, and requests an early audience.

The letter to the Second King of Siam is to be found in *L. B.*, vol. 1, pp. 16–17. This letter is not so long as that to the First King. In fact, it plainly refers the Second King to that other letter for more complete information.

The treaty concluded by Townsend Harris gives the names of the two kings thus:

First King: Phra Bard Somdetch Phra Paramendr Maha Mongkut Phra Chom Klau Chau Yu Hua;
Second King: Phra Bard Somdetch Phra Pawarendr Ramesr Mahiswaresr Phra Pin Klau Chau Yu Hua.

declined to be saluted, as he was not on board officially. He went over the ship and examined everything very minutely and made many very sensible and shrewd remarks. He is the father of the Siamese navy, as he built all the ships they have which are after European models.

He told me I must let the King know how many swords and guns and big ships we have, which would greatly alter his tone. Still I have hopes of getting a treaty on terms that will be satisfactory, and without any bluster.

Two Americans came down with the Minister,— Captain Duvall[98] and Mr. Porter, both recently from China. Captain Duvall brought me a letter of introduction from Mr. Keenan, U. S. Consul at Hongkong.[99]

After taking some refreshments the Prime Minister and suite left for Bangkok.

The little steamer had the private flag of the King,—

---

[98]Writing from Shimoda on Apr. 4, 1859, to Mr. E. E. Rice, United States Commercial Agent at Hakodate, Townsend Harris says (*L. B.*, vol. 4, p. 32):

"Your friend Captain Duvall died miserably in the jungles of Siam, where he had gone on a gold hunting expedition. The story about his brave conduct while in command of one of the Siamese ships-of-war was nothing but fiction. He never held any such command, nor was he ever in Siamese employ."

[99]General James Keenan, of Pennsylvania, U.S. Consul for Hongkong, 1854–57. He was nominated Feb. 2, 1854, in place of F. T. Bush, resigned; reported, Feb. 8, 1854; consented to, Mar. 14, 1854. (Hasse *Index*, pt. 3, p. 1707.)

Tyler Dennett (*Americans in Eastern Asia*, p. 283) points out that General Keenan carried the American flag over the walls of Canton when Admiral Michael Seymour (British) attacked the city (Oct. 29, 1856), but that no mention of this fact was made in the official reports to the Department of State. (*Cf.*, too, Lane-Poole and Dickins's *Life of Sir Harry Parkes*, vol. 1, p. 239.)

This act of General Keenan, then, constitutes another, and an earlier, instance of Commodore Josiah Tattnall's "Blood is thicker than water," uttered on the occasion of the British reverse at the Peiho forts in northern China, on May 28, 1858—and both these gentlemen were therefore technically guilty of breaking the official neutrality of the United States. (For the full details of General Keenan's deed, see 35–2, S. Ex. Doc., no. 22, pt. 2—in Serial no. 983—pp. 1383–99.)

viz., on a red field the royal crown supported on each side by state umbrellas, closed.

Mr. Mattoon remains on board the ship with me until the King shall send down for me.

Wednesday, April 16, 1856. Nothing from Bangkok to-day. Had much conversation with Mr. Mattoon regarding my mission. He thinks I shall have no difficulty in getting the same terms as the English obtained. Has given me the characters of the two Kings and principal nobles.[100] We expect to be sent for to-morrow in the small steamer to proceed to Paknam and from thence we shall go up to Bangkok in the King's state barges.

The tide on the bar is about twelve feet. Lowest water on the bar is in March, when it is only thirteen feet at high water. The highest is in November, when eighteen feet is found.

Vessels can always lie in the roads, as no storms of a serious kind ever occur. No hurricane or typhoon was ever known in Siam.

Cambodia is now tributary to Siam, but a portion of its territories have been seized on by Cochin-China on the east and Siam on the west.

Chantibon produces most of the spices and fine gums

---

[100]Townsend Harris had taken pains to procure information on these points before leaving New York City. (See *Journal*, entry for Sept. 21, 1855.) It is almost certain (from a study of the handwritings) that the Rev. Dr. Samuel R. House (who had been a missionary to Siam for many years) was the author of the four-page unsigned document (*L. & P.*, vol. 2, no. 61), which Mr. Heusken (Townsend Harris's secretary) endorsed: "Biography of the King of Siam, his family and prime ministers."

The Rev. S. R. House must also have penned for Townsend Harris a similar document (*L. & P.*, vol. 2, no. 18), giving him a list of good books on Siam, and making suggestions regarding such practical details as the supply of paper, envelopes, tape-ribbon, and presents for the two kings, which last he actually assisted Townsend Harris in selecting. (*L. B.*, vol. 1, pp. 1, 76.)

of Siam. Black pepper is lately become an article of cultivation there, and enough might easily be produced to take the place of the Sumatra pepper.

The white elephant is an object of veneration, but not of worship. It is considered as a fortunate possession for a king—bringing to him good luck. The Siamese annals state that the Burmese once made a successful war on Siam, to obtain five white elephants.

Divorce in Siam is the simple will of the husband— who can even sell his wife as a slave. The father can always sell his son, no matter what his age, etc. Marriage is a simple sale of the girls, as the sum paid is only considered as her dower, when the family is rich. When it is poor, they use a part or the whole of the purchase money for the payment of their debts.

No marriage ceremony is performed. At a feast given on the occasion, a priest comes and eats before 12 M., as he cannot eat after noon. He says some prayers on the occasion, but it cannot be called a benediction or making a contract. Slavery[101] is deprived of some of its evils by the laws of Siam. The slave can work for himself, provided he pays his master a certain per cent. on the sum paid for him. He can also redeem himself by paying the original purchase money, but the owner may add any costs he may be put to by the slave, such as running away, sickness, or by his failing to pay the sum due to his master when working for himself.

A slave may keep any property which he has acquired

---

[101]Townsend Harris's interest in slavery is easily understood when we remember that his mission to Siam and Japan took place in the years immediately preceding the Civil War.

by his own labor or other means. So, also, the wife can trade on her own account, and her husband or his creditors cannot touch it.

Sodomy is very common, as is also bestiality. Neither is punished with any severity, and never except in the case of a priest.

Adultery is very common, but almost escapes without punishment, except when the female belongs to the royal family or some of the very high nobles, in which case the male offender is punished with death.

Thursday, April 17, 1856. Nothing new to-day, nor anything from Bangkok. Very hot.

Friday, April 18, 1856. I have a letter[102] this morning from the Minister of Foreign Affairs acknowledging the receipt of my letter of Sunday and explaining that the bamboo house prepared for me is according to strict Siamese etiquette of the most honorable kind, as it is new and has never been occupied.

He also writes that he will send out for me on Monday to take me to Paknam, or, according to its name in the court language, Samut-phra-kan, at which place I am to meet twenty-two royal boats to take me and my suite up in high honor to Bangkok.

Write to the Minister in reply. (See copy this date.)[103]

---

[102]The manuscript original of the translation of this letter (by the Rev. Mattoon) is still extant. (*L. & P.*, vol. 2, no. 25.) It is dated as follows: "This communication was written on Thursday the 12th of the increasing Moon, the fifth month of the year of the Serpent, corresponding to April 17th, 1856."

William M. Wood is authority for the statement that on April 17th Townsend Harris received presents from the King. (*Fankwei*, p. 159.)

[103]*L. B.*, vol 1, p. 17. The substance of the letter from the Minister for Foreign Affairs(*L. & P.*, vol. 2, no. 25) and of Townsend Harris's reply is given in this *Journal* entry.

Concerning slavery. On the death of the father, the eldest son succeeds to his rights. When only minors are left, an uncle can sell his nephews and nieces, especially if they have lived with or have been supported by him.

Saturday, April 19, 1856. The little steamer came down to-day, and Mr. Parkes in her paid me a visit. I had much conversation with him. He finds much delay in getting a full understanding as to the *meaning* of the Treaty, and some efforts have been made to change some of the articles in Schedules A and B of the Treaty. He is now having the line four miles distant from the walls (within which foreigners may lease but cannot buy houses and grounds until they have resided ten years in Siam) measured and marked, and when this is done the Treaty is to be proclaimed by the Siamese Government.

He fears that I shall find my new house too small and says I will require both that and the one erected for the French Embassy.

Mr. S. Parkes recommended me to apply for the house occupied by the late Phra Klang. I got Mr. Mattoon to write up to his friends to move in the matter.

Mr. Parkes informs me that I will meet a most friendly reception from the Siamese, but that I must be prepared for many and some very unreasonable delays which will greatly try my patience.

After taking some refreshment, Mr. Parkes went over the ship and saw her armament, machinery, etc., etc., and left at half-past two. We gave him a salute of eleven guns, although as Consul he only is entitled to nine guns, but Captain Bell had been informed that Mr. Parkes had been saluted with that number by the *Auckland* when he disembarked at Bangkok.

The weather is very hot. The thermometer ranges about 82° at night, and from 88° to 90° during the heat of the day. A pleasant breeze springs up about 2 P. M. and blows until 4 A. M.

I am told the heat at nights is more oppressive on board ship than it is at Bangkok, although the thermometer rises to 96° there during the day.

It is an old saying here that those who come here for business should bring one ship loaded with patience, another loaded with presents, and a third ship for carrying away the cargo.

Mr. Mattoon has made a careful translation of the Foreign Minister's letter to me (*i.e.,* the Phra Klang).

About 8 P. M. heavy clouds arose in the north (in the direction of Bangkok), and the lightning was very vivid for more than an hour with an occasional sound of distant thunder. The lightning was almost all vertical, descending quite to the edge of the horizon. Some bolts were of a deep red, others yellow in color. Mr. Mattoon thinks the storm was over Bangkok. It is the beginning of the rainy season.

Sunday, April 20, 1856. Mr. Mattoon preached a most excellent sermon at half-past ten to the ship's company. He had an attentive audience, and was earnest and clear in his discourse.

The schooner sent down for the presents anchored

near the ship this morning, but they will not be put on board till to-morrow.

Boats came off from her with eggs, fowls, onions, plantains and a few mangoes for sale. About noon another boat from Paknam came alongside with a present of dried fish and cocoanut oil, as a present from the King to the ship's company. The boat had two rudders, one on each quarter.

I shall send up in the schooner one case of cordials, one ditto cherry brandy, the "diplomatic trunk,"[104] and two barrels of flour, which I borrowed from the ship and am to return it in Hongkong. I take the flour to make bread for the party, as neither bread nor flour is to be had at Bangkok.

Monday, April 21, 1856. At 7 A. M. the little steamer, *The Siamese Steam Force,*[105] with two Cochin-Chinese boats, each rowed by thirty men, came alongside and brought five nobles, one of the third rank and four of the fourth rank. Of the latter, one went on board the schooner, one to each of the Cochin-Chinese boats, and one to the steamer, where the other third rank noble remained. A joint note was received written in the name of the Phra Nai Wai, etc., explaining that the boats were sent to convey part of my suite, for fear the steamer should be too much crowded. The steamer had two flags

---

[104]This trunk was recently in the possession of Mrs. Sarah C. W. Harris, of New York City, who died Feb. 5, 1927.

[105]Under the caption "A Royal Siamese Machinist" (Prince T. N. Chau Fa Khromakhun Isaret Rangsan), the New York *Tribune* gives an interesting account of the building of a Siamese steamer entirely by native talent. (*Tribune,* morning ed., Saturday, April 7, 1849, p. 2, col. 3, quoting from the *Singapore Free Press* of Oct. 19, 1848.) William M. Wood, *op. cit.,* p. 153, identifies this Prince as the then Second King of Siam.

on the bow: the flag of Siam, a white elephant on a blue field; the other was the particular flag of the King,—his crown, supported on each side by royal umbrellas,—and was hoisted on the stern. The boats, which were some fifty feet long, had each four flags on the stern, red, blue, pink, white.

The schooner came alongside, and the articles heretofore noted and the packages of presents were all put on board and the marines sent to the two boats. After leaving Penang a large number of the marines were on the sick list, but as soon as it was known that a guard of marines was to go up to Bangkok, they all speedily recovered.

At 10:20 A. M. we started, the ship saluting me with seventeen guns.

The air was from the north and, as our course was also north, it made a fine refreshing breeze, which was most grateful after the great heat we had suffered in the ship. As we passed H. M. Surveying Schooner,[106] she saluted us by dipping her flag, which courtesy was answered by the band playing "God Save the Queen."

About eight miles from the ship we entered into the pass between the fishing stakes. These are stout saplings and from the strong tide which was then running were constantly swaying to and fro. Large quantities of shell fish were adhering to the poles. The white ibis, or paddy bird of the Indian Archipelago, were collected in numbers. Some perched on the stakes, others in larger

---

[106]The *Spartan; cf.* above entry for Apr. 14, 1856. Willian M. Wood, *op. cit.,* p. 160, ascribes this interchange of courtesies to H. M.'s Brig *Saracen.*

numbers were collected on the little patches of sand, seen here and there. At the very entrance of the river was a building roofed with tiles and standing some ten feet above the water on strong posts. On the staff was a flag with blue, red and blue in horizontal stripes and having the white elephant. This building is a sort of lookout, and is also a refuge for benighted persons in boats. About three miles above is Paknam. This place is strongly fortified with long lines of batteries on both banks and on an island nearly in the middle of the river. The batteries appear to be in good order, and are well supplied with guns. The position of these defences appears to be judiciously selected, but of this only a military man could judge. A short distance above the fortified island is a very pretty pagoda, crowning another islet. It does not contain any images, but is a place of great resort at certain seasons of merrymaking, when it is covered with cloths of various colors.

On approaching the landing place a number of flags were seen fluttering in the wind. Soldiers were seen under arms, and a large number of people collected. As soon as we had anchored, a person in a tawdry uniform with the black hat of the West on his head came on board and invited me to land, which I did, in company with the Commodore, my secretary and some three others. As I ascended the steps, the guard, which lined both sides of the brick pathway, presented arms, and the bugles made a most diabolical noise. The uniform was red pantaloons and jacket, black shako, cross belts and bare feet.

About fifty yards from the landing was a building, open on all sides, and built after the exact manner of the Pondoppo of Java, and in its interior consists of three stages or degrees, the upper one occupying more than half of the whole area, and is the post of honor.

It was here that Mr. Balestier met the first instance of uncivil treatment, as he was stopped on the second stage, and there he was compelled to take the refreshments offered to him.[107] I was aware not only of the custom, but also of the manner [in which] Mr. Balestier was treated, and was determined not to submit to such treatment, had it been attempted. But my reception was quite different. I was met on the upper stage by the Phra Nai Wai and a brother of the Prime Minister, who was of higher rank than the Phra Nai Wai. They were very cordial, shaking hands and inviting me to be seated, etc., etc.

The Phra Nai Wai requested the band might land

---

[107]Mr. Joseph Balestier went up the River Menam on Apr. 3, 1850. In his long report to the Hon. Daniel Webster, Secretary of State, dated Washington, Nov. 25, 1851, he tells the story as follows (32–1, S. Ex. Doc., no. 38—in Serial no. 618—pp. 10–11):

"At the second port, about midway between the mouth of the river and the capital, where preparations had been made on a large scale to receive the embassy, I was informed that the commanding officer or governor of the place was taken suddenly ill, and I was attended by men of low rank, who seated me on the second platform of the building I was in, thereby intimating to the crowd that I was a person of inferior rank; for, in that country, officers of high rank occupy the upper platform of the floor; those of inferior rank, the second platform; and, finally, the third or lowest part of the floor is resorted to by persons of low rank. It was only after I returned to my barge that I was made aware of this rule of etiquette, and, consequently, of the affront put upon me . . ."

This episode had already been reported by Mr. Balestier to the Hon. Clayton, Secretary of State, but much more briefly and with minor differences. (*Ib.*, p. 51, dated U. S. Flagship *Plymouth*, Gulf of Siam, Apr. 30, 1850.)

and play during the meal which they had provided, and that when the marines came up (their boat was about a mile astern when we arrived) that they also might land.

We soon after sit down to a table abundantly supplied with soup, fish, poultry, pork, vegetables, etc., etc., followed by plenty of fruits and various preparations in sugar, etc.

The Phra Nai Wai proposed to salute the American Flag with twenty-one guns, and borrowed an ensign to hoist on the Fort during the salute, and requested that we should order another American flag to be hoisted on the little steamer during the same period. All of which was done, and when the salute was over the band struck up "Hail, Columbia." The Siamese of all ranks are greatly attracted by our band, and, when the men went to another building, they were followed by large crowds to see them eat, etc. I here saw the Siamese women for the first time. Their scanty clothing is almost the same as that of the men, except a cloth which is thrown over the neck, with the ends falling down over their bosom which it partially conceals, when the wind does not blow it about. They have the same ungraceful way of cutting the hair,—*i. e.,* very short except on the crown of the head, where it is about three inches long and stands up like bristles. On examination, we found the Kanyu[108] boats were not of the style usually sent when similar persons are to proceed up to Bangkok, and Mr. Mat-

---

[108]There is a town of this name in northern China; and perhaps the reference in the text is to some kind of Chinese boats.

toon was of [the] opinion that they did not expect us to use them, or rather, they expected we would prefer going up in the steamer; which, in fact, was the case, for on our transit from the ship to Paknam we had canvassed the matter, and we agreed that it would be more agreeable to go up in the steamer which would reach Bangkok before six o'clock, P. M., while the boats would probably not reach there before eight o'clock. Mr. Mattoon formed his opinion of their intentions from the fact that the boats were not decorated with cloth of gold, banners, etc., etc., as is usual on such occasions, and also because the number was not as great as that named by the Minister of Foreign Affairs in his letter to me,—*viz.,* twenty-two.

The Phra Nai Wai inquired after my health and age, and the health and age of the President, and some other and similar questions. He told me that when I embarked I should be saluted with seventeen guns.

I then ordered the marines, band and servants to go on board and afterwards embarked myself, receiving similar honors as on my landing. Soon after the steamer got under way, the promised salute of seventeen guns was fired from one of the forts on the left bank of the river. Some of the guns seemed by the report to be very heavy pieces. The powder appeared to be poor, as the smoke from a single discharge was almost equal to the smoke of a whole salute from the frigate.

A lively scene was now seen. The Kanyu boats, some of them full fifty feet or more long, with high prows and sterns, propelled by the paddles of some fifty men, all shouting and striving not only to pass each other but the steamer also. The strife was animated, as you could see by their countenances and eyes, while the air seemed to be filled by a whirlwind of arms, paddles and naked, screaming savages.

The tints of the green are very beautiful and rich, among which the light pea green of the mangrove arrests the eye from the moment you get near enough to the land to distinguish shades of color, and this continues up the river for some distance, but is now (above Paknam) mixed with the deeper greens of the *casuarina littorea* and *nipah* palms, from which [come] the *ataps* so largely used in the Indian Archipelago and the peninsula for making and covering their houses. It is a pretty palm, and is difficult to distinguish from the young cocoanut, but it never grows up into a boll with a verdant head of waving fronds, but remains lowly and lovely and most useful to man. It is impossible to overestimate the advantages which are drawn from the common varieties of the palm.

It furnishes materials for building the house and the boat, with cordage and sails for the latter; fishing lines and seines; refreshing and cooling drinks in the hottest day; it furnishes oil and champagne wine, with as much brandy as may be desired. Its produce of sugar resembles the maple of our country, while it forms an important part of each meal, furnishing the vessels in which both food and drink are placed. The above are all *literal,* and no doubt other uses are made which do not at present occur to me.

We now went on rapidly, as we had wind, tide and steam all in our favor.

A few miles above Paknam and you begin to meet with the houses of the Siamese peasantry. These are generally very neat and far superior to the house occupied by the same class in India and China and, of course, to those of the Malays. The houses are elevated on posts some six feet above the ground, which [not only] secures a greater degree of dryness (an important consideration in a damp country), but [also] secures the inmates from the carbonic acid gas or malaria which is exhaled during the night and collects on the ground until it is some feet in depth. Most travellers give as a reason for this elevation of the house so far above the ground that it is a means of protection against reptiles and noxious animals and insects. This reason is no doubt quite satisfactory to those who like to have their nerves agitated by the dangers they *read of,* but careful examinations prove that in this case (as in most analogous ones) it is a better reason than childish fear of snakes and toads that induces them to build their houses some height above the ground. But to return to the house— the roof is quite as steep as a French château; the sides are covered in with very neat panel work made of very small pieces of wood, indeed the smaller the prettier in Siamese eyes. The roof is covered with a neatly made thatch made from the *nipah* palm. About ten miles from Paknam the river makes an extraordinary curve or curves quite like that in the Connecticut River at Mount Holyoke. It is about twenty miles around this bend, but the Siamese have cut a canal, practicable for boats, in the direct line of the river, which saves some ten miles of distance, but we were compelled from the size of our conveyance to follow the river. During the dry season, —*i.e.,* from December to May, a dam is erected across the lower end to prevent the salt water from entering the canal and thus injuring their cultivations; but during the rains such is the volume of rain water that the river is always fresh even down to Paknam, and ships some four miles from the mouth are said to take fresh water from the surface during this season.

The entrance to this canal is near a sugar plantation and just below the fort of Paklat. On arriving at Paklat the steamer was stopped, and a number of boats came alongside bearing an abundant supply of the various fruits in season from the Commander of the place. It was here that Mr. Balestier landed for the second time on his way up, as is usual when the transit is made in boats. Above the fort is the great iron chain which the Siamese stretch across the river in times of danger, and is thought by them to be a perfect barrier to the river. The chain is on and attached to logs to float it to its place, and powerful windlasses are erected on the left bank to heave it across and to its place.

When Sir James Brooke[109] came up, the chain was

_____

[109]Sir James Brooke (1803–68), born at Benares, India—another of the famous empire builders of Great Britain. He later became the Rajah of Sarawak, on the northwest coast of Borneo. (An interesting sketch in *Dict. Nat. Biogr.*)

In 1850 he was commissioned to conclude a treaty with Siam, but he was received (only a few months after Mr. Balestier, *L. & P.*, vol. 2, nos. 31 and 61) with hostile demonstrations, and negotiations were broken off in a manner that

stretched across and he was taken through a small canal which the Siamese cut around the end of the chain.

The scenery was now beautiful in the extreme, the tide being a spring, and nearly high water hid all the mud banks. Trees hung over the stream in many places with their branches touching the water. Here we saw, in addition to those noted before (except the mangrove), the cotton tree, the feather bamboo, areca[110] and cocoa palms, *pandanus spiralis,* with others unknown to me. The light of the declining sun had its rays softened by thin clouds and seemed to give life and freshness to everything which, with the delicious coolness of the air, seemed like a paradise after the dreadful heat we had endured at the anchorage outside the bar.

Boats of all sizes, from the tiny affair of some seven feet long by fifteen inches wide, holding a single person, up to those paddled by some fifty men, were seen darting about in all directions. Here was a boat laden with wood or coal propelled by a Chinaman standing erect and facing the bow; *pushed* two oars and seemed to be indifferent about us or our craft. *There* were boats of the Siamese who all squatted as we approached, out of respect. Hundreds of neat cottages were seen peeping through the rich foliage, with frequent *wats* or temples, near which clusters of priests in their yellow robes were seen, while men, women and children would occupy every post of vantage to see us and hear the band. Now

made matters more difficult for those who followed him—namely, Sir John Bowring, Sir Harry Parkes and Townsend Harris. (Lane-Poole and Dickins, *op. cit.,* vol. 1, p. 190; Bowring, *Siam,* vol. 2, pp. 209–10.)

[110]The areca or betel-nut palm.

we began to meet the floating houses which are erected on a raft of bamboos some two feet above the level of the water. These houses have a neat appearance, and, when kept in order, are far preferable to the houses occupied by the laboring classes in Europe and America. I omitted to note that when we stopped at Paklat to receive the presents of fruit, the head man asked, as a favor, that the band might play, and appeared much pleased with the music.

We now began to find the wats larger and finer. Raft houses more frequent and the number of boats larger. Presently we saw the masts of square-rigged vessels, and, to our sincere pleasure, the "Star Spangled Banner" waving in the gentle evening breeze.[111] One must be far from home and among strangers to appreciate the intense emotions that fill the heart at the sight of the national flag. Abstractly, it is but so much bunting of divers colors, but as a flag it represents country and home and friends and all the dear thoughts that are associated with those ideas.

The flag was hoisted on the ship *Ianthe,* which was receiving some repairs, preparatory to loading a cargo for China.

I have before noted the fine ships which the Siamese have built, and I now saw a new specimen—it was the complete fusion of the junk of China with the ship of the West. Her foremast was rigged as a ship, the main hoisted the enormous single sail of the junk, while the

---

111Wood, *op. cit.,* p. 160: "On our way in, we passed several merchant ships at anchor, all of which were being loaded by Mr. King, an enterprising American merchant of Bangkok. . . ."

mizzen was bark rigged; the bow was open and had its two enormous goggling eyes of the junk, but out of the open space projected the bowsprit and jib booms of the ship of the West.

About 6 o'clock we came in sight of the Portuguese Consulate, which had hoisted its flag in our honor; and, a short distance above, a high flagstaff with a new bamboo-house pointed out our new residence. As soon as we had anchored, a boat came off and a Portuguese as interpreter welcomed me and desired me to land. On ascending the steps from the river I was welcomed by the Phra Klang in a very cordial manner. Here I also met Dr. Bradley[112] of the American Presbyterian Mission, also Mr. D. O. King,[113] and Mr. Stone, both Americans. The Phra Klang now invited me to enter the house. I

---

[112]The Rev. D. B. Bradley, who is also referred to as belonging to the American Missionary Association (*L. & P.*, vol. 2, no. 61, p. 4), and to the Congregational Mission (Wood, *op. cit.*, p. 190). As in so many other cases in the Far East, the Rev. Bradley was at the same time both missionary and physician. For the story of his vain effort to cure the Queen of the First King of Siam, see Wood, *op. cit.*, pp. 248–51; and Bowring, *Siam*, vol. 2, pp. 411–21.

[113]David O. King had established himself at Shanghai, where he served as Consul for Prussia. Some time before the date of this *Journal* entry, he had freed some Siamese vessels that had been captured by the Chinese at Shanghai, and the King of Siam had in gratitude appointed him Consul and Commercial Agent of Siam at Shanghai. (*L. & P.*, vol. 2, no. 23, Mr. King to Townsend Harris, Bangkok, Jan. 28, 1856; and *L. & P.*, vol. 1, nos. 30, 32.)

Naturally, Mr. King soon desired to visit the country which he officially represented. He reached Bangkok some time in Nov., 1855. Writing from Canton on Dec. 18, 1855 (*L. & P.*, vol. 1, no. 25), S. Drinker warns Townsend Harris against Mr. King:

"I wish you were at Siam now. David King from Shanghai has gone down there to try and get the King's business at Shanghai. I am afraid he will be meddling in your business with the King, and making a treaty on his own hook."

Mr. King's own letter to Townsend Harris (see above) is a tirade against the Prime Minister of Siam, and the latter's attitude towards Mr. King is therein portrayed as so hostile that there was small danger of Mr. King's obtaining a treaty "on his own hook."

found a large room intended as a public and dining room. Back of this, two large bedrooms with Chinese bedsteads of a rich description, good beds, pillows, bolsters, or Dutch wives, and silk mosquito curtains. These rooms were appropriated to Commodore Armstrong and myself. Four other bedrooms, each with two beds, properly furnished, accommodate eight of the officers.

Two of our company went to the house of Mr. Mattoon, and the purser went to the house of Mr. D. O. King (an American merchant who has established a branch of his house here, having others at Canton and Shanghai). I found the house to be airy and clean, having some appliances for comfort in the shape of bathing rooms and water closets, but I have no private room for writing or conversation, except my bedroom, which has a doorway but no door. I closed it after a fashion with a small flag, which was brought up for our procession.

After looking around the house and getting over the bustle of arrival and landing baggage, I went to see the quarters of the marines, band and servants, etc., etc., which are very comfortable, and each man is supplied with a good mattress made of quilted cloth wadded with cotton, and to each man are given two sheets.

This over, the Phra Klang came to my room bringing a man of Portuguese descent (who is, as he told me, a general) as interpreter.[114]

He spoke but very little English, but by speaking

---

[114]This must be the strange individual who is called Gabrielle by William M. Wood (*op. cit.,* p. 162).

Spanish I got along pretty well. The Phra Klang was anxious to know how far my instructions went and what we wanted, etc., etc. I avoided giving him any particular information, saying that my mission was of the most friendly kind; that the President had a great esteem for the King and was anxious to strengthen the ties of friendship already happily existing, and to increase the intercourse between the people of the two countries, etc., etc.; and finally that, when I met the Ministers together, I would more fully explain matters, as I could then have the assistance of Mr. Mattoon, who was competent to interpret correctly between us.

The Phra Klang asked me if I had a copy of our treaty with Japan.[115] I replied that I would send him a copy when I reached China, as I was unwilling that they should see that treaty at present. We continued in conversation until near eight o'clock, when dinner was served. We sat down to a table handsomely spread with French porcelain, white and gold, and plenty of new table silver of English make. The food and fruit were abundant, but the cooking was bad, meat almost raw and everything surcharged with onions, garlic and leeks.

Soon after, some of the men were seized with cholera morbus; which is not to be wondered at, as they had eaten fruit and drunk cocoanuts to an unreasonable extent, one man having drunk one hundred cocoanuts between Paknam and Bangkok. In addition to all this, they ate heartily of fresh pork at Paknam, and drank of the very bad water at this place. Now, to all this, add

---

[115]The treaty concluded by Commodore Perry, Mar. 31, 1854.

exposure to the sun for some hours and the only wonder is, not that some were sick, but that all were not so.

I went to bed about ten o'clock and was long kept awake by the excitement of the day and the novelty.[116]

List of Suite:
Commodore Armstrong
Lieutenant Lewis   U. S. N.
    "   Rutledge   "
    "   Carter   "
    "   Tyler   U. S. Marine Corps
Fleet Surgeon Wood   U. S. N.
Assistant Surgeon Daniels   "
Purser Bradford   "
Chief Engineer Isherwood   "
Mr. H. J. C. Heusken   Secretary to Envoy
Mr. Van den Heuvel   "   " Commodore
16 Marines   U. S. N.
 8 Bandsmen   "
 1 Quarter Master   "
 4 Servants
 2 Apprentices

In all 42 persons.

Tuesday, April 22, 1856. It rained in the night, and we find a prospect of a rainy day, and in fact it rained very steadily until three P. M. Seven persons were found sick this morning, three officers and four marines. One of the latter was considered as being dangerously ill, but happily he and all the others were in the way of recovery before night.

[116]The voyage up the River Menam and the arrival at Bangkok are described at full length in Wood's *Fankwei*, pp. 159–74.

105

Mr. Mattoon was also ill. He came to me about ten o'clock. He says that the King is decidedly indisposed to receive me in the same manner he did Sir J. Bowring, and that the President's letter must be sent to him through the nobles and that then he can appoint persons to receive me. I learn that he has been much annoyed by the number of letters which Mr. Parkes has written to him, or rather the labor it has thrown on him, and that he declares he will not receive any more. In fact I am informed by Mr. Mattoon that Mr. Parkes took a letter this morning to the Prince (the King's brother)[117] to be forwarded to the King, and that the Prince refused to forward it until Mr. Parkes informed him that it was simply an answer to some questions about the presents, etc., etc., which the King had asked through a messenger, and that, being unable to give an answer then, the messenger went away and thus Mr. Parkes was compelled to write. On this the Prince consented to take the letter to the King.

I wrote to the Phra Klang (see copy),[118] requesting a private interview with the King, etc., etc.

During the morning the following American missionaries called on me:

---

[117]The King's younger half-brother and favorite. His full name, as it appears on his visiting card (*L. & P.*, vol. 2, no. 63) is: Prince Pra Chau Nong Ya Ter Krom Luang Wong Sa Tirat Sanit. The treaty later concluded by Townsend Harris has it: Krom Hluang Wongsa Dhiraj Snidh.

[118]This letter (*L. B.*, vol. 1, p. 19) not only requested a private audience with the King, but also that this audience should take place before his public reception. Townsend Harris expressed his desire to be accompanied on this occasion by Mr. Heusken and the Rev. Mattoon, and to receive permission to present a copy of the President's letter.

Mr. Telford,[119] Mr. Ashmore[119] and Mr. Chandler[120] of the Baptist Mission, and Mr. Bradley of the Presbyterian Mission.

I feel somewhat dispirited by the unfavorable mood of the King and fear it will cause me much delay, if not defeat my object,—but *Nil desperandum* is my motto; and, by unchangeable good humor, I hope to shame them into kinder treatment, and the King is said to [be] very capricious in his moods and he may as suddenly turn around in my favor. The greatest difficulty exists in the fact that the King is totally ignorant of the power and greatness of the United States, and he will remain in that state unless I can have a private interview and convince him that we are to be both feared and respected. Captain Smith and a surgeon from the steamer *Auckland* called; and in the evening Mr. King, Captain Duvall and Mr. Porter, all Americans, called on me.

About seven this evening Prince George Washington,[121] son of the Second King, called on me, having

---

[119]The Rev. Robert Telford and the Rev. William Ashmore were both members of the Chinese Department of the Baptist Mission. Mr. Ashmore was shortly to leave Siam for China on account of the ill health of Mrs. Ashmore, and his last service in Siam was held (in the Chinese language) on Sunday, May 4, 1856. (Wood, *op. cit.*, pp. 193, 213.)

[120]Mr. John H. Chandler was a type founder and printer and a member of the Siamese Department of the Baptist Mission. (*L. & P.*, vol. 2, no. 61, p. 4.)

Stephen Mattoon, Samuel J. Smith, and John H. Chandler were among the six American missionaries who had signed a letter exculpating and defending Mr. Joseph Balestier on the occasion of the failure of his negotiations in 1851. Said letter of defence was signed by every American citizen resident in Bangkok (*i. e.*, the six missionaries) and by the only English firm doing business there—that of Daniel Brown. (32–1, S. Ex. Doc., no. 38—in Serial no. 618—pp. 14–15, 75.)

For a brief account of the American missions in Siam, read Bowring, *Siam*, vol. 1, pp. 381 ff.

[121]A young man eighteen years of age. (Wood, *op. cit.*, p. 210.)

107

the Rev. Mr. Smith of the Baptist American Mission as his interpreter.[122] He had with him a Siamese officer of the rank corresponding to ours of major, and some other persons, among others a soldier of his father's.

He brought me a kind message from his father, with his regrets that he could not see me until after my public reception, and that, as soon as I had been received in audience by the First King, he should expect to see me often, etc., etc. He also brought a message to the Commodore and his officers requesting them to visit him privately, as he could not receive them publicly until I had had my audience.

The Prince now asked for a musket, and one being brought, he ordered the Major[123] to put the soldier through the manual, which he did, giving all his orders in the English language. The performance was very creditable, both to the soldier and to his officer.

At the Prince's request a marine was put through the manual by a sergeant. The band played "Hail, Columbia," etc., etc., much to the Prince's satisfaction.

A good deal of conversation then passed, but all political subjects were carefully avoided. The Prince left about nine o'clock, and I then retired; had a good rest. The weather was rainy during the night and so cool that I was glad to have warm clothing over me.

---

[122]Samuel J. Smith, a member of the Siamese Department of the Baptist Mission. For the services conducted at his house (in Siamese) on Sunday, May 4, 1856, see Wood, *op. cit.*, pp. 193, 210, 213–14. (*Cf. L. & P.*, vol. 2, no. 61, p. 4.)

[123]Meaning the Siamese officer who accompanied Prince George Washington; while the "soldier" similarly refers to the Siamese soldier just mentioned as belonging to the Second King.

Wednesday, April 23, 1856. The schooner came up this morning, and I had the trunk and two cases of cordials brought to me. The two barrels [of] flour were sent to Mr. Mattoon's, and the twelve large cases I put in the godowns of Mr. D. O. King (see note to him).

Mr. A. F. Moor, Portuguese Consul, and his secretary[124] called on me. He is a very pleasant person and speaks English with great fluency.

Mr. Mattoon came in and informs me that the King declines a private interview before my public one, and refers me to his Ministers. He says that Sir John Bowring was an old correspondent of his and that he admitted him to a private audience, not as envoy, but as an old friend. Mr. Mattoon also informs me that the King wishes me to deliver the President's letter to the Nobles, who, after examination, will, if it be in proper terms, deliver it to him. *We shall see about this.* Mr. Mattoon suggests that I should see the Minister of Foreign Affairs, the Prime Minister and the Prince, to which I assented, and we go about 4 P. M.

Mr. Parkes called on me, and we had a long and pleasant conversation. He has a prospect of being detained here quite as long as I am.

The Second King has sent me a most kind letter, accompanying a present of eighty-seven large dishes of the most beautiful fruits of Siam. The quantity is enormous —in fact, quite enough for the appetite of full five hundred men. It came down in boats finely decorated and under the charge of a high noble, who spoke excellent

---

[124]The Consul's secretary was J. Da Silva. (*L. & P.*, vol. 2, no. 61, p. 4.)

English. This kingly present called forth the warm applause of the Commodore and all the gentlemen of my suite. The grammar of the letter was perfect, and the calligraphy quite puts all ours to shame; each letter is as perfectly formed as though it had been written by a writing master and, moreover, was all the King's, both matter and manner.[125]

SECOND KING'S LETTER

[The royal device]

To HIS EXCELLENCY TOWNSEND HARRIS
Envoy Plenipotentiary of the U. S. Am. to Siam, &c.

DEAR SIR:

Your kind favor of the 15th Inst., announcing your safe arrival off the Bar, has been received.

It affords me pleasure to welcome you and your suit[e] to our country.

Please accept the accompanying fruit.

I am anticipating the pleasure of seeing you in due time, of which you shall be informed.

With best wishes for yourself, and the gentlemen of the Steamer, believe me,

Yours truly,

P. S. PHRA PIN KLAU CHAU

YU HUA.

Second King of Siam, &c.

Palace of the Second King,
Bangkok, Siam, April 22nd, 1856.

---

[125]The original here quoted in full is *L. & P.*, vol. 2, no. 33. (See illustration.)
Townsend Harris answered this letter on Apr. 23rd, expressing his appreciation of the King's welcome and gift. (*L. B.*, vol. 1, p. 21.)
It may here be mentioned that Commodore Perry, too, corresponded with this Second King of Siam. (See 33–2, H. Ex. Doc., no. 97, vol. 2, pp. 191–97.)
Also, beginning with this letter of the Second King, the entries in the manuscript *Journal* are for some pages written by Mr. Heusken, Townsend Harris's

A HOLOGRAPH LETTER FROM THE SECOND KING OF SIAM
Dated, Palace of the Second King, Bangkok, Siam, April 22, 1856.

This evening[126] I started accompanied by Dr. Mattoon, Dr. Wood, Lieutenant Carter and my secretary, in two barges to pay a private visit to the Phra Klang, Minister for Foreign Affairs. His Excellency received me very kindly, offered us segars and thea [tea],[127] usual reception in Siam. His palace is built in a mixed European, Chinese style, the reception room [is] covered with carpets, and furnished with chairs, sofas, large mirrors, etc.[128] I explained to him the nature of my mission, the extent of my powers, titles etc. [He] inquired after the usual form of addressing the President. I told him his title was merely "The President of the United States," this being the highest rank in our country and equivalent to that of Emperor or King. He suggested that, Siam being a small country and the United States a good, friendly and powerful nation, to include in the treaty to be made an article wherein the United States should bind themselves to act as arbiter in case of any difficulty arising between Siam and any other nation. I replied that the United States would al-

---

secretary. Mr. Heusken was a Hollander, and, though not perfect in his English, had been hired as secretary by Townsend Harris with a view to his future services in Japan, where a knowledge of the Dutch language would be and was essential.

[126]Meaning at about 4 P. M. (See above in this day's entry.)

[127]Mr. Heusken had originally spelled this word "thee," then changed it to "thea"—a confusion due to his knowledge of French.

[128]This visit to the Minister of Foreign Affairs is more fully reported by Mr. Wood, *op. cit.*, pp. 174–77. The Minister himself is thus described (*ib.*, p. 175):

"The Prah Klan, about forty years of age, was a heavy, solid, sober-faced man, dressed in a blue figured silk mantle, fastened around the waist by a yellow silk sash, and received us in an easy and dignified manner, but seemed disappointed that a larger number of officers had not come, and immediately inquired the reason."

ways willingly act in the above mentioned capacity, and consider it as the highest honor that could be paid to the wisdom and power of their government; so even they offered to act as mediators between the now belligerent powers of France, England, Turkey and Russia; and that, by making it an Article of the Treaty, would infer that the Government of the United States were only willing to act in the capacity of arbiter *conditionally,* which, considering it as a high honor they are always ready to accept, makes the Article in question quite superfluous.

From there we called on Krom Luang Wong [Sa] Tirat Sanit, the King's brother and Chief Physician to the royal family.[129] His Highness seems to be fifty years old, has a very benevolent face, his features are quite Bourbonic and [bear] a striking resemblance to those of Louis XVI. After explaining to him my titles and mission, he kindly suggested to write a note to the Phra Klang, [asking] on which of the nobles I had to call before my public audience to the King in order to give no offence to His Majesty and to conform myself to the rules of Siamese etiquette. He spoke about the Siamese being a jungle people, and not so advanced in civilization as the nations of the West, hinted at Mr. Balestier's mission and said the old bridge being a bad one, he was confident that the new one was strong and sufficient to

---

[129]We have already given the full name of Prince Krom Luang. Again Mr. Wood gives a full description (*op. cit.,* pp. 177–78), and says of the Prince (*ib.,* p. 177):

"Prince Wongsa was a short and very fat man, with a broad, benevolent and somewhat jocular face, though at the time of our call the expression was rather sad."

carry us over, anticipating the good result of the Treaty. [He] was highly delighted at making Dr. Wood's acquaintance (he, the Prince, having received some years ago a doctor's diploma[130] from the New York faculty), and requested to consult him on his brother's disease. I told the Prince I had heard of him many and many times before I ever dreamt of visiting his country, and left him most favorably impressed with his reception and manners.

Paid a visit to Khun Phra Nai Wai, Prime Minister.[131] The magnificence of his house exceeded my

---

[130]Mr. Wood more accurately says that Prince Krom Luang was a member of the New York Academy of Medicine (*op. cit.*, pp. 150, 177, 247); while Max von Brandt states that in the Prince's reception room there hung his diploma as an M. D. from Philadelphia (*Dreiunddreissig Jahre in Ost-Asien. Erinnerungen eines deutschen Diplomaten*, 3 vols., Leipzig, Georg Wigand, 1901, vol. 1, p. 255).

[131]This is an error for Phra Kalahom. Compare Wood, *op. cit.*, pp. 178–82. This officer was, by general consent, considered the chief diplomat of the Siamese Court.

We have already ascribed to the Rev. Dr. Samuel R. House document *L. & P.*, vol. 2, no. 61. On page 3 thereof he says:

"The Prime Minister, Chau P'ya Pra Kalahom, or P'ya Sri Suriwongsa as he is sometimes called, understands English but little, and with him an interpreter will be necessary. He is a man of great ability and shrewdness—the very embodiment of Siamese address and intrigue—has a great deal of energy of character—to his enterprise Siam owes her numerous square-rigged merchant vessels that have taken the place within the last sixteen years of her junks, and to him mainly, alone I had almost said, is owing the success of the late British negotiations for a liberal treaty. . . ."

So much for a characterization of his official conduct. Mr. David O. King, the enterprising American merchant who had recently established himself at Bangkok, gives equally interesting sidelights on his personal conduct and influence, in the course of a letter to Townsend Harris, written at Bangkok on Jan. 28, 1856 (*L. & P.*, vol. 2, no. 23, pp. 2 and 4):

". . . but the country is really ruled by the Prime Minister, a wily, deep, rapacious fox; and, as the King was placed on the throne by his family, they have gone on increasing in wealth and importance until they now fill every post of importance in the land; with all their wealth and influence they are extremely jealous of foreigners. . . . This Prime Minister's family were at the bottom of the ill treatment Mr. Balestier received here. . . ."

most sanguine expectations. It is built quite in the European style, large mirrors, encased in frames richly gilt, cover the walls; pendules, thermometers, engravings of the London Exhibition, and the illustrated battles of the everywhere-to-be-found Emperor Napoleon. His antechamber leads into a spacious hall supported by pillars, his bedroom [is furnished] with silk mosquito nettings and crimson curtains of state. A Sharpe's rifle hangs on the wall; fine bath and washing rooms. His house must be two hundred feet deep,—the annexed brick houses of his retainers, which form a whole street, not included. His Excellency received me in as dignified a manner as any Prime Minister of a European Court. He was suffering from his nervous system and apologized for not receiving me at my arrival at the house prepared for my reception. He made the same remarks about mediation as the Phra Klang had previously done. I told him that my conditions for the Treaty were entirely based on that made with the English, with a few exceptions. He replied that so much as they possibly could concede was conceded to the English; that he had no fear of the Treaty [not] being made to the satisfaction of both parties; but, no such a thing as *law* being known in Siam, he was afraid of its conditions [not] being kept. I told him it would prove beneficent to both nations. He replied he was perfectly well aware of that, [but] to make the people understand it was another question. His most ardent desire was to make the people *happy*. He confessed their *ignorance* and *inferiority* to the nations of the West. I told him to hope and persevere and good

114

would come of it at last. [I] threw out a hint about the tin mines,—if American citizens found and worked them, to pay 10 per cent.; he was satisfied to include this in the Treaty. Workmen, Chinese or Siamese, could always be found when paid high wages. He was afraid the Siamese were too indolent. I made a comparison with the pepper trade on the coast of Sumatra, how much better it might be got in Siam. He told me the taxes were too high to sell it, but even at the price, taxes included, he calculated it would amount to considerable. I assured him the Siamese pepper would find eager buyers. [I] hinted I wanted no monopoly in opium trade. On being asked if there were often changes in the dynasty, he uttered the real republican sentiment that kings who claim their title by right of birth, often forget they originated from the people, consider themselves as superior beings and don't lend an ear to the sufferings of their subjects,—so there was often a change at the fourth generation of princes of the same dynasty. On taking leave, the soldiers were drawn out. On gliding down the peaceful waters of the Menam, silvered by a bright moonlight, in our stately gondolas pulled by thirty oarsmen, one would almost fancy to be on a visit to the city of St. Marcus, and if, instead of floating bamboo-houses and Chinese shops lighted with fanciful paper lanterns, the stately palaces of Venice's patricians had lined the shore, the illusion would have been complete. A fine effect was produced by the graceful pagodas with their fine tapering spires, shaming in elegance the most refined works of Grecian architecture. Each king builds himself a pagoda for his memory.[132]

Thursday, April 24, 1856. Received a visit[133] from the Prime Minister, Minister of Foreign Affairs, and Prince Krom Luang Wong Sa Tirat Sanit. Entertained them with music and had the guard drawn out when they left. Sent my secretary with a letter to the Minister of Foreign Affairs before he called, inquiring[134] when I should be received by the King, and also as to what princes and nobles I could visit with propriety before my public reception.[135]

At the visit before noted, I was told I was to have my audience on Wednesday next, and also that I was requested to visit two princes to-morrow morning.

In the note of yesterday evening at the Foreign Minister's,[136] it is omitted that I was then informed that the President's letter would be received in the same manner as was that of Her Britannic Majesty. This was most welcome news to me, as it quieted my mind about an absurd question which ruined the mission of Mr. Balestier.

I gave Prince Wong Sa, etc., a copy of my full

---

[132]Heusken had written "for his last resting place"; Townsend Harris corrected it to "for his memory." Though it is quite certain that Townsend Harris wrote the original draft of his *Journal* (he at least jotted down the rough notes), his secretary seems to have been permitted a good deal of liberty in writing the clean copy of the *Journal* into the blank books in which it has come down to us.

[133]Compare Wood, *op. cit.*, pp. 182–83.

[134]Beginning with this word, the manuscript is again in Townsend Harris's hand.

[135]See *L. B.*, vol. 1, p. 21.

[136]Referring to the series of visits which he paid on Apr. 23rd, setting ou at about 4 P. M. (*v. s.*).

powers.[187] The company remained with me until half-past twelve M.

I then called on Mr. Moor, the Portuguese Consul, all the Baptist missionaries, Mr. Parkes, Mr. Mattoon, and Mr. King.

Friday,[138] *April 25, 1856.* Paid a visit[189] to Somdet Oong Noy, Chief Councillor, and the chief of the old party opposed to progressive principles. His Excellency received me, however, in the most cordial manner. Our band played several national airs; the Somdet's table was bountifully furnished with the beautiful fruits of Siam, a golden teapot and golden water-monkey and several other dishes and boxes made out of pure gold and mounted with precious stones. We had an opportunity of seeing some of the ladies, wrapt in yellow scarfs. They gave us some Siamese music, which from a distance sounded rather sweet and contrasted favorably with the ear-deafening noise given us by his band of male musicians. The Somdet seemed very favorably inclined to the Americans, and willing to concede to them all the privileges obtained by the English. Paid a visit to Somdet Pia Yumarat, Chief Justice, who received me very well and presented me and each of my suite with an ornamented water-monkey brought by him to Bangkok when second in command in a military expedition to Laos, a distant province of

---

[187]These "full powers" for Siam are dated Sept. 8, 1855, and are signed by President Franklin Pierce and Secretary of State William L. Marcy. The original document is at The College of the City of New York.

[138]Beginning with this word, the manuscript is written in Heusken's hand.

[189]Wood, *op. cit.,* pp. 185–88.

the Siamese Empire. Visited Dr. Mattoon, where Prince Wong Sa sent me word to call on him, if convenient.[140] His Highness, having observed the quality of our sugar was not a very good one, made me a present of a superior quality, which, however trifling the value may be, was a fine attention of a man of his rank and station.

Saturday, April 26, 1856. Paid a visit to the French Bishop,[141] who bade me a cordial welcome and expressed in a toast his hopes that my mission might prove beneficial and glorious to my country; he said that patience, which he learnt I had, was a cardinal virtue here, and [which] Mr. Balestier, had not; etc. Visited Mr. Moor, the Portuguese Consul, and the Baptist missionaries. This evening the Bishop sent me a copy of his Siamese dictionary. I returned him my best thanks for this beautiful present in a letter. The Somdet Oong Noy[142] paid me a visit to-day accompanied by his son-

---

[140]What took place at this visit is related below, in the entry for Saturday, Apr. 26, 1856.

[141]Mgr. Jean Baptiste Pallegoix, Bishop of Mallos and Vicar Apostolic of Siam, 1840–62. By letter dated Bangkok, Apr. 26, 1856 (*L. & P.*, vol. 2, no. 36), he sent Townsend Harris a copy of his dictionary *de la langue Thai*—a gift which Townsend Harris acknowledged by letter of the same date (*L. B.*, vol. 1, p. 22), praising the dictionary as "a noble monument of your Lordship's learning and industry."

The Bishop's modesty in describing his dictionary of 30,000 words—a life work (he had arrived in Siam about 1830)—may be judged from the full title of the work: *Dictionnaire siamois—latin—français—anglais*. He wrote also: *Déscription du royaume Thai ou Siam*, Beaune, 1853 and Paris, 1854. (*Cath. Encycl., s.v., Siam.*)

[142]Wood, *op. cit.*, pp. 188–89. Sir John Bowring, in speaking of the Commissioners with whom he had had to deal, thus describes Somdet Oong Noy (*Siam*, vol. 2, pp. 226–27):

"The Commission was composed of the Somdetch om Fai, the first regent, and his brother, the Somdetch om Noi, the second regent of the Kingdom. These occupy the highest official rank. The second Somdetch [om Noi] is the receiver-general of the revenues, and was notoriously interested in the existing system, by which production, commerce, and shipping were placed

in-law, and about twenty of his slaves, treasure bearers and music band. I am told, I am the first foreign minister to whom the Somdet ever paid this attention, he being considered one of the proudest nobles of the realm and having an instinctive antipathy against all foreigners and foreign nations.

I[148] availed myself of the occasion to introduce some statistics of our country. Told him we had two millions of militia—three millions of firearms—forty thousand cannon—fifteen thousand merchant ships. Our gold mines yield over fifteen hundred piculs of gold annually. He said Siam had gold mines, etc. I told him that many very rich tin mines, not worked, were in Siam, and that Americans would come and work those, as well as coal and other mines, if permitted. That they would not require to purchase, but would lease, paying a rent of 10 per cent. of the product. I was glad to present this matter to him, in this casual manner, to let it work on his mind, as I mean to bring it into the Treaty if I can, and desired he might have previous notice 'of it. He did not seem to receive it very favorably, but he is astute and cunning and would not let his sentiments appear, whether they [were] favorable or not. He asked

at the mercy of the farmers of the various revenues, who paid the price of their many and vexatious monopolies either to the Royal Treasury, or to the high officials through whom those monopolies were granted. The two Somdetches had been long the dominant rulers in Siam. Their names will be found in all the commissions and councils by which have been thwarted the attempts made by various envoys from Great Britain and the United States to place the commercial relations of Siam with foreign countries on a satisfactory basis."

[148]Beginning with this word, the manuscript is again written in Townsend Harris's hand.

if we raised sugar in the United States, and I answered some, but not all we wanted. He then asked why no American ships had been here for eighteen years? I answered that the duties were too high; that they could buy sugar cheaper in Manila (which was the fact owing to the old monopolies); that twenty American ships loaded each year at Manila. That in order to have a good trade in Siam, the merchant must live here and pick up his cargo by detail, by the catty and picul, as there were no large markets where a cargo could be purchased at once, etc., etc. He asked about the size and population of Japan, and its size as compared with Java, Ceylon, England and the United States. He asked me to send him a fine Japanese sword from Japan, giving me the length, scabbard, etc., etc., not being very delicate, although it is to be a present from me.

When at Mr. Mattoon's on Friday evening, I had some conversation with Mr. King about details which it was desirable to introduce into our treaty, etc., etc. I was then (about 9 P. M.) sent for by the Prince, who wished to see me. It appears that when Sir John Bowring was here he told the Siamese that the governments of the United States and France had been informed of the treaty that he came to make, and they would make common cause in demanding and (as I understood) in enforcing it.

I was asked if this was true? When the President first knew of the treaty made by Sir John? When the President was informed of the accession of the present

Kings? etc., etc. (see letter on file).[144] To all of which I replied that I did not know, as I was absent from the United States when these things took place, and that my government had not given me any information on these points. I was also asked when I was appointed to come to Siam. I answered, in September, 1855. I then gave the Prince a copy of the President's letter to the King, and begged him to observe my willingness to grant every request they had made of me, as I had also done by giving them a copy of my full powers.

The Prince then introduced the subject of the United States being the friend of Siam, in case of any trouble with any of the Western powers (meaning England). To this I replied as I had before done to the Prince and Foreign Ministers.

While with the Somdet Oong Noy on Friday morning, he strongly recommended Mr. Mattoon as the best person to be American Consul, saying he knew the Siamese language, customs, etc., etc. That he was a discreet good man; that they had full confidence in him; that *he never lied;* and that he never got angry, all of which I assented to and believe him the best person for that place that the government could select.[145]

---

[144]This is *L. & P.*, vol. 2, no. 35, dated at the Ancient Royal Palace, Bangkok, Friday evening, Apr. 25, 1856. In addition to those mentioned in the text, there were in this letter other questions (asked in the name of the First King), which endeavored to connect Townsend Harris's appointment as Envoy to Siam with the knowledge of Sir John Bowring's success that had reached the United States.

The endorsement on page 4 of this letter reads: "received from the Prince in person and answered verbally informing him I was appointed in September, 1855, and to the other questions [I answered] that I had no knowledge."

[145]See below, *Journal* for May 28, 1856, and note 191.

Sunday, April 27, 1856. This morning received a present from Somdet Oong Noy of a large number of very sweet cocoanuts (the finest I ever drank), and the fruit of the Palmyra palm: the size of a small cocoanut, rich purple color like the eggplant.

When opened, a fine tender fruit is found, like very young nipah palm. It is oval and flat in shape, about three inches long and two wide and three fourths in thickness—taste, cool and refreshing.

I argue favorably from these attentions from the Somdet, as [he] has never before done the like, and is considered as the head of the "Old Siam" party and policy. Still, nothing certain can be relied on such attentions, as he is most astute and cunning, and possesses a large share of the duplicity of an Oriental diplomatist.

The Second King has to-day sent me a present of mangoes of two kinds. One of the sorts, the durian mango, is the finest I ever tasted. These were grown in the King's garden.[146]

Attended divine service at the house of Dr. Bradley of the Presbyterian Mission.[147] All the missionaries and most of the white population were present, numbering between thirty and forty.

Service is held at the house of each of the missionaries in turn, following the alphabetical rule.

---

[146]Descriptions of and anecdotes connected with the durian (that strange but most delectable of Oriental fruits which at first is so positively repellent) are to be found in Wood, *op. cit.*, pp. 187–88; Edmund Roberts, *Embassy*, p. 333; U. V. Wilcox, in *Japan* for Mar., 1926, p. 20, etc., etc.

[147]Dr. Bradley's note inviting the members of the Townsend Harris suite to attend services at 4:30 P. M., is *L. & P.*, vol. 2, no. 37. (*Cf.* Wood, *op. cit.*, pp. 190–91.)

I am told there are five inflections or tones on each word in Siamese, and that while in sound there is but a very small difference, in sense there is a large one. I am also told that the word for angel and teapot is the same, and the difference of meaning is produced by the delicate inflection.

A missionary preaching to a Siamese audience was horrified at hearing his congregation burst out into the most uproarious laughter. On demanding the reason he was told that he had said, "And the Lord sent his teapot unto Joseph" in place of "sent his angel," etc., etc.

It now rains regularly every afternoon, at four to six o'clock, and continues during the night. The days are pleasant, as the sun is slightly obscured by clouds, but there is no rain in general.

Monday, April 28, 1856. Heavy showers during the night, which continued until ten this morning.

Composed my address to the King. Find it hard work to reconcile my republican ideas with the strong language of compliment I *must* use.

Mr. Mattoon came in at 11 A. M. Says the Prince wishes to see me this evening to arrange the ceremonial of my presentation, etc., etc.

Mr. Mattoon informs me that my audience is again postponed until Thursday, 1st of May. The reason for this is that the Siamese consider this an unlucky month for the transaction of business, and although Thursday is not a new month with them, yet, as it is so with us, they think that may remove the unlucky influence.[148] They say they are unwilling to detain me until their month is over.

I am to go to Mr. Mattoon's, in order to see the Prince at four o'clock.

Opened the cases containing the presents[149] of books and portraits. All in good order except one book, which was injured by a nail which had been carelessly driven into the box. The fireflies here are very abundant. In a tree in front of my bedroom they congregate in great numbers, and at night they seem to assume most singular forms—now like a huge bird, then a dancing jack, etc., etc.; but the most singular thing about them [is] that the light emitted by them was all *simultaneous,* an instant flash and the same period of darkness. The period was about the time of an ordinary pulse, say eighty per minute. This unity of action obtained among *all the insects,* from the lowest branches to the topmost spray. For fear my senses might deceive me, I called the attention of Commodore Armstrong and Dr. Wood to the sight, and they received the same impressions as myself. I have before seen the same thing at Penang.

When in Java, I was travelling one hot and very dark night; my road lay through paddy fields most of the way; the rice was then headed out.

On this occasion I saw more of these firefly insects than I had ever seen before. Then I saw a very singular effect of the light from them. The impulse appeared to

[148]Compare Wood, *op. cit.,* pp. 182, 200.

[149]The two complete lists of the presents for the First and the Second King respectively are to be found in *L. & P.,* vol. 2, nos. 41 and 42; and in Appendices II and III.

proceed from one side of the paddy field and advanced in a regular line and at a rapid rate across the breadth of the field, so that it was like waves of light moving regularly across it. I frequently stopped my carriage to see this beautiful sight. It was continued for miles through the various rice fields that I passed that night.

Called on Prince Wong Sa by his request at 5 P. M. and made arrangements in detail for my reception, etc., etc., etc.

The Prince informed me that the Second King will receive me on next Friday, the day after the First King's [reception].[150] I do not now enter the details of these arrangements as they may possibly be altered.

The Prince also told me that I had made a most favorable impression on Somdet Oong Noy; that the Somdet said he liked my appearance and my mode of talking. I told the Prince that I was very glad to hear this, as I feared the Somdet would be my chief obstacle, etc., etc. He told me not to fear, that he and the Somdet were old friends and that he would bring him over to me, etc., etc.

Tuesday, April 29, 1856. Opened the case containing the oval mirror for the Second King in order to get out some prints which are to be divided between the

---

150Compare Wood, *op. cit.,* pp. 200–201. The rough draft of the details here agreed upon is in Townsend Harris's hand (*L. & P.,* vol. 2, no. 40). Earlier in the day, Mr. Mattoon had written Townsend Harris that the Prince was detained at the palace of his sick brother, and that therefore it was uncertain whether Townsend Harris would be able to call on the Prince that afternoon (*L. & P.,* vol. 2, no. 38) ; but later in the day, Mr. Mattoon hurriedly sent Townsend Harris a very brief note (*L. & P.,* vol. 2, no. 39) announcing that the Prince had returned to his home. Thus Townsend Harris's call was made at 5 P. M., instead of at 4 P. M., as originally scheduled (see above).

two Kings. I was quite relieved on opening this case to find the mirror quite safe and the gilding as bright as when I saw it in New York. I had feared that the concussion of the ship's guns in firing salutes might have broken the plate (as is often the case), but all was safe.

Indeed, I owe this probably to the kindness of Commodore Armstrong, who gave orders that no *shotted* guns should be fired for exercise while the mirrors were on board, although the standing orders of the Navy Department require that the men shall be exercised at target firing as often as (I think) once a month.

An unlucky mistake has occurred. I had a cask containing cut-glass globes, chimneys, etc., etc., for a pair of chandeliers, which I am to present to the First King, but instead of this cask one containing glass for my use when I arrive in Japan came up. I availed myself of the kindness of Mr. King who instantly dispatched a whale boat to the *San Jacinto* for the proper package, and I expect it will arrive to-night, so that it will be in good time.[151] The other package was returned to the ship by Mr. King's schooner which goes down in the morning.[152]

Mr. Chandler has kindly taken charge of the opening and arranging the presents for the Kings, and, as he is perfectly competent, it takes a great charge off my mind, and I cannot sufficiently thank him for his aid.

[151]The necessities of the case were explained by Townsend Harris in a letter to Captain Bell, who had been left on board the *San Jacinto* while Commodore Armstrong was in Bangkok with Townsend Harris. (*L. B.*, vol. 1, p. 22.)

[152]Meaning that the wrong package would go down the river the following morning—*i. e.*, Wednesday, Apr. 30, 1856.

Went to dine at Mr. Mattoon's with Dr. Wood and Lieutenant Carter. The Commodore does not like to go out; but, being sent for, went to the Second King's for a private visit, taking with him some five of our suite, the band, and half a dozen marines. He stayed until 8 P. M. and returned much pleased with his visit. After dinner at Mr. Mattoon's, went to visit the fine wat near his house. The buildings at a distance look very beautiful. The green and yellow tiles of the roofs; the hooked ornaments representing the tails and wings of dragons, which decorate all the terminal points of the roofs and gables; the pagodas with their beautiful outlines and, at a distance, apparent gorgeousness of detail in color and adornment; the delicate spires which spring up in every direction; abundant statuary of men and beasts and birds, real and imaginary; the finely placed houses for taking the air near the water; the grounds so well laid out and kept and bearing every variety of sacred or flowering tree—all these form an *ensemble* not easily forgotten.

But many of these things look best at a distance. The ornamental work of the pagodas, so beautiful in form, color and detail, falls off into coarsely wrought figures of men, beasts and flowers, made of mortar and broken bits of porcelains. How much like the scenery of a theater, so gorgeous by gaslight, so rough and coarse by daylight!

A visit to the interior of the wat,—*i. e.,* the principal one, for there are several in the enclosure, showed us something better. The court was crowded with grand figures of genii brought from China. In the arcades or cloister surrounding the court of this wat, we counted one hundred and thirty golden figures of Budh in his posture of meditation.

The wat has some fine columns of marble and a rich pavement of the same. The doors and windows were richly decorated with the elaborate drawing and tracery of the Siamese, all done in gold. Inside, the walls were covered with paintings, descriptive of the life and actions of Budh and his principal apostles. Before the throne were a great number of votive figures, four of which bore royal umbrellas, two of which were of gold and two silver, all solid. As you leave this wat the roof and gable covering the main gate is worthy of observation, and for beauty and richness of detail is fully equal to anything I ever saw. It is composed of representations of fruits, flowers, etc., etc. Here also you see the cool marble seats erected under the shade of a *ficus religiosa,* which from its coolness seems to invite quiet and repose. The Buddhist gentlemen have a marvellously good eye for all such spots. Afterwards we returned to Mr. Mattoon's, took tea, and then our departure for our home, which was some two miles distant down the river.

Neale, in his Munchausen history of Siam (London, 1852),[153] says that the floating houses of Bangkok are

[153]*Narrative of a Residence at the Capital of the Kingdom of Siam, with a Description of the Manners, Customs, and Laws of the Modern Siamese,* by Frederick Arthur Neale, formerly in the service of His Siamese Majesty. London, 1852, 1 vol., 8vo. This was one of the works on Siam recommended by Consul Bradley, of Singapore, in his letter of Jan. 30, 1856 (*L. & P.,* vol. 1, no. 28).

seventy thousand in number, and that the whole of Bangkok (except a few named houses) is built on rafts. From all I see and from all I can learn, I think there are seven thousand, not seventy thousand floating houses in Bangkok, and I *know* that more than nine tenths of the whole city is built on terra firma.

I learn that Neale was actually in Bangkok for a few weeks, and this increases my astonishment at his gross errors in matters of fact, that required no great labor to ascertain the truth. In America we call Baltimore the Monument City, New York the Empire City, and Cincinnati Porkopolis. In the East, Calcutta is called the City of Palaces (I think the City of Large and Dirty Houses would be a more correct name). Now, I think Bangkok should be called the City of Flagstaffs. From every palace, from every wat, from the house of every noble, you see them springing up in every direction by hundreds, if not by thousands.

A very bad feature is the gambling houses. This vice is legalized and farmed out. It is said there are more than three hundred of these hells among the floating or raft houses, and on the mainland they are said to be numbered by thousands. Neale represents the raft houses as forming streets, crossing each other at right angles. I cannot find *anywhere* more than *one tier* of raft houses.

Wednesday, April 30, 1856. Settled the order of our procession for to-morrow for my audience, which is as follows:

Thursday,[154] *May 1, 1856.* The boats will arrive about 11 A. M., when the procession will be formed as follows:

1. The President's letter in a special boat;
2. The Envoy, Interpreter and Secretary in a boat bearing the American Flag;
3. Commodore Armstrong in a boat;
4. The gentlemen of the suite according to their rank in as many boats as required;
5. The band in a large boat;
6. The guard in a large boat;
7. On arriving at the palace landing place, a salute will be fired which will be returned by the band playing "God Save the King";
8. After landing, the procession will be formed again in exactly the same order as in the boats, with the exception that the American Flag borne by the Commodore's coxswain, and supported by two boys, will be placed between the band and the guard; all gentlemen will be carried on chairs;
9. On arriving at the Hall of Justice, the band, Flag and guard will halt, and the remainder of the procession will proceed on to the Audience Hall;
10. On arriving at the Audience Hall, the procession will be formed in four lines, as follows: Commodore Armstrong, Mr. Harris, Mr. Mattoon, Mr. Heusken; Dr. Wood, Lieutenant Rutledge, Purser Bradford, Lieutenant Carter, Mr. Isherwood, Lieu-

---

[154]Beginning with this word, the manuscript is again written in Mr. Heusken's hand.

tenant Tyler, Dr. Daniels, Mr. Van den Heuvel, Dr. Bradley, Mr. Chandler, Mr. King.

By request of the King the three last mentioned gentlemen join the procession.

11 The procession, having fairly entered the Hall, will halt, and make one bow, being uncovered; it will then proceed up the Hall in the same order to a place marked by a table, when the procession will halt, and, after bowing again, the gentlemen will be seated, Commodore Armstrong occupying a cushion on the left in front.

Mr. Harris will then place the President's letter (which he has borne from the entrance of the Hall) on the table and remain standing by it. On receiving a signal he will advance and present the President's letter to the King, after which he will return to his place and, still standing, will read his speech, on the completion of which (which will be known by his bowing and handing a paper to Mr. Mattoon) the gentlemen will please rise again, bow and be reseated.

12 In marching up the Hall and in being seated, gentlemen are requested not to crowd on the rank in front, and to cover their file leader.

Mr. Harris does not know whether the chairs will be borne singly or two or more abreast.

This afternoon the Second King's son came with a message from his father; being overcome with fatigue I could not receive him.

Thursday, May 1, 1856. We left the house of [the] Embassy at 1 P. M. in the order before alluded to, except that the guard and band preceded the President's letter. There were scarcely boats enough, the boat for the presents being intended likewise for me, which I declined, and took passage in another. In order to honor us an oarsman gave at every ten or twelve strokes a loud yell, which was responded [to] by the others with a low growling noise. Arrived at the palace of Somdet Phra Paramendr Maha Mongkut, Major King of Siam, we were carried in sedan chairs to the reception hall, where some refreshments were served to us. All along the road we passed through a double file of soldiers, dressed in a most fantastic manner. Some companies were armed with long poles, furnished at the top with a round knife, others with battle axes, crossbows, old flint muskets. Some wore long gowns and looked like women, others looked like the Swiss montagnards of a Chatham theater. Twenty elephants, each with a howitzer on its back, of Spanish manufacture of two centuries ago. A salute was fired of twenty-one guns. Arrived at the Hall of Justice, the nobles, who had escorted me from the House of Legation, fell on their knees as soon as the door was opened, made three salaams and preceded us up to the throne, crawling on hands and knees, among a crowd of nobles all prostrated in the same manner, and dressed in rich gowns interwoven with gold. Everyone had the insignia of his rank,—*viz.,* a gold betelnut box, gold teapot, swords, etc., near him. The Hall of Justice is a large building of immense height, built in the form of a cross, the centrum supported by four slender and most graceful looking pillars, rather in the Egyptian style. Between the four pillars, the white state umbrella of nine stages; at the upper end of the hall, the throne richly carved and gilt. The throne has no steps, the King entering it outside the hall, and has no communication whatever with the hall but the opening of the throne where the King is seen sitting. His crown consists of a blue velvet cap surrounded by rich precious stones and mounted with a yellow feather. He had in his hand a sword presented to him by the United States. On each side of the throne two state umbrellas of seven stages and ten others of five stages. Immediately under the throne, four swordbearers and two guards armed with a rifle. Two cushions were provided for the Commodore and myself, my suite had to sit or lie down on the floor, covered with rich Smyrna carpeting. Having gone through the ceremonial as alluded to in the program and presented His Majesty with the President's letter[155] (I could hardly hand it to him, the throne

---

[155]On Sept. 20, 1855, W. Hunter, Assistant Secretary of State, wrote a letter to Townsend Harris (*L. & P.*, vol. 2, no. 17), then at New York, in which he stated that a package would be forwarded containing Townsend Harris's Instructions and Other Papers (*L. & P.*, vol. 2, nos. 1–6 incl.), and also the originals of the President's letters to the King of Siam and to the Emperor of Japan. Secretary Marcy's first dispatch to Townsend Harris, dated Sept. 12, 1855, seems to have had enclosed therein copies of these two letters (*L. & P.*, vol 2, nos. 14 and 15 respectively).

For the text of President Pierce's letter to the First King of Siam, dated Sept. 12, 1855, see Appendix I.

During the visit which Townsend Harris paid to Prince Krom Luang on Monday, Apr. 28, 1856, at 5 P. M. (see above), the details of his audiences with the First King and the Second King had been agreed upon. The presents (the more bulky ones) were to be sent to the Palace on Wednesday, Apr. 30th, the day preceding the audience; the books and pictures were to be taken by Townsend Harris on the day of the audience; while the complete list of the presents was to be placed under the silk cover of the President's letter (*L. & P.*, vol. 2, no. 40).

For the complete lists of the different sets of presents for the two Kings (*L. & P.*, vol. 2, nos. 41 and 42), see Appendices II and III. Wood, *Fankwei*, pp. 201–07, gives a good account of this audience.

being so high), on a signal given I read my address as follows:

"May it please Your Majesty,

I have the honor to present to Your Majesty a letter of the President of the United States containing a most friendly salutation to Your Majesty, and also accrediting me as his representative at your court.

"I am directed to express, on the President's behalf, the great respect and esteem that he feels for you, and his warm wishes for the health and welfare of Your Majesty, and for the prosperity of your dominions.

"The fame of Your Majesty's great acquirements in many difficult languages and in the higher branches of science, has crossed the great oceans that separate Siam from the United States, and has caused high admiration in the breast of the President. The United States possesses a fertile soil and is rich in all the products of the temperate zone. Its people are devoted to agriculture, manufactures and commerce. The sails of its ships whiten every sea; its flag is seen in every port; the gold mines of the country are among the richest in the world.

"Siam produces many things which cannot be grown in the United States, and the Americans will gladly exchange their products, their gold and their silver for the surplus produce of Siam.

"A commerce so· conducted will be beneficial to both nations, and will increase the friendship happily existing between them.

"I esteem it a high honor that I have been selected by the President to represent my country at the court of the wisest and most enlightened monarch of the East, and if I shall succeed in my sincere wish, to strengthen the ties of amity that unite Siam and the United States, I shall consider it as the happiest moment of my life."

134

The King opened a commonplace conversation; asked how many treaties had been made between the United States and Eastern nations; how long the actual President would remain in office; the number of our states, etc. Gave to me and each of the officers his visiting card. After the audience we partook of a dinner dressed up in the European style, and returned to our house at sunset. At the end of the audience a large curtain is drawn concealing the throne from our sight in three strokes, and at every stroke the crouching nobles make a salaam by raising their joined hands to their foreheads. During the audience segars were handed to us by the King's nephew on his knees.

Friday, May 2, 1856. Left in the same order as yesterday for the Second King's palace; had a salute of twenty-one guns. His soldiers were in much better order than the First King's. Some, dressed in the European style, preceded us as a bodyguard and were the best drilled troops I ever saw. The field pieces in firing the salute were beautifully served. The Hall of Audience is less splendid than the First King's. I was pleased to see some of the highest peers I had seen at the First King's present at his brother's audience, as Prince Wong Sa and Somdet Oong Noy. My address reads as follows:

"May it please Your Majesty,
"I am to deliver to Your Majesty a most cordial and friendly salutation from the President of the United States, and to assure you that the President is aware of the kind manner in which Your Majesty has received the Americans who have visited Siam for many years past. The United

States does not hold any possessions in the East, nor does it desire any. The form of its government forbids the holding of colonies. The United States therefore cannot be an object of jealousy to any Eastern power. Peaceful commercial relations, which give as well as receive benefits, is what the President wishes to establish with Siam, and such is the object of my mission.

"A new state of the American Union has lately sprung into existence, from which the voyage to Siam can be made in one month.

"This makes the United States the nearest neighbor that Siam has among the Caucasian races and is a strong reason for uniting the two nations.

"The fame of Your Majesty's great acquirements in languages and in the higher branches of science (acquirements so unusual among Oriental nations) has reached the United States and has caused great admiration. If I can succeed in my earnest wish to draw more closely the bonds of friendship that unite Siam and the United States, I shall esteem it as the happiest event of my life."

The King inquired after our health, said he knew all the names of the Presidents with the exception of the late President and wanted to know the actual Vice-President's name. The audience over, we partook of our dinner and returned.[156]

Saturday, May 3, 1856. The officers not yet invited to the Second King's private audience went to-day to see His Majesty.[157] Dined at Prince Wong Sa's without our host,[158] he being detained at the First King's audience.

---

[156]Wood, *op. cit.*, pp. 207–08.

[157]Wood, *op. cit.*, pp. 208–10.

[158]Being obliged to attend this "political dinner" at Prince Krom Luang's, even though the Prince was detained elsewhere, Townsend Harris missed the

Monday, May 5, 1856. Commodore Armstrong left this morning in the steamer *The Siamese Steam Force* accompanied by Lieutenant Rutledge, Lieutenant Carter, Chief Engineer Isherwood, Assistant Surgeon Daniels, Commodore's secretary Van den Heuvel and some marines.[159] I paid visits to all the Ministers and called this evening on the Somdet.

Tuesday, May 6, 1856. Arrived Captain H. Bell, Lieutenant Williamson, Lieutenant Bryant, Master Bowen, Assistant Surgeon Semple and Captain's clerk Ashe.[160]

Wednesday, May 7, 1856. The Second King sent word for the newly arrived officers to call on him, which they did and remained till late in the evening.

Friday, May 9, 1856. The First King gave a festival called Rak-na, or festival of opening the agricultural labors of the year. A large roof, stuck on poles, was erected for the performances, during which the King, sitting on an estrade surrounded by the princes of the royal blood, transacted business. Under the estrade the most wealthy and noble dignitaries of the realm attended the performances, all kneeling from the beginning to the end. On my arrival the King told me that the commission for the commissioners appointed for me was drawn up in Siamese and now in the act of being translated into

---

dinner party given by the Rev. and Mrs. Bradley to Townsend Harris and the officers of his embassy, the gentlemen and ladies of the several missions, and to Mr. and Mrs. Harry S. Parkes (*L. & P.*, vol. 1, no. 37).

[159]Townsend Harris had arranged for their departure by writing three letters on Saturday, May 3, 1856: one to the Rev. S. Mattoon (*L. B.*, vol. 1, p. 23); a second to the Minister of Foreign Affairs (*ib.*); and a third to the First King (*ib.*, p. 24).

[160]Wood, *op. cit.*, p. 220.

English. Chairs were provided for us. Refreshments consisting of Siamese sweetmeats, fruits, wines, coffee, seasoned meat and segars, duly served. On the King's expressing a wish for our band being sent for, this was complied with, and our band and the King's orchestra, vocal and instrumental, played together different tunes at the same time, which created a most barbaric confusion, the singing women each [being] armed with two long flat sticks, which they struck every time together, accompanying this with some lamenting cries just the same as the poor girls in New York on a wintry night produce by crying "Hot Corn." So much for the singing part. The instrumental consisted of different drums, bells and wooden hautboys, if this name may be given to them. The stage itself was in the centrum of the building; no decorations except an artificial mountain, or clouds, I could not make out. The play was a prince being in love with a princess and seeing in a wood a young girl sent out by the princess to cut a very rare plant; some sacrifices by the princess and her court to an idol, etc., etc. The performers are all young girls from eight to fourteen years of age; trained for their profession from their most early childhood, have a wonderful flexibility in their arms which they bend, without twisting them, in the wrong way. The dances consist in very slow but graceful movements especially with the arms, and instead of dancing as in our ballets on the uppermost end of their toes, they slowly proceed on the downmost part of their heels. They were all painted white and had black wigs on, gold dresses and crowns with dragon

138

wings glittering with precious stones. Some looked very well, their limbs exceedingly well rounded off and well proportioned. Had generally very small feet supporting a well formed and, according to the lines of beauty, in thickness increasing leg. I remarked a good deal of precision in their combined movements. Every time the performers entered or re-entered the stage, they crawled first, until arrived opposite the King's seat, and made the usual Eastern salutation. The King presented our band with four piculs each, which I first refused, but on his repeated request complied with.

The word "wat" means all the ground within the enclosure of their temples, houses where the priests live, detached buildings, etc., etc.

Omitted [161]:

Sunday, May 4, 1856. Attended divine worship at the house of Mr. Mattoon.[162]

Monday, May 5, 1856. Wrote to the King,[163] urging the appointment of commissioners to meet me, stating I had been twenty-two days in the country. I learned in the evening that a grand row had taken place, about the business of Mr. Parkes who had so wearied the King by his letters, etc., that he got enraged, blew up all his court and ended by closing the palace gates against all the world. My letter was not presented until

---

[161]Beginning with this word, the manuscript is again written in Townsend Harris's hand.

[162]An invitation had been received from the Second King for the officers to visit him privately; but it was not accepted on the ground that it was Sunday (Wood, *op. cit.,* pp. 215–20). We shall see that also in Japan Townsend Harris made it a rule never to conduct any official business on Sunday.

[163]*L. B.,* vol. I, p. 25, which was presented on May 7th (see below).

Wednesday, May 7, 1856, when I was told the King would give me a private audience on Thursday or Friday, and then would inform me who were the commissioners, etc., to treat with me. This promised private interview ended in merely inviting me to visit his theater.[164] When I entered, he invited me to the foot of the estrade on which he was walking about, shook me by the hand and said, *"good-bye,"* which is his English for "How d'do."

Saturday, May 10, 1856. Am told the Royal Commission is now being translated, as the King has now a strange fancy for executing public documents connected with Americans and English in the English language. This must cause more delay[165] and I *think* is so intended.

I am convinced I shall not be able to do *anything* until the English have left. The Siamese cannot entertain two ideas at the same time.

Sunday, May 11, 1856. Attended divine service at the house of the Rev. Mr. Smith who read a capital sermon by the Rev. Mr. Williams of the Baptist Church, New York.

Monday, May 12, 1856. Mr. Chandler sends down for my secretary to assist him in copying the Royal Commission, which he has only completed translating this morning.[166]

---

[164]On Friday, May 9, 1856. (See above, and Wood, *op. cit.,* pp. 240–44.)

[165]This delay is the theme of *L. B.,* vol. 1, p. 26 (Townsend Harris to Commodore Armstrong, May 7th); of *L. & P.,* vol. 1, no. 36 (the Commodore's answer, May 11th); and of *L. & P.,* vol. 2, no. 45 (Mattoon to Townsend Harris, May 8th).

[166]Mr. Chandler's letter (*L. & P.,* vol. 2, no. 44, written early in the morning of May 12th) expresses the hope that Townsend Harris will send Mr. Heusken

Mr. Chandler is an excellent, good man; what he docs, he does well, but he is not reliable as to *time*.

With Captain Bell, the officers and marines visited the great wat in the palace enclosure. Found an endless number of idols (over seven hundred it is said), six hundred priests and *the* idol *par excellence* of the world. It is a recumbent Budh, of the enormous length of one hundred and fifty feet, richly gilt, and the soles of the feet a perfect bijou of decorative mother-of-pearl work. I never saw anything of the kind more beautiful. The figure is pretty well proportioned. It reclines on the right side, supporting the head on the right hand—the elbow being bent to a right angle.

Subsequently visited the temple where worship is performed. Rich gold and silver state umbrellas, etc., etc., before the altar. The decorations of the temple were rich and in good taste.

The patterns were rather elaborate than grand, with a detail that bore the closest inspection.

Numberless pagodas of all sizes decorated the numerous courts through which we passed.

The courts neatly paved with sandstone flags neatly cut; large figures in granite from China representing gods, heroes, men, genii, animals, rostral columns, Chinese triumphal arches, fine bronze griffins and num-

---

to make two English copies of the document appointing the Treaty Commissioners, which Mr. Chandler is nearly through translating from the Siamese.

Mr. Wood states (*op. cit.,* p. 230) that it was thought negotiations would be opened on this day (May 12th), but that it was found a mistake had been made in the translation.

berless similar objects, which would require weeks to examine and describe. In the courts ornamental trees and shrubs were frequent. Artificial ponds, with ditto rocks, in the best Chinese manner, are also there. The sides and roof of the building called the "Library" are a gem of Siamese decorative architecture. The court and floor of one of the temples is paved with marble tiles from China, of the cool dove color. This wat covers many acres of ground and is kept *very clean,* not a usual thing in Siam.

In this enclosure stand the three pagodas before noted as erected by the Kings of the present dynasty. A fourth is in the course of erection by the present King. As to these pagodas, which show so prettily from the river, I can justly say that a close inspection does not add to their beauty. Here we saw the Budh in the jungle where his wants were supplied by wild animals. An elephant presents him with water, a baboon gives him fruit— both animals being in the attitude of adoration.

Next went to the wat on the opposite side of the river, near Mr. Mattoon's, which I have already described.

Dined and passed the evening at Mr. Mattoon's. At 9 P. M. the Prince sent for me. He says the Royal Commission will be signed to-morrow and that I shall meet the Commissioners on Wednesday. Mr. Parkes is to leave early on Thursday morning. When he is gone I shall think business has commenced with me.

Tuesday, May 13, 1856. Breakfast with Mr. Telford. Complete *pro forma* of Treaty as I wish it, and give it to Mr. Mattoon to finish the little that remains to be translated. The forts on both banks of the river, just above the embassy, are called Phra-cha-mit and Pit-patch-nuck. It is these forts which mark the limits above which men-of-war are not to pass. In front of Phra-cha-mit I this morning saw a human right hand, which had been cut off at the wrist, stuck on a bamboo and drying in the sun. I am told that forgery is punished by cutting off a part or the whole of the hand, which is then stuck up at this place.

Full one half of the children die before they are one year old, owing to the unwise mode of treating them. I have seen a Siamese woman pull her nipple from the mouth of her child and insert the end of her lighted cigar.

Visited Phra Klang with Captain Bell and his officers. White elephants modelled in clay, well done.

Pull up river with Mr. King, go up five miles, beautiful scenery. Visit paper mill. Paper from bark of tree, macerated in lime water, afterwards comminuted and spread on frames made of bamboo splints. Creeks or canals every fifty yards—bridges—steep ascent—then a slab or pole—no hand rail—frequent falls.

I to-day saw the offerings or consecration of the *lingum*. It is formed of clay, natural size. Is placed in small shrines near the river. Its accurate form makes its exhibition a filthy one. I am told they are to be found everywhere. They are [offered] as a means of recovery from the venereal [diseases], for a continued virility, or as a thank offering *for* recovery.

143

Returning down the river at eight o'clock P. M., the scene was very beautiful. The air, cool and balmy, was loaded with the perfume of flowers. The moon silvered over every object and softened the harsher features of them. Boats of all descriptions were darting about. The deep drum of the wat was booming its call for prayer. Tom-toms were marking the seats of mirth and pleasure. High up in the air twin lights marked the walls of the Palaces of the Kings. Now an immense blaze of light, with the clashing of musical instruments, called our attention to some cause of more than ordinary merry-making.

On drawing near, we found two large buildings, open on all sides, were illuminated by every possible means known to the natives. Single lights, chandeliers, pyramids of lamps, vessels filled with a resinous gum and set on fire—all these and other means were used to procure a perfect illumination. A full band of actors, dancers and musicians were exercising their calling, to give pleasure to the crowds that were assembled.

The occasion was the cutting [of] the long hair of a boy some ten or twelve years old. It is something like a mark of approaching puberty, this having the hair cut so as to form the round crest or comb on the top of the head, and may be said to resemble the *toga virilis* of the Romans.

This crest of hair is only cut off in cases of mourning or when a man becomes a priest.

Wednesday, May 14, 1856. This was the day the Prince had fixed for me to meet the Siamese Commissioners, but in the morning he sent to me to say he could not give me the meeting, as His Majesty had not drawn up the full powers. The King resembles Sully's description of James I of England,—"The most learned fool in Christendom." His Majesty is pedantic beyond belief, and that too on a very small capital of knowledge. Add to this the fact that he is much given to women, and a solution is found for the delay of all useful business. It may be said that [he] resembles Solomon only in the chapter of wives and concubines.

This afternoon visited an old and respectable noble, —Boudin. It was at his house that Mr. Roberts was lodged when he was in Siam. After the usual routine questions and answers, we were invited to enter a new building, where a sumptuous repast in Chinese and Siamese styles of cookery, served up in European dishes, was set out. Among a vast variety of other things, we had bird-nest soup, *bêche-de-mer,*[167] sharks' fins, eggs from Japan and many preparations of fowl and fish which we could not name. A dessert of fruit followed of the finest descriptions.

Spent the evening at Mr. Mattoon's, where all the white persons had assembled to meet Mr. and Mrs. Parkes who are to leave in the morning.

The evening was a lovely one, and our band added much to the pleasure of the occasion.

---

[167]*Bêche-de-mer,* or sea cucumber, as it was called, because of its shape. Like sandalwood, it was in great demand in China in the early days of our Pacific trade. For a description of the various kinds of these sea slugs of the South Seas, read Greenbie and Greenbie, *Gold of Ophir,* p. 49, note.

Thursday, May 15, 1856. This morning Mr. Williamson, Mr. Bryant and Mr. Bowen go back to the ship in company of Mr. Parkes, etc.[168]

I am quite unwell, having many boils, etc., etc., indigestion, etc.

The Second King sent for me this morning. I did not go, being too unwell.

Friday, May 16, 1856. This morning I have the welcome news that I am to meet the Commissioners this P. M. at the house of the Prince. Four o'clock is the hour fixed on.

At[169] the meeting with the Commissioners,[170] found

---

[168]Sir Harry S. Parkes had brought back from England the ratified copy of the Treaty with Siam concluded by Sir John Bowring on Apr. 18, 1855.

On Tuesday, May 13, 1856, he had signed a series of Supplementary Articles (given in full in Bowring's *Siam*, vol. 2, pp. 230–47). On Wednesday, May 14th, he had had his audience of leave (Wood, *Fankwei*, p. 230), and on Thursday the 15th he left Bangkok

On the same day (May 15th), an audience was granted to the Portuguese Consul, who had been waiting for this privilege more than a year (Wood, *ib.*), and on the 16th, the American negotiations began to make progress— which fully bears out Townsend Harris's presentiments in this connection— namely, that business would really commence with him only after the departure of Mr. Parkes (see above, entry for May 12, 1856).

[169]Beginning with this word, the manuscript is again written in Mr. Heusken's hand.

[170]The original document appointing the five Commissioners to negotiate the Treaty, and granting them full powers, is *L. & P.*, vol. 2, no. 47, dated May 16, 1856.

At the top of page 1 (of this six-page document) are two rectangular stamped seals: the left-hand one bears (in addition to Siamese printed writing) the Latin legend, *Maior Rex Siamensium,* written by hand of the First King; the right-hand seal bears (in addition to Siamese printed writing beneath the Arabic numeral 120) the Latin legend *Secundus Rex Siamensium,* written by the hand of the Second King.

At the end of the document (on p. 6) there are two elliptical seals: the left-hand one bears across the face of it the signature of the First King, as follows: "S.P.P.M. Mongkut, the First King of Siam"; the right-hand seal similarly bears the signature of the Second King, as follows: "S. P. Pawarendr Ramesr, the Second King of Siam."

The handwritings of these two sets of seals not only correspond from the one set to the other, but are also to be compared with the handwritings in

that the Phra Kalahom, who had always affected to entertain the most friendly feeling towards Americans, was my chief opponent: wished to have the article about opium,[171] which I left out as contrary to the wishes of my government, inserted; the article stipulating protection to Siamese subjects[172] when in the United States, erased as unnecessary,—considering the Siamese living in foreign countries as *cut off* from the Siamese nation. The reason this article appears in the English Treaty is that, the English having possessions adjoining and in the neighborhood of Siam, many of their subjects are living there and engaged in trade. My three amendments to the English Treaty were all rejected.[173]

They were decidedly opposed to American citizens and actual residents of Bangkok having residing agents in any part of the Siamese dominions,[174] and their being

---

L. & P., vol. 2, no. 48 (by the First King) and in L. & P., vol. 2, no. 33 (by the Second King).

The "full powers" of Townsend Harris for negotiating a treaty with Siam were dated Sept. 8, 1855, and were signed by President Pierce and Secretary of State Marcy. The original document is now at The College of the City of New York.

[171]Bowring's Treaty (Apr. 18, 1855), Art. VIII, says, in part (L. & P., vol. 2, no. 29):

"Opium may be imported free of duty, but can only be sold to the Opium Farmer or his agents," etc., etc.

This portion of the British Treaty appears verbatim in Art. VII of the American Treaty as adopted by the Senate—which was Art. VIII in Townsend Harris's original draft (L. & P., vol. 2, no. 53).

[172]Bowring's Treaty, Art. I. In Art. I of the American Treaty this matter was replaced by clauses promising to Siamese vessels on the high seas the aid of American men-of-war without, however, committing a breach of neutrality; and to Siamese vessels in foreign ports the aid of the American consuls at said ports.

[173]L. & P., vol. 2, no. 54. These amendments formed part of six propositions advanced by Townsend Harris (L. & P., vol. 2, no. 55); the other propositions finally found place in the Treaty.

[174]This was the substance of Amendment 1.

allowed to visit the coasts adjacent to the Menam and islands under their annual pass without procuring a special passport for that purpose.[175] Willing to grant the lease of mines, but only for a period of five or ten years. On my representing that it would be an absurdity for a man spending say 150,000 piculs in laying shafts, labor, etc., etc., and when at last the mine began to yield being obliged to give it up, they would not yield;[176] wished to have the Treaty take effect eighteen months after its date,[177] and consuls appointed at the same time. I told them the Treaty was in operation now, and I had a right of appointing a consul at once in virtue of Mr. Roberts's Treaty.[178] Insisted on having an Article inserted [of] the United States being arbiter in case of differences with other nations, and American men-of-war rendering the same assistance to Siamese vessels which they would render to vessels of their own nation in case of piracy, etc., etc.; postponed for consideration. The reason they gave for rejecting my amendments was, "they would willingly grant them, but by doing so had to give

[175]This was the substance of Amendment 2.

[176]This was the substance of Amendment 3.

[177]Art. XI of the Treaty as adopted by the Senate (Art. XII in Townsend Harris's original draft) provided that the treaty "shall take effect immediately." The Siamese had a precedent for their desire to postpone in Art. XII of the British Treaty signed by Sir John Bowring on Apr. 18, 1855, which provided that that Treaty should take effect from Apr. 6, 1856—almost a whole year after it was signed and sealed.

[178]Mr. Roberts's Treaty (1833), Art. X:

"If hereafter any foreign nation other than the Portuguese shall request and obtain His Majesty's consent to the appointment of Consuls to reside in Siam, the United States shall be at liberty to appoint Consuls to reside in Siam, equally with such other foreign nation."

The "such other foreign nations" was in this case Great Britain, by virtue of Sir J Bowring's Treaty.

other nations an equal share." I proposed having my amendments drawn up as Additional Articles, as granted exclusively to Americans in reciprocation for the assistance given to their vessels by American men-of-war. They replied that whatever they granted to Americans, they had to grant to other powerful naval powers, as France and England.

Adjourned, appointed to meet next Tuesday, promised me a copy of Mr. Parkes's explanations.[179] Applied for a private interview with the King for to-morrow.

Saturday,[180] *May 17, 1856.* Quite unwell—many boils and gastric derangement.

Desired Mr. Mattoon to say to Prince Wong Sa that I would withdraw all the amendments I had offered and take the Treaty as it stands in the English version, except the clause about consuls.

Sunday, May 18, 1856. Attended service at the house of the Rev. Mr. Telford.

Very unwell.

Monday, May 19, 1856. Still unwell. Sent for by the Prince this afternoon,[181] who said they would consider my amendments, and hoped to give me satisfaction. The Americans are in error in supposing Mr. Roberts's

---

[179]See above, entry for May 15, 1856, and note 168. For another account of this day's negotiations, see Wood, *op. cit.,* pp. 230–31.

[180]Beginning with this word, the manuscript is again written in Townsend Harris's hand.

[181]The Prince made his wishes known to the Rev. Mattoon, who wrote to Townsend Harris (*L. & P.,* vol. 2, no. 46). It was the Prince's desire to learn thoroughly Townsend Harris's views, in order to present them to the nobles that evening. Townsend Harris was closeted with him from 1 P. M., when the Prince returned from the First King's Palace, to 9 P. M.

Treaty secures [for the United States] every concession that may be made by the Siamese to any other nation.

It secures any reduction of duties and the right to appoint a consul, when that right is granted to any nation except Portugal, but it does not put the United States on the footing of the most favored nation. With the Prince to 9 P. M.

Tuesday, May 20, 1856. At the Prince's, who produced a most absurd farrago of nonsense which he wished to have introduced into the Treaty. It is a history of Siamese diplomacy for the last thirty years, giving the names of the nations sending and the envoys sent, etc., with a great deal more of similar matter.

I told the Prince that it did not comport with the dignity of the United States to have the name of any third nation, or of its envoys, inserted in a mere commercial treaty; that I came to negotiate for my own country on terms of equality; that I could not take anything as a favor and because it had been granted to England, etc., etc. Could not bring him to any definite point on any subject. Left at 8 P. M.

Wednesday, May 21, 1856. All the Commissioners present. They had all the talking to themselves, as they would only hear Mr. Mattoon interpret [not] more than half a dozen words of my reply when they would all open on him. The Prince is not as cordial as formerly.

The Prime Minister advanced a proposition which will serve to show *their* ideas of reciprocity. He said, "We love the Americans, for they have never done us or anyone else in the East an injury"; that they were not seeking conquests in the East; [that] the American missionaries had been of vast use to them, teaching many valuable arts, etc., etc. The English, on the contrary, were rapacious tyrants who were seizing on the whole of Asia. They had made the Treaty with Sir John Bowring, not because they liked the English, but because they feared them.

"Now," said the Prime Minister, "you who are our friends and whom we esteem, surely you will not ask as much from us as we were forced to give to our enemies?" I told him that we acted on a different principle; that we treated our friends best and not worst; that their friendship would be a sorry thing for us if we were not allowed as much as they gave their foes.

I discover the Commissioners *cannot* do any single thing without first consulting the King. The Prince more cool than he was last night.

Left at half-past ten P. M.

Thursday, May 22, 1856. This afternoon meet all the Commissioners again at the house of the Prince. A stormy time at first. They tried every possible means to get me to give up the English Treaty as a basis,—arguments, taunts, sneers and bluster, all were tried on me, but I refused to move. They then refused to grant the three concessions I asked,[182] except on terms which would destroy them. Thinking quite time enough had been wasted, I gave them my ultimatum,—*viz.,* the Treaty as I had given it to them in Siamese, striking out the reciprocity clause from Article I and inserting that United

---

[182]The three amendments referred to above.

States ships-of-war and United States Consuls should aid and assist Siamese vessels so far as could be done without a breach of neutrality.

After much and very useless talk, they agreed to give me an answer on Saturday evening.

Left at 9 P. M.[183]

Friday, May 23, 1856. Much better in health, go out with Mr. Telford to visit some of the wats.

Saturday, May 24, 1855 [1856]. At 5 P. M. meet the Prince. He proposes to insert the preamble of the Treaty made by Mr. Roberts. I object that it is not good English, being ungrammatical, and that it would be laughed at.

The object of this is to get me to glorify the Kings[184] more than was done in the English Treaty, which would, as they think, exalt them in the eyes of England and France. I steadily refuse, and at last, after much ill humor on the part of the Prince, he agrees that the Treaty be engrossed in triplicate, as I gave it in on Thursday last.[185]

---

[183]On the same day as this "stormy" conference, the First King sent a kind autograph letter to Townsend Harris, accompanying a gift of sweet tamarinds "grown at Northern Laos Country" (*L. & P.,* vol. 2, no. 48)—a courtesy which Townsend Harris acknowledged on the following day—(*L. B.,* vol. 1, p. 28).

[184]The Preamble of Mr. Roberts's Treaty is not in bad English—certainly there are no ungrammatical constructions in it. And as for glorifying the Kings, the only expression that might be so construed is the reference to "His Majesty the Sovereign and Magnificent King," and the other minor high-flown expression that the commercial intercourse thereby established would continue "as long as heaven and earth shall endure." The rest of the Preamble of the Roberts Treaty is written in as plain and matter of fact English as that of the Bowring and Townsend Harris Treaties, though differing from the stereotyped form in which such documents were drawn up by the middle of the century.

[185]Meaning as finally agreed upon on May 22nd. The treaty negotiations were really brought to a close at the meeting of May 24th (see also Wood, *op. cit.,* p. 232), and it was on this day that Townsend Harris announced that he would leave on the 31st of May.

My mind is greatly relieved and I hope this is the end of my troubles with this false, base and cowardly people. To lie is here the rule from the Kings downward. Truth is never used when they can avoid it. A nation of slaves, each one must crawl prone on his belly in the presence of some superior, and in turn he strives to increase the number of *his* prostrate inferiors. This custom causes them to seek the company of those inferior to themselves. I never met a people like them, and hope I may never again be sent here. The proper way to negotiate with the Siamese is to send two or three men-of-war of not more than sixteen feet draft of water. Let them arrive in October and at once proceed up to Bangkok and fire their salutes. In such a case the Treaty would not require more days than I have consumed weeks.

Sunday, May 25, 1856. Attended service at the house of Dr. Bradley. I am now quite recovered.

Monday, May 26, 1856. Sent paper to the Prince so that both versions shall be on the same kind of paper.

Mr. Heusken busy with the copies of the Treaty.

Mr. Mattoon came at 11 A. M. to say for the Prince that he wanted still to change the preamble of the Treaty to that used by Mr. Roberts. I again refused, saying we had already nearly finished two copies. Mr. Mattoon tells me the Treaty is to be executed on Thursday at the Hall of Justice.

I omitted in Saturday's journal to say that the Phra Klang came in to the Prince's on Saturday evening, and that I then gave him notice I should leave on Saturday the 31st, and requested him to let me have the steamer.

At 3 P. M. a letter from Mr. Mattoon[186] saying the Prince wished me to write a letter giving my reasons for declining to take Mr. Roberts's preamble, so that he might show it to the King. I wrote accordingly. (See copy.)

At 6 P. M. another note[187] requesting that in one of the three copies of the Treaty I would name the Kings of Siam first; agreed to.

Tuesday, May 27, 1856. The Second King, with a large retinue of boats, visits the forts in our vicinity. Salute him with our band. The Prince passed in his boat. Captain Bell took off his hat and bowed to him. The Prince only gave him an angry stare in return. The King, I am told, bowed very politely to all. This afternoon the Prince requested me to delay my departure until Monday, saying the King had not the letter to the President ready, nor could he give me an audience of leave, as he had engagements for all the time. These were mere childish pretences, as plenty of time exists between this and next Saturday morning to do all they require, and moreover I told the Prince *last* Saturday that I must leave next Saturday. I accordingly sent word that I should much regret not having an audience, but it was absolutely necessary I should leave on Saturday, as the bread was running short in the ship, and that if I did not go before Monday I should lose the June

---

186*L. & P.*, vol. 2, no. 50, which contains also Prince Krom's detailed suggestions as to the arguments which should appear in Townsend Harris's reply. This reply Townsend Harris wrote on May 27, 1856, addressing it to the Rev. Mr. Mattoon (*L.B.*, vol. 1, p. 28).

187*L. & P.*, vol. 2, no. 49, also from the Rev. Mr. Mattoon.

mail fom China. Finished the copies of the Treaties and compared them.

Wednesday, May 28, 1856. Sent my secretary with my copies of the Treaties to the Prince's that he might have them compared and then attach the two versions together. Mr. Heusken engaged at this until 4 P. M.

The Prince in trouble wishes me to write him a letter with my reasons for not staying over until Monday.

Wrote it and sent it to Mr. Mattoon. The reason the Prince wishes this in black and white is that he may show it to the King, as they are such a set of unsanctified liars that the King would not believe him without some proof like this. In my letter (see copy),[188] in addition to what I said yesterday, I wrote that the King's letter to the President could be given to the *consul,* who would forward it in a proper manner. This is the first hint I have given of my intention to appoint a consul.

This evening I made out a commission[189] for Mr. Stephen Mattoon, a native citizen of the State of New York, as American Consul for the Kingdom of Siam, to reside at Bangkok. Also wrote a letter to the Minister of Foreign Affairs, informing him of Mr. Mattoon's appointment and making the usual requests.[190]

Both these papers were dated the 30th of May, as I wished them to follow the signing of the Treaty.

I consider Mr. Mattoon as peculiarly well fitted for the office of consul. He speaks the language like a native,

[188]*L.B.,* vol. 1, p. 31.
[189]*L.B.,* vol. 1, p. 34, which, however, he dated May 30, 1856.
[190]*L.B.,* vol. 1, p. 32.

he knows the people well—their manners, customs, laws, prejudices, etc., etc., having lived here nearly ten years.

He is of a mild quiet temper, firm on any point of principle, and winning in his manners. His reputation for veracity is well established, and the Siamese never doubt his word. He is popular with both of the Kings and the nobles.[191]

Thursday, May 29, 1856. This being the day fixed for signing the Treaties, I went to the Old Palace (the residence of the Prince) and met all the Commissioners except the Prime Minister. The Treaty was then sealed with all our seals and afterwards signed,—making one hundred and eight seals and as many signatures. This took over three hours. The Prince then delivered to me two copies of the Treaty and I gave him one, at which moment a salute of twenty-one guns was fired from the Prince's battery or fort. All was smiles and good humor.[192]

---

[191]To this estimate of the Rev. S. Mattoon, we should add that of Wood (*op. cit.,* p. 194) :

". . . and part of the chain of these successful events was the planting of American missionaries in Siam, for the confidence reposed in them extends to kindred Western people. It was very evident that much of the apprehension they felt in taking upon themselves the responsibilities of a treaty with us would be diminished if they could have the Rev. Mr. Mattoon as the first United States Consul to set the treaty in motion."

See also, *Journal,* Apr. 26, 1856.

[192]And so ended Townsend Harris's negotiations for the Treaty with Siam. Some years later, in the course of a letter to Robert Chilton of the Department of State, dated Yedo, Aug. 8, 1860 (*L. B.,* vol. 5, p. 12), Townsend Harris made the following disillusioned reference to his present success:

"Are you aware that the only acknowledgment of my services in making the commercial Treaty with Siam (May, 1856) is contained in Dispatch no. 8, dated August 19, 1858, in which I am informed that printed copies of the Treaty would be transmitted to me?"

On July 16, 1856, the Second King wrote to Commodore Perry (then in

I then announced to them that I had appointed Mr. Mattoon American Consul which, contrary to my expectations, was very well received. They all congratulated both him on his appointment and me on my fortunate selection.

I was agreeably surprised at this, as I expected a contest with them on this point, although I had the clear right to make the appointment, and it was for their interest to have him immediately. Another message from the King. He wishes me to leave on Saturday evening so that I can have an audience in the morning. I proposed that he should give me an audience on Friday night. After this the Second King sent to ask me to visit him on Friday night; he was informed of the state of my engagements with the First King.

Friday, May 30, 1856. Signed Mr. Mattoon's Commission and sent it to him; also thirteen cards under cover, P. P. C., addressed to various persons here.

The First King came down at noon to visit the forts Phra-cha-mit and Pit-patch-nuck; as he turned into the Ban-kok-noy, by the Residence, the band played "God save the King," and, in company with Captain Bell and the others of my suite, I went to the landing platform and there made our bows to the King, who returned the same in a cordial manner.

Went up to Mr. Mattoon's and settled my accounts

America) and spoke of Townsend Harris's Treaty as follows (33–2, H. Ex. Doc., no. 97, vol. 2, p. 408):

"The American Envoy had the honor of making a liberal treaty of commerce and friendship, which I trust will prove mutually advantageous."

with him.[193] At two P. M. the Second King sent for me to visit him, which I promised to do after dinner. The First King sent me word he would give me my audience of leave early to-morrow morning, and that his boats should be sent for me at 7 A. M.

At 5 P. M. went to [the] Second King with Mr. Mattoon, Dr. Wood and Mr. Lewis; Dr. Semple and Mr. Heusken joined me an hour afterwards. I found matting spread for me to walk on from the outer gate of the Palace up to what the King calls his English House. I was most kindly received by the King, who speaks excellent English, showed me a great many books, prints, arms, chemicals, etc., etc., all of European or American origin; a curious clock showing the hour of the day, day of the week, *idem* of month and month of the year and finally the age of the moon. The hour of the day was marked on a lapis lazuli globe, elevated above the clock and revolved on a pivot, while the red tongue of a green and gold serpent marked the actual hour. This complex piece of work is kept in order, cleaned, etc., etc., by the King himself. Had a good deal of conversation about the United States, the Presidents, and the officers of the *Peacock* who were here in 1833. The King remembered not only the name of every officer, but also his baptismal name, and asked after most of them.

He handed me a receipt[194] for the presents I brought

---

[193]It being the end of the month, Townsend Harris settled accounts with Mr. Heusken (*L.B.*, vol. 1, p. 84) and (on the assumption that "May 3" should read "May 30") also with Mr. Mattoon, to whom he paid the sum of $500 for his services as interpreter (*L.B.*, vol. 1, p. 82).

[194]*L.B.*, vol. 1, p. 45, dated May 29, 1856.

him from the President, and also gave me a list[195] of the contents of four cases he had put up containing presents from him to the President. The cases were very neatly marked and, as he said, done with his own hands.

He gave us tea, coffee, and chocolate, fruit, sweet-meats, etc., etc., making the tea, etc., himself—asking each one how he liked to have it, with or without milk, etc., etc. Two of his wives were present while we were in the tea room and joined freely in the conversation, but they were prostrate on the floor, literally grovelling on all fours. Left about half-past seven and returned to my quarters, and packed up everything so as to be ready for an early start to-morrow morning

Saturday, May 31, 1856. Up at five o'clock. Bathed for the last time in fresh water. Put up all night articles, etc., etc., and took breakfast at six o'clock.

The boats from the King, instead of coming for me at seven o'clock, did not reach me until after eight o'clock.

Started in company with Captain Bell and Dr. Semple; stopped for Mr. Mattoon and Lieutenant Lewis, reached the upper landing at ten minutes before nine, found armchairs for Captain Bell and self, and ordinary sedans for the others. About one quarter the number of troops were out now that were present when I had my first audience. We went to the Hall of Justice, where I was kept waiting nearly two hours before I was admitted, although the King knew that this delay would probably prevent my reaching the *San Jacinto* to-night.

Was received in the old Audience Hall—a finer in-

[195]*L.B.*, vol. i, p. 43, also dated.May 29, 1856.

terior than the other where I was first received. A very large number of nobles and princes was present. The King was seated on a low throne about two feet above the floor. He asked me how soon I should leave, whether I went to China direct or via Singapore. Spoke about his regret at not having time! to write to the President or to prepare presents for him. As to the last, I told him the letter and presents could be delivered to the Consul who would forward them in a proper manner, etc., etc. This brought up the appointment of Mr. Mattoon as Consul, and the King said he thought only the President could appoint, as the Commission was to be signed by him. Told him that all envoys, as well as commodores, could fill vacancies or new consulates for the time being, —i. e., during the pleasure of the President.

He then conversed aside with the nobles in a low tone about this matter, and finally ordered the Pia Yumarat, or Lord Mayor[196] as he calls him, to prepare a proclamation acknowledging Mr. Mattoon's appointment.

Soon after, the King rose and told me he would grant me a private audience, and would send for me as soon as he was ready.

Soon afterwards he sent for me, Captain Bell and Mr. Mattoon. We were conducted to a small house fitted up and furnished in European fashion. Here he welcomed me with a shake of the hands and saying, "Good-bye." After we were seated he poured out a glass of wine for each of us and took one himself, giving as a

---

[196]Townsend Harris has already referred to this person as Somdet P'ia Yumarat, the Chief Justice (see *Journal*, Apr. 25, 1856).

toast the President of the United States, wishing him health and happiness and hoping that the Treaty just concluded would lead to mutual advantages, etc., etc. He then asked when the new election for President would take place, when the new President would be sworn in, etc., etc.

He gave me a blue velvet envelope which he said contained my *Credentials!* and requested me to open and read them. There were two papers: one a receipt[197] for the presents; and the other an apology for not sending presents and writing a letter to the President, with a short history of the negotiations.[198] The last document must have taken twice as much time as would have sufficed for writing to the President direct.

So much for his excuse of "want of time." I was now delayed over an hour by the most frivolous and pedantic conversation I ever listened to, and satisfied me he was quite as weak-minded as pedantic. He enumerated all the languages he could speak—the various sciences he has a small smattering of—the learned societies of which he was a member, and the various individuals he corresponded with in various parts of the world, and honored me by asking me to correspond with him from Japan. It was now half-past twelve and I was most anxious to get away. But no—I must wait while he wrote a gossiping letter to Sir John Bowring, informing Sir John that I would show him my credentials, as he persisted in calling the two papers in the blue pocket. At last, as there

---

[197]*L. B.*, vol. I, p. 41.
[198]*L. B.*, vol. I, p. 37, and Wood, *op. cit.*, pp. 232–34.

must be an end to all things, I got away a little past one o'clock. I went down for the steamer in the King's boat, but, as the tide was strong against us, did not reach her until two P. M. I omitted to mention that at this interview I gave the King the *Nautical Almanac* for 1856, 1857 and 1858; and just before I left, he gave me a silver gilt segar case filled with segars. I shall smoke those and send the case to the Secretary of State.

On board the steamer I received a letter from the Phra Klang to Governor Marcy, giving the Siamese official account of my arrival, transit from the ship, salutes, boats and boatmen, with the dresses of the latter and all the other *important* matters which are gravely written in the archives of Siam. With this was a translation.

At twenty minutes past two we hauled down the flag, which I gave to Mr. Mattoon, received three hearty cheers from our countrymen whom we left there—returned the cheers—the band played "Hail, Columbia," "The Star Spangled Banner" and "Yankee Doodle," and so we left Bangkok,[199] greatly to our satisfaction. On we went in the little steamer *Royal Seat Siamese Steam Force* for half an hour, when we had to stop to *fix* the machinery. Then on again for another half hour—another stop and another fix. Before this, it was clear that we could not reach the *San Jacinto* to-night, so we took it all quietly.

Arrived at Paknam at seven P. M. The Governor received us with all respect and kindness, gave us tea, coffee, cakes and fruit at once, and then had a hearty

---

[199]Compare Wood, *op. cit.*, p. 263.

meal prepared which was ready at eleven P. M., but only a few ate, as most of us preferred sleeping, which we did very comfortably. No mosquitoes, and the air was quite fresh.

Sunday, June 1, 1856. Up at five A. M. The Governor had tea and coffee for us, and showed me a fine lot of fruit which he had prepared as a present for me—there were some thirty trays of it.

Started at half-past five A. M.; when outside were overtaken by a heavy thunderstorm. The rain was very heavy. No compass on board, and it was so thick nothing could be seen at one hundred yards from us, so we had to come to an anchor.

Soon afterwards the fog lifted and we saw the *San Jacinto,* and finally and happily got on board at half-past seven o'clock.

Some bills had to be adjusted and paid, and arrangements made about two Siamese boys that the Prime Minister has put under the charge of Commodore Armstrong to learn English, etc., etc. One of the lads is the son of his nephew and grandson of the Somdet.

At noon precisely we got under way. Something wrong about the machinery, as we only go about four and three-quarters miles per hour.

Monday, June 1 [2], 1856. Steaming along very slowly; see Pulo Way; squalls of rain and wind E. of South.[200]

Tuesday and Wednesday, June 3 and 4, 1856. En-

---

[200]On this day Townsend Harris wrote Dispatch No. 5 to Secretary of State Marcy, which gives the complete history of his mission to Siam, and a careful outline of the Articles of the Treaty (*L. B.,* vol. 1, pp. 46–57).

gaged in making copies of various papers to be sent with the Treaty. Heavy rain Wednesday.[201]

Thursday, June 5, 1856. This evening finish copying papers. Last evening saw Pulo Obi; and this morning, weather fine but a dead calm until noon when the wind comes out from S. W

It is now clear we shall not reach Hongkong in time for the mail, which is to leave Tuesday the 10th current at two P. M.[202]

Friday, June 6, 1856 Sight Pulo Condore. Dead calms.

Saturday, June 7, 1856. At noon stop engines for repairs. No matter about this, as I find I cannot save the mail.

Close to Pulo Supatu.

Sunday, June 8, 1856. Engines started at two A. M. Day very hot. Thermometer, 87°. No wind.[203]

---

[201]On Wednesday, June 4th, Townsend Harris wrote Dispatch No. 6 to Secretary Marcy, marked "Confidential" (*L. B.*, vol. 1, pp. 58–65). He explains the initial delay as due to the "inferior" titles borne by the President of the United States and by himself as contrasted with those of Queen Victoria and Sir John Bowring; sketches (unfavorably) the character of the First King; and gives a vivid picture of the fear of the English entertained by the Siamese.

On this same day (June 4th), Townsend Harris's thoughts turned to the work ahead of him in Japan, and he wrote to Commodore Perry (33–2, H. Ex. Doc., no. 97, vol. 2, p. 191):

"I should have mentioned before that both the Kings of Siam inquired after you and your welfare. They are both aware of your services to your country, and of your opening Japan, and I do not hesitate to say to you that *your* expedition to Japan was one of the great causes that led to the English and American Treaties with Siam."

[202]On June 5, 1856, Townsend Harris wrote Dispatch No. 7 to Marcy, in which he described the mineral and other resources of Siam, the chief articles of import and export, and the manner of carrying on business in that country. (*L. B.*, vol. 1, pp. 66–69)

[203]On the following day, Monday, June 9, 1856, Townsend Harris wrote Dispatch No. 8 to Marcy. While informing him of the appointment of the Rev. Mr. Mattoon, Townsend Harris launches into a eulogy of his appointee, and urges adequate remuneration and proper housing. (*L. B.*, vol. 1, pp. 69–72.)

Tuesday, June 10, 1856. The mail leaves Hong kong to-day at two P. M., and here we are about four hundred miles off.

Wednesday, June 11, 1856. At noon we are 185 miles from Hongkong. We shall not, probably, reach there before eight P. M. At five P. M. wind breezes from N. E. Set square sails.

Thursday, June 12, 1856. We have had a fine wind from N. E. all night, and when I went on deck at seven A. M. found the *Asses Ears* in sight. Eight A. M. Chinese pilot came on board.

Find my knowledge of the coast of some use, as Captain Bell often refers to me. English frigate in sight at 9 A. M. standing out.

When she sees us, she wears and runs towards Hongkong, keeping us close company.

At one P. M. anchor near E. Point opposite Coal Depot. U. S. Sloop *Levant* here. I am soon visited by General Keenan, U. S. Consul, Mr. Bradley from Singapore, Mr. Armstrong[204] and Rev. Mr. Johnson. Get my letters and papers—a large bag of them.

General Keenan invites me to take up my quarters on shore with him, which I gladly accept, and go on shore at four P. M.—fine large rooms and cool situation.

Friday, June 13, 1856. The excitement of arriving here and reading my letters (which was not completed till one A. M.) prevented my sleeping, and I got up at six A. M. quite worn out.

Visit the Governor Sir J. Bowring with Commodore

[204]Of the banking firm of Armstrong & Lawrence (see note 41).

Armstrong, Captain Bell and Captain Smith[205] of the *Levant*. Pleasant interview. Accept invitation to breakfast with him on Tuesday at eight and a half A. M.

Mr. Drinker[206] and Mr. Strachan call on me this evening. Go to bed at eight and a half P. M. and at once to sleep.

Saturday, June 14, 1856. From previous fatigue and want of sleep I did not awake until I was called at half-past nine. This prevented doing any work until noon. Hard at work all day writing.[207]

Tuesday, June 17, 1856. Breakfast with Sir John Bowring, Commodore Armstrong, Captain Bell, Captain Smith of *Levant*. Dr. Parker present.[208] Heavy rain.

Sir John gives me the late Dutch Convention with Japan to copy.[209]

---

205 William Smith, of Kentucky.
Midshipman, Mar. 4, 1823; Passed Midshipman, Mar. 23, 1829; Lieutenant, Mar. 3, 1831; Commander, Sept. 12, 1854; Commodore, July 16, 1862; Retired List, Jan. 19, 1865; died, Apr. 29, 1873. (Hamersly, *List*, ed. 1901.)
He commanded the *Vixen*, of the Home Squadron, 1851–52; the *Levant*, of the East India Squadron, 1857–58. (Hasse, *Index*, pt. 3, p. 1530. In pt. 2, p. 889, *s.v.*, *Levant*, however, it is stated that Smith commanded the *Levant* from 1855 to 1858.)

206 Sandwith Drinker. See note 40.

207 On this day Townsend Harris received a letter also from the Rev. D. J. Macgowan, dated Ningpo, June 8, 1856 (*L. & P.*, vol. 1, no. 39), in which the latter compares the Siamese and the Japanese, urges Townsend Harris to visit all the ports on his way to the "Rising Sun," and asks him to procure for him some Japanese books.

208 Peter Parker, the missionary-physician who was at various times Secretary, Interpreter, and Chargé of the American Legation in China, and finally Commissioner. In a letter to Townsend Harris dated Canton, Dec. 18, 1855 (*L. & P.*, vol. 1, no. 25), Mr. Drinker says:
"People think Marcy had much better made you Commissioner to China than old Parker, which appointment gives general dissatisfaction."

209 In his Dispatch No. 9 to Marcy (*L. B.*, vol. 1, pp. 73–75, dated Hongkong, July 3, 1856), Townsend Harris says that Sir John (now Governor of Hongkong) had favored him with an authentic copy in French of the Convention,

Sunday, June 22, 1856. It has rained steadily and heavily for the last nine days. Do not go out at all except on Tuesday 17th.

Hard at work the whole week getting my papers ready for Mr. Bradley.[210]

Monday, July [June] 23, 1856. Send by W. C. Bradley, Esq., the following letters, under cover to N. Dougherty:

Joseph Evans	June 4,	1856
Commodore Perry	" "	"
H. Murray	" 25	"
Mrs. Langlois and Mouse	" 2	"
" " " "	" 25	"
Miss Caroline D. Langlois	" "	"
E. P. Russell	" 16	"
R. L. Crooke	" "	"
N. Dougherty	" 7	"
" "	" 14	"
" "	" 25	"
Mrs. Richard Schell	" 14	"
P. M. Wetmore	" 9	"
" " "	" 25	"

and that he was therewith transmitting to the Department a translation of the same.

Three days later (on Friday, June 20, 1856), Sir John Bowring kindly furnished Townsend Harris with more information of great importance—a statement concerning the fish trade of Siam and the Dutch monopoly of trade with Japan (*L. & P.*, vol. 2, no. 64).

[210]For earlier history of Consul Bradley, see note 55. The wish which he expressed in his letter to Townsend Harris dated Jan. 30, 1856 (*l.c.*), was answered, for here we see him about to return to the United States as special bearer of dispatches. His special passport, signed by Townsend Harris, is dated June 20, 1856 (*L. B.*, vol. 1, pp. 88–89); his Instructions, June 25, 1856 (*L. B.*, vol. 1, pp. 87–88).

Henry Grinnell	June 8, 1856
B. A. Harris[211]	" 16 "
W. L. Marcy (private)	" " "

The following per mail:

Mrs. Eliza Harris[212]	" 4 "
Captain McDonald	" 18 "

The rain has happily ceased to-day, and Mr. Heusken started for a visit to Canton and Macao. I learn from Commodore Armstrong that it will require twelve to fifteen days' more work to get ready to start for Japan.

Tuesday and Wednesday, June 24 and 25, 1856. Fair weather. Greatly disappointed in not being able to get over to Macao.

Thursday, June 26, 1856. 5:30 P. M. start for Macao in J. B. Endicott's[213] new steamer *Lilly*. Reach there in four hours, fifteen minutes. Find a large party at Mr. Drinker's, where I stop.

---

[211]Miss Bessie Anne Harris, niece of Townsend Harris, who for so many years cared for the *Letters and Papers* of her uncle and who finally presented the valuable collection to The College of the City of New York—an institution which under the name of *Free Academy* was founded by Townsend Harris in 1847. See *The Establishment of The College of the City of New York as the Free Academy in 1847. Townsend Harris, Founder,* by Mario Emilio Cosenza, published by The Associate Alumni of The College of the City of New York, 1925.

[212]Perhaps the reference is to Elizabeth Mayer, the second wife of John Watson Harris, one of Townsend Harris's older brothers and his business partner before he left for the Far East.

[213]Captain James B. Endicott, for many years residing near Canton. While Captain of the American ship *Ruparell,* five Malays of his crew killed (Dec. 24, 1854) a Chinaman on shore at Cumsingmoon in a fight over women (35-2, S. Ex. Doc., no. 22, pt. 1—in Serial no. 982—pp. 540-60). Later Captain Endicott commanded the *Spark* (*ib.,* p. 560: Jan. 19, 1855).

Friday, June 27, 1856. Still fine weather. Call on French Legation, or [viz.],

Comte René de Courcy, Chargé d'Affaires
Comte Kleczkowski, of French Legation[214]
Mr. P. Stewart[215]
Governor Guimaraes, Governor of Macao[216]
Mrs. Loureiro
J. B. Endicott (no see)
Mrs. Hunter
S. B. Rawle—very sick—paralysis[217]

Saturday, June 28, 1856. Receive calls from Comte de Courcy, Comte Kleczkowski, Governor Guimaraes, Mr. Stewart, Mr. Troplong, French Consul [at] Manila [and] fiancé de Katy.[218] Mr. Heusken reaches here from Canton.

---

[214]Comte Michel Kleczkowski, Secretary of the French Legation. When M. de Courcy returned to Europe in 1857 (*L. & P.*, vol. 1, no. 62), Kleczkowski became First Secretary, and he served in this capacity under M. de Bourboulon, the French Minister Plenipotentiary in 1858 (*L. & P.*, vol. 1, no. 87).

Kleczkowski afterwards became Chargé d'Affaires at Pekin and, on his return to France, was made Professor of Chinese at the *Ecole Nationale des langues orientales vivantes*. In 1876 he published at Paris, in 2 volumes, a *Cours graduel et complet de Chinois parlé et écrit*.

[215]Mr. Patrick Stewart, whose house is mentioned in the story of Captain Keppel's rescue of a young and foolish Englishman, who had been imprisoned at Macao in 1849 by orders of Governor Amaral (33–2, H. Ex. Doc., no. 97, vol. 1, p. 301).

[216]Isidoro Francisco Guimaraes, an officer of the Portuguese Navy and His Faithful Majesty's Governor of the Province of Macao, Timor and Solor.

[217]S. B. Rawle, of Pennsylvania, U. S. Consul for Macao from 1856 to 1858. He was nominated on Mar. 11, 1856, in place of R. P. De Silver, resigned; consented to, Mar. 17, 1856. (Hasse, *Index*, pt. 3, p. 1742.)

He was a member of the firm of Rawle, Drinker & Co., Hongkong. (*L. & P.*, vol. 1, no. 136, W. W. Whittlesey to Townsend Harris, dated Chicago, Feb. 4, 1859.)

[218]The reference is to Catherine Ann Drinker, oldest of the four children of Henry Sandwith Drinker. Miss Drinker married Mr. Thomas Allibone Janvier on Sept. 26, 1878. She died rich in years and in honors, on July 19, 1922.

169

Write to-day the following letters:

> C. C. Currier dated July 3, 1856
> S. N. Greene   "   "   "   "
> William Hunter "   "   "   "

Wrote to Armstrong & Lawrence requesting them to ship four cases of presents for the President from the Second King of Siam to the Collector of the Port of New York, and to take five bills of lading. Also wrote to Captain Bell asking him to order the delivery of the four cases of presents now on board the *San Jacinto* to Messrs. Armstrong & Lawrence. A slight shower this morning, but weather still very fine.

A Chinese brought a *wildcat* for sale to me. It was in a basket of openwork covered and lashed in a manner that of itself was a curiosity. The legs were so lashed that they were as stiff as sticks; muzzle lashings enough to hold a dozen mad dogs—the poor creature could not open its mouth nor move a limb. It *could* wink and that was all. The body was very long—of a dirty yellow and spotted precisely like a leopard, except the spots were nearly round instead of angular in shape. On examination I found [that] the pencil of hair on the tip of the ear, and which I had always seen in wildcats, was wanting, and I expressed a doubt about the originality of the *wildness,* but I was groaned down. The basket, as I said before, was open; you could *see,* but not touch.

On hearing the groans, I made a more careful survey and lo! the spots were *forged!!!*

The Chinaman had procured a species of resin, very

dark colored, and with this and the aid of a *hot iron* had made the spots!—manufactured out of a poor harmless "roof scrambler" a fierce wildcat! I tore the basket open, and the *forgery* was soon made manifest, and I gained great applause.

Monday, June 30, 1856. Still enjoying the delicious weather on the Praya Grande at Macao. Heard a story of a countryman who commanded an American clipper loaded for London. While going down the China Seas, his dearly beloved wife died. He did not like to let the fishes feed on her. He was a temperance man and had no spirits on board. What to do?

On reflection he remembered he had some *cassia oil* on board. The recollection inspired the man! He procured a large water cask in which he *headed up* the remains of his dear wife, and then *filled up the cask with cassia oil!* It was worthy of the best days of Egyptian embalming. His triumph in cheating the fishes assuaged his grief for his loss, and he ate a hearty dinner. The man was consoled. On his arrival in London, he went at once to the consignees of the oil, and like an honest man told them what he had done and asked, "What's the damage?" In reply he was told £1,000!!!! He was near joining his truly *dear* wife. It appeared that the oil had from various causes been very high in China and had come to an excellent market in London. In the end he paid £900, $4,500.

It is said that he then drew forth the remains of his wife and had her buried in London. And it is *also* said that he carefully put up the oil *in its original jars* and took it home with him to America, where peradventure it is now being consumed in various shapes.[219]

Wednesday, July 2, 1856. Remained at Macao until six P. M. Went on board *Lily*. Mr. Heusken nearly left behind. Started at seven twenty-five; went Cap-Sing-Moon passage, arrived at eleven twenty-five P. M., and at 12:00 at my quarters with General Keenan.

Thursday, July 3, 1856. Go on board *San Jacinto*. She expects to sail Monday [the] 7th. Meet the Commodore on shore. General Keenan has a new *jurisdiction case*. Attend to various matters. Write Nos. 9 and 10 to [the] Department,[220] also write P. M. Wetmore, New York.

Friday, July 4, 1856. Attend to closing dispatches for Mr. Bradley and the duplicates to be forwarded by the August mail.

General Keenan has a large dinner party in honor of the day. Do not attend, as I wish to avoid all such affairs which are sure to run into excess of noise and drinking. Twenty-two sat down to table, and some of them remained until two A. M. of the next day. The *San Jacinto* was finely decorated with flags and fired a national salute at noon.

---

[219]On this day, President Franklin Pierce nominated Townsend Harris Consul General for Japan (S. Ex. J'l, vol. 10, p. 112).

[220]Dispatch No. 9 (*L. B.*, vol. 1, pp. 73–75) tells of his arrival at Hongkong; of the repairs to the *San Jacinto;* of the receipt from Sir John Bowring of a French translation of the Dutch Convention with Japan, etc., etc.

Dispatch No. 10 (*L. B.*, vol. 1, pp. 75–85) gives an accurate account of his disbursements to date, under the three headings of presents for the Kings of Siam, expenses of the Mission to Siam, and salary of Mr. Heusken.

Dispatch No. 11 of same date (*L. B.*, vol. 1, p. 86) encloses duplicates of the Siam Treaty, and of former Dispatches Nos. 5–10 incl.

There are many American ships in the harbor, and were finely dressed and most of them fired salutes. A poor man lost his left and three fingers of his right hand in firing on board the *Sam Willets*.

Saturday, July 5, 1856. Give to C. W. Bradley, Esq., American Consul at Singapore, the dispatches and Siamese Treaty with his passport[221] as special bearer of dispatches and letter of instructions, and also gave to General Keenan the duplicates of the Treaty and my letters to be forwarded by the mail of August 10th.

Hired a cook and his mate at sixteen dollars per month for the two; a tailor and washman at fourteen dollars *per mensem* each. I am to furnish them their food on board ship and after my arrival at Shimoda, and after one year, if they do not wish to stay longer, I am to give them a free passage to Hongkong.

Busy in picking up a few articles of furniture—hard to be obtained.

The word now is that the *San Jacinto* will be ready to sail on Monday evening next.

Sunday, July 6, 1856. Visit *San Jacinto*. Learn she cannot leave before Wednesday next. Mr. Dixon, of China, sends me a *North China Herald* of June 21st, with account of a visit to Nagasaki and Shimoda by some Americans (Mr. Cunningham,[222] late Vice-Consul at Shanghai, among others). Great compliants of high

---

[221]This passport was signed by Townsend Harris, and is dated June 20, 1856 (*L. B.*, vol. I, pp. 88–89).

[222]Edward Cunningham: U. S. Vice-Consul at Shanghai, 1852–54; Acting Consul, 1856 (Hasse, *Index*, pt. I, p. 458).

prices and unwillingness to give supplies or permit trade. The following are the quotations of prices:

	Shimoda	Shanghai
Firewood per picul	278 cash	300 cash
Chickens each	672 "	180 & 200 "
Eggs "	18 "	6 "
Sweet potatoes per catty	11 "	10 "
White rice per picul	4,440 "	3,500 "
Brown sugar per picul	$16½	$5½
Beans per catty	15 cash	10 cash

Exchange: 1,600 cash per Mexican dollar;
1 ichibu given for $1, or 66 2/3% discount.

They offered to barter silver watches and revolvers, but were not allowed to do so, it being plain the authorities prevented the traffic.

San Jacinto will not leave before Wednesday morning, 9th instant.

See Book No. 3

Journal No. 3

Commencing July 7, 1856
Ending February 25, 1857

Journal No. [3]

Monday, July 7, 1856. Write to H. Redfield, Esq., Collector of the Port of New York,[223] enclosing to him a bill of lading for the presents for the President from the Second King of Siam. Also to W. L. Marcy,[224] giving him a copy of the above letter and also a bill of lading. Make various calls: Sir John Bowring, C. Anstey, Esq., Attorney General, Captain Twiss, R. A., C. Turner, Esq., Barrister, and several others. See about some purchases.[225]

Tuesday, July 8, 1856. Settle my accounts with Armstrong & Lawrence by giving them a draft on Purser Bradford for $525. Engage a butler or head boy at fifteen dollars per month—but fear he will not go as he cannot get security for the advance, and without that he cannot or will not go. Finish all my affairs at two P. M., and

---

[223]Hemon J. Redfield. The letter itself(*L. B.*, vol. 1, p. 87), however, is dated July 8th. The four cases containing the presents for the President of the United States were shipped by the *Redgauntlet*.

[224]Dispatch No. 12 (*L. B.*, vol. 1, p. 86), likewise dated Hongkong, July 8th.

[225]On this day, President Pierce's nomination of Townsend Harris as Consul General to Japan was received by the Senate, read, and referred to the

return to my quarters at Consul Keenan's. Weather *very* hot; covered with prickly heat.

Wednesday, July 9, 1856. This morning the butler Assam completed his security and I advanced him three months wages or forty-five dollars. Go on board at eight A. M. Find the engineers have not yet completed their work, so that we cannot get away to-day. All my people come on board.

Thursday, July 10, 1856. The *San Jacinto* got under way at five A. M., but after running one mile came to a dead stop. Cause—the propeller has lost the keys that confine it on the shaft—has slipped down so far that it overlaps the outer stern post to which it gave several blows that shook the whole ship. It has been determined to put the ship into dock at Whampoa for repairs. She is to be towed up[226] there on Saturday next by the steamers *Canton* and *Willamette*.[227]

A trying delay for me. I am losing some fourteen

Committee on Commerce (S. Ex. J'l, vol. 10, pp. 112, 115). And at the other end of the world, on the following day (Tuesday, July 8, 1856), the French mission concluded a treaty with Siam; *cf.* the extract quoted above (note 84) from Consul Bradley's letter dated Singapore, Jan. 30, 1856 (*L. & P.*, vol. 1, no. 28).

[226]For an account of this "tow" on Saturday, July 12th, and of the chagrin of the Americans as they passed the British Frigate *Nankin,* see Wood, *Fankwei,* p. 274. The chagrin was due to the fact that, in order to enter the dock at Whampoa, the *San Jacinto* had to be lightened so as to draw not more than sixteen feet of water. All coal, water, provisions and even the guns had to be removed; and we can all feel the chagrin of the Americans when, not moving proudly on her own steam, but "humbly dragging in the wake of two steamboats," the *San Jacinto* had to pass in review, as it were, and the band of the British Frigate *Nankin* struck up "Hail, Columbia." No wonder the intended compliment felt like a satire!

[227]The American ship *Willamette,* Captain William Curry. On the evening of Jan. 31, 1856, she was towing a Chinese junk from Hongkong to Canton. When near the second bar inside the Bocca Tigris, she was fired upon by several mandarin boats. (Consul O. H. Perry to Dr. Parker, Canton, Feb. 16, 1856: 35-2, S. Ex. Doc., no. 22, pt. 2—in Serial no. 983—pp. 755-57.)

dollars per day salary besides the wages of my servants, some sixty dollars per month.[228]

Friday, July 11, 1856. Rainy. Go over to Macao[229] in the *Lilly.* Leave at four P. M. and arrive at eight twenty. Captain Hildreth of the American ship *Sancho Panza* on board.

Monday, July 14, 1856. The weather has been so showery and uncertain since my arrival. I have not made any visits to-day; it sets in for a storm apparently. Barometer, 29.55, wind fresh from N. N. E.

Tuesday, July 15, 1856. Blowing quite sharp. Barometer, 29.38, much rain; wind veers from N. N. E. to S. E. by S. Impossible to go out.

---

[228]On this day, Townsend Harris also wrote to Secretary Marcy (*L. B.,* vol. 1, pp. 89–90), informing him that the *San Jacinto* had to be put into dock for repairs, and impatiently adding that he would avail himself of the first opportunity of a passage to Japan without waiting for the *San Jacinto.*

On July 10th, also, the overland mail left Hongkong in the steamer for the Red Sea; and on board the steamer was Consul Charles William Bradley, Sr., special dispatch bearer to far-off Washington, D. C., taking home the Treaty just concluded with Siam (Wood, *op. cit.,* p. 273). And so, after seven years of service in the Far East—as U. S. Consul successively at Amoy, Ningpo, and Singapore—Bradley started on the long-wished-for journey home. His earnest plea had been written to Townsend Harris on Jan. 30, 1856 (*L. & P.,* vol. 1, no. 28):

"I am not advised, Sir, whether you have brought a Secretary in your suite; but, if not, I shall be much obliged if you can give me that post, and send me home as bearer of the Treaty. . . . I *must* return to the United States during the coming Spring—(my salary of $1,000 *per annum* being too little, by half, for a decent but most economical subsistence,)—and if I can be sent there in the capacity of which I have spoken, it will save me the expense of a voyage,—a matter which I can illy afford."

[229]At Macao Townsend Harris stayed with the Drinkers, who had a summer home in that city and a winter home at Hongkong. It was on one of these visits to Macao that Townsend Harris presented to Miss Catherine Ann Drinker ("Kat") the small clay model of the white elephant which had been given to him by the Second King of Siam. At the same time Townsend Harris gave her a copy of the Second King's autograph. Almost forty years later (on Mar. 7, 1905), Mrs. Thomas Allibone Janvier (née Miss C. A. Drinker) presented this model of Siam's white elephant to the American Geographical Society, in New York, where the present writer found it. (See also the *Janvier Letters* in the manuscript collections of The New York Public Library.)

Thursday, July 17, 1856. The blow appears to be over, but it is still wet. Squalls and showers. Wind S. by E. to S. by W.

Get a letter from Captain Bell, saying the *San Jacinto* got up to Whampoa on Sunday morning and would go into dock on Friday or Saturday following. Also letter from Captain Endicott.

Wrote to Captain Bell by the *Lilly* which went up this morning. Barometer, 29.55.

Wetmore & Co. of Canton, Shanghai, Foo-chau and New York, have stopped payment.[230]

Report says it was entirely uncalled for, that Mr. Roberts could easily have procured all the money he wanted. Some say it has been purposely done by Roberts. The House is said to be solvent. Hear of the death of a Mr. Randall Cunningham, a young man in the House

---

[230]The founder of the house was William S. Wetmore, whose uncle (Samuel Wetmore) was the partner of Mr. Edward Carrington of Providence, Rhode Island—in those days the largest shipowner and East India merchant in the United States. Young William S. Wetmore in 1824 became a member of the great house of Alsop, Wetmore & Cryder, in Valparaiso, Chile, and in Lima, Peru. In 1831 he retired from the firm with a large fortune, returned to the United States, and then went to China. At Canton he established, together with Joseph Archer of Philadelphia, the house of Wetmore & Co., and succeeded to the large and profitable business of Nathan Dunn & Co. (Barrett, *Old Merchants*, vol. 2, pt. 1, pp. 293–300.)

In a long letter to Townsend Harris, dated Hongkong, Apr. 3, 1857 (*L. & P.*, vol. 1, no. 62), Mr. S. Drinker says of the failure of Wetmore & Co.:

"I am not sure whether Nye had failed before you left for four million. Wetmore also failed through the rascality of Roberts. He found he was not to be included in the new firm and failed with $32,000 in the treasury. The old folks were most savage and immediately sent out L. Sheppard Wetmore and paid in full. Moore died owing the concern $30,000. By the failure poor Lamson lost all."

And again, on June 15, 1857, Mr. Drinker writes (*L. & P.*, vol. 1, no. 69):

". . . also poor old Davis [is dead], of Wetmore & Co., formerly; and that House has resumed under the style of Wetmore, Williams & Co., and in the circular state the House was never insolvent. They accuse Roberts of a fraudulent failure. They have paid off every dollar and have a surplus."

of Heard & Co., at Foo-chau. He was killed by the Chinese in a street row, for improperly interfering.[231] When will men learn to mind their own business?

Saturday, July 19, 1856. Rain, rain, constantly raining. I cannot get out for any exercise, and my health suffers accordingly. I learn the rain has extended all along the coast, but the wind has not been so heavy as at Macao. It is still squally. Mr. Drinker comes over this evening from Hongkong in the new steamer *Shamrock*. The *Lilly* also down from Canton—nothing new from the *San Jacinto*.[232]

---

[231]Townsend Harris had the name wrong. The murdered man was Howard Cunningham, of Boston, Massachusetts. All the necessary references to the government documents are to be found in Hasse, *Index*, pt. 1, p. 320. The main details are best told in a communication by Commissioner Parker to Wang, Viceroy of the Min and Cheh Provinces, Foo-Chow-foo. This letter is dated U. S. Legation, Foo-Chow, July 22, 1856, and in it Parker says (35–2, S. Ex. Doc., no. 22, pt. 2—in Serial no. 983—p. 882):

"Being informed of some difficulty in the removal of some property [furniture] from the old hong of Messrs. Heard & Co. [in the western part of Nantae] to the new one [in the eastern suburbs], Mr. Comstock, the head of the firm [in Foo-Chow], went to the street to ascertain the state of the case, and, on seeing one of the men in his employ beaten by the men in the street, very quietly asked them to desist; he was pushed down, and then knocked down, but, fortunately escaping, ran to the United States Consul, informing him of what had occurred. Soon after, Mr. H. Cunningham, another gentleman in the house of Messrs. A[ugustine] Heard & Co., [and Mr. Vaughan] went into the street, and, as it is believed [because he died without being able to tell], he, knowing that Mr. Comstock had preceded him, on arriving at the spot after he [Comstock] had fled to the consulate, seeing his chair but not seeing Mr. Comstock, supposed him to be in the crowd, and therefore he rushed in to rescue him, and not to take part in the difficulty between the Chinese [the hostile clans of Foo-Chow and Canton men—the latter of whom were in the employ of Heard & Co.]. In this most commendable effort to afford aid to the head of the house he was cruelly murdered [July 3, 1856], and I request your Excellency will not again represent it as 'joining the Chinese in a fight.' "

The whole affair must have been presented to Townsend Harris only in the aspect characterized by the closing phrase. (*Cf.* also the statement by Dr. Parker to Secretary Marcy, dated July 26, 1856. *Ib.*, p. 868).

[232]The *San Jacinto* on this day went into drydock at Whampoa. See *Journal,* July 10, 1856; and *L. & P.,* vol. 1, no. 40, a letter from Captain H. H. Bell, dated Whampoa, July 21, 1856, to Townsend Harris, then at Macao.

Monday, July 21, 1856. Mr. Drinker went over to Hongkong this morning at seven o'clock in the *Shamrock.*

Called on the Governor of Macao and Mrs. Spooner. Did not see either. Then to Mr. Hunter's,[233] Mr. Rawle's and Mr. Stewart's. Saw all. The bi-monthly mail from Hongkong to England is re-established.

Write to N. Dougherty, to go by the mail on the 24th instant from Hongkong.

Write to General Keenan, U. S. Consul, and Armstrong & Lawrence, all at Hongkong.

Tuesday, July 22, 1856. Commodore Armstrong and Dr. Wood come down from Canton this afternoon. Receive letter from Captain Bell.[234] The *San Jacinto* went into dock on the 19th. Captain Bell writes that it will require two weeks for repairs to the propeller and another week to get ready for sea. Received letter from Mr. Heusken; he is at Canton. Have been reading Huc's *Journey from the Great Wall to Canton*—full of lively sketches, gross credulity and astounding errors.[235]

---

[233]Very probably this is the Mr. W. C. Hunter who in Oct., 1854, recommended Captain S. Drinker (Townsend Harris's great friend) for the hiring of vessels and enlisting of men and soldiers to exterminate the pirates and robbers in the townships of Shawan and Kau-Tong. For the failure of this contract and for the resulting lawsuit, read the statement by Leang King Kwa and other documents in 35-2, S. Ex. Doc., no. 22, pt. 2—in Serial no. 983—pp. 704–12.

[234]*L. & P.*, vol. 1, no. 40; see note 232.

[235]The Abbé Huc, variously referred to as Missionary Apostolic in China, and Missionary Priest of the Congregation of St. Lazarus. The text may refer to Huc's *Recollections of a Journey through Tartary, Thibet, and China during the years 1844, 1845, and 1846*, published at New York, by D. Appleton & Co. in 1852, in two volumes. Indeed, Townsend Harris may have obtained this work in New York on Oct. 8, 1855, the day when he bought, at Appleton's, books and maps for the Kings of Siam to the value of $182 (*L. B.*, vol. 1, p. 1).

Wednesday, July 23, 1856. Call on Commodore Armstrong, Mr. Troplong and the French Legation— only leave cards at the last two places.

Commodore Armstrong, Dr. Wood and Mr. O. H. Perry, U. S. Consul at Canton, call on me to-day.

Write to Captain Bell, now at Whampoa, in answer to his letter of 21st inst. and send it per hands of Mr. Perry, who goes up in the morning. Weather again threatening. Wind N. Barometer, 29.50 and falling. Clouds heavy, with occasional spurts of rain.

At night, wind heavy with much rain. Barometer fell to 29.35 at eleven P. M.

Thursday, July 24, Friday 25, Saturday 26, and Sunday 27, 1856. Constant and heavy rains with a gale of wind from N. by W. to S. S. E. Twelve houses have fallen in consequence of the walls being sapped by the water, and a large number are damaged.

On Saturday night a house fell in Senate Square killing a woman and child. A second child which was on the same bed with the woman and child escaped without any injury. Friday evening went to a quiet party at Mr. Hunter's. Got home at midnight.

Monday, July 28, 1856. Calm and no rain, but the weather is not yet settled. The wind hangs in the N. E. quarter. I learn that the rice crop of this vicinity is more than half lost, and it is said that even greater damage has been felt in the eastern provinces. Wrote Armstrong & Lawrence that I had drawn on them in favor of José María de Fonseca for fifty dollars. He paid me par for my draft. Four P. M. rain again set in

Thursday, July 31, 1856. The rain has continued since Monday, with strong winds. Sad accounts from the country. Houses are falling in all directions. Rice lands are all overflown. Crops supposed to be half lost. Rice has advanced in price at retail 100 per cent.

Receive letter from Mr. Lewis, First Lieutenant of Frigate. Says the repairs will be completed and the ship come out of dock on Saturday, 2nd [of] August.

Receive my newspapers from New York up to 20th of May, also a letter from Lieutenant J. N. Guest, U. S. N.[236]

Friday, August 1, 1856. No rain, but still cloudy. Wind S. by W. Make some calls. Write to Captain Bell and Lieutenant Lewis. Rain at four P. M.

Saturday, August 2, 1856. Advance five dollars to Assam my butler, and give him leave for two days to go to his village to see after his family, his house having fallen.

Showery all day.[237]

Monday, August 4, 1856. Last night the Dutch bark

---

[236]*L. & P.*, vol. 1, no. 35, dated Washington, D. C., Apr. 15, 1856. Lieutenant Guest must have been an intimate friend, for he thanks Townsend Harris for gifts sent from Paris to his little daughter "Nan," and expresses himself familiarly on other matters:

"I sometimes think I should like to be your companion in your Japan exile. . . . The grand question in our party ranks is touching the nominee of the [Democratic] Cincinnati Convention in June. . . . Buchanan stock rises daily. . . . We are sure to have a Democratic President, old fellow, so you can stay in Japan as long as you like."

Townsend Harris's appointment as Consul General for Japan was confirmed by the Senate on this day—July 31, 1856 (S. Ex. J'l, vol. 10, p. 131); and Townsend Harris resigned his office of Minister Resident to Japan when Lincoln, a Republican, became President.

[237]The *San Jacinto* came out of drydock on this day (*L. B.*, vol. 1, p. 90, Dispatch No. 14 to Secretary Marcy, dated Hongkong, Aug. 9, 1856).

Banka, having on board 270 coolies for Havana, was burned to the water's edge, in Macao Roads, about four miles from the Praya Grande. It is rumored that 120 lives were lost.

Fine weather yesterday and to-day.

Tuesday, August 5, 1856. Captain Bell writes to Commodore Armstrong that the *San Jacinto* came out of dock on Saturday and will be ready for sea on Thursday the 7th inst. Made arrangements to go over to Hongkong to meet the *San Jacinto* on Thursday next.

Mr. Heusken, who has been at Canton since the 15th of July, writes me he should go to Hongkong yesterday.[238] Write him that the *San Jacinto* will come down to Hongkong on Thursday.

The inquiry into the loss of the *Banka* by the Governor of this place finished to-day.

There is no doubt the ship was purposely set on fire by the Chinese coolies, who were composed of the worst class of this district—vagabonds, thieves and pirates. It was proved that the Chinese threw all sorts of combustibles on the fire, which *was kindled under the cabin.*

Soon after the fire was discovered, the Captain ordered his crew to fire their muskets and pistols on the Chinese, and then two carronades, loaded with canister shot, were run in board and fired among the coolies who thronged the spar-deck.

It appears the coolies were dissatisfied and were trying to desert. The Captain knew this and had all the crew

---

[238]*L. & P.,* vol. 1, p. 41, dated Canton, Aug. 2, 1856. Mr. Heusken said, "I am going to-morrow to Hongkong," which would make him arrive at Hongkong on the 3rd, and not on the 4th, as Townsend Harris says.

armed. It is proved beyond doubt that the Captain, four of the crew, and 120 Chinese were lost. A sad affair, and is one other black page in the history of this new form of the slave trade.[239]

Rain sets in again at 4 P. M., with bright lightning all night.

Wednesday, August 6, 1856. It is clear that the Captain and all the crew of the *Banka* were more or less intoxicated when the fire broke out on board the bark.

Had the proper police been observed, the fire would have been discovered as soon as it was set. My tailor has been gambling, lost all his money, and now impudently demands one month's wages. I, having already advanced him three months, refused. Soon afterwards he sent the butler to inform me that he had not only lost his money, but had pawned all his clothes and even his sleeping mat and blanket, and asked for five dollars to redeem them. I again refused, but will take them out of pawn to-morrow and keep them until I get him on board ship.

Steady rain this morning. Wind W. S. W. Barometer, 29.50. Get papers from Shanghai up to the 1st inst. Strange to say, prayers are offered, processions made, etc., etc., at Shanghai *for* rain, as it appears they are suffering from a drought.

Thursday, August 7, 1856. Mrs. E. E. Spooner, wife of Mr. D. N. Spooner,[240] of the house of Russell &

---

[239]For a shorter account of the destruction of the *Banka* at Macao, see Wood, *Fankwei,* p. 295.

[240]Daniel N. Spooner, Vice-Consul of the United States at Canton, 1853–56. (Hasse, *Index,* pt. 3, p. 1715.)

Co., sent me seventy-five dollars to purchase articles of Japanese manufacture for her. I have before this received orders amounting to thousands of dollars for similar purposes, but this is the first one that was accompanied with money, and assuredly it will be the first one to be attended to. Mrs. Spooner's letter explains what she desires me to procure for her, in general terms.

Wrote to Armstrong & Lawrence that I had drawn on them for twenty dollars in favor of José Maria de Fonseca, of Macao.

Weather still rainy. The *Spark* came in at six P. M. from Canton, and was circulated to go over to Hongkong in one hour after her arrival, but as the weather is so bad, she is detained until after to-morrow morning. Commodore Armstrong has also been detained here, and will not join the *San Jacinto* before to-morrow.

Friday, August 8, 1856. Up at five A. M. Start for Hongkong at seven-twenty in the *Spark*. Weather wet. Arrive at twelve o'clock. Go up to house of General Keenan. Fear I shall not get away from here before Wednesday next.

Rain in the evening.

Saturday, August 9, 1856. Get up late, after a good long sleep. Breakfast at ten A. M. Mr. Heusken joins me at eleven A. M.

Write W. L. Marcy, Dispatch No. 14[241]

---

[241]Dispatch No. 14, *L. B.,* vol. I, pp. 90–91. After informing Secretary Marcy that the *San Jacinto* has been repaired, Townsend Harris expresses the hope that his next dispatch will be dated Shimoda. He adds that the Dutch Govern-

N. Dougherty, New York
C. Huffnagle, U. S. Consul General, Calcutta.

Request Mr. Huffnagle to send me six bottles of sweet sliced chutney, and six bottles curry powder, and send to Armstrong & Lawrence, Hongkong, who will pay for the same.

The *San Jacinto* came down at eleven A. M.; but, having anchored at some distance from my lodgings and under the Kowloon shore, I did not hear of her arrival until three P. M.

On looking over my copy of "Instructions to Consuls," I find that *four leaves,* beginning at page 148 and ending with page 152, are omitted by the binder, and that they contain forms Nos. 1 to 9 inclusive. I must have copies made from the copy of General Keenan.

Rain in showers all day. Walk five miles on the verandah in the evening. My tailor has absconded— sent to every gambling house and other disreputable place, but he cannot be found.

Sunday, August 10, 1856. Get up at eight after a very bad night. Rain and fog. Go on board the *San Jacinto*. Learn she will leave to-morrow evening or Tuesday morning at daylight. Called on the security

---

ment steamer *Medusa* (Captain Fabius) had left Hongkong for Nagasaki a few days before, bearing (presumably) the ratified Convention which the Dutch had concluded with Japan.

The reference is to the *Preliminary Convention of Commerce* signed by the Japanese authorities and by Curtius at Nagasaki on Nov. 9, 1855. For the text of this Convention, see J. H. Gubbins, *The Progress of Japan*, App. 8, pp. 245–50; and J. M. Tronson, *Personal Narrative of a Voyage to Japan*, etc., pp. 44–51.

of my tailor for the forty-two dollars I had advanced him,—when he went out and in twenty minutes brought the man to me tied hand and foot. I ordered him to be sent on board and wrote to Captain Bell, requesting him to receive the tailor and not permit him to leave the ship without my permission.

Wrote to Mrs. Drinker, dated to-morrow, and to Armstrong & Lawrence, informing the latter that I had ordered some chutney, etc., from C. Huffnagle, Esq., U. S. Consul General at Calcutta, and requested them to pay for the same.

Also requested them to mark the *postage in cents* on all letters and papers for me; to ask from time to time of the Commodore when a ship would go to Japan; and to send my letters, etc., by her. Also requested them to inform Mrs. Drinker at Macao when a ship was going to Shimoda.

Monday, August 11, 1856. The tailor did not go on board yesterday. Had him sought for again and at last got him on board.

To charge him three dollars for absence at Macao and one dollar for the same reason at Hongkong.

Send the butler and my luggage on board at one P. M. Visit Mr. Strachan,[242] Armstrong & Lawrence and Mr. Drinker. Go on board at four-thirty P. M. Near the *San Jacinto,* the English seventy-four gun ship *Minden* lay; she is now used as a hospital ship. It was on board this ship that the words of "The Star

[242]He is just mentioned in *L. & P.*, vol. 1, no. 62; and in *ib.*, no. 39, Ningpo, June 8, 1856, the Rev. D. J. Macgowan tells Townsend Harris: "Mr. Strachan makes a friendly notice in his Register of your [Siam?] mission."

Spangled Banner" were composed.[243] The music is an old English air, "Anacreon in Heaven." The *Minden* was one of the ships that bombarded Fort McHenry in Baltimore Bay. As usual, the purser cannot close his business to-day. Note: pursers are always behind time. Rain in showers to-day.

Do not finish coaling and water until nearly midnight.

Tuesday, August 12, 1856. Purser not ready until one P. M., when we get under way[244]—in a shower, of course. The screw works much more smoothly than before the last repairs. As we run out of the passage eastward, we run into and out of our last rain for to-day. As soon as we are out clear of Hongkong Island, we get the true monsoon from S. W., and all sail is made.

Weather pleasant for the rest of the day. I counted eight tide rips between nine and ten-thirty P. M. Left Hongkong by the Ly-moon passage.

Wednesday, August 13, 1856. Fine weather and the ship going along very well—eight knots per hour. Mr. Heusken begins to copy our back work. My cook sick. Ask Dr. David to see him. Run, 168 miles.

Von Siebold[245] says that coal exists in the Island of

---

[243]See *The Americana, s. v., "Star Spangled Banner."* It is interesting to note that the miniature of Townsend Harris as a young man, painted on ivory by John Wesley Jarvis in 1823, was exhibited at the Loan Exhibition of Colonial, Revolutionary, and Historical Relics for the benefit of a fund to erect a monument over the grave of Francis Scott Key.

[244]Wood, *op. cit.,* p. 295.

[245]Dr. Philipp Franz Von Siebold, born in Würzburg, Bavaria, Feb. 17, 1796. In 1823 he was appointed physician to the Dutch Factory at Deshima. Associating with the people for six years as closely as possible because of his medical practice, he became intimately acquainted with all things Japanese. He gave lectures and examined patients at the houses of the Japanese interpreters; later he was granted permission to open a medical school at Narutaki, a suburb of Nagasaki; and he also publicly practiced his profession beyond

Kyushu. At Koyanosi he saw a coal fire. At Wukumoto he visited a coal mine. Although he was not permitted to descend the shaft for more than sixty steps, he saw enough to convince him that the shaft was well and judiciously worked. He was told the lower *strata* were several feet in thickness, and the size of the blocks he saw drawn up confirmed the statement. The coal is bituminous, and is converted into *coke* for use by the Japanese. Run, 166 miles up to noon. [In] P. M. breeze freshens. At six P. M. are making eleven and a half knots per hour. At midnight were up to the Pescadores Islands. A large sea on after five P. M. Lovely evening— bright moon—planets like young suns, and a fine cool breeze.

Thursday, August 14, 1856. Sea began to go down and wind to fail at three A. M. At seven sight the Island of Formosa. See a brig and two other sail. Weather thick and warm; threatens rain; wind very light.

The distance run to-day from observation to observation, 227 nautical miles, actual distance 242. Barometer at two P. M. down to 29.32. Rain. Wind died away at 6 P. M. Showery all the evening.

Friday, August 15, 1856. Calm and showery. Six A. M. saw a junk at anchor; this morning, ten A. M., see

---

the walls of Deshima. See the encyclopædias; but especially *Osada's Life of Takano Nagahide,* translated and edited with an introduction by the Rev. Dr. Daniel Crosby Greene, in *Transactions of the Asiatic Society of Japan,* Vol. XLI, pt. 3, Aug. 1913, pp. 401–03; and Richard Hildreth, *Japan and the Japanese,* pp. 488–90, and *Japan as It Was and Is,* pp. 488–90.

Siebold wrote many books, chief of which was *Nippon: Archiv zur Beschreibung von Japan,* etc., in 5 quarto volumes of text and 6 folio volumes of atlas and engravings—a work on which he toiled from 1832 to 1851. He died Oct. 18, 1866.

a number of cases floating—lower a boat to pick them up—prove to be li-chi and other dried fruits—quite spoiled. Dr. Wood pays me thirty-five dollars formerly lent to him. Run to-day, 174 miles. Discovered a man floating on a raft made of bamboos. He was brought on board and proves to be a Chin-chew man who sailed from Canton fourteen days since in a junk bound for Shanghai. Four days since, suffered from a typhoon, which tore the junk to pieces and finally sank, carrying twenty-nine men in her. He says he was the only one who got on the raft and that he was on it two days. Both these statements were doubtful. The raft was large and well made and must have taken a number of men some time to make it. He was not as much exhausted as he must have been had he been forty-eight hours on the raft without food or water. The packages we picked up belonged no doubt to this junk.[246]

Two and a half P. M. discovered a junk dismasted. We run down to her. She proves to be a junk from Canton to Shanghai, sugar laden, value $8,000. Has lost her mainmast and rudder. Says she was in sight of land four days ago when she met a typhoon which blew her off her [course]. Has no compass—wanted to be towed in to the land again. This we could not do. Gave her a compass[247] and sailing directions for the Island of Agincourt,[248] south fifty miles.

While lying by this junk discover another wreck—

[246]Wood, *op. cit.*, pp. 296–97.

[247]Wood, *op. cit.*, p. 297.

[248]This island is just off the northern end of Formosa, or Taiwan.

apparently European, under jury foremast. Run for her; but, on reaching her, we found she was a Shantung mandarin junk of nine guns and fifty-three men. The commander said the junk was leaky and wished to be taken off with his crew,—which was done and the junk set on fire.[249] Before this last work was completed, another dismasted junk was discovered about six miles off. On reaching her, we found [she] was a large Whampoa junk, laden with sapan wood and sugar, and bound to a port in the Yangtse Kiang, near Nankin.

She had nearly two hundred souls on board, and was riding easily at anchor! one hundred and fifty miles from land. She had the ordinary wood anchors and coir cables.[250] These latter are so buoyant that they will float on the surface of the water, which enables them to anchor great distances from land and in very deep water. Our Whampoa friend desired us to tow him to the Yangtse Kiang, but not being able to do so we gave him a spar and a topsail.[251] No one wished to leave the junk. The females of the family of a high mandarin, in Shantung, were passengers on board the junk. It was half-past eight P. M. before all this was done, and we again steered on our course. Just before midnight another dismasted junk was discovered; and, on nearing her, piteous cries were heard for relief, from her. She

---

[249]Wood, *op. cit.*, p. 298.
[250]Buoyant cables made from the fiber of the cocoanut husk.
[251]Wood, *op. cit.*, pp. 297–98.

was boarded and found to be a Bangkok junk, last from Hongkong and bound to Shanghai, with a crew of forty-three persons, and out of water. She did not want anything else. Gave twenty small casks of water, which was an ample supply. Fifteen of the crew wished to leave the junk for the *San Jacinto,* but the Captain of the junk objected, so they were refused. It was half-past three A. M. before the relief of this junk was completed and we again stood on our course.

All these junks state that they were near the coast of China, and four days ago were blown off in a typhoon. I should state that the last junk relieved was *at anchor.* Showery all night.

Saturday, August 16, 1856. The first junk relieved yesterday had a crew of fifteen. When told we could tow them in, the crew desired to be taken on board the *San Jacinto,* but the Captain and owner both said they would not leave the junk. Commodore Armstrong said he would willingly take on board the whole of them, provided the master of the junk was consenting to it, but he had no right to interfere between him and his men, for that would be in fact to encourage mutiny— that the Captain was the best judge of what he could do, and that his opinion was of more weight than that of the crew, and that, as the master refused to let his men leave, he (the Commodore) could not take them. On leaving her the crew went down on their knees to the boarding officer, imploring him to take them out of the junk; and, when his boat left, they raised frantic cries and with actions expressive of despair implored our return—but the Captain of the junk still held to his first resolution.

I learn that the Commodore's action in this matter is strongly condemned by the Fleet Surgeon and the Purser, and that I am supposed to be the adviser of the Commodore in the matter. It is due to him to say, that he acted without advice or suggestions from anyone in the matter; and, in my opinion, he acted both wisely and discreetly, and that it is a serious thing to interfere between the master of a ship and his crew, when the only ground of such interference is the fears of the latter, and also when such interference causes the loss of both vessel and cargo. In the case of the large junk, her condition was worse than that of the one referred to, yet not a soul wished to leave her, although she had over one hundred passengers who were free to go wherever they pleased, and they were told we would take them on board, yet not one accepted the offer.[252]

Another misfortune to our machinery like the one that took place when we were leaving Siam. One of the air pumps is crippled thereby and takes in much atmospheric air, destroying (partially) the vacuum. Our run from this cause, and over twelve hours detention with the junks, is only sixty-nine miles for the last twenty-four hours. I cannot help thinking that these accidents to our machinery arise in some degree from carelessness among the engineers. It appears that, in both these cases, water had collected in the air pumps, and, on the machinery being started, the packing of the stuffing

---

[252]For more details on wrecked Japanese junks, see Wood, *op. cit.*, pp. 296–98.

box was blown out. I also think there was neglect in not examining the condition of the screw when we arrived from Siam. Indications that *something* was wrong were plain to every one, and yet, with nearly a dozen engineers on board, no advice or suggestion for any examination was made.

Sunday, August 17, 1856. As heavy rain as I ever saw in any part of the world. Very thick. Wind variable from S. E. to N. W., changing in an instant. Barometer, 29.50. Run, 126 miles. The weather looks very bad.

P. M. weather looking wild—large sea getting up. Barometer at eight P. M., 29.38. We are no doubt in the S. E. part of a typhoon, having run north of it. Its vortex now probably bears S. W. from us. Ship rolls very deep. Capsized in my chair; hurt my left hip and leg, and break my Ceylon chair.

Ship behaves well—does not take in any water— showery all night, with now and then a sight of the moon.

Monday, August 18, 1856. At four A. M. wind came out from S. W. At seven A. M. made land nearly ahead. Proves to be Tokara Sima of the Linschoten group.[253] Wind strong with slight showers. Soon see three other islands, N. E. Nine A. M. wind moderates —make sail on ship—sea gradually going down and weather improving. Barometer, 29.61. Hard work to

---

[253]Takara Shima, of the Linschoten Islands. In Japanese, the word *shima* (or *jima*) means *island*. The names of Japanese geography are spelled in such a variety of ways that, for the sake of consistency, we shall follow the spelling of the *Century Atlas* whenever possible.

write, the screw shakes the ship so much when going ten knots. Distance run, 142 miles. Latitude, 29° 18′ N., longitude, 129° 46′ E. See the Island of Akui-sima.[254] Conflicting emotions caused by the sight of these Japanese possessions. My future brought vividly to mind. Mental and social isolation on the one hand, and on the other are important public duties which, if properly discharged, will redound to my credit. A people almost unknown to the world is to be examined and reported on in its social, moral and political state; the productions of the country—animal, vegetable and mineral—to be ascertained; the products of the industry of the country found out, and its capacity for commercial intercourse, what are its wants, and what it has to give in exchange. A new and difficult language to be learned; a history, which may throw some light on that of China and Korea, to be examined; and, finally, the various religious creeds of Japan are to be looked at. These various matters offer abundant occupation for my mind, and will surely prevent anything like *ennui* being felt if I only give myself heartily to the work, and if that *sine qua non* of all earthly occupation—*health*—be vouchsafed to me by the Great Giver of all good.

The weather in the afternoon and evening was delightful—a fine cool breeze—a bright day and a bright moon at night. Water as blue as azure—was indeed like the *Pacific* on which I had sailed so many miles.

Tuesday, August 19, 1856. Rested badly—could not drive Japan and my duties, on which I am so soon to

[254]Aku, or Akuseki Shima.

195

enter, from my mind. Tried every plan to induce sleep, not forgetting Dr. Franklin's air bath, but I did not sleep until after four A. M. and was called at six o'clock, as we breakfast at seven.

The ship has been going on well during the night, averaging about ten knots per hour.

Morning bright and beautiful, wind continues fair, but is not so strong as last night.

See an albatross—the first I have seen since I last left the coast of California in the month of October, 1850. The bird looked almost like a friend, certainly like an old acquaintance.

We are to-day about seventy miles E. of the coast of Kyushu,[255] but the water is like a desert, so far as man is concerned—not a ship, junk, boat, or craft of any kind is visible—and this too when near the coast of an empire more populous than the United States! What a contrast to the whirl of life on the opposite side of the Pacific! I shall be the first recognized agent from a civilized power to reside in Japan. This forms an epoch in my life and may be the beginning of a new order of things in Japan. I hope I may so conduct myself that I may have honorable mention in the histories which will be written on Japan and its future destiny.

Our run to-day was 219 miles and we are about 380 miles from Shimoda, where we hope to arrive on Thursday the 21st inst.

Latitude, 32° 13′ N., longitude, 132° 36′ E.

Centre Island,[256] in the Harbor of Shimoda, from sur-

---

[255]Kiusiu, or Kiushiu, or Kyushu.

of things in Japan — I hope I may so
conduct myself. that I may have honorable
mention, in the Histories which will be
written on Japan & its future destiny. ✗
  Our run to day was 219 miles and we are
about 380 miles from Simoda, where we hope
to arrive on Thursday the 21st instant
Lat: 32° 13' N. Long 132° 36' E. —
  Centre Island in the Harbour of Simoda
from surveys made by Lt. Silas Bent. U.S.N.
is situated Lat 34° 40' N. Lon 138° 50' :
  A mistake has been discovered in working
the time & our Longitude, instead of that noted
above was E 133.20' & the run was 255
miles — Distance from Simoada about.
344 miles — A strong current sets in
to the Channels forming the Islands Kinsw &
Sitkoff — so strong was it. that from 6 here
we steered due E — Another
lovely night. bright moon & stars, with a
delightful breeze; the air. full of oxygen,
so different from the Tropics. I feel the
stimulating & bracing effects of it unbilly —
  The mountain "Sisi Jama" 8000 feet high on
the N Coast of Japan is covered with snow the
year round. while "Foosie Jama" 12500 is
bare during 5 months — Came. the cold wind
from Kamtskatka. on the W — while the E is
protected from them by the range of mountains.

At the top of the page may be read his hope to receive honorable mention in the
"Histories which will be written on Japan."

veys made by Lieutenant Silas Bent, U. S. N., is situated latitude 34° 40′ N., longitude 138° 50′ E.

A mistake has been discovered in working the time; and our longitude, instead of that noted above, was E. 133° 20′, and the run was 255 miles. Distance from Shimoda about 344 miles. A strong current sets in to the channels forming the islands Kyushu and Sitkoff.[257] So strong was it that from 6 P. M. we steered due East. Another lovely night, bright moon and stars, with a delightful breeze. The air full of oxygen, so different from the tropics. I feel the stimulating and bracing effects of it sensibly.

The mountain "Siri Jama,"[258] 8,000 feet high on the west coast of Japan, is covered with snow the year round, while "Foosie Jama,"[259] 12,500, is bare during five months; cause: the cold wind from Kamchatka on the west, while the east is protected from it by the range of mountains which runs through the Island of Niphon, and the winds from N. E. to S. W. are tempered by the vast expanse of the Pacific Ocean.

---

[256]The Survey of the Harbor of Shimoda made by Flag-Lieutenant Silas Bent is given in full in the official account of *The Japan Expedition,* 33–2, H. Ex. Doc., no. 97, vol. 2, pp. 383–85. On p. 384, Centre Island is said to receive its name from its being the point from which the treaty limits are measured. This island may be seen in the illustration facing p. 425; and is clearly indicated also in the chart of the Harbor of Shimoda in Plate 13 of the same volume.

[257]Shikoku. In at least two places in the official account of Perry's expedition this island is called Sikok (33–2, H. Ex. Doc., no. 97, vol. 2, map facing p. 354; and Plate 2–3). But much nearer the spelling used by Townsend Harris is the form Sikopf, found in the map facing p. 364 of the same volume.

[258]Shiroyama or Hakusan (Hakuzan; or Haksan, as in Plate 2–3, *op. cit.*). Mt. Haku, meaning the "White Mountain" (Griffis, *Townsend Harris,* p. 30), is on the boundary line between the provinces of Kaga and Echizen. In Japanese, *Yama* (the same as *Jama,* with the "J" pronounced as in the German language) and *San* mean mountain.

[259]Fuji Yama.

197

Wednesday, August 20, 1856. Fine morning. Wind very light. We steered due east all night, but at daylight, having got out of the influence of the *indraught,* we steer N. E. half E. We hope to see Cape Idsu[260] this evening, but it is doubtful if we make it before morning as the weather is so light. Commodore Armstrong desires me to purchase some Japanese articles for his wife, would like the "rare and beautiful." These purchases to be made as opportunities offer, and he will take them on his next visits. See numbers of albatross this morning. They are of the brown back and white head varieties, and are called "Gories" or "Quaker" albatross by whalers. They are not of the largest kind as seen off Cape Horn.

Run, 181 miles, and 130 miles from Shimoda.

In the afternoon we pass quite a number of Japanese junks. They are small—say forty tons—one large square sail and a small lug sail on a short foremast—no mizzen. Sails are made of some kind of white cloth and have various black marks—like private signals.

This is a common mode among the Chinese fishermen of marking the vessels belonging to each company or *hu-wi.*

We ran for some of the Japanese junks at first, desiring to speak them—but they showed such evident alarm and anxiety to avoid us that we gave it up, and they would sheer off so as to allow us to pass them at one or two miles' distance. We shall be up to Cape Idsu (ten

---

[260]Idzu.

miles from Shimoda). about two A. M. to-morrow, if nothing happens in the meantime.

Dr. Wood, the Fleet Surgeon, has given me a *torniquet* for use in case of an accident to Mr. Heusken or myself, and some instructions regarding the use of *quinine*. At nine P. M. meet many sail, which it is difficult to avoid, so stopped engines and hove ship to for the night.

The ship lies-to very nicely. Squalls of rain during the night.

Thursday, August 21, 1856. Six A. M. find ourselves in sight of land, which proves to be Cape Ome-Saki.[261] Large numbers of fishing boats, near seventy; [I] like the appearance of the Japanese, clean and well-clad, cheerful looking, pretty fish-boats.

At seven and a half A. M. under way. Showery. Write letters announcing my arrival to the Governor of Shimoda[262] and Minister of Foreign Affairs[263]—sending to the latter a letter from Mr. Secretary Marcy. Mr.

---

[261]Omaesaki, or Omaye Saki—Cape Omaye. In Japanese, the word *Saki* or *Zaki* means *Point, Cape*. This Cape is called Omaesaki in Plate 2–3, referred to above.

[262]*L. B.,* vol. 1, p. 92. Townsend Harris announces that the *San Jacinto,* commanded by Commodore James Armstrong, etc., etc., has arrived, bearing him as the Consul General for Japan; and he encloses two letters for the Minister of Foreign Affairs, hoping that the Governor will forward them to Yedo as quickly as possible. The letter is dated "U. S. Frigate *San Jacinto,* Shimoda Harbor."

The Dutch translation of this letter is to be found in *L. B.,* vol. 1, pp. 94–95

[263]*L. B.,* vol. 1, pp. 91–92. Townsend Harris announces his arrival and encloses: (a) a letter from Secretary Marcy to the Minister of Foreign Affairs, notifying the latter of Townsend Harris's appointment; and (b) a Dutch translation thereof. Townsend Harris's own letter to the Minister closes with an expression of the sincere friendship existing between the two nations.

The Dutch translation of this letter is to be found in *L. B.,* vol. 1, pp. 93–94. For the effect of these letters upon the Yedo authorities, see James Murdoch, *A History of Japan,* vol. 3, p. 624.

Heusken makes Dutch translations of these various letters. When at the mouth of the harbor, a boat with the American Flag at the bow and Japanese flags (stripes white, black, white, horizontal), came off bringing a pilot,[264] who soon took us into the petite harbor of Shimoda.[265] It is rather a *bight* than a harbor, and not more than three vessels like the *San Jacinto* can moor at the same time in the *inner* harbor. The *outer* harbor is nothing more than a roadstead. Soon after we anchored, three officials and two Dutch interpreters[266] came off from the Governor, with his compliments on my arrival, asking after my health, how long a passage I had, etc., etc., offering to supply water and food to the ship. They also asked when I proposed to land. In reply I said that, as the weather was wet, I would not land

[264]"This boat brought us a pilot, a short, full-faced, respectable individual, in straw sandals, blue stockings. . . . This functionary drew from the folds of his gown a box in which, carefully protected by several wrappers, was his commission as pilot for American vessels, given him by Commodore Perry, and printed in English and Dutch, by the 'Japan Expedition Press.' He spoke but a few words of English, and none of us spoke Japanese, but he gave us to understand, by the waving of his hand, when we were to go to starboard, or port, or ahead." (Wood, *Fankwei,* pp. 299–300.)

The three pilots appointed by Commodore Perry were Yohatsi, Hikoyemon, and Dshirobe. Their Commissions were signed by Silas Bent, Flag-Lieutenant, and were approved by Commodore Perry, at Shimoda, June 22, 1854. (33–2, H. Ex. Doc., no. 97, vol. 1, pp. 487–89; and Article 8 of the Additional Regulations, *ib.,* p. 480.)

[265]The Japanese chronicle of this momentous event says, very simply and pithily:

"During the same [7th] month an American named Harris arrived at Shimoda in Idzu, bearing a letter. He stated that he was entrusted by his nation with full powers, and that he was instructed to reside in Japan. He also requested leave to present his credentials to the Shogun." (*Kinsé Shiriaku: A History of Japan from the First Visit of Commodore Perry in 1853 to the Capture of Hakodate by the Mikado's Forces in 1869.* Translated by Sir Ernest Mason Satow, Yokohama, 1873, p. 6.)

[266]Meaning, of course, two Japanese officials who had learned the Dutch language.

to-day; but, if the weather was fair, would do so on the morrow, asking what hour it would suit the Governor to receive my visit. In reply to this they said they would ask the Governor and make known his answer to-day.

When asked what "provisions" could be furnished, they said "the Governor would answer." I asked if a house had been prepared for me? They said again "the Governor would answer," adding that Shimoda was a very poor place; that it had not yet recovered from the effects of the earthquake of December, 1854, when every house in the place except fourteen was destroyed.[267] These persons soon after left. Some of the officers went on shore this afternoon and were much pleased with the appearance of the little place and the people. The houses are all new and fresh looking. They found quite a lot of coal here for us, say some two hundred tons. At five P. M. the officials again came off and said that the letter I had given them for the Governor of Shimoda was then being translated, and that the two for Yedo had been already sent off and that it would take five days for them to reach Yedo; that the Governor would be ready to receive my visit at one P. M. of to-

---

[267]This earthquake occurred on Dec. 23, 1854. It was felt on the whole coast of Japan, did some injury to Yedo, completely destroyed Osaka, and caused great ruin at Shimoda. At this last place the real damage was caused by a great tidal wave, which first receded and then engulfed the town. The Russian Frigate *Diana*, Admiral Count Euphemius Poutiatine, happened to be in the Harbor of Shimoda and was so seriously damaged that it sank shortly afterwards. The holding-ground of the harbor was entirely swept away by the waves, leaving no bottom but naked rocks. (See 33–2, H. Ex. Doc., no. 97, vol. 1, pp. 509–11; vol. 2, p. 210; Captain Sherard Osborn, *A Cruise in Japanese Waters*, 2nd ed., pp. 107–11; and David Murray, *The Story of Japan*, p. 8, note 3.)

morrow. The interpreters were in constant trepidation and fear, and large drops of perspiration stood on their foreheads, while every word of question and answer was written down by two of the party. The Commodore is quite unwell this evening.

Friday, August 22, 1856. The officers off again this morning to inquire after the Commodore's health; and, finding he was too unwell to go on shore to-day, they said the Governor begged to be excused from seeing me to-day, as he was unwell, etc. I said to-morrow would do as well. They asked if the Commodore would be well enough to go with me to-morrow. I answered I could not say, but that my visit was entirely independent of the Commodore; that, when he was well enough, he would himself call on the Governor. I found that it was their plan to delay my visit until the Commodore was well enough, so that they might afterwards deny having received me on my individual account, but solely as one of the Commodore's suite, and this was proved by their saying that when the Governor was well enough to see me he would send me word. I then said this was a matter concerning the dignity of my government, that the Governor should write to me excusing himself on account of illness, and that I would send that letter to my government, and leave it for its adjustment.

This proposition greatly embarrassed them.

The Governor was sick, therefore no letter was required. I insisted. They then offered to write to that effect themselves; this I declined.

I finally closed the discussion by saying that if the

Governor wrote his excuse to me before noon of to-morrow, I would be satisfied, but that otherwise I should come on shore to-morrow at one o'clock to visit him. The Governor sent off ten *bonita* and some small cray-fish as a present to the Commodore. Captain Bell gave them some seeds of a creeper and a large sort of squash, which they at first accepted; but, when they were just leaving the ship, they brought them back to the cabin, their courage having failed them. They went ashore, promising to let me know to-day about the visit to the Governor, etc. Visited the village of Kakizaki,[268] opposite Shimoda. The temple of this place—Yoku-shen[269] of the Shinto sect—is set apart for the accommodation of Americans. The rooms are spacious and very neat and clean, and a person might stay here for a few weeks in tolerable comfort. Near this temple is the American cemetery,[270] which contains four neat tombs and prettily fenced in. It is very small, only about fifteen feet by ten feet. Kakizaki is a small and poor fishing village, but the people are clean in person and civil in manner. You see none of the squalor which usually attends poverty in all parts of the world. Their houses are as clean as need be. Every inch of ground is cultivated, as the ground is very [rolling], rising up in

[268]The name means *Oyster Point* (Griffis, *Townsend Harris*, p. 36, note 1).

[269]Though the name of this temple is not given, its location is clearly indicated by the word *Temple* in the chart of the Harbor of Shimoda, Plate 13 in 33–2, H. Ex. Doc., no. 97, vol. 2.

[270]See Plate 13, *op. cit.* When Perry visited Shimoda, one of the sailors of the *Powhatan* fell from aloft and died soon after. A burial place was accordingly provided by the Japanese, located near the village of Kakizaki. See 33–2, H. Ex. Doc., no. 97, vol. 1, p. 425, and the illustration facing that page and entitled "Shimoda from the American graveyard."

pinnacles of lava or indurated clay ejected from volcanoes, and so steep as not to be arable. It is a pity goats
are not introduced here. These pinnacles afford fine
grazing for goats, and their habits of climbing would
make them at home on them. Their milk would be
nutritious food, and cheese might be made from it also,
and this would be an object to the Japanese even though
they might not eat the flesh. The views from the ship
present a series of serrated hills rising up to fifteen hundred feet high—most of which are covered with fir,
spruce and cedar trees.[271]

The Temple Rioshen at Shimoda is also set apart for
the use of Americans—perhaps I may have to reside in
it until a house can be prepared for me.

Late this afternoon the officers again came off, but I
declined to see them, so Mr. Heusken heard what they

---

[271]This was the first visit of Townsend Harris on the soil of Japan. In connection therewith, it is interesting to read the grim humor of the hope expressed by William M. Wood, *Fankwei*, pp. 300–01:

"As the knowledge of Japan seems to stop with old Kampfer [Kaempfer],
I am not sure that there would be any great want of charity in hoping that
the Japanese would give our Consul General [Townsend Harris] and his
observant secretary [Heusken] a cage journey throughout their sealed empire. Of course we should promptly avenge their wrongs, shake down the
walls of exclusion, and make peace by shaking hands with Siogoon on his
throne in Yedo, and then, for once, we should know all about modern Japan.
Indeed, the interesting revelations and observations the prisoners would be
able to make, the wonderful stories they would have to tell, might go far to
shorten the duration of our national anger."

The diplomatic tact and skill of Townsend Harris will be demonstrated
more and more clearly as this story is unfolded—a story that is very far removed indeed, from the "cage journeys" in Mr. Wood's mind. He was thinking of those grim days of the captivity of the Russian Captain Golownin and
his companions (1811–13), or of the mutinous sailors of the New Bedford
whaler *Lagoda,* who were the cause of the relief expedition of the U. S.
Steamer *Preble,* Commander James Glynn, in 1849.

had to say and reported it to me. The purport was that the Governor was really unable to see me to-morrow, and they offered to bring a doctor's certificate to that effect and earnestly begged me to postpone my visit until another day. I caused them to be told that I was most anxious to do all I could to oblige the Governor, and that I wished to be on friendly terms with him. I would, therefore, consent to postpone my visit until Monday, that no visits could be paid on Sunday or any business transacted on that day. They were also told that Commodore Armstrong would not visit the Governor until after I had seen the Governor, and that we should not come together to pay a visit to the Governor. The officers were most urgent to see me, and their anxiety on this point appeared to increase with my refusals, but I persisted, and at last they left quite chapfallen. It is now understood that I am to visit the Governor on Monday at ten A. M. Some of the officers have been on shore and report a very pretty bazaar has been opened with a great display of lacquered ware, etc., etc.[272]

Saturday, August 23, 1856. Go on shore with Captain Bell and Mr. Heusken. Visit the Temple Rioshen. It is badly placed for hot weather, being at the foot of a steep hill that shuts out the S. W. wind entirely, and is surrounded by stagnant pools and other disagreeables.

We afterwards visited six or seven other temples.

---

[272]For a description of this bazaar and of the manner of conducting business there, see Wood, *op. cit.,* pp. 304–09.

are all built after one pattern; some a little larger
n better order than the others, and having more
:able situations, but beyond this they are exactly
. We afterwards walked up the valley some two
miles. Saw a large enclosure containing some twenty
detached buildings—all new, and in fact some were not
yet completed. I learn this is the residence of the
Governor. In the afternoon I went again to Kakizaki.
I find the temple there has been cleaned out, apparently
to prepare it for my reception. I have thought much
about my accepting this temple for my residence. The
building is as good [as], if not better than any of the
others, but it is isolated, and the approach is through
the narrow and crooked alleys of a very poor fishing
village. I should here be unseen and unknown to the
people, and to go to market my servants in bad weather
could not cross in a boat, and the road to go and return
would be nearly five miles. Again,—the Treaty says, and
my commission says, I am to reside at Shimoda. Now,
Kakizaki is not Shimoda. I, therefore, think I shall
refuse this temple as my place of residence.

Weather delightful. Barometer, 30.10. The air is like
that of the United States, full of oxygen.

Sunday, August 24, 1856. Do not leave the ship. In
the afternoon the Japanese come off and desire to see
me; I decline to see them or to hear their message, for
the reason that it is Sunday. They urge me at least to
hear their message, saying it is very important and from
the Governor. They also say that when Commodore
Perry was here, he made no difference for Sunday,

etc., etc.[273] I adhere to my previous determination, telling them (through Mr. Heusken) that they can come off to-morrow morning as early as they please and then state their message.

Monday, August 25, 1856. The officers came off at 8 A. M. with a message that the Governor will be ready to receive me at ten o'clock. At that hour, go on shore accompanied by Captain Bell and some ten others. I go in the Commodore's boat, having my secretary with me. The three boats preceded me so that the officers could land and form in order before I landed. When my boat had pulled well off from the ship a salute of thirteen guns was fired, waking up the grandest echoes among the hills. On landing I found the streets thronged with persons collected to see us pass. I was conducted to a new building nearly in the center of the town. As I shall hereafter have both time and better knowledge of this building and of the manners and dress of the people, I shall not now describe anything beyond my interview with the Governor. I was politely received by the Governor and Vice-Governor. Asked after my health, when I left the United States, etc., etc. They asked in whose honor the salute was fired and were told

---

[273]This statement of the Japanese does not agree with that in the official report of the Japan Expedition (33–2, H. Ex. Doc., no. 97, vol. 1, p. 240):

"The next day was Sunday (July 10, [1853]), and, as usual, divine service was held on board the ships and, in accordance with proper reverence for the day, no communication was held with the Japanese authorities."

Later in the day, Perry refused to receive on board some Japanese officers. Strenuous military preparations were made on land:

"Everything, however, remained on board the ships tranquil and without interruption, as befitted the Christian day of rest."

that it was in mine, when I perceived that I instantly rose in their estimation. The Governor said he should like to *see* such guns fired, whereupon Captain Bell invited him to visit the ship on Saturday next, as they are now painting on board and he feared they might soil their clothes. Refreshments were served up in Japanese style. The cooking was excellent and served up with extreme neatness and cleanliness. I am much prepossessed in favor of their cooking. I asked the Governor when I could see him on business. He said I could enter on business then if I pleased. I replied that it would not be good breeding to enter on business on a visit of ceremony. He then said the Vice-Governor would attend me the next day, at the same hour and place, and that the Vice-Governor could act as well as [he] himself, etc., etc.

Our visit lasted nearly two hours, and we were all much pleased with the appearance and manners of the Japanese. I repeat, they are superior to any people east of the Cape of Good Hope.[274]

Tuesday, August 27 [26], 1856. I omitted yesterday to state that a superior interpreter appeared at my interview. He is attached to the office of the Minister for Foreign Affairs; a good interpreter, of most agreeable manners and a true courtier. Seven scribes recorded our sayings and doings yesterday. To-day ashore at ten with

---

[274]At the end of this entry, we desire to emphasize the importance of this date. Here was the first day of real negotiations between Townsend Harris and the Japanese—a day of momentous importance not only for the United States, but even more so for the Empire of Japan, which began to make her entry into the family of Western nations.

". . . A courteous and amicable reception was given to a resident representative of a foreign power, and that power one of the youngest among nations." (Wood, *op. cit.,* p. 309.)

Mr. Heusken. Met the Vice-Governor and the person from Yedo, who evidently has come down since our arrival was reported there, although they say the journey cannot be made under five days from here to Yedo. My interview was long and far from satisfactory. To sum it is all I shall attempt. They did not expect the arrival of a Consul,—a Consul was only to be sent when some difficulty arose, and no such thing had taken place. That Shimoda was a poor place and had been recently desolated by an earthquake; that they had no residence prepared for me; that I had better go away and return in about a year, when they hoped to have a house ready. The Treaty said that a Consul was to come if *both* nations wished it; that it was not left to the simple will of the United States Government.[275]

Would I land at Kakizaki, and take up my residence at the temple there, and leave the question of my official residence to be settled by future negotiations? Yedo was also in a ruinous condition from an earthquake ten months since, therefore they could not offer me a house there while building one here.[276]

---

[275]Perry Treaty, Art. XI:

"There shall be appointed by the Government of the United States consuls or agents to reside in Shimoda at any time after the expiration of eighteen months from the date of the signing of this treaty; provided that *either* of the two governments deem such arrangements necessary."

The Japanese text, unfortunately, had it that *both* governments had to deem it necessary to appoint a consul. (J. H. Gubbins, *The Progress of Japan*, pp. 68–69.)

[276]"This great earthquake is graphically described in a well-illustrated book, entitled *The Tribulations of Ansei* (year period, 1854–59). Most of the dead, alleged to number 104,000, were buried in or cremated near the one enlarged temple-yard of E'Ko In, where also the alleged 166,000 victims of the seismic disturbances of 1656 had been interred or inurned." (Griffis, *Townsend Harris*, p. 43, note.)

The foregoing is the substance of their remarks and propositions, made and renewed and changed in every possible form and manner during three mortal hours. I need hardly write that I courteously but firmly negatived all their propositions. They earnestly protested against the idea that they refused to receive me, or that they meant in any way to break the Treaty. They at last begged to adjourn the business until to-morrow at the same hour, to give them time to consult. The sales in the bazaar cannot be much under two thousand dollars. The prices are most exorbitant. They appear to raise them at each new arrival of a ship here. Ordered spars to make my flagstaff; one of fifty feet, twelve inches by eight, and the other thirty feet long, seven inches by four inches, and four small pieces.

Wednesday, August 27, 1856. On shore at ten A. M. by appointment, to meet the Governor or Vice-Governor, but neither of them made his appearance. Ten persons were present, including the Yedo official. They said the Governor was very ill the previous night with a violent headache, so they were unable to consult with him. They then said that the Treaty provided for a Consul, but not a Consul General; that the Additional Articles had not been sent out as ratified;[277] that they expected the Government of the United States would send out an Ambassador with the ratified Articles, and then enter on negotiations about sending a Consul.

---

[277]The "Additional Regulations" were concluded by Commodore Perry and the Japanese Commissioners at Shimoda, June 17, 1854 (33–2, H. Ex. Doc., no. 97, vol. 1, pp. 479–81).

I told them I was surprised that the Vice-Governor should not appear after making an appointment with me; that I considered it as want of respect, and that I must decline entering into any conversation about my affairs with anyone but the Governor or Vice-Governor; that I would go on board the steamer and consult with Commodore Armstrong, and then he would determine whether he would take me up to Yedo and there get satisfaction.

The officer from Yedo said he was of higher rank than the Governor and asked why I should object to negotiate with him. I replied that I could only know the official authorities of the place, and with them only have any official intercourse; that for himself I had a high esteem, based on what I had seen of him, but that personal feeling could not give him that *status* which my official business required. They urged me to proceed in the matter, but to some questions they put, I said I had no answer to give them. They constantly renewed, and urgently, the request that I would proceed with them.

I as constantly declined. They then said they would report on what had occurred to the Governor, and requested me to meet them to-morrow at the same hour to meet the Vice-Governor. I told them that, as the Vice-Governor had broken his appointment with me, I could not consent to make another appointment, until I had some explanation or apology for his absence of this morning.

That I wished the Governor or Vice-Governor to

write me a letter and send it to me on board the steamer, stating whether they would receive me in Shimoda or not, and whether they would assign me a house to reside in; that I desired this letter to be sent to me either to-day or to-morrow morning.

They were anxious to know whether I was resolved to go to Yedo if not received here. I said that would be settled after consultation with the Commodore. They were greatly agitated when I mentioned the going up to Yedo.

Thursday, August 28, 1856. The Vice-Governor, the high person from Yedo and a large suite came off this morning. The Vice-Governor explained his absence yesterday by saying the individual from Yedo was of higher rank than[he]himself and had full powers from the government to act in my matters. He then said that he was ready to receive me with all the honors due to my high place, and to assign me the only place that was habitable for my residence—the Temple of Jocksend[278] at Kakizaki; that Kakizaki was in point of fact a part of Shimoda, subject to the same governor, magistrates, police, etc., etc.; that the name was only local to distinguish it as a part of Shimoda, as the suburbs of Western cities receive distinctive local names; that the Goyoshi was, as its name indicated, an "imperial seat" built solely for the reception of strangers of distinction who came to Shimoda; that the

---

[278]Townsend Harris time and again writes foreign names phonetically. *Jocksend* represents *Yokushen,* with the accent on the first syllable, and with the *J* of *Jocksend* pronounced as in German. This is Gyokusen-ji.

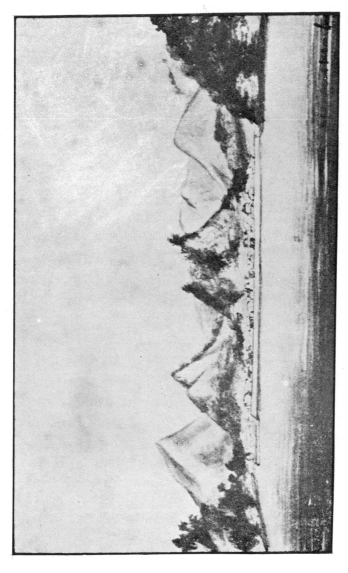

VIEW OF SHIMODA, FROM KAKIZAKI

From a drawing in India ink by Mr. H. C. J. Heusken, whose signature in the lower right-hand corner is clearly legible in the original. This drawing was enclosed by Townsend Harris in a letter to "Kate" Drinker (later Mrs. Thomas Allibone Janvier), dated Shimoda, Japan, November 21, 1856. For this letter and drawing, see the Janvier *Letters and Papers*, in the Manuscripts Division of the New York Public Library.

Governor had no power to use it for himself, or to authorize its use by others; that I must see how deplorably the place had been injured by the earthquake; that, as to the temples in Shimoda, they were all actually occupied as places of worship and for cemeteries; that it would be an outrage on the feelings of the people who worshipped there, or who frequently went there to offer [prayers] at the graves of their ancestors, to find the place used for secular purposes; that the temple at Kakizaki was not of this character; that its purpose was the accommodation of parties who went out to make a religious holiday; that its occupation by me would be inconvenient, but would not be a desecration; that the Government at Yedo could not give me any other answer, even if I went up there in the steamer; that my residence was to be considered as only temporary and until they could erect a proper building for me, and that they would adapt the building, as much as they could, to my wants; finally, that they had offered me the best they had, and, if I did not accept it, I could not say they had refused to receive me or to furnish me with quarters. I told them I would send my answer on shore in two hours by my secretary.

Accordingly, I instructed Mr. Heusken to say to the Governor that I was most anxious to avoid any difficulties; and, although I feared my Government might blame me for accepting a residence at Kakizaki instead of Shimoda, I would accept it with the full understanding that a suitable house was to be prepared for me as soon as possible, and that I must have a boat and men constantly at my command for my use while there.

I also gave notice that I should want two large boats on Saturday to take my things on shore, and men to take them from the landing to the house, with proper persons to watch them until I came on shore, etc., etc.

In the afternoon a spar thirty feet long, seven inches by four inches, was sent off to me; price, five dollars; and word was sent that to get the spar fifty feet long, they must go to the mountains to cut it and would require three or four days to get it, and that would cost eighty dollars. Sent the carpenter on shore to select the best one he could find, even if short of the fifty feet.

Friday, August 29, 1856. Mr. Heusken goes on shore with the carpenter to aid him in selecting a spar, etc., and afterwards to go over to Kakizaki to indicate what alterations, etc., are required in the temple to fit it for my residence, etc.

The Governor informs me that *three* rooms in my house will be required for Japanese officers who are to be with me night and day "to await my pleasure." I return a message that I require *all* the rooms, and that under no circumstances would I permit any Japanese (except servants) to be in my house, or even to enter it without my permission. The carpenter comes off at three P. M. saying he cannot find a stick that will answer for my flagstaff. Mr. Heusken at six P. M. informs me that the Japanese say they have cut three trees that will answer, but they cannot be got to the ship before Monday morning. The authorities have agreed to give me all my rooms, and to withdraw their threatened police force.

Dr. Wood, Fleet Surgeon, tells me a story which strongly illustrates the determination of the authorities to prevent the *people* from having any intercourse with us, except what is unavoidable. While in the bazaar a man came to him for medical advice for a cutaneous affection; after examination, the doctor wrote a prescription and gave it to the man, telling him (through the interpreter) to take the paper on board the *San Jacinto,* when medicine would be given to him which would cure him. The man, with many thanks, took the paper and went away. An hour afterwards he returned, sweating like a bull and looking much alarmed. He came to the doctor and gave him a paper, which he found to be the prescription. The doctor made signs that he should take the paper to the ship; the man shook his head and again forced the paper into the doctor's hands, making significant motions with his finger that his head would be cut off if he took the paper to the ship!!![279]

For the last three days the thermometer has stood as high as 84°, but the air is so pure, and the barometer being at 30.10, I do not feel it as much as I did 78° at Hongkong, or in fact anywhere in the tropics. A shower at eleven P. M. I have been making lists of my packages on board and preparing to send them on shore on Monday, at which time boats are to be sent for them with

---

[279]Mr. Wood concludes his version of this occurrence with the remark that the native's argument was powerful and conclusive. (*Op. cit.,* p. 307.)

proper officers to protect them from damage or plunder.

Saturday, August 30, 1856. Busy writing letters until one P. M. After dinner the Yedo officer came off with five others. The Governor sent his compliments to me and requested me to visit him at the Goyoshi at ten A. M. of Monday. I accepted. They then asked if the Commodore would come off with me. I said I presumed he would if well enough, and as he was better to-day I had no doubt he would come. They then asked when the Governor could visit the ship, and Tuesday was suggested. I discovered that the invitation to me was a ruse to get the Commodore to visit the Governor *first,* and then the Governor could visit the ship. I told them frankly that, by the rule of our country and all Western etiquette, the commander of a ship or squadron makes the first visit, and the reason the Commodore had not already visited the Governor was the illness of the Commodore in the first place, and then afterwards the illness of the Governor. This gave them great satisfaction.

The Commodore came in afterwards and he accepted the invitation for Monday, and at the same time told them that he should have gone with me at my first visit. This startled and pleased them, for they evidently had not forgotten that he had told some of them that *he would not visit the Governor until after I* had been received.[280] Then it was settled that the Governor would visit the ship on Tuesday at eleven A. M. I was requested not to

[280]See above, *Journal,* Aug. 22, 1856.

land until as late a day as possible, in order to give them the utmost time to prepare the temple for my reception. Wednesday morning was named, and they then told me that they would be there to receive me in due form.

I am compelled to pay $78 for a spar to make my flagstaff,—an enormous price!

Learn that some great personage has arrived at the residence of the Governor, as a long procession was seen by some of our officers, preceded by heralds bearing the coat-of-arms, then a number of *norimons,* one very large[281]—a led horse—servants bearing luggage, etc., etc.

Sunday, August 31, 1856. A lovely day. Write many letters. Japanese come off to see me. I refuse to see anyone on Sunday. I am resolved to set an example of a proper observance of the Sabbath, by abstaining from all business or pleasures on that day. I do not mean I would not take a quiet walk, or any such amusement. I do not mean to set an example of Puritanism, but I will try to make it what I believe it was intended to be—a day of rest

Captain Bell says we found *blue water* in the Gulf of Siam (the upper part) while the soundings are only thirty to forty-five fathoms. This proves clearly that *deep* water is not a necessary condition for *blue* water.

Monday, September 1, 1856. List of letters bearing

---

[281]Griffis (*Townsend Harris,* p. 50, note 1) explains that "The large norimono or palanquin of officers of rank had the needlessly large and heavy bearer's beam *curved* on top."

date to-day and sent to Russell & Co., Shanghai, by the *San Jacinto*, to be forwarded as directed:[282]

Armstrong & Lawrence
General James Keenan
Charles Huffnagle
C. C. Currier
Mrs. S. B. Drinker
D. J. Macgowan
S. Drinker
Henry Grinnell
P. M. Wetmore
Robert C. Murphy
Baring Brothers & Co.
Joseph Evans
Commodore M. C. Perry
Mrs. Langlois
Sir John Bowring
Wm. Hunter, Ass't Sec'y State
Richard Schell
N. Dougherty
Russell & Co., Shanghai

[282]1) To Armstrong & Lawrence, at Hongkong (*L. B.*, vol. 1, pp. 95–97), Townsend Harris sends an order for supplies and provisions of various kinds, relates incidents of the voyage from China, and describes the harbor and the village of Shimoda.

2) To Charles Huffnagle, U. S. Consul General for British India, at Calcutta. Acknowledged by letter dated Calcutta, Nov. 18, 1856 (*L. & P.*, vol. 1, no. 45).

3) To S. Drinker. Acknowledged by letter dated Hongkong, Apr. 3 and 4, 1857 (*L. & P.*, vol. 1, no. 62).

4) To Robert C. Murphy, U. S. Consul at Shanghai. Acknowledged by letter dated Shanghai, Oct 7, 1856 (*L. & P.*, vol. 1, no. 44).

5) To Baring Bros. & Co., London (*L. B.*, vol. 1, p. 99). Townsend Harris says that his drafts for salary payments will be calculated from Aug. 21, 1856—the day on which he arrived at Shimoda and consequently entered upon his duties as Consul General to Japan.

6) To Sir John Bowring, Governor of Hongkong. From Sir John Bowring's answer to this letter (*L. & P.*, vol. 1, no. 43, dated Hongkong, Sept. 27, 1856), it is evident that Townsend Harris had described to

At ten A. M. go on shore with Commodore Armstrong and a suite of officers. At the Goyoshi meet the new Governor and Vice-Governor, [and] the other Governor. It appears there are two Governors and two Vice-Governors for this place. They pass six months in Shimoda, then six in Yedo. The new one arrived in pursuance of this rule. The conversation began with complimentary inquiries about health, etc., etc. Then I was asked what was the secret object of my Government in sending me to Japan. I answered that I knew nothing beyond the fact of my appointment and our treaty rights.

I was asked if I should go to Hakodate? I replied that would depend on circumstances. If I was wanted there, I should go. They then run over all the old objections, and civilly ask me to go away; and, on my declining to do so, they asked the Commodore if he had no power to take me away. That was answered by saying that he was a military man. His orders were to bring the Consul General to Shimoda and land him there, and then his part was done. They asked would he take a letter from the Japanese Government to the American Government explaining their embarrassed position, and asking for my removal. The Commodore answered that all communications for his Government from the

him the charms of change and of climate at Shimoda, had complained of its unsuitability as a port, and had invited him to visit Shimoda.

7) To Russell & Co., at Shanghai (*L. B.*, vol. 1, pp. 98–99). Asks if they will negotiate his bills upon the account opened in his favor at Baring Bros. & Co., London, by the Secretary of State of the United States, for his salary of $5,000 per annum.

Japanese would of necessity come through the Consul General.

Next, would the Commodore write to his Government, explaining the reasons why the Japanese refused to receive the Consul General? This question, covering as it did a positive intention to refuse me, excited much surprise and received a positive negative.

I was then asked would I forward a letter from the Japanese Government to the American Government? I answered I would if it was written by the Minister of Foreign Affairs. Would not the Governor of Shimoda do as well? He had full powers to treat with me; therefore it was the same thing. I replied that it might be the same thing to them, but it was not in our eyes. Would I write to my Government asking for my own removal? This was declined. It was now twelve o'clock—two mortal hours having been frittered away in renewing and twisting the foregoing into all possible forms. Refreshments were served. The Governors retired for a short time; and, after their return and the tiffin being over, the Commodore and his suite, except Fleet Surgeon Wood, retired, leaving me with the doctor and my interpreter. They now took another turn,—apologized for delaying and wasting so much time in trivial questions, but their excuse was their want of knowledge of such matters. That it was a new thing, etc., etc. They asked me if I had any new negotiations to propose? I answered none at that time. Did I intend to make new regulations about sailors who were shipwrecked, or should I change the place of the consulate without giving notice to them? I answered, "No." They inquired what were my powers and privileges as a Consul? To which I gave a short synopsis of both. They then begged me again to write to my Government the strong objections they had to receiving a Consul at this time, stating that they had opened Shimoda to the Dutch and Russians, and that they would send a Consul here as soon as they knew I was received here (this was news).[283] I replied that I could not write any formal letter; that, if I did, it would not be attended to on such a point; that I should, as a matter of course, give my Government an account of all that had occurred here, but they might be sure it would not elicit any reply; that, if they wanted to communicate with the Government of the United States, let their Minister of Foreign Affairs write a letter, and he might depend on receiving a speedy answer.

---

[283]The Russian Treaty with Japan was signed at Shimoda, Jan. 26 (Feb. 7), 1855. Art. III of this Treaty opened up to Russia the three ports of Shimoda, Hakodate, and Nagasaki. Art. VI provided that the Russian Government could appoint a Consul (when it should deem it necessary) for one of the first two of these ports,—therefore, either for Shimoda or Hakodate; while in the Explanatory Articles (agreed upon the day the Treaty was signed), it was distinctly stated (*ad* Art. VI) that Russia was to appoint her Consuls beginning with the year 1856 (J. H. Gubbins, *op. cit.*, pp. 236–38).

The Preliminary Convention between The Netherlands and Japan was signed at Nagasaki, Nov. 9, 1855. Art. IV of this Convention provided that, in case one or more ports of the Japanese Empire were then opened or would thereafter be opened to one or more other nations, exactly the same privileges were immediately to be granted to The Netherlands.

This Article of the Preliminary Convention was repeated almost verbatim in Art. IV of the final Dutch Treaty with Japan signed at Nagasaki, Jan. 30, 1856. (See J. H. Gubbins, *op. cit.*, pp. 246, 251; compare, too, the short note from the Japanese authorities to Donker Curtius, given *ibid.*, p. 266, and answering a communication from the latter regarding the port of Shimoda, said Japanese note being dated in the 8th month—Hachigwatsu—of the 4th year of Ansei.)

Since the Perry Treaty of Mar. 31, 1854, opened the ports of Shimoda and Hakodate to the Americans (Art. II), by virtue of Art. IV of their Treaty also the Dutch were therefore to be permitted to come to Shimoda.

They said their laws forbade it. Here for the third or fourth time, they begged me not to be offended with them. They were acting under orders. The matter was new to them, and from their ignorance it appeared the more alarming. It being now near two, I prepared to leave them.[284] I should remark that at tiffin time I was told the boats were ready to go to the frigate to bring off my luggage, and asked if they should go. I answered in the affirmative. Now this fact took place during a discussion in which they had, in fact, declared they would not receive me, and it convinced me they were acting a part in which they did not even hope to succeed.

The people are of a genial disposition and are evidently inclined towards intercourse with foreigners; but the despotic rule of the country, and the terror they have of their so-called *inflexible* laws, forbids them to express their wishes.

I do not like the looks of the new Governor; he has a dark, sullen look, like a bandog, and I fear I shall have trouble with him. I much regret the change.[284a] Got on board near three P. M., and commenced at once sending off my traps. All of the supplies—furniture and some

---

[284]For a parallel account of this day's interview, see Wood, *op. cit.*, pp. 309–17. This day's discussion is typical of the many that were to follow. Townsend Harris's task was one of peculiar difficulty, because, as J. H. Gubbins points out (*op. cit.*, pp. 68–69), he was the first foreign representative to deal with the Japanese Government *on equal terms:*

"In that capacity he had to bear the brunt of obstruction so ingeniously and constantly exercised that, had he not been plentifully endowed with patience, he must have relinquished his task in despair."

[284a]The new Governor was Inouye, Shinano-no-Kami, who soon became one of Harris's best friends.

heavy luggage—was sent off, and all in pretty good order except a hat in a leather box, which was destroyed.

Tuesday, September 2, 1856. The new Governor and the old, and [the] Vice-Governors, our Yedo friend and a large suite came on board at ten A. M. Men were exercised at the guns and went through all the manœuvres of an action. Marines put through the manual and marching, etc., and a salute was fired. Then to table; and their performances in the way of eating and drinking were noteworthy. What was not eaten was carried away. Ham, tongue, salt beef, and such preserved food as is found on board a ship, seemed all of it to suit their appetites. The new Governor was cold and rude; not even the raw brandy which he and others drank seemed to warm his heart, or thaw him towards us.[285]

They asked when I would land, and were told tomorrow at five P. M. I was informed that two officers of rank would be sent to escort me to my new residence. The spar for my lower flagstaff only reached the ship at one P. M. The carpenter says it shall be done to-morrow.

Wednesday, September 3, 1856. Go on shore and select spot for flagstaff to stand. Return and write letter to Secretary of State, twelve foolscap pages.[286] Four

[285]Wood, *op. cit.*, pp. 317–18.

[286]Dispatch No. 15, *L. B.*, vol. 1, pp. 105–16. This long letter announces his arrival and then gives an outline of all that had happened since Aug. 21st—practically a synopsis of the entries in the *Journal* thus far. Townsend Harris's kindly policy towards the Japanese is clearly enunciated near the end of this dispatch:

"I have deemed it prudent to let a few weeks elapse before I open to the Japanese the matters contained in your Instructions. I wish to let the alarm

P. M.; instead of the flagstaff being ready at noon, it is not yet completed, and there is a fair chance it will not be sent ashore to-night. Mr. Heusken was taken ashore to interpret about the bills, etc., with a positive promise he should be brought back at half-past twelve. At half-past two P. M. he procured a shore boat and came off. So much for promises. I decide to land to-day, so send off all my remaining traps; and, attended by two officials, leave the ship at five P. M., having taken a kind leave of all. As I left the ship the men manned the rigging and gave me three hearty cheers. The men in my boat responded, and a counter cheer of two more came from the ship, and then the band on the quarter deck struck up "Hail, Columbia." I was both flattered and touched by this mark of attention.

It showed at least that I had so conducted myself while on board the *San Jacinto* (off and on five months) that I had secured the good will of all on board—and so I came on shore for my final landing in Japan. On reaching my temple, I found the Vice-Governor and a suite of officials awaiting my arrival to welcome me, which they did in very good terms, at the same time showing me a present of fowls, eggs and lobsters from the Governor. Two things I must note which caused me some regret in the *San Jacinto:* the first, that Commodore

occasioned by my arrival subside; to convince them by my quiet conduct of my friendly disposition; and, by such friendly intercourse as I may have, establish a kindly feeling towards me."

On the very day that Townsend Harris penned these sentiments of "quiet conduct," "friendly disposition," and "kindly feeling," Sir Michael Seymour, in command of the *Barracouta,* the *Winchester,* and the *Pique,* forced an entrance into the inner harbor of Nagasaki. (J. M. Tronson, *Personal Narrative of a Voyage to Japan . . . in H.M.S. Barracouta,* pp. 397–99.)

Armstrong was again quite unwell with considerable fever; and the other, that he and Captain Bell refused to permit me to pay anything for my mess while I was on board, saying I had not cost the mess one cent extra; that I never drank any wine, nor had called for any different cookery; that I had not given any trouble, nor added to their expenses. They therefore declined receiving anything from me. This was contrary to agreement as, before I left New York, I agreed with both the Commodore and Captain Bell that I should be allowed to pay my share of the mess. We were up until after midnight in getting copies made of my dispatches. The spar came on shore just at dusk, too late to put up my staff.[287]

Thursday, September 4, 1856. Slept very little from excitement and mosquitoes,—the latter *enormous* in size. At seven A. M. men came on shore to put up my flagstaff. Heavy job. Slow work. Spar falls; break cross-trees; fortunately no one hurt. At last get a reinforcement from the ship. Flagstaff erected; men form a ring around it, and, at two and a half P. M. of this day, I *hoist* the "First Consular Flag" ever seen in this Empire. Grim reflections—ominous of change—undoubted beginning of the end. Query,—if for the real good of Japan?[288] The *San Jacinto* left at five o'clock,[289]

[287]Wood, *op. cit.*, p. 318, wrongly states that this task was completed on Sept. 3rd.

[288]An interesting chapter might be written on this query of Townsend Harris's, for it is a thought which occurred time and again to the early visitors and representatives to Japan from the Western powers.

[289]The *San Jacinto* left for Shanghai, where she arrived on Sept. 11, 1856 (35-2, S. Ex. Doc., no. 22, pt. 2—in Serial no. 983—p. 963: Commissioner Peter Parker to Consul Caleb Jones).

saluting me by dipping her flag which was answered by me, and then she left me "alone in my glory," not feeling very sad, for in fact I was too busy in opening boxes, searching out eatables and mosquito nets, to think of being downhearted. Go to bed at eight P. M. and sleep well.

Friday, September 5, 1856. Busy all day in opening packages, arranging contents, ordering various articles from the Japanese. Get an old belfry made into a nice pigeon house in which I installed my four pairs of pigeons. Clear all day.

Saturday, September 6, 1856. Same employment as yesterday. Am getting things to look a little comfortable. Find that the *ichibu* is equal to 1,600 seni or cash. This takes two thirds off the prices of everything I buy, as the Japanese have only allowed us 1,600 seni for the dollar, although the dollar weighs three times as much as the *ichibu*,[290] consequently is worth 4,800 seni.

Moriama,[291] the Yedo official, visited me to-day on a

---

[290]This word, spelled in such a variety of ways in the early accounts, stands for *ichi-bu*, meaning *one bu*, or part. "To talk of 'a hundred *ichibus*' is as though a Japanese were to say 'a hundred one shillings.'" (Lord Redesdale (Mitford), *Tales of Old Japan* (London, 1908), p. 262, note 1.)

[291]Moriyama Yenosuke (Mr. Mountain Grove), a Samurai and chief interpreter of the Foreign Office of the Shogunate at Yedo. He took a prominent part in all the early contacts between Japan and foreign nations, and is constantly mentioned in all the narratives of the first visitors to Japan. His first appearance on the stage of the diplomatic relations between the United States and Japan is dated Sept. 2, 1848, when he visited the imprisoned sailors of the whaler *Lagoda*, at Nagasaki. One of these sailors, Robert McCoy, in the sworn statement of their captivity, made on Apr. 30, 1849, to Commander James Glynn, of the *Preble*, calls our interpreter Moreama Einaska (32–1, S. Ex. Doc., no. 59—in Serial no. 620—p. 17).

Moriyama was involved in so many important historical events that a biography of him would not only make an interesting monograph, but would constitute a valuable contribution to the history of our Japan relations. A good beginning could be made with Lewis and Murakami, *Ranald MacDonald*, p. 208, note 237; *cf.* also the index.

THE U. S. CONSULATE AT SHIMODA IN 1856

From a drawing in India ink by Mr. H. C. J. Heusken. This drawing gives the earliest and only authentic view of the grounds of the consulate, of its buildings, and of the flag-staff flying the first consular flag ever seen in Japan. See *Journal*, Thursday, September 4, 1856.

mere visit of friendship, as he said. Gave him "cakes and champagne."

My tailor is proving to be a desperate character. He will not work and says he does not care how much I cut his wages. He is the first Chinese I ever saw who was indifferent on this point.

I gave him a serious lecture. Told him if he expected to eat that he must work; that I had the power of putting him in jail and causing him to be fed on very spare diet, and also might order him to be whipped every day; that I would give him until Monday to reflect which he would take,—work, wages and good food,—or prison, hunger and whipping.

Hear a curious insect of the cricket tribe to-night. Sound was precisely like a miniature locomotive at great speed. Bats in rooms. See enormous *tête de mort* spider; the legs extended five and a half inches as the insect stood. Unpleasant discovery of large rats in numbers, running about the house. Light showers in the night.

Sunday, September 7, 1856. No work to-day. Hoist my flag, which is to be flown on Sundays, holidays— Japanese ditto—and when foreign ships are here. The Japanese were much pleased when I told them I would hoist my flag in honor of their holidays, and gave me a list for six months. The wind fresh all day from the west. Thermometer 84°, but there is so much vitality in the air that one does not feel oppressed by the heat. My flag badly made, the wind has whipped out the end hem and frayed the bunting in many places three inches

—so badly is all government contract work done. The sealing wax sent me from the Department is so bad it will not run or even drop. It appears to be composed of rosin and tallow, no wax or shellac in it. When a stick is lighted it will burn to the end like a pitch pine splinter. No rain.

Monday, September 8, 1856. Weather same as yesterday. Get on very slowly in fitting up the house with shelves, closets, tables, etc., etc. Every carpenter that comes to do anything is attended by an officer. It may be to keep him from stealing, but more likely to prevent any communication between us. I have required my poultry to be all hens or pullets. They inform me that in Japan fowls are always hatched in pairs—one cock and one hen—therefore, they must give them to me in the same manner. Send to each of the first Governors two five-pints of champagne, one quart brandy, two quarts whiskey, one cherry bounce and one anisette. This afternoon we discover a Russian cemetery with three tombs of the same patterns as the Americans'. They are of persons who belonged to the Russian Frigate *Diana,* and died in 1854 and 1855. One tomb is evidently that of an officer, but I cannot read the letters to make out his name or rank.

This tomb is decorated with *two crosses* deeply cut in the stone. One is four inches, the other about sixteen inches long. The presence of these crosses serves to prove that the Japanese of the present day have not that excessive hatred of the cross that was said to animate them formerly. On Saturday last I showed Moriama my

Mitchell's *Atlas,* the frontispiece of which contains a colored engraving of the "Landing of Columbus," in which a large cross is prominently engraved. Moriama paid no attention to it, or rather said nothing.

Spalding says that he asked a Japanese for his autograph, which he was about to write in his (Spalding's) prayer-book, but, discovering a cross in the frontispiece, he with great trepidation refused to write.[292] No rain.

Tuesday, September 9, 1856. I applied on Friday last (5th) for two boys as house servants. Am told to-day that they must write to Yedo about them. Get measures of distance from Japanese (see record book).[293] Weather fine, but little wind. Thermometer at noon 82°, but it is not oppressive. I am anxious to get my house arranged, so that I may begin to wander about the country and see how it looks, which I cannot now do, being constantly wanted for directions, etc., etc. At nine o'clock a heavy thunder shower. The lightning was as vivid as I ever saw out of the tropics, and the thunder appeared to be interminable, so long

---

[292]J. W. Spalding, *The Japan Expedition,* New York, Redfield, 1855, pp. 222–23:

"They would present their fans on which they desired some sentiment to be written. . . . Their own cards were presented. . . . They were very polite in writing names in Japanese characters in our books. I requested one to write a name on the title-page of a Book of Common Prayer, which happened to have a steel engraving of the cross upon it. He had dipped his camel's-hair pencil into his portable inkstand, passed the point through his lips, and was about to write when his eye rested upon the cross; he instantly shook his head, threw the book upon the table, nor could he be induced to touch it again."

[293]We do not know what Townsend Harris meant by *Record Book.* There is extant, however, his manuscript copybook entitled *Common Place Book,* on p. 8 of which are found not only the Japanese measures of distance, but also the cloth measure.

were the echoes prolonged among the hills. The thermometer marked 81° during the whole shower. There was not much wind with the shower, which lasted forty minutes. At eleven P. M. another shower, without lightning.

Wednesday, September 10, 1856. Quiet rain set in, in showers at three A. M. and continued until eleven A. M., closing with some few claps of thunder. The wind then came from [the] east and the thermometer fell to 70°.

Much trouble with the lock of the iron chest. Procure mechanics to open it; and, after removing a load of mortar placed over the lock, find it cannot be repaired. *Caution:* Never buy an iron chest with a *patent* lock of Mr. Gaylor's or any other man's make, especially if you are going to a semi-civilized country. I can close and bolt the chest, but not lock it. It is a protection from fire (*soi disant*), but not from thieves.[294] Moriama and suite visited me this afternoon. He said he came from the Governor to inquire if I was frightened by the thunder of last night—a Japanese ruse. He quietly diverged to the subject of Japanese servants, which I had asked for last week. Said there were none at Shimoda; must write to other places; that they had to reflect on every new proposition a long time; that they could not decide as quickly as the men of the West, etc., etc. I replied that I believed that servants could at once be procured for me in Shimoda; that it was treating me

---

[294]This perverse iron chest had been purchased in New York from the Japan Contingent Fund. "Sepr. 24th [1855]. Paid J. E. Van Antwerp for an Iron Safe for the Consulate at Shimoda $87.75." (*L. B.*, vol. 1, p. 5.)

improperly to leave me to wait on myself. I showed him my blistered hands, which had *so become* by my being compelled to do work in fault of proper servants. He then begged me to give them some more time to procure them (*i. e.,* to invent lies to deny them if they think best to do so). I said I did not wish to appear impatient, and would wait for the remainder of the week. I complained of the very great delay there was in executing my orders. I had for many days been expecting a number of slight things to be done (naming some of them), and, although time enough to do them four times over had elapsed, yet none of them had been done; that I felt that I was neglected and expected it would be remedied.

He at once began blowing up the officers who were with him and gave me some of their excuses. A greater tissue of lies was never heard. The matter was closed by an assurance on his part that I should have the matters attended to in the morning. After this he got quite jolly on champagne. At ten P. M. the thermometer marked 77°. Wind east.

Thursday, September 11, 1856. A fine breezy morning. Thermometer, 75°. Wind N. E.

Men are here working on various matters for my house. Had a *flare-up* with the officials, who told me some egregious lies in answer to some requests I made. I told them plainly I knew they lied; that, if they wished me to have any confidence in them, they must always speak the truth; that, if I asked anything they were not authorized to grant, or about which they wished to consult, let them simply say they were not prepared to answer me, but that to tell lies to me was treating me like a child, and that I should consider myself as insulted thereby; that in my country a man who lied was disgraced, and that to call a man a liar was the greatest insult that could be given him; that I hoped they would, for the future, if they told me anything, simply tell me the truth, and that I should then respect them, which I could not do when they told me falsehoods. Send Moriama an *Atlas* as a present.[295]

Friday, September 12, 1856. As lovely a morning as I ever saw. The wind fell before daylight, and we have light airs from the west with a sky so blue it looks like ultramarine. Thermometer, 79°. The Vice-Governor and Moriama, with the usual suite.

The object of the visit was my demand for two boys as house servants. It was a rare scene of Japanese deceit, falsehood, flattery and politeness. I at last got them cornered, and they were compelled to promise me to supply my wants by the 16th. They fought hard to have the boys leave at sunset and return at daylight, but I was firm and carried my point. I may here remark that at all these visits they readily drink all I offer them,—wine, cordials, brandy, whiskey, etc., etc., and many of them drink more than enough. Spirits of all kinds they drink raw.

Saturday September 13, 1856. To-day is the anniversary of the Patron Saint[296] of Shimoda, and is one of

---

[295]Very likely his copy of Mitchell's *Atlas*, which he had showed Moriyama on Sept. 8, 1856.

[296]Ushijiwa no Jinja (Griffis, *Townsend Harris*, p. 64, note).

their greatest holidays; but, as my house is not in order, I remain at home arranging books, etc., and trying to eradicate the cockroaches, which I have brought from the *San Jacinto* by thousands. They are a pest of the most disagreeable kind. Mr. Heusken went out to see what was doing, and says he saw a large procession bearing a metal mirror and pieces of white paper (emblems of the Shinto religion); a large drum borne by three men was beaten by one. The fashion of the drum was like the Chinese,—*i. e.,* a cylinder with one parchment head. He did not see any change of dress; a number of persons were throwing themselves into extravagant attitudes and shouting or screaming loudly. The procession went to a temple where a large quantity of holy water was showered on them by the attending priests. After their devotions they visited another temple, after which he left. He did not see any of the theatricals referred to by Kaempfer, Fischer, and Heer Doeff. A fine day. Wind from west. Thermometer, 84°.

Sunday, September 14, 1856. A smart thunder shower at five A. M., but the day has been a fine one. Some of my Chinese servants went out to walk. They were followed by three policemen. They offered to purchase some fruit, but were refused, and finally, on asking for a drink of water from a man who was by a well, he refused, and ran away with the drinking vessel.

Monday, September 15, 1856. Commenced raining at four A. M. with a raw wind from north, although the thermometer is 82° in our open rooms, but protected from the wind. I expect the Governor to visit me to-day,

233

as I wrote him on Saturday asking him to order the proper officer to receive from Mr. Heusken $500 in silver coin, and to give him the *same* weight of Japanese silver money.[297] I am sure he will refuse, as they have heretofore refused to take the dollar for more than their *ichibu,* or quarter of a tael of silver. The value of the tael is about $1.36. The *ichibu* is therefore worth 34 cents. We have heretofore paid nearly 200 per cent. over price,—from their only allowing us 34 cents for our dollar. But this must have an end, and I am fully instructed by my Government to insist on our money being taken at its proper value.

In the afternoon Moriama and the third Governor and suite visited me, bringing two boys of the ages of fifteen and sixteen years. Their names are Ske-zo and Ta-ki-so;[298] the latter I take for my servant, and the other for Mr. Heusken.

On showing Kaempfer's work on Japan to the Governor, he at once pointed out the place of his and Moriama's house in Yedo, showing the general correctness of the plan of that city. I tried in various ways to get at the population of Yedo from them, but without any success. They said it was a large place; that there was such a large number of persons going and coming daily, that it was out of their power to state the population, etc., etc. Complained to the Governor that my servants on

---

[297]In the same letter (*L. B.,* vol. 1, pp. 116–17), Townsend Harris states that he had received a letter from Captain Bell complaining of the poor quality of the coal that had been furnished the *San Jacinto,* and transmits the Captain's desires as to future supplies.

The Dutch translation of this letter is to be found in *L. B.,* vol. 1, pp. 99–100.

[298]Sukézo and Takézo (Griffis, *Townsend Harris,* p. 65).

Sunday last had been followed by policemen; that they had been refused fruit which they offered to buy, and even denied a drink of water. I remonstrated sharply against such conduct as disgraceful, inhospitable, etc., etc., and they promised that the matter should be inquired into. Constant rain until four P. M. Got some fine, ripe grapes and persimmons to-day and am promised a regular supply, so long as they are in season. They have constantly denied to me having any such fruits here, and it was only after my cook had seen them in the streets on Sunday and I charged them with falsehood about fruit that they would bring them to me.

Tuesday, September 16, 1856. A fine bright morning. Sky as blue as sapphire. Wind light from northwest. Thermometer, 76° at eight A. M. At eleven o'clock go out for a walk. The paths lead over towards Yedo Bay, and the views were enchanting. Sky clear—water blue— whitecaps cresting the waves. High lands on the opposite side of Yedo Bay (northeast side) dimly seen. Japanese junks with their large square sail scudding merrily before the wind. Ground here is cultivated *wherever water can be procured to irrigate* it. It appears to be equally rich on the steep hillsides as on the little plains. A streamlet of water is found running down the gorge between two hills. The ground is cut into terraces, then the water is led from the highest part right and left from the stream to the upper terraces, thence it trickles down to the next, and the next, until all the terraces have been watered down to the foot of the hill. I never saw such fine crops of rice, or rice of so good a quality as here. Rice is

235

the chief produce; some maize, millet, a little wheat, barley and buckwheat are also grown. A great variety of pulse and lentils are also grown. I see [that] many oleaginous seeds of whose names I am ignorant are also cultivated. A bulbous root—the *taro* of the South Seas—is also grown here. We pursued our pleasant walk until we reached the highest hill in this vicinity,—say some 2,800 feet; and from that we could just see the top of the celebrated Fusi Yama, the highest mountain in Japan, which is 12,500 feet high and not many miles from Yedo.

It is said that this mountain is always crowned with snow, but the distance from which we viewed it was too great to permit us to say whether it was so covered or not. This mountain is the most celebrated spot in Japan. It is the seat of their most terrible volcanoes. It is celebrated in the histories of their gods as the scene of many remarkable events, and its picture figures on everything that is highly decorated.[299]

---

[299]The annual celebration at The College of the City of New York known as Charter Day took place in the year 1925 on May 20th. The speaker of the day and the guest of honor was His Excellency Tsuneo Matsudaira, who had courteously consented to unveil a bronze tablet of Mr. Townsend Harris. Having read the Ambassador's address, Baron Takashi Masuda, who, at the age of fourteen, had served in the Bureau for Foreigners, was stirred to write his *Reminiscences of Townsend Harris,* which he sent to the Japanese Ambassador at Washington, who, in turn, caused them to be translated and then, with exquisite courtesy, presented them to the writer.

From these manuscript *Reminiscences* we quote the following interesting lines:

"Before the departure of Harris from Japan, Mr. Ando [Tsushima-no-Kami] said to him, 'I wish to express my sincere gratitude for your friendly advice on our international policy, and although I am very anxious to give you a present, I am sorry that there is nothing I can give you which is equal to the value of the help you have been to us. I wish I could give you Mt. Fuji, but I am sorry that it is impossible.' "

Remembering the rôle played in Japanese mythology, history, legend, and art by the famous Fujiyama, we realize that Ando Tsushima-no-Kami was offering the very heart of Japan to the man who had won it.

We reached home at three P. M. much pleased with our walk. Our distance out [and] in was about eight miles. Very nice grapes are furnished to us to-day at the rate of about two cents per pound. Pears, shaped like apples and of the exact color of russets, are also brought; not good to eat raw, as they are hard, dry and tasteless, but they cook very well. Persimmons, fully ripe, are now brought to us. Our poultry has been taken with some disease during the last few days and is dying off rapidly —while we are afraid to eat any of it that is not apparently sick, for fear it may have the seeds of disease in it. I charge the Japanese with selecting all the sick fowls they have and bringing them to me. They deny it, and say the poultry all around is dying off in the same manner.

Cleaning up exterior of house. Oven, extraordinary affair—*cut out of solid stone!!* New paper on our windows, by the way of glazing them anew.

Wednesday, September 17, 1856. Not pleasant this morning. Cloudy. Wind N. E. Thermometer, 74° at eight A. M.

Tuesday, September 23, 1856. Yesterday at four P. M. the wind began to blow fresh from E. S. E., with rain. The wind continued to freshen until at eight P. M. it became a heavy typhoon which continued up to midnight, when it moderated. The wind at four P. M. was S. S. E., and continued to haul to S. S. W., at which point the gale was heaviest. After midnight the wind stood at W. N. W.

I was under much apprehension that my house would

be blown down, as it shook in every post and beam, and swayed to and fro as the heavy gusts struck it. My kitchen was partly unroofed. Flagstaff blown over so as to stand at an angle of 65°. In the harbor every junk was cast ashore and many lives lost and much property destroyed. In Kakizaki, full one half the houses were blown down and some persons killed. The landing jetty and breakwater at Kakizaki are totally destroyed.

At Shimoda, the bazaar part of the Goyoshi is totally destroyed, and a large amount of beautiful lacquer and inlaid ware lost. One hundred houses blown down and twenty lives lost. The Japanese say it was the severest storm ever known at this place.[300]

Wednesday, October 1, 1856. The Dutch Steam Frigate *Diana* [*Medusa*], Captain Fabius, arrived here to-day from Hakodate en route to Nagasaki.[301] I went on board and was kindly received by Captain Fabius, who gave me a salute of eleven guns on leaving.

Captain Fabius informs me that a mine of superior coals has been discovered at Hakodate, which will greatly reduce the price of that article at that place be-

---

[300]Mr. Heusken's *Diary* says that this storm took place during the night from the 20th to the 21st of September. (G. Wagener, *Aus dem Tagebuche Hendrik Heusken's*, in the Tokyo *Deutsche Gesellschaft für Natur—und Völkerkunde Ostasiens, Mittheilungen,* June, 1883, vol. 3, p. 376.)

On Sept. 25th, Townsend Harris wrote to the Governor of Shimoda (*L. B.*, vol. 1, pp. 117-21), protesting at the merely verbal answer given to his written communication of Sept. 13th (see *Journal* for Sept. 15th), refuting the Japanese arguments for refusing to provide him with Japanese coins, and renewing his battle for evaluating the dollar at three *ichibus.* (The Dutch translation of this letter is to be found in *L. B.*, vol. 1, pp. 101-04.)

Finally, Heusken mentions a letter dated Sept. 25th and sent to Yedo to the Minister of Foreign Affairs (Wagener, *op. cit.,* p. 376). This is an error for Oct. 25th.

[301]See Heusken's *Diary, loc. cit.*

sides giving a superior quality. Captain Fabius also says that two steam vessels are now being constructed in Holland for the Japanese, which are to be paid for as follows: say one-fifth part in each of the following articles —copper, lacquer ware, etc., wax, camphor; and money or bullion for the remaining 20 per cent.

Dutch mechanics of every branch connected with shipbuilding have been brought out for the Japanese, and they are now giving instruction to the Japanese in all the various branches above referred to at Nagasaki.[302]

It appears that for some years the Dutch have received a part of the returns of their annual cargo in money or bullion.

The King of Holland has, as it is said, written a letter to the Emperor of Japan, strongly urging him to open his kingdom to the commerce *of all nations.*[303]

---

[302]Here is the beginning of the building of the mighty fleets of Japan! We are strongly reminded of the prophetic words of the imprisoned Russian Captain, Golownin, who, from observations made more than forty years before, had written (*Memoirs,* 2nd ed., 1824, vol. 3, pp. 33–34):

"However deeply a horror of everything foreign may be impressed on the Japanese and Chinese government[s], yet a change in their system is not inconceivable: necessity may compel them to do that to which their own free will does not impel them! Attacks, for example, like that of Chwostoff, often repeated, would probably induce them to think of means to repel a handful of vagabonds who disturbed a nation. This might lead them to build ships of war on the model of those of Europe; these ships might increase to fleets, and then it is probable that the good success of this measure would lead them also to adopt the other scientific methods which are so applicable to the destruction of the human race."

[303]Dr. Daniel Crosby Greene, *Correspondence between William II of Holland and the Shogun of Japan, A. D. 1844,* in *Transactions of the Asiatic Society of Japan,* vol. 34, part 4 (June, 1907), pp. 99–132. In this scholarly article, Dr. Greene gives both the versions through which the letter had to pass before it could reach Shogun Iyeyoshi: the original Dutch text, on pp. 104–09; and the Japanese translation, on pp. 124–29. The English version appears on pp.110–14.

Friday, October 3, 1856. The *Diana* [*Medusa*] sailed to-day for Nagasaki. As she will not go to Hong-kong I do not write by her.

Saturday, October 4, 1856. I am fifty-two years old to-day. God grant that the short remainder of my life may be more usefully and honorably spent than the preceding and larger portion of it.[304]

Sunday, October 5, 1856. The American Schooner *General Pierce* arrived here from Hakodate. Left no American vessels there, as it is too early for them. She comes here to complete her trading.[305]

Both the *Diana* [*Medusa*] and *General Pierce* were in the typhoon of the 22nd ult.[306]

Thursday, October 9, 1856. The *General Pierce* left to-day. Wrote by her to:

The letter of the King of Holland was dated Feb. 15, 1844; *Japonice,* the 27th day of the 12th month of the 14th year of Tempo.

To return to the *Journal.* Oct. 1st being the beginning of a new quarter, Townsend Harris duly sent an order for supplies to Armstrong & Lawrence (*L. B.,* vol. 1, pp. 104–05); and, on the matter of his salary for the broken quarter ending Sept. 30, 1856, he wrote to Russell & Co., at Shanghai (*L. B.,* vol. 1, pp. 121–23), and to Baring Bros. & Co., at London (*L. B.,* vol. 1, pp. 123–24).

[304]Townsend Harris lived to the age of seventy-four. He died of congestion of the lungs at 263 Fourth Avenue, New York City, on Monday, Feb. 25, 1878. His funeral took place at Calvary Church, Fourth Avenue and 21st Street, on the morning of Thursday, Feb. 28, 1878. He is buried in Greenwood Cemetery, Brooklyn, N. Y.

This entry in his *Journal,* written in Townsend Harris's own hand, settles the moot point of the exact date of his birth, which is variously given in the encyclopædias, and which is wrongly given even on his tombstone.

[305]The *General Pierce* arrived with a cargo of ammunition, which the Japanese did not permit to be landed because it was found to be too old (Heusken, in G. Wagener, *op. cit.,* p. 376). She left on Oct. 9th, bound for Hongkong (*L. B.,* vol. 1, p. 125).

[306]Compare above, entry for Sept. 23, 1856, and note 300.

On Oct. 7th, Townsend Harris had an interview with the Governor of Shimoda, at which he discussed the currency question. (*L. B.,* vol. 1, p. 126.)

240

The Secretary of State
N. Dougherty
P. M. Wetmore
S. Drinker
S. B. Drinker
Armstrong & Lawrence

and Russell & Co., of Shanghai, sending a bill for my salary up to 30th ult. on Baring & Co. for them to negotiate.[307]

Wednesday, October 22, 1856. I have not been well since the 17th of September. I am suffering from a bad wound in my left foot caused by treading on a large nail, and also from a total loss of appetite, want of sleep and depression of spirits.

I attribute all but the wound to two causes: first, inability to take exercise in the open air; and second, smoking too much. The latter I must break off. As I am now much better, I shall begin to go out for exercise and

---

[307] 1) To the Secretary of State: Dispatch No. 16 (*L. B.*, vol. 1, pp. 124–25). Townsend Harris reports that he has already made progress in the matter of evaluating the dollar, which makes him feel sure that the making of a commercial treaty is only a question of time. Furthermore, the storm of Sept. 22nd proves that Shimoda is an unsafe harbor and should be exchanged for another.

2) To S. Drinker: Acknowledged by letter dated Hongkong, Apr. 3 and 4, 1857 (*L. & P.*, vol. 1, no. 62).

3) To S. B. Drinker: Mrs. Susannah Budd Drinker, whose maiden name was Susannah Budd Shober.

4) To Armstrong & Lawrence: *L. B.*, vol. 1, p. 124, which speaks of finances and supplies.

Though not mentioned in the *Journal*, on this day Townsend Harris wrote at least two more letters:

5) To the Governor of Shimoda (*L. B.*, vol. 1, p. 126), going over the ground covered during the interview of Oct. 7, 1856, and again maintaining that the silver dollar was worth three silver *ichibus;*

6) To Captain H. H. Bell, in answer to one from him regarding the poor quality of the coal that had been furnished the *San Jacinto* (*cf. L. B.*, vol. 1, p. 116, Townsend Harris to the Governor of Shimoda, Sept. 13, 1856; and see above, *Journal* for Sept. 15th, and note 297). We have not found this letter to Captain Bell. Both this lost letter and Townsend Harris's letter to Captain Bell of Dec. 10, 1856 (likewise lost), are acknowledged by Captain Bell by letter dated Whampoa, Jan. 10, 1857 (*L. & P.*, vol 1, no. 54).

hope to be in robust health again. The climate here is delightful.

The thermometer since September 16th has not been above 80° nor below 61° Fahrenheit.

The Japanese have three times sent me the flesh of what they call a wild hog.[308] I find on examination that it is the baibarossa, or *hog deer* of India and the Indian Archipelago, and I am much surprised to find it so far to the north. The flesh is peculiar. It is very tender, juicy and of an excellent flavor. The taste is something between delicate veal and the tenderloins of pork. I am promised a full supply during the cold weather, which will be a great relief to my housekeeping. The typhoon destroyed all the grapes, but I have been well supplied with a great variety of the persimmon, some as large as a pippin and all of good quality. Chestnuts have also been sent to me.

To-day a horse was brought to me to examine the saddle, bridle, etc. They are queer affairs, but I have ordered a horse and trappings to be sent to me from Yedo,—not only for actual use, but to give me increased importance in the eye of the natives. For the same reason I have ordered a *norimon*.

The Japanese officials are daily becoming more and more friendly and more open in their communications with me. I hope this will grow and lead to good results by and by.

My poor pigeons have all been killed in one night by

---

[308]See comment by Griffis, in *Towniend Harris*, p. 71, note.

my cat. I have sent up to Yedo for more. The *itats,* a species of large weasel, is a sad enemy to my hencoops.

Thursday, October 23, 1856. A lovely day. The weather is as balmy and mild as in New York in October, but we have no smoke or haze in the air, and at night the thermometer does not fall below 60°. Took a walk of some five miles. The country is very beautiful— is broken up in steep volcanic cones, but every possible spot is terraced and cultivated like a garden. The labor expended in cutting down the rock to form some of these terraces is something wonderful. My walk led me first to Vandalia Point, the most southeastern part of the land. From this I had a view of the vast Pacific, and it was a curious thought that, looking due south, there was no land between me and Australia, some five thousand miles!

Turning more to the eastward I saw the Island of Oho Sima,[309] with its volcano smoking on its summit. The day is almost calm, so the smoke arose like a mighty pillar for thousands of feet. It then spread out forming a vast white cloud.

This volcano has been in action for some centuries, and occasionally treats us here to an earthquake, as it did in December, 1853,[310] when a mighty wave rolled in on Shimoda, encountering as it entered a flourishing town of some eight thousand to ten thousand souls. When the wave receded, it left only fourteen houses standing;

---

[309]Oshima or O Shima (Great Island), also known as Vries Island.

[310]A slip of the pen for Dec., 1854; see above, *Journal* for Aug. 21, 1856, and note 267.

all the rest,—temples, bazaars and a large number of the inhabitants,—were swept into the bay by the reflux of this mighty wave, which was said to have been thirty feet high. Four times it returned, but the deed of destruction was perfected by the first one. I passed through the village of Satora on the Yedo Bay, thence, through another village back of Kakizaki whose name I do not know, home. I saw to-day cherry, peach, pear and persimmon trees, grapevines, ivy, althea,—*the last just putting out new leaves. Blue* privet—very pretty; many ferns; pine trees in variety; cedar, spruce, fir and camphor trees. *Camellia Japonica* forms the jungle here and is cut for fuel.

I saw a few bushes of the common rose, but no flowers were on them. Among flowers whose names I know I found: blue bell, Canterbury ditto, Scotch thistle—the first I ever saw in the East—heart's-ease, yellow shamrock, daisy and others whose forms are familiar but whose names I do not know, and then many that were strange to me. How much I wish I was a botanist.

The fine clear bracing air, the high cultivation you see everywhere, combined with views which are of the most picturesque kind and which are constantly changing, make a walk here a thing to be desired and long remembered.[311]

---

[311]While Townsend Harris was thus living Arcadian days, events of great importance were taking place in China. On Oct. 22nd, Captain Andrew Hull Foote, of the U.S.S. *Portsmouth,* landed eighty of his men at the Canton Factories to protect Americans and their property; on the 23rd, British troops were landed, and Sir Admiral Michael Seymour captured all the Canton Forts, from the Bogue Forts up, took also the Factories, and demanded an interview with Yeh. A few days later the walls of Canton were breached, and Captain Foote issued a proclamation of American neutrality. For these and many other

Friday, October 24, 1856. The Japanese brought me the entire carcass of what I have supposed to be the baibarossa, but it proves to be simply a wild hog. It has seven molars on each side of the upper jaw, while the baibarossa has only five. The incisors are not developed scarcely at all, or have been broken off. The baibarossa has four incisors on the upper jaw; again, the baibarossa has two large tusks which protrude through the upper jaw and sweep backwards in a curve which brings the points nearly in contact with the skin just below the eye. This *boar* had only small tusks in the lower jaw.

Walked to the top of the hill that overlooks the harbor, about one thousand feet high; has a wooden cannon, about twelve pounder, bore. It is strongly bound with bamboo hoops from end to end, the hoops are close together. Here also are two old iron guns, nine pounders, bearing the shield of the Dutch East India Company. These guns are only for signals. A lookout house is erected here and a guard is always here from daylight to dark. It commands a vast range of vision, and a ship could, in clear weather, be seen some twenty miles off.

On my return I met a mountain-priest,—one of a class whose vow binds him to ascend all mountains he can meet with. He bears a staff surmounted with a circle of iron; within is a trident like that of Siva, four loose rings are attached to the circle, two on each side. These make a jingling noise when the priest shakes his staff.

---

stirring details of the capture of the Barrier Forts and of Canton, see the very lòng letter by Captain Bell to Townsend Harris, written at Whampoa over a series of days and dated Jan. 10, 18, 26, 28, Feb. 20, 25, 1857 (*L. & P.*, vol. 1, no. 54).

I get 4,800 of the small copper coin of Japan for one dollar. Ten of these given to the priest produced a long prayer and a great jingling of his rings.

The priest was of a good pleasant countenance and very robust in appearance.

Saturday, October 25, 1856. The Vice-Governor visited me to-day. He borrowed the *Treaties of the United States with Foreign Nations,* for the purpose of having it translated. It will be a heavy work for them, as they will have to do it by means of a dictionary in English and Dutch.

The two Kamis, who are Governors here, are to visit me on Thursday next. I have visited the prison of Shimoda. It corresponds generally with Golownin's description of the prisons at Hakodate and Matsmai,[312] but what he calls cages are simply cells made of squared joists of timber, placed some three inches apart. I am sure they are larger and not so solitary as the stone cells in the prisons of the United States. Imprisonment as a punishment for the Japanese is unknown. The punishments are either death or whipping, and the accused is only in prison until he can be tried. The Japanese code is somewhat sanguinary. Death is inflicted for murder, arson, burglary, grand larceny and for violent deportment towards a father.

The parent cannot put his children to death; but, on

---

[312]Wassily Michailovitsch Golownin, a Captain in the Russian Navy. The reference is to his famous work: *Memoirs of a Captivity in Japan during the Years 1811, 1812, and 1813, with Observations on the Country and the People.* Second edition, in 3 vols., London, Henry Colburn & Co., 1824. There are, of course, other editions.

complaint of disobedience of his children, the government will punish the child with whipping or death, according to the nature of the offence. The Japanese declare that infanticide of legitimate children is unknown in Japan. In cases where the parents are too poor to bear the incumbrance of an additional child, the government makes an allowance to them for the purpose. Paupers are placed with their relatives, and an allowance made for their support; but, if the pauper goes out begging, the allowance ceases. There is no law to prohibit begging, and in fact it would be difficult to frame one in a country where all the priesthood, besides a large number of monks, hermits and nuns, live solely on charity. There were three prisoners in the jail awaiting trial: two for gambling, and one for a small larceny. They were to be tried to-day, and will either go home acquitted or else well whipped to-night. Whipping is inflicted with a small bamboo or rattan over the shoulders or back. The Japanese cannot understand our imprisonment for punishment. They say for a man to be in a good house and have enough of food and clothing cannot be a punishment to a large portion of men, who only care for their animal wants and have no self-respect; and, as they never walk for pleasure, they cannot think it hard to be deprived of wandering about.[313]

---

[313]On this day, also, Townsend Harris wrote to the Japanese Minister of Foreign Affairs (*L. B.*, vol. 1, pp. 127–29), stating that he had a letter from the President of the United States for the Emperor of Japan, and that he had concluded to go to Yedo, accompanied by his secretary, Mr. Heusken. He further requested that all necessary arrangements be made for this visit; sends a Dutch translation of his Treaty with Siam, and makes the tempting statement that, when in Yedo, he will inform the Japanese Government of the intentions of the British Government toward Japan.

Monday, October 27, 1856. A lovely day; bright, clear sky and the thermometer at 72°.

Took a walk over the hills and up the valley of Shimoda, making a circuit of some ten miles, part of it on the road to Yedo. This is simply a foot or bridle path of some six to eight feet wide, and is only practicable on foot or on horseback. Every new walk I take shows me more and more of the patient industry of the Japanese, and creates new admiration of their agriculture, while the landscape from the top of the hills, overlooking the terraces rising one above another like the steps of a giant staircase and running over the rich fields of the valley and terminating with a glimpse of the blue water of the sea, forms a series of charming landscapes which are well worthy the pencils of able artists. So far as buildings or monuments are concerned, there is nothing to mark the age of the country.

There are no venerable ivy-grown ruins, no temples bearing the marks of the tooth of time on their stones. The temples and houses are from necessity built from wood or bamboo wattles plastered with clay, as a stone edifice would be very dangerous in a country so frequently visited with violent earthquakes.

In my rambles over the hills I have met with some proofs that Shimoda has been settled for many centuries —I mean in the stone quarries. The stone is a soft and light colored sandstone which is easily wrought.

In many places you see the face of the quarry in a smooth perpendicular wall of one hundred fifty to two hundred feet high, cut down in quarrying the stones.

The great number of these quarries, their vast size and the fact that the débris in many places is covered with trees of the largest size, all go to prove the antiquity of the place. This stone is used for foundations, for flagging, for ovens and cooking places; for tombstones, for altars, for images, and, in fact, for all the purposes (except houses) that stone can be applied [to]. I see that some of it is shipped away to other places.

The cotton here is a second crop which springs up just before the first is taken from the ground; the stool and bolls are small and the latter few in number, but the staple is long, strong and fine. The hemp of Japan is probably the best in the world. It is water rotted, and for this purpose a small rivulet is dammed up to give sufficient depth to immerse the hemp, which is neatly put up in cylindrical bales of some thirty-two inches long by fourteen in diameter.

There are quite a number of water mills on the principal stream of Shimoda. They are driven by *undershot* wheels, and are used for grinding rice, buckwheat, etc. Rice being the staple food of the country is, of course, the chief occupation of the mills. The water is sadly mismanaged, and a small increase of labor would convert many of the mills to an *overshot* power, but they appear to be either ignorant of the difference of power, or indifferent as to its application.

There are deer, wolves, hares and wild monkeys among the hills of this place.

I was much moved to-day on finding in the woods a bachelor's button. This humble flower, with its sweet perfume, brought up so many home associations that I was inclined to be homesick,—*i. e.,* miserable for the space of an hour. I am trying to learn Japanese. I have begun with some words to my servants and can give them all the orders necessary for my attendance.

Tuesday, October 28, 1856. Another lovely day, which I improved by walking some eight miles, skirting the shores of the Bay of Shimoda, and from Vandalia Point turning east until I came on the village of Sazaki, —a very ancient place, to judge by the vast number of heavy stone terraces for supporting temples, houses and gardens. The aggregate labor is very great, and all this among a village population of five hundred to six hundred souls. Thence I walked over the hills, and so along to the village of Satora on the Bay of Yedo. From here we cross over to Kakizaki by a valley which runs entirely across the peninsula, save a small hill just back of my residence. In this route I passed through the village of Wenoyama, celebrated for its terraces cut out of the living rock.

I do not know what to think of the seasons here. I have before mentioned that the althea was putting out new leaves, being before completely bare. To-day I found flowers on the tea shrub and also *cherry blossoms.*

Found a new variety of heliotrope and mayflower both in blossom, besides many flowers quite unknown to me. To-day I saw a *camellia Japonica* grown into a large tree. The boll was quite twelve inches in diameter, and the tree thirty to forty feet high.

I wish I could send bouquets of the wild flowers of Japan to some of my female friends.

Neither flowers nor fruits appear to be cultivated anywhere in this vicinity. The last crop of rice is now being harvested, and they are planting sweet potatoes on all the cotton grounds. We have had sweet potatoes ever since the 21st of August.

The cotton boll of Japan is divided into three cells, each containing three or four seeds, mostly four.

These rambles over this broken country, climbing the steepest of possible hills, descending on a similar plane, is improving my health very much. My appetite improves and I begin to sleep better, though not as well as I could wish.

Certainly a more genial climate than that of Shimoda, so far, is not to be found in the world. All that is wanted to make me quite happy is society. I hope when I have made some further progress in the language I shall find some pleasure in the society of the upper classes here. By a law of Japan no high officer can invite me to his house.[314] He may make friendly visits to me, but he can

---

[314]Townsend Harris's comment proves that the relations between him and the Japanese had developed to the point where a friendly visit to his home was no longer a matter of idle speculation. In fact, only two days later—on Thursday, Oct. 30, 1856 (see below)—he was visited by the two Governors of Shimoda, accompanied by the Vice-Governor. This was indeed a red-letter day; for, as Treat says (*Early Diplomatic Relations between the United States and Japan*, p. 59), on this day (Oct. 30, 1856) commenced "the process of instruction in Western affairs—beginning with an account of the coast-surveying operations of the maritime powers."

An even more significant day, however, was Tuesday, Feb. 24, 1857; for, on that day, Townsend Harris was at last freed from the regulation of having to meet the high officers at the Shimoda Goyoshi, and was permitted to enter on terms of parity the home of two Japanese Daimyo, the Governors of Shimoda—namely, Inouye, Shinano-no-Kami, and Okada, Bingo-no-Kami. (*Cf.* also *Journal* for March 7, 1857.)

only see me in return at the Goyoshi, a sort of "Hôtel de Ville" or City Hall.

Wednesday, October 29, 1856. The Japanese are much surprised to see me bathing in *cold water,* and particularly when the thermometer stands at 56°, as it does this morning.

The Japanese are a *clean* people. Everyone bathes every day. The mechanic, day laborer, all male and female, old and young, bathe every day after their labor is completed. There are many public bath houses in Shimoda. The charge is six seni, or the eighth part of one cent! The wealthy people have their baths in their own houses, but the working classes all, of both sexes, old and young, enter the same bathroom and there perform their ablutions in a state of perfect nudity. I cannot account for so indelicate a proceeding on the part of a people so generally correct.

I am assured, however, that it is not considered as dangerous to the chastity of their females; on the contrary, they urge that this very exposure lessens the desire that owes much of its power to mystery and difficulty.

Toko Juro, one of my interpreters, says that Yedo contains more than a million of houses, and that the city is twenty-four Japanese ri in circumference. This is more than fifty-eight miles, English measure. In my walk to-day I visited a cove lying to the south of Shimoda, but quite secluded on a pretty cove [sic]. In front of a decayed old temple (*mia*), I found two statues bearing marks of a higher antiquity than anything I had seen in Japan.

The figures represent a short, thickset human being, the lobes of the ears long and resting on the shoulders. Most of the features were so much obliterated by time, that it was difficult to determine whether they were taken from Japanese, Chinese or Indian types. But the most singular thing about them was that they were shadowed by two cobras capello,—after the same manner that Siva is so often represented in India. The tale runs in India that one day Siva was about perishing from excessive heat, no shelter or shade being obtainable; on a sudden, he felt a sense of grateful coolness and a shadow was spread over him. On looking around he discovered that two enormous cobras were standing erect behind him; and, having spread or inflated their hoods to the greatest possible extent, they approached their heads together and then hung over him. For this benevolent act the cobra became sacred to Siva and his followers to this day. But no trace of any such worship can be found in Japan, nor is the serpent known here.

The Japanese imperial flag is white, black and white in horizontal stripes of equal width.

The *national* flag of Japan is an orange sun (without rays) on a white field.

Thursday, October 30, 1856. This will be remembered hereafter as an important day in the history of Japan. The laws forbidding the Imperial Governor of a city to visit any foreigner at his residence is to-day to be broken, and I am to receive the two Governors, with the Vice-Governor, in a friendly and informal way.

They arrived about noon with a large suite, but only

four came into my private apartments with the two Governors and Vice-Governor. These Governors are of the highest rank of any men in Japan after the vassal Princes, being *no-Kami,—i. e.,* men so learned that nothing can be taught them, and so sublimated in goodness that they rank in name—*Kami*—with the demi-gods or saints of Japan. This word—*Kami*—has a variety of meanings,—*e. g.,* demi-god, noble, paper and hair.

Moriama was the interpreter on the occasion.

The Governors were very anxious on the subject of coast surveys, and inquired where Lieutenant Rodgers[315] was, whether he would return here to survey; whether the American Government had given orders for any new expedition to survey the coasts, etc., and if I knew what the English intended doing in the matter of surveys, etc., etc.

I told them that Lieutenant Rodgers had returned to the United States, and that I did not know of any intended expedition here for a similar purpose, and that the English had no such squadron out here at present. They wished me to promise to order off any vessels that might come here for such a purpose, but I told them that would be out of my power. I then informed them that the United States Government and all the other governments of the world expended large sums in sur-

---

[315]Lieutenant John Rodgers, who was in command of the United States Surveying Expedition to the North Pacific Ocean, consisting of the U.S.S. *Vincennes,* the *Fenimore Cooper,* and the steamer *Hancock.* He was Midshipman, Apr. 18, 1828; Passed Midshipman, June 14, 1834; Lieutenant, Jan. 28, 1840; Commander, Sept. 14, 1855; Captain, July 16, 1862; Commodore, June 17, 1863; Rear-Admiral, Dec. 31, 1869; died May 5, 1882. (Edward W. Callahan, *List of Officers of the Navy of the United States;* T. H. S. Hamersly, *General Register;* and Griffis, *Townsend Harris,* p. 81, note.)

veying their coasts and harbors, and that those surveys were published with charts so that any nation in the world could have them; that the whole world was surveyed except Japan; that these surveys made many books, and that all shipmasters purchased these books (for they were sold freely to all) before they went on any voyage to a part of the world that was new to them; that all this was done for the security of ships, it being the great object of all civilized nations to encourage commerce, which next to agriculture was the great spring of prosperity of nations; that, for the same reasons, both America and England (as well as other nations) had hundreds of lighthouses on their coasts, and the channels leading into their harbors were carefully marked out with buoys, etc., etc. All of this astonished them much, and appeared to remove some of their anxiety, although at the beginning they told me that it was a matter of life and death to them, as they must perform the *hara-kiri,* or "happy dispatch" (suicide), if the surveys went on.

Moriama has been fasting for some fifty days on this account, but he was so much consoled by what I said that he ate flesh most heartily. He thanked me warmly for my friendly deportment towards them, and got down on his knees and prayed fervently for my welfare. My company partook of my refreshments (which were prepared in our manner) without any hesitation, and by their eating showed their approval. They drank punch, brandy, whiskey, cherry bounce, champagne and cordials, but the punch and champagne were their favorite drinks.

The last Governor warmed entirely and showed himself (like the other Japanese) of a most genial temper. They did not eat or drink to excess in any respect, and their conduct during the whole visit was that of well-bred persons. I made the second Governor a present of a Colt's pistol of five discharges, with which he was much pleased. After staying about four hours they took their leave with abundant thanks for my hospitality. This P. M. they brought me a leg of *real venison*. It is excellent, tender, juicy and well flavored.

Tuesday, November 4, 1856. Yesterday it rained steadily all day and only cleared up at daylight this morning. At eight A. M. we had an earthquake. It seemed like a heavy blow, which shook the house as though some ponderous thing had fallen, and was accompanied with a corresponding sound. Two or three light vibrations followed the great shock. The weather was clear and calm, and the adjacent volcano on Oho Sima did not show any increased action.

The sound and vibrations seemed to come from the S. E. and proceed towards the N. W. Got my stove in order. It is a poor affair; it will not draw. The plates warped and cracked the first time a fire was kindled, although only a handful of charcoal was put in. I have now a smoky house, but luckily no scolding wife.[316] The stove appears to be a patent one and made by Abbott & Lawrence of Philadelphia. So miserable is it that bituminous coals go out even when the blower is up. Let

---

[316]See *Proverbs*, 10:26; 21:9 and 19. It may be added that Townsend Harris never married.

me avoid all the works of Abbott & Lawrence as I would those of the evil one. A fine wild boar brought to me to-day. I take the saddle. It is the best flesh meat in the world!!

Wednesday, November 5, 1856. A lovely day, superior to the American Indian summer, the sky clear and blue and the air balmy. At midday the thermometer stands in the shade at 62° to 65°. During the month of October the average temperature taken at eight A. M., noon, four P. M. and ten P. M. was as follows: mean, 64 35/100; highest, 77°; lowest, 51°. The weather was as follows:

Heavy rain	three days
Showery	five "
Cloudy	five "
Fine	eighteen

Thirty-one days.

Walked to-day about five miles up the Valley of Shimoda and nearly all the way by the banks of Shimoda River, or creek, as we would call it in America. I have no doubt from the size of the stream that the Valley must continue some fifteen or twenty miles further. The scenery is of the same character as heretofore described in my previous walks. The hamlets are almost continuous. You are never out of sight of a temple. The people are now in the middle of the rice harvest; and, except the rice fields, the ground is covered with green crops. Most of the deciduous trees have lost their leaves, but many of them are putting forth new ones.

257

I saw to-day some specimens of artemisia, but not equal to those of China. I do not see here any specimens of flower gardens of which so much has been written by Kaempfer and others. But this is a poor place, where all are poor and have enough to do to live without looking to the ornamental.

But they live comfortably, are well fed according to their wants, and are abundantly clad, and their houses are clean, dry, and comfortable.

In no part of the world are the *laboring* classes better off than at Shimoda.

Visited a hot sulphur spring about three miles from Shimoda. A tank about twelve feet square, paved and lined with stone, contains the water which bubbles out between the interstices of the stone. The water is beautifully clear, about three feet deep, and is about $150°$ Fahrenheit in temperature. Some few bubbles of gas arise to the surface. The whole tank is covered with a building, and is a favorite bath for the Shimodeans. No charge is made for its use. It is held in high repute for its medical properties in cutaneous and rheumatic affections. Rice is cleaned from the straw by a machine exactly like the *hetchel* used for cleaning flax with us. This is done by the women and children. They take a small number of rice straws (not over thirty), draw them through the iron teeth which stand upright on a board. They are six inches long and they are usually some twelve in number. The straw is drawn once or twice through these iron teeth, which effectually strips every grain of paddy from the straw.

The process is a slow one, but the straw is of more value than time; and, as the former is uninjured by this process, it is not likely the Japanese would adopt a more rapid process, if the straw would be injured thereby.

Thursday, November 6, 1856. The thermometer at eight A. M. stood at 50°, being the lowest point it has reached as yet.

I still continue my cold baths, much to the amazement of the Japanese.

Walked to-day around the point "Vandalia" to Suzaki, thence over the hills to Satora and home. Lovely weather. Saw many blossoms on the cherry trees. Saw some fine specimens of camphor trees. They grow wild about the hills of Shimoda.

Friday, November 7, 1856. Two hours of dirty work with my wretched stove. Happily I cannot make it worse by any experiments I may try with it, and some lucky hit may improve it.

Went in a boat to a sand beach about three miles south from Shimoda, where I landed, and then had a fine ramble over the hills and through the valleys. What a field for an artist! Every half mile gives a new view well worth drawing. The weather is balmy, clear and pleasant.

As usual the hamlets are most numerous in every valley or cove along the shore. Saw a village called Kisami or "the place of assured assistance." Saw some new varieties of artemisia. The Japanese name of this flower is *keraye.*

The sandstone is curiously hollowed out by the action

of the water in every place around here, and the Japanese have aided nature by cutting out stones for use from these places; thus, in the course of time, curious grottoes, caves or chapels are created,—and they are sometimes used as *mias* or small temples, at others as receptacles for fuel, boat gear, etc., etc. The general formation is either lava, sandstone, or else a conglomerate or pudding stone, composed of the débris of various rock, lava, sand and alumine,—the whole cemented so as to form a compact stone. It is the contents of craters which have been vomited forth by the projectile force of steam, gas or whatever composes that terrible force in volcanoes.

Saturday, November 9, 1856.[317] The Russian Corvette *Olivuzza,* Commodore Possiet and Commander Korsacoff.[318] She brought with her a schooner built by the Russians at the River Amur for the Japanese, and is a present, as I understand.[319] The schooner is built on the same lines as the one before seen by me, and makes an aggregate of *five* schooners (all on the same model) now owned by the Japanese.

Commodore Possiet is the bearer of the Ratified Treaty made with Japan and will probably remain here

[317]The correct date is Saturday, Nov. 8, 1856.

[318]Townsend Harris was very careless in the spelling of proper names, even in the case of Mr. Heusken, his own private secretary. The names of the two Russian officers were Captain Constantine Possiet (of the *Olivuzza*) and Captain W. Rimsky Korsacoff—captains of the first and the second rank in the Imperial Navy, respectively.

[319]Similarly, in commemoration of the Treaty between Great Britain and Japan (concluded Thursday, Aug. 26, 1858), Lord Elgin, in the name of Queen Victoria, presented the Tycoon with a charming little screw yacht of 318 tons and mounting six guns, called the *Emperor.* The Japanese later renamed her the *Dragon.*

some weeks.[320] I went on board the corvette soon after she anchored, and was much pleased with the officers. The corvette is a poor affair, old in age and older in model. She is armed with old-fashioned carronades, and looks to me like one of the old ships of the Russian American Company,[321] although she now wears the imperial flag. I was *not* saluted by the corvette. I also went on board the schooner. She has a pretty cabin, very handsomely furnished; has oilcloth on the floor, tables of fine woods, and the hangings are of mazarine blue velvet.

She is commanded by Lieutenant Kolaxaltsoff. I presume she is intended as a present on the exchange of ratifications.

---

[320]The Treaty between Russia and Japan had been signed at Shimoda by Admiral Poutiatine, on Feb. 7, 1855 (Russian style: Jan. 26th; Japanese style: 21st day, 12th month, 1st year of Ansei). Ratifications were exchanged at Shimoda on Dec. 7, 1856. For the French text of this Treaty and of the Explanatory Articles accompanying it, see John Harrington Gubbins, *The Progress of Japan*, pp. 235–39.

While Admiral Poutiatine was negotiating the Russian Treaty early in 1855, Commander H. A. Adams of the *Powhatan* (who had returned from the United States with the ratified Perry Treaty) was likewise negotiating with the Japanese authorities, and the Ratifications of the Perry Treaty (concluded Mar. 31, 1854) were exchanged at Shimoda on Feb. 21, 1855—exactly two weeks after Japan had concluded the Treaty with Russia. The Shogunate, therefore, was fast accumulating a great deal of valuable experience in dealing with foreign diplomats. These earlier dealings, indeed, constituted a preliminary course to the thorough-going and long-continued instruction they were about to receive over a series of years from the American Townsend Harris—the first representative of any country to be accredited to the Island Empire.

[321]This is a reference to the Russian American Fur Company, established in the reign of Catherine II. All the islands lying between Kamchatka and the then Russian part of the Northwest Coast of America were granted to them in perpetuity. The principal depot of the Company was Alexandria (on Kodiak Island), so named after Alexander I, who had greatly extended the privileges of the Company and had declared himself their immediate patron.

Many of the early contacts between Japan and Russia are linked with the names of Resanoff, Chwostoff, Davidoff, etc., and with this Company's pursuit of the fur trade; similarly, our own early contacts with Japan were due to the American seaman's pursuit of the whale.

Commodore Possiet promised me a copy of the Russian Treaty with Japan,[322] and, in return, I am to give him the American and [the] Dutch Treaties with Japan, and the Treaty with Siam which I made when at Bangkok.[323]

The Japanese have excellent provisions for *watching* fire, although the appliances for extinguishing it are not so good. In every street of length, there is a small building occupied by the fire police, who perambulate the streets in turn from dark to daylight, and they warn the people to be cautious about fire by striking two pieces of bamboo or some resonant wood together; and, on hearing this noise, all are reminded to be careful. Doeff[324] says that once, when he was in Yedo, a fire broke out which burned over ground 9 miles long by 1½ miles wide, equal to 13½ square miles, equal to 8,640 acres

[322]Which Townsend Harris received on Nov. 11th.

[323]The American Treaty referred to was the one concluded by Commodore Perry on Friday, Mar. 31, 1854.
The American Treaty with Siam was concluded by Townsend Harris at Bangkok on Thursday, May 29, 1856.
At the time Townsend Harris penned these words, there were only two agreements between The Netherlands and Japan:

1) A preliminary Convention, concluded by Jan Hendrik Donker Curtius, and signed at Nagasaki on Nov. 9, 1855. (English Text in J. H. Gubbins, *The Progress of Japan*, pp. 245–50; some good notes and remarks, in J. M. Tronson, *Personal Narrative of a Voyage to Japan*, etc., pp. 47–51.)

2) A Treaty of Commerce, likewise signed at Nagasaki, on Jan. 30, 1856 (Gubbins, *op. cit.*, pp. 250–55).

[324]Hendrik Doeff, Warehouse Master and Superintendent (*Opperhoofd*) at different times, from 1799 to 1817, of the Dutch Factory on the Island of Deshima, in the Harbor of Nagasaki. His memoirs were published under the title: *Herinneringen vit Japan*, Haarlem, 1835, 4to.
The great fire at Yedo here referred to and described by Doeff broke out on Apr. 22, 1806, at 10 A. M.: Charles MacFarlane, *Japan*, p. 349; Richard Hildreth, *Japan and the Japanese*, pp. 447, 451–52; *Quarterly Review*, July, 1836 (vol. 56), p. 420.

American measure. In American cities, where the lots are larger than in Japan, this extent of ground, after taking out the streets, would give the enormous aggregate of 1,038,800 building lots! (120 lots to the acre.) Now, supposing only half the number of lots were built on and allowing only 5 persons to each building, it would give the astounding number of 2,597,000 persons who were rendered houseless by this fire.

All the accounts I can gather of the extent and population of Yedo are so extravagant that I cannot give them credence. The Government of Japan carefully conceals all the statistics of population, agriculture, commerce, manufactures, and of the military. I am, however, convinced that what is called Yedo covers, or rather includes, a greater extent of ground in its *enceinte* than any city of the world; but whether this space is all built on or not I cannot decide.

Monday, November 10, 1856. The Russian officers, —Captain of the First Rank Possiet (he is not Commodore), Captain of the Second Rank Korsacoff, and Lieutenant Kolaxaltsoff,—I find them very agreeable persons and very friendly.

We had much conversation about Japanese affairs, but nothing worthy of particular note except that the ratification of the American Treaty was *not signed* by the Ziogoon, or, as we [call] him, the Emperor, but by the Chief of the Government. The ratification stated, in terms, that it was signed by the Chief by the express order of the Ziogoon.

I learn that the Ziogoon has written two letters to the

King of Holland, and Captain Possiet informs me that within the last eighteen months the Japanese officials have written nearly fifty letters to the Russians.

The Captain promises to loan me a barometer and some other instruments until mine arrive from Hongkong, and I am to turn them over to the Russian Consul who is expected to arrive here next spring. I am told the Russian Consul for Japan speaks English very well, and that he is very friendly to the Americans. I am inclined to think he will bring a family with him.

After the foregoing, I had a visit from three of the young gentlemen of the ship. I am very much pleased with them; their dress was neat, and their address superior.

Tuesday, November 11, 1856. Captains Possiet and Korsacoff, the Lieutenant commanding the schooner, and three other young officers dined with me to-day. Previous to this I had a visit from two of the young officers. They spoke French very well. I never passed a more agreeable evening. The Russians behaved like polished men of the world, and at my table they did not merit the charge so often brought against them of being hard drinkers. They ate with good appetites (and my dinner was both good and abundant), and took their wine in moderation. I do think the same number of American or English officers would have drunk twice the quantity of wine the Russians did. Captain Possiet informed me that the Vice-Governor told him that he wished him not to pay any money at present, for that the American Consul General had made a demand on the

Government to have a just value put on the dollar, and that they expected a favorable answer in a few days.

Captain Possiet brought me a copy of the Russian Treaty with Japan, which I have had translated from the Dutch (he gave me a Dutch translation), and shall send it to the Secretary of State.

My company left me at an early hour, say half-past nine, and went on board. It was a glorious night, with a bright moon and clear, blue sky.

Wednesday, November 12, 1856. I was starting from my house to visit the Russians, when the sound of the corvette's guns told me that the Governors of Shimoda were visiting the ship. I therefore went over to the Goyoshi which is opened in a temple just behind Rioshen, and examined the wares they have opened for the Russians. I saw some new things, and a greater quantity of articles with the fine rattan work.

I told them they would do well to have some bronze articles, some fine porcelain, and some of their prettiest toys against the arrival of another American ship, as those things would be liked by the officers.

I went on board the corvette a little after four P. M. (the Japanese having previously left). Captain Possiet kindly offered me one of the boats of the *Diana* as a present. I thanked him for his kind offer, but the boats are all too heavy for my use, as none of them pulls less than six oars. I told the two Captains my washman should wash their linen for them, if they would send it on shore, as the Japanese do not know how to wash. I also said that I was sorry I could not offer the same compliment to all of the officers, but my washman had no assistance.

Captain Possiet is to send men on shore to set up the rigging and stays of my flagstaff in the morning. He also promises me some potatoes and spirits of turpentine, neither of which is to be had in Shimoda.

Captain Possiet said the Japanese had again to-day referred to the money question, and repeated that they soon expected a favorable answer.

The Japanese all say that their country must sooner or later [be] opened to foreign commerce, and that they are anxious to have the period arrive.

Thursday, November 13, 1856. The Russians came on shore this morning early to arrange my flagstaff. The Captain Possiet made me a visit quite alone. He desires that our visits should be without ceremony, and as between friends; that I should make myself at home with him, and he will do the same with me. All this I was quite willing to accede to. We had much conversation about the harbor of Shimoda, its insecurity, its small size, the incapacity of Shimoda to furnish supplies even to one ship-of-war, and the total absence of a commercial population. We agreed on the absolute necessity of an exchange of Shimoda for another port.

Captain Possiet gave me a copy of a letter he wrote, by order of Admiral Poutiatine, after the wreck of the *Diana* frigate,[325] on the subject of the harbor of Shimoda, to the Japanese authorities.

---

[325]The *Diana* was the Russian frigate in which Admiral Poutiatine had come to Shimoda to negotiate his Treaty with Japan (concluded Feb. 7, 1855; see above).

The Western Pacific Ocean, at the end of 1854, was the scene of tremendous

Captain Possiet informs me that, had the *Diana* not met with her misfortune, she would have examined a number of harbors on the east coast of Japan, and he is of opinion that an exchange would have been made of Shimoda for some more eligible place. The Russian

disturbances—from Japan to the Bonin Islands (see the letter by Messrs. Reed and Dougherty to the editor of the San Francisco *Herald*, reprinted in the New York *Herald* of Oct. 15, 1855, p. 1, coll. 5–6).

The Harbor of Shimoda was visited by a terrible storm which lasted from Dec. 13 to Dec. 18, 1854, and which left the *Diana* almost a complete wreck. The even worse earthquake which shook Japan on Dec. 23, 1854 (a week later) hopelessly crippled not only the *Diana*, but the entire village of Shimoda and its harbor, rendering the latter absolutely unfit as an anchorage. (For a splendid description of this storm, see Captain Sherard Osborn, *A Cruise in Japanese Waters*, 2nd ed., pp. 107–11; David Murray, *The Story of Japan*, p. 8, note 3; and *Kinsé Shiriaku*—translated by Sir E. M. Satow, ed. 1873—p. 51. The latest description of this storm and earthquake written prior to Townsend Harris's arrival at Shimoda, is by the American Commander H. A. Adams, in Perry's *Narrative*, 33–2, S. Ex. Doc., no. 79, vol. 2—in Serial no. 770—p. 210.)

A few references to the subsequent fortune of these shipwrecked Russians give a clear insight into the dangers of travel in those days. After the storm, the *Diana* foundered at sea as she was being towed around to Toda (or Hey-da) Bay for repairs (Satow, *Cambridge Modern History*, vol. 11, p. 830). The Japanese of Shimoda immediately gave their willing aid to the Russians in building a new ship, the *Heda*, in which the latter planned to return to Russia (Mechnikov, *L'Empire Japonais*, vol. 4, p. 649).

In the meantime, our enterprising Americans, Messrs. Reed and Dougherty, had, immediately upon hearing of the conclusion of the Perry Treaty, chartered the schooner *Caroline E. Foote,* and had loaded her with all manner of ship chandlery, intending to carry full supplies for the American whale ships which (they thought) would immediately flock to, and pass the winter at, the splendid port of Hakodate—the opening of which was provided for in the Perry Treaty. The *C. E. Foote* sailed from Honolulu on February 13, 1855, and arrived at Shimoda on March 15th. There they found the shipwrecked Admiral Poutiatine, Captain Possiet, and the rest of the officers and crew of the *Diana*. The date for the opening of Hakodate was still in the future; and so, after some negotiations, the cargo was landed; and the *Foote,* having been chartered to the Russians, sailed for Petropaulowski with Admiral Poutiatine and other officers and men of the crew. (New York *Herald,* morning ed., Monday, Oct. 15, 1855, p. 1.)

Later, the brig *Greta* (Mr. Lühdorf, supercargo), of the Bremen Free State, visited Shimoda, and the rest of the officers and men of the *Diana* sailed away in her. On Aug. 1, 1855 (during the Crimean War, that is to say), they were captured by the English man-of-war *Barracouta* when near their destination, and were finally taken to Ayan, in Siberia, which had recently been taken by the English from the Russians. (J. M. Tronson, *Personal Narrative of a Voyage to Japan*, etc., pp. 139–43, 146–47, 227; and Henry Arthur Tilley, *Japan, the Amoor and the Pacific*, p. 222.)

sailors finished work on my flagstaff about four P. M., when they left. I gave them a dinner, with plenty of brandy and tea, and I gave one dollar to each of the five men who were employed in the work.[326]

This evening Captain Possiet sent me a bag of Hakodate potatoes, about one picul in weight. A great addition to my housekeeping.

Friday, November 14, 1856. I dined with Mr. Heusken on board the Corvette *Olivuzza*.[327] Captain Possiet gave me a salute of thirteen guns, although by the rules of the Russian service a consul general is saluted with eleven guns. Captain Possiet told me that he gave me thirteen guns so that I should not receive less than he gave the Japanese Governor of Shimoda.

I passed a very agreeable evening. The more I see of the Russian officers the more I am pleased with them. They are polished in manner and exceedingly well informed. There is scarcely one of them that does not speak two or more languages.

They speak in high terms of French generals and soldiers. They say the first have skill equal to any in the world, and the last are unsurpassed in military courage and enthusiasm. The English, on the contrary, they put directly opposite: generals without skill, and men without one of the prerequisites of a soldier, except mere bulldog courage; that to deprive an English army

---

[326]*L. B.*, vol. 1, p. 135: "Paid to 5 Russian sailors for setting up flagstaff, $5." (This memorandum is, however, dated Nov. 15th.)

[327]Townsend Harris must have enjoyed this dinner heartily; for, writing to Commodore Possiet the next day, he complained of a headache caused by his overeating (*L. B.*, vol. 1, p. 129).

MONUMENT DEDICATED TO THE MEMORY OF TOWNSEND HARRIS

This monument was erected in the courtyard of the Gyokusen-ji, near Shimoda,—the home of the first American accredited representative to Japan. It was unveiled on Saturday, October 1, 1927. The front of the monument bears the English text; the back, the Japanese text. The *Journal* entry carved on the monument is that for September 4, 1856, commemorating the hoisting of the first consular flag ever seen in Japan.

of its full supply of food and comfortable quarters is to demoralize it; that an English soldier dreads an attack on his belly more than a blow aimed at his head. A current remark at Sebastopol during the siege was that A or B had been out on so many occasions of sorties; the question was instantly asked against which force? If against the English, the querist would shrug his shoulders and say, "That was nothing"; but if against the French, he would say, "Oh! then [he] had something to do."

Constant conversations are held by Captain Possiet with the Japanese on the subject of finally and fully opening Japan to the commerce of the world. All agree that it is only a question of time, and Moriama Yenosky[328] goes so far as to place it less than three years distant.

All these things will help to prepare the way for me in my attempt to make a treaty which shall at once open Japan (at different dates for different ports) to our commerce.

I left the ship about eight P. M.; a bright moon shining; and a fresh breeze from the N. E. brought the thermometer down to 50° Fahrenheit.

Saturday, November 15, 1856. Wrote a chit to Captain Possiet sending him a few pounds of coffee, a Siamese sarong, and specimens of the three silver

---

[328]The name of this historic interpreter is variously spelled. William S. Lewis and Naojiro Murakami, in their very beautiful and scholarly work, *Ranald MacDonald* (publ. by The Eastern Washington State Historical Society, Spokane, Wash., 1923), use both *Moriyama Einosuke* and *Murayama Yeanoske*.

coins of Siam which are circulated in that country.[329] I also sent a set of coins to Captain Korsacoff,—*viz.*, one tical, one salung, one fuang.

I am glad to find anything I can present to the Russians as a small return for their favors to me.

In the afternoon, was visited by Captain Korsacoff and the surgeon of the corvette. This afternoon the Japanese brought me two small dogs, which are very fine ones.[330] They have the round, bullet-shaped head, short nose and large protuberant eyes of "King Charles spaniels," but the ears are small and short, and the hair on them is also short, otherwise they resemble those dogs closely, and I do not doubt they are the original stock from which those spaniels were bred.

Sunday, November 16, 1856. I regularly read the service of the Protestant Episcopal Church of the United States every Sunday.[331] I am probably the first

---

[329]*L. B.*, vol. i, pp. 129–30, which, in addition to the information given in the *Journal*, also thanks the Commodore for his hospitality on board the *Olivuzza* the night before.

While these social pleasantries were going on at Shimoda, the British were having trouble with Yeh, the Chinese Commissioner at Canton. Also the United States Squadron was fired upon (Nov. 15, 1856), and in the following days Commodore James Armstrong silenced the Barrier Forts on the river between Whampoa and Canton. (The best and most minute description of the American action on this occasion is the very long letter—still unpublished—to Townsend Harris by Captain H. H. Bell, of the U.S.S. *San Jacinto*: *L. & P.*, vol. i, no. 54.)

[330]These dogs Townsend Harris forthwith named *Yedo* and *Miako*, in honor of the two capitals of Japan—that of the Shogun and that of the Emperor, respectively. These names, as well as a longer description of the dogs themselves, are given by Townsend Harris in a letter to Miss Drinker: see the Janvier *Letters and Papers*, folder 2, letter no. 1, in the Manuscripts Division of the New York Public Library.

[331]The writer has seen the Prayer Book used by Townsend Harris while in Japan. It has been rebound in red morocco. On one of the flyleaves in the front of the book, and on the left-hand side, is written "Townsend Harris, New York," in Townsend Harris's own handwriting. On the same page, and

resident of Japan who ever used that service. How long will it be before that same service will be used in Japan in consecrated churches?

It is to me one of the pregnant facts that grow up daily under my observation, and which are the natural result of my residence here in a *protected* capacity.

The Japanese brought me this evening the finest specimen of a male golden pheasant I ever saw. I shall measure it to-morrow. Beak to end of tail feathers, forty-four inches; tail, thirty inches; wings from tip to tip (across body), twenty-six inches.[332]

Monday, November 17, 1856. The Japanese brought me a very extraordinary production. It is a stone about six inches by three inches of irregular form, having some six pipes standing perpendicularly on it, somewhat like a coral formation, and out of these pipes spring bunches of what appear stiff horsehair, or rather like strong spun glass. This substance is of a snowy whiteness, is elastic and quite strong. I supposed at first it was artificial; but, on examination, I found it to be natural.

On putting the fibers into the flame of a candle, they fly into minute pieces with some little noise. The pieces sparkle to the eye, no smell accompanies the burning;

---

underneath the above, there is another entry, stating that the book was the property of Mrs. Helen Kearny Harris Vreeland, grandniece of Townsend Harris. This precious Prayer Book of the man who (to use his own words) was "probably the first resident of Japan who ever used that service" was (in 1927) in the possession of Mrs. Henry Devereux Whiton (née Gwendolen Whiton Harris), of Glen Cove, Long Island.

[332] This pheasant was destined to be the *pièce de résistance* at the dinner which Townsend Harris gave to Commodore Possiet and his officers on the night of Wednesday, Nov. 19th (*L. B.*, vol. i, p. 131).

the remainder is hard, gritty and quite like minute particles of lime. The Japanese name for it is *hoszuki,*—horsehair shell.

I should have noted before that the fibers are from twelve to eighteen inches in length, and the sockets from which the bunches spring are some five inches high; but the Japanese tell me that when taken out of the sea the tube covers *all* the fiber, except about one inch, and that they remove a part of it to show the beauty of the fiber. I am inclined to think this an entirely new marine production. I *know* it is a very beautiful one. The Japanese say it is found in the Bay of Yedo near Uragawa, but I place but little reliance on their statements.

The Governor has sent special word to the village of Satora that all should go to work to procure me specimens of the marsupial fish, which is said to be found there.[333]

Tuesday, November 18, 1856. I wrote to the Governor yesterday urging a reply to my letters on the subject of the currency.[334] To-day the Vice-Governor, a high official, and my old friend Moriama Yenosky, came to visit me. They apologized for their long ab-

---

[333] On this day, Townsend Harris also wrote the following letters:

1) To Commodore Possiet, inviting him, Captain Korsacoff, and four other officers (to include the surgeon) to dinner on the night of the 19th, at 6 P. M. (*L. B.,* vol. 1, p. 131);

2) Two letters to Secretary William L. Marcy, both on financial matters (*L. B.,* vol. 1, p. 156, Dispatch No. 17; and *ib.,* pp. 155-56, Dispatch No. 18).

[334] *L. B.,* vol. 1, pp. 130-31, in which Townsend Harris emphasizes the fact that his former two letters on the currency question (dated Sept. 25th and Oct. 9th) are still unanswered; and, considering the time elapsed, he hopes that he may soon be in a position to inform his Government of the favorable settlement of this vexed question.

sence saying the arrival of the Russians had kept them much occupied, etc., etc. They brought me a cage containing six pretty tame pigeons, a present from the Governor, and they told me that he had written to Yedo expressly for them, as they are scarce in Japan.

I knew the visit of ceremony and the present were all a pretence, and that something else was behind, and a short time brought it out.

They (as if casually) said my letter of yesterday to the Governor had been at once forwarded to Yedo by a "Special Post"; and that, as soon as an answer was received, the Governor would let me know it. I told them I was happy to see them at all times, but I could not consent to receive verbal answers to, or notices of, my written communications. I told them that I knew that the Ziogoon had written at least two letters to the King of Holland; that the high officers of Japan had written more than thirty letters to the Russians, within the last two years; and that numerous letters had been written also to Captain Fabius of the Dutch Steam Frigate *Medusa* when he was here.[335]

That I could not consent to be treated with less formality than they had shown to the Russians and Dutch, and therefore I must insist on written answers to my letters.

Wednesday, November 19, 1856. Commodore Possiet, his First Lieutenant, Surgeon and two junior officers dined with me. Captain Korsacoff could not come, as both he and the First Lieutenant cannot both

---

[335]See above, entry for Oct 1, 1856.

leave the ship at the same time. I had a nice dinner, and the party was a very pleasant one. The Commodore says that the Japanese only give 1,500 seni among themselves for the *ichibu,* while they allow 1,600 to foreigners. The Russian ruble is taken by them at 1,200 seni—the same ratio as the dollar at 1,600.

Thursday, November 20, 1856. The Russians send me two barometers, but they are only marked for 730 millimeters, a little over twenty-eight inches, consequently of no use except when the height of mountains is to be measured.

The Commodore sends me as a present a new kind of thermometer—on the principle of the expansion and contraction of metals by heat and cold. It is in the form of a large sized watch, and both back and front are covered with a thick plate of glass. The metal acts on the small end of a quadrant, fixed on a pivot, and the periphery is cut into ratchet teeth which work a cogwheel, moving a needle indicator. It is graduated for Reaumur, Centigrade and Fahrenheit. It is one of the prettiest things of the kind I ever saw. Made by Richter at St. Petersburg. I am informed that the horsehair shell is only found in *detachea tubes.* These the Japanese fasten together in clusters on a stone so naturally that it is almost impossible to detect it on a close examination.

Friday, November 21, 1856. Busy in writing letters to go by the corvette.[336] Captain Korsacoff visited me.

[336] Some of the letters bearing the date of the 21st were:

1) *L. B.,* vol. 1, pp. 132–33, to Commodore Possiet, returning thanks for the thermometer and the two barometers received the day before;

Wants me to cash some bills for them. This I cannot do, but offer to lend him $1,000 to be returned at Hongkong on the corvette's reaching that place, to my agents Armstrong & Lawrence.

The Japanese sent me yesterday some singing birds which I asked for about the 10th of September—so long does it take them to determine whether any new demand of mine shall be granted or refused. The birds are a pair of canaries, of course these are exotic birds, although they now breed them in Japan; a pair of bullfinches; a pair of birds much like a small sparrow in form, but the tail is very short, plumage a mixture of yellow, green and black; and a curious bird called the mountain bird. Its plumage is very pretty, has a black hood, a mask and ruff of tawny, wings a bright steel and black, breast a dull red, or rather Spanish brown. Its bill is long and sharply pointed. It feeds on hard seed, and in breaking the shell it makes a constant noise like the hammering of a woodpecker. As the cages are too small I ordered new ones made. To-day I am told that three of the four cages wanted must be procured from Yedo, as they cannot be made in Shimoda. I ordered some four quires of a soft cheap paper for waste, blotting, etc., etc., and to-day I am told that the

2) L. B., ib., p. 134, to Armstrong & Lawrence at Hongkong, praising the climate of Shimoda and giving them an order for household supplies and sundries (for the list of these, cf., ib., pp. 189–90) ;

3) And, most important of all, a very long letter to Catharine Ann Drinker, who many years later married Mr. Thomas Allibone Janvier. In this letter Townsend Harris describes the climate, the geography, and the people of Shimoda, and gives lengthy extracts from his own Journal. Above all, he describes his house—the first American Consulate in Japan. (See the Janvier Letters and Papers, folder 2, letter no. 1, New York Public Library, Manuscripts Division.)

paper must be ordered from Yedo, as the quantity desired cannot be had in Shimoda! ! !

Whether this is an untruth, or that the place is so deplorably anti-commercial that four quires of common paper cannot be furnished, I cannot say. Nor can I see any object they have in telling a falsehood about it, as it is to be furnished.

Saturday, November 22, 1856. The Russians have presented to the Japanese all the guns that were on board the Frigate *Diana*. They consist of:

    18 short 24-pounders
    30 long 24-pounders
     4 Paixhan 68-pounders, shell guns.

The Russians are assisting the Japanese in getting up all the fittings necessary for mounting the guns properly, such as screws, quoins, etc., etc., all of which were lost when the *Diana* sank.[337]

Monday, November 24, 1856. The Goyoshi people came to inform me that my cook and tailor went to the apothecaries' shops in Shimoda yesterday, and asked for opium, and were told they had none; but, the Chinese characters being on the drawers, they discovered it and demanded it in my name and with a show of violence. They took the whole they found in two shops, which was all the opium there was in Shimoda. They said to me that opium was only used as a medicine,

---

[337]On this day, Townsend Harris wrote:
1) *L. B.,* vol. 1, p. 133, to Mrs. Drinker, at Macao, introducing Commodore Possiet, who will shortly visit that city on his way back to Russia;
2) *L. B., ib.,* p. 134, to Mr. Patrick Stewart, at Macao, likewise introducing the Commodore.

and that it was unjust that two men should have the whole of it, particularly as it was not wanted for medical purposes. They respectfully asked that I would order the Chinese to restore the greater part of it. I gave orders that the whole should be taken from them. Mr. Heusken got a lump of some six ounces from the tailor, but the cook had dissolved his in water to refine it in the Chinese way, so as to make it fit for smoking, and refused to give it up. I went to him myself; he was very surly, and after some time brought me a dish containing a small quantity of sediment and water. I demanded the filtered liquid, and it was not until I had given him his choice between a prison and the surrender of the drug that he gave it up. The lump was restored to the Japanese, but they said they could do nothing with the solution, so that was *thrown away*. I directed the officers to tell the shopkeepers that my people were not to be supplied with opium, saki, or any kind of intoxicating beverage.

Tuesday, November 25, 1856. Evacuation day in New York! What recollections of my "soldier life" this day brings up! My marching up and down Broadway, Bowery, Hudson Street, Greenwich Street—to the Battery, to the Park, and there firing off "real guns," as Mr. Mantilini said. Commodore Possiet visits me. He took a long walk on Friday, twelve miles to the village of Matsusaki on the bay to the west of Yedo Bay, and he remained there all night. He speaks in such high terms of the beauty of the road that I shall take the same walk, as soon as the Russians leave here. He

277

had a message from the Governor on Monday, requesting him to give orders that none of the officers should sleep on shore. The Commodore told them that he would give orders to his officers that if any of them went to a greater distance than seven ri, then they must not sleep there, but that, within the distance of seven ri, he claimed the right for himself and all other Russians to sleep on shore as often as it suited their convenience.[338]

To-day finish a letter of fifteen sheets to my friend General Wetmore.[339] The Japanese bring my breeding cage for my canary birds.[340]

Wednesday, November 26, 1856. I have taken a violent cold; have pains in my head, bones; and some little fever. Take some Brandreth's pills, and diet.

I do not give up to it, but employ myself in writing letters to go by the *Olivuzza.*

---

[338]Art. V of Perry's Treaty (concluded Mar. 31, 1854) for the first time established the principle that shipwrecked men and other citizens of the United States "shall be free at Shimoda to go where they please within the limits of seven Japanese miles (or ri) from a small island in the harbor of Shimoda marked on the accompanying chart hereto appended."

[339]In the entry for Dec. 10, 1856, Townsend Harris gives the date of this letter as Dec. 9, 1856. Commodore Possiet's delay made it possible for Townsend Harris to add to this letter, and very likely he then redated the entire letter.

[340]Other letters bearing this day's date were:
1) *L. B.,* vol. 1, pp. 157–60, Dispatch No. 19, to Secretary Marcy, in which Townsend Harris informs Mr. Marcy of Commodore Possiet's arrival as the bearer of the ratified Russian Treaty, of which he encloses an English translation; and adds that the Russians agree with him that the port of Shimoda is absolutely unfit either for supplying ships or for commercial purposes;
2) *L. B.,* vol. 1, pp. 160–68, Dispatch No. 20, to Secretary Marcy, in which Townsend Harris points out that the friendship of the Japanese is increasing, as are also the prospects of an early abandonment of their exclusion policy, giving four evidences of the changing times. Very significant, too, is his report of the intentions of Sir John Bowring (Governor of Hongkong, and recently appointed Plenipotentiary to Japan) to impose a new treaty on the Japanese, whether peaceably or forcibly.

Moriama Yenosky came to see me, as he said, with a message from the Governor. Three horses have been offered, but none suits the Japanese; one is too old and clumsy, one too young and vicious, the third is too ill-looking for me.

The Governor is a good judge of a horse and has promised to select one that will suit. He says he is responsible for my personal safety to both the American and Japanese Governments, and if I should be killed by a vicious horse, he would have to perform the *hara-kiri*. I told Yenosky that I would be satisfied with any horse the Governor might select, etc. Commodore Possiet and Mr. Heusken took a walk southwest from Shimoda, and were followed by a Gobanyosi. The Commodore, in a decided and stern manner, ordered him to go about his business and not to follow him; and the man left them. But soon afterwards he reappeared and pertinaciously kept with them. The Commodore then seized the man and gave him a thorough shaking, and when he was released, the Gobanyosi started off running like a deer and no more appeared.

The First Governor's name is Inowouye
    Sinano no Kami.
The Second Governor's name is Okado Bingo
    no Kami.
First Vice-Governor's name is Matsmoura
    Chiwousiro.
Second Vice-Governor's name is Wakana
    Miwosabra.[341]

[341] These names are better written as: Inouye, Shinano-no-Kami; Okada, Bingo-no-Kami; Matsmura Chiwusiro; Wakana Miwosabra.

Thursday, November 29 [*27*], *1856.* Somewhat better to-day; medicine has operated well. Busy writing letters to go by the Russian corvette.

Japanese bring me a basket of fine grapes to-day, which came from Kyushu. They look and taste like the Malaga muscatel grape, and have the same bloom on them. The price, 1,800 seni for about twelve pounds. Cheap enough.[342]

Saturday, November 29, 1856. Quite recovered, and am still occupied with my letters, of which I have five to write to the State Department, and one of them explaining my action in trying to get to Yedo is of necessity a long one.[343] I keep copies of all my letters to the State Department in my [private letter book,— which see.[344] My washman washed some clothes for

<hr/>

[342] A slight proof of the very practical aid which the American Townsend Harris (as Dean of the Diplomatic Corps in Japan) now gave to Commodore Possiet of Russia (as, later on, in far greater measure, to Lord Elgin of Great Britain, and to Count Friedrich von Eulenburg of Prussia) is the fact that on this day (Nov. 27, 1856) he sent the Russian Commodore four books on Japan—having already sent him a copy of Kaempfer's famous work. These books were a good selection, to wit:

> J. W. Spalding, *The Japan Expedition*, New York, Redfield, 1855. (A volume on the Perry Expedition.)
> Charles MacFarlane, *Japan*, New York, George P. Putnam & Co., 1852.
> Richard Hildreth, *Japan as It Was and Is*, New York, J. C. Derby, 1855.
> Richard Hildreth, *Japan and the Japanese*. (Which edition is uncertain.)

These books, to which Townsend Harris refers very briefly (*L. B.*, vol. 1, p. 135, Memorandum), undoubtedly were from among the books which he had procured for his own use when in New York in Aug. and Sept., 1855.

Similarly, Commodore Possiet, who had learned of Townsend Harris's indisposition, was equally courteous in offering him the services of the ship's surgeon. (*L. & P.*, vol. 1, no. 47, dated Friday, Nov. 28, 1856.)

[343] This was *L. B.*, vol. 1, pp. 160–68, Dispatch No. 20, outlined above, see note 340.

[344] The passage which I have enclosed in square brackets ("private letter book . . . table purposes," Nov. 29 to Dec. 1, 1856) was written on a different kind of paper by Miss Bessie A. Harris. This sheet, numbered 113, is inserted in the original manuscript *Journal* of Townsend Harris in place of a page that was carefully cut out, and that must have been numbered 113

Commodore Possiet and Captain Korsacoff, for which they sent him three dollars. I direct him to refuse to take the money, not from any feeling of pride, but I wish to make them all the returns I can for their kindness to me; and his case is different from that of the Russian sailors, to whom I made a present for their labor. *He* is my private servant. *They* are in the employ of the Sovereign of Russia.[345]

Monday, December 1, 1856. Engage another servant, Kooski. His duty will be to scrub floors, sweep the compound, bring coals and do all the coarse heavy work about the house; is to come at sunrise, eat his food (which he is to furnish himself) here, and leave after sunset; wages 400 seni *per diem.* Present to the officers of the Russian corvette three bottles of Surat

recto, and 114 verso. In other words, the material bracketed in this *Journal* entry gives Miss Harris's text, replacing a much longer original by Townsend Harris. What was in the passage thus deleted?

Miss B. A. Harris made a manuscript copy of the entire *Journal,* which copy is now in the possession of The College of the City of New York, together with the original. In her copy, Miss Harris did not hesitate to correct words misspelled in the original, to change "would" to "should," etc., to recast entire sentences, and to delete remarks that were somewhat too uncomplimentary or that, in her opinion, were for various reasons to be suppressed! For instance: she omits entirely the entry for Jan. 21, 1857; and the entry for Jan. 8, 1857, in her version, ends thus: "but words will not do—I must have acts."

[345]The intimacy and the coöperation between the Russian and the American representatives were growing apace. On this day, Commodore Possiet wrote to Townsend Harris telling him that he (the Commodore) was to see the Governors of Shimoda at noon, and asking Townsend Harris for the *status quo* of the currency question (*L. & P.,* vol. 1, no. 48).

On the same day Townsend Harris answers that he will be glad to inform Commodore Possiet of all his (Townsend Harris's) conversations with the Japanese; that he has not discussed the currency question with the Japanese since Possiet's arrival; and that late in the afternoon he will either call in person or send his secretary, Mr. Heusken, to get the news of Possiet's visit to the Japanese authorities (*L. B.,* vol. 1, pp. 136–37).

This is a perfect, and the earliest, example of the coöperation among the foreign representatives in Japan, which later almost became the general rule.

oil,[346] they having none; have been using common, Japanese oil for table purposes.]

Visit the corvette, but am soon interrupted by a lot of Japanese officials who come to see the Commodore on the subject of boat landings. Commodore Perry's Additional Articles provided that certain landing places should be provided at Shimoda and Hakodate,[347] and the Japanese now wish to confine us to landing at these places alone. I resist the propositions, as does the Commodore. On my return home I send to Commodore Possiet letters of introduction to:

Patrick Stewart, Esq., Macao, dated November 22, 1856
Mrs. Drinker   "   "   "   "   "

I also send to Captain Korsacoff letters of introduction addressed to:

Patrick Stewart, Esq., Macao, dated November 22, 1856
Mrs. Drinker   "   "   "   "   "
Mr. Sandwith Drinker,[348] Hongkong, dated December 1, 1856.

---

[346]Surat is a district in the province of Bombay, India.

[347]Article II of the Additional Regulations (signed at Shimoda, June 17, 1854): "Three landing-places shall be constructed for the boats of merchant ships and whale-ships resorting to this port; one at Shimoda, one at Kakizaki, and the third at the brook lying southeast of Centre Island" (J. H. Gubbins, *The Progress of Japan,* p. 230).

[348]Of the letters here mentioned, those introducing Commodore Possiet to Mr. Stewart and to Mrs. Drinker have already been noticed (under their proper date). The two introducing Captain Korsacoff have not been found, but must have been practically identical. "Not found" also is the letter addressed to Mr. Sandwith Drinker, who, by letter dated Hongkong, April 3 and 4, 1857, answers five of Townsend Harris's letters, dated Sept. 1, Oct. 9, Nov. 25 (21st?), Dec. 1, and Dec. 10 (*L. & P.,* vol. 1, no. 62).

There is extant also a letter by Captain W. Rimsky Korsacoff of this date (Dec. 1, 1856, *L. & P.,* vol. 1, no. 49), which expresses appreciation of Townsend Harris's offer of assistance (see *Journal,* Nov. 29, 1856), and also acknowledges receipt of the two letters of introduction just mentioned.

Get a further supply of the nice grapes from Kyushu. I find they have no pips or seeds.

Tuesday, December 2, 1856. The Third Governor, or Governor of Kakizaki, visits me to-day. His visit is on the important subject of the oil furnished for my lamps, which I have had difficulty in procuring of a good quality, or rather a regular supply of a good article, as on some days we have a capital article sent; then will follow some that will not burn for two hours. Told the [Third Governor] it was wanted for my lamps and not for eating.

He promises a full supply of what I want now [that] they fully understand my wishes. I told the Governor that it was high time the jetty or boat landing of Kakizaki was repaired; that it was destroyed on the 22nd of September, more than seventy days ago, that all the materials for its repair were still there, and that it was a great neglect to leave it so long. He promised it should be immediately attended to.[349]

In order to have a clear understanding about the orders I give, I have procured a book in which I write every order, and there are columns left in which to enter

---

[349]Townsend Harris describes the terrible damage caused by the hurricane of Sept. 22, 1856, in his entry for Sept. 23rd. He is consistent in the date of the typhoon here and elsewhere in his correspondence—*e. g.*, to Secretary Marcy (*L. B.*, vol. 1, p. 158) and to Captain H. H. Bell (*L. B.*, vol. 1, p. 143). Mr. Heusken, however, says that the storm took place during the night from the 20th to the 21st of Sept. (*Diary*, in Wagener, *op. cit.*, p. 376.)

The *Diary* was written by Mr. Heusken in French; the text just referred to is in German; and it was published the following year in an English translation in the *Japan Mail*, Jan., 1884.

It would be a great good fortune and a distinct boon to students of the early diplomatic days in Japan to find and to publish the entire *Diary* of the martyred Heusken, the first secretary of the American Legation in Japan.

the name of the interpreter to whom the order was given, with the date of it, and another column for the date at which it was executed. By this means I shall know whether my orders have been given by Mr. Heusken, or forgotten by him, and also whether the interpreter neglects them after he has received them. So far it works to a charm, and I have had more done in the last two days than in the previous fortnight.

Still busy writing letters to go by the *Olivuzza*.

Wednesday, December 3, 1856. Captain Korsacoff calls to see about my barometers, to try to get them into working order. I fear it is a bad job.[350]

Still occupied with my letters.

I have had a very bad cold and sore throat for the last four days. This arises from the habit Mr. Heusken has of *never* putting any fuel on the fire. During the day I attend to the fire myself and it is well kept up, but in the evening I get busy, and, as Mr. Heusken is on the side of the fire, I neglect it; and, being made with charcoal, it soon goes out, and with our paper windows and loose joints of the house, it soon becomes like sitting out of doors. I believe that Mr. Heusken only remembers when to eat, drink and sleep,—any other affairs rest

---

[350]Though he does not mention it in his *Journal,* Townsend Harris on this day wrote on this very subject to Lieutenant Maury, U.S.N., at the Hydrographical Bureau, Washington, D. C. (*L. B.,* vol. 1, pp. 137–40).

In this letter, Townsend Harris states that when in Washington in Aug., 1855, he had been unsuccessful in obtaining meteorological instruments from either the Navy Department or the Smithsonian Institution (*cf.,* his letter to Joseph Henry, of the Smithsonian, *L. & P.,* vol. 1, no. 18, dated Aug. 20, 1855). He now renews his application, and sends Lieutenant Maury readings of the thermometer, and observations on winds, rains, etc., at Shimoda from Sept. 15th to Nov. 30, 1856—material that was quite new to our Hydrographical Bureau.

very lightly on his memory. Busy to-day in writing letters.

Thursday, December 4, 1856. Commodore Possiet and two officers came in this evening about half-past seven, having taken a long walk on the side of Yedo Bay. They were very hungry, and I gave them such refreshments as my poor larder offered.

They told me that they had seen some thin plates of *ice* in a high bleak place. The first I have heard of, as at my house the thermometer has not fallen below 42°.

The Commodore told me that coals of a fair quality had been discovered at three points on the Amur River and also in the Island of Sakhalin, adding another important source of this important mineral.

Friday, December 5, 1856. The Commodore sends me word that the ratified treaties are to be exchanged on Sunday next, and invites me to "assist" on the occasion.

I much regret that I cannot attend. I am suffering from a very severe cold and great hoarseness; but the most important reason is that I cannot consistently "assist" in any such matter on a Sunday. From the time of my arrival I have refused to attend to any kind of business on that day,[351] and after a short time the Japanese ceased to ask it of me. Should I now join the Russians, I shall contradict all my previous acts on this account, and lose my character for *consistency,* a point that cannot be too carefully watched in dealing with

---

[351]Compare the entries for Aug. 22, 24, and especially 31, 1856.

people like the Japanese. They delight to convict a man of inconsistency.

Sunday, December 7, 1856. About eight last night we had several distant, but very heavy claps of thunder with some vivid lightning, which preceded violent squalls from the west, and heavy rain succeeded, which continued through the night. The barometer fell from 30.50 to 29.72. About the same time I had a violent exacerbation of bile; severe vomiting for two hours, and purging which lasted all night. It was a bright clear morning, with a true old-fashioned American northwester, blowing a gale.

The corvette fired a salute as the Commodore landed about eleven A. M., and at one fired a salute of twenty-one guns in honor of the exchange of ratifications.[352]

The Russian, American and Japanese flags were hoisted from the three masts, from noon until sunset.

After the exchange was completed, the Commodore and the Japanese commissioners proceeded to the place where the guns of the Frigate *Diana* were placed.

The guns have been neatly furbished up and a double guard of honor composed of Russians and Japanese were mounted over them. The guns were then formally presented to the Japanese. The commissioners then attended the Commodore to the corvette, where they received a salute and a dinner, and thus completed the ceremonies of the day.

Monday, December 8, 1856. The Third Governor, Moriama and some others visited me to-day. After kind

---
[352]See note 320.

messages and inquiries on behalf of the Governors, they said they had been ordered to inform me of the exchange of ratifications, etc., etc. Moriama was quite communicative and oracular; said that a great change was impending in Japanese affairs (as it relates to foreign intercourse), and that it would surprise all, when it took place, from its suddenness, etc., etc.

The Governor and Moriama told me that the largest Japanese vessels were about 200 tons burden, and that, enumerating all vessels of 60 tons up to 200 tons, the aggregate number was about 100,000!! This aggregate was so astounding that I made them repeat it in different forms, so that I might be sure there was no misunderstanding as to their meaning, but they all adhered to it, remarking that if they had counted all their craft of 50 tons down to fishing boats, the number would be enormous.

They said they had seen 700 junks all over 60 tons in Shimoda Harbor at one time!!

If these figures be correct, the tonnage of Japan exceeds that of any nation in the world.

Tuesday, December 9, 1856.   Up at seven A. M. to go on board the corvette to see the Commodore before he meets the Japanese to-day on the subject of the currency. I got him to agree that he would refuse to pay, except on the basis I had named,—*viz.,* one dollar to pass for three *ichibus;* that he would pay that amount to them; and, if they were dissatisfied, he would place the difference in my hands (until the arrival of a Russian Consul) to await the final settlement of the question. I am much pleased with this, as it will greatly strengthen my demands for the adjustment of the question. Am told the corvette will leave on Friday next, and am invited to dine with them for the last time on Thursday next. I shall send two pairs of nice, pet fowls (for Mrs. Stewart[353] of Macao) on board the ship on Wednesday, and embark my rascally tailor on Thursday. The Commodore is anxious to get away, as this strong northwester, which still blows, causes the ship to drag, and she is so situated that she cannot "cut and run."

Busy closing up letters to go by the ship.[354]

Wednesday, December 10, 1856. Begin to make up my mail. It consists of letters as follows:[355]

Secretary of State, five, Numbers 17 to 21.
S. Drinker, two, November 21st and December 1st

---

[353] Wife of the Patrick Stewart mentioned in the entry for Dec. 1, 1856.

[354] On this date, Townsend Harris wrote a second letter to Armstrong & Lawrence, at Hongkong (*L. B.*, vol. 1, pp. 141-43; *cf.*, p. 190), which, therefore, went off together with that of Nov. 21, 1856 (*q.v.*).

In addition to routine matters of accounts, Townsend Harris urgently begs Messrs. Armstrong & Lawrence not to permit opium to be sent to any of his servants in Japan. This, of course, was the result of the incident described by him under date of Nov. 24, 1856. Townsend Harris was playing fair with the Japanese: he now extended to China the same interdict which he had only two weeks before given to the Goyoshi of Shimoda, and which later he incorporated in his Treaty of Commerce and Navigation (concluded July 29, 1858), Art. IV, in the historic words, "The importation of opium is prohibited," etc.

[355] Of the twenty-three letters here listed, eleven have been outlined above under their respective dates—namely, those addressed to Secretary Marcy (5), Armstrong & Lawrence (2), Miss Kate Drinker, Lieutenant Maury, Captain Bell, and Sir John Bowring. The remaining twelve have not been found.

The answer, however, to Townsend Harris's numerous letters to Mr. Sandwith Drinker is extant (see above, note 348). Likewise, the letter to Mrs. Patrick Stewart (of Nov. 21, 1856) must have told her that he would send the gifts mentioned in the present entry of the *Journal;* while still another letter to Captain Korsacoff dated this day (not listed in the *Journal*) begged him to take these gifts to Mrs. Stewart at Macao (*L. B.*, vol. 1, pp. 140-41).

I. Harland	November 21, 1856			
Dr. Lorraine	"	21	"	
Armstrong & Lawrence	"	21	"	
" "	December	9	"	
General Keenan	November	25	"	
Mrs. Stewart	"	21	"	
Mrs. Spooner	"	30	"	
Mrs. Drinker	"	30	"	
Kate Drinker	"	21	"	three sheets
Joseph Evans	"	29	"	
Lieutenant Maury	December	3	"	
Captain Bell	"	10	"	
P. M. Wetmore	"	9	"	sixteen sheets
N. Dougherty	"	9	"	three sheets
Sir John Bowring	"	10	"	
S. Drinker (for gun)	"	10	"	

Send on board the Russian corvette a double coop with two pairs of pet fowls for Mrs. Stewart of Macao. Also send twenty-five catties each of rice and paddy, and some gravel for the fowls.

Thursday, December 11, 1856. Send my tailor[356] on board the Russian corvette. He had the impudence to ask me to give him a good character! Who can ever hope to fathom the want of moral principle in a Chinese? Captain Korsacoff called this morning and I loaned him $1,000,—1,000 Mexican dollars to be repaid in the same coin to my agents Armstrong & Lawrence at Hongkong, the Captain taking duplicate receipts

---

[356]In the letter which this tailor took aboard with him (*L. B.*, vol. 1, pp. 152–53), Townsend Harris gave Captain Korsacoff some good advice as to how to treat the "rascally" servant.

for the payment, one of which he is to forward to me.[357]
The weather is the most lovely ever seen at this season
of the year in a similar latitude. The sky is as blue as
a sapphire, and a light air from the west raises the
thermometer to 53°. Last night the thermometer fell
to 38°.

My *black pet hen* commenced to incubate on the 9th
inst., therefore I shall look for some chicks from her
about New Year's Day.[358]

Friday, December 12, 1856.   Dine on board the corvette. After dinner see the process of *lacquering* performed on some boxes of Commodore Possiet.

Saturday, December 13, 1856.   Go on board the corvette to see her off, but the wind being so unfavorable she
could not get out of the harbor. Not feeling well, I bid
adieu to all and go on shore.[359]

Sunday, December 14, 1856.   The corvette went to
sea early this morning.[360] The Commodore paid one-

---

[357]Townsend Harris's letter of this date to Armstrong & Lawrence (*L. B.*,
vol. 1, p. 154) gave them the necessary instructions in connection with this
loan.

[358]On this day, Townsend Harris acknowledges receipt from Commodore
Possiet of a mountain barometer, for delivery to the Russian Consul when
he should arrive in Japan (*L. B.*, vol. 1, p. 153).

[359]Owing to the different valuation set upon the Russian and the Japanese
currency, Commodore Possiet and Townsend Harris finally agreed (in the
course of this visit of leave) that the Russians pay their accounts according
to their own reckoning and leave the balance in Townsend Harris's hands
against the time when the currency question should be properly adjusted
(*L. & P.*, vol. 1, no. 50, Commodore Possiet to Townsend Harris, Dec. 13,
1856).

Further financial dealings just previous to the departure of the Russians
obliged Townsend Harris to write a second note to his agents at Hongkong,
Armstrong & Lawrence, in which he revised the figures in the letter written
on Dec. 11, 1856, to read $1,835.50 (*L. B.*, vol. 1, p. 155, dated Dec. 13, 1856).

[360]Heusken's *Diary* states that the corvette sailed on December 15th (Wagener, *op. cit.*, p. 376).

third of the Japanese bill for pilotage and boat hire,[361] and sent the other two-thirds to me to await the final settlement of their accounts. I am quite ill. I find my complaint to be "Saint Anthony's Fire." Face and forehead much swollen, and burning hot and itching.

Thursday, December 18, 1856. Have drenched myself with purgative medicines, but my complaint is but little relieved.

To-day the Vice-Governor called; and, being anxious to settle the question about the guards, I admitted him. I demanded the immediate removal of the people who have been in my compound from the day of my arrival. The Vice-Governor said he would report it to the Governors. I complained that the shopkeepers of Shimoda would not sell anything to my people or even give the prices. I added that I had before complained of this and had been promised redress, but things went on just as they did before. I also demanded ten silver *ichibus* to make presents to my Japanese servants on Christmas Day, according to the custom of my country. The Vice-Governor said that orders to the shopkeepers should again be given. As to the *ichibus,* he must report that to the Governors.

Saturday, December 20, 1856. At last my horse has arrived. It is not a high mettled racer, but will answer my purpose. The price is nineteen *kobangs,* about

---

[361]On Commodore Perry's visit to Shimoda, three Japanese pilots were appointed and the scale of charges agreed upon—on June 22, 1854 (Perry, *Narrative,* 33–2, S. Ex. Doc., no. 79, vol. 1, p. 488, note).

The Pilot Regulations for the Harbor of Shimoda were signed the next day—June 23, 1854—and the English and the Dutch versions thereof are given *ib.,* p. 487, note.

twenty-six dollars. The saddle and bridle are real curiosities and cost thirty *kobangs,* about forty-two dollars, or about 60 per cent. more than the horse! The groom to attend the horse costs me seven *ichibus* per month, about one dollar [and] seventy-five cents. The horse is shod with *straw sandals,* which last about an hour on the road.[362]

Monday, December 22, 1856. I am refused the ten *ichibus.* I am told I must give orders on the Goyoshi, and the money will be paid to the bearer of the order. I reply that such a proposition is offensive and must not be renewed, and I do not get the money. I renew my complaint about the guards and demand their imme-

---

[362]The Englishman Robert Fortune visited Yedo after Nov. 30, 1857, and enjoyed Townsend Harris's hospitality. In his book (*Yedo and Peking,* London, John Murray, 1863, pp. 200–01) he gives this interesting anecdote:

"Mr. Harris related an amusing circumstance connected with the shoeing of horses in Japan, which illustrates the ready way in which the people of the country adopt foreign customs when seen to be improvements on their own. I have already had occasion to mention the marked difference which exists between the Chinese and the Japanese in this respect. 'Oula custom' —old custom—is the barrier to every foreign introduction in China, while the Japanese adopt with promptness every improvement which is set before them. When Mr. Harris first went to reside in Yedo, his horse was shod with iron shoes in the usual way. Up to this time the horses of the Japanese either wore straw shoes, or were not shod at all. One day an officer came to Mr. Harris and asked him to lend him his horse, and to be good enough to ask no questions as to the purpose for which the animal was required. This strange request was good humouredly complied with, and the horse, after being away for a short time, was duly brought back. The officer to whom it had been lent came to the American Legation a few days afterwards, and told Mr. Harris, as a great secret, that the Prime Minister had sent for the horse to examine his shoes; and now, he said, the Minister's horse had been shod in the same way, and all the horses of the other officers were likewise being shod!"

We are indebted to Mr. Fortune for this delightful anecdote for which Townsend Harris found no room in his *Journal*—for those were the busy, fruitful days of his first visit to Yedo, when he was giving daily lessons to the Japanese authorities in everything pertaining to the politics, finance, and international law of the Western World (*cf.* below, *Journal* for Oct. 5, 1857).

diate removal. I am told it must be referred to Yedo for settlement.

Tuesday, December 23, 1856. Mr. Heusken walked out to-day alone and unarmed. On the road he met a Japanese wearing a coat-of-arms on his sleeve. As soon as he saw Mr. Heusken, he flourished a long stick he had in a threatening manner and then drew his sword, which was also flourished. Mr. Heusken at first halted and then, being unarmed, turned back. [I] directed him never to go out unarmed again.

Thursday, December 25, 1856. Merry Christmas! How happy are those who live in lands where these joyous greetings can be exchanged! As for me, I am sick and solitary, living as one may say in a prison— a large one it is true—but still a prison. I will here note where I have been on Christmas Day for the last eight years:

Christmas, 1849, at sea in the North Pacific Ocean
" 1850 " Manila
" 1851 " Pulo Penang
" 1852 " Singapore
" 1853 " Hongkong
" 1854 " Calcutta
" 1855 " Ceylon
" 1856 in Japan

The weather here is as fine as one could desire. The fields are very green with wheat which has been largely planted or "sowed," and the camellias begin to appear.

Friday, December 26, 1856. Moriama Yenosky has gone to Yedo to see about the currency question and to

293

try to hurry a decision. I have given notice that I will not allow any spies to come into my presence or even on my premises; that, when they wish to see me, I will only receive the principals and interpreters, excluding spies and secretaries. The Japanese term for spy is "a looker across."[363]

Wednesday, December 31, 1856. The last day of the year. How many events of great importance to me have occurred during this year! I am very low spirited from ill health and from the very slow progress I am making with the Japanese. However, I must keep up my spirits and hope for the best. My pet hen has presented me with five chicks,—the merest mites of chickens ever seen. The weather this month has been very fine. The thermometer was as follows: mean for the month, 48 9/10; highest, 69°; lowest, 36°. First white frost, December 12th. Rain on no days, showers on four days, clear twenty-seven days.

January 1, 1857. Happy New Year! What a busy day in dear old New York, what universal joy appears on the faces that throng the streets,—each hurrying along to get through "his list of calls." It is a good custom and one that I hope will never be given up. How many friendships are then renewed which, without the occurrence of this day of "oblivion of neglect," would otherwise die a natural death. I pass the day in calling, in imagination, on my friends; but, as to Japan, not a soul has darkened my door. I could only exchange greetings with Mr. Heusken, and present my Chinese

---

[363]The *Metsuke,* or (with the honorific prefix) *Ometsuke.*

servants with the expected *cumshaw*.[364] All my New Years since Christmas, 1849, were passed in the same place as my Christmas, except New Year's Day of 1855, which was at Benares in northwestern India; the preceding Christmas was at Calcutta.[365]

Saturday, January 3, 1857. Assam, my butler, goes to Shimoda. Is refused a few cakes he wished to buy for refreshment.

Monday, January 5, 1857. Vice-Governor calls to say that orders have been given to all the shopkeepers to give prices or sell anything my people may ask for. I asked when those orders were given? He said they had been frequently given, but were specially renewed eight days ago. I then told him what had occurred on Saturday, and added that I did not believe one word they said; that it was an infraction of the Treaty, etc., etc. I also told him that I demanded the instant removal of the guards; that their presence made me in reality a prisoner and was a gross outrage and open violation of the Treaty.

The poor Vice-Governor shook in every joint, and

---

[364]Anything given as a present or as a tip. The word itself is a corruption —a pidgin (*i. e.*, business) English pronunciation of the word "commission," current in China.

[365]On this day, Townsend Harris wrote:

1) Two routine letters to James Guthrie, Secretary of the Treasury (*L. B.*, vol. 2, p. 10, Dispatches Nos. 1 and 2);

2) Three letters to Secretary of State Marcy—of which two merely sent duplicates of former Dispatches (*L. B.*, vol. 2, pp. 11 and 12, Dispatches Nos. 22 and 23), and the remaining one transmitted an account of disbursements under the head "Contingent Expenses in Japan," for the quarter ending Dec. 31, 1856 (*ib.*, p. 12, Dispatch No. 24);

3) A letter to Baring Bros., at London, informing them that he had drawn upon them for £258. 5. 3.—his salary for the quarter ending Dec. 31, 1856 (*L. B.*, vol. 1, p. 174).

295

the perspiration streamed from his forehead and that of the interpreter. I also complained of the insult to Mr. Heusken, and demanded the arrest and punishment of the offender. The Vice-Governor begged me to believe that everything should be done to give me satisfaction that lay in their power; that they wished to keep the Treaty faithfully, and that he would hurry over to the Governor's at once, etc., etc.

Tuesday, January 6, 1857. Invited to meet the Governors at the Goyoshi to-morrow. Although quite ill I consented.

Wednesday, January 7, 1857. Went to the Goyoshi at noon and there met Bingo-no-Kami and Shinano-no-Kami, or the Prince of Shinano and Prince of Bingo, the two Governors of Shimoda. The two Vice-Governors were present, but *no secretaries.*[366]

The business commenced by the Governors informing me that they had been directed to give an answer to my letter of October 25th to the Minister of Foreign Affairs. I inquired if it was a written answer? They said it was not. I told them I must decline any verbal answer (delivered by a third person) to a written letter from me. They asked if I objected to their rank? I told them, "No." They told me that the laws of Japan forbade the writing of letters to foreigners. I told them I knew better; that letters had been written by the highest officials, and even by the Emperor himself, to Commodore Perry, to the Russians, and to the Dutch; that to assert such palpable falsehoods was to treat me like a child;

[366]For the full names of these officials, see *Journal* for Nov. 26, 1856, and note 341.

and that, if they repeated it, I should feel myself insulted. They not opening any other matter, I then repeated what I had told the Vice-Governor on the 5th about the guards and the shops, and enlarged upon it, telling them that it was not only a breach of the Treaty, but a violation of the laws of nations, and that my Government would never submit to such treatment. The Governors were in great trouble. They gave me their private word of honor that the complaints about the shopkeepers should be instantly attended to, and begged me to wait until they could write to Yedo about the officers which are stationed at my house; that I mistook their nature; that they were there simply to protect me against intrusion from the Japanese; that the Shimoda people were very rude, and would be sure to give me cause of offense if the officers were not there to keep them away; and closed by saying they had no power to remove the officers, but must refer to Yedo.

In reply I told them they could not disguise the fact of my being under guard by a mere change of name; that I had no fears of the Shimoda people, who I knew were friendly when not under the eyes of their officials; that I would not consent to the delay of one day longer as to the guard; that more than three months had elapsed since I had requested their removal; and finally, so long as they remained, I declared I should consider myself a prisoner and would not leave the compound, and that I would write to my Government the manner in which they had treated me. The trouble of the Governors increased. Finally they told me the officers should be removed. "When?" said I. "Very soon," was the reply. "How many days?" They hesitated. I repeated firmly that, now [that] I had so strongly brought the matter up and that they had consented to the removal of the guards, every day they remained was a new outrage, and they must abide the consequences. They then said that the officers should be removed to-morrow. Knowing their duplicity, I told them the removal must be real and not nominal; they must not post them near, or even in sight of, my house; that, if they made any such attempt, I should consider it as an aggravation of the wrong already done me.

They assented to the justice of my remarks and said the officers should be brought back to the Goyoshi.

They then said they hoped I would not let what had passed interrupt the good feelings heretofore existing between us; that they were most anxious to give me every proof of their friendship, etc., etc.

I told them they had a queer way of showing friendship and hospitality; that I had been in the country four months and a half, and had never yet been invited to enter the house of a Japanese,[367] and that they had even refused to dine with me on my New Year's Day, making a flimsy excuse; that in my country New Year's Day was kept as it is in Japan, by making friendly visits,

---

[367]In his *Journal* for Oct. 28, 1856, Townsend Harris had expressed the hope that he would some day find pleasure in the society of the upper class—if only he could be invited to the home of some high officer (*cf.* above, and note 314). On this day (Jan. 7, 1857) Townsend Harris makes what are certainly some very pointed remarks on the subject. Mr. Heusken, the inferior officer, managed to visit the home of a Japanese gentleman as early as Jan. 21, 1857; while Townsend Harris himself finally received full recognition—both official and social—on Tuesday, Feb. 24, 1857 (*q.v.*, and also Mar. 7, 1857).

etc., etc., but not a single Japanese came near me on that day, and closed by saying that in America such conduct would be called inhospitable.

I then asked if the man that threatened Mr. Heusken had been arrested. They said they did not know who it was; therefore, could not arrest him. I told them the person was one of a small class; that he had a crest on his clothes and wore a sword; and that, if they did not arrest him, I should have a right to think the person was acting either under direct orders from them, or according to their secret wishes, adding that hereafter we should go out armed and any insult would be promptly punished by us, since they were either unable or unwilling to punish such persons.

I then remarked that with such a system of espionage as they had, I well knew that everything that occurred to us in our walks was reported to them.

I then inquired about the currency question and received the old reply, "Waiting for decision from Yedo." I told them that it had the appearance of a determination on their part to postpone the question indefinitely. They eagerly assured me that it was their wish to close the matter as speedily as possible. So, after four hours of stormy debate, I went home, where I was agreeably surprised to find the officers and guard packing up to leave, and, in effect, they did leave in the evening. So much for showing them a bold face.[368]

---

[368]On the very day that he was thus firmly maintaining his stand in Japan, Townsend Harris was elected Corresponding Member of The China Branch of The Royal Asiatic Society, whose headquarters were at Victoria, Hongkong: *L. & P.*, vol. 1, no. 53.

Thursday, January 8, 1857. Quite ill. Write a letter to Minister of Foreign Affairs about the verbal answer offered to me (see private letter book).[369] Bingo-no-Kami, one of the Governors, goes to Yedo to-day. I suppose in consequence of the flare-up of yesterday. I am determined to take firm ground with the Japanese. I will cordially meet any real offers of amity, but words will not do. They are the greatest liars on earth.[370]

Monday, January 12, 1857. There is a fine show of a bulbous flower around my house. It has but little scent, is of a pale yellow, and is, as I think, a species of jonquil. It gives a cheerful look to everything. The camellias are increasing in number and the wheat fields are as green as emeralds. I noted in October that the althea was putting out new leaves. These fell after the frost of December. The Japanese cannot pronounce the letter L, but substitute the letter R. This is exactly the reverse of what the Chinese do. *They* cannot articulate the R,

---

[369]This was a very important letter (*L. B.*, vol. 1, pp. 172–74). In addition to what is stated in the *Journal,* Townsend Harris with this letter begins to lay down very definite lines indeed of the course he is going to pursue to obtain a treaty from the Shogunate. He rather vaguely hints at dire calamities that are threatening Japan and that emanate from a government other than that of the United States. He concludes with the statement that already it may be too late; and therefore urges that the authorities make arrangements without delay for his visit to Yedo, where he may confer with them on these impending dangers.

[370]In spite of this inauspicious beginning, a thoroughly sincere and mutual esteem gradually grew up between the Japanese authorities and Townsend Harris. Indeed, when Townsend Harris resigned his position, the Shogunate made every effort to retain their first and best friend, and expressed their deep regret at his going. (Letter by Kuze, Yamato-no-Kami and Ando, Tsu-shima-no-Kami, to Secretary William H. Seward, dated May 5, 1862: *Diplomatic Correspondence,* 1862, pt. 2, p. 812.)

For some sane remarks on this subject, see J. H. Longford, in Jas. Murdoch, *A History of Japan,* vol. 3, p. 627, note 1.

but substitute the L for it. Thus, instead of rice, they say lice. This may be added to the many other proofs that the Japanese are not a cognate people with the Chinese. The English preposition *of* becomes *no* in Japanese. Example: *Shimoda-no-Minato,* Bay of Shimoda; *Yedo-no-Mitisi,* the road of Yedo; *Shinano-no-Kami,* Prince of Shinano. It is a singular coincidence that this is the very word used in the South Sea Islands. When Captain Cook was in Ulietra, one of the Friendly Islands, the chief asked him the name of his burial place. Cook told him, "Stepney." The chief then repeated many times to his people, "Stepney Marai *No* Toote," "Stepney is the burial place of Cook."

Thursday, January 15, 1857. Ill, ill, ill. I have cured the "Saint Anthony's Fire," but I am constantly wasting away in flesh.

I have a relax that takes me every four or five days, and continues about the same time. I am most careful in my diet, but all is of no avail. I use exercise now in my compound, walking from five to six miles every day. My liver acts well, and what it is that ails me I cannot say. I left Penang on the 2nd of April last, and am now forty pounds lighter than I then was.[371]

We are well supplied with wild boars' hams, some

---

[371]On Apr. 2, 1856, Townsend Harris left Pulo Penang on the *San Jacinto,* on the way to Bangkok to negotiate the new Treaty with Siam.

It was surely due to Townsend Harris's well-founded anxiety over his frequent illness that almost exactly a week later than the present entry, on Jan. 23, 1857, he appointed Mr. Heusken Vice-Consul,

"to discharge all Consular Duties within the Consulate of the United States of America within the Empire of Japan, during such period as I may be absent or unable to discharge the Duties of said office in Person." (For the full text of this Document, see *L. B.,* vol. 1, p. 175.)

venison, plenty of fine golden pheasants, and large and good hares.

Friday, January 16, 1857. Walked to Vandalia Point, but the climbing the steep hills knocks me up. I have no wind. I must continue my exercise in the compound.

Sunday, January 18, 1857. First snow seen on the hilltops. I cannot sleep nor can I study. I have laid aside the Japanese entirely, my reading is unsatisfactory; I have a craving for something I cannot define.

Wednesday, January 21, 1857. First ice seen at my house. Mr. Heusken reports some queer examples of Japanese manners. To-day he entered the house of a respectable Japanese, who received him quite cordially, gave him tea, etc., etc. He then began to inquire the names of various things in English—parts of persons—hand—arm—eye. I should have noted that there was present the mother, wife and daughter of the man, who [had] gathered around so as to see and hear all.

After asking many names of things, the man opened his dress and taking his privities in his hand—in sight of all the females—asked the names of the various parts in English! On another occasion Mr. Heusken went to the Hot Springs and found three men, entirely naked, lying in the tank; while he was looking on, a young female some fourteen years of age came in, coolly stripped herself to her "birthday suit" and lay down in the bath in close proximity to a young fellow of some twenty years of age. I asked the Vice-Governor if this promiscuous bathing was not rather injurious to the chastity of

302

their females. He said it sometimes did so happen. I then inquired what a man did when he married a female who was supposed to be a virgin, but on consummation he found she was not one. "Nothing," replied the [Vice-] Governor. "What can he do?" and then naïvely added, "I was once served in that way myself, but what could I do? It was not my fault."

Monday, Tuesday, Wednesday, January 26, 27, 28, 1857. Festival of the Japanese New Year. Everyone released from labor; all in their best clothes; faces shining with saki and everybody paying visits of ceremony to everybody. Persons of rank put on their *camissimo* or dress of ceremony on these occasions.[372] I went out on Thursday to see the decorations of the houses. Evergreens, rice in the straw, oranges, radishes, etc., etc., were festooned about the front of every house. Before each house was a pine or cypress branch planted in the ground to represent a tree, while at the base of the tree a quantity of firewood some fourteen inches long was set on end, forming a bulk of some seven feet in circumference. The fuel was kept in its place by straw ropes. At some houses wheat straw was neatly twisted into the form of a cornucopia, in others the universal shoe of Japan,—*i. e.,* a straw sandal,—was hung up. Everyone appeared under the influence of saki, while but few were intoxicated and none quarrelsome.

Saturday, January 31, 1857. To-day closes the first month of the year. I wish I could say that my health and spirits were as good as the weather is fine, as the follow-

[372]The *Kami-shimo.* or ceremonial dress of Old Japan.

ing summary will show: mean temperature for the month, 45 1/10; highest, 54°; lowest, 32°. Rain two days, showers one, cloudy three, fine twenty-five days. A good return for the month of January in latitude 35° north. All writers on Japan speak much about the fogs. As yet I have not seen one. Ice formed on the 21st, 22nd, 23rd and 29th of this month.

Monday, February 2, 1857. Ice this morning at the Consulate three quarters of an inch thick, but it is much sheltered; while in the valley, where the north wind has a fair sweep, it freezes oftener and harder than at the Consulate.

Friday, February 6, 1857. I made an effort to-day and walked some seven miles up the valley of Shimoda, as it is level ground. This was in part a new walk to me, never having gone so far before in that direction. The vegetation improves as you recede from the seacoast, and I found the bamboo quite green in many places. Hamlet succeeds hamlet in quick succession; the houses, temples and cultivation all of the same character as at Shimoda. The hills are equally steep; sometimes they all but close the valley, only leaving a passage for Shimoda-no-gawa, or Shimoda River.

Tuesday, February 10, 1857. A violent attack of cholera morbus,—being the third I have had since last December, and it has so happened that I ate *potage à la purée* on each of those days. I shall, therefore, with great regret give it up. First snow on the level ground to-day, about one inch, but it soon melted and by eleven o'clock was all gone.

Monday, February 16, 1857. Bingo-no-Kami, now at Yedo, sends me from thence a present of English walnuts and dried persimmons. They call the latter figs and, indeed, the best quality of them is very like a good dried fig. I am daily expecting his return here, when I hope I shall be able to bring our pending matters to an amicable conclusion.

Thursday, February 19, 1857. Rain, sleet and snow. Learn that Bingo-no-Kami, with one of the Vice-Governors and Moriama Yenosky, chief interpreter, has returned from Yedo.

Friday, February 20, 1857. The Vice-Governor and Moriama call on me on their return from Yedo.

Saturday, February 21, 1857. Bingo-no-Kami, one of the Governors of Shimoda, calls on me on his return from Yedo. After the usual compliments, he presented me with two pieces of Japanese crêpe, a really good article, and a Japanese sword!! It was in a common, white wood scabbard, and had a handle to slip on of the same. In fact, was simply a *packing case.* He told me the blade was one he had worn for some years; that it was by the first swordmaker of Japan, etc., etc.; that, having procured another blade, he had shifted the scabbard and mountings to it, and therefore presented me with the blade; that *no foreigner* had ever before obtained such a blade, etc., etc.; and to all this I made the required replies. The blade is really a superb one[373] and

---

[373]On the occasion of his Audience of Leave (Apr. 26, 1862), the Tycoon presented Townsend Harris with another splendid sword, which Townsend Harris, in his turn, later presented to Lieutenant General U. S. Grant for having saved "my beloved country from the ruin that threatened her." (See the manu-

has the "shark teeth mark" the whole length of it. This, I am told, is not a mere surface mark, but extends through the metal like the *pamom* in some Malay krisses. The Governor invited me to visit him and Shinano-no-Kami, at their private residence, which I accepted. He then asked me if I would have European or Japanese cookery. I selected the latter. So I am at last to see the inside of their residence.[374]

Tuesday, February 24, 1857. *Norimons* were sent at nine this morning, but I did not leave until eleven, when I proceeded with quite a train of attendants. The *norimon* is a horrible affair. The only position you can assume is to sit on your heels, Japanese fashion, or else cross-legged. It is only four feet long and about three and a half feet high. I was received with all formality by the two Governors in an ante-room. I was then conducted to an inner apartment furnished with *seats,* braziers, etc., etc. After drinking a cup of tea and smoking three whiffs of tobacco, I was again conducted to the room of my entertainment. This room, out of compliment to me, was furnished with seats and tables. On the table before me were pipes, tobacco, a brazier, etc., etc. My seat was on the left of the Governor and close to the *toko,*[375] or sacred place, and consequently the seat of honor. The meal consisted of fish cooked in every pos-

script letter, *L. & P.,* vol. 1, no. 322, dated Union Club, New York, Nov. 15, 1865; and General Grant's courteous answer, *ib.,* no. 323, dated, "Headquarters Armies of the United States, Washington, D. C., Nov. 23, 1865.")

[374]See above, *Journal* for Oct. 28, 1856, and Jan. 7, 1857, and notes 314 and 367.

[375]The *toko-no-ma.*

sible Japanese way, and fish *raw;* the latter cut from a large fish which was brought to me to see. It was in a large dish, decorated with a mast and sail, the colors of the latter indicating welcome.

A pâté made of lobster was very nice; sweet potatoes and radishes served up in various forms were the vegetables. Contrary to my expectations, neither rice nor bread was served with the dishes. Some ten courses were served, all brought to me in wooden cups brightly lacquered. On a table placed across the foot of the room was a dwarfed cedar tree, decorated with storks cut out of radish and neatly colored. These were fastened to the tree by springs of twisted wire, which continued any motion for a long time. Flowers also, both real and artificial, were used to decorate the dishes of cakes, bonbons, etc., etc., which were also placed on this table. I was told the storks were a wish for my longevity, and that the various flowers had a complimentary meaning in them. After all the fish dishes were done, rice was served without salt or any other condiment. Saki was the beverage, but I plead ill health and only drank tea. When the heavy part of the meal was over, Shinano-no-Kami had brought to him the prettiest toy tea-making apparatus I ever saw. It was in a neat, plain, wooden case, which when opened displayed a tiny furnace for boiling water, teapot and two cups, a jar of tea, mats for the teapot and cups, a scoop for the tea, and a curious machine for heating the tea over the fire before it is put in the water. Shinano-no-Kami then proceeded to boil the water, measure and heat the tea, place it in pot, pour on the boiling water, and then pour out a cup and hand it to me with his own hands; whereat all the Japanese fell into immense admiration, and then the matter was expounded to me,—that the making of tea by the Prince of Shinano and serving it with his own hands was a proof of friendship only given to those of exalted character and position, and I was requested to view it in that light, whereupon I agreed so to regard it. Then Shinano requested my acceptance of the whole concern as a proof of his great regard, and this was also agreed to.[376]

The conversation now took the usual Japanese turn. The lubricity of these people passes belief. The moment business is over, the one and only subject on which they dare converse comes up. I was asked a hundred different questions about American females, as whether single women dressed differently from the married ones, etc., etc.; but I will not soil my paper with the greater part of them, but I clearly perceived that there are particulars that enter into Japanese marriage contracts that are disgusting beyond belief. Bingo-no-Kami informed me that one of the Vice-Governors was specially charged with the duty of supplying me with female society, and said if I fancied any woman the Vice-Governor would procure her for me, etc., etc., etc.

I was asked if their people could receive some instruction in beating the drum when the next man-of-war came. I replied I had no doubt the commander would be willing to gratify them on that point. They said they had

---

[376]This was the *Cha-no-yu*, the tea ceremony so characteristic of Japan.

brass drums copied from the Dutch. They asked me about the various signals given by beat of drum, which I answered as well as I could. Then—oh, shame! They asked me if *we* had not a beat of the drum as a signal to our soldiers to go to the houses of *ill fame,* and I emphatically replied no. They evidently did not believe me; for, said they, "We know the Dutch do so at Nagasaki, and all your armies are much the same." I gladly took my leave at three P. M. and reached home quite jaded out.

Omitted :[376a]

Monday, February 23, 1857. I applied to the Japanese to fire a salute for me on "Washington's Birthday"; but, as it fell on Sunday, I wished the salute to be on Monday.[377] This was agreed to, and this morning they

---

[376a]Townsend Harris thus indicates that he omitted to write the entry for February 23rd in its proper, chronological order.

[377]Again Heusken's *Diary* differs slightly from that of Townsend Harris in wrongly dating the firing of this salute on Sunday the 22nd (Wagener, *op. cit.,* p. 376).

The friendly policy here followed by the Japanese was quite in accord with the advice given them by the Dutch in the beginning of 1857, to the effect that the Japanese should not enter on a policy of hostility with the foreigners lest they go the way of China ten years before (Wagener, *op. cit.,* p. 375). And it was at just about this time (some time between Jan. 25 and Feb. 22, 1857) that "the ex-Chiunagon of Mito declared his unwillingness to have any further share in public affairs. This resolution was attributed to his dissatisfaction with the course pursued towards foreigners by the Bakufu" (*Kinsé Shiriaku,* transl. by Sir E. M. Satow, ed. 1873, p. 7).

In connection with the salute here fired by the Japanese in honor of Washington's Birthday, we are reminded of the astonishment felt by the officers of Commodore Perry's expedition, when they first, on Monday, Feb. 20, 1854, talked with the Japanese and learned that the name of George Washington not only was not new in Japan, but, indeed, that it was a name already respected and esteemed.

Dr. Francis L. Hawks, in Perry's *Narrative of the Japan Expedition,* expresses himself thus (33–2, S. Ex. Doc., no. 79, vol. 1, p. 333):

"They seemed perfectly acquainted with the name of the great father of our country, and expressed a desire to participate in celebrating the occasion [Wednesday, Feb. 22, 1854], asking to be permitted to come off to see the guns fired. They were, of course, politely invited, and [were] requested to

sent over two handsome brass howitzers, exactly copied in every respect from one Commodore Perry gave them; every appointment about the gun, down to the smallest particular, was exactly copied: percussion locks, drag ropes, powder or cartridge holder and all.

The cartridges were made of paper, and for wads they used wood. The firing was good, quite as good as I have seen among civilized persons.

Judging from the report, their powder is much better than that of the Chinese or Siamese. The Japanese say they have made 1,000 howitzers like those used at the salute!! But they are great liars, consequently you do not know when to believe them.

Wednesday, February 25, 1857. Met the Governors at the Goyoshi at noon to-day. They brought in, with great ceremony, a box which was reverentially placed before me. Then a Vice-Governor opened the box, which I

---

bring their ladies with them; the latter part of the invitation they, however, jeered at as a very amusing but quite an impracticable joke."

Writing many years later, in Sept., 1890, Mr. John S. Sewall (who in 1853 and 1854 had been Captain's Clerk on the *Saratoga* in the Japan Expedition) gave a very good explanation of this knowledge of George Washington on the part of the Japanese. He asks (*The invincible armada,* in *The New Englander and Yale Review,* Sept., 1890, pp. 207–08):

"Whence came all this knowledge? We naturally credited it to the Dutch, the only nation besides the Chinese which had for the last three centuries maintained its hold upon the good graces and the commerce of Japan. But it appears that the Japanese printers had been in the habit of reprinting in Japanese the manuals and text-books our missionaries had prepared for the use of their schools in China. Their [the Japanese] knowledge of America came straight from Dr. [Elijah Coleman] Bridgman's *History of the United States,* which had been published in China, and which had enjoyed what Dr. Bridgman had never dreamed of, a wide circulation in the Mikado's dominions. That book had already prepossessed them in our favor."

There is further interesting material on this small *History of the United States.* It had a truly wonderful adventure, and its fate constitutes a shining example of the Biblical behest to cast one's bread upon the waters.

found to contain five pieces of a very poor satin damask, which I was told was from five members of the Regency at Yedo,—one piece from each person. This over, another box was brought which, as I was told, contained an answer to my two letters to Yedo, and at last they mustered courage to open it and unfold a sheet of paper about five feet long by eighteen inches wide, written quite full and bearing the seals and signatures of the following Princes who are members of the Regency:

Hotta Bittsyu-no-Kami
Abé Isen-no-Kami
Makino Bizen-no-Kami
Kuze Iamato-no-Kami
Naito Ku-no-Kami

with a Dutch translation of the same, which they placed in Mr. Heusken's hands.[378]

I directed Mr. Heusken to put the letter and translation in the box and close it. The Governors wished me to have it translated into English at once. This I declined, saying I should prefer having it done at leisure, and that in the meantime I should like to hear their answer on the currency question. Now ensued a scene quite Jap-

[378]This letter (written in classical Japanese) is in the possession of The College of the City of New York. It is endorsed (in Townsend Harris's own hand) : "Letter from the Council of State, Yedo, February 1857." It was signed by: Hotta, Bitchiu-no-Kami; Abé, Ise-no-Kami; Makino, Bizen-no-Kami; Kuze, Yamato-no-Kami; Naito, Kii-no-Kami.

In addition to what is stated in the *Journal,* the original letter pointed out that the Shogunate had appointed special Governors for the ports of Shimoda and Hakodate from the moment these ports had been opened to foreign trade; and that, inasmuch as Yedo placed complete confidence in these Governors, Townsend Harris should communicate with them, for this would be the same as if Townsend Harris were to communicate directly with Yedo.

This letter from the Great Council was written in answer to Townsend Harris's two letters dated Oct. 25, 1856, and Jan. 8, 1857. Townsend Harris wrote a dignified protest to the Great Council on Mar. 28, 1857. (See above notes 313 and 369.)

anese, which occupied full two hours. The substance of it was that they admitted the justice of my demand in part, but said my offer (five per cent.) to pay for recoining was not sufficient; that they should lose by it, and they therefore begged me to reconsider it and make them an increased offer. I asked them what was the cost of coining money in Japan? They gravely replied twenty-five per cent.!! Twenty-five per cent. I told them it was simply impossible; that the cost in Europe and America for such labor was not one per cent.; that I would bring competent moneyers from the United States who would do the whole work for five per cent., or even less. They said the laws of Japan forbade the employment of foreigners about their coinage.

I endeavored to elicit a direct offer from them, but without success. Among other statements made by them was this: that gold and silver before coinage had no value; that it was the mint stamp that gave it its value, etc., etc. I told them their Government had an undoubted right to deal with the precious metals produced in Japan as they pleased, but they had no such right over a foreigner, and that to attempt to exercise such a right over him would in effect be a confiscation of his property; that they might stamp pieces of paper or leather, and compel their own subjects to take them in lieu of gold and silver, but they could not expect the foreigner to take them in exchange for his merchandise, or to have his coin measured by the intrinsic value of such worthless tokens. This ground was traveled over and over again, the Japanese always reasoning in a circle and trying to

312

gain their point by simple pertinacity. I passed four weary hours and left at four P. M., appointing the next day to meet again. On reaching home, Mr. Heusken translated the Dutch copy of the letter, and found it to be a simple announcement that all business was to be transacted with the Governors of Shimoda or Hakodate, and not one word in reference to the President's letter to the Emperor of Japan, of which I told them I was the bearer.

See Journal No. 4.[379]

---

[379]The title-page of the fourth volume of the manuscript *Journal* reads: "Journal No. 4. Commencing February 26th, 1857, and Ending December 7th, 1857." (In Townsend Harris's hand.)

Journal No. 4

*Commencing February 26, 1857, and
Ending December 7, 1857*

Thursday, February 26, 1857. On reaching the
Goyoshi to-day, the Governors asked me if I had pe-
rused the letter from the Regency, etc., etc., and said they
had something to add, which was that they had full powers to receive from me any propositions I had to make,
and to treat on all the matters referred to in my two
letters to the Minister of Foreign Affairs,[380] and then began to question me as to certain matters contained therein. I told them I was not yet ready to *answer,* but rather
to *ask* questions, and that I wished to know the nature of
their powers. Could they give me answers at once on all
matters I might propose without waiting to hear from
Yedo? They assured me in the most solemn manner that
they could. I then asked could they make a new treaty
without such reference? Their answer soon proved what
I before suspected,—that, in any minor matter, they
could decide, but, on any important one, they could only
hear and report. I then said, "I have some matters under
the Treaty which properly come under your jurisdic-

---

[380]See above, *Journal* for Oct. 25, 1856, and for Jan. 8, 1857, and notes 313
and 369.

tion, and will now proceed to open them." They wished to renew the discussion of the currency, but I told them, unless they had some new matter, or a distinct proposition to make, I should prefer leaving that for the present.

I then stated that the Port of Nagasaki had been opened to the Russians as a place where their ships could obtain necessary supplies and coals for steamers,[381] and I demanded the same rights for the Americans. This was finally agreed to.[382] My next was, that American ships in want of supplies and not having money, that goods should be taken in payment.[383] They said this was already granted by our Treaty.[384] I told them, if that was the case, of course they could have no objection to reaffirming it, and this was agreed to.[385] My next was that Americans committing offences in Japan should be tried by the Consul and punished if guilty ac-

---

[381]The Treaty between Russia and Japan (signed at Shimoda, Feb. 7, 1855) provided for the opening of the three ports of Shimoda, Hakodate, and Nagasaki. Art. III of the Treaty continues as follows (J. H. Gubbins, *The Progress of Japan*, p. 236):

"Dans ces 3 ports, les navires russes pourront réparer leurs avaries, s'approvisionner d'eau, de bois de chauffage, d'aliments et autres objets nécessaires, de charbon de terre même, là où il s'en trouverait; ils paieront tous ces objets en monnaie d'or ou d'argent, ou à défaut d'espèces, en marchandises de leur chargement."

[382]This matter became Art. I of the Convention of Shimoda, concluded by Townsend Harris on June 17, 1857. Indeed, this article is a translation of the corresponding portions of the Art. III just quoted from the Russian Treaty.

[383]This represents the rest of Art. III of the Russian Treaty; compare Art. V thereof.

[384]The Perry Treaty (concluded Mar. 31, 1854) provided in Art. VII:

"It is agreed that ships of the United States resorting to the ports open to them [at that time only Shimoda and Hakodate] shall be permitted to exchange gold and silver coin and articles of goods for other articles of goods," etc.

[385]This matter became Art. V of the Convention of Shimoda.

cording to Japanese laws.[386] To my great and agreeable surprise this was agreed to without demur. I next told them that I demanded the right for Americans to lease ground, buy, build, repair, or alter such buildings at their pleasure, and that they should be supplied with materials and labor for such purposes whenever they might require it. I told them I founded this claim on the 12th and 13th Articles made with the Dutch at Nagasaki on the 9th of November, 1855, by which all the ground at Deshima was leased to the Dutch and the buildings sold to them; and that they also had the right to build, alter or repair, etc., etc.;[387] that I claimed those same privileges under the 9th Article of the Treaty of Kanagawa.[388]

---

[386]This is a slip of the pen for "according to Americans laws." This matter became Art. IV of the Convention of Shimoda, and was later repeated in Art. VI of the Treaty concluded by Townsend Harris on July 29, 1858. "Consular Courts" thus agreed upon (already to be found in Art. VIII of the Russian Treaty and in Art. II of the Dutch Treaty of Nov. 9, 1855) were to be the cause of endless and most serious trouble till abolished by treaties concluded many years later. (For the United States, compare the Treaty of 1894, Articles I and XVII.)

[387]The Treaty between The Netherlands and Japan, concluded by Jan Hendrik Donker Curtius, reads (Gubbins, *op. cit.,* pp. 247–48):

Art. XII—
"Except the outer wall, the guard-houses, and public buildings of Deshima, all the dwellings and warehouses shall be sold, through the intervention of the Governors of Nagasaki, to the Netherlands Factory, and the ground of Deshima let. They shall be under the direction of the highest Netherlands officer dwelling there, and be maintained at the cost of the Netherlands Factory."

Art. XIII—
"For the performance of the necessary repairs, the building or pulling down of warehouses or dwellings, or for making alterations and improvements therein, the Netherlands Factory shall be at liberty to employ Japanese tradesmen and to buy Japanese materials, for which payment shall be made in *kambang* money. Previous notice of these operations shall be given to the Governor of Nagasaki."

[388]Perry Treaty, Art. IX:
"It is agreed that if at any future day the Government of Japan shall grant to any other nation or nations privileges and advantages Which are not

317

The Governors were amazed. They never heard of any such convention.[389] It did not, it could not, exist. When, where and by whom was it made? I told them. It was not known to the Government at Yedo; had never been ratified, and therefore had never gone into effect. I then read the 29th Article which declared the Convention should go into full effect on the 1st of January, 1856, and extended the time of exchange of the ratifications to the 9th of November, 1857;[390] but the ratifications had been exchanged, and that I had with my own eyes seen the ratified Japanese copy. They then asked where the ratifications were exchanged, and where it was I saw it?

I told them Captain Fabius of the Dutch Navy brought the Dutch ratification to Nagasaki in August or September last, and that when he came here in the Frigate *Medusa* he had the ratified Convention on

---

herein granted to the United States and the citizens thereof, that these same privileges and advantages shall be granted likewise on the United States and to the citizens thereof, without any consultation or delay."

The introduction of this "most favored nation" clause in the Perry Treaty is said to have been due to Dr. S. Wells Williams, for many years a missionary-printer in China.

[389]Meaning, of course, the Treaty concluded with the Dutch at Nagasaki, Nov. 9, 1855 (see below).

[390]The pertinent portions of Art. XXIX of the Treaty with The Netherlands, read (Gubbins, *op. cit.,* p. 250):

". . . and the ratifications signed by high officers empowered thereto on both sides, shall be exchanged at Nagasaki within the space of two years from the date hereof [Nov. 9, 1855].

"All the stipulations of this Convention come into immediate operation with the exception of the following Articles:

"Art. I. The freedom therein granted comes into operation on the 1st December, 1855, and Articles IX, XII, XIII, XIV, XVIII, XX, and XXVI come into operation on the 1st January, 1856."

board, and that what I held in my hand was an authentic translation of it.[391]

Now, will it be believed that during all this time (more than one hour) the Governors had an authentic copy of that very Convention lying before them in a dispatch box? It was so; and all this barefaced falsehood was a fair specimen of Japanese diplomacy.

They then took new ground. The Dutch had been in Japan more than two hundred years; that these were old matters and had no relation to the present state of affairs. I replied that I claimed none of the rights the Dutch had before the Treaty of Kanagawa was signed; that I only claimed the same new rights as had been

---

[391]The *Medusa*, Captain Fabius, had been at Hakodate; and, on the way to Nagasaki, stopped at Shimoda on Oct. 1, 1856, sailing away for Nagasaki on Oct. 3, 1856 (see above *Journal,* under these dates).

Though the Preliminary Convention of Commerce concluded with the Dutch on Nov. 9, 1855, went into operation in the manner provided in Art. XXIX (from which we have just quoted), it was never duly ratified. (Gubbins, *op. cit.,* p. 66). Only a short time elapsed before the Dutch signed at Nagasaki a second Treaty of Commerce—Jan. 30, 1856. Townsend Harris, in his discussions thus far with the Governors of Shimoda, quotes entirely from the Dutch Treaty of Nov. 9, 1855. It would seem, therefore, that when Captain Fabius visited Shimoda in Oct., 1856, he was quite generous in giving Townsend Harris the text of the Dutch Treaty of Nov. 9, 1855, because he was aware that this Treaty had already been superseded by the one of Jan. 30, 1856; and the terms of the latter Treaty he seems to have felt himself bound to keep secret until such time as the ratifications thereof should have been exchanged. This last took place at Nagasaki, Oct. 16, 1857, about eight months after Townsend Harris's present discussion with the Japanese.

In other words, Townsend Harris, not knowing the full facts, was at a disadvantage with the Japanese Governors, who, in their manœuvring for diplomatic position, could well adhere to their statement that the Dutch Treaty of Nov. 9, 1855, had never been duly ratified and that therefore, to all intents and purposes, it did not exist. And, of course, they did not give the slightest inkling of the existence of the later Dutch Treaty of Jan. 30, 1856.

Townsend Harris finally received a copy of the Dutch Treaty of Jan. 30, 1856, and from the Governor of Shimoda himself, only on Wednesday, Nov. 18, 1857—on the eve of his departure for his audience with the Tycoon at Yedo. (See his entry in the *Journal* for that date, and his remarks on this very point of leasing ground and buying buildings at Deshima.)

319

granted to the Dutch; that under the old regulations the Dutch lived in Deshima simply on sufferance, had no written rights and were liable to be ordered away at any moment, but the Convention of November 9, 1855, placed them on new and secure ground. They had acquired fixed and indefeasible rights, and among others that of permanent residence in Japan.

Again the ground was shifted. The privileges granted to the Dutch were in effect to the Dutch Government, represented by a factory, and not to the Dutch burghers at large; that as I had told them the Government of the United States never engaged in trade, of course it could not have a factory; and, as a natural consequence, the claim on my part was ill founded. I replied that it was a privilege of trade and residence granted to Dutchmen, no matter whom they represented; that the effect was the same, whether they traded for themselves or for the Dutch Government.

Four o'clock having arrived, I left them to meet again to-morrow at the same hour.[392]

Friday, February 27, 1857. At the Goyoshi at noon. The Governors opened the business by travelling over the same ground as yesterday (on my last proposition)[393]

---

[392]While Townsend Harris was thus ably presenting the point of view and the claims of the United States, his good friend Nathaniel Dougherty, in far-off New York City, was drawing up a memorial in behalf of Townsend Harris, praying compensation for him ($12,000) for the successful conclusion of the American Treaty with Siam. This memorial was presented to the Senate on Friday, Feb. 27, 1857, by another friend of Townsend Harris—Senator William H. Seward. It was referred to the Committee on Commerce, and ordered to be printed (34–3, S. Misc. Doc., no. 52, pp. 1–2).

[393]Namely, "the right for Americans to lease ground, buy, build, repair, or alter such buildings," etc.

for nearly two hours, not one new idea or argument being started. At last, when they questioned the correctness of my translation, I suddenly asked them to give me a copy of [the] 12th and 13th Articles according to their version, which they promised to do—apparently for the moment forgetting their denial of any knowledge of such a Convention only yesterday.

I next claimed the right to have purchases made for me by any person I mighty employ, and that payment should be made directly to the seller without the interference of any Japanese official.[394] I also claimed that the limits of seven ri and five ri at Shimoda and Hakodate did not apply to me as Consul General, but that the whole Empire of Japan was included in my Consulate.[395] The arguments with which I supported this claim will be found at large in my private letter book.[396]

There was less falsehood in their replies to this point than there was to the preceding one, but this arose from the want of opportunity rather than the want of inclination. Two hours were thus consumed. and I left at four

---

[394]This was breaking new ground. The Russian Treaty (of Dec. 7, 1856) distinctly said in the Explanatory Articles (ad Art. V):

"Les Russes . . . effectueront le paiement ou l'échange des marchandises dans le dit entrepôt par l'entremise des employés japonais." (Gubbins, op. cit., p. 238.)

Townsend Harris won his point, and this matter became Art. VII of the Convention of Shimoda.

[395]This matter became Art. VI of the Convention of Shimoda.

[396]These arguments were indeed given "at large" in the lengthy letter which Townsend Harris addressed to the Governors of Shimoda, dated Mar. 13, 1857 (L. B., vol. 1, pp. 182–88, and vol. 2, pp. 1–3).

Incidentally, this reference, made on Feb. 27th, to a letter that was written on Mar. 13th, is but one of many proofs that Townsend Harris first wrote a rough copy of his Journal and copied it into the present manuscript volumes some time thereafter—in the present case, two weeks later at least.

P. M., they promising to send me their version of the 12th and 13th Articles of the Dutch Convention.

Saturday, February 28, 1857. At home all day, and very glad to rest after the vexing labors of the last three days. The weather this month was as follows: thermometer, mean 45 5/10; highest, 63°; lowest 32°. The thermometer is noted at eight A. M., noon, four and ten P. M.; but at four A. M. on the 11th, the thermometer stood at 28°. Ice on 2nd, 3rd and 11th; and it snowed on the 10th and 25th. It rained four days, showers on four days, cloudy four days and clear sixteen days. The mean of the coldest day this winter was 36 25/100 on the 2nd of February.

Monday, March 2, 1857. Moriama Yenosky comes here to-day with their version of the 12th and 13th Articles of the Dutch Convention. They agree in every essential with my version!

Moriama informs me he was promoted one step when last at Yedo, and has a place in the Revenue Board. He says his name is now changed to Moriama Tatsitsio, in place of Moriama Yenosky; that each time a man rises a step in office, he takes a new name. He introduced the "currency question" by saying how very anxious he was to have it settled, and tried to persuade me to open the question with him. He assured me that he knew of his own knowledge it did cost twenty-five per cent. on all their coinage; and, on being pressed, he admitted that a whole army of officers were quartered on the mint; that some of them had very large salaries, etc., etc. I inferred from what he said that the mint is a sort of pension estab-

322

lishment for the Empire. On inquiring of him as to the revenue of Japan, I could get no satisfaction; nobody knew, most of the dues were paid in rice. But this I did learn: that all the lands in the imperial domains are crown property, and the tenants are perpetual lease-holders; the rent paid varies from forty per cent. to thirty per cent. and twenty per cent. of the gross product of the land. All rents are estimated as rice; although wheat or any other cereal or green crops are raised, it is all estimated as rice. The tenant may pay his rent in kind or in the money value of the place on the day he pays it. This applies to the imperial domain. As to the domains of the vassal princes, I could not get any satisfactory answer. No publication of any kind as to public affairs is ever made in Japan. The head of a department knows only what belongs to that department; and under such a jealous government as this, surrounded by spies on every hand, he may well tremble even at the idea of seeking information that does not directly and officially pertain to him. For these reasons nothing can be accurately known as to the amount of their army, or navy, or police, or the number of officials, or of the paid spies. The same remarks will apply to their tonnage and the action of trade. As to the latter I much doubt if the Government keeps any statistics of its action.[397]

Tuesday, March 3, 1857. Met the Governors. The

---

[397]On this date, Senator William H. Seward wrote to Secretary Marcy, asking (among other things) whether the Department of State would recommend additional compensation for Townsend Harris for his services in concluding the Treaty with Siam (*L. & P.,* vol. 1, no. 59). On the same day, Secretary Marcy gave a favorable answer (*ib.,* no. 55).

currency question was introduced, and they at last made a distinct offer. They said that heretofore the dollar had been taken by them for 1,600 seni (or cash) ; that this was not right. They proposed to weigh coins brought here by Americans—gold coins with Japanese gold coins, and silver coins against Japanese silver coins— weight for weight, and from the amount of Japanese coin to deduct fifteen per cent. to pay for the loss of melting and coining. I told them the demand was unreasonable and that I could not agree to it. They then asked me to give them a counter proposition. I accordingly made three distinct offers:

1st. The dollar in silver to pass by tale for three *ichibus* or 4,800 seni;
2nd. Weighing the coin as proposed by them and deducting five per cent.;
3rd. That inasmuch as they said their coin was composed of pure silver or pure gold and without alloy,—that, if that statement was correct, I would allow them *ten per cent.* discount, and that any alloy found in their coin should be deducted from that allowance, and that any increase of alloy in the coins brought by Americans, over the present standard, should go to swell the discount.

The third proposition was instantly rejected with such manifest trepidation that I am convinced that their coin contains a large amount of alloy. They also said that to weigh the coin would be more just than to have it pass by tale, as from wear or other causes old coins

324

were never as heavy as new ones. We then went over the ground again on my two last propositions. At last I told them I had something of great importance to communicate confidentially, and to them alone. To my great surprise the room was at once cleared of all but the two Governors and Moriama Tatsitsio. I then read to them an extract from a letter to me from the Secretary of State, which was to the effect that, if the Japanese sought to evade the Treaty, the President would not hesitate to ask Congress to give him power to use such arguments as they could not resist. The fluttering was fearful—the effect strong. They thanked me for the confidence I had placed in them by reading that part of the Secretary's letter, and asked if they might communicate the same to their Government. I told them they could do so. They then asked me to give them a written translation of the paragraph so that they might make a correct translation. This I declined, but told them I would have it translated and that Moriama might use that paper in my presence to translate it to them, but that the paper must be returned to me. This ended our proceedings for the day at half-past four P. M.[398]

Wednesday, March 4, 1857. Met the Governors at noon. The room was cleared and I then handed them the Dutch translation referred to yesterday, and it was carefully translated into Japanese by Moriama, and then the paper was returned to me. Travelled over the debates of yesterday, like a horse in a mill. I finally demanded a

---

[398]Secretary Marcy's letter to Senator Seward (dated Mar. 2, 1857) was read to the Senate and was ordered to be printed (34–3, S. Misc. Doc., no. 55, p. 1).

categorical answer to the three points open,—*viz.,* currency, residence of Americans, and the Consular rights. They requested me to place all my propositions in writing. This I declined, telling them that, once I had placed my name to a paper, it could not be modified and that I wished to leave a door open by which we might arrive at a solution of the questions. It was finally agreed that Mr. Heusken, as from himself, would give them an unsigned paper containing the substance of my demands, the paper to be sent to the Governor's residence in the morning of to-morrow, and that we should meet again for the dispatch of business on Friday, the 6th inst.

Friday, March 6, 1857. Met the Governors at the usual place,—*i. e.,* the Goyoshi.

I asked them if they were prepared to give me answers to the points remaining unsettled, and soon found they were anything but ready. They said these were important matters and must be calmly considered; that the Japanese took a great while to consider every question; that in this respect they differed from the Americans, who decided promptly on all questions.

The currency question again came up and was again gone over for the twentieth time. At last I told them my mind was made up and that I would not allow more than five per cent. for re-coinage; that their demands were exorbitant, etc., etc.; that their plea that it cost twenty-five per cent. I had fully met by offering to have it done for five per cent., and that it appeared as though the Government wished to squeeze the Americans who came here, etc., etc. This elicited a direct offer

326

on their part of taking our coins at six per cent. discount. To show how great a step this was in our favor, it should be remembered that heretofore the dollar passed for 1,600 seni, but the last offer of the Japanese would give 4,670 for the dollar, or nearly two hundred per cent. more than they formerly allowed.

I refused to advance from the five per cent. The Governor, the Prince of Shinano, rose from his seat and came to me; and, while standing, begged me as a personal favor to him to yield the one per cent. of difference; that they were most anxious to have the matter settled, but that it was impossible for them to go further than they had done, and (*mark this*) that, if they took the coin of the Americans at less than six per cent., the Government would lose by the operation of re-coinage. Contrast this with their solemn assurance that it cost twenty-five per cent. to coin the money of Japan. The mendacity of these men passes all human belief. We finally adjourned to some day next week. I am really ill, yet I am forced day after day to listen to useless debates, on points that have been exhausted, and are only varied by some new phase of falsehood!

Saturday, March 7, 1857. On looking over my *Journal* for February 25th, I find I have omitted two important matters. On the 4th of October, 1855, the Secretary of State wrote me[399] that the Navy Department had

---

[399]Townsend Harris made two copies of this Letter of Special Instructions (*L. & P.*, vol. 1, no. 21; and vol. 2, no. 21). In addition to what is stated in the text, Secretary Marcy suggests an additional article to the Perry Treaty, which should establish the right of temporary residence in Japan; discusses the currency question, and the establishment of a Consulate at Hakodate; and closes with the hope that the Japanese will reciprocate in kindly feelings and

received dispatches from Lieutenant Rodgers to the effect that Reed and Dougherty, two Americans who had gone to Japan to establish themselves there, had been ordered away from Shimoda and refused permission to land at Hakodate.[400] Lieutenant Rodgers also wrote that the Japanese version of the seventh Article of Commodore Perry's Treaty contained the words "such as may be necessary for them" in connection with the agreement to permit Americans to make purchases of goods in Japan. I was informed by the Department that these words were not contained in the English, Dutch or Chinese versions of the Treaty, and I was directed to inquire into the matter and see if they were actually inserted in the Japanese version.

I asked the Governors if they had an authentic copy of the Treaty of Kanagawa; and, on their answering in the affirmative, I requested them to turn to the seventh

that consequently Townsend Harris will succeed in procuring greater privileges than were procured by the Perry Treaty.

The question of residence was completely settled by Article II of the Convention of Shimoda (June 17, 1857), which provides "that American citizens may permanently reside at Shimoda and Hakodate," etc.

[400]Messrs. W. C. Reed and T. T. Dougherty (and party) had left Shimoda in the American schooner *Caroline E. Foote*, Captain A. J. Worth, early in June, 1855. Arriving at Hakodate, they tried in vain to land and establish in that city their store for general ships' supplies for the American whaling fleet—in vain, in spite of the help rendered by Lieutenant John Rodgers, who had arrived at that port a few days before them in the U.S.S. *Vincennes*, of the U. S. Surveying and Exploring Expedition to the North Pacific Ocean. (See Lieutenant Rodgers's letters to Messrs. Reed and Dougherty written at Hakodate, June 19 and 25, 1855.) The *C. E. Foote* therefore left Japan on June 27 or 28, 1855; put in at Guam for supplies on July 15th; and left on July 31st for San Francisco, where she arrived safely on Sept. 17, 1855, bringing: firstly, dispatches from Admiral Poutiatine, who had just (Feb. 7, 1855) concluded the Russian Treaty with Japan; and, secondly, the first cargo ever imported directly from Japan to the United States. (Read the copious correspondence of this unsuccessful commercial venture to Japan by Messrs. Reed and Dougherty in the New York *Herald,* Morning ed., Monday, Oct. 15, 1855, p. 1, columns 2–6; and see above, note 325.)

Article of the Treaty, and then asked them if the words above noted were contained in it. They at once said they were not in the Article. I then told them that, when Lieutenant Rodgers was here, the Governor had assured him that those words were contained in the Japanese version of the Treaty.

With unmoved faces they assured me they never heard of any such statement; that the Governor could not have said so, and that there must be some mistake about it. I then complained of the ordering away of Messrs. Reed and Dougherty from Shimoda and refusing them permission to land in Hakodate. They answered that that was wrong, that they ought not to have ordered them away from Shimoda, nor have refused them permission to land at Hakodate.

I also omitted a description of the interior of the houses occupied by the Governors. These are some twenty to thirty buildings in one grand enclosure, all of which are occupied by the various officials of this place. The houses are all of wood covered with tile roofs. The sides of each room are a series of paper windows some six feet high, and have sliding shutters to close them in during storms or cold weather. The houses are very open and are only warmed by charcoal braziers. The rooms are covered with very soft and beautiful mats. These mats are the same size all through Japan,—*i. e.,* six feet long and three feet wide. At the outer door the Japanese take off their straw shoes and walk into the house in their stockings, consequently the mats are always clean. The mat serves as a seat by day and a bed by night.

In cold weather they wrap themselves in a thickly wadded blanket made with sleeves; a wooden pillow three inches high supports the *neck* (not the head), and prevents the hair being tumbled. At their meals a stand of lacquered wood about one foot high and some eighteen inches square serves as the table of each person, and their food is served entirely in wooden vessels, except tea and saki, which are drunk from porcelain cups. No sofa, chair, table, sideboard or other furniture is to be found in the rooms. In the bedrooms some chests or cabinets contain their clothes, arms, books, etc., etc. The walls are sometimes decorated with paper hangings, with trees, flowers, storks, etc., drawn on them, but generally they are the plain wood or simple figured paper. Their wardrobe is always a small one, as the quantity of clothes required or rather allowed by their sumptuary laws is limited. I do not think the world contains a people so truly frugal and plain in matters of diet and dress as the Japanese. No jewelry is ever seen on a man. Gold is chiefly used to decorate their swords. In some particular cases, gold brocades are used with scarlet or yellow, but these are rare cases. They form the exception and not the rule. The colors of the dress are either black or gray; the material for the nobles is of silk, [for] all others it is cotton. They are a people of but few wants.

Sunday, March 8, 1857. A cannon from the Signal Hill announced a foreign ship at noon to-day, and caused emotions of sincere pleasure. On ascending a height near the Consulate I saw the blessed Stars and Stripes flying from a barque, which was standing towards the inner harbor, having a signal for a pilot flying, and the pilot was seen pulling off to her, but as the pilot neared her she filled away, stood off until she was fairly in Yedo Bay, and then stood southward.

What does it mean? It was like the *Flying Dutchman*.

Monday, March 9, 1857. At nine this morning the barque again made her appearance and anchored in the outer harbor. Mr. Heusken went on board, and when he returned he brought with him Captain Homer of the Barque *Messenger Bird,* from Boston via the Sandwich Islands and Guam. Mr. Edward F. Hall, the supra-cargo, presented a letter of introduction written by the Hon. David L. Gregg, U. S. Commissioner to the Sandwich Islands.[401] Captain Homer has his wife and two children on board—one an infant born at sea off the Caroline Islands.

Mr. Hall having come via San Francisco, I got newspapers up to the 8th of November, or six months later than my last dates. So, Mr. Buchanan is President. When I last saw him in London on the 31st of October last, I told him that I had no doubt he would be the next President.[402] I am glad to hear it, and trust that under his administration peace and quiet will settle on

[401]Mr. David L. Gregg had been consulted by Messrs. Reed and Dougherty (who, it will be remembered, had sailed for Japan from Honolulu on Feb. 13, 1855) and had expressed his opinion that they were quite within the terms of the Perry Treaty in trying to establish themselves at Hakodate.

[402]Townsend Harris had visited James Buchanan, then Minister to London, on Oct. 31, 1855, when, on his way back to the Far East as Consul General to Japan, he had gone to the American Legation to have his passport viséd. (See note 16.)

the land; as the newspapers were only from the 20th of October to the 8th of November, there is a large hiatus in details, and Mr. Hall being only eighteen years of age could not give me many particulars. Mr. Hall informs me that he has an assorted cargo and wishes to trade here, and that he shall then proceed to Hakodate and thence to the Amur River, at which last place he is to establish himself in business as a ship chandler. I told him that I was still negotiating with the Japanese about the currency, and told him he could depend on not losing over six per cent. on the money he should expend here, which gave him great satisfaction.

Sent word to the Governors that I wished to see them to-morrow.

Tuesday, March 10, 1857. Met the Governors. Told them the arrival of a ship required a settlement of the currency question. They stuck at the six, and I at the five per cent. I proposed that this ship should settle at the six per cent., but that it should not be used as a precedent.

They said they required ten days to settle the currency question, as they must send to Yedo. They then opened on ground that even astonished *me,* used as I am to Japanese falsehood. They roundly declared the Dutch Convention did not exist, that it was a false report. I told them with some sternness that I had seen it with my own eyes, on board the Dutch Frigate *Diana* [*Medusa*] in October last. They then said it had not been ratified. This I also stopped by saying that it did bear the ratification of the Japanese Government. This

332

point was asserted and re-asserted by them time and again and as often met by a plain statement of the truth by me.[403]

Now came a new turn. They said the 12th and 13th Articles had been stricken out of the Japanese copy.

In reply I asked, if that was so, how was it that they gave me a correct version of the 12th and 13th Articles from their copy? Bingo-no-Kami said he got a copy made for himself when at Yedo before it was acted on by the Government. I asked to see his copy, when lo! it was a *printed,* and not a manuscript copy! I called their attention to this fact, but they made no reply.[404]

I then said that the evidence of the authenticity of my version was quite satisfactory to me, and that it would be so to my Government, who would act on it as authentic.

They then repeated that those two Articles never went into operation, etc., etc. I told them that Captain Fabius of the Dutch Navy had informed me that the buildings at Deshima had been sold to the Dutch, and the ground

---

[403]See above, *Journal,* Feb. 26, 1857, and the discussion in the notes on this moot point, especially note 391.

[404]The document in the hands of the Governors of Shimoda must have been a printed copy of the first Dutch Treaty—that of Nov. 9, 1855. Therefore, the text of Art. XII and XIII was bound to be the same as that in the copy which Townsend Harris had received from Captain Fabius. The Japanese naturally made no reply, because the only reply possible under the circumstances would have revealed the existence of the second Dutch Treaty, in which (as was justly maintained by the Japanese) the privileges granted in Art. XII and XIII of the first treaty had been withdrawn.

(Articles XII and XIII of the Dutch Treaty of Nov. 9, 1855, became Art. XII of the Treaty of Jan. 30, 1856.)

leased to them. They vehemently denied the truth of that statement.

I told them that negative proof was nothing against credible, positive testimony. It was now past four, and I closed a very stormy interview with an appointment for the next day.

Wednesday, March 11, 1857. I went yesterday on board the *Messenger Bird,* and saw Mrs. Homer, a nice person indeed, with a bouncing baby in her arms. This *home sight* almost made me *homesick.*

At the Goyoshi at half-past eleven. The Governors again wished to open the currency question. I told them if they would give me satisfaction on the other unsettled points, I would satisfy them in the matter of the currency. After a great deal of debate, in which, however, they did not repeat the barefaced assertions of yesterday, they requested me to put the two claims of residence of Americans and consular rights on paper, and give them time to consider about it, as it was a matter of much gravity, etc., etc. I assented to this and so closed our business for the present. Again visited the barque, and after chatting for an hour went home.

Captain and Mrs. Homer and Mr. Hall are to breakfast with me on Friday noon.

Friday, March 13, 1857. Breakfast party as above. Walk to a place where [we] can see Oho Sima.[405] Day fine, and pass it most agreeably. Company leave at five P. M.

In the evening write letter to the Governors on the two

---

[405]Oshima.

points, which I support with a few of the strongest arguments (see private letter book).[406]

Saturday, March 14, 1857. Mr. Heusken has translated Mr. Hall's lists of merchandise and goes with him to assist as his interpreter.

Sunday, March 15, 1857. I have never been so ill for seven years as I am to-day; vomited a quantity of fresh blood.

Monday, March 16, 1857. Gave Captain Homer a list of some supplies I wish to purchase from him.[407]

Thursday, March 19, 1857. I have been and still am very ill. Earthquake at ten P. M. Heavy rumbling sound; house rattles. Comes from S. S. E. and goes N. N. W. Lasts about three seconds.

Saturday, March 21, 1857. Better to-day. Weather fine. Wheat grows beautifully. Japanese busy in planting potatoes, etc. I have a camellia tree in my yard which is some twenty feet high. It is now in full flower, and has perhaps thousands of flowers out—the finest

---

[406]See above, *Journal*, Feb. 27, 1857, and note 396. This very long letter ends with the following threat (*L. B.*, vol. 2, p. 3):

"Your Excellencies will bear witness of [to] my anxious efforts to secure the present friendly relations between Japan and the United States, and how carefully I have avoided giving offence myself, or allowing any member of my family to do so. It is my earnest hope that, after a careful examination of what I now communicate, you will give an evidence of your wish to preserve the friendly relations between the two countries.

"At the same time candor compels me to say, as I now say to Your Excellency [sic], that a refusal of these two points will endanger the good feeling now happily existing and may lead to results that I am sure Your Excellencies would deplore as deeply as I should lament."

On this day, ratification of Townsend Harris's Treaty with Siam was advised by the Senate with Amendment (S. Ex. J'l, vol. 10, p. 256).

[407]On this day, Townsend Harris's Treaty with Siam was ratified by the President.

sight of the kind I ever saw. It commenced blooming abou⁺ the 5th [of] January, and is now in full flower.

Monday [Sunday], March 22, 1857. Mr. Hall cannot sell anything to the Japanese, and no wonder, for his prices are most exorbitant.

Tuesday, March 24, 1857. Mr. Hall has completed his purchases. Instead of over three thousand three hundred dollars which they would have demanded under the old rates, he paid them about one thousand one hundred and fifty dollars; this saving of over two thousand dollars is owing to my action.

Wednesday, March 25, 1857. Get a portion only of my supplies from the *Messenger Bird,* the remainder is stowed either quite forward or quite below a large quantity of cargo. This is bad management. A vessel on such a voyage should have her cargo so stowed that any portion of it may easily be got at, so as to be ready for trade, however small, at any port.[408]

Thursday, March 26, 1857. Pay my bill to Mr. Hall in silver at very high prices, and in return he wished to pay me in gold, which entails a loss of seventy-five per cent. to me here in Japan, as their ratio of gold as to silver is only three and one seventh to one, instead of sixteen to one, as with us. It takes a New England man to do such things.

Saturday, March 28, 1857. Moriama called and wished to discuss the two points, which I decline. In answer to my questions as to the state of public opinion at

---

[408]Here Townsend Harris is speaking from personal experience. See Introduction.

Yedo regarding intercourse with foreigners, he says that, taking ten persons in authority, three would be in favor of opening the country at once, two would be in favor but with delay, three would refuse so long as force is not used, but would yield to such a demonstration without fighting, and two would fight to the last. Moriama says the Prince of Shinano wishes to call on me to-morrow. I request the Prince to excuse me on Sunday, but that I shall be very happy to see him on any other day of the week.[409]

Sunday, March 29, 1857. The Barque *Messenger Bird* went to sea early this morning, bound to Hakodate and the River Amur.

Monday, March 30, 1857. The Prince of Shinano visited me to-day. He was attended by a very large train, but only a Vice-Governor and the interpreters were admitted to my private rooms. I have completely broken up the system of having a cloud of secretaries and spies crowding into my private rooms. All are delighted except the writers and spies. Gave the Prince a Colt's revolver, one of three that was put into the case of arms I purchased for the Kings of Siam in lieu of discount.

Tuesday, March 31, 1857. This has been a fine

---

[409]This reservation of Sunday is quite in keeping with Townsend Harris's early expressed resolve to keep holy the Sabbath Day. (See *Journal*, entries for Aug. 22, 24, 31, Dec. 5, 1856, and Feb. 15, 1858.)

On this day, Townsend Harris wrote to the Governors of Shimoda, acknowledging receipt of their letter of Mar. 26th (?). He expresses surprise that they must needs refer to Yedo the two points which he had raised by letter of Mar. 13, 1857; and states his belief that they are simply trying to procrastinate. Such delay he considers tantamount to a denial of the points raised. He closes with the statement that he is daily expecting the arrival of an American man-of-war, by which he will have to send reports to the United States (*L. B.,* vol. 2, pp. 4–5).

month. The mean of the thermometer was 51 6/10; highest, 63°; lowest, 38°. Had rain on five days, showers on four, cloudy two, clear twenty.

This month the wind sometimes had southing, the first time for sixty-four days.

Wednesday, April 1, 1857. Dispatch letter dated March 28th to Council of State in reply to their letter received February 25th (see private letter book).[410] I have delayed writing this letter so long in the hope of bringing things to a quiet close here.[411]

Friday, April 3, 1857. Busy putting seeds in my little garden; have doubts about their vitality. Governors wish to see me. Go to Goyoshi at two P. M. They

---

[410]*L. B.*, vol. 2, pp. 5–9. On Feb. 25, 1857, Townsend Harris received from the Council of State a letter in reply to two of his—namely, to those dated Oct. 25, 1856, and Jan. 8, 1857. In his reply of Mar. 28, 1857, Townsend Harris repeats the arguments of his two former communications (see *Journal*, entries for those two dates, and notes 313 and 369); points out the great discourtesy of the Japanese Government in insisting on receiving the President's letter through the Governors of Shimoda—a discourtesy which he forgives on account of their ignorance of Western procedure; says that he cannot make communications through the Governors of Shimoda, because they have not been given full powers; and that he will reveal his knowledge of the intentions of the British Government only at Yedo.

He again closes (as in his letter of even date to the Governors of Shimoda, note 409) with a statement designed to bear pressure—namely, that he is daily expecting the arrival of an American man-of-war, by which he will have to send reports home.

[411]Of this date, also, are the following routine reports:

1) To Hon. James Guthrie, Secretary of the Treasury:
   Dispatch No. 3: *L. B.*, vol. 2, p. 11
   "   No. 4: "   "   "   " " "
   "   No. 5: "   "   "   " pp. 14–15
2) To Hon. William L. Marcy:
   Dispatch No. 25: *L. B.*, vol. 2, pp. 12–13
   "   No. 26: "   "   "   " p. 15
3) To Baring Bros., of London: *L. B.*, vol. 2, p. 13.

These dispatches transmitted reports for the quarter ending Mar. 31, 1857; that to Baring Bros. was a draft for his salary for the same quarter—£258. 5. 3.

wish to know the contents of my letter to Council of State. Sorry, but it would be improper in me to disclose it. They ask the meaning of certain words in [the] 12th Article of [the] American Treaty.[412] I ask for a piece of ground for a garden, which is promised.

Saturday, April 4, 1857. Busy enclosing duplicates of dispatches to Department of State, also returns of fees to Secretary of Treasury for quarters ending 31st December[413] and March 31st. Send to Secretary of State my accounts of contingent fund for the same quarters.

Monday, April 6, 1857. Moriama calls about garden spot. Have given me the piece asked for, about one eighth of an acre. Rent six *ichibus per annum,* or two dollars and ninety-seven cents.

Tuesday, April 7, 1857. Moriama again. Brings me a gardener, the occupant of the land I have hired. Have a chat with Moriama as he is quite alone and therefore more communicative. He says that I will soon have an answer to the two points, and that it will be satisfactory to me;[414] that I must not hurry them too much;

---

[412]Art. XII of the Perry Treaty is the last Article, and deals with the manner of ratifying the Treaty itself.

[413]For the reports for the quarter ending Dec. 31, 1856, see *Journal,* Jan. 1, 1857, and note 365.

[414]The long letter in which Townsend Harris presented his "two points" to the Governors of Shimoda was dated Mar. 13, 1857 (*L. B.,* vol. 1, pp. 182–88; and vol. 2, pp. 1–3). The "two points" were: first, that American citizens should be allowed to lease ground, buy, build, repair, or erect buildings for their use at Shimoda and Hakodate (Townsend Harris basing his claim on what he at this time supposed to be the ratified Treaty concluded with the Dutch on Nov. 9, 1855); and, second, that the American Consul General should be allowed to make purchases anywhere in Japan and without the intervention of Japanese officers.

Compare Townsend Harris's reference to these "two points" in *Journal,* Apr. 20, 1857. Also, see above, *Journal,* Feb. 27, 1857, notes 393, 394, 396; and Mar. 13, 1857, note 406, where the closing vigorous paragraphs of this long letter are quoted.

that but a short time need elapse before a commercial treaty can be negotiated, etc., etc. He says the letter to me was signed by the whole of the High Council of Regents,[415] the power next [to] the Ziogoon; that there is another council of five to seven persons who are under the Regents. The Regents are not hereditary officers, they are appointed by the Ziogoon and hold office during his pleasure alone; that the story of an appeal lying to [resting with] the Princes of the Empire when there is a difference of opinion between the Ziogoon and his Regents (when the defeated party, if a Regent, performs the *hara-kiri;* if the Ziogoon, he resigns), is not true; no appeal from the Ziogoon exists,—his veto is final. If a Regent proposes a measure which is negatived by the Ziogoon, no harm arises; but if he renews the recommendation and it is again rejected, *then* the Regent does perform the *hara-kiri*.

No reports of the Treasury, War, Marine or Commerce. The results are only known to the Ziogoon and Regents and the heads of each department. Moriama says "it would be considered impolite for a person to make any inquiries concerning a department with which he is not connected." The English of it is that he *dare* not make such inquiries. I put down the information I get from time to time from [the] Japanese. I know there is much falsehood, but I cannot at the time separate the true from the false.

---

[415]This was the letter which Townsend Harris received on Feb. 25, 1857. See note 410.

Simonoski, one of the interpreters, told Mr. Heusken that all the buildings at Deshima had been sold to the Dutch.[416]

Wednesday, April 8, 1857. Plant four rows of Irish potatoes in my new garden. The seed grew at Hakodate. A peach tree in my compound just begins to bloom. The blossom is very double, and of the color and size of the "Cinnamon Rose" of the United States. Cherry trees in full bloom, but no fruit comes from the peach or cherry blooms. Why, I cannot say. My grand camellia is still in fine bloom. Busy filing papers and making out my remaining quarterly reports. Men employed to recover the mats that have become worn or soiled. These mats may properly be called mattresses. They are made on a frame and composed of layers of mats, the coarsest at the bottom, until they are about two inches thick. The ordinary exterior cover has quite the appearance of Chinese matting. They make a very good bed.

Easter Sunday, April 12, 1857. I have kept a very good account of the festivals of the church since my arrival here. It has served to bring up many pleasant recollections and association of ideas in my mind. The day is a lovely one; the fields around me are green with the waving wheat, or finely decorated with flowers. An

---

[416]The significance of this remark is that it served to confirm Townsend Harris in his wrong opinion of the *status quo* of the Treaty concluded with the Dutch at Nagasaki, on Nov. 9, 1855, and particularly in his belief in the concessions supposedly made by Art. XII and XIII thereof. (See above, *Journal,* Feb. 26, 1857, and notes 387–391, 393.) The concessions which Townsend Harris assumed had been granted to the Dutch by those two Articles are included in the "two points" he himself was now seeking to obtain from the Japanese.

abundance of violets grows about here. Thermometer, 69°.

Monday, April 13, 1857. A strong wind and driving rain from the S. W. serve to inaugurate Easter Monday at Shimoda.

Moriama calls on me, nominally to see me, but in reality to settle the wages of my two Japanese boys, which is at last settled at six *ichibus* per month, or about two dollars. The Vice-Governor last December wanted me to pay them sixteen dollars per month.

Moriama tells me as a most profound state secret that the Prince of Satsuma is father-in-law to the Ziogoon. I knew this last October. Moriama says that, although the Ziogoon has the supreme power to appoint or displace the members of the High Council, yet he is *influenced* by a cabal of six persons or families, to wit: three princes of the blood, and three powerful nobles; among the latter is the Prince of Satsuma. In other words, that an oligarchy governs Japan. Moriama says that Japan will be opened to foreigners within the year.

He admits that the Japanese are now negotiating a commercial treaty with the Dutch,[417] but I should greatly distrust the provisions of a treaty so made. The Dutch are altogether too fond of monopolies to make a treaty suited to the present wants of the commercial world.

Moriama informs me that the guns presented to the

[417]In his *Journal* for Apr. 15, 1857, Townsend Harris states that Moriyama said that the Japanese were *not* negotiating a commercial treaty with the Dutch.

Japanese (fifty-two in number)[418] have been taken to Yedo; that eight or nine of them are to be mounted on a corvette they have built on the Western model. The corvette is 120 feet keel.

Tuesday, April 14, 1857. The chief of the Goyoshi came to see me to-day. At last they have brought me my accounts for seven months. The total looks alarming, as it is 2,087,009 of their coins, but luckily that is fully liquidated with the sum of $447. My servants (*i. e.,* the Chinese) are the heaviest item of my expenses here, as their wages amount to more than $700 *per annum,* that is for four men, and I also give them their food and lodging, while for five Japanese I pay $132 *per annum* and they board themselves.

The Goyoshi man also brought me a Japanese dictionary and promises in a few days to bring me some school books, works of fiction and history. In my account for the last seven months are many things that I shall not have to renew, such as furniture, *norimon,* horse, etc., etc., all of which amount to $144,—so that leaves about $300 as my expenses for seven months. But my bread, tea, sugar, spices, pickles, coffee, etc., etc., are all brought here and are a very considerable item. I think however that $2,000 *per annum* will cover all my expenses; but, had I not brought them to terms about the currency, I should have found my salary insufficient for my support.

---

[418]These were the guns that had been removed from the crippled Russian Frigate *Diana* before she set sail from the Harbor of Shimoda for that of Toda (or, Hey-da), whither she was going for repairs. (See note 325. For the caliber and names of these guns, etc., *cf. Journal,* Nov. 22, 1856.)

Wednesday, April 15, 1857. Moriama visited the Consulate to-day. I had proposed to the Governors that, when the next American man-of-war came here, salutes should be exchanged after our fashion.

Moriama says the Governor would be much pleased by such a mark of friendship as would be indicated by a salute of the Flag of Japan, but proposed to return it in the Japanese manner,—*i. e.,* after the salute, to send a high officer dressed in his *camissimo,* or robes of ceremony, to return thanks for the salute. I told him that would hardly be satisfactory; that our custom was to give gun for gun, the ship being a visitor to salute first, and then to have it returned from the land.

I told him that I was anxious that the Japanese should take their place among the civilized nations of the world, and that all these small things were so many steps in that direction. I then entered at large into the system of salutes, and explained the manner in which they were given and returned.

The Governors having expressed a wish for books on all branches of military and naval science, as taught at West Point and at the Naval School, I sent them word that, if they would address me a letter on the subject, I would at once forward it to the Secretary of State, and that I had no doubt the books would be at once sent. Moriama then said that he wished to ask me a question, and that he wanted me to consider it as a dream,—*i. e.,* to forget it. The query was: "Suppose the Governors of Shimoda should wish to make a commercial treaty with you, what would you do?" I replied that I should first

344

ask to see their full powers, and if those were satisfactory, that I would then show them mine, and after that we would go to work at a treaty at once. He said if that was so, that they had misunderstood me, that they supposed that I would only negotiate at Yedo and with the High Council.

I told him that they had confounded two things; that what I had to say confidentially as from my Government could only be said at Yedo, so also the President's letter could only be delivered by me at Yedo and in the imperial presence, etc.

That negotiations were a different thing; that I was ready to negotiate with any person of proper rank who could show me the requisite full powers, etc., etc. He declared that they were not negotiating with the Dutch a commercial treaty; that, as soon as they were ready to negotiate on that point, they would negotiate with me.

Moriama says that almost all the books of Japan are simple reprints of Chinese classics, such as Confucius, Mencius, etc., etc.; but that I shall have copies of such purely Japanese works as they have. My young pigeons fly from the parent nest and "sit up for themselves," being thirty-six days old.

Moriama says that firearms were first introduced into Japan 300 years ago; that they were first introduced in the South, at the Island of Tanagasima;[419] that a pistol to this day is called Tanagasima by the Japanese. The place and date both serve to support the assertion of

419 Tanegashima, an island south of Kyushu.

345

Mendez Pinto that he first taught the Japanese the use of firearms.

Saturday, April 18, 1857. I have been overlooking my accounts from the Japanese, which they have now rendered to me for the first time. Although they charge me double prices for everything they furnish to me, yet my bills to them for food, fuel, lights, etc., etc., will not exceed $500 *per annum.* My servants are the heaviest charge, as I am compelled to pay three times the wages to my Chinese servants that they receive in China. My servants cost me nearly $700 *per annum.* To this I must add, for my full expenses, the cost of flour, tea, sugar, hams, butter, lard, bacon, salt, beef, pickles, spices, etc., etc., etc., which will amount to some $500 *per annum* more. But Mr. Heusken pays me $365 *per annum* for his board, washing, etc., which reduces my expenses to less than $1,500 *per annum.* Clothing, books, and the wine I must use when I have guests will probably leave the full outlay about $1,750 *per annum.*[420]

My servants consist of a butler, cook and his mate, washman, two house boys, one water carrier, one sweeper, one gardener, one groom,—in all ten persons, and not one that I can do without.

I am well supplied with fine pheasants at about sixteen cents each, and so large that one makes an ample dinner for Mr. Heusken and myself.

---

[420] The attention to financial matters both here and in the entry for Apr 14th was doubtless due to the numerous reports Townsend Harris had had to prepare on matters financial, both for Secretary of State Marcy and for Secretary of the Treasury Guthrie, for the quarter ending Mar. 31, 1857 (see above).

The day is a lovely one. How I wish my dear friends in New York were here to enjoy it with me.

I am much concerned at the non-arrival of the *San Jacinto*. Commodore Armstrong promised to be here in March, and now more than one half of April has slipped away.My last letters from the United States were dated March 17, 1856. More than thirteen months ago. How much may have happened in that time. My health is not good. On the 16th I had a violent attack of cholera morbus and I have an almost constant relax.

I wish the frigate would arrive that I could have some medical advice.

Monday, April 20, 1857. A miserable wet day. Send word to the Governors that I wish to meet them at the Goyoshi to-morrow at noon. I wish to engross the Articles already settled with them, and have them make their translation, as the last is always a work of much time, and thus I shall be able to expedite the whole matter the more promptly when I get a decision on the "two points." My hen pigeon that has just raised a pair of young, commenced hatching a new nest to-day. Sharp work, as her last brood came out of the shell on the 12th of March, or thirty-nine days ago. In my previous statements of my expenses of living here, I have entirely omitted *rent*. As yet I have not paid any, but when I shall occupy a house specially built for me, I shall of course have to pay it. This item will probably bring the total to a little over two thousand dollars *per annum*.

Tuesday, April 21, 1857. Met the Governors at noon at the Goyoshi. Agreed to settle the wording of the points already agreed on. Told them I should write them a formal letter requesting them to give me their version of the seventh Article of the Treaty of Kanagawa, as, when Lieutenant Rodgers was here (May, 1855), they had interpolated the words "Such as may be necessary for them" after the words "agreeing to trade."[421] I told them I should also ask them for an explanation of the sending away of Reed and Dougherty from Shimoda and refusing them permission to land at Hakodate in 1855.[422]

I inquired when I was to receive an answer on the "two points"? They could only repeat that they were anxiously looking for it to arrive here from Yedo. I found the matter of salutes, mentioned to Moriama on the 15th, is a perplexing matter to them, so I let it rest where it is for the present. I requested the Governors to order the Goyoshi officers to answer certain questions which I had received from my Government concerning cotton, its production in Japan, etc., etc., which they promised should be done. I called their attention to the breakwater of the jetty now erecting at Kakizaki; that it is so short, that at low water of spring tides it will not give anv protection to boats.[423] I left at two P. M. After

---

[421]Townsend Harris is quoting Art. VII of the Perry Treaty loosely. The only place where the quoted words could be interpolated is after the words "for other articles of goods." (See also *Journal*, Mar. 7, 1857.)

[422]For the story of the unsuccessful venture of Messrs. Reed and Dougherty, see notes 325 and 400.

[423]It will be remembered that the hurricane which swept over Shimoda on Monday, Sept. 22, 1856, had totally destroyed the landing-jetty and breakwater at Kakizaki. Townsend Harris had appealed to the Additional Regulations concluded by Commodore Perry, and had, on Dec. 2, 1856, insisted with the

my return home wrote the letter to the Governors as referred to in the beginning of this entry, and settled the wording of the Articles.

Wednesday, April 22, 1857. The seeds I brought from the United States will, as I fear, prove to be a total failure. I put eighteen sorts in the ground on the 3rd inst., but only some few peas have as yet come up. It will be a sad drawback to my comforts if they should fail. To-day put in the ground a few grains of corn, watermelons, cucumbers and eggplant seeds procured from the Japanese. Twenty grains of corn and seven watermelon seeds were all I could procure! They said all their seeds were planted.

My canary has hatched a new brood of young.

Friday, April 24, 1857. My canary has again abandoned her nest. I cannot account for her unnatural conduct. I separated her and the male the moment she commenced to incubate, and have not only kept him out of sight but out of hearing. I can only suppose I have fed her *too high*. She had yolk of egg every day.

Saturday, April 25, 1857. I have given some lessons in English to the Imperial Surgeon, who attends the Governors here. I did this at their request. I found him very apt. He has been absent for some weeks to visit his sick father at Yedo, and to-day came to renew his lessons. I did not give him anything but a letter to the Governors, in which I told them that I should be very happy to give instruction in English, after I had been per-

Third Governor, or Governor of Kakizaki, that this boat-landing be repaired, receiving from him the promise that it would be immediately attended to. (See notes 300, 347, 349.)

349

mitted the full exercise of my rights as Consul, but, so long as I was denied any of those rights, I must decline the lessons.[424] I cannot see what it is that keeps away Commodore Armstrong. If I had a vessel of war here, I should have speedy answers to my demands on the two points, but I feel sure they will not be settled so long as no ship-of-war comes here.

The Commodore promised to be here in March, yet April has nearly passed away and no ship has come.[425]

My last letters from the Department of State were dated in October, 1855,[426] more than eighteen months ago. It is too long a period to leave me here alone, and some order should be given to ensure more frequent communication with me.

Monday, April 27, 1857. The rhododendron, althea, is now in beautiful flower, colors chiefly pink. I have planted some of them in the cemetery where the four Americans are buried.

Flowers of the peony,—*China poppy, flowered peony* and *"Tree Peony,"*—brought me to-day. Very splendid.

---

[424] *L. B.*, vol. 2, p. 17.

[425] Aside from the natural desire to see his countrymen—a desire rendered more acute by his isolation—Townsend Harris must have felt real diplomatic concern at the long delay in the arrival of the *San Jacinto*. He had held the threat of its arrival over the heads of the Japanese in two recent letters—both written on Mar. 28, 1857: one, to the Governors of Shimoda, in connection with the "two points"; the other, to the Council of State at Yedo (see notes 409 and 410).

If, after he had thus brought pressure to bear, no American man-of-war should appear to give added weight to his words, Townsend Harris would soon have "lost face" with the Japanese negotiators. It was not until Tuesday, Sept. 8, 1857, that a vessel of the United States Navy finally appeared at Shimoda—the sloop-of-war *Portsmouth,* Captain Andrew Hull Foote.

[426] This was the Letter of Special Instructions, dated at the Department of State, Oct. 4, 1855, which enclosed the necessary documents referring to the Reed and Dougherty case. (See note 399.)

Moriama calls for verbal explanations about the wording of the Articles already agreed on. Fihd it is a cunning attempt to interpolate words of different meaning. Moriama says very coolly that "it is a very different thing to *say* a thing or to write it." In other words, they are always at liberty to deny anything they have said or promised, so long as it is not in writing.

Tuesday, April 28, 1857. Plant some more potatoes of the seed procured from Hakodate. Those planted on the 8th inst. are coming up. The Japanese say the season is unusually backward and the weather colder than they ever knew in April. The thermometer averages much lower than I expected for this month in the latitude of 35° north. All the winds from the northward are quite chilly. The Seville orange trees in front of my house do not show a single leaf as yet.

Busy to-day in making indexes of the correspondence and documents of the Consulate. Have now got all my papers in perfect order, and only await the arrival of a ship to dispatch a large amount of correspondence. I feel sure that what I have accomplished will give satisfaction. I have settled the currency so that one dollar goes as far almost as three did when Commodore Perry left the question. I have opened the Port of Nagasaki to American ships wanting supplies.

Americans are only to be amenable to American authority for offences committed in Japan.

American ships in distress and who have no money can pay for all necessary supplies by barter.

The great point of residence of Americans is still

351

pending; and, although it may not *now* be admitted, yet I have placed it on a footing which must ultimately secure it. The consular rights and franchises stand on the same ground as the rights of residence.

I have fought the battles; and, although *I* may not receive the victory, yet victory will come and will be owing to my labors.[427]

Wednesday, April 29, 1857. Moriama visits me and brings the Dutch version of the Articles agreed on. I find it correct at last. One would think the translation of a paper to be a simple process, but it is not so with the Japanese; for, besides their duplicity and constant efforts to vary the substance, they are so absurd as to wish to have every word placed in the Dutch version exactly in the order it stands in the Japanese. It is very difficult to explain to them the idioms of language, or the grammatical structure of it, or to get them to see that, although the placing of the words does not correspond with theirs, yet the meaning is the same. Their knowledge of Dutch is imperfect. They have learned the language as spoken by traders and sailors, and the Dutch they use is not only that of two hundred and fifty years ago, but it is limited to the subjects above referred to; hence we have great difficulty in conveying an abstract idea to them, and it is almost impossible to speak figuratively to them.

The Japanese have *fixed days* for their change of clothing. The *law* settles the matter beforehand, and

---

[427]In this entry, Townsend Harris outlines the Convention signed two months later at Shimoda—on June 17, 1857.

no inclemency of weather can postpone the change.

The following are the periods and changes of their dress for our year 1857:

On the first day of the fourth month, April 24th, they threw off their wadded clothes and put on unwadded ones, but of thick materials.

On the fifth day of the fifth month, May 23rd, they will put on their summer clothing.

On the first day of the ninth month, October 18th, they will resume the same clothing as that put on on the 24th of April.

On the ninth day of the ninth month, October 26th, they will put on their winter clothing. This is made of the same material as the previous change, only it is thickly *wadded* with cotton or silk wadding.

As a specimen of the cool mendacity of the Japanese, even about things that are tangible to the sight, I note the following: the Island of Oho Sima is in plain sight of Shimoda and some twelve or fifteen miles distant from us, so that it comes within the limits of *seven ri,* or sixteen and five-eighths miles as settled for the Americans. Yet the Governors coolly tell me that Oho Sima is *twenty-five ri,* or fifty-nine and three-eighths miles distant from Shimoda!!

Kaempfer speaks of a superior fish, said to be taken in Yesso, which the Japanese call *sukee,* but he could not find out what kind of fish it was. I have discovered that it is *salmon.*

Thursday, April 30, 1857. The thermometer this morning at daylight was as low as it has been at any time this month,—about 43°. The temperature has been very low for such a latitude.

My health is very unsatisfactory. I am unable to cure my acid stomach arising from indigestion. I have reduced my food to bread, rice and the flesh meat we get here, having left off butter, oil, fruit, and all vegetables except potatoes. Still my indisposition continues and I am constantly growing thinner and thinner. I walk every day from six to eight miles. Perhaps the machine is wearing out, and these are premonitions of the approaching end. I have slept comparatively well for the last ten days.

The thermometer has stood as follows: mean for the month, 57 2/10°; highest, 67°; lowest, 43°; rain on four days, showers two days, cloudy three days, and fine twenty-one days. Light earthquake on the fourteenth of April.

Friday, May 1, 1857. May Day! A fine day indeed. Thermometer, 69°. Mr. Heusken brought me a bunch of violets which gave out a fine fragrance. Generally the flowers here have but little perfume. Moriama brings a letter from the Governors in answer to mine of [the] 22nd of April.[428] It is anything but what I expected, and quite different from what they said to me at our con-

---

[428]There is no mention of such a letter in *Journal*, Wednesday, Apr. 22, 1857. The entry, however, for Tuesday, Apr. 21st, does speak of such a letter. Townsend Harris had wrongly dated the latter entry "Tuesday, April 22nd," correcting it later to "April 21st." In other words, the reference in the entry for May 1, 1857, was made back to the earlier date before Townsend Harris corrected the earlier date from the 22nd to the 21st.

The text of this letter to the Governors is not found; but its contents are pretty well indicated in *Journal*, Apr. 21, 1857. The answer of the Governors (undated) was received May 1, 1857 (cf. also Townsend Harris's letter to Shinano-no-Kami, dated June 3, 1857: *L. B.*, vol. 2, p. 18).

versations on the subject in February last. It is all of a piece with their falsehood and duplicity. I do not think that any Japanese ever tells the truth, if it can possibly be avoided. He prefers using falsehood when the simple truth would answer just as well.

The Japanese cycle consists of twelve years which are named as follows:

1st	Year	Ne	or the	Rat
2nd	"	Oo-s	" "	Bullock
3rd	"	Tora	" "	Tiger
4th	"	Uh!	" "	Hare
5th	"	Tat's	" "	Dragon
6th	"	Mi	" "	Serpent (1857)
7th	"	Um-ma	" "	Horse
8th	"	He-'tsu-zi	" "	Sheep
9th	"	Sarru	" "	Monkey
10th	"	Tory	" "	Cock
11th	"	E-noo	" "	Dog
12th	"	E	" "	Boar

The Japanese divide the day into two parts, each six hours long,—the day is six hours and the night six hours,—but, as the length of the day and night is constantly changing, so the Japanese hours vary in the number of our minutes which they contain. Thus, at the Equinoxes, the hour in Japan both night and day is 120 minutes; but, on the twentieth of June, the *day* hour at Shimoda is 143 minutes long, and the night hour is 97 minutes. On the twentieth of December, the length of the hours is reversed from what it was in June, as the day hour is 97 minutes and the night hour becomes

143 minutes. They have a mode of equalizing this monstrous difference between the Equinoxes and the longest and shortest days, but it is very inexact. The hours begin to count from the meridian, or twelve o'clock noon, or midnight, so that six o'clock of our time becomes the sixth hour with them. The following is the name they give to divisions of time, corresponding with our hours:

12 o'clock	with	us	is	the	Japanese	9th hour
1	"	"	" " "	"	8½	"
2	"	"	" " "	"	8	"
3	"	"	" " "	"	7½	"
4	"	"	" " "	"	7	"
5	"	"	" " "	"	6½	"
6	"	"	" " "	"	6	"
7	"	"	" " "	"	5½	"
8	"	"	" " "	"	5	"
9	"	"	" " "	"	4½	"
10	"	"	" " "	"	4	"
11	"	"	" " "	"	3½	"

And from 3½ hours it rises at once to 9 hours, so that there is no 1, 2, or 3 o'clock with them. The Japanese have no names for the signs of the zodiac, nor do they designate or distinguish days by any particular name; nor do any number of days receive any distinctive terms,—e. g., "a week," etc.

They say the "fifth day of the 10th month of the year of the Dragon." Our "Friday, May 1, 1857," would read in Japanese "the seventh day of the fourth month of the year of the Serpent."

Saturday, May 2, 1857. I have made another trial of some of my garden seeds by putting them in a most favorable position for sprouting, and afterwards they can be transplanted if they germinate.

A most lovely day. Thermometer, 70°.

Tuesday, May 5, 1857. It is now eight months and three days since the *San Jacinto* left here.[429] Commodore Armstrong promised me he would be here again in six months. I am a prey to unceasing anxiety. I have not heard a word from Washington since I left the United States, say October, 1855.[430]

What can be the cause of this prolonged absence of an American man-of-war? Where are the English? Where the French? And, above all, where is the Russian Consul? He should have been here before this. I am only nine days distant from Hongkong, yet I am more isolated than any American official in any part of the world.

I have important intelligence to send to my Government—intelligence that will give an immediate spur to our trade with Japan; yet here it remains, month after month, without my being able to communicate it to my Government, or enabling my countrymen to benefit by it. The absence of a man-of-war also tends to weaken my influence with the Japanese. They have yielded nothing except from *fear,* and any future ameliorations of

---

[429]The *San Jacinto* had left Shimoda for China on Thursday, Sept. 4, 1856 (*cf. Journal*), and had arrived at Shanghai one week later—Sept. 11th. (See letter by Commissioner Peter Parker to Consul Caleb Jones, Shanghai, Sept. 13, 1856, in 35–2, S. Ex. Doc., no. 22, part 2—in Serial no. 983—p. 963; *cf.* p. 1206.)

[430]See note 425.

our intercourse will only take place after a demonstration of force on our part.

I will not suppose this apparent neglect arises from indifference or idleness on the part of our naval commanders out here. I, therefore, am left a prey to all sorts of imaginations as to the detaining causes.[481]

Wednesday, May 7 [6], 1857. My young fowls have commenced laying eggs at the age of eighteen weeks. I do not know how soon they usually begin the great business of their lives "to increase and multiply," but it appears to me that this is a tender age to take up the "cares of maternity."

I have the greatest difficulty in breeding fowls, pigeons and birds. For enemies I have the cats, the rats, the foxes, the weasels, the itats (a ferocious brute of the weasel tribe), hawks, owls and crows.

Out of three nests my pigeons have only raised one,— *i. e.,* one pair. I had a fine nest of thirteen eggs, which would have been hatched in three days, when the brood hen was almost murdered by a rascally tomcat; so the poor thing refused to go back to the "post of danger," and gave me another lesson on the folly of "counting our chickens before the eggs are hatched."

I have recorded the shortcomings of my canary, and how she cruelly abandoned two nests of her callow young. She is now incubating a third nest of eggs, and I have put her on a *low diet,* and separated her from her mate, hoping by these measures to keep the "devil of

---

[481]Not only the American men-of-war, but also those of the allies, were waging the so-called Second Opium War in China. For a few details of the American participation in these hostilities, see note 311.

concupiscence" out of her little body, until her young can feed themselves. The cat in Japan is from the Indian Archipelago, as is proved by its having the preposterous screw tail that peculiarly marks the cats of that part of the world. They are capital mousers and are afraid of nothing in the shape of a quadruped.

Saturday, May 9, 1857. We have had six days of the most unpleasant weather I have experienced since I arrived here. It has either rained or been cloudy for a week.

Moriama brought me to-day $283.50, American gold, which was paid to the Japanese by the purser of the *San Jacinto.* I redeemed it (as he promised to do) by giving them silver for it; but, instead of paying them a silver dollar for each gold dollar, I give them a silver *ichibu* for each dollar of gold.

I have called on the Governors of Shimoda to redeem the promise they made me before I landed,—that "all my supplies should be furnished at the same rates as were charged to the Japanese." I am satisfied that I have been constantly and systematically overcharged, and I sent to the Governor a list of prices at which I am charged, and against these I placed the prices that I have obtained from time to time from Japanese who are not connected with the Government.

The difference is very great.[432]

For the last few weeks I have seen the only attempt

---

[432]There is extant a memorandum in Townsend Harris's hand (a Dutch translation of which was sent to the Governors) of his objections to the prices he had been charged. The memorandum is dated May 2, 1857, and was sent the same day (*L. & P.*, vol. 1, no. 65).

of Japanese boys at amusement of any kind. They have no games, no plays, do not congregate together, have no hoops, no skip ropes, no marbles, no tops, and, I fear, nothing else; but I have been relieved by the sight and *sound* of *kites* lately. I say sound of kites; they affix some thin slips of bamboo on the back of the kite, which give out a sound like the Æolian harp; and, the kite being made to *plunge* violently, gives out the sound constantly.

Monday, May 11, 1857. Went over to the Goyoshi to select some articles for Mrs. S. N. Spooner,[433] who gave me seventy-five dollars in August last to invest for her. I was not pleased with the articles offered to me. I think we have overrated the habit of the Japanese in making elaborately fine articles of any kind. The genius of their government seems to forbid any exercise of ingenuity in producing articles for the gratification of wealth and luxury.

Sumptuary laws rigidly enforce the form, color, material and time of changing the dress of *all;* so, as to luxury of furniture, the thing is unknown in Japan. I do not hesitate to say that the house of a Prince of the Empire does not contain half the value of furniture that you will find in the house of a sober, steady mechanic in America.

Simplicity and frugality is the great maxim of this country, and it is enforced in a most surprising manner. It would be an endless task to attempt to put down all

---

[433]See note 240.

the acts of a Japanese that are regulated by authority. This is no country for modistes, tailors, jewelers and the whole army that batten on the imaginary wants of the West.

I have said nothing about my health lately. I have left off the use of tobacco, and have come down to plain boiled rice, fish and chicken,—but all is of no avail. I use a great deal of exercise, but it cannot reach my liver, and that is the source of my trouble. Oh, for a foreign ship to come here with a good doctor!![434]

Saw the first land crab to-day since last October. I suppose I may put this down as a proof that the summer has now actually commenced.

The large *Camellia Japonica* in my compound, which first showed its blossoms on the 5th of January, is now going out of bloom. It has been a splendid sight and has, I have no doubt, produced some *thousands* of roses!

Wednesday, May 13, 1857. For the purpose of ascertaining whether gold is really as cheap in Japan as the Japanese pretend, I ordered two mustard spoons to be made of pure, unalloyed gold. They wished me to give them coin to make the spoons from. This I declined, as it would defeat the object I have in view.

After some days, a formal message was sent to me by the Governors, stating that, by the laws of Japan, gold could only be used to ornament their swords, and that its use by the people in any other form was ab-

---

[434]This worry concerning his personal health was a very weighty reason to be added to the diplomatic concern that he felt over the long delay of the *San Jacinto* (see note 425).

solutely prohibited.[435] A greater falsehood was never uttered. It is true that the Japanese use but few ornaments, or indeed articles of luxury of any kind; but gold *is* used in weaving brocades, in decorating saddles, in making a small chain which secures a small basket which contains a cloth with which they wipe perspiration from their faces, and for women's ornaments.

I told the messenger to say to the Governors that I knew that gold was used for many purposes besides swords; but, even if that was not the case, it was nothing to me, as I was not a Japanese, nor bound by Japanese law.

Moriama comes to say that Bingo-no-Kami has received orders to go to Yedo and that he is to leave early to-morrow morning; that he is unable to call in person to take leave of me, and begs me to excuse his apparent neglect. I send him messages wishing him a pleasant journey to Yedo and a favorable reception on his arrival.

Thursday, May 14, 1857. I have received a circular from the United States Patent Office asking for a great variety of information about cotton, the whole being put in the form of twenty-seven questions. These I had translated and gave them to the Japanese, requesting them to give me the desired information. To-day I have their return. It is a beautiful specimen of Japanese craft, cunning and falsehood. Their great object appears to be to permit as little to be learned about their country as

---

[435] W. E. Griffis quotes the following extract from a Japanese source: "The use of gold or silver in making utensils of all kinds was prohibited"—in 1855. (*Townsend Harris*, p. 155, note.)

possible; and, to that end, all fraud, deceit, falsehood and even violence, is justifiable in their eyes. It is true that this is the most difficult country in the world to get information; no statistics exist; no publications are made on any subject connected with industry. No man makes experiments to improve his implements, or to increase the product of his lands by new modes of culture. As his father sowed and reaped, so does he; and if the crop is large, it is his good fortune; if it be poor, it is his misfortune. As in everything else in Japan, the motto is *Quieta non movere;* the cultivator never measures his produce to see how it compares with that of his neighbor, or with his own on previous years. He is entirely ignorant of the mode of culture or crops produced at places not twenty miles distant from him. The great mass of the people are literally tied to the spot on which they were born. Of course, government officials, priests, pilgrims, etc., are exceptions. It may be that some few of the traders may go from place to place in pursuit of their calling, but such men, in Japan, have no eyes for anything but their traffic.

Saturday, May 16, 1857. I ordered a small belvedere to be erected on the top of a hill near the Consulate, so that I might enjoy the cool air during the hot season, and also have a view over the whole of the harbor. To-day they brought me some plans and elevations very neatly done, with estimates of the cost of the work. It seems to be a most important matter to them, as they have been a number of days about it and many persons were engaged on it. I was satisfied with their plans and accepted them. The price is fifteen dollars.

I am collecting specimens of natural history,[436] but they are but meagre, *as the Japanese will not bring me one,* on the national principle of concealing everything.

Tuesday, May 19, 1857. To-day I paid the Japanese for the gold I received from them on the 9th inst., as well as for a draft on me from Purser Bradford of the *San Jacinto.* In this case I paid them one *ichibu* for each dollar of the account, and my dollars were weight against silver *ichibus,* deducting five per cent. for recoining. This made my *ichibus* cost me thirty-three and eighty-three one-hundredth cents each. The allowance of five per cent. is not a fixed one. I offer them five per cent., they ask six. When the *Messenger Bird* settled her bills, she paid at the rate of six per cent.[437] I am to settle all my bills since my arrival here at five per cent. The next settlement is to be at six, and so on, five and six at each alternate payment, until the matter is finally closed. The amount of the accounts settled to-day was $452.50, but I paid it with $153.50, thus saving $299!! The wheat in the vicinity begins to assume a golden hue, and will soon be ready for harvesting. I find that the Japanese *do* use a few incense sticks in their temples. They

---

[436]In collecting these specimens, Townsend Harris must have had in mind his best friend, Mr. Sandwith Drinker, then in China, who was a member of The Academy of Natural Sciences of Philadelphia. In fact, in a letter dated Hongkong, Apr. 3 and 4, 1857 (but which was received only on Oct. 20, 1857), Mr. Drinker asks Townsend Harris for some specimens of Japanese ferns, etc., that he may send to the Academy (*L. & P.,* vol. 1, no. 62).

[437]The *Messenger Bird* left on Sunday, Mar. 29, 1857 (*q.v.*). For the terms of the settlement, see *Journal,* Mar. 9, 1857.

are made of some fragrant material, but are far inferior to those of China; and, as to number, what a contrast with China! There one may say truly that hundreds of thousands are burned every day in a city like Canton.

They are kept up night and day, and the perfume is as obvious as possible the moment you approach a Chinese town.

Thursday, May 21, 1857. Nine months to-day since I arrived in Japan, and I am still without any communication with home. Where is Commodore Armstrong?[438]

The Japanese brought a horse for Mr. Heusken to-day. It is dearer than mine, although not so good looking, but this is Japanese custom, always advance the price, but *never lower it.*

Saturday, May 23, 1857. The weather is very bad indeed, almost constant rain and a raw unpleasant wind from the northeast.

The Japanese say that "the oldest inhabitant" does not recollect such a miserable *May* as this is. We have, however, enjoyed eight months of as fine weather as anyone could wish for, so we may put up with the present without grumbling.

Tuesday, May 26, 1857. To-day I have a reply from the Governors about the prices charged to me by the Goyoshi people.[439]

---

[438]See above, May 5, 1857, and note 429.

[439]See above, May 9, 1857, and note 432. The letter of the Governors, written in Dutch, is *L. & P.*, vol. 2, no. 68. In his reply to the Governors, dated Monday, June 1, 1857, Townsend Harris takes note of their refusal to alter the prices to conform to those paid by the Japanese (as promised); and he gives notice that he will demand from the supreme Government of Japan repayment of all overcharges(*L. B.*, vol. 2, pp. 17–18).

It is plainly and unequivocally a full support of the Goyoshi rascality in all of its ramifications.

They do not regard the promise they gave me last August as worth the breath it cost them to utter it. However, to *lie* is, for a Japanese, simply to speak.

Wednesday, May 27, 1857. To-day being the fifth day of the fifth month is a great festival among the Japanese, and is attended to by abstaining from labor, putting on their best clothes, and by flying their musical kites, which sometimes remind you of a distant organ.

I do not see any special religious attendance. I must say that I never was in a country so abounding with priests, temples, *mias,* statues, etc., etc., where there was so great indifference on religious subjects as there is in Japan. I believe all the higher classes are in reality *atheists.*

These festivals are kept on the first day of the first month, the third day of the third month, and on the fifth day of the fifth month. These (I think) are the principal festivals of the Japanese except those of the new and full moons, neither of which is observed by abstaining from labor.

My canary left her nest, leaving her eggs unhatched, although she had *set* for twenty days. On breaking the eggs I could not discover any sign of young in them; apparently the eggs were not impregnated by the cock bird.

Friday, May 29, 1857. The wheat harvest is now being actively carried on. On counting the grains I find from five to sixty grains in one head.

Moriama informs me that Bingo-no-Kami is not to return to Shimoda, having been appointed "Superintendent of Repairs" at Yedo. His successor is not a Kami, but will be made one before he comes here. He is said to be a mild and amiable man. If so, I am glad to change Bingo-no-Kami for him, as the former is anything but a friend to foreigners, and besides he is the most *inveterate liar* I ever met with.

At a temple on one of the hills near the Consulate, the Japanese mariners make an *ex voto* offering of the tuft of hair which completes their headdress. This is in consequence of some vow made in a moment of peril, and when he arrives safely he cuts off the hair and hangs it up, although it is a great sacrifice to a Japanese to cut it off.

Sunday, May 31, 1857. I have walked this month, for exercise, over three hundred and fifty miles. I have entirely quit the use of tobacco in all its forms. I have brought down my diet to plain boiled rice and a little fowl. I tried fish for some days, but that was worse than the fowls. I cannot eat bread, either fresh or of the American biscuit. I have taken any quantity of blue pill, but all is of no avail. I suffer horribly from acid stomach and am getting leaner day by day. What is very singular is that my appetite is uncommonly good; but, my digestion being so much out of order, my food does not do me much good. The weather this month has not been as pleasant as on the previous ones. The mean temperature was 64°; highest, 73°; lowest, 55°. Had rain eleven days, showers two days, cloudy six days, fair twelve. We had an earthquake at 8:30 A. M. on the 2nd of May.

Where, oh, where is Commodore Armstrong? I am sick and weary of looking out for him.

Monday, June 1, 1857. The Japanese have said that strawberries grew around here, and that, as soon as they were ripe, I should have a good supply of them. At last they brought me some *itsigo,* or strawberries. They prove to be a kind of *raspberry,* of a pale straw color and of an insipid taste, quite without aroma or flavor; and these are their promised *strawberries.*

I have found in the woods a fruit of the size, shape, color, leaf, etc., etc., of the real strawberry, but the fruit is not edible, having a decidedly unpleasant flavor. I saw the same fruit in the north of China, during my wanderings there in 1853. The varieties of the laurel family here are almost innumerable. I am sure a botanist would find many new things here to repay his trouble. How often do I regret my ignorance of botany. Generally speaking, however, wild flowers are not abundant here, and scarcely none are cultivated, and but few have any scent.

How much I miss that Queen of Flowers, the Rose that is now in full bloom in New York; I should not be sorry to have a few sprigs of *champacka* from Penang, the tuberose from Macao, or the jessamine from Calcutta, to please my sense of smell.

Tuesday, June 2, 1857. Moriama brings me Mr. Portman's Dutch version of the Treaty of Kanagawa, as well as *their* Dutch version made from the Japa-

368

nese.[440] I wish to have a copy to save the trouble of constant reference by means of letters asking for copies of parts of Articles. Moriama says that in reality Bingo-no-Kami is in disgrace, as his new appointment is two grades lower than the post of Governor; that his salary is a mere trifle compared with what he enjoyed here, and that he is now excluded from all knowledge of foreign affairs, nor can he even have interviews with the members of the High Council. The causes of this disgrace are said to be various; but the chief one was that he did not agree better with me, the Government apparently holding him responsible for all my complaints, and for my recalcitrations against their various attempts to restrain me and deprive me of my just rights. Bingo-no-Kami did not carry his honors meekly. He was (to the Japanese) haughty and overbearing, and did not practice the usual Japanese *suaviter in modo*—hence he had made many small enemies, who no doubt did all in their power to prejudice him with the Government at Yedo.

The only real outcasts in Japan are tanners, who also make all work that has any leather about it. They live in villages by themselves; they cannot intermarry with any other class, nor can they enter the house, eat or drink, even with the poorest Japanese. Voluntary beggars are outcasts while they continue beggars, but

---

[440]Mr. A. L. C. Portman, a native of Holland, had been Dutch interpreter for the Perry Expedition. Later, he was of great service on the occasion of the visit of the first Japanese Embassy to Washington, in May, 1860; and, after Mr. Heusken had been slain by the Japanese (Jan. 15, 1861), he became the Dutch interpreter for Townsend Harris at Yedo.

they can restore themselves to society whenever they please. Of course religious mendicants are not outcasts. Public executioners are *not* outcasts. They are of the body of the soldiery, and associate with their equals in rank, without reference to their calling.

Malformations and distortions of the spine, etc., etc., are known in Japan. Infants malformed *are not put to death;* on the contrary, the poor rickety child appears to receive a double portion of affection from its mother.

As a general principle a Japanese may follow any calling he likes, as he is not *compelled* to follow the trade of his father, although he generally does so. Japanese cannot remove from their district to another, except on special permission from the Government, and those permissions are rarely granted. A man wishing to perform a pilgrimage must procure a passport for that purpose, which runs from one to eight months, according to distance.

Merchants trading from city to city must also obtain passports. There are no internal octroi, or transit duties in Japan.

Oasaca, Oaxaka or Oasaka is, according to Moriama, a fine town of from five hundred thousand to eight hundred thousand inhabitants. It has a large and secure harbor and enjoys a large commerce. It communicates with *Miako* by means of a river which is navigable with boats 60 (sixty) feet long.

The thin porcelain so much admired by foreigners is only made in Fizen. There are three places in this island celebrated for this fabric, the most noted of which are Imari and Firando. The first named is the best. *Mikado* is the only title of the Spiritual Sovereign. *Dai-ri* means "Spiritual residence,"—*i. e.,* residence of the Mikado, who is "brother to the sun and father of the moon."

Ziogoon is the only title of the political ruler of Japan. It means "General of the Kingdom, Lieutenant General, or Generalissimo of the whole Empire."

Tuesday, June 2, 1857 (continued). Took a walk to the southwest of Shimoda towards Cape Idzu. It is of the same character as the other parts seen. Every possible spot is cultivated, and as many inhabitants as can be, supported. I find that what I considered as jungle on the steep hillsides, is actually all planted. Trees, bamboos, rushes, etc., etc. All are renewed as they are cut off for use. No spot is neglected. I have never seen a person that had the appearance of *want* marked on his countenance. The children all have faces like "full moons," and the men and women are quite fleshy enough. No one can for a moment suppose (after seeing the people) that they are not well fed.

Every day increases my regret that I have no knowledge of botany. I am sure there are many curious plants here, and have no doubt that many are quite new.

I saw to-day a peach tree nine inches high which had some full grown fruit on it. The peaches are not ripe, therefore I cannot speak as to their quality; but the appearance of them is not in their favor. The Japanese, like the Chinese, pluck and eat the fruit before it ripens.

Wednesday, June 3, 1857. Walked up the valley of Shimoda towards Matsusaki.[441] Visited a new hot spring. It is arranged as a bath house like those before described, but the water is much warmer and more strongly impregnated with sulphur. I found a woman in the bath with her child. She was not in the least discomposed, but gave me the usual "Ohio" (good-morning) with a smiling face. Her skin was very fair, nearly as white as a Circassian. On my return homewards I called on the Prince of Shinano and passed a very agreeable hour with him. He presented me with some superior tobacco from Yedo, but, happily, I do not now use it. On my walk home I picked up (on the beach) some *pure white fuci.* I find nothing in my books analogous to this. It was not an isolated specimen, as abundance of it was found. It is quite as white as the best quality of the celebrated "Edible Bird's Nests."

The quantity of edible seaweed (*fuci*) that is collected at Shimoda is quite large, and it appears to form one of their articles of export to Yedo.

The trees about Shimoda are chiefly laurels, arbutus, and the varieties of the pine family.

Saturday, June 6, 1857. To-day I paid the Japanese my account for my household expenses, including some articles of furniture, a horse, saddle, etc., etc., a *norimon,* together with the Government bill for my flagstaff material,[442] the accounts of my Chinese ser-

---

441Matsuzaki.

442For the "First Consular Flag" ever raised in Japan, see *Journal*, Sept. 4, 1856.

vants, and also for seventy-five dollars of lacquer articles purchased for Mrs. S. N. Spooner. The accounts begin about the 30th August, 1856, and end May 22, 1857. The total presents the alarming amount of 3,476,594. But these are Japanese seni, and I settled the whole for $699.

Had I paid the accounts on the basis admitted by Commodore Perry, the amount would have been $2,173, so that $1,474 was saved by my arrangement of the currency with the Japanese.

Monday, June 8, 1857. I omitted to enter the arrival here of the new Governor, who comes in place of Shinano-no-Kami. His name is Nakamora Dewa-no-Kami, or Nakamora, Prince of Dewa. I have at last carried every point triumphantly with the Japanese, and have got everything conceded that I have been negotiating for since last September. Among my papers will be found a copy of the Convention[443] which contains the following provisions:

1st Opens the Port of Nagasaki to American ships;
2nd Gives the right of *permanent residence* to Americans at Shimoda and Hakodate, and the right to appoint a Vice-Consul at the latter port;
3rd Settles the currency, so that where we paid $100 we now pay only $34.50;
4th Americans to be exclusively under the control of their Consuls and to be tried by American law;
5th Concedes the right of the Consul General to go where he pleases in Japan, and to be furnished with Japanese money to enable him in person, or by his servants, to make his purchases without the intervention of any

---

[443] The text of this Convention of Shimoda will be found in Appendix IV.

Japanese official. This is even more than I was instructed to ask for by my special instructions dated October 4, 1855.[444] No class of Americans is named in the second Article, so that missionaries may actually come and reside in Japan.

Am I elated by this success? Not a whit. I know my dear countrymen but too well to expect any praise for what I have done, and I shall esteem myself lucky if I am not removed from office, not for what I have done, but because I have not made a commercial treaty that would open Japan as freely as England is open to us.

Besides, it is so easy to criticize, and so agreeable to condemn. It is much more pleasant to write imbecile, ass or fool, than to say able, discreet and competent.

Wednesday, June 10, 1857. The rice is now being rapidly transplanted, and, as the crop begins to be harvested in October, it gives about four months for the growth of the rice crop from the time of transplanting, or five months from the time the paddy is placed in the sprouting grounds.

Wednesday, June 17, 1857. To-day we signed the Convention,[445] having been some nine days in settling

[444]See notes 399 and 426.

[445]Only two days before this, on June 15, 1857, the ratifications of Townsend Harris's Treaty with Siam had been exchanged at Bangkok, by Charles Wm. Bradley, Sr., who bore credentials signed by President James Buchanan. For this, and for the letter written (in English) by the First King of Siam to accompany the ratified Treaty, see Wood, *Fankwei*, pp. 236–40; for former Consul Charles W. Bradley, Sr., see notes 55 and 210.

Returning to the Convention of Shimoda, it should be noted at once that when the Shogun later informed the Emperor at Kyoto of what he had done, the latter was pleased to accord his consent, and it is so stated in the Shogun's address to the Emperor delivered in Nov., 1865 (Francis O. Adams, *The History of Japan*, vol. 2, p. 25), even though the Choshiu clan rightly complained that the Shogunate had not received the sanction of the Emperor *beforehand* (Gubbins, *The Progress of Japan*, p. 169).

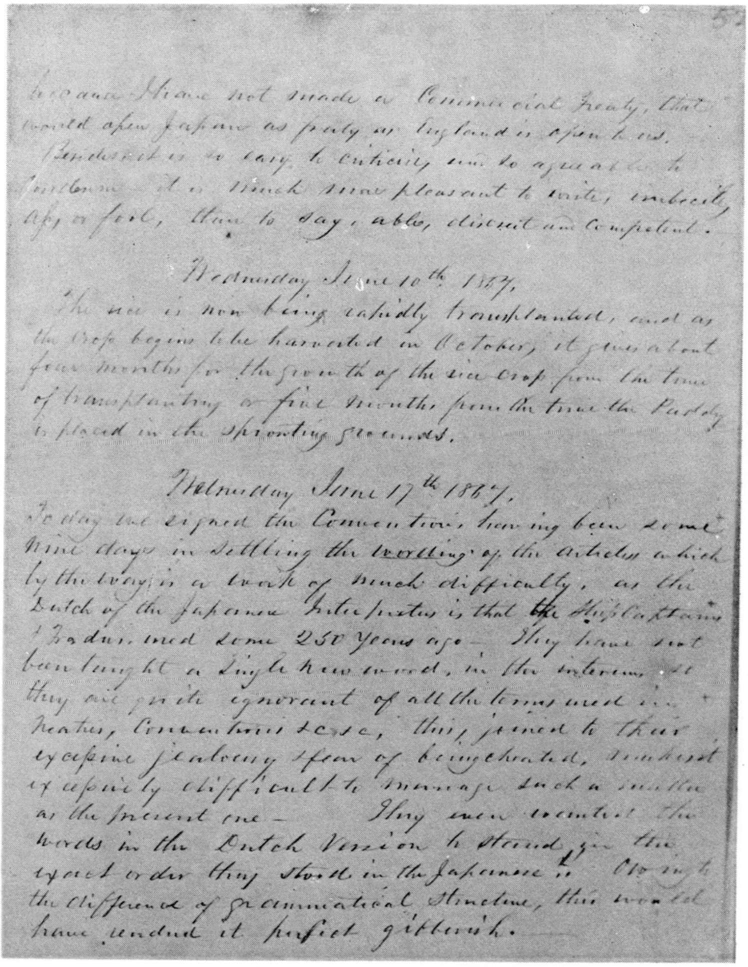

because I have not made a Commercial Treaty, that would open Japan as freely as England is open to us.
Remember it is so easy to criticise, and so agreeable to condemn, it is much more pleasant to write, imbecile, ass or fool, than to say, able, discreet and competent.

Wednesday June 10th 1857.
The rice is now being rapidly transplanted, and as the crop begins to be harvested in October, it gives about four months for the growth of the rice crop from the time of transplanting or five months from the time the Paddy is placed in the sprouting grounds.

Wednesday June 17th 1857.
To day we signed the Convention, having been some nine days in settling the wording of the Articles which by the way is a work of much difficulty, as the Dutch of the Japanese Interpreters is that the Ship Captains & traders used some 250 years ago. They have not been taught a single new word in the interim, so they are quite ignorant of all the terms used in Treaties, Conventions &c &c, this, joined to their excessive jealousy & fear of being cheated, renders it excessively difficult to manage such a matter as the present one. They even wanted the words in the Dutch Version to stand in the exact order they stood in the Japanese! Owing to the difference of grammatical structure, this would have rendered it perfect gibberish.

TOWNSEND HARRIS'S MANUSCRIPT JOURNAL, VOL. 4, P. 52

This illustration shows his comment on having concluded the Convention of Shimoda: June 17, 1857.

the *wording* of the Articles, which by the way is a work of much difficulty, as the Dutch of the Japanese interpreters is that of the ship captains and traders used some two hundred and fifty years ago. They have not been taught a single new word in the interim, so they are quite ignorant of all the terms used in treaties, conventions, etc., etc. This, joined to their excessive jealousy and fear of being cheated, makes it excessively difficult to manage such a matter as the present one. They even wanted the words in the Dutch version to stand in the exact order they stood in the Japanese!! Owing to the difference of grammatical structure this would have rendered it perfect gibberish.

Monday, June 22, 1857.   I have been in correspondence with the "Council of State" since October 25, 1856, concerning a letter from the President of which I am the bearer,[446] and I have had a great many interviews with the Governors of Shimoda of late, concerning the manner in which that letter should be delivered, as well as certain communications which I wrote them I was charged with should be made. They wished the letter to be delivered here in Shimoda and the communications made to the Governors, while I demanded to go to Yedo, have an audience of the Ziogoon, and there deliver the letter, and afterwards make the communications to the

[446]Townsend Harris's letters to the Minister for Foreign Affairs, up to this point, were dated Oct. 25, 1856; Jan. 8, 1857; and Mar. 28, 1857; for the first two, see those entries in the *Journal* and notes 313, 369; for the letter of Mar. 28, 1857, however, see entry for Apr. 1, 1857, and note 410.

On June 18, 1857, Townsend Harris wrote Dispatch No. 7 to the Secretary of State, by which he forwarded copy of the Convention of Shimoda, with a lengthy discussion of its various Articles: *L. B.*, vol. 2, pp. 29–35.

proper Minister. I have not heretofore, nor shall I now enter these matters at large in my *Journal,* but my private letter book contains copies of all my official letters; and there, and in my files of papers, full details of these matters will be found.

The Governors now produce an imperial mandate under the "Seal and Signature Royal," commanding them to receive the President's letter and bring it to Yedo, and they are quite dumbfounded that I refuse to yield to the mandate.

Tuesday, June 23, 1857. To-day I received an official and also a private letter from Mr. "E. E. Rice, U. S. Commercial Agent at Hakodate," announcing his arrival at that place, and that he had "hoisted his flag." His private letter to me is a curiosity in composition and orthography. It will be found in my files under date of May 17, 1857.[447] He writes me that two ships under the American Flag are there from Hongkong, and that the supercargo Mr. Lühdorf[448] has some things for me,

[447]This letter of Mr. Rice is not to be found among the *Letters and Papers* of Townsend Harris. The earliest extant letter by Mr. Elisha E. Rice is one written in Aug., 1857 (*L. & P.*, vol. 1, no. 68), in answer to the two letters written to him by Townsend Harris on July 6, 1857.

Mr. Harris is very charitable when he styles Mr. Rice's letter "a curiosity in composition and orthography." The bare and unpleasant fact is that all of Mr. Rice's letters have a sentence and paragraph structure, a grammar, capitalization, punctuation, and spelling that are absolutely impossible and appalling, and that are as difficult to decipher as a text in palæography.

[448]We have already spoken of Mr. Lühdorf as supercargo of the *Greta* (see note 325). Since that time, when he had been an actor in the famous cases of the shipwrecked Russian Frigate *Diana* and of the rebuffed Americans, Messrs. Reed and Dougherty, he had been appointed supercargo of the American ship *Esperanza,* which had brought papers, letters, and stores from Hongkong to Hakodate, where she stopped on her way to the Amur River. It was the *Esperanza* that brought to Hakodate all the letters which Townsend Harris finally received on Oct. 20, 1857. Mr. Lühdorf left Hakodate June 10, 1857. (*L. & P.*, vol. 1, nos. 62, 68, and 70.)

which Mr. Rice promises to forward to me, if they are landed at Hakodate, but he does not say one word about letters.

This is most tantalizing. I am now more than ten months in Japan, and have not as yet received a single letter from the United States. As no direct communication is allowed by sea between Shimoda and Hakodate by Japanese junks, my supplies might as well be at Hongkong as there. I have been out of flour, bread, butter, lard, bacon, hams, sweet oil, and in fact out of every kind of foreign supply for more than two months. I am living on rice, fish and very poor poultry, as no game of any kind has been brought to me for the last three months.

My health is miserable, my appetite is gone, and I am so shrunk away that I look as though a "Vice-Consul had been cut out of me." Where, oh! where is Commodore Armstrong?[449]

---

[449]In his Dispatch No. 7 to the Secretary of State (*L. B.*, vol. 2, pp. 29–35, dated June 18, 1857), Townsend Harris again gives vent to his feeling of isolation (*ib.*, p. 35):

". . . In this connection I beg to remark that I have not received any dispatches from the Department since I left the United States (October, 1855).

"When at the Department of State in September, 1855, I was informed that a man-of-war would visit Shimoda every three months. Commodore Armstrong informed me that he had not received any orders directing him to revisit Japan, but that he would either come here, or send a ship in March, 1857. What the causes are that have prevented the dispatch of a ship I do not know.

"I need not point out the importance of my having the means of communicating with you as often as three times a year. The voyage from Hongkong to this port is only ten days, and from Shanghai seven days.

"The occasional presence of a man-of-war here would be of benefit to our interests, even if she only remained a week."

When Lord Elgin and Mr. Laurence Oliphant visited Townsend Harris— on Tuesday, Aug. 10, 1858—the latter speaks thus of Townsend Harris's iso-

Tuesday, June 30, 1857. Only one earthquake this month and that was on the tenth.

The report of the weather is as follows: thermometer, highest, 80°; lowest, 59°; mean, 70.8°; extreme daily range, 10°. Rain seven days, showers six days, cloudy three days, fine fourteen days.

Saturday, July 4, 1857. I never felt more miserable and wretched than on this day. Ill in health and in want of everything but low spirits, of which I have an abundant supply. I had a national salute of twenty-one guns fired in honor of the day by the Japanese,—I paying the expense, which was less than two dollars. Dear New York! How I wish I could pass the day there among my friends.

Monday, July 6, 1857. I have now abandoned all

---

lation (*Narrative of the Earl of Elgin's Mission to China and Japan*, New York, 1860, p. 345):

"For disciples of Zimmerman, notwithstanding, or lovers in a Petrarchian state, Japan offers greater attractions, probably, than any other country in the globe, but neither Mr. Harris nor Mr. Heusken seemed altogether to appreciate them. A well-stored library, and a few rooms comfortably fitted up, gave an agreeable air of civilization to the establishment; but what can compensate for two years of almost entire isolation and banishment from communion with one's fellow-men? Except upon the rare occasions of Shimoda being visited by some foreign vessel, these two gentlemen had not seen a creature with whom they could exchange an idea. They had been for eighteen months without receiving a letter or a newspaper, and two years without tasting mutton—sheep being an animal unknown in Japan. Still, this exile had not the effect of disgusting them with the country of their banishment. Mr. Harris spoke in terms even more eulogistic than those universally employed by the Dutch of the Japanese people. His residence among them, under circumstances which compelled him to form intimate relations with them—for they were his only companions—only served to increase his high opinion of their amiable qualities and charming natural dispositions. He told us numerous anecdotes illustrative of this. . . ."

On June 27, 1857, Townsend Harris received a copy of a letter of the Shogun addressed to Inouye, Shinano-no-Kami and Nakamura, Dewa-no-Kami, investing them with full powers to negotiate with Townsend Harris at Shimoda: *L. & P.*, vol. 2, no. 69, dated "5th year of Ansei, Mi, 5th month."

hopes of seeing Commodore Armstrong, and I accordingly have made an effort to send some letters through the Japanese to Hakodate, hoping Mr. Rice may be able to forward them. I wrote to the Secretary of State, N. Dougherty, and to Commodore Armstrong, S. Drinker, and Armstrong & Lawrence. My letters were very short and very guarded, as I do not doubt the Japanese will open them. Although the distance from here to Hakodate is under six hundred miles by land, yet the Japanese consume thirty-five days in conveying a letter there. My letters to Mr. Dougherty, General Wetmore, and to my private friends in New York are not copied, nor are those to S. Drinker at Hongkong, or any other purely private letters.[450]

---

[450]Among the *Letters and Papers* of Townsend Harris, the following letters referring to this general period have been found:

1) To Shinano-no-Kami: June 3, 1857, protesting against the opinion of the Governors of Shimoda that the expulsion of Messrs. Reed and Dougherty was justified (*L. B.*, vol. 2, pp. 18–19).

2) To the Governors of Shimoda: June 29, 1857, pointing out that the "full powers" which they had received from Yedo were not sufficiently comprehensive to warrant his entering upon negotiations for a treaty (*ib.*, p. 20).

3) To Secretary of Treasury, Dispatch No. 8: June 30, 1857, sending mail via Hakodate and complaining of his isolation (*ib.*, p. 36).

4, 5) To the Secretary of State, Dispatches Nos. 6 and 7: July 1, 1857, being routine reports on shipping and fees received for previous quarter (*ib.*, p. 38).

6) To Baring Bros., of London: July 1, 1857, advising them of his draft for salary (*ib.*, p. 21).

7, 8) To the Secretary of State, Dispatches Nos. 9 and 10: July 1, 1857, being routine reports on the funds in his charge (*ib.*, pp. 37–38).

9) To Commodore Armstrong: July 6, 1857, praying for the arrival of a ship (*ib.*, pp. 25–26).

10, 11) To E. E. Rice: July 6, 1857, giving him general information and instructions (*ib.*, pp. 21–25).

12) To Mr. Lühdorf: July 6, 1857, at Hakodate, urging him to touch at Shimoda on his way back from the Amur River to Hongkong (*ib.*, p. 27).

13) To Armstrong & Lawrence: July 6, 1857, asking them to send things hereafter direct to Shimoda, etc. (*ib.*, pp. 27–28).

Wednesday, July 8, 1857. Shinano-no-Kami started to-day for Yedo for the purpose of reporting my refusal to deliver the letter of the President anywhere but at Yedo, or to anyone but the Emperor. They assure me that it is quite preposterous to even think of an audience of His Majesty, as the laws of Japan forbid it. As it happens, they also told me that the Council of State could not write to any foreigners (the laws forbidding it) ; and, as the Council has written to me, I am shrewdly inclined to think that they will be found equally pliable in the matter of an audience.

Tuesday, July 14, 1857. This has really been a *shocking* day—to make a poor pun. We had twelve shocks of earthquake—the first and sharpest one occurred at two A. M. and lasted about two minutes. It shook my bed so violently that it made it creak. Happily but little damage was done. Eleven shocks followed at intervals during the day, the last occurring at seven and a half P. M.

I could not perceive any sensible effect on the barometer or thermometer, nor did an ordinary pocket compass show any particular perturbation, beyond what would be produced by a jar of similar force produced

14)   To Charles Huffnagle, U. S. Consul General for British India, residing at Caicutta: July 6, 1857, sending him a copy of the Convention of Shimoda, and explaining his adjustment of the currency question (*ib.,* p. 39).

15, 16, 17, 18)   To Charles C. Currier,   U. S. Consul at Penang;
    To Charles W. Bradley,   "   "   " Singapore;
    To John Black   "   "   " Point-de-Galle, Ceylon;

    To U. S. Consul at Hongkong: these four are exact copies of the letter to Mr. Huffnagle (*ib.,* p. 39).

19)   To Hon. Peter Parker, U.S. Commissioner for China: July 6, 1857: same as above (*ib.,* p. 40).

380

by any other means. I do not make any entries of my walks and wanderings. In fact, I am too miserable to go out. I have a horse, but I do not use him, as it is impossible for any but a Japanese to use their saddles, and mine is snugly lying at Hakodate, thanks to Commodore Armstrong.

Thursday, July 23, 1857. The cannon from the lookout hill was fired at noon to-day, and it caused such joy as only can be felt by those who have been living isolated, as I have been, for the last eleven months. Mr. Heusken ran like a deer to the top of the signal hill, and came back breathless and streaming with sweat, to say that there was a ship in sight, about ten miles south of the harbor; that as the wind was not very fresh she would not come in for some time. He started again for Vandalia Point (the most southern point) to watch her approach. At four P. M. he returned quite down-hearted. The ship had disappeared in the blue haze at a little after one o'clock and had not reappeared; she appeared to be standing about northeast. We are now in doubt what it can mean, but think she must be bound here, else why approach so near?

Friday, July 24, 1857. Up at daylight and off to the east hills that command a view of the Bay of Yedo and the South Pacific.

Alas! No ship could be seen; whoever she was, it was clear she was not bound to Shimoda. I never had anything to try my philosophy so hardly as this.

I am inclined to think she was *not* the *Flying Dutchman* (as suggested nationally by Mr. Heusken) but

381

simply a whaler, fishing along the coast. I wish the "blubber hunter" had kept a few miles further from land and spared us the excitement of hope and the bitter disappointment that followed.

Monday, July 27, 1857. Made a present of my third and last revolver[451] to Dewa-no-Kami. I am sorry to hear of the death of Abé Ise-no-Kami at Yedo. He was the second member of the Council of State and very influential.

He was always represented to me as a man of great intelligence, and one that fully understood the power of the United States and other Western nations, and above all was convinced that the time had arrived when Japan must abandon her exclusive policy, or be plunged into the miseries of war. He is a great loss to the liberal party of Japan.[452]

Friday, July 31, 1857. Weather report this month: Thermometer, highest, 84°; lowest, 66°; mean, 76.1°. Extreme daily range, 7°.

---

[451]The first revolver had been number 9 of the presents made to the First King of Siam; and the second had been number 5 of those to the Second King of Siam: See Appendices II and III.

[452]Abé, Ise-no-Kami, was succeeded as Prime Minister (or Head of the Council of State) by Hotta, Bitchiu-no-Kami. This succession was a very fortunate one for Townsend Harris, because Lord Hotta was in favor of opening the country. One of his first acts was to address a letter to the Daimyo, in which he stated (Shunkichi Akimoto, *Lord Ii Naosuke and New Japan*, 1909, pp. 142–43):

"I presume the opening [of] the country for foreign trade is ore scheme very eminently fitted to increasing wealth and armaments on the profits of foreign trade in the prevailing circumstances."

Indeed, he faced the issue even more squarely when he put this question to the clan lords:

"Whether our intercourse with foreign nations should be conducted with neighborly feeling of good will or with that of enmity, regarding them as our enemies?"

382

Rain five days, showers five days, cloudy three days, fine eighteen days

Earthquakes on the 3rd, 14th, 26th and 30th,—together, sixteen shocks.

Saturday, August 15, 1857. Mr. Heusken, having extemporized a saddle and bridle, has been riding for some time past. As he is somewhat inexperienced in riding, he has laid his horse up with a sore back and I lent him mine until he should recover. The second time he rode out with him a difference of opinion arose between Mr. Heusken and the horse,—the latter wishing to return and Mr. Heusken to go on. Then ensued a trial of force vs. obstinacy, which ended in the horse slipping his shoulder and thus disqualifying himself from ever being mounted again. I ordered the poor brute killed, but no one would perform the butcher's part. As I had parted with my last revolver, I could not shoot him, and I could not bring myself to cut his throat like a butcher. At last by great good luck I succeeded in giving him away!!

Think of that! Ye Knackers of London and Masters of the Abbatoir at Montmartre and manufacturers of "real bologna" sausages in Germany! What a country it is for you, where it is considered a favor to accept a horse as a gift with full privilege to "look in his mouth."

Friday, August 21, 1857. Happy day! I get a package with a dozen newspapers and some China letters from Mr. Rice. He writes me that he will forward my packages about October next by a Japanese schooner (American model), which will leave about that time.

What a relief to have this slight glimpse of the outer world, although I do not get any American letters. This day is the anniversary of my arrival in Japan. One year here, and not a single letter from America. My last letters were dated February, 1856. Eighteen months ago! How much may have happened in the meantime, whom among my old friends has death removed?

I suppose my letters must be packed up in a box which was not known to Mr. Rice, or he would have sent letters in place of newspapers. What has become of the American men-of-war of the East India Squadron?[453]

Thursday, August 27, 1857. The Japanese inform me that all the American ships left Hakodate in June, so my letters sent there cannot go by them. I have made duplicates of all those letters and sent them to Nagasaki, writing to Mr. H. Donker Curtius, requesting him to forward them by one of his ships.[454] I placed them under cover addressed to the U. S. Consuls at Batavia, Shang-

---

[453]For the answer to this question, see *Journal* for Sept. 8, 1857.

[454]The letter to Mr. Curtius is *L. B.,* vol. 2, pp. 41–43. Townsend Harris begged him to send the enclosed letters to Mr. Alfred A. Reed, U.S. Commercial Agent at Batavia, if a Dutch ship were going there; otherwise, to any port in China by the first opportunity. Townsend Harris enclosed for Mr. Curtius also a copy of the Convention of Shimoda.

Some of the letters written by Townsend Harris on this day and sent to Mr. Curtius to be forwarded are:

1) *L. B.,* vol. 2, p. 41: to the Secretary of State, Dispatch No. 11, to the effect that he is sending the present dispatch (enclosing copy of Dispatch No. 8) by way of Nagasaki and Batavia; and complains that he has received no letters from the Department.

2) *L. B.,* vol. 2, pp. 43–44: to Commodore Armstrong at Hongkong, enclosing copy of letter of July 6, 1857; and again lamenting the fact that he has received no letters from either the United States or China since the *San Jacinto* left.

3) *L. B.,* vol. 2, pp. 44–45: to Mr. Alfred A. Reed, begging him to forward the enclosed five letters (of which the above were two) *via* Singapore.

hai, or Hongkong, requesting Mr. Curtius to send them to China if any one of his ships was bound there.

The Prince of Shinano returned from Yedo on the 14th, and I have had many interviews with the Governors on the subject of the President's letter.

See my letter book **for full** details of these interviews.[455]

Monday, August 31, 1857. Health wretched. I weigh about 130 pounds. Weather report: thermometer, highest, 87°; lowest, 67°; mean, 77.7°. Extreme daily range, 10°.

Rain four days, showers four days, cloudy none, fine twenty-three days.

Warmest day was the 7th. Mean temperature, 83.25°.[456]

Monday, September 7, 1857. At noon to-day the signal cannon again gave us the joyful news that a for-

---

[455]Shinano-no-Kami had left for Yedo on July 8, 1857, to confer on the matter of the delivery of the President's letter (*L. B.,* vol. 2, p. 78). On the very day of Shinano's return to Shimoda, Aug. 14th, Townsend Harris had an interview with the two Governors, at which Shinano suggested that Townsend Harris should at once, and at Shimoda, make the communications he had previously referred to, and that he should then proceed to Yedo, be received by the Council of State, and deliver the President's letter to Hotta, Bitchiu-no-Kami. These proposals were rejected by Townsend Harris (*ib.,* pp. 79–80).

Of the "many interviews" mentioned in the text, there is reference to one on Aug. 27th, in the course of which Townsend Harris referred to Father Valignani, etc. (Wagener, *Aus dem Tagebuche,* etc., p. 378. An outline of these negotiations, beginning with Jan., 1857, is to be found in Townsend Harris's long Dispatch No. 13 to Secretary Lewis Cass, dated Sept. 11, 1857: *L. B.,* vol. 2, pp. 73–85). At the conference of Aug. 28th, Townsend Harris submitted to Shinano-no-Kami a list of the Dutch Superintendents of the Factory at Deshima that had been received in audience by the Shogun in ancient times. Other conferences were held on Aug. 31st, and on Sept. 1st, 2nd, and 4th. (Wagener, *op. cit.,* pp. 378–79; and *L. B.,* vol. 2, pp. 45–46.)

[456]A weather table for the period from January 1 to Aug. 31, 1857, is given in *L. B.,* vol 3, p. 148.

385

eign ship was in sight. Mr. Heusken went over his old ground, and on his return informed me that a heavy ship was standing in for the harbor; that, as the wind blew the colors *end on,* he could not make them out. It was a comfort to think that she was coming here, although we did not know what flag she wore,—at all events she was from a civilized land.

It was now one year and four days since I was left here by the *San Jacinto,*[457] and full six months had run beyond the time that Commodore Armstrong had promised to visit me. That it was not the Commodore was clear, as it was a sailing ship. The wind fell provokingly light, and at seven P. M. the boom of a heavy gun came from the ship. Mr. Heusken volunteered to go to her, although she was some ten miles off. He accordingly started and did not get back until

---

[457]See *Journal,* Sept. 4, 1856.

What a really "joyful" week this must have been for Townsend Harris! The arrival of the *Portsmouth* and the following days of poignant excitement made him forget to enter in his *Journal* quite the most important step won thus far in his long drawn out negotiations with the Japanese. We quote from the long Dispatch No. 13 to Secretary Cass (*L. B.,* vol. 2, p. 82):

"On the 7th of the present month, the Governors requested me to meet them, and at this interview, to my agreeable surprise, they yielded every point they had so strongly contested for eight months. They said they were ordered to inform me that I was to proceed to Yedo with every honor; that on my arrival I was to have an immediate interview with the Prime Minister; and, on the first ensuing fortunate day, I should have a public audience of the Ziogoon, and, at that audience, I should deliver the President's letter."

This complete success was won on Monday, the 7th; on Tuesday, Sept. 8th, the *Portsmouth* anchored in the Harbor of Shimoda, and Townsend Harris, for the first time since Sept. 4, 1856, beheld the countenances of his fellow countrymen and heard news of his own land. The lonely exile who, for "one year and four days," had truly been a man without a country, at last enjoyed the communion of his people. His state of mind must almost have been a refutation of the Horatian

". . . *nihil est ab omni*
Parte beatum."

386

Tuesday, September 8, 1857, at one A. M. The ship proves to be the United States Sloop-of-war *Portsmouth,* Captain A. H. Foote,[458] eighteen days from Shanghai, where he left Commodore Armstrong in the *San Jacinto,* and where he *has been* nearly three months, at the distance of seven days steaming from me. The *Portsmouth* did not expect to visit Japan when she left Hongkong, so that all my letters from home that have been received since April last[459] are still at Hongkong. She brought me letters from Captain Bell and the officers of the *San Jacinto* only.[460] I was up all night eagerly reading the newspapers and the few letters she brought to me. The ship came up at noon and at two P. M. the Captain came to see me.[461] He was much pleased when I showed him the Convention of June 17th, and said that all would be surprised at my success. He told me that he had great difficulty in getting the Commodore's consent to come here, and I believe it was only obtained by some medical ruse, by which the ship was

---

[458]This was Captain (later Rear-Admiral) Andrew Hull Foote. He had brought Charles William Bradley, Sr., to Bangkok to exchange the ratifications of Townsend Harris's Treaty with Siam (Paullin, *Proceedings of the United States Naval Institute,* vol. 37, p. 417; see above, note 445; and *Journal,* Sept. 10, 1857); and in Oct. and Nov., 1856, he had taken a very prominent part in the storming of the Barrier Forts at Canton (see above, note 311).

[459]It was in Apr. 1857, that the *Esperanza,* one of Pustan's ships, had sailed from Hongkong for Hakodate, having on board letters, papers, and supplies for Townsend Harris (*L. & P.,* vol. 1, no. 70). These were the letters and newspapers which were so long detained at Hakodate by Mr. Rice, and a few of which Townsend Harris so joyfully received on Friday, Aug. 21, 1857. (See *Journal,* Aug. 21, 1857; and June 23, 1857, and note 448.)

[460]The letter from Captain Bell was, very likely, *L. & P.,* vol. 1, no. 71, dated Shanghai, Aug. 21, 1857.

[461]Writing in the *Journal of the Royal Asiatic Society,* vol. 1, p. 130, Captain Foote says: " Mr. Harris, our Consul General, welcomed us with that emotion, which the seclusion, for a year, from one's countrymen naturally inspires."

ordered here for the health of the crew. Captain Foote told me he had the most stringent orders not to enter the harbor of Shimoda; that he was to stay the shortest possible time here, and an ungracious addendum was made,—that he would probably have to bring me away.

It appears that Commodore Armstrong has been occupied from December to June in protecting the British Colony of Hongkong, thus enabling Admiral Seymour to employ more of his force in active hostilities against the Chinese. He found himself able to send a ship to Manila to inquire about some Americans who are imprisoned there under a charge of murder, and he was also able to send another to Singapore to inquire into,— what? A case of salvage!!! However, let him pass with this addition. I informed Captain Foote that all my dispatches from the Government were at Hakodate, where they had remained since last May,[462] and that, as he was going there, I asked him to touch here on his return and give me my letters. It would seem as though the Commodore had foreseen this request, for he positively ordered Captain Foote on leaving Hakodate to stretch out one hundred and fifty miles from land, while his direct route would have carried him about twenty-five miles south of Shimoda.

Captain Foote invited me to visit his ship to-morrow to receive a salute and to dine with him. He then went over to the Goyoshi to look at the lacquer ware, Mr. Heusken attending him as his interpreter. Employed

[462]Again Townsend Harris refers to the mail brought to Hakodate by the *Esperanza* (see notes 448 and 459).

until a late hour of the night on my correspondence.

Wednesday, September 9, 1857. The Purser of the *Portsmouth* has brought me $1,000 from Purser Bradford, which I lent to the ship September 1, 1856, and which I have sadly wanted since.[463] Captain Foote kindly offers to advance me as much money as I may want, taking my draft on my agents at Hongkong, which is a great favor to me, and I gladly accepted $500., giving my draft on Russell & Co., Hongkong, to whom I have sent my money in lieu of Armstrong & Lawrence, with whose conduct I am much displeased.[464] The Purser will also exchange the gold I took from the Japanese, which had been paid to them by the Purser of the *San Jacinto*.[465]

I told Captain Foote and his officers that I was deeply mortified that I could not invite them to dine with me, as in reality all I had to offer them was rice, fish and tough chickens. They begged me not to mention it, as they had been fully prepared to find me suffering from privations, owing to the manner in which I had been neglected. Went on board at two P. M., and had my salute of thirteen guns from the heavy sixty-eight pounders, which were loaded with full charges and not with the

---

[463] There is no mention of this loan in the *Journal* entry for that date.

[464] Some of the details of these financial matters may be learned from the letters which Townsend Harris wrote (on Sept. 10, 1857) to Messrs. Russell & Co., of Hongkong (*L. B.*, vol. 2, pp. 55–56), and to Messrs. Davis & Lawrence, likewise of Hongkong (*ib.*, p. 57); and on Sept. 11, 1857, to Messrs. I. Hunt & Co. (*ib.*, p. 112).

[465] This transaction consisted in redeeming from the Japanese the sum of $283.50 in gold which Purser Bradford of the *San Jacinto* had given them (*L. B.*, vol. 2, pp. 49–51, Townsend Harris to Mr. Bradford, dated Sept. 11, 1857, and written in answer to one from him that had been brought to Shimoda by the *Portsmouth*).

usual reduced charge which is used for saluting. A pleasant dinner in the cabin, with Captain Foote and his First Lieutenant Mr. Macomb, son of Major General Macomb, of Plattsburg memory.

I am to go with Captain Foote and his officers to visit the Governor to-morrow, and afterwards dine in the ward room. Returned home at five P. M., and went to work and wrote to a very late hour.

Thursday, September 10, 1857. To the Goyoshi at eleven A. M. and had a pleasant visit, which lasted about an hour.[466] Captain Foote and his officers are very busy in making purchases, and they are delighted at only paying thirty-four and a half cents for what cost the *San Jacinto* officers one dollar. Mr. Heusken is constantly occupied with them, which retards my writing sadly. Went on board ship at one P. M. and remained until five, having dined in the ward room. The *Portsmouth* appears to be a very happy ship. I learn from Captain Foote that he took Mr. C. W. Bradley with the Siamese Treaty to Bangkok, and that the ratifications were exchanged. The Senate struck out the fifth Article,[467]

---

[466]We have a description of this visit by the pen of Captain Foote himself (Paullin, *Proceedings of the United States Naval Institute*, vol. 37, pp. 396–97):

"We were received with great courtesy and apparent cordiality. They enquired with a good deal of interest how the President and Government of the United States regarded Japan; about the war in China, its cause and probable result; and expressed the hope that, at some future period, the Japanese would visit America for the purpose of education and obtaining a knowledge of many things in which they acknowledged their deficiency. I stated to the governors that our men-of-war in future would no doubt visit Japan more frequently, as the occupation of the squadron in looking out for our interests in China had prevented a vessel being in Shimoda and Hakodate during the past year."

[467]At the meeting of the Senate of Wednesday, Dec. 17, 1856, Mr. James M. Mason, of Virginia, moved that the Siam Treaty be referred to the Committee

which nearly lost the Treaty; but the Consul, Mr. Mattoon, accepted all the provisions of the Article (which related to passports) as a police regulation. I am pleased to learn that the Treaty is working admirably. Ships have already loaded for New York and San Francisco, and a large quantity of American tonnage is employed in the trade between Siam and China. Many of the finest American clippers have loaded in this manner at the Menam. Captain Foote has kindly permitted the Purser to supply me with flour, butter and pork from the ship's stores, I paying for them, and a great favor it is, in two senses: first, to be able to get them at all; and second, the price is only about half what they would have been at Hongkong. I cannot find words to express my thanks to Captain Foote and the officers of the *Portsmouth* for the generous manner in which they have divided their own private stores to help me in my distressed situation. Captain Foote supplied me with a quarter box of superior tea, two jars of lard, and a bag of prepared hominy. From the ward room I received half a dozen fine Virginia hams and five smoked tongues. I had nothing to give them in return but barren thanks.[468]

on Foreign Relations, and printed (34–3, Sen. Ex. J'l, vol. 10, p. 163). On Jan. 16, 1857, Mr. John Slidell, of Louisiana, reported it without amendment (*ib.*, p. 175). On Mar. 9, 1857, the Treaty was again referred to the Committee on Foreign Relations (35, Special Session, Sen. Ex. J'l, vol. 10, p. 227). On the 11th, Mr. Mason reported it with an amendment (*ib.* p. 237), and finally, on Mar. 13, 1857, Mr. Mason moved that the Senate advise and consent to the ratification of the Treaty after striking out the original Art. V (quoted in full, *ib.*, p. 256). On Mar. 16, 1857, the Treaty was ratified by the President.

[468]Townsend Harris expressed his sincere thanks to Captain Foote in a letter written on the day of the *Portsmouth's* departure, Sept. 12, 1857. This letter is in the Ford Collection of manuscript letters in the New York Public Library.

In this letter Townsend Harris also gives Captain Foote important infor-

Mr. Heusken will be employed until noon to-morrow with them at the Goyoshi, in settling their accounts; and, as the ship must leave at daylight on Saturday morning, I have but very little time to get my letters ready. I returned home at five P. M. and worked until a very late hour writing.

Friday, September 11, 1857. Captain Foote visits me this morning. I gave him my pet dog Yedo, as he could not get one of the kind here.[469] I sent a fine Japanese sword to Captain Bell and some crêpes to Commodore Armstrong. Captain Foote had several orders for Captain Bell, which I was anxious to pay for, but Captain Foote would not permit it. I have some Japanese blades that are now being mounted, and I promised to send one to Captain Foote. I also gave him some trifling articles, and I much regret that I had nothing for him or his officers that was worthy of their acceptance.

Mr. Heusken returned at noon and we went to work on our correspondence, and continued so occupied until midnight.[470]

---

mation on the coal available at both Shimoda and Hakodate, and begs him to take on board the *Portsmouth* the letters and packages for Townsend Harris which had so long remained at Hakodate (see notes 448, 459, and 462).

[469]For Townsend Harris's two dogs, *Yedo* and *Miako,* see note 330.

[470]On this day Townsend Harris wrote two dispatches to Secretary Cass and a private letter to Mr. Rice:

1) *L. B.,* vol. 2, p. 64: Dispatch No. 12, enclosing duplicate of former Dispatch No. 11 that had been sent by the doubtful and uncertain route of Nagasaki–Batavia (see *Journal,* Aug. 27, 1857, and note 454).

2) *L. B.,* vol. 2, pp. 73–85: Dispatch No. 13, in which Townsend Harris, taking advantage of the certainty of the delivery of the letter by the *Portsmouth,* not merely tells of the various avenues by which he had tried to communicate with Washington, but gives a careful outline of his negotiations with the Japanese, beginning with Jan., 1857.

3) *L. B.,* vol. 2, pp. 57–61: to Mr. E. E. Rice, at Hakodate.

Saturday, September 12, 1857. Mr. Heusken finished his copying at four A. M. and, having made up our mail,[471] he went on board the *Portsmouth* at five A. M. The wind being light, the ship did not get clear of the south point until three P. M.

The visit of the ship has thrown me into a state of intense excitement, as may well be imagined. I have not had three hours of consecutive sleep since the signal was fired announcing her approach.

Before the *Portsmouth* sailed I sent on board a coop of twenty fowls for the ward room and two pigs, one for the cabin and one for the ward room. I put on board the *Portsmouth* a fine lacquered tea tray, and a coop of six fine pet fowls for Lieutenant H. H. Lewis of the *San Jacinto.*[472]

Thursday, September 17, 1857. I have been wretchedly ill ever since the departure of the *Portsmouth,* but am now a little better. I received to-day, through the Japanese, some newspapers from Mr. H. Donker Curtius, the Dutch Superintendent at Nagasaki. The envelope was marked August 28, 1857, or one day after I wrote to him. These papers were, therefore, only twenty days en route from Nagasaki, while thirty-five days is the usual time employed.

Monday, September 21, 1857. Wrote to Mr. Cur-

471The copious correspondence that went by the *Portsmouth* has been noted above, *passim.* There remains only to refer to *L. B.,* vol. 2, pp. 53–54, to Messrs. Russell & Co., of Shanghai, thanking them for their kind offer to advance him funds.

472Lieutenant Henry H. Lewis: Midshipman, May 1, 1828; Passed Midshipman, June 23, 1838; Lieutenant, Oct. 28, 1842; dismissed, Apr. 20, 1861. (Callahan, *List;* Hamersly, *General Register.*)

tius, thanking him for his papers.[473] I am much better in health. The Governors request me to meet them tomorrow at the Goyoshi.

Tuesday, September 22, 1857. At the Goyoshi this morning at eleven o'clock. The Governors informed me that they had received letters from Yedo relating to the President's letter; that after many anxious consultations it was finally settled that I am to go to Yedo, in the most honorable manner; and, after my arrival, I am to have an audience of the Ziogoon, and then present the letter of the President![474] I expected that something would follow this, some objectionable proposition that I could not accept, which would throw the responsibility of the

[473]This letter is *L. B.*, vol. 2, pp. 68–71. The Singapore newspapers thus received from Mr. Curtius for the first time informed Townsend Harris of the great Sepoy Rebellion in India. In return, Townsend Harris informs Curtius that a steamship company has been formed to ply between San Francisco and China, stopping at Nagasaki; congratulates him on the Dutch Treaty concluded with the Japanese on Jan. 30, 1856; tells him that he (Townsend Harris) has written to Yedo for a copy, and hopes that Curtius will send him a copy too. He concludes by saying that he will keep Curtius informed of all that transpires.

In his letter to the Council of State (also dated Sept. 21, 1857: *L. B.*, vol 2, pp. 65–67), Townsend Harris frankly tells them that he has learned from the European papers brought him by the *Portsmouth,* that the Japanese had concluded a second Treaty with the Dutch, and asks for a copy. He adds that the communications from Yedo do not close with the customary expressions of friendliness and respect; and concludes with the statement that, if they do not see fit to employ such phrases, he too will be obliged to omit them in the future.

This was still another of the many instances of well-nigh endless patience on the part of Townsend Harris, coupled with a goodly portion of firmness and dignity.

[474]There is an irreconcilable contradiction in this entry. The *Journal* here distinctly says that this information was given to Townsend Harris on Sept. 22, 1857; whereas the subject-matter of this entry is already fully discussed in Dispatch No. 13 to Secretary Cass, dated Sept. 11, 1857, where the historic interview is clearly assigned to Sept. 7, 1857. (See *Journal* under this date, and note 457. Heusken's *Diary* assigns the event to Sept. 23rd: Wagener, *op. cit.,* p. 380.) Unfortunately, this very historic letter—the first ever sent for such a purpose by the Shogunate—is not to be found among the extant *Letters and Papers* of Townsend Harris.

non-delivery of the letter on me, but nothing of the kind occurred. They wished me to agree to start and stop at certain hours and at certain places, saying that accommodations suitable for me could only be found at such places, etc., etc. I informed them that I should be willing to agree to such hours as might prove best, and to stop where I could be best accommodated, but I could not bind myself beforehand to any hour or march; that I must not only be free in my action, but that the escort attending me must be under my command, exclusively; that they would find me, as a reasonable man, quite ready to adopt any proper suggestions on those points on the road, but I could not be bound up to comply with their regulations before I knew what might occur, etc., etc. To which they at once assented. The manner in which I am to salute the Ziogoon is to be the same as in the courts of Europe,—*i. e.,* three bows. They made a faint request that I would prostrate myself and "knock-head," but I told them the mentioning such a thing was offensive to me. The Governors informed me that Shinano-no-Kami was ordered to Yedo for the purpose of assisting in the arrangements to be made for my visit. They said that a great deal was to be done in the way of preparations, and that it would probably require some two months to complete the arrangements. In the meantime, they will consult with me in preparing my retinue, etc., etc.

Monday, September 28, 1857. Shinano-no-Kami, with Moriama Yenosky, started yesterday for Yedo. The Commissary of Shimoda came to-day to take orders for procuring the men I shall want, and preparing their dresses.

I shall not take any of my Chinese with me, as the Japanese have a great dislike to the Chinese, and I do not wish to be associated in their minds with the Chinese or any other people. I shall, therefore, only be accompanied by Mr. Heusken and my two Japanese house servants from my family. My own train will consist of some forty porters bearing my luggage, cooking utensils, bedding, etc., etc., and by the following, who will all have the arms of the United States on their dresses, as the coat-of-arms is worn by the Japanese,—*viz.,*

20 *norimon* bearers	1 sword
12 guardsmen	2 swords
2 standard bearers	2 swords
2 shoe and fan bearers	2 swords
2 grooms	1 sword
2 quinine,[475] or commanders of the foregoing.	

All except the grooms and *norimon* bearers are to have silk dresses.

I am to be attended by the Vice-Governor of Shimoda, the Mayor of Kakizaki, the Commissary of Shimoda, and by the private secretary of Dewa-no-Kami. They will have, together, a tail of some one hundred and fifty or more men, so that the whole train will form a body of not far from two hundred and fifty.

Wednesday, September 30, 1857. My health is much improved. I attribute this to my improved diet, as I am

---

[475]That is: *Gokenin.*

now well supplied with delicate China pork, my sow having littered thirteen pigs on the fifth of August last. I have no doubt that the agreeable termination of the vexed question of the reception of the President's letter has also been of great service to me, as it has removed an immense pressure from my mind. I cannot help hoping that I shall be able to do something satisfactory in the way of a commercial treaty before I leave Yedo.

The weather report for the month is as follows:[476] Thermometer: highest, 85°; lowest, 62°; mean, 75.4°. Extreme daily range, 12°. Rain four days, showers three days, cloudy two days, fair twenty-one days.

The report for the twelve months beginning October 1, 1856, and ending September 30, 1857, is as follows: Thermometer: highest, 87°; lowest, 32°; mean, 61.2°. Hottest month, August; mean, 77.7°. Coldest month, January; mean, 45.1°. Coldest day, February 2nd; mean, 36.25°. Hottest day, August 7th; mean, 83.25°.

Rain fifty-one days, showers forty-one days, cloudy thirty-three days, fine 240 days.

Wind, Northerly and Easterly	107	Showing wind with a Northerly board	184 times
" " " Westerly	77	" " " " Southerly "	142 "
" Southerly " Easterly	19	" " " " Easterly "	126 "
" " " Westerly	123	" " " " Westerly "	200 "
Calm	39		
	365		

[476] The Wind Table for the period Jan. 1 to Sept. 30, 1857, is given in *L. B.*, vol. 3, p. 149. This table Townsend Harris sent to the Rev. E. W. Syle (*L. B.*, vol. 4, p. 172), a missionary at Shanghai of the Presbyterian Episcopal Church, and the first person later to be invited by the Japanese to go to Japan as a teacher of the "American" language (*L. & P.*, vol. 1 no. 102, dated Nagasaki, Oct. 6, 1858).

On Oct. 1st, Townsend Harris wrote the usual routine reports: Dispatches Nos. 14 and 15 to Secretary Cass (*L. B.*, vol. 2, pp. 72 and 98); Dispatch No. 10 to Hon. Howell Cobb, of the Treasury (*ib.*, p. 72); and the customary draft notification to Baring Bros., of London (*ib.*, p. 64).

Sunday, October 4, 1857. My birthday.[477] I am fifty-three years old. My lease is rapidly running to its close. God grant that the short remainder of it may be usefully and honorably employed. My health is better than it was a month ago, but far, very far from being as good as it was this time last year. Shall I ever see New York and my dear American friends again? *Doubtful,* but God's will be done, I can say truly and heartily.

Monday, October 5, 1857. I have got a new horse, and to-day got on horseback for the first time in Japan, having extemporized a saddle, bridle, etc., etc. I was pleased with the exercise but, alas! Shimoda is no place for equestrian exercises. It is all up and down; no roads, but mere footpaths; and, in a great many places, these are so steep that a regular staircase is made of stone steps, and at a giddy angle, particularly when you look down.

When the *Portsmouth* was here, Mr. Heusken got his horse shod by a smith that was on board. This proceeding produced a great sensation among the Japanese. They never saw anything of the kind before. They put a *straw sandal* on the hoof; and, as this seldom lasts an hour, the groom that follows on foot always carries a quantity of new ones to replace those that give out.[478] The Japanese are no horsemen; both hands are employed in holding the reins; they have no martingale, the horse therefore carries his head very high with his nose stuck out straight. They therefore have no command over him. Usually the groom leads the horse by a

[477]See note 304.

[478]For an interesting anecdote regarding the "great sensation" caused by horses so properly shod, see *Journal*, Dec. 20, 1856, and note 362.

third rein put on for that purpose. The Governors were very fearful for my safety; they assured me that the Japanese horses were so vicious, that my life would be in danger if I attempted to ride in any different manner from their mode. They said their horses all would bite and kick. No wonder, when one knows the manner in which they use the poor brutes. *Every month* the horse is burned in his belly in a quincunx,—*i. e.,* as the spots are placed to mark five on dice; then he is burned in the roof of his mouth in the same manner. Can we wonder that this monthly application of red hot iron should spoil the temper of a horse?

Mr. Heusken's performances on horseback, and my riding, have raised us to a pinnacle of glory among the Japanese. In 1848 Lieutenant-Colonel May, of the U. S. Horse Artillery, rode his horse up the stone steps and into the hall of Barnum's Hotel [at] Baltimore, and then rode him down again. The feat was considered so wonderful that it was glorified in the newspapers from the Rio Grande to the St. Croix. If Colonel May could see the staircase I ride up and down, he would decline hearing his exploit mentioned again.[479]

Saturday, October 10, 1857. I am every day called on to see something the Japanese are preparing for my journey, or to give some new directions.

Saturday, October 17, 1857. I have selected a variety of such things as I have that will probably be acceptable as presents to the Ziogoon and the Ministers

[479]On this day, Townsend Harris wrote to Curtius, at Nagasaki, expressing his gratification that Curtius would open a correspondence with him (*L. B.,* vol. 2, pp. 92–93).

at Yedo. They consist of champagne and sherry, wines, cordials and cherry brandy; books of natural history, richly illustrated; telescope; barometer; rich astral lamp; richly cut decanters; preserved fruits, etc., etc. I am having these carefully packed up, and the Japanese prove to be very handy at such work. I have been almost daily occupied in seeing to clothing, etc., etc., preparing for my people. The coat-of-arms is very neatly done, and the motto *E pluribus unum,* the eagle, arrows, and olive branch quite perfect. I am informed that the news of my visit has spread like wildfire over the country and, as they express it, "millions will go to Yedo to see the grand entry of the American Ambassador." They *will* call me that name instead of Plenipotentiary, as the former has the grandest sound to their ears. They tell me that printed accounts of me, illustrated by drawings, are circulated by thousands.[480] These are not in the form of newspapers, but are analogous to the "broad sheets and little books" that preceded that mighty engine,— the newspaper.

Tuesday, October 20, 1857. At last, and fourteen months after my arrival in Japan, I have received my letters and supplies from Hakodate, from which place they were conveyed in a schooner to Yedo, and from thence were sent to me in a Japanese junk. *Thank God for them.* I find letters from my kind and sincere friend N. Dougherty of the following dates: July 22nd, August

---

[480]Griffis, *Townsend Harris,* p. 176, note: "These were the *nishiki-yé* or 'brocade pictures,' drawn on and printed from wooden blocks, and gaily colored, being xylographs. These pictures are usually made in three parts, which are pasted together, making one piece."

THE PRESIDENT OF THE UNITED STATES OF AMERICA.

TO ALL WHO SHALL SEE THESE PRESENTS, GREETING:

KNOW YE, That, reposing special trust and confidence in the abilities and integrity of *Townsend Harris of New York* I have nominated, and, by and with the advice and consent of the Senate, do appoint him CONSUL GENERAL of the UNITED STATES OF AMERICA, for *Japan to reside at Simoda*

and do authorize and empower him TO HAVE AND TO HOLD the said office, according to law, and to exercise and enjoy all the rights, pre-eminences, privileges, and authorities, to the same of right appertaining, during the pleasure of the PRESIDENT OF THE UNITED STATES, for the time being. And I do hereby enjoin all captains, masters, and commanders of ships and other vessels, armed or unarmed, sailing under the flag of the said States, as well as all other of their citizens, to acknowledge and consider him, the said *Townsend Harris* accordingly.

AND I DO HEREBY PRAY AND REQUEST *His Imperial Majesty the Emperor of Japan His* GOVERNORS and officers to permit the said *Townsend Harris* fully and peaceably to enjoy and exercise the said office, without giving or suffering to be given unto him any molestation or trouble; but, on the contrary, to afford him all proper countenance and assistance; I offering to do the same for all those who shall, in like manner, be recommended to me by *His Said Majesty*

In testimony whereof, I have caused these letters to be made Patent, and the SEAL of the UNITED STATES to be hereunto affixed. Given under my hand, at the City of Washington, the *thirty first* day of *July* in the year of our Lord one thousand eight hundred and *fifty Six*, and of the Independence of the United States of America the *81st*.

Franklin Pierce

BY THE PRESIDENT:

W L Marcy

SECRETARY OF STATE.

TOWNSEND HARRIS'S SECOND COMMISSION AS CONSUL GENERAL FOR JAPAN
Dated, Washington, D. C., July 31, 1856.

16th, September 22nd, October 15th, November 12th, November 26th, all 1856, and March 18, 1857. From my other dear and valued friend, General Wetmore, I have letters dated June 9th, July 21st, and November 10th, 1856.

I received in all twenty-eight letters,[481] but not one word from the Department of State[482] about my Treaty with Siam,[483] or one word in answer to some of mine that it was important *to me* to receive answers.

All the letters from the Department were printed circulars,[484] except one dated August, 1856, and relating

[481]Not one of these seven letters from Mr. Nathaniel Dougherty and of the three from General Prosper M. Wetmore has been found. It will be remembered that Townsend Harris himself informed us that his letters to Mr. Dougherty, General Wetmore, and other private friends in New York and elsewhere were not copied into his *Letter Books* (*Journal,* July 6, 1857). Similarly, not all the letters received from his friends are to be found in his *Letters and Papers.* There are extant, however, a great many of the letters included in this total of twenty-eight.

[482]From the Department of State, Townsend Harris received Secretary Cass's dispatch dated Mar. 6, 1857, which informed him of the appointment of Mr. Cass to the office of Secretary of State. In acknowledging receipt of this communication, Townsend Harris concludes with the familiar cry: "Your letter is the first that I have received since I arrived in Japan" (*L. B.,* vol. 2, pp. 98–99, dated Oct. 20, 1857).

On the same day, and together with the communication from Secretary Cass, Townsend Harris received also the second copy of his Commission as Consul General for Japan, signed by President Franklin Pierce and Secretary William L. Marcy, and dated July 31, 1856.

This second copy of his Commission has the title "Consul General" printed in full in the body of the text, and the wording differs here and there from that in the first copy of the Commission, dated Aug. 4, 1855, and signed by President Pierce and by W. Hunter, the Acting Secretary of State. The second copy was issued to Townsend Harris because his appointment as Consul General was confirmed by the Senate on July 31, 1856 (S. Ex. J'l, vol. 10, p. 131). Both originals of these Commissions are now in the possession of The College of the City of New York.

[483]See note 467.

[484]In his Dispatch No. 19 to Secretary Cass, dated Oct. 20, 1857 (*L. B.,* vol. 2, p. 100), Townsend Harris acknowledges receipt that day of the following circulars from the Department:

1) Statutes at Large for 1855–56.

to a debt contracted by two Americans, Reed and Dougherty, with the Japanese.[485] Nor am I more fortunate in receiving answers to my letters [which] I wrote to Henry Grinnell and Joseph Evans.[486]

Saturday, October 24, 1857. I find that the President was strongly inclined to reward my services in making a commercial treaty with Siam, by removing me from my office of Consul General at Japan. It appears that the Treaty reached Washington on the 17th of September, 1856, and on the same day the New York *Times* published what *it said* was the actual Treaty. The President held that it was I and I alone that communicated it to the *Times,* and was for my instant removal. This was only prevented by the friendship of Governor Marcy and the untiring labors of my kind friend General Wetmore.

The President appeared to think the best mode of proceeding would be to punish me first, and *then* call

2) Act to regulate the Diplomatic and Consular Departments, Aug. 18, 1856.
3) Regulations for Consular Officers, 1856.
4) List of fees chargeable by American Consuls.

[485]This letter from the State Department was dated Aug. 19, 1856; it was numbered 34; was signed by Secretary William L. Marcy; and authorized a special credit on bankers for $3,000 to cover the debt incurred by Messrs. Reed and Dougherty. (For a copy of this letter, see *L. & P.,* vol. 2, no. 65; *cf., L. B.,* vol. 4, p. 38; for the Reed and Dougherty affair, see above, notes 325 and 400; and Mar. 7, 1857, and notes.)

[486]On this day Townsend Harris wrote to Secretary Cass acknowledging receipt of Circular No. 16, dated Nov. 8, 1856; and stating that he had duly filled in the enclosed bond for $10,000, which he was therewith sending to his agent in New York, Mr. Nathaniel Dougherty (Dispatch No. 18: *L. B.,* vol. 2, p. 99). In his letter to Mr. Dougherty, of even date, Townsend Harris requests him to attend to all the details as soon as possible (*L. B.,* vol. 2, p. 106).

On Oct. 21, 1857, he wrote Dispatch No. 20 to Secretary Cass (*L. B.,* vol. 2, pp. 100–01); and on the 22nd Dispatch No. 21 (*ib.,* pp. 101–02). For Joseph Evans, see note 52; to Henry Grinnell, Townsend Harris had written on June 8, 1856: see *Journal,* July 23, 1856.

on me for my defence. This mode of procedure is quite common among Oriental despots, but I am inclined to think that the Western rule is to hold every man innocent until he is proved to be guilty. Had the President, in his ardent desire to punish the guilty, given orders to compare the publication in the *Times* with the *official* copy in the State Department, he would at once have seen that the *Times's* version could not have emanated from me, nor from anyone who had an opportunity of copying the Treaty!!!

The *Times* uses the words "American *subjects*" in twenty places; the Treaty reads, "American *citizens*."

The Preamble is entirely omitted.

Article 1. The last clause is not in the Treaty, and omits a very important provision.

Article 2. Omits a reference to the Treaty made by Mr. Roberts in 1833.

Article 3. The closing paragraph is not in the Treaty.

Article 8. Omits an important provision regarding the prohibition of the export of rice, besides also omitting a reference to the Treaty of 1833.

Article 9. The closing paragraph not in the Treaty.

Article 12. Alters the sense of the original entirely, as the Treaty went into operation the moment it was signed. The Regulations of Trade, which form an integral part of the Treaty and consist of six articles, are omitted.

Various verbal alterations run through the whole Treaty as published in the *Times*. I wonder the *Times* correspondent was so inexact, as he could easily have procured an accurate copy.

After I had engrossed the English version of the Treaty, the Siamese asked to have it for the purpose of comparing it with their version; and, as they were bound to accept the English version (see Regulations, Article 6) as the original, their request was reasonable and could not be refused. It was some days in their possession, and their chief interpreter showed it freely to all who desired to see it, and I was told it was seen by Americans, English, French and Portuguese residents, and a single tical would have purchased the right to copy it. Everyone who has had anything to do with Oriental Courts knows that the idea of secrecy as attached to negotiations is absurd. The thing is unknown and is impracticable. Monsieur Montigny,[487] the French Plenipotentiary, succeeded me at Bangkok about two months after my departure. He set out with a full determination to keep his negotiations and the results a profound secret, and how did he succeed?

Mr. Mattoon, U. S. Consul at Bangkok, wrote to me under date September 15, 1856, as follows:

"There was an attempt made on the part of the French to have everything secret, utterly refusing to discuss any question in the presence of others than French and Siamese. The attempt was perfectly futile in such a place [as] this, even had there been any reasonable motive for secrecy. The Treaty was on its way to Washington and London nearly, or quite, as soon as to Paris."

---

[487]He concluded a Treaty with Siam on July 8, 1856. It was on his nomination that Townsend Harris, on Sept. 23, 1859, was elected a member of the *Société Impériale Zoologique d'Acclimatation* of Paris (*L. & P.*, vol. 1, no. 233). Mr. Mattoon's letter, from which Townsend Harris quotes in this entry and which he had received only four days before (Oct. 20, 1857), is *L. & P.*, vol 1, no. 99

Wednesday, October 28, 1857. Moriama appeared at my house this morning, having just returned from Yedo. He brought a message from Dewa-no-Kami, requesting to meet me at the Goyoshi at noon to-day. Moriama brought me a box containing files of the Singapore *Free Press, Illustrated London News,* and *Java Bode,* which were forwarded to me from Nagasaki on the 14th of August by Mr. H. Donker Curtius by sea, and had (of course) passed by Shimoda and been taken to Yedo. Moriama informed [me] that it was true that publications had been made concerning my visit, and added that the Government had suppressed them, as they contained so many mis-statements. On going to the Goyoshi, Dewa-no-Kami showed me various ground plans of the buildings where my audience was to take place, and explained their views of the ceremonies to be had, etc., etc. I accepted the whole program with one exception. They proposed that, after my audience was over and I had retired, I should return to the Audience Chamber, not as the representative of the President, but in my private capacity; that, instead of proceeding to the place I formerly occupied, I should stop at the place where I made my first bow; that the Ziogoon would then address me, to which I was not to reply, but simply bow and retire.

It struck me that there was some petty scheme of glorifying themselves at my expense in this proposition, and I avoided it by saying that I could not divest myself of my character of Plenipotentiary which had been conferred on me by the President, and that, so long as the

President pleased, I must maintain that character. They were evidently chagrined at this and tried to persuade me to alter my decision, assuring me that it was meant as a personal honor to me, etc., etc. I replied that I was gratified for the intention; and that, if the Ziogoon wished to see me at a private audience, I would cheerfully attend him, but that it must always be in my official character.

To-day I am told that *Ziogoon* is not the proper appellation of their ruler, but that it is *Tykoon. Ziogoon* is literally "Generalissimo," while *Tykoon* means "Great Ruler." The genius of the people shines out in this. For more than a year I have spoken and written *Ziogoon* when referring to their ruler, and they never gave me any explanation; but now, when I am on the eve of starting for Yedo, they give me the real word.

My departure is fixed for Monday, November 23rd. They proposed Friday, November 20th, but as that would cause me to pass Sunday among the hills, I declined it and fixed on Monday, which will cause me to pass my Sunday at Kawasaki, a town about fifteen miles from Yedo, on the banks of the river that brought up Mr. Bittinger, Chaplain of the *Susquehanna,* when he made his dash at Yedo in 1854.[488]

---

[488]It was on Mar. 14, 1854, that Mr. Bittinger had been prompted by his curiosity to see more of Japan and to walk beyond the usual four or five miles permitted by the Japanese authorities to the men of Perry's squadron. He had pushed on from Yokohama to Kanagawa, and then to Kamasaki (or, Kawasaki), where he was overtaken by a messenger from Commodore Perry ordering him back to his ship immediately. (Perry, *Narrative,* in 33-2, H. Ex. Doc., no. 97, vol. 1, pp. 359-60.) On Oct. 28, 1857, Townsend Harris wrote Dispatch No. 24 to Secretary Cass: *L. B.,* vol. 3, pp. 5-6.

Friday, October 30, 1857. To-day is the anniversary of the first visit paid to me by the Governors of Shimoda; and, according to appointment, Dewa-no-Kami, or the Prince of Dewa, visited me attended by one of the Vice-Governors, the Mayor or Prefect of Kakizaki, the Commissary of Shimoda and his private secretary, besides a large train of officers, guards, etc., etc., but the above were all that were admitted into my private rooms. After an hour of pleasant chat we sat down to a very good dinner provided in our style, and they did full honor to my cheer, both solids and fluids.

As soon as this was done, the dishes were removed and I gave them a second one in Japanese style. Still they ate, but nature has its limits; they did what they could, but fell far short of their first performance. They left me at five P. M., full of fun and good cheer. Their conduct at table would have passed in any society of New York, Paris or London.

An enormous umbrella has been added to the paraphernalia of my *tail* for Yedo.

Saturday, October 31, 1857. I am truly grateful for improved health. I begin to recover a little of my lost flesh.

Weather report for the month:

Thermometer: highest, 79°; lowest, 54°; mean, 65.8°. Extreme daily range, 14°. Rain one day, showers six days, cloudy two days, fine twenty-two days. Last year October was: thermometer, highest, 77°; lowest, 51°; mean, 64.3°. Extreme daily range, 15°. Rain three days, showers five, cloudy five days. Fine eighteen days.

Monday, November 2, 1857. Moriama gave me the following as the prices at which copper and camphor are sold to the Dutch at Nagasaki, with the mode of calculating the money. The seni and *ichibu* are real coins, the others are mere imaginary Chinese coins and are only used in the accounts of the Dutch.

10 seni make 1 candereen; 10 candereen make 1 mas; 10 mas make 1 tael; 16 mas 1 ichibu, but in account with the Dutch, the tael is reckoned 11 mas, and the ichibu at 1 tael 5 mas.

Copper	per picul in a/c	,	8 ichibus &	50 seni
"	" " "	silver,	4 "	" 25 "
Camphor "	" "	a/c ,	0 "	" 600 "
"	" " "	silver,	0 "	" 300 "

It strikes me that there must be some misunderstanding in the above. Either the picul is short weight, or the price is erroneous.

Moriama says the copper costs the Government ten kobangs per picul,—that is Macoto, day–nigh, or a great——[?]

Tuesday, November 3, 1857. The poor despised *porgy* of New York here becomes a capital boiling fish, weighing frequently seven to ten pounds. The same character attends him in the South Pacific, in Australia, New Zealand and other parts. He is called a "snapper," in Australia.

Wednesday, November 4, 1857. A beautiful day. Thermometer, 70°. Rode down towards Cape Idsu as far as was possible on horseback, and over roads that would startle any English steeplechaser. The country looks far more beautiful than it did at this time last year, as the typhoon of September 22, 1856, destroyed nearly all [the] vegetation. Rice crop is about one-third harvested and looks very well. Buckwheat in full bloom.

Saturday, November 7, 1857. I paid my bills to the Goyoshi for my bills with them for four months, amounting to 754 *ichibus,* or $260; but this covers a good deal of carpenter's work and other extras. My bills with the Japanese for supplies will be about $700 *per annum.* To this add supplies from Hongkong, say $500, servants $650, gives a total of $1,850 *per annum,* less $365 *per annum* paid by Mr. Heusken as his share of household expenses,—leaving my outlay about $1,500 *per annum.* But, at the rate of exchange against the United States, which varies from thirty to forty-five per cent., I can remit to New York some $6,000 *per annum* as my savings out of a salary of $5,000! Besides, I have made a little sum of about $2,500 by taking from the Japanese foreign gold at the rate at which they took it,—*i. e.,* 34½ cents per dollar. This I send to Hongkong to be disposed of by remittance to New York or for sale, as may be most for my interest.

Wednesday, November 18, 1857. I have got everything packed up and ready for my journey to Yedo,[489]

---

[489]Among other things, Townsend Harris had prepared two letters of Instructions which were to be used during his absence from Shimoda: one addressed to any United States Naval Commander that should visit Shimoda (*L. B.,* vol. 2, pp. 86–89); the other to any merchant captain (*ib.,* pp. 89–90). He had, furthermore, issued a warrant to the Japanese authorities for the arrest of any of his Chinese servants that might attempt to leave Shimoda while he was away at Yedo (*L. B.,* vol. 3, pp. 6–7, dated Nov. 3, 1857), and had, in a covering letter to Dewa-no-Kami, provided for the comfort and security of the American Consulate (*ib.,* p. 7).

which is to begin on Monday next, the 23rd. Visited the Prince of Dewa at Nakamura to take leave of him before my setting out, according to Japanese custom. The Governor gave me a copy of a Treaty made with the Dutch in January, 1856. It is only a recapitulation of the substance of the Dutch Convention of November, 1855, *except* it withdraws the right of the Dutch to lease the grounds and buy the buildings at Deshima.[490]

Friday, November 20, 1857. Went to the Goyoshi at the special request of the Governor, who gave me copies of Additional Articles made with the Dutch, October 16, 1857, and with the Russians on the 24th of the same month.[491] The only points of importance in these Articles are those contained in my Convention of June 17th. A curious Article is inserted in the Dutch papers,—*viz.,* "The Dutch shall have the right to exercise their own, *or the Christian religion,* in the buildings occupied by them at Deshima." It would appear from this Article that the "Dutch religion" is not the Christian religion.[492]

---

[490]See notes 387–391, inclusive, and 393.

[491]For the Additional Articles to the Dutch Treaty, and for other material connected with the ratifications that were exchanged on Oct. 16, 1857, see Gubbins, *The Progress of Japan,* pp. 255–66.

For the Supplementary Treaty with Russia signed at Nagasaki, see *ib.,* pp. 239–45. The full text of this Supplementary Treaty, written in the Dutch language, is to be found in *L. & P.,* vol. 2, no. 70. Admiral C. E. Poutiatine, who had negotiated the Russian Supplementary Treaty, sailed from Deshima for Shanghai on Tuesday, Oct. 27, 1857 (*L. & P.,* vol. 1, no. 74). On November 20th, Townsend Harris wrote Dispatch No. 25 to Secretary Cass, forwarding copies of these Treaties and discussing their contents: *L. B.,* vol. 3, pp. 22–24.

[492]Additional Articles, Art. XXXIII (Gubbins, *op. cit.,* p. 262): "The Netherlanders are at liberty to practise their own or the Christian religion within their buildings and at the burying-places appointed for them."

It seems to us that the phrase "or the Christian religion," instead of being (as Townsend Harris says) an alternative to the phrase "their own [religion],"

Sunday, November 22, 1857. This morning I received a package from Mr. J. H. Donker Curtius, Dutch Commissioner at Nagasaki, in answer to my letter of August 27th. He sends me copies of the Dutch and Russian negotiations of October last, and a copy of the *Overland Mail* of August 10th. All of which are very acceptable.[493]

Monday, November 23, 1857. At eight this morning I start on my journey to Yedo. I went on horseback; the morning was very fine, and the idea of the importance of my journey and the success that had crowned my efforts to reach Yedo, gave me a fine flow of spirits. The American Flag was borne before me, and I felt an honest pride in displaying it in this hitherto secluded country.[494]

At Nakamura (about one mile from my house) I joined the main cavalcade, and we started in the following order. My avant courier was Keekoona,[495] a mili-

---

is in apposition to it and explains its meaning. We feel sure that the Dutch so meant it. Indeed, in the postscript to a letter dated Deshima, Nov. 6, 1857 (*L. & P.*, vol. 1, no. 76), Curtius says to Townsend Harris: "The Japanese have agreed, too, to abolish the custom of trampling the cross of our Lord." Occurring as it does in a letter which speaks of the recently concluded Additional Articles, this postscript sounds very much like a commentary on Art. XXXIII, and we think it fair so to consider it. Townsend Harris received Curtius's letter on Nov. 27, 1857, when he had reached Odawara on his journey to Yedo; but, in spite of this postscript, he had not changed his mind on the meaning of the phrase in question by Jan. 25, 1858, *q.v.*

Before passing on, it should be emphasized that the words of Curtius quoted above constitute the first authentic statement of the abolition of the odious custom of trampling on the Cross—the *Fumi-yé;* and, further, that this important statement appears in a brief postscript: *Servus servorum Dei!*

[493]See letter by Curtius to Townsend Harris, Nov. 6, 1857: *L. & P.*, vol. 1, no. 74.

[494]For the history and significance of this flag, see Appendix V.

[495]The Japanese words in this entry should be written: Kikuna; Shi-ta-ni-iro; Kago, Kabi-ya. (Griffis, *Townsend Harris*, ad loc.)

tary officer with a rank corresponding to captain. He had his horse and *norimon* and the usual bearers and attendants, but before him went three lads each bearing a wand of bamboo with strips of paper attached to the top; they cried out, alternately, *Stanee-hiro,* that is, "Sit down," "Sit down." They kept some four hundred yards in advance, and their cry sounded quite musical.

Next to Keekoona came the American Flag guarded by two of *my* guards. Then I came on horseback with six guards, next my *norimon* with its twelve bearers and *their* headman; bearers of my shoes, etc., etc. Then Mr. Heusken on horseback with two guards, then his *norimon,* bearers, etc., etc. Next followed a long retinue bearing packages containing my bedding, chairs, food, trunks, and packages containing presents; my cook, and *his* following. The Vice-Governor of Shimoda followed, with his train, then the Mayor of Kakizaki, and lastly the private secretary of the Governor of Shimoda. A Dutch interpreter was carried in a *cango* in Mr. Heusken's rear. The whole train numbered some three hundred and fifty persons.

All the bearers of luggage, etc., etc., were changed every two ri, or about five miles, and I was glad to see that these men were all paid for their labor.

My "standard bearer" was clothed in a long *kabyya,* or gown made of brown and white calico, of a particular pattern, and open at the sides like a herald's coat, from the hip downward.

My guards were clothed in silk dresses, and had the

THE FIRST AMERICAN FLAG MADE IN JAPAN: NOVEMBER, 1857
This flag is now framed and is hanging on the wall of the Director's Office, in the Townsend Harris Hall
High School.   See Appendix V.

arms of the United States on the right and left breast
of their upper garment; each man wore *two swords*.
The *norimon* of Japan appears to have been made after
the model of the iron cages said to have been invented
by Cardinal Balue, in the reign of Louis XI of France.
They are so low that you cannot stand upright in them,
and so short that you cannot lie down at full length. To
one who has not been accustomed to sit with his legs
folded under him, and the whole weight of his body
pressing on his heels, the posture is more painful than
can be easily imagined. I previously had a *norimon*
made for me, which was six and a half feet long (like the
palanquin of India), which enabled me to avoid the torture of the Japanese *norimon*.

The packages containing my bedding, clothing, etc.,
were covered with black cotton cloth with the arms of
the United States neatly put on them. The other packages were neatly put up and had a little pennon with the
United States arms flying from a short bamboo, which
was placed upright on each package.

My *norimon* bearers were dressed in dark blue, with
the arms of the United States *on the back*. These were
picked men (twelve for me and eight for Mr. Heusken),
and very tall for Japanese. My men wore a peculiar
ornament, which is prohibited to any below the bearers
of princes. It is made of cotton cloth, gummed very
stiffly and folded back and forth in folds about three
inches wide. It is about thirty inches long, and has one
end stuck in the girdle at an angle below the right
shoulder, with the upper end projecting a little beyond

413

the right side of the body. Across the upper end two white stripes run diagonally across all the folds.

The motion of the body causes the folds to open and close, something like the action of a fan, and is considered as being *very beautiful* by the Japanese. My route to-day was only fifteen miles; it continued along the river of Shimoda, the ground gradually rising and the river diminishing to a mere thread of water, until we crossed a hill some four hundred feet high which separates the watershed of Shimoda from the Valley of Nasimoto.[496] Our midday halt was at Mitskoesi.[497] The last part of the ride gave us the sight of some noble cypress and camphor trees,—one of the latter was of enormous bulk, and the Japanese said it was many hundred years old. Nasimoto is a small village of about one hundred houses, very prettily situated. My quarters for the night were in a temple which commanded a most beautiful view of the hills and valley, and of the village which lay some one hundred and fifty feet abruptly below us.

I have remarked that throughout the Catholic and Pagan world, the most picturesque positions are always selected for churches and temples. I found that much attention had been paid to the *path* (for it cannot be called a road) over which I passed to-day. Bridges had been built over every stream, the pathway mended, and all the bushes cut away so as to leave the path clear. At the temple I found that a bathroom and water closet had

---

[496]Nashimoto.

[497]Mitsukuri (Griffis, *Townsend Harris,* p. 185).

been built for my special use, and every attention paid to my comfort.

Tuesday, November 24, 1857. Started at eight A. M. Our route to-day was over the mountain Amagi, which is some 3,500 feet above the level of the sea. The path was very difficult,—so much so that I was compelled to leave my horse and enter my *norimon;* and it was no easy matter to carry that, even with eight men bearing it, as the road was sometimes at an angle of 35°, while the zigzags were some of them not so long as the pole or beam of my *norimon,* which is twenty-two feet long. Amagi is clothed with noble trees, consisting of cypress, pine, camphor and others of the laurel family, besides many of whose names I am ignorant. The *orchidea* were numerous, and offer a rich harvest to the experienced botanist. We halted on the top of Amagi, whence we had a fine view of Shimoda, Oho Sima and its volcano, with the Bay of Suruga, the Gulf of Yedo, etc., etc. The descent is not quite so abrupt as the ascent was, and about two-thirds of the way down I mounted my horse once more. As I descended, the valley opened and gave some beautiful views; on the *south* side of Amagi I saw a very pretty cascade.

Passing through a village, I saw some camellias which were already in full bloom, both white and red, but the flowers were all single.

Passing through the village of Yugasima[498] to go to my quarters at a temple, I turned to the right from the

---

[498]Yugashima.

road and in a few moments I had my first view of the Mountain Fusi Yama.[499]

It is grand beyond description; viewed from this place the mountain is entirely isolated and appears to shoot up in a perfect and glorious cone, some ten thousand feet high; while its actual height is exaggerated by the absence of any neighboring hills by which to contrast its altitude. It was covered with snow, and in the bright sun (about four P. M.) it appeared like frosted silver. In its majestic solitude it appeared even more striking to me than the celebrated Dwhalgiri of the Himalayas, which I saw in January, 1855. I found the temple at Yugasima prepared for me in the same manner as that at Nasimoto.

Wednesday, November 25, 1857. Left Yugasima at eight A. M. and, as our road lay over a plain, I mounted on horseback.

As I proceeded the plain widened, until in many places it was three miles across it. The scene was very pleasing. The plain was covered with a heavy crop of rice, of which the harvest had just commenced; and it reminded me of the golden wheat fields of old Ontario. The houses of the people, the mode of cultivation, the dress of the people, and all minor particulars were exactly like Shimoda. We halted at noon at a hamlet called Ogiso;[500] and when I mounted my horse I pushed on in company with Keekoona and Mr. Heusken more rapidly than my attendants could do. This brought me to

---

[499]Fujiyama.
[500]Ohito.

the town of Missima[501] at three P. M. This town is on the *Tokido,*[502] or great road of Japan, and is the route travelled by the Dutch when they go to Yedo. I may here remark that the Dutch have not been to Yedo for the last ten years, their *tribute* having been delivered at Nagasaki to the Japanese. The Dutch thus avoided the great expense of the journey; but this has not relieved them from the presents they made on the occasion of those visits, as they are regularly demanded and given at Nagasaki.

Missima contains about nine hundred houses, and the description of it by Kaempfer in 1696, after making due allowance for high coloring, will apply to it now. It had a fine temple situated in a fine square and surrounded by noble trees, but it was totally destroyed by the great earthquake of December, 1855. I went to see its ruins; and, in my walk, I was surprised at the numbers of the people, which were apparently far more numerous than the whole population of the place. On asking for an explanation, I was told that the time of my arrival was known many days ago, and that all those who could procure permission had come to Missima to see me; that some had come more than one hundred miles. The people were perfectly well behaved, no crowding on me, no shouting or noise of any kind. As I passed, all knelt and cast their eyes down (as though they were not worthy even to look at me). Only those of a certain rank were

---

[501]Mishima.
[502]Tokaido.

allowed to salute me, which was done by "knocking head" or bringing the forehead actually to the ground. In the temple grounds are some fine tanks swarming with fish. A small pagoda of three stories was so much shaken by the earthquake that it totters to its fall. Even the bridges leading over the small canals of the temple grounds, with the stone wall which surrounded the enclosure, have all been overturned.

My rest place to-night was at a *honjin,* or rest house for persons of the highest rank, such as the princes, etc. Even the Vice-Governor of Shimoda could not stop here. There are two or three classes of houses of entertainment for persons of rank and government officers, and these are distinct from the public hotels, which are also of various grades, but all are open to those who have money to pay the higher prices. I found myself very comfortable. In the rear was a garden, with dwarf trees, miniature mountains and other rock work; diminutive ponds with bridges over which nothing grosser than a fairy could walk, etc., etc.

In criticizing Kaempfer's description I must bear in mind the difference there is in the standards of splendor, etc., as they existed in 1696 and in 1857. What was splendor when he left Holland about 1685 would not be entitled to any adjective of praise in 1857.

So, when he speaks of stately castles, noble palaces, and magnificent temples, we should remember what class of buildings elicited those terms of praise one hundred and seventy years ago. I have had Fusi Yama in view all day, but alas! like many other things in this world, the nearer approach does not add to its beauty or grandeur.

It is now connected with a range of hills, one of which, Hakone, is some forty-five hundred feet high, which takes away the air of solitary majesty which the view from Yugasima has. " 'Tis distance lends enchantment to the view." To-morrow I have to cross over the mountain Hakone,[503] and, as the road is very bad for horses, I shall proceed in my *norimon*. Dignity (even if health permitted) forbids my going on foot, which I should prefer to riding in my *norimon*.

Thursday, November 26, 1857. As our march to-day is a weary one, I start at half-past seven. I stop in the suburbs to visit a temple. It is approached by a noble flight of eighty-five stone steps. There was nothing to mark the difference between this and a Chinese Buddhist Temple except that the Japanese affair was less gaudy and much cleaner than its Chinese fellow. We were now on the great road of Japan; it is from thirty to forty feet wide and is bordered by very noble cypress, pine, fir and camphor trees. Many of the cypresses are of extraordinary size. The typhoon of September 22, 1856 (see my *Journal* of that date)[504] made sad ravages among these fine trees. I found marks of its effects almost every hundred yards. We soon began to ascend the spurs of Hakone. The road up the mountain is paved with flat stones; and, from the total absence of wheel carriages, or

---

[503]Not to be confused with Hikone.

[504]The reference to this typhoon actually occurs in the entry for Sept. 23, 1856; *cf.* note 300.

of horses that are shod with iron, the stones are quite polished and so slippery that it is dangerous riding a horse over them. The ascent is bad, but not so vile as that over Mount Amagi. Near the top of the mountain I was taken to a temple built by Yeyas,[505] the founder of the present dynasty of Tykoons. From the top of Hakone we had a fine view of the City and Bay of Suruga. Fusiyama was quite near, and altogether a different affair from the glorious view at Yugasima. A short distance on the north side of Hakone, and about one mile from the top, stands the village of that name. Here is the celebrated pass into the Yedo district, and a rigid search is made of every *norimon,* and each person is examined as to his passport.

Here the Vice-Governor of Shimoda, after a vast deal of circumlocution, informed me that, when the great Princes of the Empire passed here, the door of the *norimon* was opened and an officer looked into it, without stopping the bearers; that it was a mere ceremony, but the ancient laws required it, etc., etc.

I replied that, as I was not a Japanese subject, and being as I was the diplomatic representative of the United States, I was free from any such search; that they knew what was in my *norimon,* and could inform the officers at the pass that there was nothing forbidden in it. The Vice-Governor tried for some time to change my determination, and at last proposed that I should ride through on horseback, and then permit the search of the empty *norimon.* I decidedly declined this, telling

505Iyeyasu Tokugawa.

him that it was the search under *any form* that I objected to. He then said that we must stop until he could send to Yedo for instructions, which would only take five days. I told him I should not wait five days nor five hours; that if the search was insisted on I should at once return to Shimoda. The poor Vice-Governor was in great tribulation and finally went to the guard house, and after a delay of two hours returned with word that it was all settled and that I should pass unmolested. The *honjin* where I stopped was on the bank of a pretty lake about two miles long, but it is notorious for its insalubrity. The water here is very bad, and the cold winds that rush down the sides of Fusi Yama are well calculated to produce sickness. Directly north of the "Gate of the Pass" is a temple which contains in its court some noble and colossal copper figures of Buddh. About two thirds of the way down the mountain I stopped at a perfect little bijou of a "rest house." Everything was in miniature. The house was new and nothing could exceed its cleanliness. A miniature garden adorned the rear, and from a wall of rocks some tiny cascades tumbled down like threads of silver, with a pleasing murmur. The trees were dwarfed into the smallest of possible sizes and into the queerest of forms. Some tiny canals were filled with water of crystal clearness, and the bottoms were paved with white pebbles. In these canals some enormous gold and silver fish were swimming. One of them was more than two feet long. A carp of some thirty inches long was the patriarch of this finny family. A number of small tortoise (the Japanese emblem of longevity) lazily crawled on some tiny rock work and over bridges of some eighteen inches' span.

Among other refreshments served to me were *living* fish and tea leaves made up with sugar as bonbons. The sweetmeats were in great variety and of excellent quality. Owing to the loss of time I did not reach Odowara[506] until long after dark, but I was not sorry for the delay, as the effect of my train with an immense number of flambeaux made from bamboos presented a curious and novel appearance, as it wound and turned in the descents of the mountain, making a figure like the tail of an imaginary fiery dragon. Beyond the walls of the town I was met by the officials, with an army of lanterns of all imaginable sizes, shapes and colors, all decorated with the arms of the owner. For nearly a mile before reaching the place I heard occasionally a hearty booming sound, the cause of which I could not divine. After reaching my resting place, these sounds increased in frequency and were now attended with a sensible jar which caused the sliding doors and windows to rattle sharply. I was told it was the surf breaking on the beach, and such I found it to be afterwards. The Gulf of Yedo is bifurcated by Cape Sagami, and the Bay of Odowara extends westerly and northerly, while the Gulf continues its course nearly north by east. The ground swell of the Pacific Ocean rolls in full majesty up the Bay of Odowara and breaks heavily on its beach. It was so late when I arrived that I could not see much of the town. I

---

[506]Odowara.

422

was told it contains 700 houses, while Kaempfer gave it 1,000 in 1696. If his account was correct, the town has lost three-tenths of its houses during the last 160 years. I should here remark that the principality of Idsu ends at Missima. Idsu, in which Shimoda is situated, is one of the poorest provinces of the Empire. It is so mountainous that only a very small portion of it can be cultivated, and it has no resources to support any large population. It has no town of 10,000 inhabitants, and the mountain Amagi cuts off the rest of the world from it, except by a painful and troublesome journey over it. The Japanese showed their astuteness in getting Commodore Perry to accept Shimoda for the Americans, as they were completely isolated by land, and they could easily keep away any undue number of Japanese craft. In fact, since I have been at Shimoda, I have never seen 150 vessels at one time in that harbor, while the Japanese assured me that a short time before my arrival it was not unusual to see 300 to 400 at a time, and that, during a gale of some days, 700 vessels had been there at one time.

Friday, November 27, 1857. Left Odowara at half-past eight, and at noon halted at Ohiso.[507] We were ferried over the river Banyugawa,[508] which is now some 200 yards wide, but in the rains of May and June it is over one mile wide. The land on either side is a mere bed of sand, and the river is filled with quicksands. These sands [and] the great width of the river during the floods,

[507]Oiso.
[508]Banriugawa (Griffis, *Townsend Harris,* p. 193).

joined to the very low banks, render the bridging of the stream very difficult. This river with the broad sands and low banks reminded me of the River Sone[509] in India. Reached Fusisawa[510] at six P. M. From Odowara to Fusisawa it is almost one continuous village, as the hamlets are only separated a few hundred yards from each other. Kaempfer speaks of the crowds of travellers, priests, pilgrims, nuns and beggars which thronged the Tokido when he was in Japan. Nothing of the kind was seen by me. I have not as yet seen a dozen travellers on the road, nor met any of the great trains that attend the princes when they travel. In the towns and villages the shops are all closed except the cookshops. The people are collected in large numbers in front of their houses and are silent and motionless as I pass. The authorities of each village conduct me to the bounds of their village, where they are relieved by those of the next. They salute me on leaving by a prostration, which is also made by my new conductors. The road has not only been repaired and put in order for my reception, but it is *actually swept* only a few hours before I pass over it.[511] The

---

[509]Son.

[510]Fujisawa.

[511]Happily, we know to-day far more than Townsend Harris himself could know of the careful preparations made by the Japanese to do him honor on his journey to Yedo. The series of Japanese documents containing the necessary instructions was entitled: *"Visit of the American Ambassador to the Castle of Yedo in the 10th month of the 4th year of Ansei* (1857)."

The original Japanese version of these documents was obtained by the American Dr. David Murray (who was then serving Japan as educational adviser) from the successor of Hotta, Bitchiu-no-Kami. Lord Hotta, in 1857, had been Chief of the Great Council, or Gorogio. Dr. Murray presented the documents to Mr. D. W. Stevens, Secretary of the U. S. Legation, who caused them to be translated into English by Mr. Thompson, interpreter of the Lega-

424

crossroads and paths leading to the Tokido are closed by ropes stretched across them. At the entrance of each village small cones formed of earth are erected, each having a small green sprig in the top of it. This is in honor of me. It reminds me of the "Shiva Lingas" of India.[512]

All the people I see are clad in their holiday costume, but, as noted at Missima, it is only those of rank that salute me. All below that rank kneel and avert their eyes from me. At each place where I halt, the front of the house is decorated with long cloths festooned over the gates and doors and with the Imperial colors,—i. e.,

---

tion. In the letter forwarding the translations to the Hon. William M. Evarts, Secretary of State, and dated Mar. 25, 1879, Mr. Stevens says:

> "It is understood that the literary executors of Mr. Harris are engaged in collecting material for his biography. I have no doubt that they would find facts worthy of notice in this account of his first visit to Yedo."

The account referred to is given in 46–2, H. Ex. Doc., no. 1, pt. 1, pp. 621–36, in Serial no. 1902. To give an idea of how thoroughly everything was anticipated, we shall outline some of the documents reported:

1) Notification to Honda, Mino-no-Kami, that the Shogun will grant an audience to Townsend Harris at an early date.
2) Appointment of Commissioners to take charge of Townsend Harris's journey to Yedo, directing them to make all ʾhe necessary preparations.
3) A special notification to ʾhe officials in charge, emphasizing the fact that, inasmuch as Townsend Harris's visit will be the first, it will necessarily serve as a precedent, and hence the need of special care!
4) Notices to the Ometsukes regarding the care of the roads, houses, and people; and to the inspectors of roads.
5) A careful plan of the route to be followed on arriving at Yedo; on entering the Shogun's Castle; on going to the house of Lord Hotta.
6) A notice to the overseer of the Buddhist and Shinto Temples in Yedo, to be ready to provide new quarters in case anything (presumably fire) should happen to Townsend Harris's abode.
7) A notice to Inouye, Shinano-no-Kami, ordering him to Shimoda to consult with Governor Nakamura, Dewa-no-Kami, relative to the approaching visit to Yedo.
8) A notice from Lord Hotta to Lord Honda, asking him to notify Yedo when Townsend Harris was ready to leave Shimoda.

[512]Linga, a Sanskrit word for the phallic symbol, which represents one of the aspects under which the god Siva is worshipped in India.

425

black and white stripes; and a stake is always found placed to which my flagstaff can be attached. As I mounted my horse after being ferried over the Banyu-gawa, my vicious brute of a horse both bit and kicked me. The little finger of my left hand was very painful and I ordered some leeches to be applied. The doctor approached with great trepidation, while large drops of perspiration stood on his forehead. I asked what ailed him; he said that he had never approached any person of such exalted rank before, and he was terrified at the idea of drawing blood from me. He was told to forget all about rank, and to apply his remedy as quickly as possible. The leeches are very small and of course not very efficient. Excellent leeches are found in every part of the *tropical* East. A tank like those of Pulo Penang would be a pretty fortune to a man if he had it in New York. I have known the bites of those leeches to bleed for twenty-four hours. The doctors of Japan are of two classes: the one following the European mode so far as they understand it; the other continues the old Chinese practice. Their medicines are generally of a simple kind. No violent chemicals are used, and calomel is unknown. Rhubarb and gentian are their chief internal remedies, while the moxa or cautery with scarification, is applied externally in local inflammations, rheumatism, etc. Tropical bleeding by leeching and cupping is also used. Vaccine matter was introduced by the Dutch a few years ago. I was informed that about one-tenth of the population have been vaccinated. They do not inoculate the smallpox. Still the ignorance of the Japanese of the true mode of treating the diseases of children in particular is shown in the frightful statement made to me by the Prince of Shinano, that out of 100 children born no more than 30 reach the age of twenty years. My surgeon, having finished his labor, retired a proud and happy man; happy that he had pleased me, and proud that he had been called on to attend a person occupying my position.[513]

Saturday, November 28, 1857. Left Fusisawa at seven A. M. The road is very pleasant, as the plain gradually widens as we approach Yedo. The Tokido from Odowara runs quite near the shore, except where it crosses the Peninsula of Sagami. See many marks of the typhoon of September, 1856, along the road. Fusi Yama begins to improve in appearance as we recede from it. The villages are larger and more closely connected than on yesterday's route. The people, all in holiday costume, are kneeling on mats in front of their houses, as I pass.

At noon stop at Kanagawa, at a pretty *honjin* placed at the water side. This is an interesting spot to me as it was the scene of Commodore Perry's negotiations. From my house I look across the bay to Yokohama, the place where his fleet was anchored. I was much surprised by the sight of three ships of European build and rig, which with two schooners were lying about midway between Kanagawa and Yokohama.

---

[513]The Western, or Dutch, learning found its way gradually into Japan through the small Dutch window at Deshima. A splendid picture of this scientific infiltration in the fields of mathematics, geography, medicine, etc., is presented in *Osada's Life of Takano Nagahide,* translated and edited with an introduction by D. C. Greene, D.D., in *Transactions of The Asiatic Society of Japan,* vol. XLI, part III, Aug., 1913, pp. 379–492.

These ships have been purchased from the Dutch by the Japanese, as the beginning of a navy. To the northeast from Kanagawa I saw the steamer which the Dutch presented to the Japanese.[513a] Kanagawa has the air of a flourishing town and has much increased since Kaempfer described it. It is the nearest harbor to Yedo, and must become a place of great importance whenever Yedo shall be opened to foreign commerce. I left Kanagawa with regret and pursued my road to Kawasaki, where I shall pass Sunday. Ever since I have been in this country I have refused to transact any business on that day or even to receive a message from the Japanese.

They now fully understand my motives, and they respect me for them. The village authorities are now preceded by a body of policemen, each bearing an iron rod some half an inch thick and six feet long. Four or five iron rings are attached by eyes to the top of the rod, which make a loud jingling noise as the foot of the rod is struck on the ground by the policeman at each two or three steps. They alternate the time of striking the rod on the ground by a regular measure, and this, with the different tones of the rings, makes a species of music. The number of people seen increases. They are all fat, well clad and happy looking, but there is an equal absence of any appearance of wealth or of poverty,—a state of things that *may* perhaps constitute the real hap-

---

[513a]This was the steam paddle-wheel corvette of six guns, the *Soembing*, presented to the Bakufu by the King of The Netherlands in 1855, and renamed the *Kanko*. She was possibly the first ship to hoist the *Hinomaru*—the Red Sun on a white ground—which was at this time adopted as the national flag (Murdoch, *A History of Japan*, vol. 3, p. 616 and note 1).

piness of a people. I sometimes doubt whether the opening of Japan to foreign influences will promote the *general happiness* of this people. It is more like the golden age of simplicity and honesty than I have ever seen in any other country.

Security for person and property, universal frugality and contentment seem to be the *apparent* condition of Japan at present. Reached Kawasaki at half-past four P. M. The *honjin* prepared for my reception I found to be in a sadly dilapidated condition. Doors and windows would not close, the paper in many places broken, so that the wind played freely through the rooms, while an air of dirty slovenliness reigned over the whole. This was the first instance of a dirty house I had ever seen in Japan, and it struck me all the more forcibly as I was to pass Sunday here; the condition of the house became a serious matter, and I soon determined to have better lodgings if they could be found in the place, as the idea of lodging in a *honjin* would not protect me from the actual discomfort of the place; so, after much grave remonstrance on the part of the Vice-Governor, Mr. Heusken sallied out to look at the hotels of the place. He soon returned with word that he had found a house pleasantly situated and that it was neat, clean and comfortable. I decided at once to accept it. The Vice-Governor implored me not to think of going to a tavern, but, rather than I should do so, he would give up his quarters and go to the tavern himself. I told him I could not think of disturbing him; and, as to my dignity, *that* was my affair, and I would take good care of it. So to the

429

hotel *Mannenya,* or "the felicity of ten thousand years,"
I went, and a very good change it was, for I had a bright,
clean and comfortable house in place of the dark, dirty
and uncomfortable *honjin.* Among other reasons advanced by the Governor why I ought not to go to the
Mannenya was the very grave fact that at all the *honjins*
the floor of the room occupied by me was raised some
three inches higher than the other rooms; that to place
me on a floor of the same level as the others was to
derogate from the respect due to me; that the most
positive orders had been issued by the Tykoon that I
should receive all the marks of honor in my journey that
were bestowed on persons of the most exalted rank in
Japan, and for that reason I had always been lodged in
honjins on a raised floor which was covered with mats
of the finest quality, and bordered with a binding of a
particular pattern, etc., etc. I answered him that what
he said was no doubt very true and very proper, but he
had forgotten that I sat on chairs that raised me much
higher than even the favored floor of the *honjin,* and
that, as to the "mats and binding," my being a foreigner
would allow me to dispense with those considerations
while I was at Kawasaki, and so *that* matter ended after
consuming nearly three hours.

My cook served me up some very delicate teal and
delicious quail for my dinner. I had this man (who
is a Japanese cook) instructed in the Western manner of
cooking for some five weeks before I left Shimoda. His
cookery is inferior to Delmonico's, but much more to my
taste than the Japanese cuisine.

I pay for my food and lodgings (and for the hire of my guards and bearers, grooms, etc., etc.) while on my journey.

The Government furnishes all the coolies that are employed to transport my luggage, etc., etc.

I am informed that on my arrival at Yedo I am to be considered as the guest of the Tykoon, and that my lodgings and table will be furnished by him. This Kawasaki is the place that "brought up" Chaplain Bittinger, the Chaplain of the U. S. Steamer *Susquehanna,* when he made his dash to see Yedo, as the Japanese refused to ferry him over the River Logo, which runs on the north side of the town.[514]

The Japanese *say* that the reverend gentleman made all sorts of efforts to cross the river, and finally drew his sword, which he was flourishing with considerable energy, when Commodore Perry's positive order to him to rejoin his ship immediately reached him. The Japanese slyly added that they presumed he only flourished his sword "for amusement." It is rather a novel thing for an American clergyman to resort to his "carnal weapon" instead of relying on the "sword of the spirit."

The policemen are dressed in a uniform; the back and breast of the jacket is frequently red, sometimes blue, but in all cases it is covered with characters which look vastly like the cabalistic signs which used to decorate the robe of the astrologer. The Fire Department is an important one in Japan, and each village has one or more stations for their engines. These might be

[514]See note 488.

better named a good sized squirt. They are made entirely of bamboo and wood, and by means of arms projecting beyond the ends of the machine, they are *carried* by two men on a brisk trot to the place of conflagration.[515]

Sunday, November 29, 1857. The first Sunday in Advent. I read the whole service for this day with Mr. Heusken as my clerk and congregation. I experienced some peculiar feelings on this occasion. It was beyond doubt the first time that ever a Christian service on the Sabbath was read audibly in this place, which is only thirteen miles from Yedo, and this, too, while the law punishing such an act with death is still in force![516]

My rooms look out on a pretty garden filled with the usual miniature pieces of water, tiny bridges, and rock work with the invariable dwarfed trees. I occupy a

---

[515]It has several times been told to the writer that Townsend Harris in his younger days belonged to the New York City Fire Department, which, as everyone knows, was chiefly composed of volunteer organizations in the early 'forties. No proof of this fact has yet come to our notice. If it be true, then this and other entries of his *Journal* (*e. g.,* Nov. 29, 1857) take on a more sympathetic coloring.

[516]The earliest of these dreaded and oft-repeated edicts on the subject of Christianity in Japan was aimed against the Portuguese, Shogun Iyemitsu saying in June, 1636: "The whole race of the Portuguese, with their mothers, nurses and whatever belongs to them, shall be banished to Macao" (Lewis and Murakami, *Ranald MacDonald,* p. 127, note 137; Hildreth, *Japan,* p. 192, citing Kaempfer).

The decree of death instead of expulsion seems to have been issued in 1639. And when, in defiance thereof, a Portuguese ship from Macao arrived at Nagasaki in 1640, the entire crew (with the exception of thirteen) was killed. The survivors returned to Macao with the following written message:

"So long as the sun warms the earth, any Christian bold enough to come to Japan, even if he be King Philip himself, or the God of the Christians, shall pay for it with his head."

See Robert P. Porter, *Japan, The Rise of a Modern Power,* The Clarendon Press, 1918, p. 77; compare Captain Sir Edward Belcher, *Narrative of the Voyage of H.M.S. Samarang,* etc., p. 42; and Kenneth Saunders, *Foreign Missions in Japan,* in *Japan* for Aug., 1923, p. 22.

pavilion detached from the main house, and it is only occupied by me and my immediate attendants.

Kaempfer and all other writers on Japan state that their rooms were invariably in the rear of the house, and they all add their belief that this was done merely to prevent their seeing anything of the people, etc. Had these writers better understood Japanese customs they would have drawn very different conclusions from the same facts.

The Japanese houses of the best class are all built *entre cour et jardin,* as the French say. The buildings fronting on the street are used as offices and for the servants. A large gateway opens in the center of these buildings, and discloses a court of greater or less extent, according to the size of the house.

It is some fifteen to forty yards from the gate to the door of the real residence of the occupant, and the *most honorable* rooms are in the rear, where they open into or overlook the garden. Now, in Japan the higher the rank the greater is the seclusion in which the individual lives. This is a great and fundamental principle with them, and it therefore follows that they would of course occupy the most secluded rooms of the house, for that follows as a necessity from the principle.

I now learn, beyond doubt, that the solitude of the great road is caused by positive orders issued by the Government, prohibiting any travel over the road during my journey; and, as my route for each day was fixed some time before, they could make their arrangements, and by my punctuality the stoppage of traffic was only for one day on each day's route.[517] In the afternoon I went out for a little exercise, and visited a very noble temple situated about one and one-quarter miles from the Tokido, towards the bay. The roof is of copper (the first I have seen in Japan). There is some little gilding on the ends of the rafters and beams which project some eight feet beyond the walls and form a pent house on every side. (This is also the manner of building the roof for all kinds of edifices.)

In the temple were a multitude of lanterns, some of which were fully ten feet in diameter, and all were prettily decorated with Chinese and Japanese characters in various [colors]. I found some very good castings of copper, among the rest a shrine in the vestibule of the temple showed much merit. It was supported by figures of demons, the varied expression of whose faces was capital. On the outside of the shrine the zodiacal signs (Japanese) were well done in bas-relief. The altar shone resplendently with an infinite number of objects all in fine brass and as bright as gold. I was told they were a present from the late Tykoon.[518] The High Priest was clad in purple silk, with an embroidered alb about his neck. The attending priests were all in yellow. The temple and everything pertaining to it was exquisitely clean. The consoles and ends of the rafters and beams

[517]See note 511.

[518]Iyeyoshi, the twelfth of the Tokugawa dynasty, who died Aug. 25, 1853—in other words, soon after Commodore Perry had sailed away from Yedo for the first time. The coincidence of the Shogun's death and of the visit of the American squadron was duly noted both by those who favored the opening up of Japan, and by those who fought against it might and main—not to speak of the significance which the Shogun's death bore for the superstitious.

were carved into grotesque masks and heads, which were executed in a spirited manner.

In the courtyard in front, an enormous bronze bell was suspended. The tone of the Japanese bells is in general very fine; they are struck with a wooden pole some ten feet long and from three to six inches in diameter. The pole is suspended in a horizontal position, and the bell is struck by simply pulling back the pole and then letting it fall by its own motion against the outside of the bell.

In Commodore Perry's journal of the first night he passed in Japan, he speaks of the bells that were struck during the night, and he supposed them to be alarm or signal bells. They are still struck in the same manner, not only during the night, but the day also, and are simply to note the hour.[519]

On my return I saw a number of the largest storks I ever met with. The tameness of all kinds of wild animals

---

[519]Townsend Harris was not in a position to know exactly what took place when Perry's Squadron entered the Bay of Yedo, about 5 P. M. of July 8, 1853. In the pages of Inazo Nitobe (who undoubtedly used Japanese sources) we have a very vivid description of the terror that seized the inhabitants of Yedo (*The Intercourse between the United States and Japan,* The Johns Hopkins Press, 1891, p. 46):

"No sooner had 'the black ships of the evil mien' made their entry into the Bay, than the signal guns were fired, followed by the discharge of rockets; then were seen on the shore companies of soldiers moving from garrison to garrison. The popular commotion in Yedo at the news of 'a foreign invasion,' was beyond description. The whole city was in an uproar. In all directions were seen mothers flying with children in their arms, and men with mothers on their backs. Rumors of an immediate action, exaggerated each time they were communicated from mouth to mouth, added horror to the horrorstricken. The tramp of war-horses, the clatter of armed warriors, the noise of carts, the parade of firemen, *the incessant tolling of bells,* the shrieks of women, the cries of children, dinning all the streets of a city of more than a million souls, made confusion worse confounded."

The italics in the above quotation are ours. We cannot help feeling that Nitobe's words are a description of what must have actually taken place.

435

(even including the cautious crow) in Japan is surprising and proves that the Japanese boys are not so given to destructive habits as the Caucasian races. The stork remains here all the year round, and the wild goose takes up his winter quarters here, both of which facts establish the mildness of the climate. The weather has been very fine, for not a drop of rain has fallen or a cloud obscured the sun for the last twelve days.

I passed by some gardens which had a good show of artemisias, and some curiously trained pear trees. About six feet from the ground the branches are tied down to a horizontal frame. The new wood that grows during the summer is of course upright, but the next winter so much as is required is tied down to the frames, and the remainder cut off. In a short time this makes a verdant room, quite impervious to the sun's rays, and forms a pleasant retreat in the hot weather. The Japanese pear is not a nice fruit, in fact I cannot eat it until it has been preserved. It is from two and one-half inches to four inches in diameter, and shaped and colored exactly [like] the russet apple.

In the towns and villages I have passed through, wooden tubs filled with water are placed at short distances from each other, to use in case of fire. Here these tubs are made of copper. The firemen wear helmets; these and their hooks and ladders quite put me in mind of dear old inflammable New York[520]

Monday, November 30, 1857. To-day I am to enter Yedo. It will form an important epoch in my life, and a

---

[520]See note 515.

still more important one in the history of Japan. I am the first diplomatic representative that has ever been received in this city; and, whether I succeed or fail in my intended negotiations, it is a *great fact* that will always remain, showing that at last I have forced this singular people to acknowledge the *rights of embassy.* I feel no little pride, too, in carrying the American Flag through that part of Japan, between the extremity of Cape Idsu and into the very castle of the City of Yedo.

I left Kawasaki a little before eight A. M., and was ferried over the River Logo,[521] which even now is both broad and deep. I proceeded to-day, after much deliberation, in my *norimon.* My *wish* was to go into Yedo on horseback, and the Vice-Governor eagerly encouraged that idea. This excited my suspicions; and, after much difficulty, I discovered that none but the *Daimyo,* or Princes of the highest rank, can enter Yedo in their *norimons;* all below that rank enter the city on horseback or on foot. This fact, coupled with the Japanese idea of seclusion and respectability being equivalent terms, determined me very reluctantly to proceed in my *norimon.*

The distance from Kawasaki to Sinagawa[522] is seven and one-half English miles, and the houses form almost a continuous street the whole way. Just before entering Sinagawa I was shown the execution ground, which is at the water's edge. Kaempfer describes the sight as a very revolting one as seen by him, with human bodies

---

[521]Rokugo (Griffis, *Townsend Harris,* p. 200).
[522]Shinagawa.

lying about on the bloodstained ground, while dogs, kites and crows

> Held o'er the dead their carnival.

Nothing of the kind was seen by me, and the only indication of the place was an unusual number of kites and crows, but those congregate in a similar manner about the places for burning the dead in India, Burmah and Siam.

The *honjin* of Sinagawa was not pleasantly placed. It was at the bottom of a deep court, and, as its garden was surrounded by the blank walls of buildings, we had no prospect whatever. I was much disappointed as I expected to have found it on the water side. We remained at Sinagawa more than an hour, and at last started on the final stage of our journey.

Sinagawa is defended by seven batteries, four on the land and three built up on shoals. The latter are placed at three hundred to eight hundred yards from the shore. I am led to think that the guns of those batteries are not of heavy calibers. From here I again saw the steamer. She was about five miles in an E. S. E. direction from Sinagawa. The channel after passing Kanagawa gradually trends to N. N. E. to N. E. and by N., so that a ship of large burden cannot approach either Kawasaki or Sinagawa nearer than about five miles, as the flats extend fully that distance from the shore. This renders the batteries of Sinagawa of no avail, as her guns cannot reach to the channel. When they were first erected, the channel was near Sinagawa, and Kawasaki was a port of entry, but at present large ships cannot proceed with any advantage above Kanagawa, as that is the last *harbor* up the bay. Had the boats of Commodore Perry sounded the bay two miles further up they would have struck the flat that may be said to fill up the whole upper part of the bay, and thus prevents the approach of large vessels nearer than some six miles to Yedo.

I did not discover the "noble palaces" or "stately castles" of Sinagawa mentioned by Kaempfer. The buildings form one continuous street from Sinagawa to Yedo, and no one can tell where the former ends and the latter begins unless it be specially pointed out to him.

At Sinagawa our procession was reformed. The Vice-Governor now led the way, and all my coolies, etc., etc., were kept in line, and the whole cavalcade was nearly half a mile long. We proceeded with a slow and stately step along an unpaved street, some forty to fifty feet wide and bordered with wooden houses, none more than two stories high and mostly covered with tiles. Every Japanese town is divided into streets of one hundred and twenty yards long, and this district is responsible for the conduct of all in it. It has a captain called the *Ottono,*[523] and he has policemen under him. From Sinagawa I found that these divisions were marked in an unmistakable manner, a strong stockade is erected each one hundred and twenty yards across the street and has a pair of wide and strong gates. These gates are shut at a certain hour in the evening, and a wicket of some two feet square

---

[523]O-tono.

is opened for the passage of those who have the right to pass after the closing of the main gates. At many places in Yedo this stockade is double; that is, a second one is erected some fifteen yards distant from the regular one. When both the stockades are closed it makes quite a strong defence against anything but artillery, and is admirably calculated to stop the advance of a mob, or secure the arrest of criminals. Again, Yedo has between eight thousand and nine thousand of these streets, so that after a certain hour it is cut up into that number of little forts. From Sinagawa the people no longer knelt, nor did they avert their eyes.

The authorities made their prostrations as before, but the people remained standing. As the authorities were changed every one hundred and twenty yards, there was a constant "knocking of heads." A large proportion of the assemblage wore two swords, showing they were of some rank, and almost all had on the *camissimo* or dress of ceremony. The number admitted into the streets through which I passed formed a rank of five deep on each side of the way. Every cross-street had its stockade closed to prevent too great a crowd; and, as I looked up and down those streets, they seemed a solid mass of men and women. The most perfect order was maintained from Sinagawa to my lodgings,—a distance of over seven miles. Not a shout or a cry was heard. The silence of such a vast multitude had something appalling [in] it. Lord Byron called a silent woman *sleeping thunder*.

I calculated the number of persons that lined the street from Sinagawa to my residence at one hundred and eighty-five thousand. I called the distance seven miles; that each person occupied two feet of front in his line, and that the lines were five feet deep on each side of the way. This calculation excludes all those who were in the cross-streets or on the tops of the houses. In front of the lines of the spectators stood men about ten feet apart and armed with a long white stave like the marshals' staff in the courts at New York. These men wore clothes of various colors, some green, some blue, black, gray, etc., while the coats-of-arms were so various that it easily appeared that they were the retainers of persons of rank, who "kept the ground" in the vicinity of his residence. The people all appeared clean, well clad and well fed; indeed, I have never seen a case of squalid misery since I have been in Japan.

A large number of *officers* of police attended the procession. In addition to his two swords each one bore an iron truncheon about two feet long and one inch in diameter,—a savage and dangerous weapon in the hands of a passionate or violent man; but there was no use for them nor any apparent need of the constant cry of *Satu, Satu,*—"Keep back," "Keep back," which was constantly shouted forth by the street keepers.

In this manner I went on passing over seven bridges, the fifth was the Nippon Bas, or Bridge of Japan.[524] It is from this bridge that all distances are reckoned in this country. After passing the bridge some few hundred yards, we went on in a nearly N. N. W. direction, and after a while we reached a broad moat on the opposite

[524]Nippon Bashi, sometimes found as Nihonbashi: Bridge of Japan.

441

[side] of which rose a stone wall varying from twenty to forty feet in height according to the make of the ground. The road followed this ditch for more than a mile, when my bearers started on a full run, rushed through a gateway, across a court and ended by bearing me *into* the house.[525]

This was doing the matter in the most honorable Japanese manner. Mr. Heusken had to leave his *norimon* at the outer gate. As I got out of mine, I was warmly welcomed by my old friend the Prince of Shinano, who conducted me to my rooms and pointed out the arrangements made for my comfort. It will sound queerly when I say that these consisted of a bedstead, some chairs and tables, but the Japanese never use one of these articles. Their rooms are destitute of a single article that we would call furniture. The universal mat serves as chair, couch, table and bed. Their food is served on stands or trays from three to ten inches high, and is contained

---

[525]We cannot refrain from quoting at this point some keen remarks by Tyler Dennett, *Americans in Eastern Asia,* pp. 355–56:

"Notwithstanding the handicaps laid upon him and the obvious intentions of the authorities to thwart his purpose, we see him [Townsend Harris] entering the capital city of Yedo (November 30, 1857) five and a half months after signing the Convention [of Shimoda], with the promise that he should be permitted to deliver in person the letter from President Pierce to the Shogun. It was an extraordinary achievement in which he had surrendered no particle of the official dignity of his position and had won his way by argument and by absolute candor. The contrast between Commissioner Ward's entry into Peking and Consul General Harris's entry into Yedo is striking. The honor accorded to Harris was, however, a mark of the greater political astuteness of the Japanese Government as well as of the finer diplomatic skill of the New York merchant. Yedo had read correctly the designs of Russia, while Peking, wholly deceived, had taken the Russian envoy to her bosom; the mere intimation [by Townsend Harris] of British intentions in Japan had been alarming, while the destruction of the Taku forts in 1858 by the allied British and French forces had been dismissed by the Manchu Government with fatuous indifference."

chiefly in wooden bowls lacquered. Porcelain is only used for drinking tea and saki from. The Prince even pointed out a water closet copied from mine at Shimoda. The bathroom was close to my sleeping apartments. I had set apart for my special [use] a bedroom, sitting room and dining room.[526] Mr. Heusken's rooms adjoined mine and consisted of a bed and sitting room. In addition to this I was shown my reception rooms, which could be increased to any size by merely removing the sliding doors. In fact, every Japanese house may in a short time be converted into a single room by this simple and expeditious process. The building is very large. It is government property and was formerly used as a college.[527] It is situated within what is called "the castle"; that is, it is the outer one of four circles (rather irregular ones), the center one of which is the residence of the Tykoon. My house runs up to the road that runs along the ditch, and on the opposite side it fronts on a wide street. From my rooms I see the stone wall before men-

---

[526]When, later, the British Mission under Lord Elgin arrived at Yedo, they too were surprised to see how carefully the Japanese had forestalled their wants. Mr. Laurence Oliphant gives the following as the reason for the Japanese knowledge of European wants (*Narrative of the Earl of Elgin's Mission to China and Japan,* New York, Harper & Bros., 1860, pp. 374–75):

"They [the Japanese] had first been made acquainted with the requirements of Europeans in the matter of furniture through Mr. Harris. Prior to that gentleman's visit [to Yedo], the government had sent privately to Shimoda to have exact copies made of his furniture, so that, on reaching Yedo, he found, to his astonishment, chairs, tables, and beds, in a city where all such articles had been previously unknown."

[527]Griffis, *Townsend Harris,* p. 205, note: "In this structure, originally the 'Office for the Examination of Barbarian Books,' *i. e.,* from Europe and America, lay the germ of the present magnificent Imperial University of Tokio. . . . The edifice in which Mr. Harris lodged was on the west side of the old Kai-Séi-Jo inclosure near the Kudan, fronting the Castle moat, and not far from the Shimidzu gate. Significantly, coming from Shimoda (low field), the district in Yedo where he lived was named Kanda (high or divine field)."

tioned and the buildings occupied by two of the brothers of the Tykoon. It is a "court" part of the city, and none but persons of rank reside in it. This over, the Prince informed me that the Government had been in a fever of anxiety all day for fear of some accident; that the people were wild with curiosity to see my entry; and that, had the Government not used the most stringent measures, the people would have rushed to Yedo "by millions" (those are *his* numbers) to see me; and finally the whole of the inner gates of the city had been closed ever since the previous night to keep away the crowd and thus prevent accidents; that they were all much rejoiced at my safe arrival, etc., etc.

He then informed me that, as I came as the representative of so great a nation, the Government had appointed eight persons of distinguished rank as "Commissioners of the Voyage of the American Ambassador to Yedo." I did not exactly understand what was meant by this move. I was assured that it was solely in honor of me, and that nothing connected with their duties could give me any umbrage, etc., etc. I told him that with this explanation I had no objection to make at present. The Prince then gave me a list of the Commissioners, which was as follows:[528]

| No. | 1 Toke | Prince of Tamba |
| " | 2 Hayasi | Prince of Daigak |

---

[528]The names of these eight Commissioners (*osetsu-gakari*) were: Toke, Tamba-no-Kami; Hayashi, Daigaku-no-Kami; Tsutsu, Hizen-no-Kami; Kawase, Saiyemo-no-Kami; Inouye, Shinano-no-Kami; Uyedono, Mim-bu Shoyu; Nagai, Gemba-no-Kami; Tsukagoshi, Tosuke (Griffis, *Townsend Harris*, p. 206; *cf.* Murdoch, *A History of Japan*, vol. 3, p. 634).

No. 3 Tsoetsoe	Prince of Hizen
" 4 Kawasi	Prince of Saiyemo
" 5 Inawouye	Prince of Shinano
" 6 Woedono	Mimbosioyu
" 7 Nagai	Prince of Gemba
" 8 T'sukagosi	Tooske

Numbers 2 and 6 were Commissioners with Commodore Perry at Kanagawa in 1854.[529]

I was then informed that the next morning an Ambassador from the Tykoon would wait on me to congratulate me on my arrival, etc., etc.

The Prince of Shinano, having been informed by me that my first official step after my arrival would be to write to Hotta, Prince of Bittsu, informing him of my arrival at Yedo, that I was the bearer of a letter from the President of the United States to His Majesty the Tykoon, and asking when I could have an audience of His Majesty for the purpose of delivering that letter, etc., etc., now asked if I could send that letter by him at once.

As the letter had been previously prepared at Shimoda and only required to be dated and sealed, that matter was soon dispatched. (See private letter book for copy.)[530]

---

[529]The Preamble to the Treaty concluded by Perry mentions as two of the Japanese Commissioners: Hayashi, Daigaku-no-Kami; and Udono, Member of the Board of Revenue.

[530]This letter is *L. B.*, vol. 2, p. 93; it is followed by a Dutch translation, pp. 93–94. The original English version is dated "U.S. Legation, City of Yedo, November 30, 1857." This is, therefore, the first American communication dated from our Legation in the Capital of the Shoguns, and is, at the same time, the first of a distinguished series addressed by Townsend Harris to the different officers of the Shogunate.

A sumptuous repast (after the Japanese fashion) was now served to me and Mr. Heusken. Mr. Heusken's stands or trays were four inches high. The trays for my use were ten inches high. After the dinner was over, I told the Prince that it was my wish to pay all the expenses of my table, etc., etc., and that such was the fashion of all parts of the world; that otherwise I should not feel at liberty to order such articles of food as best suited me; that it would be a point of delicacy to eat whatever was sent without making any remarks, etc., etc. He replied that I could not be permitted to pay for anything sent to me, but he thought there would not be any objection to my people buying anything I might wish to have prepared by my cook that I had brought from Shimoda. This was just what I wished, and gave me full satisfaction. At last the Prince left me to repose after the fatigue and excitement of this (to me) important and eventful day. The distances of my route from Shimoda here are as follows:[531]

---

[531]The manuscript *Journal* (vol. 4, p. 113) does not indicate the distances in this table. We have, however, found a small scrap of very thin rice paper, on which Mr. Heusken kept note of the distances—the paper having the endorsement (in Townsend Harris's hand): "Route from Shimoda to Yedo, November, 1857."

The record is in Dutch, and reads thus (in part):

Mitsoekoeli	Nasimoto	6 Ri
Amagi	Agasima	6½
Oohito	Misima	8
Hakone	Odawara	8
Ooiso	Hoezisawa	8½
Hodogaja	Kawasaki	8
Sinagawa	Yedo	5½

446

	ri	or	English	miles
Shimoda to Nasimoto				
Nasimoto to Yugasima	"	"	"	"
Yugasima to Missima	"	"	"	"
Missima to Odowara	"	"	"	"
Odowara to Fudsisawa	"	"	"	"
Fudsisawa to Kawasaki	"	"	"	"
Kawasaki to Sinagawa	3 "	"	"	"
Sinagawa to the Nippon Bas	2 "	"	"	"

Totals

Tuesday, December 1, 1857. The "Commissioners" of my voyage to Yedo paid me a visit of ceremony this morning. Their various retinues amounted (in the aggregate) to some hundreds. Each one had his pikes, or ensigns of his dignity, borne before him, and led horses followed his *norimon.* The caparisons of the horses bore the "coat-of-arms" of the noble owner. Among others, each "following" had fan bearers, slipper bearers, cane bearers, etc., etc. Each one had his *camissimo* or dress of ceremony brought with him in neat lacquered boxes, and his "portfolio" was neatly wrapped up in silk and slung over the back of a particular bearer. After they arrived they went at once to rooms where they put on their *camissimos,* and then they proceeded to the Audience Chamber.

As soon as they were ready I was informed, and I also went there attended by Mr. Heusken, the Prince of Shinano and a long following of Japanese.

On my entry I found them drawn up in a line and standing. I took my place in front, and then we exchanged profound bows.

447

Toke, Prince of Tamba, was their *spokesman*. He began by saying that, to do proper honor to me as the representative of a great nation, His Majesty the Tykoon had sent them to congratulate me on my arrival at Yedo, and to inquire after my health; to this he added the personal respects of himself and of his colleagues. I made a suitable reply, and then each of the Commissioners was separately presented to me. As Hayasi, Prince of Daigak, and Woedono Mimbosioyu were presented, I was told that they were among the Commissioners who negotiated with Commodore Perry at Kanagawa. The Prince of Hizen assisted in making the Russian Treaty.[532]

As soon as these particular presentations were over, I told them that I was happy to become acquainted with persons of their distinguished merit, and that I hoped our intercourse would prove mutually agreeable. They returned this compliment. Then followed more stately bows, and I retired attended as on my entry. The Commissioners are rather intelligent looking men taken together, while some of them bear faces that are capital introductions to your respect. The Prince of Shinano informed me that the arrival of the "Ambassador" of the Tykoon was delayed by the wish of His Majesty to examine personally the present, which, by the laws of etiquette of Japan, was to be presented to me by the Tykoon; and he then added that, *after* it had been ex-

---

[532]The Russian Treaty referred to is the one signed at Shimoda, on Feb. 7, 1855 (Russian style, Jan. 26th), by Admiral C. E. Poutiatine; Tsoutsoui-Khizenno-Kami (Tsutsui, Hizen-no-Kami); and Kavadzi-Saiemonno-Dzio (Kawaji, Sayemon-no-jo): Gubbins, *The Progress of Japan*, pp. 237-39.

amined in the Palace, it had to be taken to the Great
Council for their examination. In answer to my inquiries, I was told that the Tykoon cannot make or receive the smallest present until they have been *examined* and *approved* by the Council of State!!! That
single statement convinced me that the Tykoon was a
mere "lay figure" of government, and that he did not
possess a single particle of political power. He is even
more restricted than was the Doge of Venice by the
"Council of Ten." Before the Ambassador arrives I
will explain a particular part of the Audience Chamber.

In all Japanese houses the upper end of one or more
of the best rooms has an alcove running across. The alcove is about three feet deep and has a floor raised about
four inches. It is divided into unequal parts—say in the
proportions of four to five or four-ninths and five-
ninths. The smaller portion contains two shelves—the
upper one of which is closed with little sliding doors;
the lower one is in two parts, one part being lower than
the other by some six inches, thus ———. The ends
are fastened to the wall and partition, and the centers
are fancifully connected by a hanging scroll.

The larger alcove is called the *toko,* and in private
houses contains the shrine of the *lares* or domestic deities.
In a building like the one I occupy it is vacant. It is a
place of honor, and seats in the room are more or less
honorable as they are in close or distant proximity to it.

A little after midday I was told of the arrival of the
"Ambassador"; and, on entering the Room of Audience, I found him to be Toke, Prince of Tamba, who

is a person occupying a high position at Court, and, so far as I could understand the matter, somewhat analogous to the office of chamberlain at the Courts in the Western world. In the *toko,* and placed on a tray of white wood, stood a box some three feet high which was tied with a broad, green, silk braid.[533] I took my place near the *toko,* while Toke stood opposite. We then saluted each other, and the Prince said that His Majesty, knowing that I had come from a far distant land, had sent him to inquire after my health and whether I had made my long journey without accident. He then added that His Majesty had sent "a small present" for my acceptance. This ended, the Prince went three steps down the room and from that place paid his personal compliments to me and made inquiries after my health. This over, he returned to his first standing, and I made a proper reply to the kind message of His Majesty and returned my thanks for this mark of his kindness. As I spoke of the present I turned towards the box and bowed.

When I began to thank the Prince for his personal civilities, he again retreated the three steps, so that he might occupy a lower position when hearing what I said in relation to himself than the one he stood in while hearing what I said in relation to the Tykoon.

---

[533]We have already described the series of Japanese documents referring to Townsend Harris's visit to Yedo (see note 511). One of those documents was addressed to the Ometski, Toke, Prince of Tamba, and directed him to deliver this very cedar chest or box of bon-bons (46–2, H. Ex. Doc., no. 1, pt. 1, p. 624, in Serial no. 1902). The same story is related by Townsend Harris in a letter dated July 3, 1858, and addressed to "My dear [N. Dougherty]": reprinted from the *Washington Union* of Jan. 15, 1859, in Littell's *Living Age,* vol. 60, Feb. 26, 1859, pp. 567–71.

As soon as the interpretation of what I last said was finished, he again returned to his original place, and we exchanged bows and thus the ceremony ended.

When I reached my private apartments the present was brought in. On opening it, it was found to contain four trays of Japanese bon-bons made of sugar, rice flour, fruit, nuts, etc. They were arranged in the trays in a beautiful manner, and the forms, colors and decorations were all very neat. The quantity was about seventy pounds of weight. I am very sorry I cannot send them to the United States, but they will not keep for so long a voyage.

In my conversations with the Prince of Shinano to-day, he enlarged on the difficulties that he had overcome and the great labor he had performed to enable me to come to Yedo. He spoke of his anxious days and sleepless nights; that care and anxiety had taken away his appetite, so that he had become lean in his person; and that his blood had frequently gushed from his nose from his great agitation; that he had done all this from his friendship for me, etc., etc. Something of this had been before hinted at, but never so fully expressed as now. I replied that I was duly grateful to him for his friendship for me; but, as he appeared to be under a great error as it regarded my visit to Yedo, I must now fully explain myself on that point. I told him that I came to Yedo as the representative of the United States and not in my private capacity; that the United States did not ask anything from the Government of Japan *as a favor;* that it only demanded its rights, and that nothing would be accepted on the ground of favor; that my mission had for its object the good of the Japanese Empire; and that it was no favor to me or to my country that they should listen to my advice, but that it was the Japanese who should feel grateful to the President for the friendship he had shown to Japan by the messages with which I was entrusted.

That for myself, individually, I had no wish to come to Yedo, and that I only came here because my official duty required it; that I hoped he now fully understood not only my object in visiting Yedo, but that he would clearly see that it was not any favor to me either in my private or in my official capacity to receive me at Yedo.

The Prince was quite chapfallen at this, as it was the evident wish of the Japanese that I should look on my reception here as an unprecedented favor to me, both personally and officially, and thus they would establish a claim on my gratitude, which might be of great use to them in the negotiations that might be commenced here.

However, the Prince confessed that my view of the matter was a just one, and that he had only looked at the question from one point of view, and that point was on the Japanese side.

I omitted in my journal of November 30th to state that we halted to rest our bearers three miles from Kawasaki at a village called Oomoorie.[534] I was taken to a

---

[534]Omori.

very pretty tea house, situated in a fine garden of plum trees. These trees are grown, not for the fruit, but for the *flowers,* which are considered as very beautiful by the Japanese, and sometimes are immensely large. The *petals* of these flowers are preserved in various ways, with sugar, salt, etc., and are made up as conserves, or drunk as tea.

The garden had the usual little ponds, canals, tiny bridges, rock work, etc. It also had a very pretty miniature temple. I was shown what to me was a very great vegetable curiosity,—that is, bamboos that were *perfectly square.* I never saw anything of the kind before, and at first supposed it was the result of artificial means, but I was assured that it was simply a natural production and that art had nothing to do with it. I saw some mallards with very beautiful plumage, almost as fine as the "Mandarin Duck" of China. They were swimming about in one of the tiny ponds of the garden.

The name of the place is *Bay-reen-kiu-sabro,* or "plum tree house," and is a favorite resort in the flower season for the Yedo people.

After entering Yedo, I observed some high structures of framework, having a platform on the upper part and a large bell hung there, exactly like the fire "lookouts" of New York, and on inquiry I found they were erected for that very purpose.

I have mentioned that, some time after passing the Nippon Bas, I struck one of the moats of the castle, and that, turning to the right, my road ran along the banks of this moat for more than one mile.

In this part of my route I passed a number of open spaces bordered with trees and quickset hedges. These are called *ba-ba,* or "horse course," and are for the purpose of military exercises of various kinds.

Wednesday, December 2, 1857. This morning at half-past ten A. M. I felt a smart shock of earthquake, not severe enough, however, to do any damage. In the afternoon I received a letter from Hotta, Prince of Bittsu, Minister for Foreign Affairs, informing me that he had received my letter and communicated its contents to his master the Tykoon, and that His Majesty had fixed on Monday next, the 7th inst., for my public audience.[534a]

The Prince of Shinano is considered as my host (I do not know but keeper would be a more correct term), and he visits me daily. To-day he informs me that the Great Council of State has heretofore consisted of five members, but, since it had been determined to receive me at Yedo, the number had been increased to six, and that the Prince of Bittsu, in addition to his position of first member of the Council, is now created "Minister of Foreign Affairs," and that all correspondence with foreign envoys will be conducted in his name. It appears that there remain eighteen of the great landed Princes of the Empire, who date from before the establishment of the present dynasty,—say about 1605; that after Yeyas, the

---

[534a]Hotta's letter, dated the 16th day of the 10th month (Dec. 2, 1857), was in answer to Townsend Harris's, dated the 14th day of the 10th month (Nov. 30, 1857). The day fixed for the audience was the 21st day of the 10th month. The text of Hotta's letter is given in 46–2, H. Ex. Doc., no. 1, pt. 1, p. 624, in Serial no. 1902.

founder of the dynasty, had suppressed the rebellion that broke out during his reign, he created over three hundred territorial princes, whose lands consisted, in part, of the forfeited estates of the revolted princes, and in part of the Imperial domains; that *all* the landed princes form that class of nobility which are called *Daimyo;* and that from the class last created (*i. e.,* the three hundred) the Council of State is chosen. None of the original eighteen Princes are eligible to that office, nor any of the *Kami* or titular Princes. The *Kami* form the next rank, and from them are selected the Governors of Imperial cities, provinces and all the high offices about the Court. These men do not possess either hereditary rank or estates. Nominally the Tykoon appoints the Council of State, Governors, etc., but in reality (as far as I understand it) Japan is ruled by an oligarchy composed of the *Daimyo* or landed hereditary Princes. But these again are ruled by the rigid and hitherto unalterable law of Japan. The families of all the *Daimyo,* all the *Kami* and of some ranks of officers, must reside in Yedo and form the hostages for the good conduct of those classes. The *Daimyo* only visit their domains at certain short periods; the remainder of their time is spent at Yedo. The *Kami* who are appointed to office out of Yedo pass from six to twelve months at the place of their appointment, and then return to pass a corresponding period of time at Yedo. None of the *Daimyo, Kami* or other officers are allowed to take any of their females with them, nor may they form any connection or have any intercourse with women while away from

Yedo. Hence the search and examination at Hakone.[535]

Thursday, December 3, 1857. Wrote to the Minister of Foreign Affairs enclosing copy and translation of the President's letter to the Tykoon. I also wrote him that I would pay him a visit of ceremony whenever he should be ready to receive me.[536] In the evening I received an answer to my letter, and he wrote that [he] would be happy to receive my visit to-morrow. (See my private letter book.)[537] Had my usual visit from Shinano-no-Kami, and a good deal of conversation ensued. He was very anxious to have me make promises not to visit about the city, saying that Yedo contained a great many bad people who might insult and maltreat me, and thus the Government would be plunged into serious difficulties with that of the United States.

I replied that I could not make any promises that would circumscribe my undoubted rights under the laws

---

[535]On the system of government here described, consult Gubbins, *The feudal system in Japan under the Tokugawa Shoguns,* in *Transactions of The Asiatic Society of Japan,* vol. XV, pt. 2 (Sept., 1887), pp. 131–42; and *cf.* pp. VII–VIII at the end of pt. 2.

[536]See *L. B.,* vol. 3, pp. 9–10.

[537]This parenthesis by Townsend Harris refers only to the letter which he wrote to Hotta (see preceding note). Hotta's reply is dated the 17th day of the 10th month, and is found in 46–2, H. Ex. Doc., no. 1, p. 624. It contains more than is reported in this entry of the *Journal.* He acknowledges receipt not only of the Japanese and the Dutch translations of the President's letter, but also of the address to the Tycoon which Townsend Harris intended to deliver at the audience; and it concludes with the appointment for the next day—the 18th day of the 10th month, or Dec. 4, 1857. It should be noted, in passing, that the President's letter was not addressed to the Tycoon, but to the Emperor of Japan.

Two important dates were now fixed—Dec. 4th for the visit to Hotta, and Dec. 7th for the audience. Accordingly, we find in the collection of Japanese documents pertaining to this visit, the necessary memorandum to this effect; and also an order issued by Lord Hotta to the Ometskis that everything connected with the Audience should be ready by 9 A. M. (46–2, H. Ex. Doc., no. 1, pt. 1, p. 624, in Serial no. 1902).

of nations; that I had no fears for my personal safety, as I had gone boldly and freely through many cities of the East where the population was of a much worse character than that of Yedo, and where I had no official character to protect me; that they must and might rely on my age and discretion that I should not do anything to cause them any embarrassment, but I must be left free to act in all respects according to the dictates of that discretion; and that I could not give them any pledge or promise of any kind that might afterwards be used by them to limit me in my freedom of action, etc., etc. I also told him that exercise in the open air was the daily practice of all Western people, and was necessary to the preservation of health; that I wished the Government to point out some place, either in the wide streets or in a *ba-ba,* where Mr. Heusken and I could take the requisite exercise. This appeared to cause much trouble, but it was so just and reasonable that he could not urge anything against my demand, except his fears of the populace. I told him he might remember that, when I demanded the removal of the guards from my residence at Shimoda, he had told me that the people of Shimoda were the worst in Japan and that the presence of the Japanese officers at my house was absolutely indispensable to protect me from outrage by day and robbery at night; that, notwithstanding his remonstrances on that occasion, I had insisted, and the guards were removed fully eleven months ago, and that he well knew that nothing unpleasant had occurred since; that I had no doubt his fears about the conduct of the good

457

people of Yedo were equally unfounded. Poor Shinano looked confused when I referred to the Shimoda affair; and in his reply said that what he then told me was by express orders of the Government, but that I might rely on the truth of what he now stated about the people of Yedo. He concluded by saying he would report my wishes to the Government and hoped to have the matter arranged to my satisfaction.[538]

Friday, December 4, 1857. I start on my visit to the Prime Minister at ten A. M., the Prince of Shinano acting as my escort. My retinue is composed in the same manner as it was on my entry into Yedo, excepting my luggage, cook, etc., etc.

I went southwardly over the same road that I came on my entry for about one mile, when we crossed the moat on a new bridge about one hundred feet long and passed through a gate into a square of some fifty or sixty feet formed by stone walls about twenty-five feet high. A gate in the wall running at right angles with the gate of entrance gave us exit from the quadrangle, and we entered into the third enclosure of the castle by a broad street, having the outer wall on our left and a line of houses on our right. After a short time we turned to our right (or westward) still proceeding through fine streets lined with the houses of the *Daimyo* and *Kami,* etc. These houses were all built of wood, roofed with tiles, and correspond to the description of a Japanese

---

[538]The dangers which threatened the life of Townsend Harris during this, the first visit to Yedo of an accredited representative from a foreign country, were very real and very serious. They will be spoken of below, under the entry for Jan. 25, 1858.

house given under date November 29, 1857. The streets were unpaved and scrupulously clean. The streets' keepers were the retainers of the Princes and each wore the arms of his master; the crowd was not so great as in passing through the city,—still, vast numbers were collected, especially when we came to the frequent open spaces or squares. The observers were the servants and retainers of the nobles and gave a lively idea of the magnitude of the households of those personages. The buildings on the street have projecting windows, like the houses at Cairo and Alexandria. Through the grass screens to these openings we saw plenty of fair faces, and it would appear that Mother Eve's failing is fully inherited by her daughters in Yedo. Every possible part of the window, from its sill to the top, was plastered with a female face; as no part of their dresses could be seen, I am unable to describe them. After a while our road turned again to the westward, and then again to the south. We passed by a causeway and short bridge over a canal. Here the water had a fall of about six feet and appears to prove that the city is built on ground that rises gradually from the shore of the bay. At length we entered a street running westwardly which brought me to a second moat and stone wall; this we crossed by a bridge about one hundred and fifty feet long, into a quadrangle exactly like the previous one, and through a gate placed at right angles to the first we entered into the second circle or enclosure of the Castle. Our route was now westward, now southward, again westward until we reached a third moat. Our route was southward

along the banks of this moat until we reached the house
of Hotta, Bittsu-no-Kami, or Hotta, Prince of Bittsu.
Measuring the distance by *time,* I made it more than one
mile from the first bridge to the Minister's house, and
less than one mile from the same bridge to my residence,
—or in other words, it was about two English miles
between my starting place and the residence of His Excellency the Minister. All the *norimons,* except mine,
were stopped at the outer gate. My bearers mended their
pace at some hundred and fifty yards from the gate, and
by the time they reached it they were at a full trot, dashed
through the gate across the court, and plumped me
down close to the edge of some clean mats that had been
placed there for my reception. On getting out of my
norimon, my "shoe bearer" gave me a new pair of un-
soiled patent leather shoes which I put on. The Japanese of all ranks enter a house in their stockings alone,
leaving their straw sandals outside. And there is a good
reason for this; for, as I have before noted, the mat serves
as chair, couch, table and bed. In the vestibule some
thirty persons, dressed in *camissimos,* were seated in
Japanese fashion, and saluted me by bringing the forehead down to the mat. I passed to the right and soon met
the "Commissioners of my Voyage," who saluted me,
and through Toke, Prince of Tamba, inquired after my
health, etc., etc. I was now conducted into a room where
I found chairs made after our pattern for Mr. Heusken
and myself, with comfortable braziers filled with burning charcoal. In a few moments two *tables* were
brought in on which were placed pipes, tobacco and fire.

Soon afterwards the Japanese great tea luxury was served to me.[539] It is made of very fine tea reduced to a powder, on which boiling water is poured and forms what may be called a tea gruel,—the taste was much better than the looks.

As soon as I had drunk my tea I was asked if I would then see the Minister; and, on my replying in the affirmative, the sliding doors were opened, and here I met the Minister. We saluted each other in silence, and he then led the way into a fourth room where I found two chairs on one side and ten black lacquered stools on the other. We again saluted each other, when the Minister courteously motioned to me to be seated, and, waiting until I was seated, he sat down himself. The Commissioners of my Voyage now entered the room and again saluted me, after which they also took their seats on the black stools.

The Minister courteously inquired about my health; and, after my reply and the requisite counter inquiry, he expressed much admiration at the long voyage I had made through so many different countries (for he perfectly understood what is called the overland route to India). I made the proper answer, adding that I considered myself as a fortunate person, as I was the first foreigner who had ever visited the great city of Yedo in a diplomatic capacity. Tables were now brought in by servants who carried them elevated as high as possible and marching with a stately step and with a meas-

[539] Again the *cha-no-yu:* see *Journal,* Tuesday, Feb. 24, 1857—the day when Townsend Harris first entered the private residence of the Governors of Shimoda; and note 376.

461

ured cadence. Then followed pipes and tobacco, tea and trays of refreshments. The trays of the Minister and myself were of the same height, both being some inches higher than those served to the others. The Minister courteously urged me to partake of his refreshments, and begged me to excuse his not smoking, as he never used tobacco. He afterwards said he did not offer me saki, as he understood I did not drink wine or saki when I could avoid it.

After some little conversation I presented him with a copy of my intended address to the Tykoon on the day of my audience, adding that I had made it very short so that no unnecessary topics should be introduced.[540] The Minister requested leave to withdraw for a short time in order to have the paper translated. He accordingly left me with Shinano-no-Kami,—the Commissioners of my Voyage going with the Minister. The interior of this house exactly corresponds with the one I occupy. The posts, *plafond* and crossbeams in which the sliding doors run are all of unpainted wood. The windows of white paper and the sliding doors or movable partitions are covered with paper hangings of the Greek scroll pattern in ultramarine blue and white patterns.

The agitation of the Japanese interpreter is beyond anything I ever saw,—he trembled all over his body as though he had an ague fit, while large drops of perspiration stood like beads on his forehead.

---

[540]In the letter to his friend Nathaniel Dougherty, Townsend Harris states (on p. 569) that Hotta on this occasion gave him a copy of the answering speech which the Shogun would deliver at the audience. (See note 533, and also the text below.)

My seat was placed nearest the *toko,* and I was warmed by a lacquer and copper brazier. In place of ashes, the brazier contained pulverized spar of a snowy whiteness neatly formed into a representation of the celebrated Fusi Yama, the top being opened like the crater of a volcano to admit the coals.

In about half an hour the Minister returned and told me that my address was quite satisfactory and at the same time he handed me the Tykoon's reply![541] showing clearly that His Majesty would utter exactly what the Council should dictate. The Minister informed me that, as the interpreters could not be admitted into the Imperial Presence, he had furnished me with a copy of the reply so that, by having it translated, the presence of the interpreter would not be required. My business being ended I rose and we again bowed, the Minister following me to the same spot where he first met [me], where we again bowed; beyond that I found my Commissioners, who again saluted me. The two who had made the Treaty with Commodore Perry inquired very kindly after him, and requested me to inform him of the

---

[541]The Tykoon's reply (handed on this occasion to Townsend Harris) must have been written either in Japanese or in Dutch. When Townsend Harris returned home, he set Mr. Heusken to work upon its translation. The original half sheet of paper upon which Mr. Heusken wrote the English version is still extant (*L. & P.,* vol. 1, no. 78), and reads:

"Pleased with a letter sent with the embassador [sic] of a far distant country, and likewise so with his discourse. Intercourse shall be continued for ever.

A true translation
H. C. J. HEUSKEN."

This version differs in only very minor details from that given by Townsend Harris in *Journal* for Dec. 7, 1857. The original manuscript by Heusken is endorsed by Townsend Harris: "Speech of the Tycoon of Japan. Received November 4, 1857." The date is, of course, a slip for Dec. 4, 1857.

fact whenever I might write to him.[542] In the vestibule I found the same persons seated who *salaamed* to me as on my entry, and from thence I once more entered my *norimon*.

The Minister[543] is about thirty-five years old, short in stature, of a pleasant and intelligent countenance; his voice is low and rather musical. I returned by the same route, and have nothing to add except that there was not the least attempt at military display of any kind. At the gateway (*i. e.,* in the quadrangle) was a small building in front of which some half dozen spears were placed, and from three to five persons were seated on the mats. The great gates have a strong look with their heavy hinges and the broad-headed bolts that half cover them; but a very slight examination shows that it is all show and no substance. The doors are made of pine or cypress. The hinges, instead of having their sockets in stone, are merely driven into pine posts, and the broad-headed studs are merely shams in form, having a little tack on the under side to hold them to the gate. A six-pound howitzer charged with powder alone would destroy any one of these gates. The bridges over the two great moats were both new. They are neatly built of wood, and the posts are crowned with copper caps. There is nothing about them worthy of remark. I was told at Shimoda that new bridges were being built on account of my visit, but I supposed it was only a Japanese . . . to excuse delay. The exterior walls and

---

[542]See note 529.
[543]Hotta Bitchiu-no-Kami.

fences of [the] Japanese are all blackened with sepia, of which fish enormous quantities are taken in Japan. The second story is made of wattles covered with clay, and this is whitened.

The tiles on the roof have a number of white stripes which are regulated by the rank of the owner. I have not as yet learned the rule that regulates them.

The *enceinte* or third wall of the Castle is nearly pear shaped, the length running north and south. My house is over against the northern and stem-end of the pear.

Saturday, November [December] 5, 1857. To-day we have rain and snow. The first stormy day since the 20th of November. Yedo is about 5° colder than Shimoda, but it has a most delightful climate. Nothing in Italy equals it.

Sunday, December 6, 1857. This is the second Sunday in Advent. Assisted by Mr. Heusken I read the full service in an audible voice, and with the paper doors of the houses here our voices could be heard in every part of the building.[544]

This was beyond doubt the first time that the English version of the Bible was ever read, or the American Protestant Episcopal Service ever repeated in this city. What a host of thoughts rush upon me as I reflect on this event. Two hundred and thirty years ago a law was promulgated in Japan inflicting death on anyone who should use any of the rites of the Christian religion in Japan; that law is still unrepealed, and yet here have I

[544]According to Townsend Harris's own prayer-book, this service consisted of: for the morning, First Lesson, Isaiah, 5; Second Lesson, Luke, ? , v. 39; for the afternoon, First Lesson, Isaiah, 24; Second Lesson, Rom., 12.

boldly and openly done the very acts that the Japanese law punishes so severely![545]

What is my protection? The American name alone, —that name so powerful and potent now cannot be said to have had an existence then, for in all the wide lands that now form the United States there were not at that time five thousand men of Anglo-Saxon origin.

The first blow is now struck against the cruel persecution of Christianity by the Japanese; and, by the blessing of God, if I succeed in establishing negotiations at this time with the Japanese, I mean to boldly demand for Americans the free exercise of their religion in Japan with the right to build churches, and I will also demand the abolition of the custom of trampling on the cross or crucifix, which the Dutch have basely witnessed for two hundred and thirty years without a word of remonstrance.[546] This custom has been confined to

[545]See note 516.

[546]Griffis, *Townsend Harris*, p. 224, note:

"This custom of trampling (*fumi*) on a *yé* (engraved copper plate with representation of the crucifix) was abolished by the Japanese government in 1853, the year before Perry's second arrival. As the *Kindai Geppio* states, 'From this year, the practice of *fumi-yé* at Nagasaki was abolished.' Most of the American sailors shipwrecked on the Japan coasts, and cared for by the government until shipped away, seem to have had no compunctions about treading on the copper plate, thereby proving they were not Portuguese."

This practice had continued for more than two centuries, and it was not abolished at one stroke. Towards the end of 1853, it was quietly allowed to lapse, no official action being taken in regard to it. In April, 1856, however, "official orders were at last formally issued to discontinue the enforcing of the annual *Fumi-yé*. . . ." (Murdoch, *A History of Japan*, vol. 3, pp. 616–17).

The clearest case of this *Fumi-yé* by Americans which occurs to the author is that of the mutinous sailors of the New Bedford whaler *Lagoda*. When finally released by the Japanese, they testified, on April 30, 1849, to Commander James Glynn, of the U.S.S. *Preble*, as follows:

Robert McCoy: "They made me trample upon it, and they made all the others trample upon it—first putting the left foot on the cross, and then

Nagasaki; had it been attempted at Shimoda, I would have remonstrated in a manner that would have compelled the Japanese to listen to me.

I shall be both proud and happy if I can be the humble

the right foot. We were afterwards told that, if we had refused to do this, we would have been put into a small iron house, from which we would never get away."

Jacob Boyd: ". . . and told us that in going into the door of the town-house, he wanted us to step on something. We inquired what it was; and he said an image, or an iron plate. In going in, they pointed it out to me on the gravelled walk, and I perceived that it was a crucifix. Seeing I was not willing to step on it, two of the Japanese took hold of me and forced me to tread on it. First I merely trod on one edge, but they pulled me back, and made me trample on it with both feet."

John Martin: "That at Nagasaki we were taken into the town-house, and on entering the door we found there had been placed on the floor a metal plate with the figure of our Saviour upon it. This they compelled us to step upon, both feet together. I saw John Bull, who was right before me, put one foot on it, and they hauled him back and made him put both feet on together."

Melcher Biffar: ". . . on going into the town-house at Nagasaki, there was a crucifix in the way, and we were told to step on it. We disliked to do it. They then told us that it was no harm; but if we did not do so, they would think we were Portuguese, and it would be told to the governor. We tried to avoid stepping on the crucifix, but a man having hold of each of our arms, forced us to trample on it."

For this and other testimony, which surely reveals a goodly degree of compunction, see 32–1, S. Ex. Doc., no. 59—in Serial no. 620—pp. 9, 20, 22, 24.

We think it fair, after quoting these passages, to add one more clear statement on this subject, from the pen of the missionary Guido Fridolin Verbeck (Griffis, *Verbeck of Japan*, p. 129):

"Herewith inclosed you will please find a picture of a crucifix, and one of Christ with the crown of thorns. They are exact copies of the two pieces that for about two hundred years have been used in the annual 'Ceremony of trampling on the Cross' in the vicinity of this place. It will be something to show in addresses on missions, etc. The ceremony is mentioned in nearly every book on Japan, as you know; but I think writers on Japan have much mistaken the object of the shameful wicked act. It was not so much, if at all, to abuse and disgrace the Saviour, as to find out who were Christians and who not. It was known that no good Christian would trample on the image of Christ; therefore, at the annual census of the people, these images were produced to discover secret Christians."

Considering, however, the penalty in store for those who refused, we are of the opinion that even some "good Christian" might have been forced to commit the act of *Fumi-yé*—unless, indeed, he were of the stuff that martyrs are made of.

467

means of once more opening Japan to the blessed rule of Christianity.

My Bible and Prayer Book are priceless mementos of this event, and when (after many or few years) Japan shall be once more opened to Christianity, the events of this day at Yedo will ever be of interest.

Monday, December 7, 1857. I started for my audience about ten, with the same escort as on my visit to the Minister, but my guards all wore *camissimos* and breeches which only covered half the thigh, leaving all the rest of the leg bare. My dress was a coat embroidered with gold after the pattern furnished by the State Department: blue pantaloons with a broad gold band running down each leg, cocked hat with gold tassels and a pearl handled dress-sword.[547]

Mr. Heusken's dress was the undress navy uniform, regulation sword and cocked hat. Our route was by the same street that I have mentioned on my visit to the Minister, but we crossed the moat by a bridge that was about half a mile from my house. The gateway with the quadrangular building was precisely like those described in my *Journal* of the 4th inst.; so also the appearance of the streets, buildings, people, etc., was exactly the same. On arriving at the second moat all were required to leave their *norimons* except the Prince of Shinano and myself. We crossed the bridge, passed the gate and quadrangle, and pursued our course, and everything was so exactly like what I then saw that nothing

[547]*L. & P.*, vol. 2, no. 7, is a scrap of notepaper, written in Townsend Harris's own hand and having the "Regulations as to the Uniform to be Worn."

Franklin Pierce
President of the United States of America

To all to whom these presents shall come, Greeting:

Know Ye that reposing special trust and confidence in the integrity, prudence and ability of Townsend Harris Consul General of the United States for the Empire of Japan I have invested him with full and all manner of power and authority for and in the name of the United States to meet and confer with any person or persons duly authorized by His Majesty the Emperor of Japan being invested with like power and authority and with him or them to agree, treat, consult and negotiate of and concerning general commerce between the United States and the dominions of His Majesty the Emperor of Japan and all matters and things connected therewith: and to conclude and sign a Treaty or Treaties Convention or Conventions touching the premises, transmitting the same to the President of the United States for his ratification by and with the advice and consent of the Senate thereof.

In testimony whereof I have caused the seal of the United States to be hereunto affixed.

Given under my hand, at the City of Washington the

TOWNSEND HARRIS'S "FULL POWERS,"
OR LETTER OF CREDENCE (Page 1)
Dated, Washington, D. C., September 8, 1855.

the eighth day of September in the year of Our Lord one thousand eight hundred and fifty five and of the independence of the United States the eightieth

By the President.

Franklin Pierce

W. L. Marcy
Secretary of State.

TOWNSEND HARRIS'S "FULL POWERS" (Page 2)

but the assurances of Shinano could convince me that I was in a different quarter. When we arrived within about three hundred yards of the last bridge, Shinano also left his *norimon;* and our horses, his spears, etc., etc., with the ordinary attendants, all remained. I was carried up to the bridge itself (and, as they say, further than any Japanese was ever carried before), and here I dismounted, giving the President's letter, which I had brought in my *norimon,* to Mr. Heusken to carry. We crossed this bridge through the same quadrangle as before; and, at some one hundred and fifty to two hundred yards from the gate, I entered the Audience Hall. Before entering, however, I put on the new shoes I had worn on my visit to the Minister, and the Japanese did not even ask me to go in my stocking feet. As I entered the vestibule I was met by two officers of the household. We stopped, faced each other and then bowed. They then led me along a hall to a room where, on entering, I found the "two chairs" and a comfortable brazier. I should here note that tobacco is *not* served among the refreshments of the Palace. I again drank the "tea gruel." The room in which I was seated was different from any I had seen before. The ceiling or *plafond* was divided into square compartments of some thirty inches, the ribs or divisions being about two inches wide and the same in thickness. It was either painted or covered with paper, —I could not determine which. The ground was a fine ultramarine, on which arabesque figures were drawn of various colors; the posts and beams were of unpainted wood; the usual height of Japanese rooms is from eleven to twelve feet. I thought these to be about thirteen to fourteen feet. I have already mentioned that a Japanese house is cut up into rooms by sliding doors or screens, and that in a short time a whole building may be converted into a single room by the removal of the screens; by this process what was hall becomes part or parts of the rooms. The height of these doors varies from five feet six inches to six feet six inches. Transverse beams are placed in those positions which are to serve as the division wall or partition of a room; a series of grooves is deeply cut in the under side of the beam [and] corresponds with shallow grooves cut in a beam of the floor placed directly under it.

When it is desired to remove a partition, the parts are lifted up until the foot is clear of the floor groove. It is then carried forward or back until the angle it forms will allow the upper part to be removed from the upper beam.

To construct a room the above process is simply reversed. The sliding doors are from four to four and a half feet wide, and they always slide past each other, so that of necessity there must be as many grooves as there are parts of the screen,—four is the usual number. The part between the upper beam and the *plafond* is variously filled. Sometimes it is with frames resembling our window sashes on which paper is pasted, and it looks exactly like a sash that is glazed with rough ground glass. Another, and the most usual mode, is to fill the space with light and neatly made lattice work. At the Palace I saw another mode of filling this space. It was (apparently) carved openwork representing birds, fruits, flowers, and arabesque ornaments, all very highly colored and producing a tawdry effect, which was the more remarkable as the Japanese do not greatly affect violent contrasts or gaudy colors. They apparently prefer the neutral tints and have a good eye for the harmony of colors. The partitions, doors or screens, were painted with passable drawings of their favorite fir tree. This description is exact for every part of the Palace which I saw, and which was equal to some seven or eight of their ordinary rooms, but on this occasion a number of rooms were thrown into one. I was now conducted to another part of the Palace. As I passed along I saw some three hundred to four hundred of the *Daimyo* and high nobles sitting in exact rows, all facing in one direction. They were all clad in Court dresses, of which more anon.

The room to which I was conducted was a large one (but [the] screen [was] made of gilt paper; I have never seen a single expensive screen made of lacquered ormolu ˙and mother-of-pearl since I have been in Japan; I think they were only made by the express orders of the Dutch); and here some of my Commissioners came to pay their respects to me in an informal manner, and some cheerful conversation passed between us. I should describe the Court dress, but to convey an intelligible idea of it is beyond the power of mere words. Drawings are indispensable to a clear understanding of it. The *camissimo,* or upper garment, differs from the ordinary one by coming down quite to the hips. The breeches are the great feature of the dress. They are made of yellow silk, and the legs are some six to seven feet long! Consequently, when the wearer walks, they stream out behind him and give him the appearance of walking on his knees, an illusion which is helped out by the short stature of the Japanese and the great width over the shoulders of their *camissimos*. The cap is also a great curiosity and defies description. It is made of a black varnished material and looks like a Scotch Kilmarnock cap which has been opened only some three inches wide, and is fantastically perched on the very apex of the head. The front comes just to the top edge of the forehead, but the back projects some distance behind the head. This extraordinary affair is kept in place by a light colored silk cord which, passing over the top of the "Coronet," passes down over the temples and is tied under the chin; a lashing runs horizontally across the forehead, and, being attached to the perpendicular cord, passes behind the head, where it is tied. The *camissimo* is without sleeves and is worn over the other garments. It is made of some highly gummed material which makes it quite stiff. Imagine a Van Dyke [collar] of two half diamonds or lozenges. The acute points project over each shoulder; from thence the line of its shape runs so as to strike the waist or girdle. The front and back are composed of box pleats, and the whole is secured by the waist girdle.

My description cannot be very intelligible, but it is the best I can give.

My friend Shinano was very anxious to have me enter

the Audience Chamber and *rehearse my part.* This I declined as gently as I could, telling him that the general customs of all Courts were so similar that I had no fear of making any mistakes, particularly as he had kindly explained their part of the ceremony, while my part was to be done after our Western fashion. I really believe he was anxious that I should perform my part in such a manner as to make a favorable impression on those who would see me for the first time. I discovered, also, that I had purposely been brought to the Palace a good hour before the time, so that he might get through his rehearsal before the time for my actual audience. Finding I declined the rehearsal, I was again taken to the room that I first entered, which was comfortably warm and had chairs to sit on. Tea was again served to me. The servants in the Palace wore black dresses, and their heads are entirely shaved. They are either priests, or wear the dress of priests.

I here discovered that one of my Commissioners, Kawasi, Prince of Saiyemo,[548] is brother of the Prince of Shinano, my host or keeper. He is a lively, cheerful person and was vastly pleased when I told [him] he looked younger than Shinano, although he is four years his senior.

He is the head of all the governors of cities and provinces, and all business from or to them passes through his office. At last I was informed that the time had arrived for my audience, and I passed down by the poor *Daimyo* who were still seated like so many statues

[548]See *Journal,* Nov. 30, 1857, and note 528.

in the same place; but, when I had got as far as their front rank, I passed in front of their line and halted on their right flank, towards which I faced. Shinano here threw himself on his hands and knees. I stood behind him, and Mr. Heusken was just behind me. On looking out I saw a small courtyard surrounded with wooden buildings one story high and covered with tiles. The audience chamber faced in the same manner as the room in which the great audience was seated, but separated from it by the usual sliding doors, so that, although they could see me pass and hear all that was said at the audience, they could not see into the chamber. At length, on a signal being made, the Prince of Shinano began to crawl along on his hands and knees; and when I half turned to the right and entered the audience chamber, a chamberlain called out in a loud voice, "Embassador Merrican!" I halted about six feet from the door and bowed, then proceeded nearly to the middle of the room, where I again halted and bowed; again proceeding, I stopped about ten feet from the end of the room exactly opposite to the Prince of Bittsu on my right hand, where he and the other five members of the Great Council were prostrate on their faces.[549] On my left hand were three brothers of the Tykoon, prostrated in the same manner, and all of them being nearly "end on" towards me. After a pause of a few seconds I addressed the Tykoon as follows:

---

[549]The American Dr. David Murray (who later was adviser to the Japanese Minister of Education) tells us that he saw the original of the Japanese memorandum, showing not only the arrangement of the rooms through which Townsend Harris was to pass, but also the spot where he was to stand during the delivery of his congratulatory remarks to the Shogun: *The Story of Japan* (in *The Story of the Nations* series), p. 327, note 2.

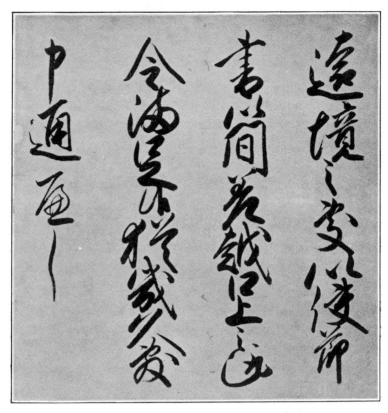

THE JAPANESE TEXT OF THE SHOGUN'S SPEECH

This speech was delivered at the First Audience granted to Townsend Harris, December 7, 1857. It is the earliest official and personal expression uttered by the Shoguns of friendly relations between the United States and Japan. See page 475.

May it please Your Majesty:

In presenting my letters of credence[550] from the President of the United States, I am directed to express to Your Majesty the sincere wishes of the President for your health and happiness and for the prosperity of your dominions. I consider it a great honor that I have been selected to fill the high and important place of Plenipotentiary of the United States at the Court of Your Majesty; and, as my earnest wishes are to unite the two countries more closely in the ties of enduring friendship, my constant exertions shall be directed to the attainment of that happy end.[551]

Here I stopped and bowed. After a short silence the Tykoon began to jerk his head backward over his left shoulder, at the same time stamping with his right foot. This was repeated three or four times. After this he spoke audibly and in a pleasant and firm voice, what was interpreted as follows:

Pleased with the letter sent with the Ambassador from a far distant country, and likewise pleased with his discourse. Intercourse shall be continued forever.[552]

For continuation, see Journal No. 5, page 60.[553]

[550]For the text of Townsend Harris's Letter of Credence (or "Full Powers") signed by President Pierce and Secretary of State Marcy, see Appendix VI. The original document is the property of The College of the City of New York. The Dutch translation of it is given in *L. B.,* vol. 2, pp. 94–95.

[551]The English and the Dutch texts of this address by Townsend Harris are given also in *L. B.,* vol. 2, p. 97. The English version of both these speeches was transmitted to Secretary Cass in Dispatch No. 26, dated Yedo, Dec. 10, 1857. (*L. B.,* vol. 3, pp. 49–56, esp. p. 55.)

[552]See *Journal,* Dec. 4, 1857, and note 541. For the Shogun's speech, as rendered into Dutch by the Japanese interpreter Moriyama, see Wagener, *Aus dem Tagebuche,* etc., p. 382.

[553]Townsend Harris had, for some unexplained reason, broken off his entries in vol. 1 of the manuscript *Journal,* on page 60, with the entry for Monday, Apr. 14, 1856. There he had noted: "For Continuation of Journal in the order of dates, see Journal No. 2." The present note, therefore, sends us back to vol. 1, pp. 60–144, of which contain the rest of the extant *Journal,* beginning with the statement: "Monday, December 7, 1857 (continued from Journal No. 4)."

[Journal No. 5

Commencing December 7, 1857
Ending February 27, 1858]

Monday, December 7, 1857 (continued from Journal No. 4). Mr. Heusken, who had been standing at the door of the Audience Chamber, now advanced with the President's letter, bowing three times. As he approached, the Minister for Foreign Affairs rose to his feet and stood by me. I removed the silk cover over the box, opened it, also raised the cover of the letter so that the Minister could see the writing. I then closed the box, replaced the silk covering (made of red and white stripes, six and seven), and handed the same to the Minister, who received it with both hands and placed it on a handsome lacquered stand which was placed a little above him.[554] He then lay down again, and I turned towards the Tykoon, who gave me to understand my audience was at an end by making me a courteous bow. I bowed, retreated backward, halted, bowed, again retreated, again halted, and bowed again and for the last time. So ended my audience, when I was reconducted to my original room and served with more tea gruel. In

---

[554]For the text of President Pierce's Letter to the Emperor of Japan, dated Washington, Sept. 12, 1855, see Appendix VII. The text there given is taken from a copy of the letter found among Townsend Harris's papers (*L. & P.,* vol. 2, no. 15). The Dutch translation of it is given in *L. B.,* vol. 2, pp. 95-96.

order to see as much as I could, I asked to be shown to a water closet. On leaving the room I found myself in a small court surrounded by wooden buildings exactly like those described on the opposite side of the house. A good deal of negotiation had been used by the Japanese to get me to eat a dinner at the Palace, alone or with Mr. Heusken only. This I declined doing. I offered to partake of it provided one of the Royal Family or the Prime Minister would eat with me. I was told that their customs forbade either from doing so. I replied that the customs of my country forbade anyone to eat in a house where the host or his representative did not sit down to table with him. At last the matter was arranged by ordering the dinner to be sent to my lodgings. I had not been long in the room last mentioned before I was requested to meet the Council of State. I found them in the place where the *Daimyo* had been seated, but who had now left the room. Hotta, Prince of Bittsu, spoke and in the name of the Council congratulated me on my arrival and audience, and then said His Majesty had ordered a present to be offered to me, which was then in the room, at the same time pointing to three large trays each holding five silk *kabyas*[555] thickly wadded with silk wadding. I thanked the Council for their kind inquiries and desired them to return my thanks to His Majesty for his present. After this, bows were exchanged and I turned and left the room going towards the vestibule; but a few yards from it I halted and turned, when the Council of State again formed line and took leave of me by a deep bow. At

[555]Kabiyas (Griffis, *Townsend Harris*, p. 231).

the vestibule I met the two officers who had first received me, and I exchanged bows with them, and then left the Palace, and proceeded to my *norimon* and returned home by the same route I had come by.

The Tykoon was seated in a *chair* placed on a platform raised about two feet from the floor, and from the ceiling in front of him a grass curtain was hung. When unrolled it would reach the floor, but it was now rolled up, and was kept in its place by large silk cords with heavy tassels. By an error in their calculation the curtain was not rolled up high enough to enable me to see his headdress, as the roll formed by the curtain cut through the centre of his forehead, so that I cannot fully describe his "crown," as the Japanese call it. I was afterwards told that this mistake arose from their not making a proper allowance for my height, as, had my eyes been three inches lower, I could have seen the whole of his headdress. This may, or may not be so.[556] The dress of the Tykoon was made of silk, and the material had some little gold woven in with it. But it was as distant from anything like regal splendor as could be conceived. No rich jewels, no elaborate gold ornaments, no diamond hilted weapon appeared, and I can safely say that my dress was far more costly than his. The Japanese told me his crown is a black lacquered cap, of an inverted bell shape. The dress of the Tykoon was differently shaped from those of his courtiers and appeared like loose robes, while his breeches were of a reasonable length. The

---

[556]Surely another reason is that, whereas Townsend Harris stood during the audience, all who had ever before been granted an audience had been obliged to approach the Shogun on their knees.

material was far inferior to the glorious "kincabs" of the Benares looms.[557]

I did not see any gilding in any part, and all the wooden columns were unpainted.

Not an article of any kind appeared in any of the rooms, except the braziers and the chairs and tables brought for my use. At the right side of the last gate I entered, a square pagoda or tower of three stories was erected. There was the same absence of military display as on my visit to the Minister. Soon after reaching my quarters the dinner followed. It was very handsome according to Japanese rules, and the centerpieces were beautifully got up. Miniature fir trees, the tortoise and stork, emblems of longevity, with tokens of welcome and respect were prominently exhibited.[558] I merely looked at it but was unable to eat a morsel, as I was seriously ill. I had taken a violent cold; had much inflammation of the lungs,[559] and now a violent ague fit attacked me. I was glad to send for the doctor of the Prince of Shinano, a very intelligent man that I had frequently seen at Shimoda. Finding I had already taken cathartic medicine, he prescribed tisanes,[560] feet in hot water, to drink freely of hot *cunju,* or rice gruel, and to put on as many clothes as I could pile on my bed, so as to promote perspiration.

---

[557]*Kincobs*—India silk brocaded with flowers in silver or gold.

[558]For the various courses of this dinner, see 46–2, H. Ex. Doc., no. 1, pt. 1, pp. 626–27, in Serial no. 1902.

[559]The record at the Greenwood Cemetery in Brooklyn (where Townsend Harris is buried), reads that he died Feb. 25, 1878, of "Congestion of the lungs."

[560]Ptisancs.

Tuesday, December 8, 1857. Still quite ill, although better than yesterday.

Write to the Minister for Foreign Affairs that I have some important communications to make which deeply concern the interests of Japan, which I will communicate to him, or to the whole Council of State. (See private letter book no. 3.)[561]

I omitted to state yesterday that the dinner sent to me was placed on some forty to fifty trays made of unpainted wood. These trays were eleven inches high for me and about five inches for Mr. Heusken. The dinner was served in the usual lacquered cups.

I was told that the trays and other utensils, after having been used by me, could never be used by any other person, and therefore they were made of unvarnished wood, this being the custom of Japan when presenting food to persons of exalted rank, etc., etc.

The fan used at the audience differs from that used on ordinary occasions. It does not open and fold like ordinary fans, but is permanently fixed and is about three inches across the top. The handle also is longer than that of the ordinary fan. Gave the letter for the Minister to the Prince of Shinano who came to me this afternoon, after his visit to the Castle. He told me that all who were

---

[561]*L. B.*, vol. 3, p. 10. More fully: This letter referred to the letter of the President which Townsend Harris had finally delivered at the audience of the preceding day, Dec. 7, 1857. Townsend Harris tells Prince Hotta that he is now ready to make confidential communications either to Hotta or to the Great Council. He adds that immediate action will be needed thereafter, and that he is ready to treat with duly appointed commissioners. The "confidential communications" hinted at in this letter, and the "important communications" hinted at in the text, both refer to the subjects discussed by Townsend Harris during his interview at Hotta's house on Dec. 12, 1857: *cf. L. & P.*, vol. 1, no. 79.

present at the audience yesterday were amazed at my "greatness of soul" and at my bearing in presence of the mighty ruler of Japan.

They had looked to see me "tremble and quake," and to speak in a faltering voice. He added that the Americans were a very different people from the Dutch. I insert this because he told it to me, and I let it pass for what it is worth, but I am hugely inclined to think that there is some admixture of "soft sawder."

Thursday, December 10, 1857. We had a shock of earthquake yesterday at nine A. M.—quite light—better to-day. Show the presents I have brought for the Tykoon; they consist of the following articles:

12 quarts of champagne, 24 pints of champagne
12 bottles sherry, 12 bottles of assorted liqueurs
1 rich astral lamp, 3 rich cut globes, extra chimneys, etc., etc.
2 very rich cut-glass decanters
1 telescope
1 aneroid barometer
2 volumes, Museum of Natural History, 1,000 plates.
5 Bramah's patent locks.[562]

Trays to place these articles on must be made before they can be presented.[563] The Prince of Shinano tells me that the person who gave maps of Japan to Von Siebold did not perform the *hara-kiri,* but was crucified; and

[562]Wi·h this rather meager and inferior list, compare the lists of official presents made to the First and the Second Kings of Siam (Appendices II and III).

[563]The cost of making these stands or trays had to be met by Townsend Harris, and is given in *L. & P.,* vol. 2, no. 91.

that a number of other persons lost their lives by their conduct on that occasion.[564]

Crucifixion is performed as follows: the criminal is tied to a cross with his arms and legs stretched apart as wide as possible; then a spear is thrust through the body entering just under the bottom of the shoulder blade on the left side and coming out on the right side just by the armpit. Another spear is then thrust through from the right to the left side in the same manner. The executioner endeavors to avoid the heart in this operation. The spears are thrust through in this manner until the criminal expires, but his sufferings are prolonged as much as possible.

---

[564]*Osada's Life of Takano Nagahide,* translated and edited with an introduction by D. C. Greene, D.D., in *Transactions of The Asiatic Society of Japan,* vol. XLI, part III, Aug., 1913, pp. 408–09:

"Although the civilization of Western Europe had seemed to be swelling to a full tide at Nagasaki ever since Siebold's arrival, an unforeseen calamity came upon the Dutch community, and forced Takano to give up the plans upon which he had set his heart.

"In the ninth month of the eleventh year of Bunsei (commencing October 9th, 1828), Siebold had completed his period of service and was planning to return home. His ship drifted ashore as the result of a hurricane, and this led to a re-examination of the cargo, with the result that there were found in his effects certain prohibited goods.

"It seems that when Siebold went to Yedo for the first time [1823], he was visited by Takahashi Sakuzaemon who had the office of Chief Librarian and Astronomer under the Shogun's government; who asked him many questions about foreign countries. Takahashi was widely read and farsighted, and, on learning that Siebold had Russian books and a map of New Holland [Australia], he thought it would be of advantage to the country if he should translate them and present them to the government; but Siebold was at first unwilling to loan the books. Finally, however, he prevailed upon Siebold to give them in exchange for maps of Japan and Yezo, together with an account of the products of the country, and these articles were found by the authorities in examining the ship.

"Accordingly Siebold was confined in Deshima, while Takahashi, the interpreters Baba Hachiro, Kichio Yoshijiro, Inomata Genzaburo and more than thirty others were imprisoned. The Shogun's physician, Habu Genseki, was also arrested on the charge that he had given Siebold clothes with the hollyhock crest, and had studied ophthalmology from him. This affair caused great excitement in the medical communities of Yedo and Nagasaki."

Shinano told me that a few years ago a very strong man lived until the eleventh spear had been thrust through him.

No man is put to death in Japan until he has confessed his guilt. After conviction, if he asserts his innocence, he is put to the *torture* until he confesses or dies or faints,— in the last case he is removed to his prison and brought to the question on another day, and this continues until he either confesses his guilt or dies under the torture. Had a long argument on the injustice of the torture as a means of eliciting truth.[565]

Saturday, December 12, 1857. Again visit the Minister for Foreign Affairs. Everything attending this visit was so exactly like my first visit that I have nothing to note except what relates to the conference I had with him. The Commissioners of my Voyage assisted the Minister on this occasion.

My private papers on "Japan" contain an exact copy of what I said on this occasion,—therefore, I do not copy it here.[566]

---

[565]On the same day, Townsend Harris wrote a long Dispatch to Secretary Cass (*L. B.*, vol. 2, pp. 49–56, Dispatch No. 26), in which, after referring to Dispatch No. 13, he narrates in great detail the story of his trip to Yedo, his entry into the Shogun's capital, the negotiations preceding the Audience, and the Audience itself. (The text of Townsend Harris's speech on that occasion, and of the Tycoon's answer, are both to be found, *ib.*, p. 55.)

[566]In 46–2, H. Ex. Doc., no. 1, pp. 627–31, we find: "Statement made by Townsend Harris in the house of Hotta on the 26th of 10th month of 4th year"—*i. e.*, Dec. 12, 1857. For additional details of this visit to Lord Hotta, see Heusken's *Diary*, in Wagener, *op. cit.*, pp. 382–83.

The manuscript source to which Townsend Harris refers is *L. & P.*, vol. 1, no. 79, which is endorsed (in Townsend Harris's hand): "Memorandum of the communications I am to make to the Council of State at Yedo, 1857." From this wording it is clear that Townsend Harris had written it all out in advance, probably before leaving Shimoda; for it will be remembered that Townsend

It related to the changed condition of the world by the introduction of steam; that Japan would be forced to abandon her exclusive policy; that she might soon become a great and powerful nation by simply permitting her people to exercise their ingenuity and industry; that a moderate tax on commerce would soon give her a large revenue by which she might support a respectable navy; that the resources of Japan, when developed by the action of free trade, would show a vast amount of exchangeable values; that this production would not in any respect interfere with the production of the necessary food for the people, but would arise from the employment given to the actual surplus labor of Japan, etc., etc.; that foreign nations would, one after another, send powerful fleets to Japan to demand the opening of the country; that Japan must either yield or suffer the miseries of war; that, even if war did not ensue, the country would be kept in a constant state of excitement by the presence of these large foreign armaments; that to make a concession of any value it must be made in due season; and that the terms demanded by a fleet would never be as moderate as those asked by a person placed as I was; and that to yield to a fleet what was refused to an ambassador would humiliate the Government in the eyes of all the Japanese people, and thus actually weaken its power. This point was illustrated by the case of China, the war of 1839 to 1841, the events succeeding that war, and the present hostilities.

Harris distinctly says (*Journal*, Nov. 30, 1857) that the letter which he on that day sent Hotta by Shinano (*L. B.*, vol. 2, p. 93) "had been previously prepared at Shimoda and only required to be dated and sealed."

I told him that, by negotiating with me who had purposely come to Yedo alone and without the presence of even a single man-of-war, the honor of Japan would be saved; that each point would be carefully discussed, and that the country should be gradually opened.

I added that the three great points would be: 1st, the reception of foreign ministers to reside at Yedo; 2nd, the freedom of trade with the Japanese without the interference of Government officers; and 3rd, the opening of additional harbors.

I added that I did not ask any exclusive rights for the Americans, and that a treaty that would be satisfactory to the President would at once be accepted by all the great Western powers. I did not fail to point out the danger to Japan of having opium forced upon her, and said I would be willing to prohibit the bringing it to Japan.

I closed by saying that my mission was a friendly one in every respect; that I had no threats to use; that the President merely informed them of the dangers that threatened the country, and pointed out a way by which not only could those dangers be averted, but Japan made a prosperous, powerful and happy nation.

My discourse lasted over two hours and was listened to with the deepest attention and interest by the Minister. He asked some questions occasionally when he did not fully understand what was said.

When I had finished, the Minister thanked me for my communication, and said it should be communicated to the Tykoon and have that consideration which it merited,

486

and that it was the most important matter ever brought before the Government.

He added that the Japanese never acted as promptly on business of importance as the Americans did, that many persons had to be consulted, and therefore I must give them sufficient time for those purposes. This was to prepare me for the usual delay of the Japanese in everything.

I replied I wished them to fully consider all I had said, and that I should be very glad to give any explanations of details whenever it should be asked.

The Minister kindly inquired after my health, courteously expressing his regret at my illness.

The usual refreshments were served, and I returned to my quarters about four o'clock.

Sunday, December 13, 1857. The second Sunday in Advent. Read the service with Mr. Heusken. I have told the Japanese that I performed my religious worship, in order that they might not say they had no knowledge of it.

Monday, December 14, 1857. I have had a long and unpleasant debate about my diplomatic rights, the Japanese insisting on their right to appoint persons to guard me from insult, injury, fire, etc., etc.

I replied that I had come to Yedo alone, therefore I wished the Government to place proper persons in the house, but that it must be done by my request and not as their right. I had in view the great importance of my not doing anything that might be quoted as a precedent whenever foreign ministers shall come here to reside.

This matter has been agitated for a number of days, and at last I carried my point, and the matter was settled as follows: he wrote me a letter stating that the Japanese Government admitted my full and complete control of the premises occupied by me, and that no person could enter the place without my permission.

I wrote in reply, first quoting his letter, and added that I wished the Government to supply me with a proper number of persons to protect me from accidents, carefully adding "but in so doing I do not admit the right of the Japanese Government to place any person in my house under any pretence whatever without my consent." (See private letter book no. 3.) [567]

Wednesday, December 16, 1857. In reply to my request for some place where I could exercise on horseback, the Japanese offered me a piece of ground adjoining my house, about five yards wide and some thirty yards long!

They then offered me another spot about one hundred feet long by seventy-five feet wide. This was also rejected. To-day the Prince told me that they had set apart

---

[567]The quotation here given is from *L. B.,* vol. 3, p. 11; but this is a letter addressed to Inouye, Shinano-no-Kami, dated Dec. 19, 1857, and written in reply to one from Inouye dated Dec. 18, 1857. The debate about his diplomatic rights (mentioned in the beginning of this entry) must therefore have been with Inouye, who likewise is the person referred to a little later by the words, "He wrote me a letter stating," etc.

All the internal evidence in the letter here cited proves that the dates are correct in the *Letter Book.* How this entire entry came to be dated Dec. 14th in the *Journal* (which is here written in Townsend Harris's own hand) is beyond comprehension. It may be that Townsend Harris made his rough copy of the *Journal* on loose sheets, beginning each new day's entry on a separate sheet; and that, because he wrote hurriedly, he misinterpreted his own handwriting, and entered under Dec. 14th the entry which rightly belonged to Dec. 19th. An added consideration in favor of this solution is that the *Journal* has no entry for Dec. 19th.

a *ba-ba* not far distant from my place, and wished me to send Mr. Heusken or to go myself and see it. Mr. Heusken examined it, and reported that it was a regular military ground, over three hundred yards long and from fifty to seventy-five yards wide, and that it would answer my purpose. On this I accepted it, and in the afternoon I went to it. It is on a plateau elevated some fifty feet above my residence and directly opposite to a bridge and gate leading to the residence of the brothers of the Tykoon. It is enclosed with a hedge and large trees. Large numbers of the people collected around the hedge and the streets by which I went to the place. They were perfectly quiet; the only noise being that of the street keepers with their eternal *"Satu, satu,"* "Keep back, keep back." To-day I sent a present of a few bottles [of] wines and liqueurs to the Minister of Foreign Affairs with a copy of Blunt's *Coast Pilot*. In my letter to him (which see) I called his particular attention to the book, and that it contained an accurate account of every harbor in the United States, West Indies and South America; that such books were printed by private individuals and sold freely to all that wanted them; that the Government encouraged such publications, as they increased the facilities of foreign commerce, which was one of the great elements of our prosperity, and that I considered it as a very proper book to place in the hands of the Minister for Foreign Affairs in Japan.[568]

[568]Here again there is a discrepancy that cannot be explained (see preceding note). This entry of the *Journal* correctly gives the substance of *L. B.*, vol. 3, pp. 15–16, which is a letter addressed by Townsend Harris to Lord Hotta and dated Dec. 24, 1857. Again, Dec. 24, 1857, must be the correct date on

Thursday, December 17, 1857. A fine ride in the *ba-ba* to-day. The Japanese wish me to agree to go to the *ba-ba* only two days in the week, and that for a single hour! as they required it every day for the exercises of their soldiers. I replied that, if the place was wanted for that purpose, I must of course give it up; and, as the times they named were unreasonable, I would hereafter take my exercise along the street running along the moat.

This did not suit at all, and at last it was settled that the *ba-ba* should be at my disposal from three P. M. every day of the week except Sunday. I may be said to be now engaged in teaching the elements of political economy to the Japanese and in giving them information as to the working of commercial regulations in the West.

This is attended with more labor than can be well imagined, for I not only give them ideas for which, as they are new, they have no adequate terms, but the interpreter does not understand the Dutch terms when he hears them. Thus I am sometimes employed for hours in trying to convey a very simple idea. It requires an incalculable amount of patience to prevent my throwing the matter up in despair. But I know that every word I utter, every new idea I succeed in conveying, is at once carried to the Council of State, so I persevere in the hope that my labors will at last produce fruit, if not for me, at least for my successor.

which Townsend Harris made these presents to Hotta, and for two reasons: the first, because this date is nearer Christmas; the second, because on Jan. 4, 1858 (*q v.*), Hotta made a return present to Townsend Harris, and in his accompanying letter said that he had read Townsend Harris's letter, "sent on the last 9th day" (*L. & P.*, vol. 2, no. 67). In the Japanese calendar Dec. 24, 1857, was the 9th day of the 11th month.

Friday, December 18, 1857. After an incredible amount of talk and difficulty, the Japanese have given me a map of Yedo. I am not to give it away or suffer it to be copied.[569]

Sunday, December 20, 1857. The last Sunday in Advent. Read service as usual. Yesterday had an earthquake—not very sharp. Quite unwell these three days.

Monday, December 21, 1857. To-day the Commissioners of my Voyage call on me for the purpose of receiving information.[570]

The chief point of their inquiries related to the object of sending Ministers to foreign countries; their duties, their rights under the laws of nations. All these questions were as clearly answered as possible.

I added that, when a Minister gave serious offence to the Court to which he was appointed, the government might suspend intercourse with him and order him to leave the country; that the usual mode was to complain of his conduct to his own government and to request his recall. The Commissioners asked questions also respecting commerce, and what I meant by trade being carried on without the interference of government officers. This I also succeeded in explaining to their full satisfaction. They said they were in the dark on all these points and

---

[569]For the fate of Siebold under similar circumstances, see note 564.

[570]Lord Hotta did not go himself, but sent five of the eight Commissioners (for whose names see note 528). The purpose of their visit was to seek further particulars on the substance of the conversation between Townsend Harris and Hotta on Dec. 12, 1857. Complementary to the brief statements here made, is the full and detailed account to be found in 46–2, H Ex. Doc., no. 1, pt. 1, pp. 631–34, in Serial no. 1902: "Account of a conversation with Townsend Harris in the Banshe Shirabejo [a kind of Foreign Office] on the 6th of the 11th month." This date corresponds to Monday, Dec. 21, 1857 (*cf.* note 527).

therefore were like children; therefore I must have patience with them. They added that they placed the fullest confidence in all my statements.

I gave them a written paper containing the *basis* of a commercial treaty which I explained to them article by article, and told them I wished that paper might be taken into serious consideration.

I then gave them champagne, which they appeared to understand and to like.

Friday, December 25, 1857. Merry Christmas! I little thought on last Christmas to pass the present one in Yedo. If I could pass one in Pekin, it would make my different places of passing the day a remarkable list.

I ask every day when I may expect an answer to my great communications.

The invariable reply is that a great many persons are to be consulted: the brothers of the Tykoon, all the *Daimyo* and some other great men; that letters have to be written and answers received, and then the old story, —"the Japanese do not decide important affairs until after long deliberation."

Wrote to the Minister for Foreign Affairs transmitting a memorandum pointing out the most obvious articles that will form the elements of foreign commerce, and showing how these articles may be increased in production, etc., etc. (See private letter book no. 3.) [571]

[571] The letter to Hotta is *L. B.*, vol. 3, p. 16; the Memorandum enclosed therein is *ib.*, pp. 17–19, and the "most obvious articles that will form the elements" of trade between the United States and Japan are lacquerware, silks, tea, and copper. The writing of these letters on Christmas Day was a rather

Sunday, December 27, 1857. Snow and a gloomy day. I cannot get one word out of the Prince of Shinano as to my prospects of success, nor a hint as to the existence or non-existence of any obstacles. This state of uncertainty joined to indifferent health greatly depresses my spirits.

Thursday, December 31, 1857. An earthquake today. I have not had a visit for three days from the Prince of Shinano, [which fact,] joined to the uncertainty that hangs over my negotiations, causes me to pass this, the last day of the year, in a melancholy manner.

I fondly hope that the year now about to commence will give me more frequent opportunities of communicating with the outer world than I enjoyed during the present one. In truth I was most shamefully neglected by the Navy in the East.[572]

Friday, January 1, 1858. I desire to return thanks to Almighty God for permitting me to see the beginning of a New Year.

With my poor health, and over half a century of years, I cannot promise myself that I shall see another. I am thankful that I have been able to accomplish so much

---

prosaic occupation, and yet a good example of the saying "the better the day, the better the deed." Indeed, only two days before, Townsend Harris had written a long (and private) letter to Mr. E. E. Rice, American Commercial Agent at Hakodate, in which, after telling of his audience and his hopes, he discusses in detail not only the two Dutch Treaties with Japan (Nov. 9, 1855, and Jan. 30, 1856), but also the Additional Articles signed by the Dutch and the Russians (*L. B.*, vol. 3, pp. 12–15). Treaty making was verily the one task of Townsend Harris's life during these busy months.

[572]And in spite of his "melancholy manner," he dutifully, on this last day of a long and weary year, wrote Dispatch No. 27 to Secretary Cass, transmitting the number and the dates of all his dispatches to the Department of State for the year 1857 (*L. B.*, vol. 3, p. 35).

as I already have done for the honor of my country during the past year, and I hope that I shall be able to effectually open this country before the present one closes. I was visited in honor of *my* New Year's Day by the Princes of Toke and Shinano; both came in dresses of ceremony and brought me some trifling presents. Had some very pleasant conversation, but nothing was said on business.[573]

Saturday, January 2, 1858. A very sharp shock of earthquake. People much alarmed, and all ran out of their houses. I am told the earthquake of December, 1856, killed over ten thousand persons in Yedo alone, and that one-third of the houses in the city were either thrown down or so much shaken that they had to be taken down. To add to their afflictions, fire broke out in an immense number of places among the ruins of the fallen houses. A very intelligent Japanese told me the motion was perpendicular and the shocks followed each other almost instantly. This is the motion that is most injurious. The billow or wave motion does but little injury, comparatively.

Monday, January 4, 1858. Hotta, Prince of Bittsu, sent me a present of some pretty lacquerware and some fine crêpes.[574]

---

[573]Townsend Harris found time on this day to write five routine dispatches to Secretary Cass (*L. B.*, vol. 3, pp. 35–36, Dispatches Nos. 1–5); two to the Hon. Howell Cobb, Secretary of the Treasury (*ib.*, p. 37, Dispatches Nos. 1 and 2); and one to the bankers Baring Bros., at London (*ib.*, p. 37).

[574]These presents were accompanied by a letter addressed "To His Excellency Townsent [sic] Harris, Plenipotentiary and Consul General of the United States of America, etc., etc., etc." It was dated the 20th day of the 11th month, Mi. A copy of the English translation of this letter (the copy being made by Mr. Heusken himself) shows that the original translation into English was

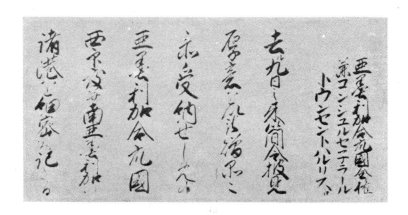

LETTER WRITTEN BY HOTTA, BITCHIU-NO-KAMI, TO
TOWNSEND HARRIS

Dated, Yedo, January 4, 1858. See Appendix VIII.

To-day I procured some specimens of the square bamboo. Earthquake to-day.

Tuesday, January 5, 1858. Earthquake.[575]

Saturday, January 9, 1858. To-day the Prince of Shinano visited me for the first time in three days. I determined to bring about a crisis, and therefore began by saying that it was now twenty-nine days since I had made some very important communications to the Minister of Foreign Affairs, of which no official notice had since been taken;[576] that they would not even name a period within which I should have a reply; that such treatment could not be submitted to; that the President had sent me to Yedo on a most friendly mission, having solely the benefit of Japan in view; that the United States asked nothing for themselves; that the trade of Japan was no object to us; that all we cared for was that our ships could make repairs and get supplies in their harbors, and that we had already got that point; that they must open their eyes and then they would see that I

---

made and signed by Moriyama Takitsiro, the interpreter. At the bottom, the letter is countersigned: "A true translation, H. C. J. Heusken." (*L. & P.*, vol. 2, no. 67.) For a reproduction of this letter, see illustration; for the text as given by *L. & P.*, vol. 2, no. 67, see Appendix VIII.)

[575]Though silent as far as this *Journal* entry is concerned, Townsend Harris on this day took another forward step in his negotiations. On Dec. 12th (*q. v.*) he had made a long and important statement to Lord Hotta. On Dec. 21st (*q. v.*) he had given further explanations to the five Commissioners who had visited him at his house. On the 25th (*q. v.*) he had actually enumerated what would probably prove to be the chief objects of Japan's trade with the United States. Finally, on this day (Jan. 5, 1858) he again writes to Hotta, saying that, judging from the delay in receiving an answer to his propositions, he must fain believe that they have not been understood. Townsend Harris therefore offers to meet Hotta and give still further explanations, emphasizing the value of a full and free discussion which need not (he points out) be considered binding on either party (*L. B.*, vol. 3, pp. 19–18 *bis*).

[576]Referring to the statement made in the house of Hotta on Dec. 12, 1857 (*q. v.*, and note 566).

neither asked nor would I accept any favors from Japan; that ten days ago I offered to give them explanations on any points on which they needed information;[577] and wound up by saying that their treatment of me showed that no negotiations could be carried on with them unless the plenipotentiary was backed by a fleet, and offered them cannon balls for arguments. I closed by saying that unless something was done I should return to Shimoda. Poor Shinano listened in evident trepidation, and earnestly assured me that no slight to the President or insult to me was intended; that, as to-morrow was my Sunday and I would not do business on that day, he could not answer me before the next day, at which time he told me I should be satisfied.

This was apparently a bold step on my part, but from my knowledge of this people I felt that I ran no kind of danger of breaking off my negotiations by what I did, and that the more I yielded and acquiesced, the more they would impose on me, while, by taking a bold attitude and assuming a threatening tone, I should at once bring them to terms.

Monday, January 11, 1858. A visit to-day from the Prince of Shinano. He began by saying that he had reported all I had said to him at our last interview to the Minister of Foreign Affairs; that the Minister admitted that I had just cause of complaint, but that the position of the Government was most difficult; that *they* were *enlightened,* and knew that what I had recom-

---

[577]This Townsend Harris really did by letter to Hotta dated Jan. 5, 1858 (see note 575).

mended was truly for the best interests of Japan, but their conviction alone was not sufficient,—they had to convince the brothers of the Tykoon, the *Daimyo,* the military, and [the] literary classes of the wisdom of following my advice; that the Minister and his colleagues had labored constantly night and day to secure the consent of the persons referred to; and that a brother of the Tykoon was in Kyushu, and they had to write to him and get his reply; and finally he said that on Friday the 15th he would inform me the day when I should have an answer.

This was much to my satisfaction, and I told the Prince that, so long as I had specific days fixed, then I could wait with patience.

I endeavored to draw from him some hints as to the probable color of the answer I should receive, but I could not elicit anything. Either he has "great powers of silence," or he actually was ignorant of the matter.

Wednesday, January 13, 1858. Slight shocks of earthquake to-day. Mr. Heusken has been much indisposed since the 8th inst. with a bilious attack.

Wednesday, January 13, 1858. Slight shocks of promise, the Prince of Shinano visited me. He said the Minister of Foreign Affairs would give me an answer to-morrow or at a later day, as best suited me, and as the matters were of the highest importance he desired to have a conference with me.

I accepted at once the day and place of conference.

Saturday, January 16, 1858. Again to the Minister's. Retinue, roads and the appearances in the streets exactly as they were on my two previous visits to him, except that there were not so many people in the streets to look at the cortège as it passed. Foreigners will soon cease to excite curiosity here. I was received in the usual manner by the [Minister], except that I thought his smile was warmer this morning than before; to-day it was more than skin deep. The Minister soon opened the conference by saying that the communication I had made verbally to him, together with the written memorandums I had sent to him,[578] and the information I had communicated to his Princes, had all been laid before His Majesty the Tykoon. His Majesty desired first to thank the President for his very kind advice and for the friendship he had thus shown for Japan. The Minister then proceeded to give me His Majesty's answer.

The demand for the residence of a Minister at Yedo is admitted.[579] The place of his residence and the rights he is to exercise shall be settled by negotiation.

The right of free trade is granted. Commissioners shall be appointed to settle the details of trade.

Three harbors having already been opened, and as Japan is a small country, the number cannot be increased; but, as Shimoda is not found to be suitable as a harbor, another shall be given in place of it, but the number may not be increased beyond three. After the Minister had ended, I told him I was much concerned at His Majesty's decision about harbors;[580] that it was im-

---

[578]See *Journal,* Dec. 25, 1857, and note 571.
[579]This later became Art. I of the Treaty concluded July 29, 1858.
[580]For the question of harbors, see *ib.,* Art. III.

possible for me to make a satisfactory treaty under such restrictions. I pointed out to him the west coast of Japan, bordering on the Japan Sea.

⨯From Hakodate to Nagasaki, following the coast line, it is quite four hundred ri (one thousand miles English), yet in all that distance not a single harbor was opened; that many American whale ships were in the Japan Sea, and it was very important for them to have a convenient harbor in that sea; that His Majesty had spoken of the small size of the Empire, but an examination of the maps of the principal parts of the world would show that Japan had a coast line far greater than the average states. I therefore earnestly recommended a reconsideration of that part of His Majesty's decision.

I was informed that the Commissioners to negotiate with me would be appointed immediately, and that the first interview should be held day after to-morrow, and that the negotiations should be conducted at my quarters. I then handed the Minister a copy and translation of my full powers,[581] and pointed out to him the necessity that the powers of the Japanese Commissioners should specify that they were appointed to negotiate with me, and not a mere general power.

I requested that a translation of the Japanese full powers should be handed to me before the meeting.

I also told the Minister that, as soon as we had gone through the formality of exchanging our full powers, I would hand the Commissioners a draft of such a treaty as would be satisfactory; that they could have it trans-

---

[581]See note 550.

lated into Japanese; and, after having duly considered it, we could then proceed with our negotiations; that this course would greatly facilitate our negotiations and thus save valuable time; adding that I had nothing to conceal, no secret motives or wishes, and therefore I could proceed in this frank and open manner. The Minister said that my course was very praiseworthy and that it gave him much satisfaction.

I have the draft of a treaty which I drew up before leaving Shimoda, and I was anxious to take the initiative in presenting a draft, as, had the Japanese presented one, it would have been difficult if not impossible to reject it entirely, and to try to amend one of their performances would have made a piece of literary or diplomatic patchwork that would have excited the laughter of all who might have the misfortune to be compelled to read it. I could not learn the number or names of the intended Commissioners. I was told the Prince of Shinano would be one, but nothing further.[582]

Monday, January 18, 1858. To-day I rigged out in full dress in honor of the signatures of the President and Tykoon which are to be exhibited to-day. I learn to-day

[582]Another account of this busy day in Townsend Harris's life is to be found in 46–2, H. Ex. Doc., no. 1, pt. 1, pp. 635–36, in Serial no. 1902. The speakers at the Prime Minister's house were Hotta, Townsend Harris, and other Japanese whom the document just cited does not name. This government publication, moreover, is wrong in translating "the second day of the twelfth month" as "February, 1858."

At this point, one should not fail to read Gubbins, *The Progress of Japan*, App. 16, pages 289–91, which are a quotation from the *Bakumatsu Gwaikodan*, or *The Story of Foreign Relations in the last days of the Shogunate*, by M. Sanabe. These few pages give an admirable picture of the complicated political activity that was going on behind the mirror.

Finally, see Heusken's *Diary* in Wagener, *Aus dem Tagebuche*, etc., p. 383.

that I am to have only two Commissioners to deal with. This pleases me, as it will prevent much interruption; although the Commissioners will have full powers, yet in reality I shall be negotiating with the whole Council of State. The Commissioners will hear my arguments, and then request time to consider them; they will repeat what I have said to the Council, who will consider the matter and then dictate what the Commissioners shall say. I feel just as sure of this as though I had been told it by themselves. The Commissioners are:

> Inowouye, Prince of Shinano, and
> Iwase, Prince of Hego[583]

At one P. M. the Commissioners appeared. They were attended by two secretaries to take down every word that was uttered.

We saluted each other standing. I then gave my full powers to Mr. Heusken, who handed it to the Prince of Shinano who opened it, looked at the President's signature and the seal, and then passed it to his colleague, who also examined it and then returned it to Mr. Heusken, who handed it to me. The full powers of the Japanese Commissioners were then given to the Vice-Governor of Shimoda who handed it to me. I opened it and looked at

---

[583]These Treaty Commissioners were Inouye, Shinano-no-Kami; and Iwase, Higo-no-Kami. In the printed copies of the Treaty (concluded July 29, 1858), they appear as "their Excellencies Inoooye, Prince of Sinano, the Iwasay, Prince of Hego."

Townsend Harris's belief that these Commissioners did not really possess full powers, but would report everything back to the Great Council, is repeated in the letter which he wrote on July 6, 1858, to General Prosper M. Wetmore. This letter appeared (without the name of the person to whom it was addressed) in the *Washington Union* of Jan. 15, 1859, and was reprinted in Littell's *Living Age* of Feb. 26, 1859, vol. 60, pp. 571–74.

the Imperial seal and signature, and then returned it.[584] Those who have read Commodore Perry's account of his Japanese Expedition will remember that the Japanese would not let their full powers go out of their hands, pretending the Imperial seal was so sacred it could not be handled by any but a Japanese, and of them only by those to whom it was specially directed.[585]

The seal was in vermilion, about two and a half inches in diameter, and composed of the old Chinese "Seal Character." This over, I handed the Commissioners a Dutch translation of my draft of a treaty. I told them that, as this treaty might contain words not well understood by their interpreters, I suggested that the work had better be done in one of the rooms of the house where we were, so that if any words or phrases were not understood they could at once have recourse to Mr. Heusken for explanation, and thereby not only would the translations be facilitated, but greater exactness would be secured. They assented at once to my suggestion. They added that, as soon as they had time to examine the translation and consider it, they would again meet me, but that it would require some days to do both. I re-

[584]A copy of the Full Powers of the Japanese Commissioners is *L. & P.*, vol. 1, no. 80. It is numbered 17 (of the "Japan Documents" of Townsend Harris) and is endorsed in Townsend Harris's hand.

[585]Perry, *Narrative* in 33–2, H. Ex. Doc., ño. 97, vol 1, p. 249 (Wednesday, July 13, 1853):

"The apologies having been made, the governor exhibited the original order of the Emperor [Shogun], addressed to the functionary who had been appointed to receive the Commodore. The Emperor's letter was short, and was certified by a large seal attached to it. This imperial epistle, which was wrapped in velvet, and enclosed in a box made of sandal-wood, was treated by the governor with such reverence that he would allow no one to touch it."

quested the Commissioners not to read the Treaty piecemeal as it was translated, as the various Articles had such relations with each other that they must be read together and not separately; that to read it as it was translated would give very erroneous ideas, and thus perhaps prejudice might arise that it would be difficult afterwards to remove. They at once assented to this. The original draft of the Treaty will be found among my private "Japan papers."[586]

Wednesday, January 20, 1858. Received a letter from Mr. Rice, U. S. Commercial Agent at Hakodate.[587] He wants "women and must and will have 'em."

[586]This precious document is not among the extant *Letters and Papers.*

[587]*L. & P.*, vol. 1, no. 72, dated Hakodate, Dec. 15, 1857. It is marked "Private," and was written in answer to Townsend Harris's letter of Oct. 27, 1857; and was in turn answered by Townsend Harris on Feb. 1, 1858.

In addition to what is stated in the *Journal,* Mr. Rice says in this long letter that he refuses to accept the site for a foreign settlement chosen by the Japanese; emphasizes the importance of Hakodate as a resort for whalers; and describes Russia's designs upon it. He then complains of discrimination in favor of the Dutch, and appeals to Townsend Harris to remedy the situation, etc., etc.

The passage referred to by Townsend Harris reads:

"The men want women and rum (and have got both in a few instances) and the Japanese people are perfectly willing except [the] officials, who constantly follow every American when on shore, which is very annoying to our people; and I fear when a large number of ships comes here next spring that serious difficulties will follow unless the government gives way and complies to [with] the customs of other countries where whaleships resort. Five hundred whalemen with their officers (and they would lead them) would take and hold this place with perfect ease, and they swear they will unless there is a change. The complaint is that the Dutch have what we do not. How it will end time will tell; but one thing is certain: they must adopt a more liberal policy. The trouble is entirely with the officials."

We have already commented upon the downright illiteracy displayed by Mr. Rice in his letters. The text as given above is a reconstruction *a fundamentis.*

Townsend Harris replied to Mr. Rice by letter dated Feb. 1, 1858, marked "Private" (*L. B.,* vol. 3, pp. 18 bis–22), in which he states (pp. 20–21) that the question put by Mr. Rice had been favorably decided by the Japanese on the ground of "fear of sickness."

Busy at the translations of the Treaty. It cannot be done before Friday or Saturday.

Saturday, January 23, 1858. To-day the translations were finished. In order to be sure of the translation being correct, I had the Japanese translator read from the Japanese copy and translate orally into Dutch to Mr. Heusken, who held the Dutch version. It has been an immense labor, but my great anxiety has been that the Japanese should *fully* understand what I proposed to them.

A visit from the Prince of Shinano to-day. Some time ago I told him that if he saw a dog that had any white hair about him, he might be sure the tip of the dog's tail would be white also. This he repeated (of course) at the Castle, and it appears that each of the nobles set his retainers to search for a dog who should have some white about his body while the terminal color of his tail should be black, or at least not white. Many thousands of dogs have been examined and as yet no exception to my rule has been found. This has given me a reputation for universal wisdom that is quite amusing from its simplicity. I have omitted to note that I made presents of wines, cordials, sardines, preserved salmon and lobster, and Bramah locks to all the Commissioners of my Voyage. These presents exhausted all the articles I brought from Shimoda.

The Tykoon was much pleased with my presents and uses the astral lamp constantly. He sent me a return present of a very handsome cabinet.

The Commissioners each sent me a present of a piece

504

of brocade silk twenty-four inches wide and three and one-quarter yards long,—the pattern of a pair of such breeches as are worn by the highest ranks only.

Monday, January 25, 1858. To-day at two P. M. we fairly opened our negotiations.

In this *Journal* I shall confine myself to the main leading facts of actual transactions, omitting the interminable discourses of the Japanese where the same proposition may be repeated a dozen times; nor shall I note their positive refusal of points they subsequently grant, and meant to grant all the while; nor many absurd proposals made by them, without the hope, and scarcely the wish, of having them accepted,—for all such proceedings are according to the rule of Japanese diplomacy, and he who shows the greatest absurdity in such matters is most esteemed. They do not know the value of a straightforward and truthful policy, at least they do not practise it. They never hesitate at uttering a falsehood even where the truth would serve the same purpose.

The Preamble to the Treaty was accepted as was the first Article,—so far as to agree to receive a Minister and Consuls. They wished the Minister to reside between Kanagawa and Kawasaki, and only come to Yedo when he had business, nor should the Minister or Consuls travel anywhere in Japan except on actual business.

They then proceeded to *read from a book* what I will abridge and insert, merely to remind me hereafter of their mode of doing business.

Earthquake, nine A. M.

Monday, January 25, 1858, continued.

They began by saying that they had carefully considered the draft of the Treaty I had given them. The Empire being small, it had been determined that not more than three harbors should be opened; that Shimoda should be closed and a large harbor should be given in place of it. The opening of any harbors to Commodore Perry was a great concession and was made with much difficulty. Thus far, American ships have only been furnished with supplies and not with Japanese goods. Now, in consequence of the President's letter and the very important and friendly communications of the plenipotentiary, it has been determined to open trade with the Americans on the same terms as were contained in the Treaties just made with the Russians and Dutch!!![588] (See copies of these disgraceful papers in my private files on Japan.)[589] They offered Kanagawa and Yokohama in place of Shimoda, and, after all the *Daimyo* are satisfied with the effects of trade, another harbor should be opened. Trade to be conducted as provided for in the Dutch and Russian Treaties. Americans cannot be allowed to travel in Japan, must be confined to strict limits.

---

[588]The Treaty with Russia was concluded at Shimoda, Feb. 7, 1855 (Gubbins, *The Progress of Japan*, pp. 235–39); the Supplementary Treaty, at Nagasaki, Oct. 24, 1857 (*ib.*, pp. 239–45).

The Preliminary Convention with The Netherlands was concluded at Nagasaki, Nov. 9, 1855 (*ib.*, pp. 245–50); the Treaty itself, at Nagasaki, Jan. 30, 1856 (*ib.*, pp. 250–55); the Additional Articles thereto, again at Nagasaki, Oct. 16, 1857 (*ib.*, pp. 255–64); and, finally, the Supplement to these Additional Articles, at the same place and on the same day (*ib.*, pp. 264–66).

For additional light on Townsend Harris's knowledge of (and attitude toward) these Treaties, see above, *Journal* for Feb. 26, 1857, and notes.

[589]The full text (in Dutch) of the Supplementary Treaty with Russia is *L. & P.*, vol. 2, no. 70.

They here paused, and I replied that, by the ninth Article of the Treaty of Kanagawa, anything granted to other nations accrued at once to the Americans, and therefore did not require any treaty stipulations; that, as to those Treaties, the conditions of them were disgraceful to all parties engaged in making them; that, so far as trade was concerned, those documents were not worth the paper on which they were written; that, were I to sign any such conditions, the President would recall me in disgrace. I then demanded that the promise of the Tykoon "that freedom of trade should be granted," should be made good.[590] I added that it was mere trifling to offer to me conditions that had already accrued to us months ago; that the proposition to shut out the Minister from residing in Yedo, or wherever he pleased, was highly offensive, and that it would be far better for them to refuse to receive him than to couple his reception with such conditions, and that the Minister and Consuls must have all the rights enjoyed by such persons under the laws of nations; that I asked nothing more for them than those rights, and that I could not take any less.

The Commissioners were not prepared for this. It quite upset their plan so nicely prepared for them by the Council of State, and they were embarrassed exceedingly. They began to repeat the old story: "Japan has been closed for more than two hundred years; the people are not prepared for such great changes as you propose;

---

[590]At the Audience of Dec. 7, 1857, the Shogun had closed his very brief speech with the words "Intercourse shall be continued forever."

they must be introduced by degrees, and, as the people learn to know you better, then we can act more freely, etc., etc."

I replied that, under such regulations as they proposed, trade was impossible; that Americans might be in Japan for fifty years and make no advances towards a better acquaintance; that intercourse under such circumstances, so far from removing prejudices, would increase them,—for the Japanese would learn to despise the Americans as much as they do the Dutch.

That, from all I had observed in Japan, I was convinced that the people were actually anxious to have a free intercourse with us, and, if objection existed anywhere, it was confined to the *Daimyo* and the military, two classes of people that in all countries were opposed to any improvement in the condition of the great body of the people.

The Commissioners frankly admitted that I was right in my last statement, adding that a large class called the *Literati* or expectants of office, being entirely ignorant of everything out of their own land, were also opposed to opening the country. In explanation of this I was told that every person who had mastered the four books of Confucius and could pass the requisite examination, received a small pension from the Government, and that as officers were wanted they were selected from this class. They added that colleges were established at Yedo and in each of the provinces of the Empire; that the only books used were Confucius and the history of China; that no sciences, arts, history, or polite literature, or in fact anything but Confucius and Chinese history were taught in those institutions.

The Commissioners here had a long and animated conversation together. After it ended, the Prince of Shinano asked me if I would hear a private and confidential matter, which he wishes to communicate to me. I replied, "Most certainly." He then said that of the sons and brothers of military men, none enjoyed any rank except the eldest son; that they all received a military education, being taught the art of war, the use of weapons, etc. They had no pay, nor any prospect of advancement in life. They were supported in idleness by the head of the family, as their positions forbade their devoting themselves to any useful avocations, and they had no hope of honorable employment. Their only distinction consisted in their .right to wear two swords. From these habits of idleness many of them fell into bad courses, became dissipated, drunken brawlers and bullies; and that when their conduct became too outrageous they were disowned and cast off by their families. In this condition they form a class called *loneen,* which corresponds to bravo, bully, rowdy and loafer.[591] The Government has just discovered a plot among these *loneen* against the American Ambassador (what they intended to do to me I could not learn), and the Government had that morning arrested three ringleaders of the conspirators and had them now in prison; that it had

---

[591]The common form in English of the word *loneen* is *ronin*—as, for instance, the famous tale of "The Forty-Seven Ronin," in Mitford's *Tales of Old Japan,* and in Murdoch's *A History of Japan,* vol. 3, ch. VI, "The Forty-Seven Ronin."

given the Government the greatest possible anxiety, for, should anything happen to the Ambassador, it would be the cause of serious difficulties with the United States, besides disgracing the Government of Japan in the eyes of all the civilized world. He then added that a large body of men was now employed in patrolling around my house and in all the neighborhood, and that at night they would be in all the various courts and open spaces of the house. He then gave me the names of these three Yedo rowdies. They are as follows:

Horeye Yosi-Nosuke
Nobu-ta-Nee Ziu-ro
To-zo.

The Commissioners now resumed and said [that], from what had been told me, I must see that the residence of Foreign Ministers in Yedo would be certain to cause disturbances, and therefore it was far better for them to reside at Kawasaki or Kanagawa than in Yedo.

I thought it a most suspicious circumstance, that these *loneen* should have remained perfectly quiet for the whole fifty-five days I have been in Yedo, and should only stir at the very nick of time that the question of the residence of Foreign Ministers in Japan was to be agitated, and that they should be arrested on the morning of the very first day that the conferences were to be opened. Therefore, I concluded that, if the whole matter was not an actual "arrowsmith," it was very much like one.

I replied to all this that they did not know the material

of which foreigners were composed if they supposed that
the acts of three or three thousand *loneen* would keep
them away from Yedo; that I considered it as too trifling
a matter to call for any serious reply.[592]

---

[592]As already remarked in note 538, the dangers which threatened the life
of Townsend Harris were very real and very serious. Though he could not
learn what these *ronin* intended to do to him, Shinano-no-Kami and every
other Japanese of that day knew, and we all know to-day, that the *ronin*
intended to kill him. The record of the events that followed the coming of
the foreigner and the consequent opening of the country leaves no possible
doubt on this score. The writer has gathered a long list of these Japanese
attacks on foreigners—attacks that were cruel and of none avail, but which
are readily understood when we recollect the excited state of politics in those
early days of foreign intercourse. From the point of view of the Japanese
themselves, some, at any rate, of these attacks were due to the exalted state
of their minds and to a sense of patriotism that later history proved to be
a mistaken one.

The list of those attacks on foreigners is really appalling. To mention only
a few from the earlier years, we have:

1) On Aug. 26, 1859, at Yokohama: the attack on a Russian naval lieutenant, a sailor, and a steward, resulting in two deaths.
2) On Nov. 5, 1859, at Yokohama: the slaying of a Chinese servant in the
employ of M. Loureiro, the French consular agent at Yokohama.
3) On Jan. 29 (or 30), 1860, at Yedo: the slaying of Dankichi, the Japanese
interpreter of the British Legation, who was struck down from behind
in broad daylight close to the home of Sir Rutherford Alcock, the
British Minister.
4) On Feb. 21 (or 26), 1860, at Yokohama: the slaying of two Dutch
merchant captains.
5) In Feb., 1860, at Yedo: the attack on the valet of the French Minister,
M. Duchesne de Bellecourt.
6) In Nov., 1860: the attack on Mr. Moss.
7) On Jan. 15, 1861, at Yedo: the slaying of Mr. Heusken himself, as he
was returning home from the Prussian Legation of Count Friedrich
von Eulenburg.

These earlier attacks did not assume the tremendous importance of the later
murders of Richardson, or of Lieutenant Bird and Major Baldwin; but they
clearly show the dangerous temperament not only of the irresponsible *ronin,*
but also of men in high position. For instance, no less a personage than
Nariaki, Prince of Mito—a man of the highest lineage and a splendid irreconcilable—is reported to have exclaimed in a fit of anger: "Let Bitchu [Hotta]
and Iga commit hara-kiri, and decapitate Harris at once" (Akimoto, *Lord Ii
Naosuke and New Japan,* p. 147).

The names of the three ringleaders on this occasion were: Horei Yoshino-
suke, Nobutani Tuiro, and Tozo (Griffis, *Townsend Harris,* p. 262). Mr.
Heusken's *Diary* (in Wagener's *Aus dem Tagebuche,* etc., pp. 383–84) says that
Townsend Harris later asked that these three prisoners be set free, but that

The Commissioners were again in a quandary. At my suggestion they took up my draft and gave a general answer on each Article.

The demand for Americans to have Japanese coin, or for Japanese to receive American coin, was rejected in a most decisive manner. It was emphatically declared that no sales could be made except through Japanese officials. In this manner they went through the Treaty, rejecting everything except Article VIII.

This Article I had inserted with scarcely a hope that I should obtain it. It provides for the free exercise of their religion by the Americans, with the right to erect suitable places of worship, and that the Japanese would abolish the practice of trampling on the Cross. To my surprise and delight this Article was accepted!

I am aware that the Dutch have published to the world that the Japanese had signed Articles granting freedom of worship and also agreeing to abolish the trampling on the Cross.

It is true that the Dutch *proposed* the abolition, but the Japanese refused to sign it.

In the Dutch Treaty of January, 1856, an Article provides that "within the buildings at Deshima the Dutch

---

the Japanese Government refused to do so. Shortly afterwards they died in prison (Nitobe, *The Intercourse between the United States and Japan*, p. 65).

This attempt on Townsend Harris's life was, then, the first in chronological order—and naturally so, for he was the first "barbarian" to establish himself in Japan, first at Shimoda and now in Yedo. It is this attempt on Harris's life, too, which is the subject of a play that has become very popular in Japan —namely, *The American Messenger,* by Okamoto Kido, in which the famous actor Matsumoto Koshiro takes the rôle of Townsend Harris himself. (See the illustration in the magazine *Japan* for Jan., 1927. It may be added that the Japanese word *Taishi,* or Ambassador, literally means *Great Messenger:* E. W. Clement, in the *Nation,* vol. 106, p. 111.)

may practise *their own,* or the Christian religion." The extraordinary words *"their own,* or the Christian religion" are copied from the Treaty as sent to me by the Dutch Commissioner, Mr. John Henry Donker Curtius, from Nagasaki; and are also in the copy of the same Treaty which was furnished me by the Japanese.[593]

I have copies of every Article ever made by the Japanese with the Russians, Dutch and English, and the above is the only Article that relates to religion. (See my *Journal* for Sunday, December 6, 1857.) I told the Commissioners, as we were about to adjourn at five P. M., that it was useless to proceed with the further consideration of the Treaty until they would consent to grant the Minister the rights he enjoyed under the "Laws of Nations."

Tuesday, January 26, 1858. Commissioners come at half-past two P. M. They open the business by saying that I had misunderstood them yesterday; that they did not refuse the right of the Minister to reside in Yedo, but only recommended Kawasaki or Kanagawa as a more suitable place for his first residence. They therefore accepted the Article as it stood, so far as it relates to the Minister. They wished, however, that the Treaty should not go into effect until January 1, 1861. (It stood July 4,

---

[593]See note 546.

The Article referred to by Townsend Harris is not part of the Treaty of Commerce signed at Nagasaki on January 30, 1856. The ratifications of the Treaty were exchanged at Nagasaki, Oct. 16, 1857, and on the same day Additional Articles were signed. Of these Additional Articles, No. XXXIII reads: "The Netherlanders are at liberty to practise their own or the Christian religion within their buildings and at the burying-places appointed for them." (Gubbins, *The Progress of Japan,* p. 262.) For comment on this Article, see note 492.

1859, in my draft.) I replied that to suspend a treaty for three years was an unheard-of thing and showed a most unfriendly spirit on their part. They hastily replied that they did not mean the Treaty, only that the Minister should not be sent before that time. I answered that was even worse than the other; that the object of sending a Minister was that he could promptly settle any small difficulties that might arise, whereas, if they were neglected until word could be sent to America, they might grow into grave and serious matters. I added that the proposition manifested a spirit quite at variance with the Preamble of the Treaty.[594] They then asked me to give them my secret promise that the Minister would not be sent before that time. I told them such a promise was beyond my power, as it was the President and not the Plenipotentiary that had that matter in his power. They then requested me to write to the President, making known their wishes on this head. I told them I would write to the Secretary of State, who would make their wishes known to the President, and this satisfied them. They then insisted that the consuls should not have the right to travel in Japan "except on business." I pointed out to them that to accede to such a clause would put every consul at once in the power of each local governor, who would have the right to inquire into his business, etc.; that if the consul wished

---

[594]Especially with the words:

". . . desiring to establish on firm and lasting foundations the relations of peace and friendship now happily existing between the two countries, and to secure the best interest of their respective citizens and subjects by encouraging, facilitating, and regulating their industry and trade. . . ."

THE FAMOUS GINKGO TREE AT THE ZEMPUKU-JI (THE SHRINE OF PEACE
AND PROSPERITY) IN TOKYO

This tree marks the site where once stood the first flagstaff erected by Townsend Harris in the
Capital of Japan. Townsend Harris concluded the Treaty of Yedo on July 29, 1858; the Convention
of Kanagawa on March 19, 1859; and opened the American Legation at Yedo (Tokyo) on July 7, 1859.

to make a journey for his health he could not do so, with other objections.

They said that, as the Treaty was to be read by all the *Daimyo* and great nobles, they did not wish to have it appear that every consul had the right to travel in Japan; that the words "on business" were proposed as a mere cover to conceal the extent of the rights actually conceded; and that no governor or other official should ever inquire into the nature of the business on which a consul might be travelling. I said that implied that the consul would be willing to tell a falsehood when he wished to travel and had no official business; that such conduct was not according to our customs; that a liar was looked on with the greatest contempt, besides which it was a sin by our religion for a man to utter a falsehood.

Finding we could not agree at present on this point, I requested them to lay it aside for the present and proceed with the other Articles, which was agreed to.

Article II provides that the President will act as the mediator of the Japanese when asked to do so, and that American men-of-war and consuls should assist Japanese vessels and their crews so far as the laws of neutrality permitted.

There is nothing in this Article that requires a treaty stipulation, but I inserted it to produce an impression on the Government and people, and it had that effect. This Article was accepted without hesitation.

Article III, the Sebastopol of the Treaty, was now taken up, and the debate continued until the hour of our

515

adjournment. In the draft as proposed by me I claimed Hakodate, Sinagawa, Oasaca, Nagasaki, another port in Kyushu near the coal mines, Firato, and two ports on the west coast of Nippon, making together eight harbors, and I also claimed the cities of Yedo and Miako should be opened to the Americans.

They went over the old ground of objections so often stated before. In answer I said that to secure the peace, honor and prosperity of Japan, a satisfactory treaty must be made; that the freedom of trade was an essential part of such a treaty, and without harbors it was absurd to talk of any trade being done.

I repeated the remark I had made to the Minister for Foreign Affairs, that there was a distance of 400 ri on the west coast in which not a harbor was opened. The discussion continued until dark, when the Commissioners said that my arguments were so important they must have a day to take them into consideration, and therefore they could not meet me until the day after to-morrow. Thus making good what I have before noted,— that, in reality, I am negotiating with the whole Government and that the Commissioners can only repeat what has been told them and report what I say.

The two Japanese secretaries are constantly employed in taking down every word that is uttered.

Wednesday, January 27, 1858. I was shown some Japanese radishes of a wonderful sort. One was eighteen inches long, fifteen inches in circumference, and weighed four pound five ounces; the other *thirty-four* inches long and one and one-quarter inches diameter. Procured seed of both these sorts to send to the United States Patent Office. The Japanese preserve them by drying.

Thursday, January 28, 1858. The Commissioners arrive at half-past one P. M. They go to "the Castle,"— *i. e.,* the Council of State, at nine A. M., and leave at one; eat a hasty meal and then are ready for business. They opened proceedings by saying that half the *Daimyo* were at Yedo and the other half in the provinces, and that, when the half in the provinces returned to Yedo, the other half went to the provinces also; that the Government was compelled to consult the *Daimyo* on all important matters; and if the Government attempted to carry any important measure against their advice, it would cause "confusion,"—*i. e.,* rebellion,—therefore the Government must defer to their opinions. The answer of the Minister of Foreign Affairs on harbors was final. No doubt more will be opened by and by, but not at present. *The merchants and common people are no doubt in favor of opening the country,* but the *Daimyo* and *Military* oppose it.

The civilians at the head of the Government understand these matters better. They have learned a great deal since you have been in the country,[595] therefore they are in favor of a treaty, which they see will make the country prosper and the Government rich and powerful.

This is not a refusal to open more harbors! It is only a statement of the condition of the country. Coals have been discovered within three ri (seven and a half miles English) of Nagasaki, so that the other harbor asked for

[595]Townsend Harris is here reporting the trend of the Japanese argument.

in the Island of Kyushu is not wanted. The Island of Firato is small and poor, and only produces porcelain, therefore a port in that island is not needed. Miaco is not the true name of that city. It is Kyoto. The meaning of Miako is Capital.

(This is another instance of the extraordinary secretiveness of the Japanese; for more than three hundred years they have permitted foreigners to call it Miako,[596] instead of Kyoto!)

Kyoto is comparatively a poor place. The population, instead of being five hundred thousand as stated by Kaempfer, does not contain two hundred and fifty thousand. It is merely a city of priests and temples. No large manufactures are carried on, nor [is] any lacquerware made there. Silk is not woven in more than twenty houses. (They spoke almost contemptuously of the Mikado, and roared with laughter when I quoted some remarks concerning the veneration in which he is held by the Japanese. They say he has neither money, political power, nor anything else that is valued in Japan. He is a mere cipher.)[597]

[596]Kaempfer distinctly said that *Miako* meant simply *the town* or *metropolis:* see the quotation in Thomas Rundall, *Memorials of the Empire of Japan in the XVI and XVII Centuries,* London, The Hakluyt Soc., 1850, p. 96.

Is this not a parallel to the Roman *ad urbem,* and to the *Stamboul* of the City of Constantine?

[597]Of the relations between the Mikado and the Shogun, Masaoka says (in *Japan to America,* p. 224):

"A long time ago, Townsend Harris, the first consular representative in Japan of the United States, said, in effect, that nothing taxed his brain so much as the Mikado of Dai Nippon."

An interesting study could be made of the slow, but constantly growing, realization in the minds of the early diplomats to Japan as to where the real power rested—whether in the Yedo Shogunate, or in the remote Emperor at Kyoto.

As to Sinagawa, it is no harbor, as no large ship can come within two and a half ri (six and a half miles) of it. Kanagawa is the nearest to Yedo of any harbor, and that is already opened to you. Kanagawa Post House is seven and a half ri from the Nippon Bas[598] (eighteen and three-quarters miles English). Osaca is fifteen ri (thirty-seven and a half miles) from Kyoto.

To my surprise, after the beginning of this speech of theirs, they wound up by offering me the harbor of Nee-e-gata[599] in the province of Itsigo on the west coast of Nippon. The city has a large river running through it and contains 60,000 inhabitants. On further inquiry I found that only nine feet of water was found on the bar of the river, and from their charts the outer harbor is more like an open roadstead than a harbor.

They assured me that no good harbors like Hako-date, Nagasaki and Kanagawa could be found on the west coast; that all the harbors were so filled up with mud that vessels of large size could not enter them. They added that, if a better harbor than Nee-e-gata could be found on the west coast, it should be given in exchange for it. On these terms I took Nee-e-gata. I then told them that my way of doing business was plain and straightforward; and, to give them a proof of my friendly feelings and to facilitate our business, I would withdraw the claim to Firato,[600] one harbor on the west coast, another

[598]See note 524.

[599]Niigata, in the Province of Echigo.

[600]Townsend Harris must have put in a claim for Hirado for sentimental reasons, thinking of the olden days before the captivity at artificially built Deshima in the Harbor of Nagasaki; of the days when the Japan trade was free and open to all comers; of the days when at Hirado there mingled (in

harbor in Kyushu, making three harbors withdrawn.

That to give ample time to prepare for these changes, I would fix the opening of the various places as follows:

Yedo to be opened January 1, 1863 (with Sinagawa)
Osaca   "   July 4   1861
Nee-e-gata   "   July 4   1860
Kanagawa   "   July 4   1859
and Shimoda should [be] closed January 1, 1860
Nagasaki to be opened July 4, 1859.

In answer to their often repeated assertion that all these places would be opened by and by, I replied that between nations verbal assurances had no value; that it was written stipulations alone that were considered as of any value; that a written promise to open a harbor in four years would be far more satisfactory than a verbal promise to open it in two years.

The Commissioners said they did not see how the difficulties to Yedo and Osaca could be overcome. They thought it impossible. They therefore required a day to think of it, and would meet me on Saturday, the 30th inst.

Saturday, January 30, 1858.   Meet at the usual hour. They promptly offer to open Yedo and Sinagawa, but the Americans to reside at Kanagawa and Yokohama. The Americans only to purchase articles in a small way at Yedo. They have a class of large merchants called *toyas* who keep immense establishments and are ready

---

not too friendly an intercourse, to be sure) the Dutch from Java and the banks of the Texel, the Spanish from the Philippines, the Portuguese from Goa and Macao, and the English of the famous East India Company.

to buy anything and to any amount. These merchants will open establishments at Kanagawa where the Americans can buy and sell what they desire. They here entered into a long argument showing that the residence of Americans in Yedo for the purposes of trade was unnecessary, and then, to my great surprise, they added that the American may buy where he can best suit himself as to quality and price, and sell to whom he pleases *without the intervention of any government officer.* This is a complete abandonment of the leading principle of the Dutch and Russian Treaties, and is one of the chief points I have so long contended for.[601]

I now entered into arguments tending to show that, to expect Americans to go to Yedo from Kanagawa and to return the same day (thirty-seven and a half miles) and to do business in Yedo, was a physical impossibility; that such a regulation would prevent their selling anything in Yedo; that to limit their sales to the *toyas* was in fact

---

[601]The Explanatory Article to Art. V of the Russian Treaty (signed at Shimoda, Feb. 7, 1855) reads:

". . . Les Russes, après avoir choisi dans les boutiques les marchandises et objets qui leur conviennent et être convenus de leur prix avec les vendeurs, effectueront le paiement ou l'échange des marchandises dans ledit entrepôt par l'entremise des employés japonais." (Gubbins, *op. cit.,* p. 238.)

Additional Articles to the Treaty of Commerce (concluded Jan. 30, 1856) between The Netherlands and Japan were signed at Nagasaki, Oct. 16, 1857. Number VII states:

"After inspection of the goods for sale, the sales take place at the Treasury, which receives and takes care of the purchase money unless goods are received in payment by the sellers. . . ." (*ib.,* p. 257.)

And, finally, the Treaty concluded by Townsend Harris at Yedo, on July 29, 1858, clearly provides (Art. III) that:

"Americans may freely buy from the Japanese and sell to them any articles that either may have for sale, without the intervention of any Japanese officers in such purchase or sale. . . ." (*ib.,* p. 271.)

creating a monopoly in favor of that class; that every person of rank and wealth resided a part of every year in Yedo, while the families of all these classes resided there.

That the quantity of foreign articles sold at Yedo alone would, at the beginning of the trade, be more than all the rest of the Empire; that most of the articles were not even known by name to the Japanese; that they must first see them, learn their use, etc.; and after one person had purchased a thing, it would be the means of inducing others to buy of the same article; that, to do this, the Americans must bring their goods to Yedo to show them, and this, of course, involved the necessity of their having their warehouses and residence in Yedo.

That it was idle to think of trying the experiment of free trade so long as the Americans were excluded from Yedo and Osaca,—two of the greatest cities of the Empire, etc., etc. I offered to withdraw Sinagawa as a port, and that American ships should not go above the harbor of Kanagawa, but for this I must have Yedo and Osaca open for trade.

Monday, February 1, 1858. Meet the Commissioners at the usual hour. They open business by the following proposition: "The permanent residence of Americans shall be at Kanagawa, and, after [the] first of January, 1863, one street shall be opened in Yedo for the temporary residence of Americans to buy and sell." Nearly three hours were occupied in making, discussing various propositions regarding Yedo,—the Japanese making strenuous resistance to any concessions beyond the above. I finally made them the following proposition:

"On the first of January, 1863, the city of Yedo shall be opened to Americans for the purposes of business. The place they shall occupy for their business shall be settled by the American diplomatic agent and the Government of Japan." The Japanese take until to-morrow to consider this proposition.

Tuesday, February 2, 1858. Meet at the usual hour. The Commissioners object to the word "business" and wish the word "trade" inserted in lieu of it. As this in its literal sense would deprive the American of cook, clerk, medical aid, and in fact of all assistance, I objected to it; at the same time I told them the word used by me would not justify the residence in Yedo of any persons who were not either directly engaged in trade, or in the employ of such persons.

After a vain attempt to come to an understanding, I propose to lay Yedo aside for the present and to take up Kyoto and Osaca. They produce a map of Kyoto. (The map in Kaempfer is an exact copy.) They give the size of the city to be thirty-six and one-half streets long, or 4,380 yards, and seventeen and a half streets wide, or 2,100 yards. If their measurement be correct, the whole area of the city, including the ground occupied by the Palace of the Mikado and the Castle, both large enclosures, is 190 acres, each 4,840 square yards. Kaempfer gives the population at 500,000, which would be 2,631 souls for each acre! or less than sixteen and a half square feet of ground for each living soul.

The Commissioners said that there were insurmountable objections to opening Kyoto to the Americans as a place of residence, which were connected with their religion; that if it was only extremely difficult they would say so, but in reality what I asked was impossible; that it was no place of business, as the American Minister could satisfy himself whenever he should visit the city. To attempt to open the place for the permanent residence of foreigners would excite a rebellion; that they were sure, when I reported this to the President, that he was too good a friend to Japan to insist on a thing which was of no real value and would at the same time introduce anarchy and bloodshed into Japan. They made the most solemn asseverations that what they said was true. They then offered to open Sak-kai, a town containing 150,000 souls, situated on the Bay of Set-tsu, and distant by land only three ri (seven and a half miles) from Osaca, the second city of the Empire. Osaca lies on a river, and by that route it is five ri (twelve and a half miles) from the bay. Ships going to Sak-kai or [to] Osaca anchor nearly at the same spot; but, owing to shoals or mud banks, ships like the Americans' cannot come nearer than one and one-half ri (three and three-quarter miles) to Sak-kai or two ri (five miles) of the mouth of the river leading up to Osaca. Osaca has never been opened to foreigners as a residence, and its proximity to Kyoto renders the opening of it to them very objectionable to the Japanese. If I do not like Sak-kai, they offer me Hio-n'go on the same bay and lying ten ri (twenty-five miles) to the westward of Osaca River. It is about the same size as

Sak-kai, but it has a bold shore and a good artificial harbor, built many hundreds of years ago at a vast expense. (See next page for a rough draft of the harbor of Set-tsu.)

Tuesday, February 2, 1858 (continued). I insisted on having Osaca opened for the permanent residence of Americans. A long time was passed in debating a proposition of theirs that Americans should reside at Sakkai, but have the right to visit Osaca, to buy and sell there, and to rent houses for that purpose, etc., but not to sleep in Osaca. I strongly insisted on the unfriendly and inhospitable appearance such an Article would bear, and told them I could not understand why they should have greater objections to opening Osaca than they had to opening Yedo. I said that difficulties would constantly arise under such an arrangement, and gave as an illustration that, suppose an American late in the day should be taken suddenly and violently ill and quite unable to return to Sak-kai, the authorities of Osaca, acting under stringent orders, would place the sick man in a *norimon* and send him off to Sak-kai. On the road the man dies. The Americans, indignant at such inhumanity, would make a very strong and possibly exaggerated statement of the transaction. This would be sent to the Minister, and copies to the United States. A very serious difficulty might thus arise between the two nations. As to the vicinity to Kyoto, I was willing to let the lines run at the full distance from that city, so that difficulty was imaginary. I also told them to remember that the seventh Article of the Treaty claimed, for every well conducted Amer-

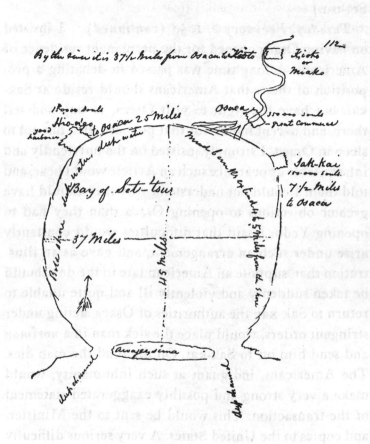

By the river it is 37½ miles from Osaca to Kioto

112

Kioto
or
Miako

18000 souls
good harbour

Hio-o'go
to Osaca 25 miles

Osaca

350 000 souls
great Commerce

mud banks or low dirt water, deep water

Bay of Set-tsu

Sak-Kai
150 000 souls

7½ miles
to Osaca

dirt free

dirt water

low land

6½ miles from dirt Shore

37 Miles

45 miles

deep channel

deep channel

Awajezsima

526

ican who had resided one year in Japan, the right to travel as freely as the Japanese. The Commissioners told me that the seventh Article and the opening of Kyoto were two impossibilities; that they could not be granted without producing rebellion. Many other propositions of the Treaty were excessively difficult, but still might be carried into effect, but the two points were absolutely impossible. And here they made a very sensible remark. They said if foreign nations would go to war with them on account of those two points they must make the best they could of the calamity, but under no circumstances was war from abroad so much to be feared as intestine commotion. Lamps had been introduced by me; and, as we had been steadily at work, the Commissioners told me I had fairly beaten them out in my powers of endurance, and they must therefore beg to be excused for the evening. I urged them to reflect seriously on what I had laid before them, remarking that the present was the turning point of the Treaty, and that one false step might utterly destroy our labors. No meeting to-morrow.

Wednesday, February 3, 1858. This morning at an early hour the Prince of Shinano called to have some private conversation.

He said there was an intense excitement among the old party at the Castle; that the concessions already made had greatly exasperated them, and he feared, if I persisted in insisting on Kyoto being opened and on the right of the Americans to travel in the country, I should run a great risk of losing the whole Treaty; that what had already been conceded excited his wonder, for when I arrived at Yedo he did [not] dream that I could use any arguments that would secure so much. He said better secure what you have obtained than risk it for the attainment of what is [of] but little or no value even if you do get it. He said that, if we would be patient and let the present Treaty work its work quietly among the people, he had no doubt the two disputed points would be granted without difficulty by the time named for the opening of Yedo; that the two points were not refused by the Government, but merely postponed to await a favorable period for carrying them into effect. He closed by saying that he was very unhappy and implored me to consider the wisdom of following his advice. I gave him to understand that, if all the other parts of the Treaty were arranged to my satisfaction, I would try to suit them on the two points.

Meet at eleven A. M. A long debate on the seventh Article. At last I offer to withdraw the objectionable clause provided they would open Osaca as a place for the permanent residence of Americans.

I also offered to limit the boundaries at Osaca in the direction of Kyoto to two ri (five miles). The Commissioners inform me that my request to have a salute fired in honor of the birth of Washington had been acceded to, and that I would be conducted to the battery on the twenty-second instant, when a salute of twenty-one guns should be fired.[602]

They added that Commodore Perry had made them a

602See note 377.

present of a brass howitzer gun; that they had made many after that model, and that the salute should be fired from their copies of the American gun.[603]

Meet again at two P. M. and take up the Articles seriatim. Three and four, accepted. Article V relates to the currency, and contained a clause giving the Japanese Government an agio of six per cent. on all foreign coin paid to them, and prohibited the exportation of Japanese coin. To my utter astonishment, they gave up the six per cent. and permitted the free exportation of their coin! and also declared that all foreign coins should pass freely in Japan. They *did* astonish me.

Article IV gives to the United States Government [the right] to land stores free of duty for the use of its fleet at Kanagawa, Hakodate and Nagasaki. By this I have secured the choice of three good harbors for our Naval Depot in the East, in a country that has the most salubrious climate in the world, where the men cannot desert, and with a power that is sufficiently civilized to respect our rights, and above all not a power with whom we might have a rupture, like England. I consider this

[603]This story of the Japanese making copies of the brass howitzer given them by Commodore Perry reminds us of one equally interesting. It is told by L. Adams Beck (*Unbroken Ways in South Japan,* in *Asia* for Apr., 1923, p. 272):

"Here too [at Shimonoseki] was the destiny of Japan again decided when the allied fleet of the United States, England, France and Holland in 1864 thrust the civilization of the West in the face of her repulsion. A relative of my own, still living, was present. . . . I stood by the swirling, dangerous currents of Shimonoseki and marvelled, remembering that to the hand of this man who still lives was given the first breech-loading Winchester rifle turned out by Japanese workmen, with the request, proudly made, that he would show it to the British Admiralty. He did this and adds: 'But I do not recall that any interest was taken in the circumstance.' Admiralties are not intuitive; one would think [that] that rifle might have interested them a little."

clause of immense importance, as now the depot can be removed from that wretched place Hongkong, and the stores out of the power of England. We finished our day's work with Article V, and adjourned until the sixth inst.

Saturday, February 6, 1858. We take up Article III. To my surprise they proposed to build a lazaretto outside the walls of Osaca for the use of any Americans that might suddenly be taken sick while on a visit to Osaca from Sak-kai,—and still excluded Americans from a residence in the city. I was indignant. On page 116 I have noted the terms on which I agreed to withdraw the two difficulties in the way of the Treaty, and it was fully understood *that* was the basis on which the matter was to be arranged.[604] I told them that their proposition was so very offensive that I would not consent to have it again interpreted to me. I taxed them roundly with bad faith, and gave them notice that I renewed the clause in the seventh Article (right to travel) and also the claim for Kyoto. The Commissioners stammered and boggled for some time, partially admitting that the proposal was none of their making, and that they would consult over it (*i. e.,* report its rejection at the Castle). They then proposed to take up the Articles of the Treaty. Article VI, agreed to. Article VII, postponed until Article III is settled. Articles VIII to XV inclusive, all agreed to with some slight verbal alterations not calling for any remark. Article XVI (The family name of the Tykoon is Minamote E-yea-Sada).[605] The Article provides for

[604]Page 116 was the page of the manuscript *Journal* immediately preceding the page bearing the present entry.

[605]Minamoto Iyesada, or Iyesata.

the exchange of ratifications, and they proposed, if I was willing, to send an ambassador in their steamer to Washington *via* California for that purpose! I told them nothing could possibly give me greater pleasure.

That, as the United States was the first power that Japan ever made a treaty with, I should be much pleased that the first Japanese Ambassador should be sent to the United States. The Article was accordingly altered and also amended so as to make the Treaty go into effect, if from any unforeseen accident the ratifications should not be exchanged by that time. The regulations of trade (except the tariff) were informally accepted. I gave them notice that I wished to introduce a clause giving the right to American ships to employ Japanese as seamen on board American ships, giving bonds to return the men to Japan within three years, except in cases of death or desertion. The Commissioners agree to meet me on Monday at eight A. M. and to work the whole day; adjourn at seven P. M.

Received a present of a very handsome round chow-chow box called by the Japanese *hogy*. It is of rich lacquer, with handsome plates of yellow chased metal, bound with a rich scarlet silk cord with heavy tassels. They carefully told me that none but *Daimyo* were allowed to use the *hogy*. It contained 260 eggs packed in black beans of a very small size.

Monday, February 8, 1858. Meet according to agreement at eight A. M. The Commissioners propose various Articles on the subject of Osaca, and at last the following is agreed on:

On the first of January 1863 the city of Yedo, and on the . . . day of . . . 18 . . . the city of Osaca shall be opened to Americans for residence and trade. The special place within which they may hire houses in each of these two cities, and the distance they may walk, shall be settled by the American Diplomatic Agent and the Government of Japan.

The Japanese showed me maps of Sak-kai and Osaca. Sak-kai contains 270 streets. Osaca contains 600 streets.

Sak-kai produces twenty-two articles, among which are metal works, silk stuffs, arms, rattan work, etc., etc.

I inform them I wish for both Sak-kai and Hio-n'go, —the latter for its good harbor, and the former from its proximity to Osaca. They positively refuse both places. I then claim Hio-n'go according to their original offer to me of either Hio-n'go or Sak-kai. They replied that offer was made by them in lieu of Osaca, and that I did not include Sak-kai or Hio-n'go in my original draft. After much debate, I tell them I will withdraw the claim, as they will be quite willing to open Hio-n'go by the time Osaca is opened. We at last fix the dates on which the various places shall be opened :

Kanagawa	July 4, 1859
Nagasaki	the same
Nee-e-gata	January 1, 1860
Yedo	January 1, 1862
Sak-kai	January 1, 1863
Osaca	January 1, 1863

Adjourned at one P. M. for their dinner, and meet again at two P. M. The whole of this P. M. was spent in a vain attempt to fix the boundaries of the various places. They were so unreasonable and so inconsistent that I could not help suspecting the champagne which I sent to them had not operated favorably. Adjourned at five P. M. to meet to-morrow at eight A. M.

Tuesday, February 9, 1858. Meet at nine A. M. Take up Articles regulating trade. In the Treaty with the Russians, the regulations were imperfect and oppressive.

Fines of the most outrageous character were imposed, and ship and cargo both were confiscated for light offences, and the innocent were thus punished for offences in which they neither participated, nor had any knowledge of, or power of preventing.[606] I pointed out the injustice of such laws to the Commissioners, and they admitted the force of my objections. They said they were entirely in the dark on the subject, not having any experience to guide them.

They said I had evidently taken much pains in drawing up the code now before them; that they thanked me for my kindness, and, as they had perfect confidence in my integrity, they would accept them.[607]

---

[606]Compare the Supplementary Treaty with Russia, signed at Nagasaki, Oct. 12/24, 1857, Art. IV, XIV, XXI (Gubbins, *op. cit.*, pp. 239–45).

[607]There is corroborative evidence in Mr. Heusken's *Diary,* though the date of his entry is February 2nd—exactly a week earlier than this of Townsend Harris's. The weight of evidence favors the date given by Townsend Harris. Mr. Heusken's *Diary* reads (Wagener, *Aus dem Tagebuche,* etc., p. 386, note 1—one of the three passages which Wagener cites in the original French employed by Heusken):

"Aujourd'hui les commissaires disent que, comme M. Harris leur assure que les regulations du commerce ont été proposées dans le seul but d'assurer le revenu du Japon, et qu'ils sont sur les bases de celui d'Amérique et d'Angleterre, ils acceptent aveuglément."

For information on Mr. Heusken's *Diary,* see note 349.

They then examined the figures of some fines that had been changed at their request from kobangs to dollars, and found them all right. I now took up the tariff.

I began by stating the objections to all tonnage dues, and showed that they only served to check commerce, were unequal in their operation, and injurious to revenue.

I then stated the objections to export duties, saying that it was a burden on the industry of their own people, was vexatious to the merchant, led to great expense to prevent smuggling, and was not of much benefit to the revenue. I then quoted the example of England and the United States, two of the greatest commercial nations in the world, neither of which levied tonnage dues or export duties. I closed by saying that commerce could bear a certain burden and no more, and, whether that was collected under one or three forms, only a certain tax could be paid; and concluded this branch by urging the simplicity and economy of collecting their revenue from imports alone. I then took up the tariff and explained the various classes and my reasons for making different rates of duties, etc., etc. They say the tariff is out of their province and must be submitted to the Chamber of Accounts They also inform me that the 14th instant is their New Year, and that they cannot meet me again before the 17th; that they usually take seven days for these holidays, but on account of my long detention here they will only take three.

It was agreed that clean copies of the Treaty should in the interim be drawn out and the amendments and alterations translated into Japanese. The Commissioners inform me that orders have been sent to Hakodate to allow women to American sailors at that port. Adjourn at half-past twelve o'clock.

Friday, February 12, 1858. The Prince of Shinano visited me to-day. He said they were all very busy in preparing their annual reports for the close of the year, but that he would pay me a short private visit.[608]

He soon afterwards introduced the boundaries of the opened places, and the right of consuls to travel in the country; and, from his frequent mention of the *Daimyo,* I am prepared to have difficulties with them on those subjects.

Saturday, February 13, 1858. Busy in writing. I find I have omitted any notice of the *loneen* since the 25th of January.

On that and the following night I was much annoyed by the noise kept up by the "grand rounds," who patrolled every half hour. As soon as the point of the residence of the Minister in Yedo was settled, the rounds and noise ceased. This adds to the belief always held by me that the whole matter was a mere "arrow-

---

[608]The Japanese authorities in general, and Shinano-no-Kami in particular, were very anxious for Townsend Harris's safety. Mr. Heusken tells us in his *Diary* that the Prince of Shinano called in the afternoon, and that his chief purpose was to beg Harris and Heusken not to go out on the streets on February 14th—the Japanese New Year's Day (Wagener, *op. cit.,* p. 386, note 2).

The excited state of men's minds over the pending negotiations and the rapidly approaching opening of the country, might easily, on such a festive day, have brought about precisely those disasters that shortly afterwards became so common—and only because these ordinary rules of precaution were in many cases haughtily disregarded. The early foreigners and diplomats who went to Japan had, unfortunately, been brought up in the far different atmosphere of Canton and the other treaty ports of China. (See *Journal,* Jan. 25, 1858, and note 592.)

smith," got up to frighten me and, failing of its purpose, it was then abandoned.[609]

Sunday, February 14, 1858. Japanese New Year's Day. The houses here are dressed up precisely in the same manner as described in my *Journal* for January 1, 1857, at Shimoda. The streets are filled with the long trains of the *Daimyo* and nobles going to the Castle to pay their compliments and carry presents.

This reminds me of the New Year's festivities in New York.[610]

Monday, February 15, 1858. The Tykoon sends presents of boiled cakes on New Year's Day to all those he wishes to honor, but, hearing I did not eat those cakes, he sent me a large basket of oranges from Kyushu. The present came yesterday, but I declined receiving it on that day—it being Sunday—and I was glad of an opportunity of showing the Japanese that not even for the Tykoon would I alter my strict rule for that day.[611] I receive presents of fans from Higo-no-Kami and others.

Shrove Tuesday, February 16, 1858. A snowstorm to-day which fell some eight inches. The sight reminded me of home and dear old New York.[612] The Prince of

609This delusion persisted in Townsend Harris's mind; but, considering the fact that he did not, and could not, know what was going on behind the "mirror" and the "fan," the delusion itself was natural enough. On the present occasion it was further strengthened by the unfortunate coincidence with the discussion on the residence of the American Minister in Yedo.

610Heusken, in his *Diary* (Wagener, *op. cit.*, p. 386), tells us that Iwase Higo-no-Kami, one of the two Treaty Commissioners, on this day brought Townsend Harris several fans as New Year presents. (See entry for February 15, 1858.)

611See note 409.

612Townsend Harris would have been cheered in the midst of these arduous negotiations had he known that in far-off Washington he was the subject of daily conversation. On Wednesday, Feb. 10, 1858, President Buchanan had

Shinano sends me word he will meet me to-morrow at noon. P. S. (18th) I was in error as to the quantity of snow,—nearly twelve inches fell on the 16th instead of eight inches.

Ash Wednesday, February 17, 1858. The Commissioners, instead of meeting me at noon, as they had appointed, did not arrive until near five P. M. They commenced by giving a history of my negotiations from the day of my audience up to the ninth inst., repeating many parts three or four times and constantly referring to the *Daimyo* and their opposition to any change in the ancient customs of the land, by permitting the residence of foreigners in Japan, etc., etc. This lasted for more than an hour, without their giving me any information as to what they desired. I plainly saw that there was a hitch somewhere. They then proceeded to say that on the eleventh inst. the Treaty, as it then stood, had been submitted to the *Daimyo* and instantly the whole Castle was in an uproar

Some of the most violent declared that they would sacrifice their lives before they would permit such great changes to be made. The Council of State had labored incessantly to enlighten these men; had pointed out to them not only the policy, but necessity there was to make the Treaty if they would avert the ruin of the Kingdom, etc. They had brought over some, but others still remained obstinate; that the Government could not at once

transmitted to the Senate the Convention signed by Townsend Harris at Shimoda, June 17, 1857. The President's Message (undated) was received and referred to the Committee on Foreign Relations. This Committee, on Feb. 16th, reported the Convention, without amendment (S. Ex. J'l, vol. 10, pp. 303, 304, 307).

sign such a treaty, except at the expense of bloodshed; that they were sure the President did not wish to bring any such evil on Japan, etc., etc.[613]

I at last discovered that they wished to delay the signing of the Treaty until a member of the Council of State could proceed as "Ambassador to the Spiritual Emperor" at Kyoto and get his approval;[614] that the

[613]For some Japanese material on the confusion caused among the *Daimyo* by the proposed opening of the country to the Westerners, read the extracts from the *Bakumatsu Gwaikodan* given in Gubbins, *The Progress of Japan*, pp. 289–91. And Heusken, under date of February 12, 1858 (*Diary*, in Wagener, *op. cit.*, p. 386, note 2) quotes the interpreter Moriyama on the wrath of the *Daimyo:*

"Moriyama ne pense pas qu'il y aura plus de difficultés sur les régulations. 'Pour l'argent,' dit-til, 'il n'y a pas de difficultés. Les Daimios ne regardent pas l'argent, les taxes et les douanes; ils ne disent rien du tout. Nous ne comprenons rien au commerce, et vous qui nous assurez sur votre honneur que les régulations sont pour le bien du Japon, nous devons vous croire. Mais pour les grandes concessions du traité, voilà des choses où le danger est avec les Daimios.' "

[614]Gubbins, *op. cit.*, pp. 71–72:

"There was no necessity for this reference. The supremacy of the Shogun in all administrative matters is clearly laid down in the constitution, or arrangement, established in 1615. Long custom had confirmed the rule then made. And before that date the Crown's concern in such matters had never extended beyond a formal recognition of accomplished facts. Moreover, the Treaty had not yet been signed, so reference to Kioto was in any case premature. But on the occasion of Perry's first visit the Shogunate, in order to conceal its embarrassment, had revived the obsolete formality of Imperial concurrence, extending at the same time its application. The same course was pursued now, and the minister who had taken the most prominent part in the negotiations, Hotta Bitchiu-no-Kami, was sent to Kioto to obtain the imperial consent. Hayashi Daigaku-no-Kami had been sent a month previously to explain matters, but the Court had signified its disapproval of the negotiations."

Leaving Yedo on January 25th, Hayashi had arrived in Kyoto on Feb. 5, 1858, accompanied by the censor Tsuda Hanzaburo as Deputy Delegate (Payson J. Treat, *The Early Diplomatic Relations between the United States and Japan, 1853–1865*, Baltimore, The Johns Hopkins Press, 1917, p. 98; and *Japan and the United States, 1853–1921*, Boston and New York, Houghton Mifflin Company, 1921, p. 39; Murdoch, *A History of Japan*, vol. 3, pp. 646–47).

Hayashi's task was to convince the Emperor's Court of the necessity of conforming to the changing spirit of the times and to gain the Emperor's consent to the Treaty. Though a memorial had been presented to the Imperial

moment that approval was received the *Daimyo* must withdraw their opposition; that they were content to take the Treaty substantially as it stood, having only some slight verbal alterations to suggest, and solemnly pledged their faith that the Treaty should be executed as soon as the Ambassador returned from Miako, which would require about two months. Having concluded this extraordinary conversation, I asked them what they would do if the Mikado refused his assent. They replied in a prompt and decided manner, that the Government had *determined not to receive any objections from the Mikado*. I asked what is the use then of delaying the Treaty for what appears to be a mere ceremony. They replied that it was this solemn ceremony that gave value to it; and, as I understood, it being known that the Mikado [had been] thus gravely appealed to, his decision would be final, and that all excitement would subside at once.

Cabinet at Kyoto in the 12th month of the 4th year of Ansei (Jan. 14 to Feb. 12, 1858), the exclusion (or Mito) party at the capital had had such great influence that no answer was given even as late as the first month of the following (or 5th) year of Ansei (Feb. 13 to Mar. 13, 1858). He was so confident of success that he told the *Daimyo* of Echizen that ten days in Kyoto would be ample time for the accomplishment of his purpose. He set out on Mar. 6th, reached the Emperor's capital on Mar. 19th, and was back again in Yedo on June 1st—"a very chastened and humbled man." (Murdoch, *op. cit.*, pp. 648–49, 652.)

When this first failure had been reported to Yedo, Premier Lord Hotta himself was sent to Kyoto. As H. Satoh says (*Agitated Japan,* Tokio and New York, D. Appleton & Co., 1896, p. 59):

"Pressed on one side by Mr. Harris, the American representative, and urged on the other side by his anxiety for his country, Baron Hotta now went in person to the Imperial Capital. There he did his best in explaining the impossibility of adhering to the old tradition, but the influence of the opposing party in Kyoto was too great. The result was that he received instructions to consult further with the princes of the Tokugawa Family and with the Barons of the land, before again submitting the question to the Imperial Cabinet."

They proposed that we should go on with the Treaty until it was completed and engrossed.

That I could amuse myself by going about, and, if I wished to make a trip to Shimoda, the Government would send me down and bring me back in their steamer. In answer I said that what they had told me was unprecedented in the history of negotiations; that it was much like the acts of children and unworthy of wise statesmen like those who rule Japan; and that it was a trifling with a serious matter, that would be sure to give the President great concern; and that it would have been far better not to have negotiated with me at all, than to refuse to sign a treaty which had cost so much labor, for so very trifling a reason, etc., etc. I added that the mere *act* of signing the Treaty might be kept as secret as they chose, as I should not divulge it in Japan. They replied that it was impossible to keep anything secret that passed between us (and I have no doubt they spoke truly); that they were acting in good faith, and I might rely that the Treaty should be executed. I finally told them I had no power to compel them to execute the Treaty; that I could not then give them an answer to their proposition, but I proposed to put that matter aside for the present and proceed to complete the Treaty, but they must clearly understand that I did not agree to accept the delay asked for. This was agreed to, and they opened the Treaty with the first Article, over which they wasted time (and with an evident intent to do so) until eight o'clock, when they said they were weary and begged to adjourn until day after to-morrow,—Friday, 19th. Their plan evidently is to spin out the time, until I either assent to their wish or the Ambassador has returned from Kyoto. I have before noted that they had agreed to fire a salute on Washington's Birthday. They now informed me the salute would be fired between Sinagawa and Kawasaki, some eight miles from my residence, adding that was the nearest place where cannon could be fired. In answer I said I could not go so far as that; that if they had any objections to firing the salute, I would withdraw my request; that a salute under such circumstances would be anything but an honor; that I had heard howitzers fired every week since I had been in Yedo; that I was so accustomed to such sounds that I could very well judge of the distance; and that the firing had frequently been within sixteen streets of my residence (one mile). They said that must have been the guns of the *Daimyo*. They then said they could themselves fire the salute. I replied they, of course, could fire when they pleased, but I should not consider it as being fired in honor of the day. They then proposed that Mr. Heusken should ride to the place. I answered that he was not the representative of the United States. They said the discount of six per cent. was to be paid by me until the new Treaty went into effect.

Thursday, February 18, 1858.   I have made no entries in my *Journal* of my having gone out of my house for any purpose, except on official business, since December 17, 1857. In fact I have not gone out of the enclosure of the premises but once since that date, and that was on the occasion of my visit to the Minister of Foreign Affairs on the 16th of last month.

My reasons for this seclusion have been twofold. I have frequently referred to the fact that the Japanese connect the idea of seclusion with high rank, and that the one is the measure of the other. The Government had proclaimed me to be, from my official position, a person of *exalted* rank, as they termed it, and caused all the ceremonies of my journey from Shimoda here to correspond with that idea. I felt that my influence with this singular people greatly depended on my maintaining that opinion. I also knew that a large majority of the *Daimyo* were violently opposed to the object of my mission, and that some were exceedingly violent. I apprehended that, were I to go out frequently for recreation, I should meet the trains of some of these persons, and that difficulties might arise from their claiming from me some acknowledgment of their rank that I might not be willing to concede. Or, that from my ignorance of their complicated etiquette, I might unwittingly give umbrage that might create much angry feeling among this class, who from an *esprit de corps* would embrace the cause of their brother *Daimyo,* whom they might suppose I had wantonly insulted, thereby creating difficulties to the object of my mission, give power to the opposition, and embarrass the Government of Japan.[615] I

---

[615]This common sense and broad-minded policy of Townsend Harris evinced a world of sympathetic understanding of the tremendous difficulties which beset the Government of Japan. And, as all students of Japanese history know, it was precisely the non-observance of these simple rules by the newly arrived Westerners that resulted in many of the murders mentioned above, among the most famous of which were those of Richardson, Lieutenant Bird, and

have taken exercise by walking some miles every day in the court on which my rooms open.

I walk from three to eight miles *per diem,* yet my health has sensibly suffered and I am become exceedingly thin. I also feel the want of food properly prepared, as my Japanese cook is extremely deficient in many points.

The Prince of Shinano visited me to-day, and we had a long talk over my business. He says that I may rely that the Government is acting in good faith and is anxious to make a treaty with me; that the mission to Miako will be successful in obtaining the assent of the Mikado;[616] and that when that assent is promulgated the opposition [of] the *Daimyo* will instantly cease. The Prince informed me that of the 18 Great *Daimyo* 4 were in favor, and 14 opposed to the Treaty; that of the 300 *Daimyo* created by Iyeyasu, 30 out of every 100 were in favor, and the remainder opposed; that the Government was constantly working on these men and, when they could get them to listen, they frequently convinced them, but many—like the obstinate of more enlightened countries—refused to listen to a word of reason, argument or explanation. This last class will only yield to the opinion of the Mikado when it shall be promulgated.

I made the following suggestion to Shinano. Let us

Major Baldwin (see note 592). It was the same lack of understanding and sympathy that at a later crisis made the foreign representatives (Sir Rutherford Alcock and Duchesne de Bellecourt) abandon Yedo for Yokohama (Kanawaga), while Townsend Harris, true to his principles and steadfast in his faith in the Japanese, remained alone in Yedo—literally and splendidly alone.

[616] As we have already seen, even Hotta's mission was not successful in obtaining the consent of the Emperor to the Treaty.

proceed and complete the Treaty as soon as possible and have it engrossed and ready for signature. Then, let the Council of State, or the Minister for Foreign Affairs, write me a letter saying that the Commissioners appointed to negotiate with me a commercial treaty between the United States and Japan had completed their labors, and that the Treaty was now ready for signature, but, for certain important reasons, the signing of the Treaty must be postponed for sixty days, on or before the expiration of which time the Treaty, as it now stood, should be signed.

Thereupon I would return to Shimoda to prepare my dispatches for my Government; that at the end of fifty days (if not before) the Government should send their steamer to Shimoda for the purpose of bringing me again to Yedo, for the purpose of executing the Treaty. The Prince was much pleased with the idea, and told me he would communicate it to the Government at once and speak to me about it to-morrow. I do not see what I can do better under the peculiar circumstances in which I am placed. If I can get the written promise of the Government, that *the* Treaty (not *a* treaty) shall be signed by a certain day, I do not see but it is as binding on them as the signature of the Commissioners to the Treaty itself.

Friday, February 19, 1858. Toke, Prince of Tamba, sent me a beautiful present of a plum tree in full bloom, having more than one thousand blossoms! The stock is four [inches] in diameter at the bottom, and eighteen inches high. Nearly thirty grafts have been inserted in the stock, and these have grown up some twenty-four to thirty inches high, and branching out give more than fifty sprays. Not a green leaf is visible, but all the sprays are covered from end to end with fragrant white blossoms.

At two P. M. the Prince of Shinano visited me and brought a beautiful China pot of bulbs of the daffodil family, in bloom. The Japanese name is "Happy Longevity," and is a favorite New Year's gift. He tells me that their laws regarding [mourning] have been greatly modified during the last two hundred years. Formerly, an officer, on the death of his father, resigned his employments and lived retired for three years. Now he does not resign, and mourns for fifty days full mourning, that is, does not attend to any business or shave his head or beard during that time. After the fifty days are expired, he resumes his duties and shaves, etc., but for one year he must not attend any festivities.

The *Daimyo* who have sovereign rule in their dominions are seven or eight, of the original eighteen of that rank. The Prince of Ca-ga (or Kaga) has the largest principality and is the most powerful and wealthy of any of his class. Not even the Tykoon may send a person into the dominions of these *Daimyo* without their consent "first had and obtained." The Japanese pretend that any officer of the Imperial Government intruding without such leave would instantly be put to death.

Did not meet the Commissioners until nearly five P. M. They informed me that the proposition I made to Shinano-no-Kami yesterday was accepted by the Government; and that the letter pledging the faith of the Government that the Treaty should be executed within sixty days from this date would be signed by Hotta, Prince of Bittsu, Minister for Foreign Affairs; and that the steamer should be sent to Shimoda ten days before that time to bring me to Yedo.[617]

---

[617]Fortunately there are extant both versions of this historic letter: first, an original copy made by Heusken of the Dutch version sent by Hotta (*L. & P.*, vol. 1, no. 81); and second, an original copy (also made by Heusken) of the English translation thereof (*L. & P.*, vol. 1, no. 82).
This letter is so important that it merits being reproduced in full:

"To His Excellency Townsent [sic] Harris, Plenipotentiary and Consul General of the United States of America, etc., etc., etc.

"The negotiations between you and the Commissioners of the Treaty of the United States and of Japan is ended, and this Treaty is completed and made ready to be signed. But from a very important cause, an embassy from His Majesty the Tycoon will be sent to Kyoto to present it respectfully to the consideration of His Majesty the Spiritual Emperor; thus it is impossible to sign the Treaty until the return of the Embassy, wherefore a time of two months will be required, on or before which time the Treaty shall be signed.

"Represented with respect.

"The 5th day of the first month of the fifth year of Ansei.

(signed) HOTTA BITSUNOCAMI.

"For Dutch translation: (signed) MORIYAMA TAKITSIRO.

"A true translation: H. C. J. HEUSKEN."

The Japanese date is equivalent to Feb. 18, 1858. Townsend Harris endorsed the letter in his own hand: "Letter from Minister of Foreign Affairs. Yedo, Feb. 18, 1858. Concerning the postponing of signing the Treaty."
There is a certain amount of confusion in these dates. The substance of this (then only proposed) letter was first outlined by the Japanese Commissioners on Ash Wednesday, Feb. 17th. On the 18th, Townsend Harris agreed with the Prince of Shinano that such a letter be written by the Minister of Foreign Affairs, and he suggested its contents pretty definitely. On Feb. 19th, at 5 P. M., the Commissioners informed Townsend Harris that his proposal of the preceding day had been accepted by the Government, and that the letter pledging the faith of the Government would be signed by Prince Hotta. This letter is again referred to on Feb. 22nd. Just when Townsend Harris received this letter, however, is not certain. We sadly miss the item "Received" (with the date) which he so frequently put into the endorsements of his letters.
Prince Hotta left for Kyoto some time after Feb. 18 (the date of this letter), arriving at the Emperor's Capital on Mar. 19th. On Mar. 4th, Townsend Harris wrote to General Cass, Secretary of State, stating that he had received Hotta's letter, and enclosing for the Department of State a Dutch original

We then took up the Treaty for final consideration, and after much consideration the Preamble was accepted. A long debate arose on the right of "All diplomatic and consular [officers] shall have the right to travel freely in any part of the Empire of Japan."[618] After much time wasted over it, I offered to strike out the whole clause, and leave those officers to claim their rights under the laws of nations. This they also objected to, wishing to restrain Consuls to their consular districts, which I as strongly refused to do, or to insert any clause which might deprive them of a right they could claim under the laws of nations. I had at one time serious doubts that the whole Treaty might be wrecked on this point. They went over the old ground of objections: the claims of the *Daimyo* to exclusive jurisdiction in their own principalities; their furious objections to any infringement of their ancient rights; and the certainty that serious difficulties would arise from the clause. At last they said that they would consent to insert [that] the Minister and Consul General should have that right,

and an English translation thereof—in other words, *L. & P.*, vol. 1, nos. 81 and 82, referred to above.

The contents of Hotta's letter run closely along the lines suggested by Townsend Harris on Feb. 18th, and it is therefore difficult to believe that this letter was written, in its present form at least, before the 18th. We are inclined to believe that the following was the sequence of events: first, that a version of this letter already existed in written form on Feb. 18th, when the Japanese Commissioners first hinted at the possibility of referring the matter to Kyoto; that it then received slight modifications, in order to harmonize with the suggestions made by Townsend Harris on the 18th; that the original date (Feb. 18th) was left untouched; and that Townsend Harris received the letter before Mar. 4, 1858, the date of his Dispatch No. 6 to General L. Cass, Secretary of State. Indeed, if we may trust implicitly a statement made by Mr. Heusken in his *Diary*, this letter was given to Townsend Harris by Shinano-no-Kami on the evening of Mar. 2, 1858 (see *Journal*, Feb. 27, 1858, and note 628).

[618]Art. I of the Treaty.

but to exclude other Consuls. I at last consented to accept their proposition, but not to insert the words "other consular officers." At last they accepted it after a struggle to get the insertion of a clause requiring the Minister and Consul General to give notice to the Government of their intention to travel etc., etc., and also to strike out the word "freely" from the connection "may freely travel in any part," etc. Both propositions were rejected by me, and finally the clause was accepted as above amended. The counterpart for "Japanese Diplomatic Agent, etc., in the United States" was made to correspond with the grant to us. The whole Article was now finally accepted. Article second: after an attempt to strike out the word "request" from the first paragraph,— "The President of the United States will at the request of the Japanese Government act as a friendly mediator," on inquiry I found they had translated the Dutch word *verzoek,* "to beg." After an explanation of the true meaning of "request," they consented to take the clause as it stands in the original draft.

The Commissioners now wished to adjourn, promising to meet me at noon to-morrow. I am told that formerly, on the death of one of the *Daimyo,* numbers of his domestics or officers performed the *hara-kiri,—i. e.,* ripping themselves up, but that custom has been abolished.

Earthquake at 11 :30 P. M.

Saturday, February 20, 1856. Snow this morning. I am told the Prince of Ca-ga "goes on" like a lunatic about the Treaty. He says [that], while the Tykoon governs by the ancient laws, he will be his subject, but, when

548

he departs from them, his allegiance ceases. (I do not by any means place full faith in what the Japanese tell me about these matters. I know enough of them to be aware that to lie is the rule; to tell the truth is the exception.)

I am told the Tykoon is in favor of the Treaty, saying that he is convinced it is for the good of the country. The smaller *Daimyo* dare not openly oppose the Government, but they shield themselves under the opinions of the greater *Daimyo*. They say that two papers will be presented to the Mikado, one in favor of the proposed Treaty, and the other against it; that after examining both, he will approve of one, and that approval is binding on all; that even those most violently opposed to the Treaty will say (if he decides in favor of the Tykoon), "God has spoken; I submit." This does not agree very well with the almost contemptuous manner in which the Japanese speak of this potentate.

I am told that large sums of money have already [been] distributed among the officers of the Mikado, and that still larger sums will be applied in the same manner.[619]

Meet the Commissioners at two P. M. and continue until seven. A very discouraging meeting, the whole time was passed in noting down their proposed amendments to the first eight Articles. Many of these are absurd,

---

[619]By comparing this entry with Heusken's *Diary* (Wagener, *op. cit.*, pp. 387–88), we are sure that the source of all this gossipy news was Moriyama, who paid Townsend Harris a morning visit. In addition to what the *Journal* says, there was also a discussion on the relative command of the Dutch language held by Moriyama and Heusken. (See also *Journal* for Feb. 21st.)

others childish, and some fatal to the working of the Treaty.

Sunday, February 21, 1856 [1858]. The first Sunday in Lent, and a lovely day. I am quite disheartened and low spirited about the Treaty. I greatly fear that I shall altogether fail in making a treaty that will be acceptable to the President.

To add to my difficulties, their Dutch interpreter is very imperfectly acquainted with the *idioms* of that language, [while] his self-sufficiency is in the exact ratio of his ignorance. The Japanese language does not possess either singular or plural, has no relative pronoun, nor is the use of the antecedent known. Neither has it any possessive case. These defects require the constant repetition of nouns and verbs, and at all times make the meaning vague and obscure. I never shall get to the bottom of the deceptions of the Japanese. I now learn that the "three brothers of the Tykoon" are merely titular brothers. They are of the family, but the removes by birth carry them beyond the list of parentage as known by us. They are the Princes of Owaru, of Izu (or Izeu), and of Mitu. These men are called the "first brothers" of the Tykoon, and he also has three "second brothers," who are also merely titular relations.[620]

---

[620]The reference is to Go-Sanké, the three Tokugawa houses descended from three sons of Iyeyasu, and from which a successor to the Shogun had to be chosen in the event of failure of issue in the direct line. The three houses were: the Owari, descended from the sixth son of Iyeyasu; the Kii (or Kishu), descended from the seventh son; and the Mito, descended from the eighth son.

The three "second brothers" constituted the Go-Sankyo—three branch houses that were added to the Go-Sanké, and from which an heir to the Shogunate had to be chosen in case no suitable heir was furnished by the Go-Sanké. These three houses were: the Tayasu, the Hitotsubashi, and the Shimizu.

550

Monday, February 22, 1858. Meet at nine A.M. Only Shinano-no-Kami present. I note the proposed amendments to the Treaty offered by him, but do not enter into any discussions about the merits of them.

They are of various classes. Some are absurd, others mischievous, and not one that is of the least benefit to Japan by adding to her security or honor. The insertion of some would make obscure what is now clear, and many would excite laughter. The tone of all the amendments is unfriendly, and haughty, and calculated to make the Treaty unacceptable.

They have not as yet decided on the tariff, consequently the subject of tonnage dues, import and export duties, and fines was all passed over, they promising an answer to those points on the 24th. The next meeting is to be to-morrow at two P. M. when both Commissioners are to be present. They promise to give me an amended copy of the letter which is to be written to me by Hotta, Prince of Bittsu, after the negotiations are closed.

Tuesday, February 23, 1858. Met both the Commissioners at one P. M.

I opened the discussions by saying that I had carefully considered all their proposed amendments. Some were a mere change of words, others rendered the meaning obscure, many will open the door for disputes and difficulties; that the change of a word in one Article sometimes required the alteration of many Articles, as all must agree; that many of the amendments showed a

(David Murray, *The Story of Japan*, p. 277; Captain F. Brinkley, *A History of the Japanese People*, The Encycl. Brit. Co., 1915, New York and London, pp. 591–92.)

very unfriendly spirit, and that the insertion of what they proposed would cause the Treaty to be rejected. I closed by saying that such amendments as were reasonable or necessary should be adopted.

We then took Article VII, concerning the limits of the various ports, and to my agreeable surprise they accepted my proposal for Hakodate and Nagasaki. They now give me Hio-n'go for Sak-kai, and the boundaries are arranged. Nee-e-gata is postponed until it is determined whether that port, or another on the west coast of Nippon, shall be accepted; and, lastly, we settled on the Nagasaki boundaries. The Treaty must be referred to for the particulars.

We then took up their proposals in the order in which they relate to the Articles and rapidly disposed of them, so that at five P. M. the Treaty was agreed on. The regulations were then taken up. They accepted the penalties, and agreed that tonnage duties should not be levied, but they gave me notice that they should levy export and import duties. I then informed them that the levying of export duties would require an alteration of Article X and the striking out of Article XI of the Treaty. Which they assented to.

They informed me that the report on the tariff and export duties could not be ready before the 25th inst., —on the morning of which day they would hand me the tariff as they propose it, and meet me at one P. M. Thus closes this *Journal* with an account of the most satisfactory day's business I ever had with them. They seemed to be in earnest and acted promptly and reasonably.[621] Two of the three theatres of Yedo were burned last night (say rather one A. M.). They stood very near to each other. A number of tea houses and private dwellings were also destroyed. The Japanese name for theater is *seebyya*.

Wednesday, February 24, 1858. (At the City of Yedo, Japan.) Do not meet the Plenipotentiaries today. Memo. obtained from Keekoona.[622] The titular brothers of the Tykoon are called,—say:

The first three are named Go-san-kio.

'I'he second three are named Go-san-kee.[623]

The whole number of *Daimyo* or nobles of first rank is 360.

The second rank, including the Kami, [are] called *Shomyo* and number 8,000. All the families of these two classes reside constantly in Yedo, and are never allowed to leave it. The retainers of the eighteen Great *Daimyo,* which are with them at Yedo, will average over 10,000. The average number of retainers of the second class, or *Shomyo,* will average 200 each.

[621]It is not clear just what Townsend Harris meant by the words "Thus closes this *Journal*." This statement appears on the cover-leaf of the manuscript volume used by Townsend Harris, which page he numbered 140. It is clear that he had run beyond the capacity of the blank-book. The words may have been intended to mean, "Thus closes this volume of my *Journal*," which would agree perfectly with the fact that Townsend Harris actually labelled his volumes, "Journal No. 1," "Journal No. 2," etc.

Unfortunately, the *Journal* as a whole practically does end at this point. The rest of the entry for Feb. 23rd seems to have been an afterthought, and was added at the foot of that same page 140. The strange thing is that the entries for Feb. 24th, 25th, and 27th are written on loose sheets of paper (numbered 141 to 144, inclusive), of precisely the same quality, size, etc. (though unruled) as the preceding pages. Townsend Harris, therefore, must have owned an additional blank-book of the same format from which he tore the additional sheets.

[622]For Kikuna, see *Journal*, Nov. 23, 1857.

[623]See note 620. Townsend Harris has inverted the order of seniority of the two groups.

This would give for Yedo a population of these two classes alone of:

Daimyo—   18 at 10,000 each is   180,000
Daimyo— 342 "   2,000 " "   684,000
Shomyo—8,000 "   200 " " 1,600,000
                                2,464,000[624]

Thursday, February 25, 1858. The Commissioners sent me their proposition for duties. With the exception of a few articles, they propose an import duty of twelve and a half per cent., and an export duty of the same amount on all articles exported, whether of Japanese or foreign production. Such an export duty would crush anything like prosperous trade.

[624]On this day of comparative leisure Townsend Harris wrote a long letter to Sir John Bowring, Governor of Hongkong (*L. B.,* vol. 3, pp. 90–96). In this letter (marked "strictly confidential"), Townsend Harris repeats the substance of this entry of the *Journal,* and describes in great detail the difficulties which attended his negotiations. The most interesting part of this letter, however, is the skillful way in which Townsend Harris quoted to the Japanese a passage from one of Sir John's own letters, written Mar. 18, 1857 (*L. & P.,* vol. 1, no. 58). Townsend Harris says that he had taken the liberty of reading to the Japanese the following extract (*L. B.,* vol. 3, pp. 90–91):

"Japan, of course, occupies much of my thoughts; and, if I had reason to know that I should have a becoming reception and a disposition to give me such a treaty as I could accept with propriety, and which would satisfy the reasonable expectations of my country and of the world at large, I have no desire to be accompanied by so great a fleet as to cause alarms and apprehensions; but, at the same time, you must be aware that commercial relations must be put on very different foundations from the present, and that it is altogether for the peace, prosperity and permanent interests of Japan to satisfy reasonable demands."

Townsend Harris passes his own comment on his reading of this extract:

"This extract forcibly supported one of the lines of argument I had adopted, and the reading of it produced a marked sensation; they eagerly asked me if the letter was signed by you. I answered that it was not only signed, but the whole letter was written by you."

The mention of great fleets, alarms and apprehensions must have aroused recollections (by no means vague in Japanese minds) of the "black ships" of Commodore Perry in 1853 and 1854, and of the opium war in China in 1842.

Met the Commissioners at two P. M. Stated my objections to their tariff. I have been anxious not to have any export duties, but I am forced to abandon the idea. We at last agreed on an export duty of five per cent. on all articles of Japanese production *exported as cargo.* The import duty is to be five per cent. on all articles required for ships, whalers, etc., etc., and some other articles, including living animals of all kinds, bread and breadstuffs, and salted provisions, etc.

Intoxicating drinks of all kinds, thirty-five per cent.

All other articles (except as below), twenty per cent.

Gold and silver, coined or uncoined, with the clothing, books, furniture, etc., of persons who come to reside in Japan,—duty free.

The duties are to be subject to revision, if the Japanese desire it, five years after Kanagawa has been opened.

I informed them that Ministers, Consuls General, etc., did not pay duty on any articles for their own use. They agree to write to the Governor of Hakodate to act with Mr. Rice in selecting the place where Americans shall erect their buildings, etc., at that place; also, that Mr. Rice is to be furnished with Japanese money. I gave them Mr. Rice's complaints about high prices at Hakodate, and they promise to inquire into it.[625]

---

[625]These complaints were presented by Mr. Rice in his letter of Dec. 15, 1857 (*L. & P.*, vol. 1, no. 72). The letter was received by Townsend Harris at Yedo, Jan. 20, 1858, and answered Feb. 1, 1858 (*L. B.*, vol. 3, pp. 18 bis–22; and note 587).

On Feb. 26th, however, and chiefly because of the negotiations that had been going on during the intervening weeks, Townsend Harris wrote two more letters to Mr. Rice, going into the details of the agreements reached on each of his complaints, and quoting part of Art. III of the Treaty then being negotiated (*L. B.*, vol. 3, pp. 24–26, marked "Official"; and pp. 27–28, marked "Private").

They still wish me to write to my Government asking that a Minister shall not be sent to Japan before January 1, 1861. They gave me notice they should write me a letter requesting that copies of the Treaty should be transmitted to the English and Russians by the Secretary of State.

We made some slight verbal amendments and then agreed that a fair copy should be made for examination, prior to its being engrossed.[626]

They still stick to the six per cent. discount on money in my case,—rather small for a government that professes to have such a contempt for money.

Saturday, February 27, 1858. Last evening gave clean copy of Treaty to the Japanese. To-day the Commissioners send me word they will require until Tuesday next (March 2nd) to examine *with the Council of State* the final draft of the Treaty. If any doubt had existed in my mind that I was in reality negotiating with the Council, and that the Commissioners had no real full powers, this significant circumstance would remove it.

They tell me it will take the steamer two days to run from Kanagawa to Shimoda (not over seventy nautical miles). If this be true, it must be a very poor affair, and will hardly take their Ambassador to San Francisco.

Busy yesterday and to-day in writing letters. One

---

[626]The "fair copy" was given to the Japanese Commissioners the following day: see *Journal*, Feb. 27, 1858.

to Mr. Rice, one to Mr. Donker Curtius, and other private letters to my friends in America.[627]

Since the 16th inst., when the snow fell so deeply, the weather has been remarkably cold for the latitude of 36°. Until to-day, the thermometer has never risen above 33°, although the days have been generally fine. A fresh wind from N. W., bringing the frosty air from Kamchatka, has constantly blown.[628]

[627]As we have just seen, Townsend Harris wrote two letters to Mr. Rice on the 26th. This reference must be to the one marked "Official." The letter to Mr. Curtius is not extant. Of the private letters to his friends it will be remembered that Townsend Harris did not keep copies. It is hoped that readers of this work will be good enough to send to the writer all such material (or copies thereof) as they may possess, for use in future works on the diplomatic relations between the United States and Japan.

[628]Here ends the *Journal* of Townsend Harris considered as a continuous narrative. We are indebted to the scanty extracts published from the *Diary* of Heusken (Wagener, *op. cit.,* p. 388) for the sad information that on this very day, Feb. 27th, Townsend Harris fell sick. On Mar. 2nd Townsend Harris was so ill that he asked to be sent back to Shimoda by boat. In the evening he signed both copies of the Treaty, retaining one and giving the other to Shinano, who in his turn gave Townsend Harris a written statement to the effect that the Treaty would be signed by the Government in two months. (See note 617.) In spite of his illness, Townsend Harris wrote a very long report to Secretary of State Cass on Mar. 4, 1858 (*L. B.,* vol. 3, pp. 58–72), which closes thus:

"Not feeling well, I shall return to Shimoda in two or three days. The Japanese send me down in their steamer, which they are to send for me in April next, to bring me again to this place."

Coincidences sometimes are of great importance, and sometimes are mere coincidences. But we cannot resist the temptation to mention at this point the fact that, at almost the same moment, Commodore Perry died of rheumatism of the heart at his home in New York City, on March 5, 1858, at 2 A. M. (Griffis, *M. C. Perry,* Boston, Cupples & Hurd, 1887, p. 390.)

On arriving at Shimoda, Townsend Harris fell very ill—so ill that there was a perfect blank in his memory. The crisis came on Saturday, Mar. 13th (Heusken's *Diary,* in *op. cit.,* p. 388). On Mar. 28th he recovered sufficiently to *know* that he was sick (Townsend Harris to Nathaniel Dougherty, July 3, 1858, in Littell's *Living Age,* vol. 60, p. 570).

This long illness is more than sufficient to explain the breaking off of the *Journal* at this point. Neither could Mr. Heusken, his faithful secretary, spare any time from his devoted nursing. It is gratifying to know that, in the course of these long negotiations and in spite of diplomatic differences of opinion, the Japanese authorities had become quite attached to Townsend Harris personally. The Council of State wrote anxious letters; the Tycoon sent presents and wishes for a speedy recovery. Harris's own words, written to a friend on July 8, 1858, are particularly touching:

"Two days after my return to Shimoda, I was seized with a very dangerous nervous fever, which soon after showed symptoms of putrid fever, and I remained in a critical situation until the first of April last.

"His Majesty the Tycoon and the Council of State manifested a deep concern on hearing of my illness. Two of the best of the Imperial Physicians, who had been taught by the Dutch surgeons at Nagasaki, were sent at once from Yedo to this place.

"The Tycoon constantly sent me very kind messages, accompanied with presents of such things as he thought might aid my recovery. Daily bulletins were sent by the physicians to Yedo, and on the receipt at that place of a bulletin stating that my case was hopeless, the doctors received peremptory orders to cure me, and that, if I died, they would themselves be in peril.

"I mention these particulars to show the kindly disposition of the Japanese. Perhaps I might add that it proved that my three months' residence in Yedo had not made an unfavorable impression on the Japanese authorities."

What a world of eloquence in these simple words! To those who have read this *Journal* and who remember not merely the political but also the social isolation visited upon Townsend Harris during his first year in Japan, no comment is necessary.

Fragments[629]

Tuesday, May 15, 1858.[630] Interview with Higo and Shinano-No-Kami.[631] Higo has a message to me from

---

[629]These additional entries are written in pencil on both sides of a large piece of Japanese paper, 16½ inches by 10.

It is clear that such a very methodical man as Townsend Harris was, must have resumed keeping his *Journal* the moment his health permitted it. The stray sheet of paper containing these Fragments represents, first of all, the rough draft of Townsend Harris's *Journal*. There are many proofs in the body of the *Journal* that Townsend Harris did not write at once in the blank-books that are extant, but first made a rough draft on scrap paper of various kinds. Furthermore, this stray sheet is written very much in the nature of brief notes that were evidently meant to be written up more fully when finally transcribed (in ink) in the blank-books of his *Journal*.

Just how many of these sheets there were, and why they were not transcribed into blank-books is a mystery that we are not able to solve. Perhaps this is the only sheet of the rough copy that in some inexplicable way remained among Townsend Harris's *Japan Papers,* and perhaps the rest were duly transcribed. If so, what has become of the missing volumes of the *Journal?*

The last entry in the connected narrative is for Feb. 27, 1858; Townsend Harris did not leave Japan until May 8, 1862, more than four years later. We are morally certain that Townsend Harris kept a *Journal* for the whole of this time. During the years that elapsed before his departure from Japan, Townsend Harris witnessed the arrival of the representatives of Great Britain, France, Prussia, Russia, and The Netherlands. He witnessed, also, the influx of the business men of these nations. He witnessed the growth of divergent, nay, conflicting, diplomatic aims; of national and international rivalries; of suspicions and hatreds. During all these latter years, which contrasted so violently with the peace and isolation of his Shimoda days, Townsend Harris, as dean of the diplomatic corps in Japan, could and did exert a steadying influence; could, thanks to his long experience and to his maturer and sympathetic judgment, distinguish right from expediency. This play of intellect upon intellect is clearly shown in his correspondence, which from this period on becomes more and more voluminous. And it would have been a consummation devoutly to be desired had his *Journal* continued up to the end of his career in Japan.

Townsend Harris, the bachelor, lived the last years of his life away from friends, away from relatives, in an unassuming boarding house at 263 Fourth Avenue, New York City. When he died on Feb. 25, 1878, he must have been surrounded by his books and papers. He was buried on Feb. 28th. What happened to his belongings in those few days before and after his death? In

Hotta, Bittsu-no-Kami. The matters at Miako are more difficult than words can express. The throne of the Tykoon has existed in full power for 300 years. During that period only three embassies have been sent to Miako, and heretofore they have only remained ten days until this time. A conspiracy exists at Miako to murder Hotta, Bittsu-no-Kami; and placards threatening his death have been posted on the walls of Miako. The population of Miako and the adjacent districts are in a state of great excitement.

The Mikado said, "When you have got the consent of the *Daimyo,* I will give my consent."[632] The Tykoon and the Council still adhere to the Treaty. Agree to wait the action of Government for twelve days.

---

the general confusion, were the concluding volumes of the *Journal* misplaced? Were the loose sheets, perhaps, lost in the general, unthinking and hasty clearing-out process that so often follows such visitations? Let us hope that somewhere someone may yet discover these precious "lost books"—books that would throw such important light on the early history of friendly relations between the United States and the Empire of Japan—a history the shaping of which, providentially, lay so largely in the kindly hands of Townsend Harris!

[630]This date really fell on Saturday. The confusion is inexplicable.

[631]After his illness was over, and though still so weak that he had to be carried aboard the Japanese steamer that called for him, Townsend Harris returned to Yedo. His Treaty was still unsigned. On May 20th, he gave the Japanese a copy of a letter which he had written to China, asking that a warship come to Kanagawa (Heusken's *Diary,* in Wagener, *op. cit.,* p. 389).

[632]This was not all the Emperor had said. Akimoto (*Lord Ii Naosuké and New Japan,* 1909, p. 153) gives the substance as follows:

"The first question Lord Ii placed on the tapis was whether the Imperial message which Lord Hotta had brought back from Kyoto should be made public. Much opposition was offered on the ground that the step was premature. Lord Ii insisted that it should be [made public] and had his way. Copies of the message were then distributed among the clan lords. The purport of this message was that the signing of the commercial treaty with the United States being too serious an affair, the views of the clan lords and nobles in general should be consulted once more. If no decision could be arrived at even then, His Majesty would proceed to the Imperial shrines to invoke the aid of the gods."

Monday, June 7, 1858. Interview with Shinano and Higo. [They] ask delay of three months, as was to be expected from my interview with the Minister of Foreign Affairs on Saturday, 5th inst.[633]

Wednesday, 8 [1858].[634] [Their] propositions re: jected. I propose two months. Letter from Council and Tykoon. [I require] them not to sign any other treaty until thirty days after [the] American [Treaty] is signed.

Thursday, June 9, 1858.[635] [They] refuse to accept two months. [They] try hard to get rid of [the] thirty days required by me before they are to sign any other treaty. I adhere, and they give way, and I give up the month, so the Treaty is to be signed on the fourth of September, 1858.

---

[633]Hotta returned from Kyoto on either June 1st or 2nd, 1858. On June 4th or 5th, the Lord of Hikone—Ii Kamon-no-Kami—was appointed to the position of the highest responsibility in the Shogunate Government, namely, that of Tairo (Akimoto, *op. cit.*, pp. 149, 152; *cf.* Gubbins, *The Progress of Japan*, p. 107). Heusken tells us (*Diary*, in Wagener, *op. cit.*, p. 389) that Townsend Harris insisted that the Japanese sign the Treaty now, but date it three months later.

[634]The original is clearly so dated. The date should be either Tuesday, June 8, 1858, or Wednesday, June 9th.

[635]Again: the date should be either Wednesday, June 9th, or Thursday, June 10, 1858.

APPENDICES

APPENDIX I

PRESIDENT PIERCE'S LETTER TO THE FIRST KING OF SIAM

(*L. & P.*, vol. 2, no. 14)

FRANKLIN PIERCE,
President of the United States of America

TO HIS MAJESTY, THE MAGNIFICENT KING OF SIAM.

GREAT AND GOOD FRIEND:

Having long been aware of the extent of Your Majesty's dominions, of the richness and variety of their productions, and of the desire of Your Majesty's subjects to receive in exchange for them the production of other countries, it has occurred to me that the existing Treaty between the United States and Siam might be so amended as to secure greater facilities for that purpose. I have accordingly made choice of Townsend Harris, Esquire, the Consul General of the United States for the Empire of Japan, and a citizen of this country, who is the bearer of the present letter, to confer upon the subject with such Ministers or other officers as Your Majesty may designate. I trust that they may agree upon the terms of a treaty which will strengthen and perpetuate the bonds of amity between the United States and Siam, as well as increase the commercial intercourse between them to their mutual advantage.

I trust that Your Majesty will receive Mr. Harris with kindness, and will place entire confidence in all the representations which he may make to Your Majesty in my behalf.

I pray God to have Your Majesty in His safe and holy keeping.

To these presents I have caused the seal of the United States to be affixed, and have subscribed the same with my hand, at the City of

Washington, on the twelfth day of September, in the year of the Christian Era, one thousand eight hundred and fifty-five.

FRANKLIN PIERCE.

By the President:
  W. L. MARCY, *Secretary of State.*

APPENDIX II

LIST OF PRESENTS FOR THE FIRST KING OF SIAM

(*L. & P.*, vol. 2, no. 41)

PRESENTS FOR THE FIRST KING OF SIAM

No. 1. Two splendid mirrors, very thick plates, measuring 80 inches by 56 inches, with frames finely carved out of solid wood and richly gilt.

No. 2. Two superior solar chandeliers, each eight lights, ormolu gildings, after the premium [prize] models of the World's Exhibition in 1851.
  36 cut glass globes for the same.
  36 cut glass chimneys for the same.
  72 dozen of lampwicks for the same.

No. 3. One compound achromatic microscope of the most approved form for the magnifying of minute objects, with three eye-pieces of different powers. Four sets of achromatic object glasses of different focuses, double mirror, moveable stage, diagonal eye-piece, condenser, dissecting instruments, box of objects; and camera lucida, by which an accurate drawing of any object viewed in the microscope may be taken.

No. 4. Solar microscope, by which a magnified image of an object is represented on a white wall or screen; has three rack adjustments, three-inch condensing lens, three object glasses of different magnifying powers, and three objects finely prepared.

No. 5. A small box containing twelve finely prepared objects for the solar microscope.

No. 6. A small box containing twelve finely prepared objects for the compound achromatic microscope.

No. 7.   A book descriptive of the objects most interesting for the microscope, with many plates.

No. 8.   One Sharpe's patent primer rifle, octagon barrel, globe sight, number 32 gauge, and German silver mounted. Two thousand of Sharpe's primers. One hundred cartridges.

No. 9.   One extra-fine finished, engraved, richly gilt, ivory handle Colt's five-inch pistol, in rich, brass-bound rosewood case, velvet lined, with fine extra-plated flasks, moulds, wrench-key, etc.; best percussion caps, powder, balls, etc., etc., complete.

No. 10.   One portrait, life size, of General Washington.

No. 11.   One portrait, life size, of President Pierce.

No. 12.   One *Republican Court or Society in the Days of Washington,* illustrated and splendidly bound, scarlet Turkey morocco, full gilt.

No. 13.   One *American Scenery, or Principal Views in the United States,* with full description; bound antique morocco.

No. 14.   One illustrated description of the works of art, etc., exhibited at the New York Exhibition, bound Turkey morocco, gilt.

No. 15.   One *Iconographic Encyclopædia, or The Arts and Sciences Fully Described and Splendidly Illustrated,* bound Turkey morocco, gilt.

No. 16.   One *Webster's American Dictionary,* unabridged, bound in scarlet Turkey morocco, full gilt and lettered, "Presented to His Majesty the King of Siam, by Franklin Pierce, President of the United States of America."

No. 17.   One colored view of the City of Washington.
One do.   do. of the City of New Orleans.
One do.   do. of the City of New York, from St. Paul's Church.
One do.   do. of the City of New York, from the Bay.
One do.   do. of the City of Boston.
One do.   do. of the Senate Chamber at Washington.
One do.   do. of the City of Philadelphia.
One do.   do. of West Point.
One do.   do. of the Crystal Palace, New York.
One tinted do. of the City of New Orleans.
One view of an express railway train.

No. 18.   One *Map of [the] United States from Atlantic to Pacific Oceans,* on rollers.

APPENDIX III

PRESENTS FOR THE SECOND KING OF SIAM

No. 1.   One splendid oval mirror, very thick plate, with frame finely carved out of solid wood and richly gilt.

No. 2.   (a) An electrical machine of the latest and most approved construction, and possessing extraordinary power, having a thirty-inch glass plate excited by four rubbers, having adjusting screws, brass conductor supported on four glass pillars set in brass sockets.

(b) A spotted Leyden jar; within, the dark is singularly luminous in receiving or discharging its electricity.

(c) A jointed discharging rod for taking out the electricity from the Leyden jar.

(d) A set of five fine-tuned electrical bells, which are arranged to be rung by the power of electricity.

(e) An insulating stool having a polished mahogany top, and glass legs set in brass sockets. By standing on this stool, a person can be filled with electricity from the machine so that his hair will stand on end and his person will give off the fire when touched by another.

(f) The quadrant electrometer for showing the intensity of the electricity by the raising of the ball.

(g) A glass cylinder containing pith balls. These are made to dance rapidly up and down by the electrical influence.

(h) One dozen extra pith balls, to supply any loss from the instruments requiring them.

(i) A thunder house, to illustrate the effect of lightning on a house if struck by it, and to show the use of the lightning rod in buildings.

(j) The man with long hair, showing that electricity will make the hair stand up.

(k) Electrical sawmill, a very curious model worked by electricity.

(l) Electrical firehouse, for showing that electricity can set on fire a house.

(m) Electrical sportsman: some feathers attached to small strings are fastened to a Leyden jar, the electricity causes them to fly in the air, the discharge of electricity from the sportsman's gun causes them to drop as if shot.

(n) Radiating feathers: several feathers attached by small strings to a brass ring on a glass stand are made to fly about by the electricity.

(o) Electrical orrery, or earth, moon and sun, made to revolve by electricity. It is mounted on a stand having a spiral within the tube, which is beautifully luminous when electricity is passed through it.

The electrical spiral tube, when electricity is passed through the spiral, is brilliantly illuminated,—a flash of light passing from each metallic spot.

(p) The electrical rotating bellglass, showing the wonderful power of electricity in causing the motion of bodies.

(q) Electrical eggstand, to make an egg luminous by electricity.

(r) Electrical mortar, to explode hydrogen gas by an electrical spark, and make a great noise thereby.

(s) Apparatus for firing spirits, ether, etc., by electricity.

(t) Electrical image plates, having adjusting rods; small images placed between these plates and electrified will dance up and down rapidly.

(u) Two pith images for using with the electrical plates.

(v) Magic picture for giving an electrical shock to a person unexpectedly.

(w) Revolving electrical chase of six horsemen mounted in a glass stand. The horsemen all move when electrified, chasing one another but not overtaking one another.

(x) An electrical battery of four Leyden jars for the accumulation of electricity in great quantity for experiments.

(y) One pound of amalgam for anointing the rubbers of the machine.

(z) An optical experiment,—color blender, for showing that the union of all colors in their proper proportion will produce white.

No. 3. One portrait, life size, of General Washington.
No. 4. One portrait, life size, of President Pierce.

No. 5. One extra-fine finished, **engraved**, richly gilt, ivory handle Colt's five-inch pistol in rich, brass-bound rosewood case, velvet lined, with five [fine] extra-plated flasks, moulds, wrench-key, etc.; best percussion caps, powder, balls, etc., etc., complete.

No. 6. One Sharpe's patent primer carabine, round barrel, 32 gauge, globe sight, German silver mounted. Two thousand Sharpe's primers. One hundred cartridges.

No. 7. One *Republican Court or Society in the Days of Washington,* illustrated and splendidly bound, scarlet Turkey morocco, full gilt.

No. 8. One *American Scenery, or Principal Views in the United States,* with full description; bound antique morocco.

No. 9. One illustrated description of the works of art, etc., exhibited at the New York Exhibition, bound Turkey morocco, gilt.

No. 10. One *Iconographic Encyclopædia, or The Arts and Sciences Fully Described and Splendidly Illustrated,* bound Turkey morocco, gilt.

No. 11. One *Webster's American Dictionary,* unabridged, bound in scarlet Turkey morocco, full gilt, and lettered, "Presented to his Majesty the Second King of Siam, by Franklin Pierce, President of the United States of America."

No. 12. One *Map of the United States from Atlantic to Pacific Oceans,* on rollers.

No. 13. One colored view of the City of Washington.
One do. do. of the City of New Orleans.
One do. do. of the City of New York, from St. Paul's Church.
One do. do. of the City of New York, from the Bay.
One do. do. of the City of Boston.
One do. do. of the Senate Chamber at Washington.

APPENDIX IV

The Convention of Shimoda Between the United States and Japan

June 17, 1857: concluded.

February 10, 1858: is received by the Senate, and is referred to the Committee on Foreign Relations.

February 16, 1858: is reported without amendment.

June 15, 1858: is again referred to the Committee on Foreign Relations.

June 15, 1858: ratification is advised by the Senate.

June 30, 1858: is ratified by the President.

June 30, 1858: is proclaimed.

Note: This Convention was executed in quintuplicate, each copy being written in the English, Japanese, and Dutch languages, but it was agreed "that the true meaning shall be found in the Dutch version of the articles." (See Arts. VIII and IX.)

For the purpose of further regulating the intercourse of American citizens within the Empire of Japan, and after due deliberation, his Excellency Townsend Harris, Consul General of the United States of America for the Empire of Japan, and their Excellencies Ino-oo-ye [Inouye], Prince of Sinano [Shinano], and Nakamura, Prince of Dewa, Governors of Simoda [Shimoda], all having full powers from their respective Governments, have agreed on the following articles, to wit:—

I. The port of Nangasaki [Nagasaki], in the principality of Hizen, shall be open to American vessels, where they may repair damages, procure water, fuel, provisions, and other necessary articles, even coals, where they are obtainable.

II. It being known that American ships coming to the ports of Simoda [Shimoda] and Hakodate cannot have their wants supplied by the Japanese, it is agreed that American citizens may permanently reside at Simoda [Shimoda] and Hakodate, and the Government of the United States may appoint a vice-consul to reside at Hakodate.

This article to go into effect on the fourth day of July, eighteen hundred and fifty-eight.

III. In settlement of accounts, the value of the money brought by the Americans shall be ascertained by weighing it with Japanese coin (gold and silver itsebues [*ichibus*]), that is, gold with gold, and

571

silver with silver, or weights representing Japanese coin may be used, after such weights have been carefully examined and found to be correct. The value of the money of the Americans having been thus ascertained, the sum of six per cent. shall be allowed to the Japanese for the expense of recoinage.

IV. Americans committing offences in Japan shall be tried by the American Consul General or Consul, and shall be punished according to American laws. Japanese committing offences against Americans shall be tried by the Japanese authorities, and punished according to Japanese laws.

V. American ships which may resort to the ports of Simoda, [Shimoda], Hakodate, or Nangasaki [Nagasaki], for the purpose of obtaining necessary supplies, or to repair damages, shall pay for them in gold or silver coin; and, if they have no money, goods shall be taken in exchange.

VI. The Government of Japan admits the right of his Excellency the Consul General of the United States to go beyond the limits of seven ri, but has asked him to delay the use of that right, except in cases of emergency, shipwreck, etc., to which he has assented.

VII. Purchases for his Excellency the Consul General, or his family, may be made by him only, or by some member of his family, and payment made to the seller for the same without the intervention of any Japanese official, and for this purpose Japanese silver and copper coin shall be supplied to his Excellency the Consul General.

VIII. As his Excellency the Consul General of the United States of America has no knowledge of the Japanese language, nor their Excellencies the Governors of Simoda [Shimoda] a knowledge of the English language, it is agreed that the true meaning shall be found in the Dutch version of the articles.

IX. All the foregoing Articles shall go into effect from the date hereof, except Article II, which shall go into effect on the date indicated in it.

Done in quintuplicate (each copy being in English, Japanese, and Dutch), at the Goyoso [Goyoshi] of Simoda [Shimoda], on the seventeenth day of June, in the year of the Christian Era eighteen hundred and fifty-seven, and of the Independence of the United States of America the eighty-first, corresponding to the fourth Japanese year of Ansei, Mi, the fifth month, the twenty-sixth day; the English version being signed by his Excellency the Consul General of the United

States of America, and the Japanese version by their Excellencies the Governors of Simoda [Shimoda].

TOWNSEND HARRIS. [L. S.]

APPENDIX V

THE FIRST AMERICAN FLAG MADE IN JAPAN

(See *Journal,* November 23, 1857)

When Townsend Harris had been put ashore by the U. S. S. *San Jacinto,* an American Flag had been given to him, and this flag had been raised with due ceremony on the flagstaff at the American Consulate at Shimoda—as described by Townsend Harris himself in the *Journal.* But Shimoda was a windy place; and, by November, 1857, the flag left by the *San Jacinto* had been torn to shreds. The best possible impression, on the other hand, had to be made on the journey to Yedo and on the Tycoon himself.

In this difficulty, Townsend Harris (or perhaps Dewa-no-Kami) must have turned to the natives of Shimoda and requested them to make a new flag for him. And they did. It was this new flag which was proudly borne before Townsend Harris on his triumphal journey to Yedo, and it is this flag of which we give a photograph, as it appeared before it was framed.

Let us look at this flag, and let us dream dreams. Count its thirty-one stars, and think of the United States in 1857—before the election of Lincoln, before the great trial of battle, before Bull Run, before the victories of Lee and of Grant. This was the American flag that was first seen in awe and wonderment by countless Japanese. Picture the thoughts of those countless men, women and children, who formed a rank five feet deep on each side of the way; who peeped from the windows and doorways of the City of Yedo for a distance of over seven miles—and all in absolute silence! Picture, if you can, the indelible impression made by this flag upon the keen and active minds of the beholders as, in the midst of the appalling silence of such a vast multitude, the Stars and Stripes were carried along slowly, and in front of a man whom the Japanese could not even see, hidden as he was in the respectable aloofness of his *norimon.*

Let us remember that Townsend Harris was the first accredited

573

representative of any foreign government to be granted an audience in Japan; that his visit to Yedo was the first ever made by an accredited representative of a foreign government to the capital of the Tycoon. Let us emphasize the fact that the flag which was borne before him on this occasion was the first American flag ever made in Japan by (perhaps) a Japanese Betsy Ross who is as yet unknown, unhonored and unsung; that this flag was not merely the first American flag, but the first flag of any foreign nation to be seen in the interior of Japan for many centuries back; and that it was the first flag of any nation officially carried into the Shogun's capital and into his very Palace.

Townsend Harris himself was, and with very good reason, devotedly attached to this flag. In a letter to Mr. Nathaniel Dougherty dated Shimoda, July 3, 1858 (Littell's *Living Age,* vol. 60, pp. 567–571), he says (p. 569):

"A new flag, made of Japanese crêpe, was carried before me. This flag is the first foreign banner that was ever carried through this great city [Yedo], and I mean to preserve it as a precious relic."

Again, in a letter dated December 23, 1857, and addressed to Mr. E. E. Rice, U. S. Commercial Agent at Hakodate, he says (*L. B.,* vol. 3, p. 14):

"The American flag was carried before me for more than 100 miles through this country. I displayed it in the streets of this great City, and it daily waves before my residence, so that we can say that the first foreign flag ever hoisted in this City was the Stars and Stripes. On the day of my audience [December 7, 1857], the Flag was borne into the great Castle and up to the gate of the Audience Hall."

And, finally, in a letter dated Shimoda, July 16, 1858, and addressed to Catherine A. Drinker (the late Mrs. Thomas Allibone Janvier), Townsend Harris says:

"On the Monday week after my arrival, I set out for the Palace. My train blazed out in new silk dresses, and a new flag made of Japanese crêpe was displayed—by the way, the American flag is the first foreign banner that was ever 'flung to the breeze' in this great city."

574

This precious relic both time and fortune have spared. A most precious relic it is—it would be difficult to find one more dear and more significant to American hearts. The writer was for ten years Director of the Townsend Harris Hall High School—the only monument in this country that recalls the memory of our first Ambassador to Japan. At the writer's instance, this historic flag was duly and properly framed, thus seconding the wishes of the great man whose name the school is proud to bear. The flag now adorns the north wall of the Director's Office and bears the following inscription:

THE TOWNSEND HARRIS FLAG

THE FIRST AMERICAN FLAG MADE IN JAPAN

1857

FRAMED BY THE FACULTY AND THE STUDENTS

OF THE

TOWNSEND HARRIS HALL HIGH SCHOOL

JUNE 1921

APPENDIX VI

TOWNSEND HARRIS'S LETTER OF CREDENCE, OR "FULL POWERS": DATED WASHINGTON, D. C., SEPTEMBER, 8, 1855

FRANKLIN PIERCE

President of the United States of America

To all to whom these presents shall come, Greeting:
Know Ye, that, reposing special trust and confidence in the integrity, prudence and ability of Townsend Harris, Consul General of the United States for the Empire of Japan, I have invested him with full and all manner of power and authority for and in the name of the United States to meet and confer with any person or persons duly authorized by His Majesty the Emperor of Japan, being invested with like power and authority, and with him or them to agree, treat, consult and negotiate of and concerning general commerce between the United

575

States and the dominions of His Majesty the Emperor of Japan, and all matters and things connected therewith; and to conclude and sign a Treaty or Treaties, Convention or Conventions, touching the premises, transmitting the same to the President of the United States for his ratification by and with the advice and consent of the Senate thereof.

In testimony whereof I have caused the seal of the United States to be hereunto affixed.

Given under my hand at the City of Washington, the eighth day of September, in the year of Our Lord one thousand eight hundred and fifty-five and of the Independence of the United States the eightieth.

FRANKLIN PIERCE.

By the President:
W. L. MARCY, *Secretary of State*

[Seal of the United States]

APPENDIX VII

PRESIDENT PIERCE'S LETTER TO THE EMPEROR OF JAPAN: DATED WASHINGTON, D. C., SEPTEMBER 12, 1855

FRANKLIN PIERCE
President of the United States of America

To HIS MAJESTY THE EMPEROR OF JAPAN.

GREAT AND GOOD FRIEND:

It has occurred to me that the existing Treaty between the United States and Japan might be so amended as to secure greater facilities for the exchange of the rich and varied productions of Your Majesty's vast Empire for those of the United States. I have accordingly made choice of the bearer of this letter, Townsend Harris, Esquire, a citizen of this country, who has already been accredited to Your Majesty's Minister for Foreign Affairs as the Consul General of the United States, to confer upon the subject with such Ministers or other officers as Your Majesty may designate. I trust that they may agree upon the terms of a treaty which will strengthen and perpetuate the bonds of

576

amity between the United States and Japan as well as increase the commercial intercourse between them to their mutual advantage.

I trust that Your Majesty will receive Mr. Harris with kindness, and will place entire confidence in all the representations which he may make to Your Majesty in my behalf.

I pray God to have Your Majesty in His safe and holy keeping.

To these presents I have caused the seal of the United States to be affixed and have subscribed the same with my hand, at the City of Washington, on the twelfth day of September, in the year of the Christian Era, one thousand eight hundred and fifty-five.

FRANKLIN PIERCE.

By the President:
W. L. MARCY, *Secretary of State.*

APPENDIX VIII

LETTER WRITTEN BY HOTTA, BITCHIU-NO-KAMI, TO TOWNSEND HARRIS

(L. & P., vol. 2, no. 67)

To HIS EXCELLENCY TOWNSENT [SIC] HARRIS, Plenipotentiary and Consul General of the United States of America, etc., etc., etc.

I have to acknowledge that I have read Your Excellency's letter, sent on the last 9th day, and that I have thankfully accepted Your Excellency's cordial presents.

The book, exactly describing all the ports of the United States of America, the West Indies and South America, is found exceedingly useful.

In acknowledgment of this favor I send you herewith a trifling present, as per list. Should Your Excellency wish to accept the same, it shall be very agreeable to me.

Represented with consideration and respect,
the 20th day of the 11th month, Mi.

(s)   HOTTA BITTSIUNOKAMI
(s)   MORIYAMA TAKITSIRO

A true translation.
H. C. J. HEUSKEN

577

APPENDIX IX

THE TREATY OF AMITY AND COMMERCE BETWEEN THE UNITED STATES AND JAPAN

July 29, 1858: concluded at Yedo.

December 7, 1858: date of President Buchanan's letter transmitting the Treaty to the Senate.

December 13, 1858: is received by the Senate.

December 15, 1858: ratification is advised by the Senate.

April 12, 1860: is ratified by the President.

May 22, 1860: ratifications are exchanged at Washington, D. C.

May 23, 1860: is proclaimed.

> NOTE: "This Treaty is executed in quadruplicate, each copy being written in the English, Japanese, and Dutch languages, all the versions having the same meaning and intention, but the Dutch version shall be considered as being the original." (See Art. XIV.)

The President of the United States of America and His Majesty the Ty-Coon [Tykoon] of Japan, desiring to establish on firm and lasting foundations the relations of peace and friendship now happily existing between the two countries, and to secure the best interest of their respective citizens and subjects by encouraging, facilitating, and regulating their industry and trade, have resolved to conclude a Treaty of Amity and Commerce for this purpose, and have, therefore, named as their Plenipotentiaries, that is to say: the President of the United States, his Excellency Townsend Harris, Consul General of the United States of America for the Empire of Japan; and His Majesty the Ty-Coon of Japan, their Excellencies Ino-oo-ye [Inouye], Prince of Sinano [Shinano], and Iwasay [Iwase], Prince of Hego [Higo]; who, after having communicated to each other their respective full powers, and found them to be in good and due form, have agreed upon and concluded the following Articles:

Art. I.   There shall henceforth be perpetual peace and friendship between the United States of America and His Majesty the Ty-Coon of Japan and his successors.

The President of the United States may appoint a Diplomatic Agent to reside at the City of Yedo, and Consuls or Consular Agents to reside at any or all of the ports in Japan which are opened for American commerce by this Treaty. The Diplomatic Agent and Consul General of the United States shall have the right to travel freely in any part of the Empire of Japan from the time they enter on the discharge of their official duties.

The Government of Japan may appoint a Diplomatic Agent to reside at Washington, and Consuls or Consular Agents for any or all of the ports of the United States. The Diplomatic Agent and Consul General of Japan may travel freely in any part of the United States from the time they arrive in the country.

Art. II.   The President of the United States, at the request of the Japanese Government, will act as a friendly mediator in such matters of difference as may arise between the Government of Japan and any European Power.

The ships-of-war of the United States shall render friendly aid and assistance to such Japanese vessels as they may meet on the high seas, so far as can be done without a breach of neutrality; and all American Consuls residing at ports visited by Japanese vessels shall also give them such friendly aid as may be permitted by the laws of the respective countries in which they reside.

Art. III.   In addition to the ports of Simoda [Shimoda] and Hakodade [Hakodate], the following ports and towns shall be opened on the dates respectively appended to them, that is to say: Kanagawa, on the 4th of July, 1859; Nagasaki, on the 4th of July, 1859; Nee-e-gata [Niigata], on the 1st of January, 1860; Hiogo [Hyogo], on the 1st of January, 1863.

If Nee-e-gata [Niigata] is found to be unsuitable as a harbor, another port on the west coast of Nipon [Nippon] shall be selected by the two Governments in lieu thereof. Six months after the opening of Kanagawa, the port of Simoda [Shimoda] shall be closed as a place of residence and trade for American citizens. In all the foregoing ports and towns American citizens may permanently reside; they shall have the right to lease ground, and purchase the buildings thereon, and may erect dwellings and warehouses. But no fortification or place of military strength shall be erected under pretence of building dwellings or ware-

579

houses; and, to see that this Article is observed, the Japanese authorities shall have the right to inspect, from time to time, any buildings which are being erected, altered, or repaired. The place which the Americans shall occupy for their buildings, and the harbor regulations, shall be arranged by the American Consul and the authorities of each place, and, if they cannot agree, the matter shall be referred to and settled by the American Diplomatic Agent and the Japanese Government.

No wall, fence, or gate shall be erected by the Japanese around the place of residence of the Americans, or anything done which may prevent a free egress and ingress to the same.

From the 1st of January, 1862, Americans shall be allowed to reside in the City of Yedo; and from the 1st of January, 1863, in the City of Osaca [Osaka], for the purposes of trade only. In each of these two cities a suitable place within which they may hire houses, and the distance they may go, shall be arranged by the American Diplomatic Agent and the Government of Japan. Americans may freely buy from Japanese and sell to them any articles that either may have for sale, without the intervention of any Japanese officers in such purchase or sale, or in making or receiving payment for the same; and all classes of Japanese may purchase, sell, keep, or use any articles sold to them by the Americans.

The Japanese Government will cause this clause to be made public in every part of the Empire as soon as the ratifications of this Treaty shall be exchanged.

Munitions of war shall only be sold to the Japanese Government and foreigners.

No rice or wheat shall be exported from Japan as cargo, but all Americans resident in Japan, and ships, for their crews and passengers, shall be furnished with sufficient supplies of the same. The Japanese Government will sell, from time to time at public auction, any surplus quantity of copper that may be produced. Americans residing in Japan shall have the right to employ Japanese as servants or in any other capacity.

Art. IV.   Duties shall be paid to the Government of Japan on all goods landed in the country, and on all articles of Japanese production that are exported as cargo, according to the tariff hereunto appended.

If the Japanese Custom House officers are dissatisfied with the value placed on any goods by the owner, they may place a value thereon, and offer to take the goods at that valuation. If the owner refuses to accept the offer, he shall pay duty on such valuation. If the offer be accepted by the owner, the purchase-money shall be paid to him without delay, and without any abatement or discount.

Supplies for the use of the United States navy may be landed at Kanagawa, Hakodade [Hakodate], and Nagasaki, and stored in warehouses, in the custody of an officer of the American Government, without the payment of any duty. But, if any such supplies are sold in Japan, the purchaser shall pay the proper duty to the Japanese authorities.

The importation of opium is prohibited; and, any American vessel coming to Japan for the purposes of trade having more than three catties (four pounds avoirdupois) weight of opium on board, such surplus quantity shall be seized and destroyed by the Japanese authorities. All goods imported into Japan, and which have paid the duty fixed by this Treaty, may be transported by the Japanese into any part of the empire without the payment of any tax, excise, or transit duty whatever.

No higher duties shall be paid by Americans on goods imported into Japan than are fixed by this Treaty, nor shall any higher duties be paid by Americans than are levied on the same description of goods if imported in Japanese vessels, or the vessels of any other nation.

Art. V. All foreign coin shall be current in Japan and pass for its corresponding weight of Japanese coin of the same description. Americans and Japanese may freely use foreign or Japanese coin in making payments to each other.

As some time will elapse before the Japanese will be acquainted with the value of foreign coin, the Japanese Government will, for the period of one year after the opening of each harbor, furnish the Americans with Japanese coin in exchange for theirs, equal weights being given and no discount taken for re-coinage. Coins of all description (with the exception of Japanese copper coin) may be exported from Japan, and foreign gold and silver uncoined.

Art. VI. Americans committing offences against Japanese shall be tried in American Consular courts, and, when guilty, shall be punished according to American law. Japanese committing offences against Americans shall be tried by the Japanese authorities and punished according to Japanese law. The Consular courts shall be open to Japanese ereditors, to enable them to recover their just claims against American citizens; and the Japanese courts shall in like manner be open to American citizens for the recovery of their just claims against Japanese.

All claims for forfeitures or penalties for violations of this Treaty, or of the Articles regulating trade which are appended hereunto, shall be sued for in the Consular courts, and all recoveries shall be delivered to the Japanese authorities.

Neither the American or Japanese Governments are [sic] to be held responsible for the payment of any debts contracted by their respective citizens or subjects.

Art. VII.   In the opened harbors of Japan, Americans shall be free to go where they please, within the following limits:

At Kanagawa, the River Logo [Rokugo] (which empties into the Bay of Yedo between Kawasaki and Sinagawa), and 10 ri in any other direction.

At Hakodade [Hakodate], 10 ri in any direction.

At Hiogo [Hyogo], 10 ri in any direction, that of Kioto [Kyoto] excepted, which city shall not be approached nearer than 10 ri. The crews of vessels resorting to Hiogo shall not cross the River Enagawa, which empties into the Bay between Hiogo and Osaca [Osaka]. The distance shall be measured inland from Goyoso [Goyoshi], or town hall of each of the foregoing harbors, the ri being equal to 4,275 yards American measure.

At Nagasaki, Americans may go into any part of the Imperial domain in its vicinity. The boundaries of Nee-e-gata [Niigata], or the place that may be substituted for it, shall be settled by the American Diplomatic Agent and the Government of Japan. Americans who have been convicted of felony, or twice convicted of misdemeanors, shall not go more than one Japanese ri inland from the places of their respective residences, and all persons so convicted shall lose their right of permanent residence in Japan, and the Japanese authorities may require them to leave the country.

A reasonable time shall be allowed to all such persons to settle their affairs, and the American Consular authority shall, after an examination into the circumstances of each case, determine the time to be allowed, but such time shall not in any case exceed one year, to be calculated from the time the person shall be free to attend to his affairs.

Art. VIII.   Americans in Japan shall be allowed the free exercise of their religion, and for this purpose shall have the right to erect suitable places of worship. No injury shall be done to such buildings, nor any insult be offered to the religious worship of the Americans. American citizens shall not injure any Japanese temple or *mia,* or offer any insult or injury to Japanese religious ceremonies, or to the objects of their worship.

The Americans and Japanese shall not do anything that may be calculated to excite religious animosity. The Government of Japan has already abolished the practice of trampling on religious emblems.

Art. IX.   When requested by the American Consul, the Japanese authorities will cause the arrest of all deserters and fugitives from justice, receive in jail all persons held as prisoners by the Consul, and give to the Consul such assistance as may be required to enable him to enforce the observance of the laws by the Americans who are on land, and to maintain order among the shipping. For all such service, and for the support of prisoners kept in confinement, the Consul shall in all cases pay a just compensation.

Art. X.   The Japanese Government may purchase or construct in the United States ships-of-war, steamers, merchant ships, whale ships, cannon, munitions of war, and arms of all kinds, and any other things it may require. It shall have the right to engage in the United States scientific, naval and military men, artisans of all kinds, and mariners to enter into its service. All purchases made for the Government of Japan may be exported from the United States, and all persons engaged for its service may freely depart from the United States: provided that no articles that are contraband of war shall be exported, nor any persons engaged to act in a naval or military capacity, while Japan shall be at war with any Power in amity with the United States.

Art. XI.   The Articles for the regulation of trade, which are appended to this Treaty, shall be considered as forming a part of the same, and shall be equally binding on both the Contracting Parties to this Treaty, and on their citizens and subjects.

Art. XII.   Such of the provisions of the Treaty made by Commodore Perry, and signed at Kanagawa, on the 31st of March, 1854, as conflict with the provisions of this Treaty are hereby revoked; and, as all the provisions of a Convention executed by the Consul General of the United States and the Governors of Simoda [Shimoda], on the 17th of June, 1857, are incorporated in this Treaty, that Convention is also revoked.

The person charged with the diplomatic relations of the United States in Japan, in conjunction with such person or persons as may be appointed for that purpose by the Japanese Government, shall have power to make such rules and regulations as may be required to carry into full and complete effect the provisions of this Treaty, and the provisions of the Articles regulating trade appended thereunto.

Art. XIII.   After the 4th of July, 1872, upon the desire of either the American or Japanese Governments, and on one year's notice given

583

by either party, this Treaty, and such portions of the Treaty of Kanagawa as remain unrevoked by this Treaty, together with the regulations of trade hereunto annexed, or those that may be hereafter introduced, shall be subject to revision by Commissioners appointed on both sides for this purpose, who will be empowered to decide on, and insert therein, such amendments as experience shall prove to be desirable.

Art. XIV.   This Treaty shall go into effect on the 4th of July, 1859, on or before which day the ratifications of the same shall be exchanged at the City of Washington; but if, from any unforeseen cause, the ratifications cannot be exchanged by that time, the Treaty shall still go into effect at the date above mentioned.

The act of ratification on the part of the United States shall be verified by the signature of the President of the United States, countersigned by the Secretary of State, and sealed with the seal of the United States.

The act of ratification on the part of Japan shall be verified by the name and seal of His Majesty the Ty-Coon, and by the seals and signatures of such of his high officers as he may direct.

This Treaty is executed in quadruplicate, each copy being written in the English, Japanese, and Dutch languages, all the versions having the same meaning and intention, but the Dutch version shall be considered as being the original.

In witness whereof, the above-named Plenipotentiaries have hereunto set their hands and seals, at the City of Yedo, this 29th day of July, in the year of Our Lord 1858, and of the Independence of the United States of America the eighty-third, corresponding to the Japanese era, the 19th day of the 6th month of the 5th year of Ansei, *Mma* [year of the horse].

[L. S.]   TOWNSEND HARRIS.

REGULATIONS UNDER WHICH AMERICAN TRADE IS TO BE CONDUCTED IN JAPAN

REGULATION I.   Within 48 hours (Sundays excepted) after the arrival of an American ship in a Japanese port, the captain or commander shall exhibit to the Japanese Custom House authorities the receipt of the American Consul, showing that he has deposited the ship's register and other papers, as required by the laws of the United States, at the American Consulate, and he shall then make an entry of his ship, by giving a written paper, stating the name of the ship, and the name of the port from which she comes, her tonnage, the name of her captain or commander, the names of her passengers (if any), and the number of her crew, which paper shall be certified by the captain or commander to be a true statement, and shall be signed by him; he shall at the same time deposit a written manifest of his cargo, setting forth the marks and numbers of the packages and their contents, as they are described in his bills of lading with the names of the person or persons to whom they are consigned. A list of the stores of the ship shall be added to the manifest. The captain or commander shall certify the manifest to be a true account of all the cargo and stores on board the ship, and shall sign his name to the same. If any error is discovered in the manifest, it may be corrected within 24 hours (Sundays excepted) without the payment of any fee; but for any alteration or post entry to the manifest made after that time, a fee of 15 dollars shall be paid. All goods not entered on the manifest shall pay double duties on being landed. Any captain or commander that shall neglect to enter his vessel at the Japanese Custom House within the time prescribed by this regulation shall pay a penalty of 60 dollars for each day that he shall so neglect to enter his ship.

REGULATION 2. The Japanese Government shall have the right to place Custom House officers on board of any ship in their ports (men-of-war excepted). All Custom House officers shall be treated with civility, and such reasonable accommodation shall be allotted to them as the ship affords. No goods shall be unladen from any ship between the hours of sunset and sunrise, except by special permission of the Custom House authorities; and the hatches, and all other places of entrance into that part of the ship where the cargo is stowed, may be secured by Japanese officers, between the hours of sunset and sunrise, by affixing seals, locks, or other fastenings; and if any person shall, without due permission, open any entrance that has been so secured, or shall break or remove any seal, lock, or other fastening that has been affixed by the Japanese Custom House officers, every person so offending shall pay a fine of 60 dollars for each offence. Any goods that shall be die-charged or attempted to be discharged from any ship, without having been duly entered at the Japanese Custom House, as hereinafter provided, shall be liable to seizure and confiscation.

Packages of goods made up with an attempt to defraud the revenue of Japan, by concealing therein articles of value which are not set forth in the invoice, shall be forfeited.

585

American ships that shall smuggle, or attempt to smuggle, goods in any of the non-opened harbors of Japan, all such goods shall be forfeited to the Japanese Government, and the ship shall pay a fine of 1,000 dollars for each offence. Vessels needing repairs may land their cargo for that purpose without the payment of duty. All goods so landed shall remain in charge of the Japanese authorities, and all just charges for storage, labor, and supervision shall be paid thereon. But if any portion of such cargo be sold, the regular duties shall be paid on the portion so disposed of. Cargo may be transshipped to another vessel in the same harbor without the payment of duty; but all transshipments shall be made under the supervision of Japanese officers, and after satisfactory proof has been given to the Custom House authorities of the *bona fide* nature of the transaction, and also under a permit to be granted for that purpose by such authorities. The importation of opium being prohibited, if any person or persons shall smuggle or attempt to smuggle, any opium, he or they shall pay a fine of 15 dollars for each catty of opium so smuggled or attempted to be smuggled; and if more than one person shall be engaged in the offence, they shall collectively be held responsible for the payment of the foregoing penalty.

REGULATION 3. The owner or consignee of any goods, who desires to land them, shall make an entry of the same at the Japanese Custom House. The entry shall be in writing, and shall set forth the name of the person making the entry, and the name of the ship in which the goods were imported, and the marks, numbers, packages, and contents thereof, with the value of each package extended separately in one amount, and at the bottom of the entry shall be placed the aggregate value of all the goods contained in the entry. On each entry the owner or consignee shall certify, in writing, that the entry then presented exhibits the actual cost of the goods, and that nothing has been concealed whereby the Customs of Japan would be defrauded; and the owner or consignee shall sign his name to such certificate.

The original invoice or invoices of the goods so entered shall be presented to the Custom House authorities, and shall remain in their possession until they have examined the goods contained in the entry.

The Japanese officers may examine any or all of the packages so entered, and for this purpose may take them to the Custom House, but such examinations shall be without expense to the importer or injury to the goods; and, after examination, the Japanese shall restore the goods to their original condition in the packages (so far as may be practicable), and which examination shall be made without any unreasonable delay.

If any owner or importer discovers that his goods have been damaged on the voyage of importation before such goods have been delivered to him, he may notify the Custom House authorities of such damage, and he may have the damaged goods appraised by two or more competent and disinterested persons, who, after due examination, shall make a certificate setting forth the amount per cent. of damage on each separate package, describing it by its mark and number, which certificates shall be signed by the appraisers in presence of the Custom House authorities, and the importer may attach the certificate to his entry, and make a corresponding deduction from it. But this shall not prevent the Custom House authorities from appraising the goods in the manner provided in Article IV of the Treaty, to which these regulations are appended.

After the duties have been paid, the owner shall receive a permit authorizing the delivery to him of the goods, whether the same are at the Custom House or on shipboard. All goods intended to be exported shall be entered at the Japanese Custom House before they are placed on shipboard. The entry shall be in writing, and shall state the name of the ship by which the goods are to be exported, with the marks and numbers of the packages, and the quantity, description, and value of their contents. The exporter shall certify in writing that the entry is a true account of all the goods contained therein, and shall sign his name thereto. Any goods that are put on board of a ship for exportation before they have been entered at the Custom House, and all packages which contain prohibited articles, shall be forfeited to the Japanese Government.

No entry at the Custom House shall be required for supplies for the use of ships, their crews, and passengers, nor for the clothing, etc., of passengers.

REGULATION 4. Ships wishing to clear shall give 24 hours' notice at the Custom House, and at the end of that time they shall be entitled to their clearance; but, if it be refused, the Custom House authorities shall immediately inform the captain or consignee of the ship of the reasons why the clearance is refused, and they shall also give the same notice to the American Consul.

Ships-of-war of the United States shall not be required to enter or clear at the Custom House, nor shall they be visited by Japanese Custom House or police officers. Steamers carrying the mails of the United States may enter and clear on the same day, and they shall not be re-

587

quired to make a manifest, except for such passengers and goods as are to be landed in Japan. But such steamers shall, in all cases, enter and clear at the Custom House.

Whale ships touching for supplies, or ships in distress, shall not be required to make a manifest of their cargo; but if they subsequently wish to trade, they shall then deposit a manifest, as required in Regulation 1.

The word ship, wherever it occurs in these Regulations, or in the Treaty to which they are attached, is to be held as meaning ship, barque, brig, schooner, sloop, or steamer.

REGULATION 5. Any person signing a false declaration or certificate with the intent to defraud the revenue of Japan, shall pay a fine of 125 dollars for each offence.

REGULATION 6. No tonnage duties shall be levied on American ships in the ports of Japan, but the following fees shall be paid to the Japanese Custom House authorities: for the entry of a ship, 15 dollars; for the clearance of a ship, 7 dollars; for each permit, 1½ dollars; for each bill of health, 1½ dollars; for any other document, 1½ dollars.

REGULATION 7. Duties shall be paid to the Japanese Government on all goods landed in the country according to the following tariff:

Class 1. All articles in this class shall be free of duty.
  Gold and silver, coined or uncoined.
  Wearing apparel in actual use.
  Household furniture and printed books not intended for sale, but
    the property of persons who come to reside in Japan.
Class 2. A duty of 5 per cent. shall be paid on the following articles:

All articles used for the purpose of building rigging, repairing, or fitting out of ships.
Whaling gear of all kinds.
Timber for building houses.
Rice.
Paddy.
Steam machinery.

Salted provisions of all kinds.
Bread and breadstuffs.
Living animals of all kinds.
Coals.
Zinc.
Lead.
Tin.
Raw Silk.

Class 3. A duty of 35 per cent. shall be paid on all intoxicating liquors, whether prepared by distillation. fermentation, or in any other manner.

588

average duty on goods into Jap. m 70%

Class 4. All goods not included in any of the preceding classes shall pay a duty of 20 per cent.

All articles of Japanese production, which are exported as cargo, shall pay a duty of 5 per cent., with the exception of gold and silver coin and copper in bars. Five years after the opening of Kanagawa the import and export duties shall be subject to revision if the Japanese Government desires it.

[L. S.] TOWNSEND HARRIS.

INDEX

INDEX

Abbott & Lawrence, 256, 257.
Abbreviations used in the notes, xix.
Abé Ise-no-Kami, 382 and 382 n.
Accounts, Harris's, 343, 346 and 346 n.;
Harris pays, 175, 372-373, 409.
Acknowledgments, ix, x.
Adams, Captain H. A., 261 n.
Adams, J. H., 51 n.
Additional Articles to Dutch Treaty
with Japan, 410 and 410 n., 411 n.
Address, Harris's, to the Shogun at
Yedo, 475; to King of Siam, Harris
composes, 123; to King of Siam, text
of Harris's, 134; to Second King,
text of Harris's, 135-136.
Aden, Harris describes, 18.
Adultery in Siam, 88.
Adventures in the Punjab, 38.
Age, Harris's, 240 and 240 n.
Agriculture, Japanese, 235-236.
Albatross, Harris sees, 196, 198.
Alcock, Sir Rutherford, 69 n.
Alley, M., Harris visits in Aden, 33.
Alsop, Wetmore & Cryder, 178 n.
Alton Locke, 37.
Amaral, Governor, 169 n.
Ambassador, Japanese propose to send,
to Washington, 531.
American Messenger, the, 512 n.
Americans in Eastern Asia, extract from,
on Harris's entry into Yedo, 442 n.
Amusements of Japanese boys, 359-
360.
Andrews, W. W., *see* Winthrop, William.
Animals, 61, 87, 249, 359.
Anna Maria, the, 73.
Anstey, the Honorable Chisholm, 31
and 31 n., 45, 46, 175.
Anti-Coningsby, 38, 40.
Appleton, John, Secretary of Legation,
27 n.
Archer, Joseph, 178 n.
Armstrong, James, Commodore, 68, 75,

76, 77, 78 n., 81, 93, 103, 124, 126, 130,
131, 133, 137, 140 n., 163, 165-166,
168, 172, 180, 181, 185, 187, 192,
193, 199 n., 205, 207, 219, 220, 224,
225, 270 n., 347, 350, 357, 365, 377,
379, 381, 386, 387, 388, 392; Harris
makes acquaintance of, 26; career of,
26 n; Harris writes to, 53; private
visit of, to Second King, 127; Governor of Shimoda sends presents to,
203; invited to visit Governor of
Shimoda, 216.
Armstrong, Mr. (of Armstrong & Lawrence), 165.
Armstrong & Lawrence, 46, 186, 240 n.,
275 and 275 n., 289, 389; Harris
settles accounts with, 175; Harris
writes to, 180, 181, 185, 187, 288 n.,
290 n.
Artemisia, 258.
Ashe, Captain's Clerk, 137.
Ashmore, the Rev. William, 107 and
107 n.
Ashmore, Mrs., 107 n.
Assam, Harris's butler, 182, 295.
Atlantic, the, Harris takes passage on,
23.
Atlas, Mitchell's, 229.
Auckland, the, 79, 81, 90, 107.
Audience with Shogun, date set for,
454; dinner served to Harris on oc-
casion of, 478, 481; fan used at, 481.
See also under Harris, Townsend,
Shogun, *and* Yedo.
Audience with King of Siam, 129-135,
133 n.; order of procession, 130-131;
Harris's address, 134.
Audience with Second King of Siam,
Harris's, 135-136; order of proces-
sion, 130-131, 135; Harris's address,
135-136.
Audience Chamber at Yedo, Harris
describes, 449.

595

596

a letter to E. E. Rice, 85 n.; awaits summons from King of Siam, 86; converses with Mr. Mattoon regarding his mission, 86; bamboo house prepared for, 88; his interest in slavery, 87 n.; has letter from Siamese Minister of Foreign Affairs, 88; replies, 88; his presents to King of Siam, 91; goes up river to Bangkok, 92–102; reception of, by Siamese, 93–94, 102; his house at Bangkok, 102–103; American missionaries call on him, 106–107; finds King of Siam in unfavorable mood, 107; is called on by Prince George Washington, 107–108; King of Siam refuses him a private interview, 109; receives letter and present from Second King of Siam, 109–110; calls on Phra Klang, 111–112; calls on Prince Krom Luang, 112–113; calls on Phra Kalahom, 113–116; is visited by Phra Klang, Phra Kalahom, and Prince Krom Luang, 116; calls on Somdet Oong Moy, 117; calls on Somdet Pia Yumarat, 117–118; visits Dr. Mattoon, 118; receives present of sugar from Prince Wong Sa, 118; calls on French Bishop, 118; visited by Somdet Oong Noy, 118–120; converses with Mr. King on Treaty, 120; discusses Treaty with Prince Wong Sa, 120–121; receives presents from Somdet Oong Noy and Second King of Siam, 122; attends divine service at Dr. Bradley's, 122 and 122 n., 139; composes address to King of Siam, 123; his audience with King again postponed, 123; calls on Prince Wong Sa, 125; makes good impression on Somdet Oong Noy, 125; dines at Mr. Mattoon's, 127; describes wats, 127–128; his audiences with Kings of Siam, 129–136; describes festival Rak-na, 137–138; writes to King of Siam, 139; invited to audience with King, 140; attends service at house of the Rev. Mr. Smith, 140; visits wats, 141–142; goes up and down the River Menam, 143–144; meeting with Siamese Commissioners, 146–147; offers to withdraw amendments to his Treaty with Siam,

149; visits Wong Sa, 150; meeting with Commissioners, 151–152; meets Wong Sa, 152; receives present from First King, 152 n.; his opinion of the Siamese, 153; gives notice of departure from Bangkok, 153; requested by Wong Sa to delay his departure from Bangkok, 154; writes letter to Wong Sa, 155; informs Phra Klang of Mattoon's appointment as Consul, 155; settles accounts with Heusken and Mattoon, 157–158 and 158 n.; visits Second King, 158–159; his departure from Bangkok, 159–162; returns to the *San Jacinto*, 162–163; describes thunderstorm, 163; returns to Hongkong, 162–165; writes dispatches to Marcy, 163 n., 164 n., 166 n., 172 n., 175 and 175 n., 182 n., 185 and 185 n.; stays with General Keenan, 165; letters sent by him June 23, 1856, 167–168; starts for Macao, 168; calls on French Legation at Macao, 169; nominated Consul General for Japan, 172 n.; prepares to leave for Japan, 173; hires servants, 173, 175, 176; stays with the Drinkers, 177 n.; reads book by Abbé Huc, 180 and 180 n.; confirmation of his appointment as Consul General for Japan, 182 n.; describes voyage to Japan, 188–200; illustrations of pages of his manuscript *Journal*, 196, 374, 527; Governor of Shimoda postpones meeting with him, 201; visits Kakizaki, 201–202; Temple of Rioshen suggested for his residence, 206; meets Governor of Shimoda, 207–208; first real day of negotiations with Japanese, 207–208 and 208 n.; has unsatisfactory interview with Japanese, 209–210; refuses to negotiate with Yedo official, 211; accepts temporary residence at Kakizaki, 213; requested to visit Governor of Shimoda, 216; meeting with new Governor and Vice-Governor of Shimoda, 219–222; his policy toward Japanese, 223–224 n.; send-off on leaving *San Jacinto*, 224; hoists "First Consular Flag," in Japan, 225; getting settled, 226; sends present to Governors of Shimoda, 226;

insists on Japanese officials telling him the truth, 231–232; complains of treatment of his servants, 234–235; tablet of, unveiled at Charter Day celebration at The College of the City of New York, 236 n.; death of, 240 n.; age of, 240 and 240 n.; describes flesh of baibarossa, 242; horse sent to, 242; his pigeons, 242–243, 273, 345, 347, 358; visits Shimoda prison, 246; begins to learn Japanese 250; development of friendly relations with Japanese, 251 n., 253; describes statues seen on walk near Shimoda, 252–253; gets American stove, 256; visits sulphur spring, 258; visits the *Olivuzza*, 261; visited by Russian officers, 263–265; offers services of his washman to the Russian officers, 265–266; dines with Heusken on the *Olivuzza*, 268; likes Russian officers, 268 and 268 n.; illustration of monument dedicated to the memory of, 268; receives dogs from Japanese, 270 and 270 n.; sends his tailor away, 288, 289; makes loan to Korsacoff, 289–290 and 290 n.; engages another servant, 281; writes to Lieutenant Maury on subject of meteorological instruments, 284 n.; visits Possiet on currency question, 287–288; complains of guards and shopkeepers, 291, 295; his horse arrives, 291–292; meets Governors of Shimoda, 296–299; appoints Heusken Vice-Consul, 301 n.; visit of, to Governors of Shimoda on their return from Yedo, 306–309; First Governor makes tea for him, 307–308; meets Governors of Shimoda, 310–313; receives answer from Regency at Yedo to his letters, 311 and 311 n., 313; discusses treaties with Governors of Shimoda, 315–320; again meets Governors on Treaty questions, 320–321 and 321 n.; reads Secretary Marcy's letter to Governors, 325; meets Governors on Treaty questions, 323, 325, 326; complains to Governors of ordering away of Reed and Dougherty from Shimoda, 329; describes Governors' houses, 329 330; meets Governors on currency question, 332, 334; writes letter to

Governors, 334–335, 335 n., 337 n.; plants his garden, 341; receives account from the Goyoshi, 343; his anxiety over non-arrival of *San Jacinto*, 347, 350 and 350 n., 357, 361 n., 365, 368, 377; meets Governors, 347–349; Moriyama brings him letter from the Governors, 354 and 354 n.; Moriyama brings him American gold, 359; objects to overcharges, 359 and 359 n.; orders belvedere erected, 363; collects natural history specimens, 364 and 364 n.; visits hot spring, 372; pays account, 372–373; his success, 373–374; abandons hope of seeing Armstrong, 379; receives letters from Rice, 383; gets letters and newspapers by the *Portsmouth*, 387; dines on the *Portsmouth*, 390; gives Foote his dog Yedo, 392; sends presents to Captain Bell and Commodore Armstrong, 392; receives newspapers from Curtius, 393; meets Governors, 394; to visit Yedo, 394–396; his birthday, 398; gets new horse, 398; illustration of his second Commission as Consul General for Japan, 400; receives supplies and letters from Hakodate, 400–401; meets First Governor (Dewa-no-Kami), 405; preparations for his audience with the Shogun, 405, 406; pays account to the Goyoshi, 409; receives package from Curtius, 411; starts on journey to Yedo, 411; describes cavalcade, 411–413; his journey to Yedo, 411–442; is injured by his horse, 426; his entry into Yedo, 436–442; arrangements made for his comfort at Yedo, 442–443 and 443 n.; his meals at Yedo, 446; visited by Commissioners, 447; dangers threatening him on visit to Yedo, 456–458 and 458 n.; explains object of his visit to Yedo to Shinano, 451–452; sends copy and translation of President's letter to Japanese Minister of Foreign Affairs, 456; describes journey to Prime Minister's house, 458–459; his meeting with Prime Minister of Japan, 461–464; presents him with copy of intended address to the Shogun, 462; Prime Minister hands him Shogun's reply, 463; illustration of his "Full Powers," or Letter of Credence, 468; his uniform at audience with the Shogun, 468; goes to audience with the Shogun, 468–469; describes Palace, 470–471; describes Court Dress, 471–472; declines to rehearse part at audience, 472–473; his audience with the Shogun, 473–477; his address to the Shogun, 475; the Shogun's reply to his address, 475 and 475 n.; debate on his diplomatic rights, 487–488 and 488 n.; refuses to dine at Palace after audience, 478; describes Shogun's appearance at audience, 479–480; leaves Palace after audience, 478–479; writes to Minister for Foreign Affairs after audience with the Shogun, 481; visits Minister for Foreign Affairs, 484; statement made by him on visit to Minister for Foreign affairs after audience with the Shogun, 484–486, 485–486 n.; teaches Japanese elements of political economy, 490; rides horseback, 490; answers questions of Commissioners of the Voyage on duties and rights of Ministers in foreign countries, 491–492; writes Minister for Foreign Affairs on foreign commerce, 492 and 492 n.; Japanese delay in replying to his communications, 492, 495–496; Japanese give reasons for delay, 496–497; his third visit to Minister for Foreign Affairs, 497–498; answer to his communications, 497–499; attempt on his life, 512 n.; drawing of harbor of Settsu by, 527; his seclusion during Treaty negotiations, in Yedo 542–544, 542 n.–543 n.; his suggestion to Shinano regarding completion of Treaty, 544; Harris's proposition to Shinano on completion of Treaty accepted, 545–546; disheartened over Treaty, 550; discusses tariff with the Commissioners, 554; receives tariff proposition from the Commissioners, 554; serious illness of, 557 n., 558 n.; his last days, 559 n.; returns to Yedo, 560.

Hayashi, Daigaku-no-Kami, 444 and 444 n., 445 n., 448; failure of, to gain Emperor's consent to the Treaty, 538 n.–539 n.

Hazlett, Captain, 49.

Health, Harris's, 15, 27, 29, 146, 149, 152, 153, 241–242, 278, 280, 284, 285, 286, 290, 291, 296, 300, 301 and 301 n., 303, 304, 335, 347, 354, 361, 367, 378, 381, 385, 393 396–397, 398, 407, 480, 481, 491, 493, 543, 557 n.

Heard & Co., 179 and 179 n.

Heerjeebhoy Rustumjee, 50.

Hemp, 249.

Hen, Harris's, 290, 295.

Henna tree, 39.

Heusken, Harris's secretary, 28 n., 50 n., 93, 106 n., 110 n., 111 n., 116 and 116 n., 117 n., 130 and 130 n., 140 n., 153, 155, 168, 172 and 172 n., 180, 183 and 183 n., 185, 188, 199, 200, 204 and 204 n., 205, 207, 209, 213, 214, 225, 233, 247 n., 260 n., 268, 279, 283 n., 284, 290 n., 294, 298, 302, 309, 311, 313, 326, 331, 335, 341, 346, 365, 378 n., 381, 383, 388, 390, 392, 393, 398, 409, 412, 413, 416, 429, 432, 442, 443, 446, 447, 457, 460, 474, 477, 481, 489, 494 n.–495 n., 497, 501, 504, 534 n., 536 n., 542, 558; drawings by (illustrations), 212, 226; Harris settles accounts with, 158 n., arrives at Macao, 170; has encounter with armed Japanese, 293, 296; appointed Vice-Consul, 301 n.; slain by Japanese, 369 n.; translates reply of Shogun to Harris's address, 463 n.; his uniform at Harris's audience with Shogun, 468; slaying of, 511 n.

Higginson, J. B., 29 n.

Higo-no-Kami, 537, 561; asks delay on Treaty, 561.

Hildreth, Captain, of the *Sancho Panza*, 177.

Hio-n'go, Harris claims, 532.

History of the United States, Dr. Elijah Cole Bridgman's, 310. n.

Hodge, J. L., 30 and 30 n.

Hogs, wild, 61.

Holland, King of, 239, 240 n., 264, 273.

Hollis, Captain, of the *Chilo*, 48.

Holograph letter from Second King of Siam (illustration), 110.

Homer, Captain, of the *Messenger Bird*, 331, 334, 335.
Homer, Mrs., 331, 334.
Hongkong, Harris returns to, in 1856, on the *San Jacinto*, 162–165.
Hongkong Government Gazette, 81 n.
Horse, Harris's, 291–292, 381.; Japanese to select, for Harris, 279; Heusken's, 365, 383.
Horsemanship, Harris's and Heusken's, 399; Lieutenant-Colonel May's, 399; Japanese, 398–399.
Horses, Japanese, 399; shoeing of in Japan, 292 n.
Horseshoes, Japanese, 398 and 398 n.
Hospitality, Harris complains to Japanese of lack of, 298–299.
Hoszuki given to Harris by Japanese, 271–272.
Hotta, Bitchiu-no-Kami, 81 n., 445, 454, 456 n., 460, 491 n., 500 n.; Harris receives letter from, 454 and 454 n.; created Minister of Foreign Affairs, 454; description of his house, 462; hands Harris Emperor's reply to his address, 463; Harris describes, 464; at Harris's audience with the Shogun, 474; letter written to Harris by (illustration), 494; sent to Kyoto to obtain Emperor's consent to the Treaty, 538 n.–539 n.; signer of letter pledging execution of Treaty, 546 and 546 n.; copy of his letter promised to Harris, 551; conspiracy to murder, 560; returns from Kyoto, 561 n.; letter from, to Harris, 577.
House, the Rev. Samuel R., 86 n., 113 n.
House, Harris's, at Bangkok, 102–103.
Houses, Governors', description of, 329–330; Japanese, 329, 433, 458–459, 469–470; Japanese, furnishings of, 442–443; floating, in River Menam, 101; floating, Bangkok, 128, 129; raft, in River Menam, 101.
Howitzers made by Japanese, 309–310.
Huc, Abbé, Harris reads book by, 180 and 180 n.
Huffnagle, Charles, 29 and 29 n., 31, 45, 77, 186, 187; appointments of, 29 n.
Hunt I., & Co., 389 n.
Hunter, Governor, 68 n.
Hunter, William, 24 n., 133 n., 170;

sends Harris notice of appointment as Consul General to Japan, 12–13.
Hunter, W. C., 180 and 180 n., 181.
Hunter, Mrs. 169.
Hypatia, 37.

Ianthe, the, 101.
Ibis, white (paddy bird), 92–93.
Illustrated London News, Harris receives files of, 405.
Imperial surgeon, Harris gives lessons in English to, 349–350.
Inazo Nitobe, extract from book by, 435 n.
Incense, 364–365.
Ino, the, 80, 81.
Inouye, Prince of Shinano, *see* Shinano-no-Kami, *and* Shimoda, First Governor of, *and* Shimoda, Governors of.
Insects in Penang, 62.
"Instructions to Consuls," 186.
Interpreter, Japanese, 462.
Interpreter, Portuguese, for Harris at Bangkok, 103–104, and 103 n.
Invocations to Buddha, 43–44.
Ipecacuanha shrub, 61.
Isherwood, Mr., 130, 137.
Iyesada Tokugawa, Shogun, x.
Iyesato Tokugawa, His Excellency Prince, acknowledgment to, x.
Iyeyoshi, 434 and 434 n.

Janvier, Thomas Allibone, 169 n.
Janvier, Mrs. Thomas Allibone, *see* Drinker, Catherine Ann.
Japan, gratitude of, to United States, 16.
Japan to America, extract from, 518 n.
Japan, Emperor of, 28 n., 247 n., 313, 371, 456 n., President Pierce's letter to, 133 n., and text of, 576–577.
Japan Expedition, the, 1, 2, 207 n.
Japan Expedition, The, extract from, 229 n.
Japan Society, acknowledgment to officers of, ix.
Japanese, curiosity of, to see Harris's entry into Yedo, 444; Harris teaches them elements of political economy, 490; right of America to employ as seamen on American ships, 531.
Java Bode, Harris receives files of, 405.
Jephcott, Sir William, 74.

Mehter, definition of, 48 n.

Memorial in behalf of Harris drawn up by Nathaniel Dougherty, 320 n.

Menam, the River, Harris describes scenery along, 100; Harris describes return down, from Bangkok, 115–116; Harris describes trip up and down, 143–144.

Mencius, 53.

Mendee, henna tree, 39.

Messenger Bird, the, 364 and 364 n.; arrives at Shimoda, 331; Harris visits, 334; Harris's supplies from, 336; leaves Shimoda, 337.

Meteorological instruments, 284 and 284 n.

Miako, *see* Kyoto.

Mikado, the, 518 and 518 n.; consent of, to Treaty, 560 and 560 n., *See also* Japan, Emperor of.

Milk tree, 60.

Miller, Mr. and Mrs., 23, 27.

Minamoto Iyesada, 531 and 531 n.

Minden, the, 187, 188.

Mines, Harris discusses, with Somdet Oong Noy, 119.

Minister of Foreign Affairs (Siamese), writes to Harris, 88.

Minister of Foreign Affairs (Japanese), 199 and 199 n.

Minister of Foreign Affairs, 208; Harris writes to, 247 n., 300 and 300 n.; Hotta, Prince of Bitchiu, created, 454; Minister of Foreign Affairs, Harris sends copy and translation of President's letter to, 456; Harris visits, 484; Minister of Foreign Affairs, replies to Harris's speech, 486–487; Harris's third visit to, 497–498.

Mirage, Harris describes, 20, 24.

Missionaries, American, call on Harris at Bangkok, 106–107 and 107 n.; Baptist, Harris visits, 117, 118.

Mississippi, the U. S. S., 35 n.

Mitchell, Mr., Sr., 48.

Mitchell, T., 48.

Mitford, Judge, 32, 34, 35.

Money, Japanese, 226 and 226 n.

Monkeys, 61.

Montigny, Monsieur, 404 and 404 n.

Montravel, Commodore, 78.

Monument dedicated to the memory of Townsend Harris (illustration), 268.

Moor, A. F., Portuguese Consul, calls on Harris, 109; Harris calls on, 117, 118.

Moriyama Yenosuke, 226 and 226 n., 228–229, 234, 254, 255, 272, 286, 287, 293, 325, 336–337, 348, 351, 362, 370, 408, 475 n.; Harris sends him an *Atlas*, 232 and 232 n.; prophesies as to opening of Japan to world commerce, 269; spelling of his name, 269 n.; visits Harris, 279, 339–340, 342 and 342 n., 350 n.; promotion of, 322; converses with Harris, on salutes, the Treaty, Japanese books, firearms, 344–345; brings Harris letter from Governors, 354 and 354 n.; brings Harris American gold, 359; brings Harris Dutch versions of Dutch Treaty, 368–369; brings Harris newspaper files, 405.

Mosquitoes in Japan, 225.

"Mount Ellenborough," Currier's bungalow, 76.

Mourning, Japanese laws of, 546.

"Moving Sand Pillars," Harris describes, 19–20.

Murphy, Robert C., 51 and 51 n.

Murray, Dr. David, 424 n., 474 n.

My Novel, 37.

Nagai, Prince of Gemba, 445.

Nagasaki, Port of, open to American ships, 351.

Nairne, Mr., 49.

Nankin, the, 176 n.

Narrative of the Earl of Elgin's Mission to China and Japan, extract from, 378 n.

Narrative of the Japan Expedition, extract from, 309 n.–310 n.

Nathan Dunn & Co., 178 n.

Natural history specimens, Harris collects, 364 and 364 n.

Nautical Almanac, Harris gives King of Siam, 162.

Navy, Japanese, beginning of, 428.

Neale, Frederick Arthur, 129; his book on Siam, 128 and 128 n.

Neem tree (Persian lilac), 39.

Negotiations with Japanese, first real day of Harris's, 207–208 and 208 n.

Nepenthe (pitcher plant), the, 62.

Netherlands, King of the, 428 n.

Rice, E. E., 555 and 555 n.; extract from letter from Harris to, 85 n;. Harris receives letters from, 376 and 376 n.; Harris sends letter to, 392 n.; Harris receives letter from, 503; extract from letter from, 503 n.; Harris writes to, 557 and 557 n.; extract from letter from Harris to, 574.

Rice, 249, 251, 257, 258–259, 374.

Richards, Mr., of the *Spartan*, 81.

Rifle, first breech-loading Winchester made by Japanese, 529 n.

Rioshen, Temple, 204, 205; suggested for Harris's residence, 206.

Roberts, Edmund, 79 n., 145, 152, 153, 178 and 178 n.

Robertson, S., congratulates Townsend Harris, 2.

Rodgers, Lieutenant, 254 and 254 n., 328 and 328 n., 348.

Roman Catholic Cochin-Chinese College, 52–53.

Ronaine, Mr., 41.

Ronin, see Loneen.

Rose, Mrs., 48.

Rose of Shiraz, 61.

Route to Yedo, 453–454.

Royal Commission, 142.

Royal Commission, Siamese, Chandler translates, 140.

Royal Seat Siamese Steam Force, 162.

Royal Umbrellas, 128.

Ruparell, the, 168 n.

Russell & Co., 184–185, 240, 389 n.

Russia, Supplementary Treaty with, 410 n.

Russian American Fur Company, 261 and 262 n.

Russian officers, Harris offers services of his washman to, 265–266, 280–281; their opinion of French and English soldiers, 268–269; dine with Harris, 273–274.

Rutledge, Lieutenant, 130, 137.

Sabbath, Harris's observance of the, 51, 122 and 122 n., 139, 140, 149, 206–207, 217, 270–271, 309, 337 and 337, n., 428, 432, 465 and 465 n., 487, 491, 496.

"St. Anthony's Fire," Harris has, 291.

St. George's Church, Penang, Harris attends, 51.

Sak-kai, Japanese offer to open, 524–525; Harris claims, 532.

Salutes, in honor of Mr. Parkes, 89–90; of American Flag, at Bangkok, 95; in honor of Fourth of July, 378; in honor of Harris, 92, 96, 135, 207–208, 238, 268, 389–390; on signing of American Treaty with Siam, 156; on Washington's Birthday, 309–310 and 309 n.; Harris explains system of American, 344; in honor of Washington's Birthday, 528, 541.

Sam Willets, the, 173.

Samshew, defined, 54 n.

San Jacinto, the Steam Frigate, 26 and 26 n., 28 and 28 n., 40, 53, 68, 74 and 74 n., 75 and 75 n., 76 and 76 n., 77, 78 n., 79 and 79 n., 83, 126 and 126 n., 159, 162–163, 172 and 172 n., 173, 174, 178, 179 and 179 n., 180, 182 n., 185 and 185 n., 186, 187, 192, 199 n., 200, 233, 234 n., 301 n., 359, 364, 386, 387, 389, 390; delayed in sailing for Japan, 176, 176 n.; Harris leaves, 224; leaves Japan, 225–226, 225 n.; Harris's anxiety over non-arrival of, 347, 350 and 350 n.; 357–358, 357 n., 361 n., 365, 368, 377

Sandstone, 259–260.

Saracen, the, 92 n.

Schooner given by Russia to Japan, 260.

Scorpion, care for bite of, 61.

Scorpions, 62.

Scott, Charles, 49, 70; Harris describes house of, 55.

Scott, Walter, 49.

Seal, Townsend Harris's, title-page.

Seals, on document appointing Commissioners to negotiate Treaty, 146 n.

Semple, Dr., 76 and 76 n., 137, 159.

Senate Square, house falls in, 181.

Sepoy Rebellion, 394 n.

Servants, Harris's Chinese, 233, 346; Harris hires, 173, 175, 176; he complains of treatment of, 234–235; refused opium, 276; Harris's tailor, 288, 289; wages of, 343, 346; Harris pays accounts of, 373; Harris's Japanese, trouble in getting, 230–231, 232; hires another, 281; wages of, 281, 342, 343; requests silver *ichibus* for presents to, 291; his cook, 430.

611

613

514; ratification of, 530–531; opening of various places, dates of, 532; trade regulations, 533; tariff, 534, 552; Japanese wish to delay signing of, 538–540; Harris refuses to accept delay, 540; letter pledging execution of, 546 n.; final consideration of, 547; Preamble of, 505, 514; acceptance of Article II, 515; opening of negotiations for, 505; Harris's reply to Japanese discourse on, 507, 508; Shogun favors, 549; Shinano-no-Kami offers proposed amendments to, 551; Harris agrees to adoption of reasonable or necessary amendments to, 551–552; agreements on, 552; Harris gives clean copy of, to Japanese, 556 and 556 n.; signed by Harris, 557 n.; date fixed for signing of, 561.

Treaty of Amity and Commerce Between the United States and Japan, text of, 578–589.

Treaty with Japan, Perry's, 5, 104 and 104 n., 209, 221 n., 261 n., 267 n., 278 n., 316 and 316 n., 339 and 339 n., 421 and 421 n., 445 n., 507; a "wood and water" treaty, 7; extract from, 209 n.; Additional Articles to, 210 and 210 n.; Additional Articles to, 282 and 282 n.; Harris complains of breach of, 297; extract from, 317 n.–318 n.; Secretary Marcy suggests additional article to, 327 n.; Japanese version of Article VII of, 328.

Treaty with Japan, Russian, 221, 260, 261 n., 265, 266 n., 278 n., 285, 286, 316 and 316 n., 321 n., 328 n., 448 and 448 n., 506 and 506 n.; 521 and 521 n.; trade regulations in, 533 and 533 n.

Treaty with the Japanese, Admiral Stirling's, 81.

Treaty of Kanagawa, see Treaty with Japan, Perry's.

Treaty with Siam, Sir John Bowring's, 51 n., 69 and 69 n., 78 n., 146 n., 151; article on opium in, 147 n.

Treaty with Siam, French mission concludes, 176 n.

Treaty with Siam, Harris's, 78 n., 79 n., 172 n.; Parkes and Harris discuss, 89; Phra Klang makes suggestion regarding, 110; Harris talks of, with Prime Minister of Siam, 114–115; Harris intends to bring leasing of Siamese mines into, 119; delays over, 140 and 140 n.; Harris completes pro forma of, 142–143; clauses in, promising American aid to Siamese vessels, 147 n.; substance of amendments to, 147 and 147 n., 148 and 148 n.; Harris's, reason given for rejection by Siamese of amendments to, 148–149; Harris's, Prince Wong Sa wishes to have "farrago of nonsense" inserted in, 150; Phra Kalahom advances proposition regarding, 150–151; Harris's, Wong Sa wants to change preamble to, 153; signing of, 156; ratification of, 335 n., 390 and 390 n., 391 n.; ratifications exchanged, 374 n.; successful working of, 391; inaccurate copy of, appears in New York Times, 402–403; Siamese ask for English version of, 404.

Treaty with Siam, Mr. Roberts's, 148 and 148 n.; Mr. Roberts's, Americans in error with regard to concessions secured by, 149–150; Preamble to, 152 and 152 n.

Treaty of Peace between France, England and Russia signed, 70.

Treaty Commissioners, 500–501 and 501 n.; See also Shinano-no-Kami and Higo-no-Kami.

Trees, 39, 45, 55, 60, 97, 100, 202, 244, 250, 259, 335, 341, 371, 372, 414, 415, 419, 421, 427, 436, 453.

Tribune, New York, 26 n.

Troplong, Mr., 169, 181.

T'sukagosi, Tooske, 445.

Tsutsu, Prince of Hizen, 444 n., 448 and 448 n.

Tuckerman, Charles K., 55.

Tulasi, legend of, 38.

Tulsi, sacred Hindu plant, 38.

Turner, C., 175.

Twiss, Horace, 45 and 45 n.

Twiss, Quintin William Francis, 45 n.

Twiss, Captain, R. A., 39 and 39 n., 175.

Tycoon, see Shogun.

Tykoon, see Tycoon and Shogun.